Myth and Knowing

MYTH AND KNOWING

An Introduction to World Mythology

Scott Leonard
Youngstown State University

Michael McClure
Washington and Lee University

Boston   Burr Ridge, IL   Dubuque, IA   Madison, WI   New York
San Francisco   St. Louis   Bangkok   Bogotá   Caracas   Kuala Lumpur
Lisbon   London   Madrid   Mexico City   Milan   Montreal   New Delhi
Santiago   Seoul   Singapore   Sydney   Taipei   Toronto

McGraw-Hill Higher Education 𝒳

*A Division of The **McGraw-Hill** Companies*

MYTH AND KNOWING

Published by McGraw-Hill, a business unit of The McGraw-Hill Companies, Inc., 1221 Avenue of the Americas, New York, NY, 10020. Copyright © 2004 by The McGraw-Hill Companies, Inc. All rights reserved. No part of this publication may be reproduced or distributed in any form or by any means, or stored in a database or retrieval system, without the prior written consent of The McGraw-Hill Companies, Inc., including, but not limited to, in any network or other electronic storage or transmission, or broadcast for distance learning.

Some ancillaries, including electronic and print components, may not be available to customers outside the United States.

This book is printed on acid-free paper.

3 4 5 6 7 8 9 0 FGR/FGR 0 9 8 7 6 5

ISBN 0-7674-1957-X

Publisher: *Kenneth King*
Sponsoring editor: *Jon-David Hague*
Senior marketing manager: *Greg Brueck*
Project manager: *Diane M. Folliard*
Lead production supervisor: *Lori Koetters*
Coordinator of freelance design: *Mary E. Kazak*
Manager, photo research: *Brian J. Pecko*
Art editor: *Cristin Yancey*
Cover design: *Sarah Studnicki*
Cover art: *"Ad Marginem" 1930, 210 (E10)*
      46 × 36 cm; water-colour; Oeffentliche Kunstsammlung, Basel.
      © 2002 Artists Rights Society (ARS), New York/VG Bild-Kunst, Bonn
      Scala/Art Resource, NY
Typeface: *10/12 Times Roman*
Compositor: *G&S Typesetters, Inc.*
Printer: *Quebecor World Fairfield, Inc.*

Library of Congress Cataloging-in-Publication Data

Leonard, Scott A., 1958–
    Myth and knowing : an introduction to world mythology / Scott Leonard, Michael McClure.
      p. cm.
    Includes index.
    ISBN 0-7674-1957-X (softcover : alk. paper)
      1. Mythology.   I. McClure, Michael, 1950– II. Title.
    BL312.L46 2004
    398.2—dc21

                        2002041074

www.mhhe.com

About the Authors

In 1986, Scott Leonard and Michael McClure met in an undergraduate critical theory course at Humboldt State University in Arcata, CA. They soon formed a friendship based on their mutual love of literature, theories about, well, everything, and excellent micro-brews. Both received their B.A.s and M.A.s from Humboldt State and both traveled east to pursue their respective doctoral studies.

Scott received his Ph.D. from The Ohio State University (go Bucks!) in 1992. He has published scholarly articles on nineteenth-century British Literature, institutional theory, and composition. He currently is associate professor of English at Youngstown State University where he teaches myth, the British romantics, and serves as director of YSU's Composition Program.

Michael received his Ph.D. from the Joint Program in English and Education at the University of Michigan (go Blue!) in 1993. He has since published fiction and poetry as well as academic articles on composition and rhetoric. He is currently a visiting assistant professor of English at Washington and Lee University in Lexington, VA.

Preface

Myth and Knowing is an introduction to myths around the world and their systematic study, written primarily for introductory college courses in myth, mythology, and world literature, with numerous generative uses in other disciplines, including first-year writing, anthropology, religion, and psychology. Although several excellent textbooks on classical mythology exist, readers wishing to explore the mythic terrain beyond Athens and Rome have not been as well served. Given an ever-growing public interest in myth and an academic climate that encourages "multicultural" approaches to traditional subjects, this lack is surprising. Yet, until now, textbooks devoted to world myth have tended to feature pallid, often sanitized versions of these sacred narratives, presented not to fire the reader's imagination nor for their inherent beauty and strangeness but to exemplify a limited range of myth types or to illustrate one argument or another about *the* interpretive key that unlocks the hidden meaning of all myth. Teachers wishing to discuss world myth in terms other than such tale-types as fertility, creation, and hero myths or to investigate with their students the psychological and cultural implications of these stories have been forced to rely on supplemental course packets and a great deal of ingenuity.

Myth and Knowing was born of a frustration that no single volume provided a broad collection of the world's myths and a thorough overview of mythology as a field of study. We have endeavored to create a book that acquaints students with traditional academic classification systems but that nevertheless puts the story itself above all else. While, like its predecessors, our text does a great deal of summarizing of the world's myths to illustrate various teaching points, it also respects the potency of myth's densely symbolic and metaphoric phrasing. We have, therefore, selected, wherever possible, translations and versions of the following stories that preserve some of the majesty and mystery, the poetry and power of their original languages.

Moreover, an important assumption guiding our efforts has been that myth—far from being merely stories about the gods and the exploits of heroes—is a vital way through which human beings orient themselves to the world. Where did we come from and what is our purpose? What happens after we die? Why is there suffering and what can be done about it? Myths provide a rich array of answers to these and many other phenomenological and ontological questions. Through the study of myths we can see diverse cultures wrestling with such fundamental questions, and we can use the perspectives thus provided as ground from which to see our own attempts to understand the nature of the divine, the nature of the self, and the obligations we have to others in new ways. Through myths each person learns what is good and praiseworthy and what is not; what is beautiful and valuable and what is not; and what is true and right and what is not. These understandings about the individual in relation to notions of the divine order and the human community are the bedrock upon which societies, religions, and individual lives are built. Encouraging students to engage imaginatively, sympathetically, yet critically with the narratives that inform belief and rationalize action in this violent and anxious world is one of the central missions of our text.

The archeological, cultural, and historical contexts provided for the stories are another distinguishing feature of *Myth and Knowing*. We feel strongly that, despite the universality of many mythic themes, the stories themselves should be presented in a way that also communicates some of a culture's unique history and qualities. While all creation myths tell us how we got here, by whose agency, and how human beings fit in the grand scheme of things, characteristic qualities of each culture inflect these stories. For example, Native American creation myths tend to dramatize the idea that everything is intelligent, that the human being is related to brothers bear and fox as well as to the rocks and trees, while Egyptian and classical Greek accounts only imply human creation in their portrayals of how the various gods gave cosmic order to primordial chaos. These distinct cosmological approaches shape a culture's social organization, religious beliefs, art, customs, and way of relating to outsiders. All cultures tell stories of origins, but the conceptual architecture built upon these foundational accounts is significantly different. Our text teaches students to look for and appreciate those differences.

Organization

We've designed *Myth and Knowing* to serve the needs of the typical semester-long course. Each of the book's chapters is, in effect, a scholarly essay that introduces students to major mythologists and their ideas, defines important terms, outlines classification systems, and specifies the terms of on-going debates. Each chapter-essay concludes with an extensive bibliography from which students can launch research projects of their own. The text begins with a historical overview of the shifting definitions of myth and clear, if brief, summaries of the major schools of mythology. Our text demonstrates that the definition of the word "myth" and its study have complex histories in which moral, religious, philosophical, and political authority has always been at stake. Myth and mythology are presented as contested fields of meaning that have shaped and been shaped by various ideological currents. Rather than assuming a consensus that doesn't exist about what can legitimately be called a myth and how we should study it, we show our readers why myth is so difficult to define and why approaches to it are so numerous. Thus, the introductory chapter furnishes students with a conceptual vocabulary and rudimentary methods for analyzing the myths that appear in later chapters.

The five chapters following the Introduction focus on specific mythic genres—creation myths, myths of the female divine, myths of the male divine, trickster myths, and myths of sacred places. The essay portions of the chapter discuss characteristic features of each genre and mine mythic treasure from around the world to provide illustrations. While we do a fair bit of summarizing and excerpting of the world's myths to illustrate various themes, characters, and analytical schemes in the essays, each genre chapter also features a collection of full-text readings upon which students and their instructors may perform close, critical readings. Each story is introduced with a map and brief remarks that provide an overview of the known archaeological, historical, and cultural facts shaping the narrative. These stories exemplify the unique rhythms, ethnocentrisms, and symbol systems of myths told in cultures around the world.

Acknowledgments

Since this text is the product of two minds, our expressions of gratitude must be both individual and collective. Scott would like to thank Christine Miletta Leonard who, in her capacity as research assistant, spent many tedious hours photocopying and scanning stories for possible inclusion in the final manuscript and who, in her capacity as loving wife, jealously guarded his writing and research time from every intrusion. Without Chris's encouragement, support, and meticulous care this project would not have been possible. Scott would also like to thank Tom Gage, now professor emeritus at Humboldt State University, in whose classroom his passion for myth and mythology was first kindled. During the fall of 1987, Tom fought through a 15-week bout with laryngitis to show his students the Semitic precursors of Greek myth, a singular display of enthusiasm for his subject and commitment to his students that continues to inspire and in form Scott's own classroom practice. To this list of worthy benefactors, Scott also gratefully acknowledges Youngstown State University and its Research Council for granting a semester's leave and a stipend in support of this project. And he would also like to thank his co-author and long-time friend Michael McClure for every day we spent on this project. Who else would have insisted that our guiding editorial principle should be that the book feature "really cool stories"? Spending the last four years talking, marveling, arguing, and laughing together about myth, mythology, and our book has truly been reward enough for our labor.

Michael would like to thank Robin Le Blanc for her commitment to the power and importance of telling and hearing the stories that, in the end, are "all you get." Also, for her wisdom that that "all" is enough.

This book has benefited at various stages from the suggestions of many scholars who were gracious enough to review the manuscript for McGraw-Hill. The following people offered helpful suggestions in the early stages of the book:

Louise Ackley—Boise State University

Ann Canale—Lindenwood University

Marvin Lansverk—Montana State University, Bozeman

Jen Wahlquist—Utah Valley State College

Robert Wolverton—Mississippi State University

Michael Sexson, Montana State University, Bozeman

David Karnos, Montana State University, Billings

Later versions benefited from the reviews of:

William Tanner, Texas Woman's University

Caryl Terrell-Bamiro, Chandler-Gilbert Community College

Andrew Buckser, Purdue University

Ann Canale and Marvin Lansverk were kind enough to review the material again just prior to publication. We owe a significant debt of gratitude to them all.

We would both like to thank our publisher, Ken King, for his vision and support during the first crucial year of this project. Nor can we say enough good things about our sponsoring editor, Jon-David Hague, whose enthusiasm for this project, particularly through the review and revision process, matched—and sometimes exceeded—our own. Jon-David's expert and elegant translations of the classical Greek materials and his wise counsel and judicious comments at all stages along the way have been invaluable. We're grateful as well to the McGraw-Hill production team, and, especially, our project manager, Diane Folliard, for her superior communication skills, patience, good humor, and sensible suggestions for handling the myriad crunch-time details that repeatedly threatened to throw this project hopelessly off schedule. Thanks as well to Karen Lyle, copyright permissions coordinator at Washington and Lee University.

And last, but most importantly, we'd like to thank the students who inspired us to write *Myth and Knowing* and whose candid feedback about the developing manuscript, questions and classroom discussion, and research interests have guided our efforts at every turn.

Contents

Myth and Knowing

CHAPTER 1 # Purposes and Definitions

THE STUDY OF MYTHOLOGY

Why Study Myths?

The study of myths—mythology—has a long, rich, and highly contested history of debate about exactly what myths *are,* what they *do,* and why they are worthy of systematic study. Because of the complexity of such considerations about myths, any short answer to the question "Why study myths?" will be, at best, only a starting place. Yet this very complexity is one of the reasons why such study can be so exciting. The study of myth is a field of inquiry that ranges from the earliest known history of humanity up to and including contemporary cultures and societies and even our own individual senses of self in the world.

Every part of this introduction (and every part of this book) should serve more as a direction for further investigation than as a fully satisfactory explanation of settled facts. In our view, (1) the intertwined nature of the uses of myths in diverse cultures; (2) the myriad ways in which myths can be seen to embody cultural attitudes, values, and behaviors; and (3) the rich rewards awaiting questioners willing to approach myths from numerous points of view are all open-ended fields of inquiry. We see this book as an invitation to enter into these fields, whether briefly or as a lifelong interest. The study of myth entails discovering a way of making meaning that has been part of every human society.

What Are Myths?

Myths are ancient narratives that attempt to answer the enduring and fundamental human questions: How did the universe and the world come to be? How did we come to be here? Who are we? What are our proper, necessary, or inescapable roles as we relate to one another and to the world at large? What should our values be? How should we behave? How should we *not* behave? What are the consequences of behaving and not behaving in such ways?

Of course, any short definition, however carefully wrought, must oversimplify in order to be clear and short, so accept this definition as a starting point only. If this definition holds up under more extensive examination of myths across the world and in our own backyards, then what a promise with which to start a book, what an answer to the opening question, "Why study myths?"

Engaging thoughtfully with the myths in this book and with research projects that go far beyond what space constraints allow us to present in this book will deepen and complicate the elements of our starting definition. For example, myths are *ancient* narratives. But they are not static artifacts. They are not potsherds and weathered bone fragments. In many cases, they are living texts with which living people continue to write or narrate or perform their unique answers to basic human questions. This never-ending quality to myth is one reason we have included in this book not only ancient or "primary" versions of myths but also more contemporary tales, such as "Out of the Blue" by Paula Gunn Allen (see pages 68–75), which take up ancient myths and refashion their constituent elements in order to update answers to perennial questions and participate in ongoing cultural self-definitions.

Modern Native Americans, for example, who take up myths from their varied heritages and retell them do so in a context that includes the whole history of their people, from their ancient roots and primordial self-definitions to their contacts with European-American culture and modern self-definitions that search for meaning in a world forever changed by that contact. Today's Irish poets, for another example, who use Celtic myths as source material and inspiration and who write in Irish, a language which came perilously close to extinction, are engaged in cultural reclamation on a number of levels, and Irish myths, ancient and modern, are an important part of that effort. Looking at examples of ancient and more contemporary uses of myths introduces their varied cultural values and behaviors to us, and, at the same time, such study helps us develop intellectual tools with which to look at and question our own ancient and contemporary mythic self-understandings. In this sense, studying myths introduces other cultures to us and, at the same time, provides us with different lenses through which to view our own.

WHAT IS MYTH HISTORICALLY?

Mythos and *Logos*

The English word "myth" derives from the Greek word *mythos* and has been distinguished from the Greek word *logos,* both terms having been translated into English as *word* or *story*. In early uses of the term—for example, in Hesiod's *Theogony* (approximately 700 BCE)—*mythos* seems to have meant divinely inspired, poetic utterance, whereas *logos* was more often associated with crafty "legalese" as well as everyday, transactional discourse. The lines that open Hesiod's *Theogony* illustrate the original distinction made between the two terms,

> The Muses once taught Hesiod to sing
> beautiful songs as he tended his flocks
> on Mt. Helicon.
> And so what follows here
> are the very first words [*muthon*]
> these goddesses said to me:

"Country shepherd, a disgrace to your name,
thinking only of your next meal:
We know how to say [*legein*] many things
that aren't true yet seem to be,
and whenever we want, we know how
to tell the truth."

Sincere or not, this is what Great Zeus' daughters said
and they gave me a staff,
snapping one verdant branch from a laurel tree
—it was amazing—and they breathed into me
the breath of divine song so that I could tell
of what will happen in the future
and what took place in the past;
and they told me to praise the immortal race
of the blessed gods,
yet always to sing of them first and last.

As you can see, Hesiod's use of the word *mythos* in this passage is meant to legitimate both the Muses' words and his own. For the ancient shepherd-poet, *mythos* is breathed from the divine and, whether a *mythos* is, literally speaking, a fiction or a truth, its origin is divine, its meaning sacred. Hesiod uses a form of the word *logos* when he quotes the muses as declaring "we know how to say [*legein*] many things that aren't true yet seem to be."

The Devaluation of *Mythos* in Ancient Times

Xenophanes and Heraclitus   Like all words, the semantic meanings of *mythos* and *logos* were not forever fixed. By the time of Xenophanes and Heraclitus (middle and late 500s BCE, respectively), Hesiod and Homer were under attack for attributing to the gods "all/The shameful things that are blameworthy among humans:/Stealing, committing adultery, and deceiving each other" (Xenophanes, Fragment B11, in Lincoln 1999). Heraclitus sneered at the gullibility of the common folk (*hoi polloi*) for believing in, among other things, the divine inspiration of poets. Heraclitus appears never to have used the word *mythos*. Rather he focuses on the term *logos,* which, according to Lincoln, "is more likely to be a discourse of written prose than one of oral poetry, and more likely to be one of argumentation than of narrative" (27). In general, the pre-Socratic philosophers appear to have said little about *mythos* and, by comparison, a great deal about *logos*—a kind of discourse which could be true or false, a means of arguing propositions, tricking someone, or accurately describing reality. The sixth-century-BCE critique of Homer and Hesiod suggests, however, that the term *mythos* was, for some, beginning to mean something like "fanciful tale."

Plato's Rational Myth   Plato (427–347 BCE) permanently complicated the definition of *mythos* by treating the ancient use of the term as synonymous with falsehood; ironically, his own use of the word, when applied to philosophical speculation about origins and the nature of reality, reaffirmed the ancient meaning as a form of truth.

Thus Plato created a new myth to "clarify" the traditional meaning of *mythos;* this reconfiguration of terms to "restore" the vitality of myth's claim to truth-telling has been borrowed repeatedly by mythologists ever since. Doniger amusingly summarizes the great philosopher's use of the term:

> Plato used the word [*mythos*] in both senses, to mean "lie" and "truth" . . . [he] "deconstructed" the myths of Homer and Hesiod, contrasting the fabricated myth with the true history. But since people have to have myths, Plato was willing to construct new ones for them, and so he invented the drama of the philosophical soul and made it a reasonable, logical myth to challenge the old myths of centaurs and so forth. He transformed ancient mythic themes to make the myth of Eros and the myth of the creation of the universe, and he actually applied the word myth (which he called *mythos,* since he spoke ancient Greek) to the story of the world that he created in the Phaedo and to the myth of Er that he created at the end of the Republic. The myths that Plato didn't like (that were created by other people, nurses and poets) were lies, and the myths that he liked (that he created himself) were truths. And this ambivalence in the definition of myth endures to the present day. (1998, 2–3)

Plato's argument, that myths about gods, heroes, and centaurs contain irrational and therefore false elements and that philosophical myths about origins were rational and therefore true, was crucial to his political and philosophical vision. Leveling a charge that has been made occasionally against art down to our own time, he argued that poets manipulate their audiences and present them with cheap imitations of reality which have the effect of making their hearers lazy consumers of stories and images rather than active seekers of the truth. In Plato's ideal political state, poets—if not banished altogether—would be subject to philosopher-kings who would have the power to censor the irrational and morally suspect elements of their *mythoi* (*mythoi* = more than one *mythos*). As Lincoln puts it,

> The space that [Plato] assigned to [the poets] is that which lies between the state and its lowliest subjects, where they craft *mythoi,* at the direction of philosopher-kings, for mothers and nurses to pass on to their charges. . . . What others had taken to be primordial revelations or undeniable truths now were treated as state propaganda, best suited for children and those incapable of adopting the discourse and practice of the ruling elite, within an emergent regime of truth that called (and calls) itself "philosophy." (1999, 42)

Euhemeros and Euhemerism   Another early doubter of myth's truth-value was Euhemeros of Messene (330–260 BCE). Like many others since, Euhemeros assumed that his ancestors were primitives who lacked the scientific method, philosophical principles, and cognitive sophistication of the "modern" world in which he lived. He believed that the ancients, who were dominated by superstition and fancy, exaggerated the facts of actual historical events and created imaginative explanations of historical events because they did not have access to better forms of knowledge. Euhemeros claimed to have taken a journey across the Indian Ocean to the land of Panchia. There, he read an inscription which stated that Kronos and Zeus were at one time living kings on earth. Euhemeros reasoned that the beneficence of these kings was so great during their lifetimes that their legends lived on in the popular imagination. Eventually, their deeds were romanticized and sentimentalized to the point that they became honored as gods—as were others after them. In short, Euhemeros believed that myths were not true per se but that they contained the kernels of historical truth. Today, *euhemerists* are those who interpret myths as primitive explanations of the natural world or as time-distorted accounts of long-past historical events. As Doty (2000) points out in *Mythography: The Study of Myths and Ritual,* the "rationalistic anthropology of Euhemeros was not paid much heed by his Greek contemporaries . . . [but] the euhemeristic attitude was revitalized and developed by Roman writers. Later it became an important apologetic tool in the hands of Christian writers who used euhemeristic analysis to demonstrate the secondary nature of the Greek pantheon" (10).

Myth of the Golden Age

Hesiod, in his *Works and Days,* tells a devolutionary tale of origins that most scholars have come to call the myth of the Golden Age. Hesiod writes of the gods on Olympus creating mortal men numerous times (current humanity is actually the fifth race of mortal men in this scheme). Each race of mortals is associated with a metal, and each is a significant comedown from the previous race (with one exception). Thus the first creation is a golden race that lived perfect, harmonious, and peaceful lives. The second, markedly inferior but still highly honored, is silver. The third, dedicated solely to might and violence, is bronze. The fourth, the one exception to the devolutionary pattern, which Hesiod calls a "better and more just" race, is not labeled by a metallic association. Finally, associated with iron, the fifth mortal race, which Hesiod laments to be part of, is a "blend of good and bad" and will suffer "growing cares" imposed by the gods (1983, 110–201).

In this myth, Hesiod articulates a common motif in which nostalgia for a "golden" past—when mortals, living in harmony with the world and with each other, did not know suffering or care—is combined with criticism of the present age—when children are hostile and ungrateful and adults are violent and morally bankrupt. This hearkening back to a time when things were still warm from the divine touch has been both a conscious and subconscious motive guiding mythologists since the time, at least, of Plato. Impelled by quests for the original human language, myth's deep structure, or myth's universal meanings, mythologists have hoped to gain a glimpse of the world as it was when the cosmic clay had not yet hardened and actions and words still had power to create physical law and shape human society. As Plato knew, myth is extraordinarily powerful; how it is defined and who gets to do the defining have far-reaching implications for what counts as knowledge and therefore far-reaching cultural and political consequences. Thus there is a great deal more at stake in the study of mythology than the exciting tales of heroes and their fantastic adventures.

The rest of this chapter will show that the meaning of myth has always been in contention. For two and a half millennia, debates over the importance and meaning of myth have been struggles over matters of truth, religious belief, politics, social custom, cultural identity, and history. The history of mythology is a tale told by idiots—but also by sages, religious fundamentalists and agnostic theologians, idealists and cynics, racists and fascists, philosophers and scholars. Myth has been

Michelangelo's "The Creation of Adam" from the vault of the Sistine Chapel. The images, scenes, and characters of myth frequently become the raw materials from which painters and sculptors, poets and prophets draw inspiration. Often these secondary elaborations, which include folktales, legends, movies, novels, and short stories, are more familiar to a people than the sacred stories which inspired them.
Source: © Scala/Art Resource, NY.

understood as containing the secrets of God, as the cultural DNA responsible for a people's identity, as a means of reorganizing all human knowledge, and as a justification for European and American efforts to colonize and police the world. Our telling of the story of mythology will, we hope, make clear that there is a great deal at stake in study of myths.

THE RISE OF MYTHOLOGY

Myth and Mythology

Until the Renaissance, the Platonic and euhemeristic notions that myths other than their own were, at best, degraded forms of philosophical truth were little questioned among the educated. This understanding of mythic truth-value did not, however, dampen popular interest in them. Even among those who, like Plato, saw nothing sacred in the old myths, enough intellectual reward was found in them to encourage consideration of and debate about *myth* and *mythology*. To be clear, we will combine our definition of *myth* with Hesiod's of a divinely inspired utterance of a literary (poetic) truth and distinguish it from *mythology,* which we define as the scholarly study of myths.

Early Christian Mythology

The early church had an important role in transmitting Plato's "demythologized" definition of *mythos* down to our own day. As we have already suggested, the early church fathers used a form of euhemerism to contrast the "false" gods of the Greek and Roman pantheons with Jesus. Doniger tells us, for example, that Justin Martyr, Clement of Alexandria, and Tertullian developed the "Thesis of Demonic Imitation," which held that the demons, perceiving that Jesus would soon come, "suggested to the poets who created [Greek] myths that they give Zeus many sons and attribute monstrous adventures to them, in the hope that this would make the story of Christ appear to be a fable of the same sort, when it came" (1998, 69–70). In this doctrine, the gods of non-Christian myths are demonic deceptions and the story of Jesus' life was not myth at all but unquestionably fact.

In addition, the term *logos,* at least in the New Testament, had come to mean something like "transcendent truth." Thus the Gospel of John opens with the famous claim: "In the beginning was the Word [*logos*] and the Word [*logos*] was with God and the Word [*logos*] was God; and the Word [*logos*] became flesh and dwelt among us" (John 1:1). Here, *logos* has the divine associations of Homer's and Hesiod's *mythos,* but there is no suggestion of an inspired poet singing his truth. Instead, the *logos* exists, like one of Plato's Ideal Forms, unchangeable and timeless, outside the corruption and flux that characterize the material cosmos and human history. *Logos* and *mythos* had switched connotative places. *Logos* now transcended the corrupting limits known to human users of language, and *mythos* was mired in associations of make-believe or, even worse, outright falsehoods designed to damn souls to Hell. This negative Platonic/Christian definition of myth prevailed for the next 1,500 years. Only when Classical Greek and Roman texts became more widely available during the Renaissance did the old myths enjoy a rebirth in literature and the arts, paving the way for a later revaluation of the stories themselves.

MYTHOLOGY DURING THE ENLIGHTENMENT

Toward the end of the Renaissance, a rage for roots swept Europe, as attested by books and essays that speculated on the primordial "Ur-language" from which all others developed after the calamity at Babel. But there was more at stake than simply establishing which language had been spoken in the Garden of Eden. European scholars hoped also to name the "Ur-people" and the true location of Eden (the Ur-place), thus bringing the prestige and presumed political power of being God's "firstborn" to their respective nations. Olender's *The Languages of Paradise: Race, Religion, and Philology in the Nineteenth Century* provides a detailed and readable history of this early search for linguistic origins. In it we learn that patriotic scholars from many nations—often using ingenious if specious linguistic comparisons—each "discovered," not surprisingly, that the original language spoken in the Garden was their own.

These early, chauvinistic researches into the world's original culture and language were precursors of the 18th-century's Volkish school, named after Johann Gottfried Herder's theory that the rural German *Volk* (i.e., folk, nation, or ethnicity) still retained much of the vitality of their nation's original character. While these early attempts to identify the source-language and the first people might strike us today as naive nationalism, they are important because they are provocative examples of mythological thinking having extensive political consequences. Herder's Volkish theories were influential in numerous settings, including the national romanticisms of the 19th century and the racist ideologies of 20th-century fascism. Noting the connection between Herder's mythology and its uses by the Nazis in the mid-20th century is not to argue Herder's Volk theories caused the Nazis' Aryan monstrosities. In other places, the notion of a "folk spirit" has led to very different behaviors and political institutions. Nevertheless, the Nazis' use of such theories does highlight our contention that mythology is not merely about quaint stories. In thinking about myths, a central question should always be "What are the potential political ramifications of this or that way of thinking about myths and their uses?"

Giovanni Battista Vico and *The New Science*

As late-Renaissance fascination with roots, scientific method, and classical texts grew into the obsession for rational order that characterized the Enlightenment, a number of thinkers began to examine what ancient myths might tell them about the very beginnings of human history. Early mythologists sifted through myth, hoping to peel away the layers of irrationality and error.

Stunningly original, *The New Science,* first published in 1725, exemplifies the key elements of mythology during the Enlightenment and thereafter. The writer of this work, Giovanni Battista Vico, claimed to have discovered the scientific principles that finally could make sense of the confused histories, geographies, and linguistics of his time. The result of his lifelong effort was an "ideal eternal history" (Vico 1968, 12) which organized the ancient accounts in Egyptian, Greek, and Roman classical literature and presented them in a rational order. Among Vico's research methods were careful attention to "hieroglyphs"—pictographic symbols such as those found in coats of arms, carvings, and military emblems—and to etymology, the study of word origins. Vico used these tools to theorize that languages and cultures experience recursive evolutionary cycles. He reasoned that human society began after the flood in a primitive state without language, moved through a heroic phase when language was identical with poetry, and culminated in our current stage in which language serves a wide variety of prosaic, transactional purposes. Eventually, Vico speculated, an upheaval will occur starting the cyclical, progressive process all over again. Thus Vico sought to rescue myth from the clutches of irrationality by reorganizing its chronology and meanings into a logical system— a system, as it happened, that used history, linguistics, iconography, and a great deal of ingenuity to align Egyptian, Greek, and Roman myths with the key beliefs of his Christian culture.

Sir William Jones's Science of Language

Though Vico's work did not enjoy wide circulation, his suggestion that languages evolve over time was reiterated much more visibly and explicitly in the late 18th-century work of Englishman Sir William Jones. Jones was a prodigy who, even in his twenties, was an international authority in five languages and possessed a respectable grasp of several others. Jones took a post in India, where he noticed remarkable similarities among the Arabic and European languages in which he was fluent and Sanskrit, the priestly language of India. Jones began to compare the roots of many key words among these languages methodically. Rather than attempting to fit his observations into the predetermined conclusion that English or another European language was the language of Paradise, Jones let the evidence take him in a different direction, suggesting instead that these similarities could be explained by the existence of "a common source [language]," which, he suggested, "perhaps, no longer exists" (Jones 1807/1984, 3:34–35).

Following Jones's suggestion, linguists methodically demonstrated that nearly all the languages of India, Southwest Asia, and Europe derive from a single ancestor language which is today known as proto-Indo-European, a language existing only in linguistic theory. This scientific approach to language study gave direction, method, and legitimacy to the search for the original *Volk* from whom all European culture and achievement emanated. As linguistic research advanced, interest in myths intensified as well. As Lincoln shows us, a translation of the Norse Eddas by Paul Henri Mallet, the counterfeit translation of the blind Gaelic bard Ossian by James Macpherson, the linguistic and mystical speculations of Johann Georg Hamann, and the books of Herder all attest to the fact that, by the middle of the 18th century, myth was widely assumed to be "a crucial resource for collective identity" and that "myths convey historic, cultural, and practical knowledge while also guarding a *Volk*'s distinctive values—and errors—against forgetfulness and change" (1999, 53).

Herder's Organicist *Volk* Mythology

Herder's work was particularly influential. Tapping into growing feelings of nationalism all over Europe, enthusiasm for the new comparative science of language, and an emergent romanticism valuing irrational forces of the mind, Herder theorized an original, divinely sanctioned unity of humanity. From this unity, Herder claimed, humans devolved into the various linguistically, geographically, and culturally separate *Volk* that we see today. While Herder saw these differences as resulting from a fall from the original divine plan, he also affirmed the importance of modern cultural distinctions. Like Vico, who theorized that language influenced human physiognomy, Herder also suggested that a people's environment shaped not only their myths, culture, and language but also their bodies and characters. His theory of an organic relationship between *Volk* and landscape had great emotional resonance not only in Germany but throughout Europe, and with very different long-range effects. For example, if, as we noted earlier, Herder's Volkish theories were seized upon to justify Nazi fantasies, in Denmark Herder's theories fueled a romantic folklore movement in which the idea of a "pure folk spirit" contributed to Danish resistance to Nazi racism.

Herder's romanticism, like that of William Wordsworth and Samuel Taylor Coleridge in England, was founded in part on a nostalgic view of rural life in which close connection to the soil and other natural elements produced simple, honest *Volk* whose language was believed to possess a spontaneous vitality and transparency of meaning not found among city dwellers. Indeed, myths were important to Herder and those influenced by him in part because it was believed that they embodied the

Volkish purity and simple power from which the "civilized" nations had been receding for centuries. Or, as Lincoln puts it, "if the environment impresses itself directly on the bodies of a *Volk,* it impresses itself on their customs and mores through the medium of myths, which *Völker* use to reflect on their surroundings and history and to transmit ancestral traditions from one generation to another" (1999, 53).

Rise of Comparative Mythology

Herder's suggestion that physical environment has a direct influence on a people's collective disposition and body type and, indirectly, on their sociocultural values gave impetus to three closely related mythological schools. The first group of theorists, who came to be called practitioners of comparative mythology, sought, using methods borrowed from linguistics, to identify myth types and trace them back to their presumed original versions. The second group, known as the "Nature School," used comparative methods to identify *the* environmental cause of a given people's myths. Thus, for example, the Solar Hypothesis proposed that all myths could be referred back to the ancients' fascination with the sun's waxing and waning throughout the year. Others found that such meteorological conditions as thunderstorms or wind formed the basis of all myth. The third group of theorists were particularly interested in Herder's suggestion that the various *Völker* had specific and defining qualities. This group came to be known as "ethnologists." It is a sobering and oft-neglected fact that mythology, in its most literal sense as the study of myths, was until World War II closely and openly identified with the "science" of race. Each of these lines of inquiry had an important influence, though often a negative one, on 20th-century mythology, and thus they merit a closer look here.

Arguably, in the 19th century the study of myths was primarily a matter of sorting out the races according to similarities and dissimilarities in their languages and sacred narratives. Herder's ideas about the organic links among *Volk,* soil, and myth were not, especially by the standards of the time, particularly racist, but a virulent and racialized strain of nationalism in Germany—as well as European colonization worldwide—fueled a widespread interest in theories accounting for racial differences. We can perhaps most quickly grasp the racial dimension of early mythology by taking a "core sample" of 19th-century German thought on the "Aryan hypothesis" about race, language, and culture. Extrapolating from Jones's theory of Asian origins for the world's largest linguistic group, a variety of German intellectuals posited the existence of a strong, technologically superior race that conquered the prehistoric world from India to Iceland, thus leaving their indelible mark on the languages, myths, and gene pool of this vast territory. This race, which they called the Aryans, provided 19th-century German nationalists with an ancient, heroic "golden age" of their own upon which to base their theories of German nationhood. If, they reasoned, Germans were actually descendants of the Aryans, then they weren't the Barbarians so vilified by the Roman Tacitus or the vassals of French-speaking Prussia, but the inheritors of an ancient patrimony of conquest, superior strength, and mighty deeds. It was, many felt, the German branch of the Aryan family's turn—even their destiny—to take a preeminent role on the world stage.

In the midst of—and to some degree creating—this fierce search for German national identity were a number of important figures. In linguistics and mythology, there were Jacob and Wilhelm Grimm whose *German Grammar* exhaustively demonstrated the relationship between their native tongue and the other Aryan languages. The Grimm brothers' famous "Fairy Tales" were one result of another line of inquiry: the search for narratives that would demonstrate that which was distinctive in the German character.

In music, there was Richard Wagner, whose famous Ring Cycle was a highly imaginative operatic synthesis of various Norse, Anglo-Saxon, and other Germanic myths about the dragon-slaying hero Siegfried. It is in Wagner that we see an almost religious devotion to the values of the Aryan *Volk.* The composer asked for and received royal patronage to build Beyreuth, which he described as a modern "temple" wherein the *Volk* could celebrate this exemplary hero's Germanic spirit. The dark side of Wagner's interest in Siegfried is revealed in his theoretical writings. In them, we find his racist thesis that Jews are physically and irretrievably "other" than the descendants of the Aryan race. For example, in "Artwork of the Future" and "Judaism and Music" Wagner goes to some lengths to argue that, because they had no homeland, Jews were incapable of producing any original art or music.

In philosophy, Ludwig Feuerbach, Ludwig Schemann, Houston Stewart Chamberlain, and, early in his career, Friedrich Wilhelm Nietzsche provide some of the clearest examples of this racist thinking among the educated elite. Nietzsche wrote with great emotional force about the importance of German art, poetry, myth, ancient religions, and native soil:

> We think so highly of the pure and vigorous core of the German character that we dare to expect of it above all others the elimination of the forcibly implanted foreign elements, and consider it possible that the German spirit will return to itself. Some may suppose that this spirit must begin its fight with the elimination of everything Romanic. If so . . . let him never believe that he could fight similar fights without the gods of his house, or his mythical home, without "bringing back" all German things! (*Birth of Tragedy* 23.138–39)

Nietzsche also coined the term "blond beast," which describes the noble (Aryan) warriors of the past as

> not much better than uncaged beasts of prey. There they savor a freedom from all social constraints . . . [and] go back to the innocent conscience of the beast of prey, as triumphant monsters who perhaps emerge from a disgusting procession of murder, arson, rape, and torture, exhilarated and undisturbed of soul . . . One cannot fail to see at the bottom of all these noble races the beast of prey, the splendid blond beast prowling about avidly in search of spoil and victory. (*On the Genealogy of Morals* 11.40–41)

Despite the complexity of Nietzsche's work and scholars' continuing debates about the degree to which his personal biases and ethnocentrism affected that work, this tale of the "noble races" and their "innocent" exercise of bloodthirsty and animalistic power—itself a prime example of mythologists reconfiguring ancient myths to create powerful modern myths—proved a sinister inspiration for German fascists in the 20th century.

As reprehensible as we now find anti-Semitism, in particular, and racism, in general, it was nevertheless a fact that respected artists, intellectuals, and academics wrote extensively about the fundamental differences in spirit and kind between Jews (and other non-Aryans) and the "Nordic tribes" descended from the great Aryan race of warriors. Even today, when such overt racism or ethnocentrism is no longer the norm, we may notice that a lingering academic bias in favor of Greek, Roman, and Nordic myth continues to influence mythology texts and course reading lists. More subtly, and to varying degrees, the writings of such eminent 20th-century figures as Sir James Frazer, Carl Jung, Mircea Eliade, and Joseph Campbell carry forward the 19th-century bias against the "primitive" races who still believed in their myths. That such understandings were not merely the accepted thoughts of the times is made evident by the fact that another major thinker on these same issues, Claude Lévi-Strauss, explicitly appreciated non-Western societies and systems of thought. Lévi-Strauss's *The Savage Mind* is, for one example, an effective and powerful argument against the dismissive attitudes too common in the works of the writers mentioned above.

Even though the Aryan hypothesis was a central concern of comparative mythology in the 19th century, there were other, less insidious lines of inquiry as well. One of Nietzsche's early influences, Adalbert Kuhn, for example, was Germany's most enthusiastic proponent of the Nature School of comparative mythology. Kuhn took Herder's earlier ideas about the integral connection between a *Volk*'s values, history, culture, and practical knowledge and their natural surroundings seriously. From this starting point, Kuhn borrowed the principles and discoveries of comparative linguists to posit an Aryan Ur-myth from which numerous cross-cultural variants emanated.

Kuhn determined that the structural features of this "original" myth were a division between earth and sky and a protagonist who mediated between these two realms by stealing something from the gods and bestowing it upon humanity. Sometimes, as in the case of Prometheus, the stolen gift was fire; sometimes it was the elixir of immortality. In all cases, Kuhn saw these variants as allegories of natural phenomena—particularly the rainstorm that bestows fire in the form of lightning and the life-giving elixir of rain which makes all life possible. Many others in Germany, France, Denmark, Switzerland, and England employed Kuhn's methods to uncover the basic plot of the Ur-myth, often reaching significantly different conclusions. Some preferred to see the Ur-myth as an allegory of the phases of the moon, others argued for the sun, still others found that prevailing winds or other meteorological conditions formed the archplot.

In England, Friedrich Max Müller was the Joseph Campbell of his time—a man of immense learning, tremendous charisma at the lectern, and a single idea about myth that he vigorously promoted long after others had found it intellectually suspect to do so. Müller argued that myth was "a disease of language" through which poetic descriptions of such meteorological features as the sunrise and the thunderstorm became distorted into the bewildering array of deities, rituals, and superstitions one finds in the world's myths. Müller's concept of mythic language echoes the devolutionary elements of the Golden Age myth. In his view, the pristine language of Paradise fell from an original unity between truth and language into the confusion of multiple and competing versions of the truth. Müller's ideas also resonate with Euhemeros in that both believed that the ancients lacked the scientific and religious sophistication of their own enlightened day and, as a result, twisted reality into the irrational pretzel-logic of myth.

The Decline of Comparative Mythology

By the middle of the 19th century, mythology was dominated by a single methodology. Whether focusing on the Aryan homeland, the relationships between environment, *Volk,* and myth, or the Ur-myth from which all myths arose, each specialist employed the comparative method. Comparative mythology, as practiced by the mid-19th century, was a matter of locking oneself in a library and reading. Comparative mythology could be cross-cultural, with the scholar comparing a story's Indian, Arabic, German, and Celtic versions; it could also specialize in the stories of a single *Volk.* Mythology relied on insights from linguistics, archaeology, and art history, but the myths themselves were regarded as static cultural artifacts from the primitive past.

Beneath the apparent methodological unity of 19th-century mythology, however, a fundamental contradiction had begun to make itself felt. On one hand, a profound longing for a simpler, more organically unified Golden Age manifested itself in the revaluation of myths and search for the Ur-*Volk.* On the other hand, an equally profound euhemerism worked in the opposite direction, manifesting itself in a nearly universal view that myths and mythmakers traded in the irrational and crudely primitive. Part of the growing rift among mythologists amounted to a debate over answers to what Segal, in his *Theorizing About Myth,* calls the "three major questions [that] can be asked of myth: what is its subject matter, what is its origin, and what is its function?" (1999, 67). Primarily, the comparatists were interested in origins and content, and they were not particularly interested in how myth functioned; or, rather, they saw explanation of natural phenomena as its sole function. Toward the end of the 19th century, as Segal demonstrates, early anthropology's view of myth emphasized function above all else. Interest in this functional approach to mythology led to the breakup of the largely bookish and tendentious study of literary myth. What emerged were various approaches toward myth driven by disciplinary concerns within anthropology, psychology, literary criticism, and the history of religions.

MYTHOLOGY IN THE 20TH CENTURY

Early Anthropology

The Golden Bough   The first of these disciplines, anthropology, came to view myth as primarily a living, oral, culture-preserving phenomenon. Led by such pioneers as Edward B. Tylor, Andrew Lang, Franz Boas, Sir James George Frazer, and Emile Durkheim, emphasis switched from textual comparisons and blood-and-soil interpretive theories to discovering the ways in which myths *function* in living societies. Sir James Frazer's *The Golden Bough* is the best-known and remains the most widely read example of the early versions of this anthropological work. *The Golden Bough,* which grew to 12 volumes, depicts the widely dispersed stories of dying and resurrecting gods as literary transformations of primitive, magical-religious rituals in which "sacred kings" were slaughtered in hopes of ensuring agricultural fertility. Frazer approached myth and culture from an evolutionary perspective, assuming, not unlike Vico, a progression from the "mute signs" of primitive magic (e.g., rituals believed to create desired effects) to the largely allegorical use of ritual in primitive religion (e.g., the substitutionary death of a "scapegoat") to the abstract symbolism of civilized religion (e.g., the doctrine of transubstantiation).

Frazer also assumed that myth was "primitive science," which attributed to the will of deities, people, or animals that which modern science attributes to the impersonal functioning of various physical laws and biological processes. While Frazer shared the new anthropological science's interests in myth's function in living cultures, he nevertheless did not completely break with comparative mythology's armchair approach.

The "Myth-and-Ritual" School   Frazer's quasi-anthropological work had wide influence and inspired, at least in part, the also quasi-anthropological "myth-and-ritual" school. This relatively short-lived branch of mythological research was intensely functionalist in its approach, caring little for the origins of myth and looking at content only as a means of demonstrating the contention that myth is a script from which early religious rituals were performed. As Fontenrose puts it in the preface to *The Ritual Theory of Myth:* "Some . . . are finding myth everywhere, especially those who follow the banner of the 'myth-ritual' school—or perhaps I should say banners of the schools, since ritualists do not form a single school or follow a single doctrine. But most of them are agreed that all myths are derived from rituals and that they were in origin the spoken part of ritual performance" (1971, n.p.).

Modern Anthropology

Another of Frazer's admirers was Bronislaw Malinowski, whose fieldwork in the Trobriand Islands contributed much to the evolving methods of modern anthropology. In a 1925 lecture given in Frazer's honor, Malinowski lavishly praised the elder writer and then proceeded to outline what has been taken, until recently, as field anthropology's gospel:

> Studied alive, myth . . . is not symbolic, but a direct expression of its subject-matter; it is not an explanation in satisfaction of a scientific interest, but a narrative resurrection of a primeval reality, told in satisfaction of deep religious wants, moral cravings, social submissions, assertion, even practical requirements. Myth fulfills in primitive culture an indispensable function: it expresses, enhances, and codifies belief; it safeguards and enforces morality; it vouches for the efficiency of ritual and contains practical rules for the guidance of man. Myth is thus a vital ingredient of human civilization; it is not an idle tale, but a hard-worked active force; it is not an intellectual explanation or an artistic imagery, but a pragmatic charter of primitive faith and moral wisdom. (1926/1971, 79)

Malinowski's outline of anthropology's view of myth contains several crucial remarks. First, the anthropologist states emphatically that myth is not an "explanation in satisfaction of a scientific interest." This view contrasts sharply with the euhemerism of Frazer, Tylor, and the comparatists, who believed to one degree or another that myths are little more than primitive or mistaken science. Second, Malinowski saw myth as profoundly "true" in the sense that it had a visible role as "pragmatic charter of primitive faith and moral wisdom." He also saw myth as real in the sense that it could be observed by the field researcher in the form of oral performance, rituals, and ceremonies, and that it visibly influenced a living people's sociopolitical behavior. As his later fieldwork makes clear, Malinowski's views are considerably broader than those of the myth-ritualists, who would have limited myth's functionality to religious ritual only.

But we can also see from Malinowski's remarks that he did not entirely part ways with his mentor. Even though the younger man claimed to have also disputed the older's evolutionary theory of culture, it is significant that he nevertheless discusses myth's role in the "primitive faith" and in the "primitive psychology" of his research subjects. It can be argued that Malinowski and his contemporaries were not explicitly dismissive of "primitive" societies, that they were even respectful of the "face-to-face" nature of such societies when compared with more institutional and "impersonal" developed ones. Yet the effects of ethnocentric assumptions make it extremely difficult to avoid such hierarchical valuations, even if there is some question about the motives or intentions of the researchers.

Nevertheless, folkloric and anthropological methodologies profoundly influenced 20th-century mythology. For example, anthropological and folklorist approaches to myth emphasize field research and have thus underscored the importance of the real-world conditions in which myths perform their functions. As a result, those working in other disciplines have come to respect myth's functions as cultural charter and socializing agent. In addition, anthropology's correlation of myths to the material, social, political, and economic facts of living cultures helps those interested in the myths of extinct cultures to understand some of the obscure references and actions in the stories they study. Moreover, the insistence of anthropologists and folklorists on examining the function of myths in *living* societies demonstrates how ignorant the 19th century's armchair mythologists had been of what so-called primitives actually *do* understand about the physical world and the degree to which they are and are not naive about the truth-value of these narratives. In short, anthropology and folklore have encouraged all mythologists to relate their theories about myth to the lived experience of human beings.

The Rise of Psychology

About the time that Frazer and the early anthropologists were beginning to turn the focus of mythology away from questions of racial identity and to replace the comparative method of the Nature School with theories of social functionalism, psychiatric pioneers Sigmund Freud and Carl Jung had begun to investigate the relationship between myth and the unconscious. Freud and Jung believed that mythic symbols—both as they are encountered in religion and as they manifest themselves in dreams and works of the imagination—emerge from the deepest wells of the psy-che. Although their conclusions about the landscape of the human mind differed, both men shared a belief that our gods and other mythic characters, as well as our dreams and works of fiction, are projections of that which the unconscious contains. For Freud, "the unconscious is the true psychical reality" (*Complete Works* 1953–1966, 612–13), but our conscious minds censor our impulses, desires, fantasies, and preconscious thoughts because they are too raw and dangerous to face unmediated. Freud saw the images that appear to us in dreams and in such imaginative works as novels and myths as tamed projections of the unconscious's ungovernable terrors. From this point of view, myths are the conscious mind's strategy for making vis-ible and comprehensible the internal forces and conflicts that impel our actions and shape our thoughts.

Jung's view is similar to but not identical with Freud's. Jung viewed the uncon-scious not as the individual's personal repository "of repressed or forgotten [psy-chic] contents" (1959/1980, 3). Rather, he argued, "the unconscious is not individ-ual but universal [collective]; unlike the personal psyche, it has contents and modes of behavior that are more or less the same everywhere and in all individuals" (3–4). Jung defined "the contents of the collective unconscious . . . as archetypes" (4). Just exactly what an archetype is psychologically is far too complex to discuss here, but, briefly, Jung defined them as "those psychic contents which have not yet been sub-mitted to conscious elaboration" (5). Indeed, Jung and Freud believed that we never see the unconscious and its contents; rather, we see only projected and therefore refined images that symbolize the things it contains.

Jung and his followers argued that such mythic archetypes as the Wise Woman, the Hero, the Great Mother, the Father, the Miraculous Child, and the Shadow are aspects of every individual psyche, regardless of gender, culture, or personal history. The healthy mind, they reasoned, learns to view the contradictory impulses repre-sented by these archetypes in a balanced pattern, or "mandala." Those with vari-ous neuroses and psychoses, however, can't balance these impulses and are over-whelmed by the unconscious's self-contradictory forces. Jung saw the universalized symbols and images that appear in myth, religion, and art as highly polished ver-sions of the archetypes lurking in the collective unconscious. Therefore, Zeus, Yah-weh, Kali, and Cybele are their respective cultures' elaborations of universally avail-able psychic material. Jung called these elaborations "eternal images" that

> are meant to attract, to convince, to fascinate, and to overpower. [These images] are cre-ated out of the primal stuff of revelation and reflect the ever-unique experience of divin-ity. That is why they always give man a premonition of the divine while at the same time safeguarding him from immediate experience of it. Thanks to the labors of the human spirit over the centuries, these images have become embedded in a comprehensive sys-tem of thought that ascribes an order to the world, and are at the same time represented by . . . mighty, far-spread, and venerable institution[s like] the Church. (1959/1980, 8)

Joseph Campbell: Literary and Cultural Critic

Whereas in the 19th century what passed for literary criticism of myth was largely a matter of antiquarians, classicists, biblicists, and specialists in dead languages reading myths and theorizing the linguistic and cultural events that explained and

connected them, in the 20th century literary approaches to myth grew more sophisticated. Important literary critics interested in reading myths include Robert Graves,
author of *The White Goddess* and *Greek Myths,* and Northrop Frye, whose *Anatomy of Criticism* makes the case that four basic motifs corresponding to the seasons (spring–comedy, summer–romance, autumn–tragedy, and winter–satire) give
shape to all literature. Many scholars wrote extensively about myth and were
influential in their disciplines, but Joseph Campbell achieved a much broader popular following.

Campbell was the best-known mythologist of the 20th century if for no other
reason than because he was able to present his ideas on television. His six-part series in the1980s with Bill Moyers, *The Power of Myth,* reached a wide audience
eager to hear about "universal human truths" in an age of increasing social fragmentation. At first glance it might seem odd to highlight Campbell's television success here, but in terms of general awareness of myth in America today and in terms
of the argument that myth has powerful resonance even in today's modern world,
Campbell's television success is precisely to the point. His first book, *The Hero with
a Thousand Faces,* continues to be widely read, and, according to Ellwood, "George
Lucas freely acknowledges the influence of reading . . . [it] and [Campbell's] *The
Masks of God*" (1999, 127–28) on his science fiction epic, *Star Wars.* Campbell
wrote voluminously throughout his life, but the ideas he lays out in *Hero* form a core
that changed little during his career—even when criticism and discoveries in other
fields urged the necessity to revisit them.

Campbell openly acknowledged the influence of Jung and Freud on his work.
Yet he never seems quite at home with Jung's *collective* unconscious. Rather, the
American mythologist always saw myth as the story of the rugged *individual* who
realizes his true nature through heroic struggle. Archetypal symbols and universals
there may be, Campbell seems to say, but mythology is ultimately and always the
vehicle through which the individual finds a sense of identity and place in the world.
Like Jung and Frazer, Campbell sought to present *the* master theory through which
all myths could be understood. In his view, there was a single "monomyth" organizing all such narratives. Ellwood summarizes Campbell's *Hero with a Thousand
Faces* in this way:

> The basic monomyth informs us that the mythological hero, setting out from an every-
> day home, is lured or is carried away or proceeds to the threshold of adventure. He de-
> feats a shadowy presence that guards the gateway, enters a dark passageway or even
> death, meets many unfamiliar forces, some of which give him threatening "tests," some
> of which offer magical aid. At the climax of the quest he undergoes a supreme ordeal
> and gains his reward: sacred marriage or sexual union with the goddess of the world,
> reconciliation with the father, his own divinization, or a mighty gift to bring back to the
> world. He then undertakes the final work of return, in which, transformed, he reenters
> the place from whence he set out. (1999, 144)

Campbell arrived at his theory of the monomyth by synthesizing insights from
psychoanalysis, methods from 19th-century comparative mythology, and analyses
typical of literary and cultural criticism. He was *not* a member of the new wave of anthropology and folklore that searched myths for references to material, political, and
social culture. Nor did he seem particularly interested in questions of translation, of

Still from *Star Wars IV: A New Hope.* According to Campbell, the hero's quest occurs in three phases: the separation, the initiation, and the return. As the hero separates himself from his home, he often encounters a helper that guards and guides him through the trials that initiate him into the true nature of reality. When he achieves mastery, he may return home to enrich his former community.
Source: Everett Collection.

variants, or in the possible social, religious, and ritual contexts of the myths he used. Rather, Campbell promoted what he called "living mythology," a nonsectarian spiritual path through which the individual might gain a sense of spiritual and social purpose and through which society might be returned to simplicity and moral virtue.

Claude Lévi-Strauss and Structuralism

At the other end of the spectrum from Campbell's individual-centered mythology is the work of French anthropologist Claude Lévi-Strauss, whose search for "deep structure" in myth had a profound influence on anthropologists and literary critics alike. Lévi-Strauss's search for the skeletal core of myth—and the related searches for organizing principles in literature carried out most famously by Vladimir Propp, Tzetvan Todorov, and Jonathan Culler—came to be known as structuralism. The influence of structuralism on the mythologies of the 20th century would be difficult to overstate, and structuralism as a critical model can be applied far beyond the boundaries of mythology or literature. It is the search for the undergirding steel that holds up the buildings of all human artifacts and endeavors, including those of meaning-making through myth and literature.

As Robert Scholes discusses the application of these ideas to literature (and, in fact, to any written text), structuralism sought "to establish a model of the system of literature itself as the external reference for the individual works it considers" (1974, 10). As such, structuralism can be seen as a reaction against 19th-century comparatist and literary approaches to myth and classical literature, especially to their subjective, even idiosyncratic, interpretations of these stories. What Lévi-Strauss and others sought was an objective way of discussing literary meaning. By borrowing from linguistics such structural notions as syntax, grammar, phonemes, and morphemes, the French anthropologist attempted to develop a model that would describe how all myths worked—and do so in a way that any literature specialist could duplicate without resorting to his or her personal impressions and imagination. With its focus on discovering an unchanging core of patterned relations giving shape to narratives of all kinds, structuralism promised to put literary criticism and anthropological investigations of myth on the firm ground of empirical science.

A quick way into the issues that structuralism wanted to raise would be to look at the work of one of Lévi-Strauss's contemporaries, Vladimir Propp, who worked almost exclusively on the Russian folktale, attempting to distinguish between constant and variable elements in that genre. After studying more than a thousand stories, he concluded that the characters in fairy tales change but their functions within the plot do not. Propp argued that fairy tales have 31 functions. For examples, Propp's folktale structures begin with (1) the hero leaves home, (2) an interdiction is addressed to the hero, and (3) the interdiction is violated. The 31 total possible plot functions include (12) the hero is tested, interrogated, attacked, which prepares the way for his receiving either a magical agent or helper, (17) the hero is branded, (24) a false hero presents unfounded claims, (30) the villain is punished, and (31) the hero marries and ascends the throne (Scholes 1974, 63–64).

Lévi-Strauss, like Propp, gathered and analyzed as many versions of certain myths as he could find, hoping to penetrate their myriad surface elements and see into a basic grammar of meaning. Working among the natives of South America, Lévi-Strauss took inventory of the various references found in each myth. Ultimately, he determined that mythic structure reveals itself through a limited number of codes. For example, "among South American myths he [distinguished] a sociological, a culinary (or techno-economic), an acoustic, a cosmological, and an astronomical code" (Kirk 1970, 43). Lévi-Strauss further determined that these codes embodied polar opposites, or "binary oppositions." Thus, within the culinary code, as the title of one of his most famous books puts it, one finds the binary of the "raw and the cooked." Within the sociological code, one would find such binaries as married versus unmarried, family versus nonfamily, and *the* people versus the other.

Lévi-Strauss concluded that myths mediate the tension created by these always-present oppositions, whether individuals within a society are aware of it or not. Indeed, Lévi-Strauss discusses the codes and structures that manifest themselves in myths in much the same way that Freud and Jung discuss the unconscious. Whereas the psychologists described the unconscious as the hidden source from which individual consciousness arises, Lévi-Strauss viewed the structures of myth and language as the hidden bedrock upon which narratives are built. In fact, he sounds more like a metaphysician than a scientist when he claims that the deep structures of narrative exist—like Plato's ideal forms or St. John's *logos*—in a realm beyond and untouched by actual stories and storytellers. As Lévi-Strauss writes in *The Raw and the Cooked* (1964), "we cannot therefore grasp [in our analysis of myth] how men think, but how myths think themselves in men, and without their awareness" (1990, 20). In other words, people don't think myths into existence; mythic structures inherent in language do a people's thinking for them, expressing themselves when people use language. Ultimately, he reduced the codes and the patterned relations he discovered among South American Indian myths to a kind of algebra, a symbol system intended to express that which was always true of these stories, regardless of such surface details as plot, character, and setting.

Mircea Eliade's Time Machine

Mircea Eliade has been described as "the preeminent historian of religion of his time" (Ellwood 1999, 79), and his ideas about the essential connection between myth and religion remain influential among students of myth. As a young man Eliade invested himself in nationalist politics. Believing in the power of myth to give a downtrodden people the courage and vision necessary to stage a spiritually motivated political revolution, Eliade became involved with a proto-fascist group called the Legion of the Archangel Michael.

Recent criticism of Eliade's political associations has begun to erode his reputation as a mythologist to some extent. However, it is important to contextualize his sympathy with a political ideology that fused, in its early days, a Christian commitment to charity for the poor and outrage at injustice with a myth of a Romania that had a special destiny to fulfill. Like so many of the 19th- and early 20th-century mythologists who explored the connection between myth and *Volk*, Eliade looked to his people's Indo-European heritage for stories that would impart a spiritual authority to a people's revolution.

In his *Cosmos and History: The Myth of the Eternal Return; The Sacred and the Profane; Myths, Dreams, and Mysteries;* and *Myth and Reality,* Eliade demonstrates his own brand of structuralism. Space, time, and objects are perceived by the religious imagination, he argues, in binary terms, as either sacred or profane. Thus such objects as icons and religious utensils, such places as temples and special groves, and such times as religious festivals are designated as *sacred.* Only certain limited activities can properly be performed with or within them. The *profane,* on the contrary, are those things, places, and times available to people without special ceremony or ritual.

Another important binary in Eliade's mythology is the distinction he makes between "archaic" and modern man. In his view, archaic peoples are more attuned than modern, history-obsessed peoples to the sacred and express this understanding more clearly in their relationships to nature and in their myths. Eliade's mythology proposes yet another opposition—that which exists between cosmic time, or the time of origins, and human history. From his perspective, moderns live in unhappy exile from the Paradise of cosmic time in which a vital connection to the sacred is natural. Myth, for Eliade, provides moderns with a vehicle through which they can periodically return to the time of origins and thus begin their lives anew. This time-machine function resembles the myth-ritualists' view that sacred narratives facilitate the putting to death of stale, profane consciousness, restoring the participants to the virgin possibilities of creation. Thus we can see that from the perspective of religious studies—at least insofar as Eliade still represents that discipline—that myth has a religious function. Like going to confession, fasting on Yom Kippur, making animal sacrifice, or doing penance, myth permits human beings, who are continually contaminated by exposure to the profane, to wipe the slate clean and make a fresh start.

Considering 20th-Century Mythology Critically

Our overview of 20th-century mythology has so far described the lenses through which myth has been studied in the past 100 years. One could easily imagine that the history of mythology presented here has been leading up to a happy ending: at last, we come to the end of the 20th century and the curtains will part to reveal state-of-the-art mythology. After millennia of deprecating myths as child's prattle and the fevered dreams of savages, after centuries of romanticizing the simplicity of our premodern past, after decades of trying to make the square peg of literature fit into the round hole of science, we have finally gotten it right. Surely we have a mythology that fairly and objectively examines the object of its study, that is methodologically but not blindly rigorous, and that duly considers history, custom, material culture, and sociopolitical and religious institutions without turning a story into a code to be cracked or a "to-do" list. But the fact is that no such mythology exists.

None of the mythologies of the past century has had it quite right—and it is instructive to see why not. Clearly, 19th-century comparative mythology was deeply flawed in its search for irrecoverable Ur-languages and highly dubious speculations about *the* German or Italian or Indian or Jewish character. The nature, ethnological, and myth-ritual schools, like Procrustes, made theoretical beds and then stretched or lopped off evidential limbs in order to achieve a perfect fit. While we owe the comparatists and their literary descendants gratitude for the thousands of myths they collected, and while we should not deny that natural environment and ritual, for example, are an important part of mythic content, we should also learn the lesson that no universal theory "explains" myth.

And we ought to ask ourselves what is to be gained from reducing all myth to a single "pattern." If we read all myths as allegories of the seasonal cycles of fertility and infertility as, for example, Frazer and Graves did, what is to be gained? Are we content to read the story of Jesus' birth, ministry, and death as one of many instantiations of the "year spirit"? Here's death and resurrection! A seasonal pattern! Is this label enough to satisfy our desire to understand mythic meanings and functions? Similarly, are we content to read all myths, as Campbell does, as yet another version of the hero's passage from home, through trial, through apotheosis, and back home again? Surely this plot line accounts for some significant events in myth, but are we content to reduce even myths of creation, fertility, and apocalypse to the story of an individual's separation, initiation, and return? What do we say after we identify, as Eliade does, the basic alienation that exists in myth between human beings and the sacred? A one-trick pony, even when the trick is pretty good, is still a one-trick pony.

But anthropology and folklore, despite the fact that they have done mythology an inestimable service by grounding it in observation-based science, are not quite the answer either. Following Malinowski, anthropologists have, to greater and lesser degrees, illuminated the relationships among myths, religion, custom, sociopolitical behaviors, and material culture. Working within this discipline, Lévi-Strauss and Propp attempted to create a completely objective typology of narrative functions through which all myths could be analyzed. To some degree, particularly in Propp's work on the morphology of the folktale, structuralism succeeded. Any student of myth can examine any number of fairy tales using Propp's model and will find that the Russian folklorist's functions are indeed present and in the described order.

Yet, for all that anthropologists and folklorists have contributed to the study of myth, their disciplined focus on the function of myths within a nexus of material, social, political, and economic phenomena has come at a considerable cost. Such concerns, as important as they are, are only partial, and they ignore the pleasures and power of narrative per se for us here and now as well as for the myth tellers and their more immediate audiences. And structuralist anthropology does not and really cannot answer one of the most important questions: So what? Once we have learned Propp's 31 elements of the folk tale, the various codes in creation myths, and the binary oppositions Lévi-Strauss claims they suggest, what do we really have? From our point of view as professors of English, anthropology's tight focus on the functionality of and within myth diverts attention away from the fundamental fact that myths are stories. We need only think of Lévi-Strauss's algebra of mythic functions or Malinowski's search for references to food, clothing, shelter, and political relationships in the myths of the Trobriand islanders to realize that something vital is lost when myth is cannibalized for its references to the "real" world. We can ask anthropologists, as we asked literary theorists, whether reducing myths to lists of material culture items or to a set of narrative functions isn't as distorting as reducing all myths to allegories of nature, the year spirit, or the hero's quest.

While anthropology and folklore focused on myth's functions and 19th- and early 20th-century literary criticism preoccupied itself largely with myth's contents, psychological approaches have contemplated those dimensions of myth and suggested a theory of psychic origins as well. Psychological approaches to myth, therefore, have been generally more holistic than others. After all, whatever else can be said about them, myths proceed from the human mind if for no other reason than the mind needs to understand "the self" in relation to the larger cosmos. For this reason, many in the latter half of the 20th century assumed that Freud's or Jung's views about myth are fundamentally sound. And the psychological approach to myth has been powerfully suggestive. Jung's archetypes, for example, offer a potent interpretation of widely distributed symbols, images, and plot lines. There's a satisfying symmetry to the notion that each individual contains and balances oppositions such as elder and child, male and female, sinner and saint. Innumerable mythic characters embody these and other human qualities. And although Freud overstates his case when he claims that myths are *nothing other* than the working out of the complex interrelationships among identity, sexuality, and family relationships, a great many myths *do* feature incest, rape, infanticide, and parricide. Myths are about relationships among the irrational, the rational, and the individual's responsibility to society, or, in Freud's terms, among the id, the ego, and the superego.

However, a principal weakness of literary, psychological, and structuralist approaches is that they are ahistorical; they don't consider the specific material and social conditions that shape myth. Indeed, most of the major mythologists of the 20th century cared little for the cultural specifics of how living myths function in the day-to-day lives of the people who told them. They cared little for cultural distinctions that might explain why one version of a myth differs from another; and, in the cases of Jung, Campbell, and Eliade, they seemed interested in myth only as far as familiarity with its presumed "core" might provide the modern individual with a return to Paradise lost—to a sense of self closely connected to the soil and fully at home in a homogeneous sociopolitical order. Thus, while the mythologies of the early- and mid-20th century demonstrated considerable genius, their lack of concern for historical and cultural context and their insistence on reading myths through analytical schema that dispensed with all but a story's most rudimentary plot structure perpetuated most of the significant shortcomings of their 18th- and 19th-century predecessors. Now, at the beginning of the 21st century, awareness of these shortcomings has bred approaches to myth that insist on the importance of context, particularly where gender, cultural norms, and the specifics of the performance events are concerned. Moreover, much like this chapter, modern scholarship has increasingly focused on mythology rather than on myth itself. We conclude with a brief survey of several of the most recent and important contributions to the study of myth and consider, even more briefly, what uses these new ideas might have for the classroom.

MYTHOLOGY TODAY

William Doty's "Toolkit"

Doty's *Mythography* concludes with a number of appendixes for "furbishing the creative mythographer's toolkit." Among these tools are "questions to address to mythic texts." Embedded in these questions is a comprehensive methodology that urges students of myth not to choose a single approach to myth but to use as many of the questions and concerns of various mythological schools as possible. Doty's questions arise from five central concerns: (1) the social, (2) the psychological, (3) the literary, textual, and performative, (4) the structural, and (5) the political (2000, 466–67). As the term "mythographer's toolkit" implies, Doty's approach to the subject is profoundly practical. Above all he is concerned with methodology and principles of analysis, and he has distilled the concerns of many fields, including sociology, anthropology, psychology, and literary criticism into a systematic series of exploratory questions and research procedures that are well within reach of most non-specialists. The questions that Doty poses for each of the five areas of concern just mentioned are particularly congenial to the kinds of thinking, discussion, and research performed in the classroom.

Bruce Lincoln's Ideological Narratives

As suggestive as Doty's questions are, other approaches to myth have been advocated recently. Lincoln, whose *Theorizing Myth* is an important contribution to the current study of myth, would define myth and mythology as "ideology in narrative form" because, as he says, all human communication is "interested, perspectival, and partial and . . . its ideological dimensions must be acknowledged, ferreted out where necessary, and critically cross-examined" (1999, 207, 208).

Ultimately, Lincoln advocates making modern mythology the study of previous mythologies. This scholarly endeavor would revolve around "excavating the texts within which that discourse [mythology] took shape and continues to thrive . . . [explicating] their content by placing them in their proper contexts, establishing the connections among them, probing their ideological and other dimensions, explicit and subtextual" (1999, 216). How students should approach myths other than those told by scholars about myth Lincoln doesn't say—though it seems plausible that his approach would be approximately the same for myth as for mythology.

Wendy Doniger's Telescopes and Microscopes

Wendy Doniger, in her *The Implied Spider: Politics and Theology in Myth,* argues for an updated and recalibrated version of the kind of comparative mythology that the Grimm brothers and Sir James Frazer practiced. Among the ways Doniger suggests improving the comparative mythology of the 19th century is, "whenever possible . . . to note the context: who is telling the story and why"; and, she argues, that context could also include—indeed would have to include—"other myths, other related ideas, as Lévi-Strauss argued long ago" (1998, 44, 45). Doniger advocates stripping individual myths to their "naked" narrative outlines—to symbols, themes, and similarities in plot—in order to manage the amount of detail that the comparatist will have to analyze. Unlike Lévi-Strauss, Doniger wouldn't reduce myth to a level where all myths look alike. Context would still matter. Accordingly, she says, we could include in our comparison the contexts of myths. Attention to the sociopolitical and performative contexts in which myths occur would, in Doniger's method, "take account of differences between men and women as storytellers, and also between rich and poor, dominant and oppressed" (46). Doniger would also have students of myth learn how to switch back and forth between the "microscope" of a single telling to the "telescope" of the world's numerous variations on a mythological theme.

Thus Doniger's comparative mythology respects the integrity of a single myth as a unique story and, at the same time, enriches our understanding of that story through comparisons with other stories with similar plots, characters, and symbolic imagery as well as through comparisons with other mythic stories with similar contexts of telling. For one example of this last sense of comparison, we might be enriched by considering myths specifically *told by* women even as we would likely be rewarded by comparing myths with women or goddesses as central characters.

Robert Ellwood's "Real Myths"

Robert Ellwood, who, like Lincoln, was one of Eliade's students at the University of Chicago in the 1960s, suggests yet another approach in *The Politics of Myth: A Study of C. G. Jung, Mircea Eliade, and Joseph Campbell* (1999). Ellwood argues that what we call "myth" does not exist. Or, to put it more precisely, modern students of myth do not study *mythos,* in Hesiod's sense of a poet "breathing" the divinely inspired utterance. Rather, what we call myth "is always received from an already distant past, literary (even if only oral literature), hence a step away from primal simplicity" (174). This is an important point for Ellwood and other modern mythologists because "official" myths like *The Iliad* and *Odyssey, The Theogony*—or the Bhagavad Gita or the Bible—"are inevitably reconstructions from snatches of folklore and legend, artistically put together with an eye for drama and meaning" (175). But "real" myths are, like one's own dreams, "so fresh they are not yet recognized as 'myth' or 'scripture,' [and] are fragmentary, imagistic rather than verbal, emergent, capable of forming many different stories at once" (175).

What students of myth study in mythology classes, then, are usually the *literary* product of many hands over the course of many generations. Even if a name like Homer or Hesiod gets attached to myths when they finally achieve their final form, they begin as folktales and campfire stories, as religious precepts, images, and rituals, as mystical revelations, and as entertaining fictional and speculative explorations of how the cosmos came into being and continues to operate. Over the generations, in the hands of gifted storytellers, a narrative capable of combining and artistically organizing these fragments and themes emerges. By the time a society officially authorizes a story as scripture or myth, the events it describes have slipped so far into the past that they can be believed—anything could have happened in the beginning—or disbelieved. Myth represents human truths in a variety of ways, few if any of which depend on mere plausibility of character or event. "To put it another way," as Ellwood says, "myth is really a meaning category on the part of hearers, not intrinsic in any story in its own right. Myth in this sense is itself a myth" (1999, 175).

READING MYTHOLOGY

Ellwood, like Lincoln, doesn't explicitly articulate a methodology by which students can analyze myths for themselves, but his suggestion that myths, like those contained in this book, come down to us in *literary* form suggests a well-established methodology: close reading and a consideration of how literary conventions inform and enable various levels of meaning.

Doty, when speaking of Müller's and Frazer's euhemerism, remarked that not only these two but "many other 19th-century [and 20th-century] scholars regarded myth almost exclusively as *a problem* for modern rationality" (2000, 11). Müller and Frazer, the myth-ritualists, the sociofunctionalist anthropologists, and the psychoanalysts have all attempted to "solve" the problem of the mythic irrational and to articulate in authoritative terms what myths "really" mean. Their efforts were not entirely wasted; they were simply too one-dimensional, too unable to engage with myth in a holistic sense. Our book takes the view that myths are *not* codes to be cracked or naive and mistaken perceptions that must be corrected. Rather, myths are literary truths told about the mysteries and necessities that always have and always will condition the human experience. These truths, these *mythoi,* have made sophisticated use of symbolic imagery and narrative strategy, have created unforgettable characters that continue to typify for us abstract realities such as love, bravery, wisdom, and treachery, and have enacted as compellingly as any modern novel the humor and horror, the ecstasy and anguish, and the fear and hope of the human drama.

One of the great strengths of the literary approach to myth is that one needn't dispense with the methods, concerns, and insights developed through other mythologies in order to pay appropriate attention to such features of narrative as plot, point of view, characterization, setting, symbols, and theme. Indeed, our understanding and enjoyment of myths is enhanced if, as Doty would say, we furnish our mythographer's toolkit with as many tools as possible. For example, by using such structural approaches as those developed by Campbell, Lévi-Strauss, and Propp we can sharpen our focus on such basic plotting issues as the events that constitute the rising action of the story, the precise moment at which the turning point is reached, and the events of the falling action that resolve the conflict or tension that gives the story its narrative energy. Yet, literary analysis offers students of myth more than charts and formulas because it also equips us with a conceptual vocabulary and specific language to understand and describe how the arrangement of a story's action and its setting affect our emotions and intellects. How, for example, are we affected by the opening lines that introduce the action in the Maya's *Popul Vu*?

> Here follow the first words, the first eloquence: There is not yet one person, one animal, bird, fish, crab, tree, rock, hollow, canyon, meadow, forest. Only the sky alone is there; the face of the earth is not clear. Only the sea alone is pooled under all the sky; there is nothing whatever gathered together. It is at rest; not a single thing stirs. It is held back, kept at rest under the sky. Whatever there is that might be is simply not there: only the pooled water, only the calm sea, only it alone is pooled (see Chapter 2, page 93).

How do we feel about the difficulty the narrator seems to have expressing a state of existence that is simultaneously nothing and yet contains a primordial sea with sleeping gods shining in its depths? What questions does this paragraph raise for us? What expectations are created and what words and phrases create them? Literary analysis of such details invites us to consider the personal connections we develop to a story and encourages us to reflect upon how a gifted storyteller (or generations of gifted storytellers) can utilize and refine language to create thought-shaping, life-defining images, ideas, and feelings within their hearers and/or readers.

Similarly, consulting the methods and insights of the comparative and psychological approaches to myth can increase our sensitivity to the universality of certain character types and to a deeper appreciation of the motives, values, and actions of the various protagonists and antagonists that people the world's sacred narratives. Through close reading of myth, we can make the crucial distinction between characterization and the more ambiguous notion of character. The characterization of

Heracles (Hercules in Latin), for example, utilizes certain stock phrases that emphasize his strength, resilience, and resourcefulness. While pinpointing precisely the language through which storytellers have depicted characters has rewards, it can be even more rewarding to articulate and debate the psychological make-up of this Greek hero's character. For instance, does Heracles's alienation from his divine father, with all the rejection and confusion that such a separation implies, create in him the determination necessary to accomplish his famous twelve labors? Are Heracles's many mighty deeds motivated by an obsessive need to prove his worth to a distant father whose fame and influence far outmatch his own? While these questions are clearly speculative and center upon a fictional entity, they nevertheless take us to the heart of literature's mysterious power over us. How fascinating that people, places, and things that may never have had a literal existence off the page, can nevertheless live in our minds as vividly as any of our flesh-and-blood acquaintances!

Likewise, we can borrow from early anthropology its insights and raw data about the prevalence of certain themes in myth. Preoccupations with such matters as the seasons, fertility, and disastrous consequences of intimate union between gods and mortals abound in myth and some anthropological studies supply us with a vast wealth of cases in point. We can also follow the lead of more recent anthropological study and generate lists of material culture items, social strata, customs, and technologies and our understanding of some of myth's most obscure references can be illuminated by this discipline's focus on the ritual and performance contexts as well as the socio-political functions of myth in living cultures.

Literary analysis, however, urges us also to consider how a narrative's uses of various material goods, social arrangements, and technologies work as symbols and icons. Returning to the *Popul Vu,* we notice that the creation of human beings is the culmination of four successive attempts, a creative process that is successful only after the correct material—maize—is used. While the scientist might view this reference as evidence that the Maya cultivated corn from earliest times, making similar observations about the tortilla griddles, domesticated dogs and turkeys, pots and grinding implements the story also mentions, the literary critic would likely emphasize the symbolic value of corn to the story. The gods' spoken word vibrating in the air, mud, and wood all prove inadequate materials for producing beings capable of intelligible speech and rational thought. However, the premier product of settled living and scientific observations about soil conditions, seeding, and the seasons is the perfect medium.

> And then the yellow corn and white corn were ground, and Xmucane [Grandmother of Light] did the grinding nine times. Corn was used, along with the water she rinsed her hands with, for the creation of grease; it became human fat when it was worked by the Bearer, Begetter, Sovereign Plumed Serpent, as they are called. After that, they put it into words: the making, the modeling of our first mother-father, with yellow corn, white corn alone for the flesh, food alone for the human legs and arms, for our first fathers, the four human works. It was staples alone that made up their flesh (see Chapter 2, page 98).

When the narrator places maize at the pivotal moment in the story when the gods' at last perfect their creation, it suggests not only were human beings the pinnacle of the creation (the fourth time is the charm!) but that the Maya viewed themselves as literal children of the corn. While such archaeological evidence as carvings of corn stalks, farming implements, and the ruins of granaries and farms are sufficient to indicate that the mastery of agrarian technology supplied the nourishment and wealth necessary to build and sustain the Maya empire, those attending to the symbolic value of corn in their mythic charter know the degree to which the Maya themselves were aware of this fact.

Like an onion, a myth has many layers. Thus we urge students of myth to familiarize themselves with the methods and assumptions of each mythology and to combine them with the methods and assumptions of literary study. Euhemerism permits us to remove one layer of the myth-onion, the comparative method another, the structuralist and functionalist approaches further layers, and psychological and literary analyses still others. We should resign ourselves to the fact that, after all our efforts, we will find at the core, quite literally, no-thing, no *single* all-encompassing explanation of myth. But, those who exert the disciplined effort to peel away and examine the social, political, historical, psychological, cultural, functional, and literary layers of the myth-onion will certainly become permeated with its distinct essence. Given the fascinating subject we study, that is reward enough.

WORKS CITED AND SUGGESTIONS FOR FURTHER READING

Belin, Isaiah. *Vico and Herder: Two Studies in the History of Ideas.* New York: Viking, 1976.

Bernal, Martin. *Black Athena: The Afroasiatic Roots of Classical Civilization.* Vol. 1: *The Fabrication of Ancient Greece, 1785–1985.* New Brunswick, NJ: Rutgers University Press, 1987.

Boas, Franz. *Anthropology and Modern Life.* 1928; New York: Dover, 1986.

Bolen, Jean Shinoda. *Goddesses in Every Woman.* New York: Harper & Row, 1985.

Campbell, Joseph. *The Hero with a Thousand Faces.* 1949; Bollingen Series 17. Princeton, NJ: Princeton University Press, 1972.

———. *The Masks of God.* Vol. 1: *Primitive Mythology.* New York: Viking, 1959; vol. 2: *Oriental Mythology.* New York: Viking, 1962; vol. 3: *Occidental Mythology.* New York: Viking, 1964; vol. 4: *Creative Mythology.* New York: Viking, 1968.

———. *Myths to Live By.* New York: Viking, 1972.

Campbell, Joseph, with Bill Moyers. *The Power of Myth.* New York: Doubleday, 1985.

Cornford, F. M. *From Religion to Philosophy.* New York: Longmans, Green, 1912.

Culler, Jonathan. *Structuralist Poetics: Structuralism, Linguistics, and the Study of Literature.* 1975; Ithaca, NY: Cornell University Press, 1976.

Detienne, Marcel. *The Creation of Mythology.* Trans. Margaret Cook. Chicago: University of Chicago Press, 1986.

Doniger, Wendy. *The Implied Spider: Politics and Theology in Myth.* New York: Columbia University Press, 1998.

Doty, William G. *Mythography: The Study of Myths and Rituals.* 2nd ed. Tuscaloosa: University of Alabama Press, 2000.

Durkheim, Emile, and Marcel Mauss. *Primitive Classification.* Trans. Rodney Needham. Chicago: University of Chicago Press, 1963.

Eliade, Mircea. *Cosmos and History: The Myth of the Eternal Return.* New York: Garland, 1985.

———. *Myths, Dreams, and Mysteries.* New York: Harper & Row, 1975.

———. *Myth and Reality.* New York: Harper & Row, 1975.

———. *Patterns in Comparative Religion.* New York: New American Library, 1974.

———. *The Sacred and the Profane.* Magnolia, MA: Peter Smith, 1983.

Ellwood, Robert. *The Politics of Myth: A Study of C. G. Jung, Mircea Eliade, and Joseph Campbell.* Issues in the Study of Religion Series. Albany: State University of New York Press, 1999.

Feldman, Burton, and Robert D. Richardson, eds. *The Rise of Modern Mythology 1600–1860.* Bloomington: Indiana University Press, 1972.

Feuerbach, Ludwig. *The Essence of Christianity.* Trans. George Eliot. Amherst, NY: Prometheus, 1989.

Fontenrose, Joseph. *The Ritual Theory of Myth.* Berkeley: University of California Press, 1971.

Frazer, James George. *The Golden Bough.* Abridged ed. London: Macmillan, 1922.

Freud, Sigmund. *The Standard Edition of the Complete Psychological Works of Sigmund Freud.* Vol. 9. London: Hogarth, 1953–1966.

———. *The Interpretation of Dreams.* London, 1900.

———. *Totem and Taboo.* New York, 1918.

Frye, Northrup. *The Anatomy of Criticism: Four Essays.* 1957; Princeton, NJ: Princeton University Press, 2000.

Gaster, Theodor. *Myth, Legend, and Custom in the Old Testament: A Comparative Study with Chapters from Sir James George Frazer's "Folklore in the Old Testament."* 1969; Gloucester, MA: Peter Smith, 1981.

———. *Thespis: Myth, Ritual, and Drama in the Ancient Near East.* 1961; New York: Gordian, 1975.

Graves, Robert. *Greek Myths.* 2 vols. 1955; Harmondsworth, England: Penguin, 1990.

———. *The White Goddess: A Historical Grammar of Poetical Myth.* 1948; New York: Octagon, 1976.

Greenway, John, and Melville Jacobs. *The Anthropologist Looks at Myth.* Austin: University of Texas Press, 1966.

Hamilton, Edith. *Mythology.* New York: New American Library, 1988.

Harrison, Jane. *Themis: A Study of the Social Origins of Greek Religion.* 2nd ed. 1927; Gloucester, MA: Peter Smith, 1974.

Hesiod. *Theogony: Works and Days: Shield.* Ed. Apostolos N. Athanassakis. Baltimore: Johns Hopkins University Press, 1983.

Hooke, Samuel Henry, ed. *Myth and Ritual: Essays on the Myth and Ritual of the Hebrews in Relation to the Culture Pattern of the Ancient East.* London: Oxford University Press, 1933.

———. *Myth, Ritual, and Kingship: Essays on the Theory and Practice of Kings in the Ancient Near East and Israel.* Oxford: Clarendon, 1960.

Hyman, Stanley Edgar. *The Armed Vision.* New York: Knopf, 1948.

Jones, William. *The Works of Sir William Jones.* 2 vols. 1807; New York: Garland, 1984.

Jung, Carl Gustav. *The Archetypes and the Collective Unconscious.* 1959; Bollingen Series 20. Princeton, NJ: Princeton University Press, 1980.

———. *Man and His Symbols.* 1964; New York: Doubleday, 1988.

Kirk, Geoffrey Stephen. *Myth: Its Meaning in Functions in Ancient and Other Cultures.* Berkeley: University of California Press, 1970.

Lang, Andrew. *Custom and Myth.* 1885; New York: AMS Press, 1968.

Leeming, David Adams. *Mythology.* New York: Newsweek Books, 1976.

———. *The World of Myth.* New York: Oxford University Press, 1992.

Lévi-Strauss, Claude. *Myth and Meaning.* New York: Schocken/Pantheon, 1979.

———. *The Naked Man.* Trans. John and Doreen Weightman. 1981; Chicago: University of Chicago Press, 1990.

———. *The Raw and the Cooked.* Trans. John and Doreen Weightman. Chicago: University of Chicago Press, 1990.

Lévy-Bruhl, Lucien. *Primitive Mentality.* Trans. Lilian A. Clare. London: George Allen and Unwin, 1922.

Lincoln, Bruce. *Theorizing Myth: Narrative, Ideology, and Scholarship.* Chicago: University of Chicago Press, 1999.

Littleton, Scott C. *The New Comparative Mythology.* 3rd ed. Berkeley: University of California Press, 1982.

Macpherson, James. *Fingal: An Ancient Epic Poem in Six Books; Together with Several Other Poems, Composed by Ossian the Son of Fingal.* Facsimile of the 1792 edition. New York: Woodstock Books, 1996.

———. *Fragments of Antient Poetry Collected in the Highlands of Scotland and Translated from the Gaelic or Erse Language.* Facsimile of the 1760 ed. Edinburgh: James Thin, 1970.

Malinowski, Bronislaw. *Myth in Primitive Psychology.* 1926; Westport, CT: Negro Universities Press, 1971.

Mascetti, Manuela Dunn. *The Song of Eve: Mythology and Symbols of the Goddess.* New York: Simon & Schuster, 1990.

Moore, Robert, and Douglas Gillette. *King, Warrior, Magician, Lover: Rediscovering the Archetypes of the Mature Masculine.* San Francisco: Harper, 1990.

Müller, Friedrich Max. *Comparative Mythology.* 1909; New York: Arno, 1977.

Neumann, Erich. *The Great Mother: An Analysis of the Archetype.* Bollingen Series 47. Princeton, NJ: Princeton University Press, 1991.

Nietzche, Friedrich. *Birth of Tragedy; and On the Genealogy of Morals.* Trans. Francis Golffing. 1956; New York: Anchor, 1990.

Olender, Maurice. *The Languages of Paradise: Race, Religion, and Philology in the Nineteenth Century.* Trans. Arthur Goldhammer. Cambridge, MA: Harvard University Press, 1992.

Poliakov, Léon. *The Aryan Myth: A History of Racist and Nationalist Ideas in Europe.* Trans. Edmund Howard. New York: Basic Books, 1974.

Propp, Vladimir. *Morphology of the Folktale.* Trans. Laurence Scott. 1968; Austin: University of Texas Press, 1990.

Raglan, Lord. *The Hero: A Study in Tradition, Myth, and Drama.* 1936; Westport, CT: Greenwood, 1975.

Scholes, Robert. *Structuralism in Literature: An Introduction.* New Haven, CT: Yale University Press, 1974.

Segal, Robert A. *Theories of Myth: From Ancient Israel and Greece to Freud, Jung, Campbell, and Lévi-Strauss.* Philosophy, Religious Studies, and Myth Series. Vol. 3. New York: Garland, 1996.

————. *Theorizing About Myth.* Amherst: University of Massachusetts Press, 1999.

Strenski, Ivan. *Four Theories of Myth in Twentieth-Century History: Cassirer, Eliade, Lévi-Strauss, and Malinowski.* Iowa City: University of Iowa Press, 1987.

Todorov, Tsetvan. *The Fantastic: A Structural Approach to a Literary Genre.* Trans. Richard Howard. Cleveland, OH: Case Western Reserve University Press, 1973.

Tylor, Edward. *Primitive Culture.* New York: Harper Torchbooks, 1958.

Veyne, Paul. *Did the Greeks Believe in Their Myths?* Trans. Paula Wissing. Chicago: University of Chicago Press, 1988.

Vico, Giambattista. *The New Science of Giambattista Vico.* Trans. Thomas Goddard Bergin and Max Harold Fisch. Ithaca, NY: Cornell University Press, 1968.

Wagner, Richard. *The Art-Work of the Future and Other Works.* Trans. W. Ashton Ellis. Lincoln: University of Nebraska Press, 1993.

Weiner, Marc. *Richard Wagner and the Anti-Semitic Imagination.* Lincoln: University of Nebraska Press, 1995.

CHAPTER 2

Creation Myths

THE BIRTH OF ORDER

Creation myths tell a special kind of story called a *cosmogony,* a word deriving from Greek that means, literally, "the birth of order." Order, in this case, refers to the organizing principles of the physical universe and the basic sociopolitical, cultural, and spiritual facts of existence that affect human beings. Many have observed that creation myths are, more or less, birth narratives. Frequently, cosmogonic myths pick up the action at a point just before the divine touch creates time and space. Before this critical moment, though there are often gods or a god preceding the world or the physical universe, the only *thing* that exists is the infinite potential of chaos. (Or should we say the chaos of infinite potential?) Not unlike the Genesis account of creation, most of the world's creation myths begin with an eternal being sleeping within or hovering in contemplation above the infinite abyss of a primeval sea. These waters represent the "chaos" of a world without physical form, where no height, no depth, no breadth, no time, and no created beings exist. All is quiet; everything rests in a state of infinite potential. At the decisive moment, potential universes give way to the one in which we actually live.

CLASSIFYING COSMOGONIC MYTHS

In Chapter 1 we noted that Mircea Eliade saw all myths as "creation stories" in the sense that people, through recitation of such stories on designated occasions, could reconnect to "primordial time, the fabled time of beginnings" (1975, 5), a notion very like that of the Australian aboriginal concept of "dreaming" and its relationship to the primordial yet ongoing "Dreamtime" (see Chapter 6, 390–91). As Eliade says, "myth tells how, through the deeds of Supernatural Beings, a reality came into existence, be it the whole of reality, the Cosmos, or only a fragment of reality—an island, a species of plant, a particular kind of human behavior, an institution. Myth, then, is always an account of 'creation'; it relates how something was produced, began to *be*" (5–6). Still, Eliade does distinguish cosmogonic stories from other types of myth, and, in *From Primitives to Zen: A Thematic Source Book of the History of*

Religions, he classifies these specialized myths into four basic types: (1) creation *ex nihilo,* in which a divinity creates the cosmos by thought, word, dream, or from bodily effluents; (2) earth-diver creation, in which a divinity sends waterfowl or amphibious animals or itself dives to the bottom of a primordial ocean to bring up mud or sand from which the world grows; (3) creation by dividing a primordial unity like earth and sky, form from Chaos, or the cracking open of a "Cosmic Egg"; and (4) creation by dismemberment of a primordial Being, like the sea monsters Yam or Tiamat in ancient Near Eastern texts, the Giant, Ymir, in the Eddas, or the various Corn mothers of the Americas. Charles H. Long, one of Eliade's students, in *Alpha: The Myths of Creation,* introduced a fifth classification, emergence myths, in which a people travels through a series of chambers or worlds until it emerges into this one.

Others have provided alternative classification schemes. Van Over, for example, suggests, rather than a typology of myth, six "basic themes":

> (1) The idea of a primeval abyss (which is sometimes simply space, but often is an infinite watery deep) . . . (2) The originating god (or gods) is frequently awakened or eternally existing in this abyss . . . (3) . . . the originating god broods over the water; (4) Another common theme is the cosmic egg or embryo . . . (5) Life [is] also created through sound, or a sacred word spoken by the original god . . . [and] (6) A peculiar theme, but quite common, is the creation of life from the corpse or parts of the primeval god's body. (1984, 10)

Maclagan suggests, in *Creation Myths: Man's Introduction to the World,* that cosmogonic narratives are patterned after the following themes: (1) inner and outer; (2) horizontal and vertical; (3) something from nothing; (4) the conjugation of opposites; (5) world order and the order of worlds; (6) descent and ascent; (7) earth body and sacrifice; and (8) death, time, and the elements. In these various schemes, we see areas of overlap, which suggests that a finite number of motifs are at work in creation myths.

Weigle's *Creation and Procreation: Feminist Reflections on Mythologies of Cosmogony and Parturition* presents the most nuanced typology of creation myths. Building upon Eliade and Long, as well as von Franz's *Patterns of Creativity Mirrored in Creation Myths* and Rooth's journal article "Creation Myths of the North American Indians," Weigle constructs a nine-part typology: (1) accretion or conjunction; (2) secretion; (3) sacrifice; (4) division or conjugation; (5) earth-diver; (6) emergence; (7) two creators; (8) *deus faber;* and (9) *ex nihilo.* We will discuss these classifications in detail shortly, but first we wish to emphasize Weigle's point that "ethnocentrism and androcentrism bias" our understanding of such classifications. Readers from Western cultures tend to rank "metaphysical or spiritual" cosmogonies like the account of Elohim-God speaking the world into existence in Genesis higher than "physical, natural, or elemental accounts of creation by accretion, excretion, copulation, division, dismemberment, or parturition" (1989, 6–7). If, however, we are self-conscious about our culture's assumptions about what is "normal," we see that at least as many cosmogonic myths have presented creation as part of a natural—even accidental—process as have conceived it as an exercise of divine and creative will. That is, many creation myths depict the birth of the cosmic order as an organic, natural, and/or evolutionary process rather than as an engineering project or the act of a master magician. Ranking one kind of myth as lower or more primitive and our own myths as higher or more cultured—as indeed all major mythologists of the past two centuries have done—derives from, as we showed in the first chapter, a racial or cultural bias. And, as Weigle would add, a pervasive sexist bias against the feminine and its associations with Nature and the body only compounds the problem we have in reading (or hearing) cosmogonic stories on their own terms. To study myth effectively, we need to free ourselves *as much as possible* from the prejudices we inherit from our cultural surroundings.

TYPES OF CREATION MYTH

Accretion or Conjunction Stories

Stories of this first type depict the birth of order as resulting from the mingling or layering of the primal elements (e.g., earth, wind, fire, and water). As Weigle describes it, myths of accretion or conjunction feature the "mingling of waters or fire and frost, the cosmic mountain rising from the sea, [and/or] random or accidental joining of elements" (1989, 6). Thus, when the warm breath of equatorial Muspell, mentioned at the beginning of the Edda, meets the hoarfrost of arctic Nieflheim, ice melts and the resulting water drops come to life, creating the evil giant Ymir. As the giant sleeps, sweat from his armpits creates the first man and woman. A Tibetan creation myth, for another example, announces that "In the beginning was voidness, a vast emptiness without cause, without end." Over time and also without cause, a gentle wind began to stir; after uncountable years, the wind grew thick and heavy, forming the mighty double thunderbolt scepter, Dorje Gyatram. The double thunderbolt, in turn, created clouds, which in their turn created a rain which fell for eons until the primeval ocean, Gyatso, was formed. Then, after everything became as still and peaceful as a mirror's reflection, the winds stirred again, roiling Gyatso until the earth-mountain heaved forth, like so much butter in a vast churn. Thus the mingling of air and water and then air, water, and the fire of the thunderbolt led to the creation of the cosmos. In a similarly "causeless" fashion, human beings arise and history begins at Sumeru, the central peak of the earth-mountain.

Into this category we add accounts of such "accidents" as that recounted by various Eskimo tribes of the trickster Father Raven—Tulungersaq—who, according to an Apatac "telling," is a "holy life power" crouching in the primordial darkness who suddenly awakens and begins to move about. Eventually, Father Raven plants the world's first vegetation. One day, to his great surprise, the first man pushes his way out of a pea pod and human history begins. Indeed, trickster gods like Raven frequently lay their hands upon primeval matter intending one thing and producing another. "There is a telling," begins a Coyote tale from America's desert Southwest, of how Coyote accidentally put the stars in heaven when he shook open a sacred pouch in search of treasure. This theme may also be found among a number of tales from peoples ranging from Central Asia to Central Europe, including the ancient Siberians, Voguls, and Rumanians. In Vogul and Rumanian tradition, for example, Satan unwittingly speeds God's creation of Earth when he lays his claws upon it in an effort to destroy it. Accretion and conjunction stories, then, demonstrate the creative potency of primal matter. Any action, whether that of wind or wave, or the earliest stirrings of a god or devil, unleashes the productive power sleeping in the primordial deep.

Secretion Stories

Cosmogonic myths following this narrative pattern will depict the cosmos as resulting from such divine emissions as "vomit, sweat, urination, defecation, masturbation, web-spinning, [and] parthenogenesis" (Weigle 1989, 6). It is interesting to note that secretion myths usually account for the creation of human or divine beings rather than for the propagation of the material cosmos. This is not to say that the four elements, landforms, heavenly bodies, and oceans that arise are *never* formed from these bodily emissions. They are, for example, when Ku'urkil, the Chuckchee's "self-formed" Father Raven, defecates and urinates, thus creating the earth and various bodies of water. But these instances are less common. Rather, divine secretions tend to create living, conscious beings who resemble the primeval creator intellectually and spiritually. For example, the Pyramid Texts of ancient Heliopolis tell of how Aten (elsewhere Atem) emerges from the primordial waters of Nun and begins to masturbate, ejaculating Shu and Tefnut. (Other versions of this myth have Aten spitting, and thus expectorating Shu and Tefnut.) The latter deities beget Geb

Sandro Botticelli's "The Birth of Venus." Tempura on canvas. Differing cultures have differing mores. Botticelli's Christianized audience would have found shocking the violent origins and frank sexuality of the classical period's Aphrodite/Venus. Thus his painting makes no reference to the violent act that gave her birth, and not only is Venus depicted as serene and modest, but a nymph waits to cover her nakedness as soon as she steps to shore.
Source: © Erich Lessing/Art Resource, NY.

(earth-father) and Nut (sky-mother) from whom all other life—and many of the most important Egyptian gods—emanate. Those familiar with classical myths will remember that Aphrodite is born when Zeus emasculates his father, Kronos, and several drops of blood from the severed genitals fall upon Ocean. Since she is the goddess of sexual attraction, Aphrodite's emergence from the blood-tinged foam metaphorically signifies the beginning of generative life on earth. Like Egyptian creation stories, the Greek *Theogony* places very little emphasis on human creation. People and the earth's flora and fauna seem to appear as a natural result of the creation of heaven and earth.

Mesopotamian traditions, on the other hand, do emphasize human creation. Typically, after due attention is paid to the creation of the heavens and the earth, the gods take counsel and determine that this great work isn't quite complete without human beings to care for it. In the poem *Attrahasis,* the story begins with the gods completing the work of creation, working together in a fashion that resembles Sumerian and Babylonian human societies in many respects. The great gods Anu, Enlil, and Enki oversee a vast "public works" project that includes digging the Tigris and Euphrates rivers. For 40 years, the lesser gods toil like day-laborers in the desert heat until they become so fed up that they form the equivalent of a labor union and demand that Enlil relieve them of their heavy "labor basket." The ever-crafty Ea/Enki has a plan: have the birth goddess Nintu create *lullu,* the first human being, who can then take over the gods' heavy labor. To accomplish this task, one of the gods, We-ila, is killed and Nintu mixes his blood, body, and "rationality" with clay and directs the Annunaki and Igigi (the great gods) to spit upon the mixture. This they do, and, through a process analogous to human gestation, Nintu waits nine months for this first man, Attrahasis, to awaken. He and his descendants flourish and assume their roles as the gods' temple servants and field hands.

Sacrifice Stories

The story of Attrahasis also contains elements of Weigle's third category because a god is sacrificed in order for the creative work to succeed. In some cosmogonies, the creator god sacrifices himself or herself or someone else to complete the work of creation. Thus, in one Chinese myth, when the cosmic egg shatters and the creator-giant Pan-Ku emerges, he grows continually for 18,000 years. During these years, by stretching his ever-growing body, he separates the lighter and brighter yin elements from the heavier and darker yang elements (i.e., he separates heaven from earth). When the universe is sufficiently expanded, Pan-Ku dies, his skull becoming the dome of the sky, his flesh becoming the soil, his bones becoming rocks and mountains, and his hair becoming vegetation. Thus his sacrifice makes life on earth possible; but, the story concludes, because the creator dies in his act of creation, people know unhappiness during their lives.

In parallel Aztec and Mayan tales, the sun and moon are created when both gods and men pay the ultimate price. In a Nahuatl version of the story, the gods, who are aware that the time of the sun's dawning and the moon's rising is near, take counsel among themselves and determine that the creation of these heavenly bodies can be accomplished only by two of their number throwing themselves on the great flaming hearth, Teotexcalli. Among the company of the gods, only Tecuciztecatl is willing to cast himself into the flames. The other gods are too afraid; but, as they look around, they spy a man, Nanauatzin, and command him to cast himself in the fire. Nanauatzin bravely answers, "It is well, O gods; you have been good to me." Interestingly, at the moment of truth, the god Tecuciztecatl is too afraid to cast himself into the searing heat of Teotexcalli. After three abortive attempts, the assembled gods tell the mortal, Nanauatzin, to try. He does not hesitate, throwing himself onto the blaze, hissing and popping as the flames consume him. More from shame than courage, Tecuciztecatl then gathers himself and finally pitches himself into the sacred hearth, but by now the flames have died down somewhat. The difference in temperature, we are told, has consequences. Nanauatzin, who cast himself on the hottest flames, becomes the sun—the more honored of the celestial lights—while the god Tecuciztecatl, who received less of Teotexcalli's vital energy, arises as the moon. From these examples, we can perhaps surmise that cosmogonies celebrating the theme of sacrifice recognize that creative effort is costly: you can't create a universe without breaking a few cosmic eggs.

Division or Consummation Stories

Creation myths that fall into this fourth category are, says Weigle, "usually associated with discriminating primal matter or a cosmogonic egg [or] with the consummated marriage of earth and sky" (1989, 7). The cosmogonic egg motif is very widespread, occurring in traditions on all six of the inhabited continents. The Hindu Rig Veda and Upanishads contain cosmic egg myths in which there was nothing in the beginning but the great primeval sea. Mysteriously, an egg appeared on the waters, eventually cracking to reveal Atman (the archetypal man-god), who then sets in motion the continually unfolding cosmos. As we saw above, the creator-giant, Pan-Ku, also emerges from a great egg before beginning his great work. In the Finnish epic, the *Kalevala*, the virgin daughter of Air, whose life of virgin solitude becomes so burdensome to her that she eventually sinks into the sea, becomes pregnant thereby, and rolls with the enormous billows of the primordial ocean for 700 years. Finally she calls out to Ukko, the highest of the gods, for help. In answer, a beautiful teal appears, flying low over the water, searching for a place to land. Alighting upon Water-Mother's knee (Air-Daughter's new name), the duck lays six golden eggs and another of iron. As she broods over them, the heat becomes so fierce that Water-Mother moves her knee, causing the eggs to fall and split open, creating the earth, sky, sun, moon, and clouds.

The consummation motif shares with cosmogonic egg myths the knowledge that tiny germs contain within them astonishing potential for organized growth. In most mythic traditions, the sky-father casts his seeds into the earth-mother in the form of rain. Thus, in the *Theogony,* Gaia, the earth-mother, emerges first from Chaos and gives birth to starry Ouranos, who immediately "covers" her and begets upon her numerous divine children, whom he does not let emerge from the womb. Eventually, with Gaia's help, Ouranos's son Kronos overcomes him, separating earth from sky through castration. Kronos himself proves no less tyrannical than his father, eating his children as they emerge from the womb. Eventually, with his mother Rhea's help, Zeus borrows his father's sharp sickle and repeats cosmic history by emasculating Kronos. But not all consummation myths are as bloody as this one. The Krachi people of African Togo, for example, tell us that, in the beginning, God Wul-bar-i was spread out not five feet above Mother earth. But he got tired of being poked by old womens' stirring poles as they pounded food in front of their huts and of having people constantly wiping their dirty hands on his white clouds and taking bits of clean blue to put in their soup pots. In disgust, Wul-bar-i eventually pulls farther and farther back from the earth, finally coming to rest in his current heavenly abode. Whether stories organized by the separation motif are filled with violent struggle or fanciful whimsy, the action emanates from a central problem: how to separate and activate the primordial elements in order for life to thrive.

Earth-Diver Stories

Most cosmogonies begin with a vast primeval sea from which creative agents emerge to organize this watery chaos. In Weigle's fifth type of creation myth, a god or his agent dives to the bottom of this primordial deep and returns with a few grains of sand or a bit of mud from which the earth and the rest of the cosmos eventually arise. Several of the stories we mentioned have earth-divers in them. For example, the Rumanian story of how Satan, despite his intentions, ultimately fulfilled God's design for earth has it that Satan is forced by God Himself to dive to the bottoms of the deep and bring back some mud. After two false starts, the devil manages to bring back a few grains under his claws, but it is enough for God to make and grow an Earth-seed. As in many Native American stories, there are beings and potential forms waiting for their appointed moment in the darkness before creation. Earth-divers and their companions wake first and notice that there is no place upon which to live or build a home. This problem usually leads to an extensive search during which the earth-diver is discovered or after which the earth-diver hits upon the solution of diving below the waves in search of a bit of land. Sometimes it is Beaver who dives to the bottom and brings back a few grains of sand on his flat tail. Sometimes it's Duck, Turtle, or Frog who brings a little mud up from the bottom.

The Maidu of California say that Turtle and Pe-i-hipe (Father-of-the-Secret-Society) were the first beings. For ages, these two floated on a raft upon the original ocean until Earth-Starter came from the sky on a feathered rope. Turtle asked him when he would make earth and if there would be people on it. When Earth-Starter asked how it would be possible for him to create earth without anything to work with, Turtle volunteered to dive to the bottom of the ocean and bring back some mud. It took six years for Turtle to make it back to the surface, and even then he managed to bring back only a few grains from the bottom. But it was enough. Earth-Starter rolled the grains around in his hands, forming a ball the size of a tiny pebble. He placed this pebble at the end of the raft and checking once, twice, three times found that it had grown as big as the earth and that instead of ocean beneath their raft, there were mountains everywhere.

Some say earth-diver myths signify a return to primal Nature—or, others say, a return to the womb—for the raw materials of life. The recurrent fact that the earth-diver manages to bring back only a few grains of sand or a tiny dab of mud from the bottom of the primeval deep—just enough to make an Earth-seed from which the world eventually grows—suggests an analogy to human birth and growth. Nothing natural in our experience begins fully formed; things begin small and grow to full stature over time, and this fact seems decisive in earth-diver myths.

Emergence Stories

Another variation on the theme of creation as an evolutionary process can be found in Weigle's sixth type of cosmogony. Emergence myths typically depict the first people or first person as journeying from an original, cramped world or womb into this world. The natives of the American Southwest tell a number of stories which depict the gradual movement of the first people up and out of the dark, cramped worlds beneath this one. A Hopi myth tells us that in the first world things were unsatisfactory because it was so dark that people kept stepping on one another and one couldn't "cast the slime from one's nose without hitting somebody else with it." So two brothers hit upon the idea of climbing a couple of canes and digging their way out of these cramped quarters. This they did, and, making a ladder, they eventually succeeded in leading their people out of the first world into a second, slightly larger one. This world and a third world, too, eventually proved too small for the growing Hopi tribe. Finally, on the fourth try, the Hopi emerged into our world where the sun and other celestial bodies had not yet been made. Then, following Death's footprints in the sand, the Hopi and several animal spirit companions eventually complete creation and have sustained it through ritual ever since.

A Navajo tale places the gods Coyote, First Man, and First Woman in the cramped and dark first world. They decide to make the journey to the second world, where they discover Sun Man and Moon Man. They soon find this second world to be too crowded and decide that they should climb the sky ladder to the third world. The third world, as it turns out, is very spacious, containing mountains, rivers, canyons, trees, lakes, and the Mountain People who welcome the strangers but also warn them not to disturb Tieholtsoti, the water monster. Coyote, the trickster, finds it impossible to leave Tieholtsoti alone and eventually kidnaps the monster's two children, wrapping them in his blanket. As a result, Tieholtsoti begins to cover the entire third world with water. Quickly, the Mountain People pile all the mountains together and make the arduous climb up into the fourth world. In this world, they find human and animal people and, despite a lengthy dispute between the men and women living there about whose role was most important to the survival of the tribe, they live in peace and security for some time. Coyote, however, still has Tieholtsoti's children wrapped in his blanket, and eventually people begin to notice that water has begun to seep up from below. Again, mountains are moved and the people climb out of danger, with Badger leading the way because his claws are sharp enough to dig through the sky. When the people arrive in the fifth world, they discover nothing but a vast sea of mud, so Locust flies around the new world until he discovers four swans, occupying each of the four directions. The swans say that the people must pass a test in order to stay in the fifth world. Locust passes this test on behalf of the people, and, just as the swans are about to give the people permission to enter the muddy fifth world, Tieholtsoti rises from the mud on a roaring torrent, demanding that he be allowed to inspect everyone's bundles. Coyote's misdeed is finally discovered, and he is forced to return the water monster's children. Tieholtsoti, in great delight, takes his children and returns to his place without further trouble. But the world is still too muddy for comfortable habitation. To remedy this, the people pray until a great wind comes and blows for four days, causing the mud to dry and form mountains and valleys, plains and swamps. As a finishing touch, the people throw Sun Man and Moon Man into the sky and the fifth world, our world, becomes a home.

From these two examples we can see that emergence myths emphasize evolutionary progress from the cramped darkness of early society to the airy brightness of civilization. In the two preceding stories, the people learn important truths before they finally arrive in our world—and even then, the world they find is not quite complete without their efforts. Tests must be successfully met, religious ritual must be learned and performed, and the people must create that which the world does not already provide.

Two Creators

This seventh category of cosmogonic myths, in which two gods create the world through cooperation or competition, occurs frequently in African and Native American mythic traditions. The Acoma Pueblo tell of two creator sisters, who were born underground, growing slowly like seedlings in the dark. When they are old enough, a spirit, Tsitctinako or Thought-Woman, tells them to be patient and that, when everything is ripe, they will emerge from the earth and complete the creation their father, Uchtisiti, began when he threw a clot of his blood into space and exerted his power to make it become the earth. After some time, the sisters discover that Tsitctinako has given them each a basket filled with seeds and carved figures of animals. Thought-Woman then instructs the sisters to give life to the figurines of Badger and Locust, who, once they come to life, dig and smooth a path for the sisters to follow up out of the earth. After emerging, the sisters set about the work of invoking the Sun and giving life to the seeds and animals in their baskets. In this version of the myth, the sisters work cooperatively. Other Southwestern Indian tribes suggest that a jealous rivalry existed between the sisters over the contents of their baskets, causing them to split up and work separately.

The African Basonge tribe tells of the rivalry of two creator gods, Kolombo mui fangi and Mwile. The latter god was the highest of the divine tribe and became angry that people kept talking of Kolombo, who claimed to have made himself. Mwile sends for this upstart and challenges him to prove his claims through a series of tests. In the first test, Mwile takes dust and spits into it, creating clay from which he fashions a living human being. "Do *that*," the high god taunts. But Kolombo is up to the challenge, duplicating Mwile's effort. "Make yours speak," demands Mwile. Kolombo at first refuses and the two quarrel. Finally, after Mwile makes his clay-man speak, Kolombo also makes the attempt, but his man can only move his lips, lacking the power of articulate speech. But humiliating his rival is not enough for Mwile.

Rather he challenges Kolombo to go into a hut and allow Mwile to burn it down around him. "If you survive this trial," Mwile says, "I will acknowledge that you, Kolombo, have made yourself." Kolombo entered the hut with his animals (for Kolombo seems more closely associated with animal than human life); once he is hidden from view, he directs two of the animals to dig a tunnel back to their village and he tells a bird to lay some eggs on the floor of the hut. Meanwhile, Mwile sets fire to the hut, hearing the eggs exploding in the inferno and congratulating himself at the thought of putting an end to the pretender, Kolombo. But by the time Mwile discovers the charred eggshells among the ashes, Kolombo is safely back in his own village. And there the story ends.

Frequently cosmogonies employing the dual-creator motif depict one god as more active or more human than the other. The Maidu earth-diver story, for example, has three characters: Turtle, Pe-i-hipe, and Earth-Starter. It is unclear from this telling what Pe-i-hipe's role in creation is. In some versions of this myth, he shouts and cries at various stages of the earth's creation, but the cries seem unconnected to the story's action. Turtle, on the other hand, has the crucial role of retrieving the mud at the bottom of the primeval ocean, but the more human Earth-Starter takes the most active role in the creation of the earth, rolling the mud into a ball and repeatedly checking on its progress. The sisters in the Acoma Pueblo story seem equally matched, but Kolombo is clearly inferior to and more closely associated with animals than Mwile. Frequently, cosmogonies featuring two creators account for a perceived hierarchy or distinction among the planet's creatures; the greater, more gifted creator makes the "noble animals" such as horse, deer, and predator cats while the lesser creator makes the dangerous and noisome creatures such as crocodile, mosquito, and fly.

Deus Faber

This eighth category of creation myths presents the creator as the *Deus Faber,* the Maker God—the quintessential architect, artisan, or craftsperson (Weigle 1989, 7). Thus the *Popul Vuh,* the story of the "Fourfold Unfolding" told by the Quiché Maya, describes the creator as "the Maker, Modeler, Mother-Father of life, of humankind, giver of breath, giver of heart, bearer, up-bringer in the light that lasts of those born in the light, begotten in the light; worrier, knower of everything, whatever there is: sky-earth, lake-sea" (Markman and Markman 1992, 105). In this tale, the dual creator makes three attempts to create men properly. As each attempt is made, the craft and technical skill of the "modeling" is emphasized. The first men were fashioned out of clay, but when the rains came these clay men melted and so another attempt was made. This time, the Bearer-Begetter carves men out of wood; these men don't melt in the rain, but they possess no mind, no heart, no memory, no power of speech and therefore cannot properly serve their creator(s). Eventually they too are destroyed, the few survivors becoming the monkeys of the forest. Finally, the Maker-Modeler grinds corn—the staple crop of the Maya—and gives it a human shape and brings it to life. Thus the first men are born. But this time, they are too perfect. They can see into heaven and everywhere in the world without moving and, like their creator(s), they understand all mysteries. Not unlike the God of

William Blake's "Elohim Creating Adam." Color print finished in ink on paper. This image suggests an intimate connection between the maker and his creation. Notice, too, that Blake depicts the awakening body of Adam as already entwined in the coils of the serpent as if to suggest that the very act of creation sets up the conditions for error and alienation from the divine presence.
Source: © Tate Gallery, London/Art Resource, NY.

Genesis who decides to cast Adam and Eve out of the Garden because "the man has become like one of Us," the Bearer-Begetter does not want man as a rival or colleague and therefore "unmakes" the first men a little, reducing their eyesight and understanding.

The Basonge myth of Kolombo mui fangi and Mwile also contains elements of *deus faber* and secretion myths in that the competing gods fashion clay models of human beings out of dust and spittle before commanding them to come to life. The Eskimos of the Bering Straits say a man and woman came down out of the sky and lived on Diomede Island for a long time, but they had no children. At last, the man painstakingly carved five dolls out of ivory and five more out of wood. He set them on his table and the next morning they were people. The dolls of ivory had become men and the dolls of wood had become women—a fact which explained to this people why men are physically stronger than women. *Deus faber* stories celebrate the astonishing intricacy and cleverness of creation. Those who watch in awe as the spider weaves its web or who have reflected in wonder upon the many delicate motions of their fingers when they pick up a coin have already experienced the motivating force behind this type of myth. In this spirit, the Psalmist of the Hebrew scriptures extolled God because in his own eyes he was "fearfully and wonderfully made" (Ps. 139:14).

Ex Nihilo

The story often considered the *ex nihilo* ("out of nothing") myth par excellence is the account in Genesis of God speaking into existence light and darkness, sun and moon, stars and earth, plants and animals, and birds and fish. God then fashions Adam from the dust and breathes life into him, thus combining *deus faber* with *ex nihilo* motifs. *Ex nihilo,* a Latin term, literally means "from nothingness" or "from spirit" and is used to describe cosmogonies in which the creator brings the world into being through speech, breath, dream, thought, or laughter (Weigle 1989, 7). When the God of Genesis uses breath to speak the universe into existence or to make Adam "a living soul," he creates "out of nothing." The Egyptian priests of Memphis, competing with their counterparts in Heliopolis, elevated not Aten but Ptah to the rank of supreme creator. In contrast with Aten's spitting or ejaculating Shu and Tefnut, Ptah, who was later associated with Greek Hephaestus and Latin Vulcan, artisan gods of great technological skill, forms all things within his heart (the seat of rationality in Egyptian belief) and then names them—a speech act that gives them being.

The Yuki of northern California tell how Solitude Walker, Taikó-mol, emerged from the foam on the primeval sea. Creating a rope, he walked along its length, revolving it in his hands and causing the rope behind him to drag up earth. He did this four times, but each time the waters overwhelmed the land. So Taikó-mol formed a new plan; he fashioned four crooks and planted them in the four directions (which formed the swastika shape that had sacred meaning for the Yuki). Then he spoke a word and the earth appeared which he lined with whale hide so it wouldn't wash away this time. But the earth was barren, so Taikó-mol created all the animals and plants from the eagle feathers in his headdress. Even then he felt that his work was incomplete. So, fashioning a house from mahogany, Solitude Walker said "tomorrow there will be laughter and singing in this house." When the sun arose the next morning, the house was full of people.

Modern Perceptions

The story of Taikó-mol has much in common with the Genesis myth. As the story begins, the Yuki creator is upon the face of the deep and, *ex nihilo,* the world appears when he utters the divine word. In addition, Taikó-mol, like the God of Genesis, first creates the earth's plants and animals, deciding to create human beings when he discovers the natural world is incomplete without them. These similarities—and those that exist between the Judeo-Christian creation story and the many other stories from so-called primitive cultures—bring us back to the caution with which we began this section: we should not let our culturally derived sense of what is normal and right distort our view of other cultures and their ways of describing what it was like "in the beginning." While our mythologist forebears were inclined to dismiss such stories as that of Ku'urkil creating the world from his own feces as crude barbarism, we should be more thoughtful. Did the Chuckchee of Siberia really believe that rivers were streams of Father Raven's urine and lakes were the leftover drops? For that matter, did the Greeks literally believe, say, that Athena was born from the head of Zeus? Those who view seminomadic and hunter-gatherer people as "savages" and "primitives" have been too willing to assume that non-Western cultures, generally, and peoples living close to nature, particularly, were capable only of childlike and literal belief. Anthropological interviews reveal a more complex picture. Yes, many people within "archaic" societies believe literally in their gods and would defend accounts of events that, to our foreign ears, sound preposterous. But within those same cultures some people take a more skeptical—or at least less literal—view. In short, levels of literalness range from fairly disinterested nominal belief to nonliteral belief to very literal belief—just as exists in "modern" Western culture. Many in so-called primitive cultures are quite capable of viewing their myths as fictions that ultimately signify the unknowability of the universe's origins.

Unwilling to credit the world's "uncivilized" societies with fully human intelligence, mythologists of previous eras assumed that post-Enlightenment rationalism could "figure out" what those stories of strange gods and barbaric events *really* meant. Some figured that those outlandish stories must have meant that the sun or the weather was completely fascinating to the unsophisticated mind of the "primitives." Some figured that the primitives couldn't distinguish clearly between the subconscious chatter of dreams and waking reality. And some figured that the primitives possessed the imaginations of the fully human but not their critical powers. But there is another, more generous, way of looking at myth. We can see that, whether taken completely literally or not, creation myths—whatever their specific features—answer some of humanity's most fundamental questions. Where did the physical universe come from? What is God like? What explains such natural phenomena as earthquakes and comets? Why does the only world we've ever known feel imperfect to us? What's the meaning of our existence? How and why did sickness, death, and other evils enter the world? When and why did human beings become alienated from the Divine and/or from nature? What explains the existence of the different nations? When and where did the world's various cultures come by their characteristic practices, beliefs, and life-giving substances?

Many people assume that cosmogonic myths have been disproved and therefore displaced by modern science. But is such an assumption reasonable? When considering questions of ultimate origin, do we find scientific answers any more satisfying than mythic ones? For all the trappings of white lab coats, powerful telescopes and microscopes, and centuries of laboratory science, do we feel any more closely connected to modern science's creation story of vast, impersonal astrophysical, geological, and biological evolutionary forces resulting in the cosmos, the earth, and those of us living on it than we do to mythic accounts? Is such a story really, for most of us, any more believable and convincing or any less mind-boggling and awe-inspiring than the Genesis story or, for that matter, the story of Earth-Starter and

Turtle dredging up a little mud and sand from the fathomless depths of the primordial ocean?

We want to be careful here. We're not saying that myth is right and science is wrong. It would be absurd to reject what modern science has discovered about the history of the cosmos. Nevertheless, we would do well to remember that cosmogonic myths are expressive forms and not—despite all the euhemerists have said—bad science. Origin myths tell literary rather than literal truths about the origin of the cosmos. Science, on the other hand, attempts to be strictly literal as it describes and measures the universe and all that it contains. We learn from scientific observation that the Earth is laughably insignificant, being only one tiny planet among countless galaxies in an unimaginably large universe that is composed almost entirely of space—that is, of nothing. We learn from cosmogonic myths that despite the unimaginable vastness of the cosmos, despite the very inconceivability of our universe's size and age, people have a purpose and a role to play in cosmic destiny. Confusion arises, however, when one takes literary truth literally—or when one assumes that people unlike oneself *must* do so.

READING CREATION MYTHS

The categories by which we distinguish the motifs operating in the world's cosmogonic myths should not be used too rigidly. As should be apparent, a great many creation myths employ more than one motif. The Yuki and Genesis cosmogonies just discussed employ both the *deus faber* and *ex nihilo* motifs. The Nordic creation myths featuring the evil giant Ymir tend to combine accretion/conjunction, secretion, and sacrifice motifs—the latter evident, for example, in the Edda in which Odin and his brothers kill Ymir and make the world from his body. Thus the nine categories just discussed shouldn't be seen as a way of pigeonholing a myth—"this is an accretion/conjunction myth; this is a sacrifice myth." Rather, these categories should lead to speculation about why certain cultures depict the creation through certain motifs. What does it signify, for example, that, in the Tibetan story, the cosmos emerges through an incredibly gradual process that was not guided by an all-powerful creator? Developing a sufficient answer to this question would require some research on your part; but to demonstrate the kind of reward that asking questions about significance can bring, we could point out that Buddhism is a nontheistic religion. That is, Buddhism sees the manifold activities of the constantly unfolding universe as "the way it is." Gods may be—or may *not* be—a part of the universe's activity, but Buddhism would say that the universe happens the way it does because that is its nature. Noting further the importance to Buddhists of meditation practice and its emphasis on breathing techniques, one might gain an understanding of how the four basic elements are thought to interact in Buddhist metaphysics. With this knowledge, the Tibetan cosmogony discussed above would show a close affinity with the Buddhist worldview. The universe begins with the gentle and rhythmic stirrings of wind—a cosmic analogy to breathing—and it takes the patience of countless "lifetimes" for the nature of the cosmos to fully reveal itself as the world we know.

Read the following myths closely. Note the motifs at work in them. Note also the objects and their uses, the various beings and the interrelationships among them, and the behaviors and apparent attitudes present in the myths, framing questions that you might want to explore through further research. As you read, keep track of the details by asking questions that will help you compare and contrast each of the narratives. What kind of tone does the narrative set (e.g., peaceful, contentious, joyful, serious, humorous, sad)? What kind of relationship is depicted between creator and the human creature? Does the narrative describe a world in which people face hard work and scarcity or light work and plenty? What kinds of religious practices are mentioned or would seem to fit in the world described by the myth? What things and activities are depicted as sacred? What symbols are used? These and many other kinds of questions can lead to a deeper understanding of the myths we present here and of myths generally.

Amma and Nummo Prepare the World

Dogon (Nigeria)

The Dogon occupy a rugged and arid territory that straddles Mali and Nigeria in West Africa. Strict taboos förbidding utterance of the Dogon cosmogony in front of women, children, and the uninitiated prevented anyone outside the tribe's elders from knowing the full account of how Amma, the creator, made mother earth and how a series of "Words" finished creation thereafter. Western observers had spent years among the Dogon recording and seeking explanations for the numerous rituals conditioning every aspect of life from how and where to dig fields for planting to how to build houses to how men and women should properly arrange their bodies for sleep each night. Yet, in all that time, they had no clear idea whether there existed a master narrative that linked and explained these rituals. Even the Dogon's neighbors considered them somewhat backward and uncultured. One day, after anthropologist Marcel Griaule had been with the Dogon for more than 15 years, a messenger came to him, requesting that he come to the home of Ogotemmêli, a blind elder. The reason for this visit, as it turned out, was that the Dogon's spiritual leaders had decided that Griaule was ready to hear the sacred creation story from the man who knew it best—Ogotemmêli. Over the course of 33 interviews, Griaule heard not only the myth but careful explanations of

Source: Adapted from Marcel Griaule, *Conversations with Ogotemmêli: An Introduction to Dogon Religious Ideas.* London: Oxford University Press, 1965.

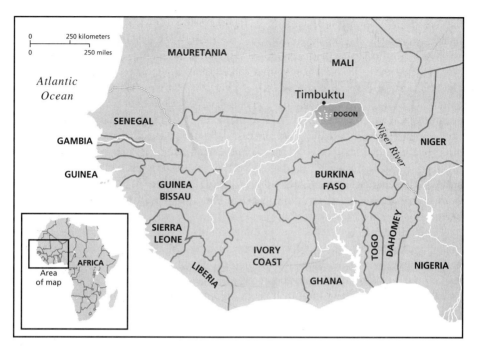

MAP 2.1 The Territory of the Dogon

[handwritten margin notes: deus faber + other elements → creates → mother earth. Appears... elders... who teaching created endures]

how Dogon architecture, textiles, iron work, agriculture, burial and marriage rituals, and a host of other practices commemorate the sacred events narrated in Dogon cosmogony.

Griaule's book *Conversations with Ogotemmêli: An Introduction to Dogon Religious Ideas* records, in circular and anecdotal fashion, the myth and explanations he heard from the Dogon elder. In this story we see the familiar pattern of an original creator god who begins the work of creation but leaves its completion to others. We have adapted Griaule's material to the linear story form with which most Westerners are familiar. The result, we hope, captures the unique symbols and fabulous complexity of the Dogon myth, a story which contains elements of secretion, conjugation, two creator, *deus faber,* and *ex nihilo* motifs.

Before anything was, Amma, the one God, rolled pellets of clay in his palms and flung them out into the darkness of space, thus creating the stars. Pleased with the result, Amma rolled out two larger clay balls, shaping them as a potter does, thus forming the sun and moon to further illuminate the darkness. The sun, they say, is a large pot—perhaps even larger than a village—which Amma heated white hot and surrounded with a red-copper spiral of eight turns. The moon's copper is white and Amma heated it only a quarter at a time.

Having made the celestial lights, the one God Amma squeezed another lump of clay between his palms and flung it out from him, as he had done with the stars. The clay spread out horizontally, beginning in the north and working to the south, thus forming the earth. Even though the world is a plate lying flat, it is also a fetus in the womb with limbs to the east and west. Lying there, head to the north, feet to the south, the earth was female. Her vagina was an anthill, her clitoris a termite hill. And she was beautiful.

Whisper now! Speak softly of the primordial error! Do not tickle even invisible eardrums when telling of Amma's great mistake! O, but the one God was lonely. O, how he ached for intimacy. He saw the earth's feminine form and was filled with desire. He approached her, ready for intercourse. But, at Amma's approach, the termite hill rose up, refusing farther passage. The termite hill exerted a masculine strength equal to God's organ. No intercourse could take place. But all-powerful God cannot be resisted. Amma cut down the termite hill and plunged himself into the excised earth.

This circumcision was without ritual, this intercourse a breach of order. Amma's act affected the course of things forever. For from this defective union was born a single being—not the twins that are natural. From this defective union was born Jackal, the deluded and deceitful son of God. Jackal was alone from birth and, because of this, he did more things than can be told.

God again had intercourse with his earth-wife; but, with the offending member gone, there was no further disorder. Water, the divine seed, entered the womb of the earth and this time twins were conceived, as is natural and right. The beings thus formed are called Nummo. They were both male and female and exist as an inseparable Pair. Their bodies were green and sleek all over like the surface of water. From head to loins they were human; below that they were serpents. Their red eyes were wide open like people, their tongues were forked like serpents. Their arms were flexible and without joints and their bodies covered with the short, green hairs of vegetation and germination. These spirits were formed of God's divine essence, made of his seed, which is simultaneously the ground, the form, and the substance of the world's life-force. They are the motion and persistence of all things. The Pair is present in all water; they *are* water—the water of seas, of coasts, of torrents, of storms, and of the spoonfuls we drink. Without Nummo, it would not have been possible to create the earth. For the earth was molded clay and water as in all things that have life. Even stones have this life-force, for there is moisture in everything.

The Nummo also produce copper. When the glorious sunburst pierces the cloudbank, the sun's rays may be seen materializing on the misty horizon. These rays, excreted by the spirits, are of copper and are light. They are water too, because they uphold the earth's moisture as it rises. The Pair excrete light, because they are also light. They were born perfect and complete with eight members. Their number is eight, which is the symbol of speech.

The Nummo, looking down from Heaven, saw their earth-mother naked and speechless from her first disastrous relations with Amma. They descended, bearing ten bunches of fibers pulled from plants already created in Heaven. The ten bunches corresponded to their ten fingers and they formed two strands of them—one for the front, one for the back. This garment was not for modesty. It symbolized the first ordering of the universe and it revealed the sacred helicoid sign in the form of an undulating broken line. For the fibers fell in coils, symbol of tornadoes, of winding torrents, of eddies and whirlwinds, and the writing motion of serpents. The coils also symbolized the eightfold copper spiral of the sun, which sucks up moisture. The fibers of the coiled strands were still moist with the freshness of the celestial plants and thus were the essence of Nummo. They were Nummo in motion, a wavy line that can be infinitely prolonged.

When Nummo speaks, what comes from their mouth is a warm vapor which conveys and is, in its very essence, speech. The coiled fringes of earth-mother's skirt were the chosen vehicle for the words with which the Spirit desired to reveal to the earth. They endued their webbed hands with magic power by raising them to their lips while they plaited the skirt, so that moisture of Nummo-speech was imparted to the fibers and the spiritual revelation was embodied in the technical instruction.

Thus clothed, the earth acquired its own primitive language. Its syntax was elementary, its verbs few. Its vocabulary was without ornament. One hears its words in breathing and the wind—in sounds of field and jungle scarcely distinguishable from one another. Nevertheless, this simple speech was a vehicle sufficient for the great work of beginning all things.

Now Jackal desired speech more than anything. He craved it so urgently that he laid his hands on the fibers of his mother's skirt—on the fibers that embodied Nummo-speech. His mother, earth, recoiled from this incestuous assault. She withdrew into her own womb; she fled into the anthill. Indeed, she became an ant, hoping to elude her son. But Jackal plunged in after her. The anthill hole was not deep enough to hide in forever. Though she struggled, the earth-mother was eventually subdued by Jackal.

This incestuous act was not without consequence. Jackal acquired the gift of speech and has ever afterward been able to reveal to diviners the plans of God. Moreover, his assault was the cause of the flow of menstrual blood, which stained earth-mother's fiber skirt. This defilement was more than Amma could bear. He rejected his earth-spouse and decided to create living beings without her. Modeling a womb in damp clay, he placed it on the ground and covered it with a pellet flung out into space from heaven. He made a male organ in the same way and, putting it on the ground also, flung out a sphere which stuck to it. The two lumps assumed organic form; they began to quicken. Members separated from the central core and bodies appeared. A human pair arose from the lumps of earth.

The Nummo Pair arrived on the scene, ready to further the action. They foresaw that the original rule of twin births was soon to disappear and that errors might result comparable to those of Jackal, whose birth was single and whose solitary state caused him to act as he did. Therefore Nummo drew two outlines on the ground, one on top of the other, one male and the other female. The man stretched himself out on these two shadows of himself and took both of them for his own. The same was done for the woman.

Thus it came about that each human being from the first was endowed with two souls of different sex—or rather with two principles corresponding to two distinct persons. In the man, the female soul is located in his foreskin; in the woman, the male soul resides in the clitoris. But man's life was not capable of supporting both beings; each person would have to merge himself in the sex for which he or she appeared to be best fitted. The Nummo Pair circumcised the man, removing the femininity of his foreskin. The excised skin, in turn, became an animal, a *nay,* which is neither serpent nor insect, even though it is classed with serpents. The *nay* was black and white, like the covering for the dead, and its name also means "four," the female number, and "sun," a female celestial being. The *nay* symbolized the pain of circumcision and the need for men to suffer in their sexual organs as women do.

The first man had intercourse with the first woman, who later bore the first two children of a series of eight. These eight were the Dogon ancestors. At the moment of birth, the pain of parturition was concentrated in the woman's clitoris, which was excised by an invisible hand and which then assumed the form of a scorpion. The scorpion's pouch and sting symbolized the female organ: the venom was the water and the blood of the pain.

Eight ancestors were born of the couple created by God. The four eldest were male, the four youngest, female. By a special dispensation, permitted only this once, the eight ancestors were able to fertilize themselves, being dual and bisexual. From them descended the eight Dogon families. Humanity was organizing itself, if only in a makeshift way. The eventual calamity of single births was mitigated by Nummo tracing the dual soul on the ground. Do not babies, even today, receive their dual souls as they are held by the hips above the drawings on the ground? Is not the superfluous soul later removed through circumcision? (male + female)

But the divine thirst for perfection could not be satisfied with things in this condition and the Nummo Pair started planning works of redemption. Nummo were aware of the terrifying effect of contact between creatures of flesh and blood and purely spiritual beings. They needed to impart reforms and instructions through human agency, within the human environment, and in forms that human beings could understand and duplicate. And so Nummo returned to earth and entered the anthill, entered the sexual part from which they were themselves the issue. Once there, they would be able to defend their mother from further incestuous attacks by Jackal and would, by their moist, luminous, articulate presence, be able to purge the earth-body that Amma had forever rejected and thus purify it for the activities of life. In the anthill, the male Nummo occupied the place of the termite-hill clitoris which Amma had cut away, while the female Nummo occupied the place of the female element, her womb becoming part of the earth-womb. The Pair thus began the work of regeneration in Amma's stead.

In those early days, men knew nothing of death and the eight ancestors lived on indefinitely. They had eight separate lines of descendants, each of them being self-propagating since each was both male and female. The four males and the four females were couples in consequence of their sexual parts. The four males were man and woman and the four females were woman and man. Each coupled and conceived within him- or herself and thus produced offspring.

When the time was fully ripe, the eldest of the eight ancestors was led by some latent knowledge to the anthill which Nummo now occupied. On his head, he wore a wooden food bowl for a head-dress, as protection from the sun. He put his two feet into the opening of the anthill and sank slowly into the earth's womb. Birth in reverse! All that remained above-ground was the round wooden bowl, still bearing traces of the food and the fingerprints of its vanished owner. The food bowl symbolized the eldest ancestors' body and human nature even as the snake's sloughed

The Dogon's primordial couple. Carved wood.
The first man and first woman gave birth to
the eight ancestors from whom the Dogon
trace their ancestry. As in the myth, this
carving depicts the primordial pair as androgynous. While they are not identical,
both figures have beards and breasts and
are approximately the same size and build.
Source: The Metropolitan Museum of Art, Gift of
Lester Wunderman, 1977 (1977.394.15).

skin symbolizes its body and ability to renew itself. Liberated from this earthly condition, the eldest ancestor was led by the male Nummo into the depths of the earth where, in the waters of the womb of the female Nummo, he curled himself up like a fetus and shrank to germinal form. The first ancestor became water, the seed of God and the essence of Nummo.

This process was the work of the Word. The male Nummo's voice accompanied the female Nummo who was speaking to herself and to her own sex. The spoken Word entered into her and wound itself round her womb in a spiral of eight turns. Just as the helical band of copper round the sun gives to it its daily movement, so the spiral of the Word gave to the womb its regenerative movement. Thus perfected by water and words, the spirit of the eldest ancestor was expelled and went up to heaven. All eight ancestors in succession had to undergo this transformation; but, when the turn of the seventh ancestor came, something powerful was revealed.

The seventh in a series, it must be remembered, represents perfection. Though equal in quality to the others, he is the sum of the feminine element, which is four, and the masculine element, which is three. Thus, he is the symbol of the total union of male and female. He is unity. And to this complete unity belongs the mastery of words, the command of language. The disappearance of the seventh into the anthill set in motion many good things.

In the earth-womb, the seventh became, like the others, water and spirit and his development, like theirs, followed the rhythm of the words uttered by the two transforming Nummo. The words which the female Nummo spoke to herself turned into a spiral and entered her vagina. The seventh ancestor learned these words inside the earth-womb. While the other ancestors had heard these words also, only the seventh mastered them and could put them to use. The seventh ancestor, therefore, received the perfect knowledge of a Word—the second Word to be heard on earth, clearer than the first and not, like the first, reserved for particular recipients, but destined for all humanity. And the second Word would give people an advantage over God's wicked son, Jackal, who knew only the primitive first Word.

The potent second Word increased the powers of the seventh ancestor, who gradually came to regard his regeneration in the earth-womb as equivalent to his capturing and possessing that fertile space. Little by little, he took possession of the whole organism, using it for his own purposes. Eventually his lips began to merge with the edges of the anthill, which widened and became a mouth. Pointed teeth emerged, eighty in all, ten for each ancestor. The earth-womb had become a mouth and the time for new instruction was at hand. But, fearing that normal men would not be able to bear direct contact with purely spiritual beings, the seventh ancestor imparted sacred instruction to the ant. From this earth-being men would receive the vital teachings.

At sunrise on the appointed day, the seventh ancestor spat out eighty threads of cotton; these he laced among his upper teeth even as a weaver prepares the loom. He did the same with his lower teeth and began to work his jaws back and forth. His whole face took part in the work. His nose studs served as the block; the stud in his lower lip functioned as a shuttle. The seventh ancestor's movements were a great teaching; he was speaking even as he wove the threads into cloth. With his forked tongue pushing the thread of the weft to and fro, the seventh Spirit wove the threads, breathing the second revealed Word into the material. By imparting the Word through a technical process, the seventh ancestor showed that material actions and spiritual forces are identical, that they must always be in cooperation.

The words that the Spirit breathed through the thread filled the interstices of warp and weft. They were one with the cloth, which is why woven material is called *soy* or "the spoken word." *Soy* also means seven to honor the Spirit who spoke as he wove. While the work progressed, the ant came and went along the edge of the anthill-mouth, hearing and remembering the words of the seventh ancestor. Having received this instruction, she passed it along to the humans living in those regions. Up to the time that the ancestors descended into the anthill, men had been living in lairs dug in the level soil. But when they discovered the food bowls of the ancestors around the opening of the anthill they noticed the ant's home as if for the first time. They realized that the anthill's design surpassed their own dwellings in comfort and safety. This revelation set the people to work constructing "anthills" of their own, complete with store-chambers for grain and numerous passageways to baffle predators and enemies. Through the second Word, human beings slowly emerged from their primitive condition. By observing the ant, human beings learned to build villages and received from her the knowledge of weaving.

On earth, order was gradually spreading; the Nummo's work of regeneration was taking hold. But there was trouble in Heaven. No one is quite sure what happened, but Spirits do not fall from Heaven except in anger or because they are expelled. It happened like this. After their transformation, the Nummo Pair had received the eight ancestors in Heaven; but, because they were the eldest, they had the rights of the elder generation. So they imposed order; they imposed a network of rules upon the eight ancestors, separating them from one another and forbidding them to visit one another. God had given the eight an assortment of grains for their food and for each of these the eight ancestors were to be responsible. But, after a while, the eight ancestors broke the rule forbidding them to meet and further transgressed by consuming each other's grain. This made them unclean in Amma's sight and the ancestors felt that their essence was incompatible with the heavenly regions. The eight ancestors therefore resolved to return to earth and bring with them anything they could find in Heaven that might prove useful to men.

The first ancestor took a woven basket with a circular opening and a square base in which to carry the earth and puddled clay required for the construction of a world-system, of which he was to be one of the counselors. This basket served as a model for a structure of considerable size which he built upside down, as it were, with the round opening, 20 cubits (60 feet) in diameter, on the ground and the square base, with sides eight cubits (24 feet) long, forming a flat roof. The entire structure was 10 cubits (30 feet) tall. This framework he covered with clay made of the earth from Heaven and in the thickness of the clay, starting from the center of each side of the square, he made stairways of ten steps each facing each of the cardinal directions. At the sixth step of the north staircase he put a door giving access to the interior in which were eight chambers arranged on two floors. The symbols embedded in the design were as follows:

The circular base represented the sun.

The square roof represented the sky.

A circle in the center of the square roof represented the moon.

The tread of each step was female and the rise of each step male and thus the four stairways of ten steps together represented the eighty original Dogon families, offspring of the eight ancestors.

Each stairway held one kind of creature, and was associated with a constellation:

The north stairway, associated with the Pleiades, was for men and fishes.

The south stairway, associated with Orion's Belt, was for domestic animals.

The east stairway, associated with Venus, was for birds.

The west stairway, associated with the so-called Long-Tailed Star, was for wild animals, vegetables, and insects.

Each step of each stairway had the representatives of various species. And each animal on each step was a line-leader behind whom were other animals of similar kind. On the first step of the west stairway, for example, stood the *walbanu,* the red antelope. Behind him stood the white, the black, and the *kâ* antelopes. All this must be described in words and it sounds impossible that so many large creatures stood on steps only a cubit wide, but everything on the steps was a symbol—symbolic antelopes, symbolic vultures, symbolic hyenas. Any number of symbols could find room on a three-foot step.

This sacred building was the <u>Granary of the Master of the Pure Earth</u>. Upon its roof the first ancestor had assembled the tools and implements of a forge, for his future task was to teach men the use of iron so that they might cultivate the land. The bellows was made of white sheepskin, its two halves joined together like twins. The hammer was a large iron block with a cone-shaped handle and a square striking surface. The anvil, similarly shaped, was fixed in a wooden beam. The ancestral smith had an iron bow and a spindle for an arrow. Aiming at the center of the moon-circle in the Granary roof and having attached a long thread of gossamer round the shaft to form a bobbin, he sunk the spindle-arrow deep within the circle. To a second arrow, the great Constructor attached the other end of the thread and shot it into the vault of the sky to give it purchase. The entire edifice became like a spindle whorl.

The Granary, then, was both a building and a dense constellation of symbols; it was the material embodiment of the third Word that would soon be revealed on earth and granaries on earth would be patterned after it. It was a picture of the new order about to be revealed as the third Word. The Granary showed in a form that could be comprehended by flesh and blood the world-system that would soon complete the redemptive work of Nummo. It was the plaited basket which had provided the ancestral Constructor with his model and which would serve in the future as the basic unit of volume. The one-cubit (three-foot) rise of the stairs on the four stairways would serve as the basic unit of length. The basic unit of area was provided by the flat roof, whose sides were eight cubits each. The Granary was also the head of the smith's hammer (which is male) and the four-sided anvil (which is female).

The Granary was the ideal realization of the anthill. It was also the sun, moon, sky, earth, and the four directions. It was the source of all seed, both animal and vegetable. It was the body of the Spirit of Water—the Nummo—and the female human body combined. Its exterior walls and inner partitions were the skeleton; the four pillars supporting the square roof were the legs and arms; the door on the north stair was the mouth; the eight inner compartments containing each of the eight types of seed given to the ancestors symbolized the stomach, gizzard, heart, small liver, spleen, intestines, great liver, and gall bladder. The round jar in the center symbolized the womb; a second, smaller jar enclosed within the first contained *Lannea acida* and represented the fetus.

Having thus completed the Granary of the Master of the Pure Earth, the first ancestor crept into the workshop of the Nummo, who are the smiths of Heaven. With a forked crook or "robber's stick," the ancestral smith stole a piece of the sun in the form of live embers and white-hot iron. In his haste, he dropped some of the embers and had to return to pick them up and was so anxious that, at first, he could not find the entrance to the Granary and had to circle it several times. Finally, he climbed the steps to the roof and stashed the stolen fire in one of the skins of the bellows, exclaiming *"Gouyo!"* "Stolen!"

Without wasting another moment, the first smith hurled the Granary along the arc of a rainbow toward the earth. The gossamer thread spun out from the top of the granary in serpentine coils, suggesting the everlasting movement of the Nummo's helicoid sign. As the Granary glided toward earth, the first smith stood ready with bellows, hammer, and bow to defend against attack from Heaven. It came in the form of a firebrand hurled by the female Nummo, which arrived with a great thunderclap. The first ancestor deflected its force with the bellows. But, because he had stored embers from the sun within the bellows, the device had acquired some of the sun's essence and so the firebrand could not prevail against it. The ancestral smith doused the flames of the firebrand, whose name was *bazu*. *Bazu* was the origin of the worship of the female fire. No sooner were the flames extinguished than the male Nummo hurled a second firebrand. But it was no more effective than the first. The second flame was named *anakyé* and was to become the origin of the worship of the male fire.

The thunder increased the velocity of the Granary and now it hurtled at top speed along the rainbow's arc. Seeing that impact was only moment's away, the first ancestor assumed a defensive posture. Then, WHACK! The Granary was on the ground. Because he was of one essence with the Nummo, the first ancestor still retained the flexible bones of their arms and legs; but, when the Granary collided with the earth, his arms and legs were broken at the level of elbows and knees. The first ancestor retained these joints ever afterwards, thus properly equipping him to perform the work of a smith. Moreover, when the Granary crashed into the earth, the symbolic humans, animals, and vegetation arrayed upon the Granary steps scattered in a great cloud of dust.

The first ancestor descended the north stairway and established a square field, 80 cubits to a side, orienting it to the Granary. This field he further divided into 80 times 80 squares and distributed these among the other ancestors whose destiny it was to remain on earth. Along the median line of the square from north to south, he built eight dwelling-houses, mixing the defiled soil with the pure mud of the Granary's walls, thus further purifying the earth. Later, as the land was gradually cleared, the impurity receded. And so it was that wherever cultivation spread, impurity receded.

To the north of the median line, the Great Constructor erected the first smithy on earth. But he could not completely impart the third Word on his own. Immediately after his arrival, the other ancestors descended along the rainbow: the ancestor of the leather workers, and the ancestor of the minstrels, each with his tools and instruments. Each of the ancestors descended in order—until the eighth ancestor broke rank and descended ahead of the seventh, the master of Speech.

What happened next determined the way the reorganization of the world would take place. Angry that the order of precedence had been broken, the seventh ancestor assumed the form of a great serpent and lunged toward the Granary to take the seeds from it. Some say the master of Speech bit the skin of the bellows. Others say that he came down at the same time as the smith in the form of the Granary itself and then became a great serpent and quarreled with the first ancestor. Still others say that upon the arrival of the Granary, the smith found the men of the eight families, and set up his smithy in their midst. When he put down the skins of the bellows, the great serpent suddenly appeared and fell upon them, scattering the millet all around. However it was, the men killed the great serpent. The smith gave them the body to eat and kept the head, taking it to the smith and burying it under his seat. That is why the seventh Nummo ancestor is present in every smithy.

From the time of the smith's coming, men had joints. Up till then, they had the flexible arm and leg bones of the Nummo which would not bend enough to do work. But arms alone—even arms with elbows—and bare hands are limited in what they can do. But in the first months after the Granary came down from Heaven, the first ancestor forged hoes of iron, thus giving man a longer arm and thus signaling that the work of agriculture was about to begin. Before this time, there were few plants and animals on earth—and nothing was cultivated for use. But, even with tools and the granary, there was no rain and thus the new agricultural order could not begin.

Lébé was the eldest man living and belonged to the eighth ancestor's family. Seven is the rank of the Master of Speech, but eight is Speech itself. Thus, Lébé was of all living beings on earth the most truly representative of the Word. It was time for the older, second Word—the word learnt from weaving—to give way to the third Word—the word of iron-making and agriculture. This new Word should have been imparted by the seventh ancestor, but he had been killed and eaten, his head buried under the seat in the first smithy. Thus, Lébé would have to pass into the same world as the seventh ancestor in order for the purposes of God to be fulfilled. So, Lébé died.

But his death was only in appearance. Just as the seventh ancestor was not really dead, Lébé could not really die. Nevertheless, they dug a grave, oriented north–south in the field not far from the first smithy. They laid him flat on his back with his head to the north, aligned exactly with the body of Earth-Mother. Nowadays, the dead are buried with proper ceremony, wrapped in the black-and-white checked cloth of the dead, males on their right sides, females on their left. They did not bend Lébé's limbs for a few moments so as to form the fetus and thus prefigure the regeneration. But, this was before people had become acquainted with death and before instructions in funerary ritual had been given.

The first sounds of the smithy were then heard. The vibrations penetrated into the depths of the earth, reaching the seventh ancestor, whom men had killed. As the rhythmic sounds of the bellows blowing up the fire and the hammer striking the anvil came down to him, the seventh ancestor Nummo took his spirit form. He rose up, human above the waist and reptile below, jerking and swaying to the rhythm of the smithy. This dance brought him to the tomb of Lébé and, working his way to the north of the grave, where the skull was, the seventh ancestor took the old man's body into his womb and gave new life to it. Then, always in time to the smithy's sounds, he expelled into the tomb a torrent of water and Lébé's transformed being. Where his body had been, water, symbol of rushing torrents and of stagnant pools, lay in a great sheet. From this underground lake five rivers flowed, one from each arm, each leg, and the head. The waters also symbolized the waters that issue forth at birth. In the Nummo's womb, Lébé's bones had been transformed into colored stones and ejected into the bottom of the tomb, forming the outline of his skeleton. Today, all priests wear round their necks the transformed bones of Lébé.

But men did not know of the old man's subterranean transformation, nor did they know it was the reason for the rains that now fell in abundance. Indeed, the first rains were for purification. The seventh Nummo, a pure spirit, in swallowing the old man, had assimilated defiled human nature and the lapsed second Word. When he released water to the rhythm of the hammer striking the anvil, he ejected a liquid which carried away impurity as well as the pure covenant stones. The rain washed this impure liquid away and thus the earth became ready for planting. The smith, who had been waiting for the rains, emerged from the smithy and taught men the art of sowing. Each family tended its plot and the eight grains, given by the one God, Amma were planted. And so the third Word was fully revealed and order was established.

As for Lébé, he was "eaten" because he was the eldest descendant of the eighth ancestor, the family of the Word. In eating Lébé, the seventh Nummo, the Master of Speech, took all that there was of good in the earlier Word and incorporated it in the stones. In eating Lébé, that which was human was permanently intermingled with the divine through the sacred stones. All that was impure was cast out with the water and carried away by the rains and spiritual truth was revealed in a technical process.

May Nummo and Lébé never cease to be the same good thing they now are! May they never lose this identity!

The Creation, from *The Eddas*

Norse (Iceland)

Between the years 780 and 1070 CE, bands of Danes, Norwegians, and Swedes (collectively known as the Vikings) were arguably the most influential power in Europe. At the height of their power, they controlled Scotland, Ireland, half of England, Iceland, Greenland, most of France, Lisbon, Cadiz, Pisa, Sicily, Novgorod, and Kiev, and they maintained trading colonies as far west as Newfoundland and New England (500 years before Columbus) and as far south and east as Baghdad. They had a pantheon of 14 major gods and conceived the cosmos as divided into three levels: Asgard (where the major gods, fertility gods, and light elves lived), Midgard (where men, giants, dwarves, and dark elves lived), and Niflheim (the underworld, where the evil dead died a second time in the fortress city of Hel). Running through and ultimately reaching above heaven is Yggdrasil, the enormous ash tree that apparently existed before the beginning and will survive after even the gods and the universe fade into the twilight of time.

Norse myths, including the creation story that follows, come to us from only a handful of sources. Thirty-four stories, written at different times by different authors, come to us from the *Codex Regius* (ca. 1270 CE) and a few others have been gleaned from the *Arnamagnaean Codex.* These poems are collectively known as the *Elder* or *Poetic Edda* (the term Edda probably derives from an Old Norse word for poem or poetry). Students of myth can be forever grateful to Snorri Sturluson, a man of letters, historian, politician, critic, and poet, whose literary efforts culminated in the *Prose Edda* (ca. 1220), a book which includes rules for Norse epic poetry and which retells a number of myths that would otherwise have been lost to us. As a Christian, Sturluson did not value the myths he was retelling as sacred truth; rather his was a scholar's and storyteller's interest and students of myth should be aware when reading the *Prose Edda* that he made artistic embellishments and devout adjustments to the original text. Nevertheless, his gifts as a storyteller were such that the retellings usually greatly exceed the imaginative power and artistic skill of other versions.

Source: "The Creation," from *The Norse Myths* by Kevin Crossley-Holland, copyright © 1980 by Kevin Crossley-Holland. Used by permission of Pantheon Books, a division of Random House, Inc.

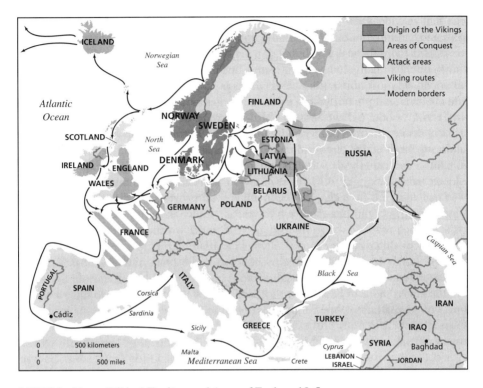

MAP 2.2a Norse (Viking) Territory and Areas of Trade and Influence

MAP 2.2b North Atlantic Regions of Norse Exploration and Settlement

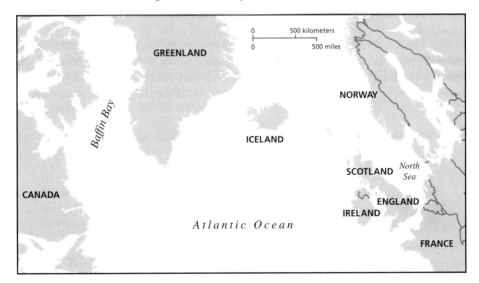

Burning ice, biting flame; that is how life began. In the south is a realm called Mus-pell. That region flickers with dancing flames: It seethes and it shines. No one can endure it except those born into it. Black Surt is there; he sits on the furthest reach of that land, brandishing a flaming sword; he is already waiting for the end when he will rise and savage the gods and whelm the whole world with fire.

In the north is a realm called Niflheim. It is packed with ice and covered with vast sweeps of snow. In the heart of that region lies the spring Hvergelmir and that is the source of eleven rivers named the Elivagar: they are cool Svol and Gunathra the defiant, Fjorm and bubbling Fimbulthul, fearsome Slid and storming Hrid, Sylg, Ylg, broad Vid and Leipt which streaks like lightning, and freezing Gjoll.

Between these realms there once stretched a huge and seeming emptiness; this was Ginnungagap. The rivers that sprang from Hvergelmir streamed into the void. The yeasty venom in them thickened and congealed like slag, and the rivers turned into ice. That venom also spat out drizzle—an unending dismal hagger that, as soon as it settled, turned into rime. So it went on until all the northern part of Ginnunga-gap was heavy with layers of ice and hoar frost, a desolate place haunted by gusts and skuthers of wind.

Just as the northern part was frozen, the southern was molten and glowing, but the middle of Ginnungagap was as mild as hanging air on a summer evening. There, the warm breath drifting north from Muspell met the rime from Niflheim; it touched it and played over it, and the ice began to thaw and drip. Life quickened in those drops, and they took the form of a giant. He was called Ymir. Ymir was a frost gi-ant; he was evil from the first. While he slept, he began to sweat. A man and woman grew out of the ooze under his left armpit, and one of his legs fathered a son on the other leg. Ymir was the forefather of all the frost giants, and they called him Aurgelmir.

As more of the ice in Ginnungagap melted, the fluid took the form of a cow. She was called Audumla. Ymir fed off the four rivers of milk that coursed from her teats, and Audumla fed off the ice itself. She licked the salty blocks and by the evening of the first day a man's hair had come out of the ice. Audumla licked more and by the evening of the second day a man's head had come. Audumla licked again and by the evening of the third day the whole man had come. His name was Buri. Buri was tall and strong and good-looking. In time he had a son called Bor and Bor married a daughter of Bolthor, one of the frost giants. Her name was Bestla and she mothered three children, all of them sons. The first was Odin, the second was Vili, and the third was Ve.

All this was in the beginning, before there were waves of sand, the sea's cool waves, waving grass. There was no earth and no heaven above; only Muspell and Niflheim and, between them, Ginnungagap.

The three sons of Bor had no liking for Ymir and the growing gang of unruly, brutal frost giants; as time went on, they grew to hate them. At last they attacked Ymir and killed him. His wounds were like springs; so much blood streamed from them, and so fast, that the flood drowned all the frost giants except Bergelmir and his wife. They embarked in their boat—it was made out of a hollowed tree trunk—and rode on a tide of gore.

accrue

Odin and Vili and Ve hoisted the body of the dead frost giant on to their shoulders and carted it to the middle of Ginnungagap. That is where they made the world from his body. They shaped the earth from Ymir's flesh and the mountains from his unbroken bones; from his teeth and jaws and the fragments of his shattered bones they made rocks and boulders and stones.

Odin and Vili and Ve used the welter of blood to make landlocked lakes and to make the sea. After they had formed the earth, they laid the rocking ocean in a ring right round it. And it is so wide that most men would dismiss the very idea of crossing it. Then the three brothers raised Ymir's skull and made the sky from it and placed it so that its four corners reached to the ends of the earth. They set a dwarf under each corner, and their names are East and West and North and South. Then Odin and Vili and Ve seized on the sparks and glowing embers from Muspell and called them sun and moon and stars; they put them high in Ginnungagap to light heaven above and earth below. In this way the brothers gave each star its proper place; some were fixed in the sky, others were free to follow the paths appointed for them.

The earth was round and lay within the ring of the deep sea. Along the strand the sons of Bor marked out tracts of land and gave them to the frost giants and the rock giants; and there, in Jotunheim, the giants settled and remained. They were so hostile that the three brothers built an enclosure further inland around a vast area of the earth. They shaped it out of Ymir's eyebrows, and called it Midgard. The sun warmed the stones in the earth there, and the ground was green with sprouting leeks. The sons of Bor used Ymir's brains as well; they flung them up into the air and turned them into every kind of cloud.

One day, Odin and Vili and Ve were striding along the frayed edge of the land, where the earth meets the sea. They came across two fallen trees with their roots ripped out of the ground; one was an ash, the other an elm. Then the sons of Bor raised them and made from them the first man and woman. Odin breathed into them the spirit of life; Vili offered them sharp wits and feeling hearts; and Ve gave them the gifts of hearing and sight. The man was called Ask and the woman Embla and they were given Midgard to live in. All the families and nations and races of men are descended from them.

One of the giants living in Jotunheim, Narvi, had a daughter called Night who was as dark eyed, dark haired and swarthy as the rest of her family. She married three times. Her first husband was a man called Naglfari and their son was Aud; her second husband was Annar and their daughter was Earth; and her third husband was shining Delling who was related to the sons of Bor. Their son was Day and, like all his father's side of the family, Day was radiant and fair of face.

Then Odin took Night and her son Day, sat them in horse-drawn chariots, and set them in the sky to ride round the world every two half-days. Night leads the way and her horse is frosty-maned Hrimfaxi. Day's horse is Skinfaxi; he has a gleaming mane that lights up sky and earth alike.

A man called Mundilfari living in Midgard had two children and they were so beautiful that he called his son Moon and his daughter Sun; Sun married a man called Glen. Odin and his brothers and their offspring, the Aesir, were angered at such daring. They snatched away both children and placed them in the sky to guide the chariots of the sun and moon—the constellations made by the sons of Bor to light the world out of the sparks from Muspell.

Moon leads the way. He guides the moon on its path and decides when he will wax and wane. He does not travel alone, as you can see if you look into the sky; for Moon in turn plucked two children from Midgard, Bil and Hjuki, whose father is Vidfinn. They were just walking away from the well Byrgir, carrying between them the water cask Soeg on the pole Simul, when Moon swooped down and carried them off.

Sun follows behind. One of her horses is called Arvak because he rises so early, and the other Alsvid because he is immensely strong. The Aesir inserted iron-cold bellows under their shoulder-blades to keep them cool. Sun always seems to be in a great hurry, and that is because she is chased by Skoll, the wolf who is always snapping and growling close behind her. In the end he will catch her. And the wolf that races in front of Sun is called Hati; he is after Moon and will run him down in the end. Both wolves are the sons of an aged giantess who lived in Iron Wood, east of Midgard.

After the sons of Bor had made the first man and woman, and set Night and Day, Moon and Sun in the sky, they remembered the maggots that had squirmed and swarmed in Ymir's flesh and crawled out over the earth. Then they gave them wits and the shape of men, but they live under the hills and mountains in rocky chambers and grottoes and caverns. These man-like maggots are called dwarfs. Modsognir is their leader and his deputy is Durin.

So the earth was fashioned and filled with men and giants and dwarfs, surrounded by the sea and covered by the sky. Then the sons of Bor built their own realm of Asgard—a mighty stronghold, a place of green plains and shining palaces high over Midgard. The two regions were linked by Bifrost, a flaming rainbow bridge; it was made of three colours with magic and great skill, and it is wonderfully strong. All the Aesir, the guardians of men, crossed over and settled in Asgard. Odin, Allfather, is the oldest and greatest of them all; there are twelve divine gods and twelve divine goddesses, and a great assembly of other Aesir. And this was the beginning of all that has happened, remembered or forgotten, in the regions of the world. And all that has happened, and all the regions of the world, lie under the branches of the ash Yggdrasill, greatest and best of trees. It soars over all that is; its three roots delve into Asgard and Jotunheim and Niflheim, and there is a spring under each. A hawk and eagle sit in it, a squirrel scurries up and down it, deer leap within it and nibble at it, a dragon devours it, and it is sprinkled with dew. It gives life to itself, it gives life to the unborn. The winds whirl round it and Yggdrasill croons or groans. Yggdrasill always was and is and will be.

From Chaos to King Zeus, from Hesiod's *Theogony*

Greek

The story that follows here comes from an ancient Greek poem called the *Theogonia,* which means "the birth of the gods." It was written by Hesiod, the second earliest of the Greek poets we know about, Homer being the earliest. Hesiod lived and wrote around 700 BCE.

The *Theogony,* as we call it, has a genuine mythic consciousness: it is more spiritual and not as thought-out as much later Greek and Latin poetry about myths tends to be. Hesiod is closer to a time when there was less distinction between the world of myth and that of daily life. The primal bond between Gaia (Earth) and Ouranos (Sky) suggests this closeness for they are, on the one hand, gods as we traditionally conceive them and, on the other, elements of nature itself. This undifferentiated mixture of the mundane and the celestial and its violent overthrow parallels human evolution. Through struggle and craft, human beings have gradually separated themselves from the merely natural and have, like Zeus, imposed a rational order on the a-rationality of the phenomenal world in order to gain the advantages of civilization.

The *Theogony* is myth at its best. The more we read this story the more we begin to see ourselves, our relationships with our parents and family, and the functions of society.

The Beginning

The very first to exist was Chaos,
and then Gaia, whose expansive lap
is the ever-safe foundation of the immortal gods
who live on the snowy peak of Olympos;
and then dark Tartaros, deep in the earth with its expansive paths;
and then Eros, the most beautiful of the gods,
whose power loosens our bones—
who controls the thoughts and decisions
of every god and every man.

From Chaos came Erebos and black Night.
From Night came Air and Day,
whom she conceived and gave birth to
from her love with Erebos.

Source: Translated for this volume by Jon-David Hague, Ph.D.

MAP 2.3 Ancient Greek World

Then Gaia gave birth to someone her equal,
the starry sky Ouranos, so that he
would cover her whole
and be the ever-safe foundation of the blessed gods.

She gave birth to the high Mountains
where heavenly Nymphs enjoy life
in mountain valleys.
But without the pleasure of love
she bore Pontos, whose stormy waves
are a barren sea. But then she
slept with Ouranos and bore Ocean
with his deep currents; then Koios and Krios;
Hyperion and Iapetos; and Theia and Rhea;
and Themis and Mnemosyne; and Phoebe
with her crown of gold;
and lovely Tethys; and after these
the youngest, most dreadful of her children, Kronos,

whose plans are crafty
and who hated his powerful father.

116–38

Kronos Overcomes His Father Ouranos

All the children that Gaia and Ouranos had
were dreadful and from the moment they were born
their father hated them.
So as soon as they were born
he hid them, not letting them see light,
deep down in Gaia, and Ouranos
enjoyed his evil. But huge Gaia,
confined and groaning from within,
thought of something cunning and evil:
Quickly making a kind of gray steel,
she forged a great sickle and showed it
to her children. She spoke to them
to give them courage though her heart was sad:

"My children, your father is wicked. But if you're willing
to listen to me, we can get revenge
for this evil and outrageous thing your father's done,
as he was the first to plan these shameful things."

This is what she said, and her children were immensely scared.
Not one of them uttered a word, but great Kronos,
whose plans are crafty, stood up and spoke these words [*mythoi*]
to his dear mother:

"Mother, I promise I'll finish this
since I don't give a damn about my father,
as he was the first to plan these shameful things."

This is what he said, and huge Gaia's heart
was very happy. So she hid him
by putting him in a bush.
And in his hands she put the sickle,
its blade like jagged teeth,
and told him the whole plan
with all its deceit.

Bringing on the night, great Ouranos came,
and eager for love, he caught hold of
Gaia on all sides
and she was stretched in every direction.
But from the bush his son stretched out
his left hand and with his right,
holding the huge sickle, long and jagged,

quickly cut his own father's penis off
and threw it back so that it went behind him:
it didn't leave his hand without purpose
as Gaia received all the drops of blood that hemorrhaged,
and when a year had passed
she produced the powerful Furies
and the great Giants, shining in their armor,
long spears in their hands,
and the Nymphs who are called Melian
throughout the expanse of the earth
and the penis he'd first cut off with the steel sickle
he threw out into the wild sea from the mainland
and it drifted in the ocean for a long time.

But then from this immortal flesh
a white foam [*aphros*] grew all around
and from within a girl was born

Both gods and men call her Aphrodite
as she was born in *aphros* . . .
                                                                    154–97

Zeus Overcomes His Father Kronos

Kronos subdued Rhea who gave birth
to famous children: Hestia, Demeter, and Hera
with her sandals of gold; and powerful Hades
who with his merciless heart lives under the ground;
and earth-pounding Poseidon Ennosigaios;
and Zeus with all his wise plans,
the father of both gods and men,
whose thunder shakes the expansive earth.

But great Kronos swallowed them down as each came out
of Rhea's holy womb and fell on their knees.
He did this so that no other royal descendant of Ouranos would
have the right to his throne.
For he'd learned before from Gaia and starry Ouranos that,
even though he was strong, it was his destiny to be
overcome by his son through the intentions of great Zeus.

So Kronos keep careful watch and swallowed down
his children while Rhea felt a pain
she couldn't forget. But when she was
to give birth to Zeus, father of both gods and men,
she asked her parents for a plan:
how she might give birth to her child

without Kronos knowing; and how one of the
Furies of her father might get revenge.

They listened to their daughter and agreed,
both of them, to explain just what was fated
for king Kronos and her son
with his powerful heart.

So they sent her to Lyktos
in the rich land of Crete when she
was just about to give birth to great Zeus,
the last of her children.
And there huge Gaia received him
on the broad shores of Crete
to nurse and raise him.
She brought him there to Lyktos first
under cover of night
and taking him in her hands she hid
him in a deep cave
in the depths of holy earth
on Mt. Aigaion with its thick woods.

She then wrapped a great stone
in baby's clothes and gave this
to the great lord, the son of Ouranos,
the king of the former gods.

He took it in his hands
and put it down into his gut,
cruel god, who didn't see
that the stone was not his son;
that his son was still alive—not troubled,
unable to be defeated;
that his son would overcome him
with his bare hands by brute force
and take revenge; that his own son
would be lord of the immortals.

And so Zeus' strength and glistening arms
and legs grew quickly.
And when a year had passed, great Kronos,
whose plans are crafty, but whom Gaia's
wiser plans deceived, spit up his children.
And first was the stone, the last he'd swallowed,
which Zeus set up on earth with its wide paths
at the sanctuary of Pytho in the valleys
beneath Mt. Parnassos:
he left it as a sign, a wonder to mortals.

453–500

Out of the Blue

Iroquois: Mohawk, Oneida, Onondaga, Cayuga, Seneca, and Tuscarora (Northeastern United States and Southeastern Canada)

Versions of this story (or parts of it) have been widely anthologized and have been attributed to most of the six nations comprising the Iroquois League after 1722 (the Tuscarora were admitted to the League at that time). Tradition has it that the League was formed through the efforts of a Mohawk, Hiawatha (not the hero of Longfellow's poem), around 1550. At the height of its influence in the 17th century, the Iroquois League controlled a vast territory that included most of the Great Lakes watershed, extending from the Atlantic coast to Michigan and from Ontario to North Carolina. Coordinating their political and military efforts through a democratic intertribal republic, each of the League's nations were represented by delegates elected from nominations submitted by the tribes' mothers. Tribal chiefs, too, owed their positions to matrilineal succession and acted with the consent and cooperation of their tribe's women of child-bearing age.

As one might expect in a society where prestige and identity are conferred through the mother's bloodline, the Iroquoian nations attributed the creation of our world to a female being who jumped into a hole in the ground of her world and emerged from the sky of ours. Indeed, one will find her referred to as Sky Woman in some anthologies. The version of the story presented here was synthesized from a number of earlier versions by Paula Gunn Allen in consultation with elders of the surviving tribes of the Iroquois League. Those interested in reading versions gathered from Mohawk, Onondaga, and Seneca sources around 1899 and in reading a 19th-century "ethnological" analysis of Iroquoian cosmology should consult Hewitt's *Iroquoian Cosmology* (1899–1900), which was reprinted in 1974.

When Sky Woman was a maiden, she was told by her dead father to go and marry a stranger. Being a strange woman, she did as he said, not taking her mother's counsel in the matter as she should have done. She journeyed to the place where the dead father had directed her to go, and there she found the man she was to marry.

Now this man was a renowned magician, a sorcerer. He heard her proposal that they marry skeptically. He said to himself, "This woman is but a girl. It would be more fitting for her to ask to be my apprentice than my wife." But he only listened

Source: Paula Gunn Allen, *Grandmothers of Light: A Medicine Woman's Sourcebook.* Boston: Beacon Press, 1991, 38–47. Reprinted by permission of Beacon Press.

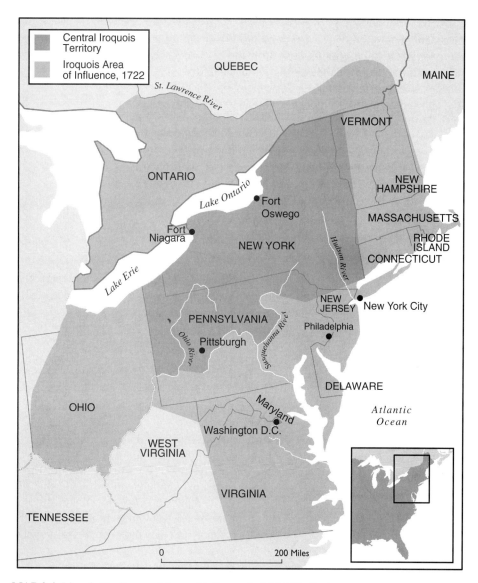

MAP 2.4 Iriquois Territory and Area of Influence in Mid-18th Century

silently to her, then he said, "It is well. If you can meet my tests, we will see if I will make you my wife."

He took her into his lodge and said, "Now you must grind corn." She took the corn and boiled it slightly, using wood he brought her for the fire. When the kernels were softened, she began to grind them on the grinding stone. And though there were mounds and mounds of stuff to be ground, still she was done with the task in a very short time. Seeing this, the sorcerer was amazed, but he kept silent. Instead he ordered her to remove all her clothing. When she was naked, he told her to cook the corn in the huge pot that hung over the fire. This she did, though the hot corn popped and spattered scalding clinging mush all over her. But she did not flinch, enduring the burns with calm.

When the mush was done, the woman told the sorcerer it was ready. "Good," he said, "now you will feed my servants." He noted that her body was covered with corn mush. Opening the door, he called in several huge beasts who ran to the woman and began to lick the mush from her body with their razor sharp tongues, leaving deep gashes where their tongues sliced her flesh. Still she did not recoil but endured the torment, not letting her face lose its look of calm composure.

Seeing this, the sorcerer let the beasts back out, then said she and he would be married, and so they were. After four nights that they spent sleeping opposite each other with the soles of their feet touching, he sent her back to her village with gifts of meat for the people. He commanded her to divide the meat evenly among all the people and further, to see to it that every lodge had its roof removed that night, as he was going to send a white corn rain among them. She did as she was told, and after the village had received its gifts, the meat and the white corn rain, she returned to her husband's lodge.

Outside his lodge there grew a tree that was always filled with blossoms so bright they gave light to his whole land. The woman loved the tree, loved to sit under it and converse with the spirits and her dead father, whom she held dear in her heart. She so loved the light tree that once, when everyone was sleeping, she lay down under it and opened her legs and her body to it. A blossom fell on her vagina then, touching her with sweetness and a certain joy. And soon she knew she was pregnant.

About that same time, her husband became weak and ill. His medicine people could not heal him, but told him that his sickness was caused by his wife. He was certain they were right, for he had never met anyone so powerful as she. He feared that her power was greater than his own, for hadn't she been able to withstand his most difficult tests: "What should I do?" he asked his advisors. They did not advise him to divorce her, because that kind of separation was unknown to them. The only death that had occurred was of the woman's father, and they did not understand what had happened to him.

After deliberating on the matter for four days, the advisors told the sorcerer that he should uproot the tree of light. Then, lying beside it, he should call his wife to come and sit with him. He should by some ruse get her to fall over the edge of the hole the uprooted tree would leave, and she would fall into the void. When she had fallen, they said, he was to replace the tree and then he would recover his health and his power.

That afternoon he went outside his lodge and pulled up the tree. He peered over the edge of the hole it left, and he could see another world below. He called his wife to come and see it. When she had come, he said, "Lean over the edge. You can see another world below." She knelt beside the hole and leaning over the edge, looked down. She saw emptiness, and a long way below, she thought that she saw blue, a shining blue that seemed filled with promise and delight. She looked at her husband and smiled, eyes dancing with pleasure. "It looks like a beautiful place there," she said. "Who would have thought that the tree of light would be growing over such a place!"

"Yes," her husband agreed. "It surely seems beautiful there." He regarded her for a moment carefully; then he said, "I wonder what it is like there. Maybe somebody could go down there and find out."

Astonished, the woman looked at her husband. "But how would someone do that?"

"Jump," the husband said.

"Jump?" She asked, looking down through the opening, trying to calculate the distance. "But it is very far."

"Someone of your power could do it," he said. "You could jump. Become the wind or a petal from this tree." He indicated the tree lying fallen next to them. "A petal could fall, gently. On the wind it would be carried. You could be a petal in the wind. You could be a butterfly, a down-gliding bright-bird."

She gazed for a long time at the shining emptiness below her. "I could jump like that. I could float downward. I could fall into the shining blue world below us."

"Yes," he said. "So you could."

For another long moment she knelt gazing downward, then taking a deep breath she stood, and flexing her knees and raising her arms high over her head she leaned into the opening and dove through.

For some time the sorcerer watched her body as it fell downward through the dark, toward the blue. "She jumped," he finally said to the council as they made their way slowly toward him. "She's gone." And they raised the tree and placed it back firmly in its place, covering the opening to the other world with its roots.

She fell. She fell so long she no longer remembered where she had come from or why she had jumped. She forgot the name of her clan and the transparent box her dead father had lain in. She forgot she had once long ago climbed up its side to sit and take his counsel, or that she had been a wise woman of such power that she had bested the most powerful of shamans in all the galaxy. She forgot the place of her home, the place of her origins. All she knew was falling. It filled her mind and it filled all the space around her until it became all that existed in creation. She forgot coming and going. She no longer remembered time or circumstance. She forgot what it was to begin, what it was to end.

There were consciousnesses, awarenesses, intelligent beings, who lived in the emptiness she fell through. None were beings such as she, but they had their own meanings, their own forms. There was a certain quality to each of them, a quality the stories have recorded as Waterfowl, Beaver, and Turtle. These beings became aware of the woman falling through the void. They watched her with their awareness for a long time, wondering. They thought about what to do, whether they should do anything.

After taking thought together, contemplating, they decided to slow her endless fall. There was a task she needed to complete, a part she was playing in the great order of the universe, and her falling was only one portion of her task. They grew aware that they also had a part to play in the great dance, the unfolding that was before them now. Seven Waterfowl moved through the emptiness and came together, forming a firm nexus of energy, a tidal whorl, a security. So arranged, they moved their thought-wings, their intelligence-net beneath her, and her fall came to rest in their arms. Not that her motion ended; they all moved together in harmony. The directionless movement, the endless drift through the nothing she had entered when the other world ended and she fell beneath the tree of light took on a coherence, a form, that connected her within the order of all that is. They stopped her fall.

For another endless time she swam with them through the waters of night. She slept then. She dreamed. In time they again took thought of their task, and of hers. They became aware of the next opening, the next coiling or uncoiling in the flow of being that is the universe as it moved toward what it moved toward.

They knew, as they contemplated, a time that she should enter another kind of motion, one that spun slowly, slowly, one as ordered and serene as the dancing of human women as it would arise out of the same pattern, the same knowing in another loop of the endless coil of creation. Beaver said, "Let me move through the reaches of space until I can find that which she needs. Somewhere there is a being that moves just so, as she will move, as we will see."

Long, long Beaver searched, using intelligence he did not know he possessed. Long, long they called, sending over great reaches of the formless sea of endlessness a sweet, haunting call like that issuing from the throats of waterfowl on earth to recall that time, that timeless place.

When the call was complete, when the search was fulfilled, an ancient being such as they but distinct in her form, her essence, as Beaver and the Waterfowl were distinct, came swimming through the void. "Lay her upon my back," she said, "as it suits the endless motion in this timeless place."

Infinitely gentle, they placed their burden upon the broad firm plane. Infinitely wondrous, they withdrew within themselves. Infinitely sensible, they made their thought complete. Beaver again: "I will seek and find that which will take its shape from her thought. I will seek that which will give her significance in her essence. I will recover that which forms the next loop in the coil of endless unfolding."

Alone with her dreaming burden, Turtle swam deeply and wide. Calmly she waited, as was the purpose of her being. After an endless place of sea change, Beaver swam within her awareness clutching a substance that was shapely in its potential, nurturing in its possibility, loving in its being. "This is the pattern of the substance she will use to make and shape the possibilities that will become her earth," he said. And so saying, he blew outward in his awareness the pattern he had remembered, and it fell about her like fur and down, like beads of rain and early light, like clear crystal notes sung in a high, cold place. Then he swam endlessly away.

The woman who fell still dreamed. She dreamed she was awash on an endless sea, adrift upon an endless sky where neither memory nor anticipation had ever dwelt. She dreamed she was held safe on a course whose purpose she did not know but whose fittingness she did not question. She sighed and sank at last into a dreamless sleep. Is it any wonder she awoke at last and saw about her endless dark and felt beneath her naked form the deep pull of Turtle's muscles pulling, pulling in a slow inexorable flow.

When she was fully awake, when her knowledge of herself and what had gone before revealed themselves whole in her awareness, she sat and gazed within. Slowly, slowly, with infinite care, she stretched out her hands and felt the pattern

Beaver had blown around her. She began to sing, a long slow song, a chant that flowed through her being in ordered variousness, in cycles of multiplicity. And as she sang, the pattern entered her thought as her being entered its being, and together they sang. As they sang, Turtle's circular swimming slowed and slowed. They entered the galaxy of stars and night. They found their way to the outer reaches of the spiral whorl, the path that life would follow after, from Turtle's back, to night, to the spiraling void, to the tree of light.

After the primordial patterns were fixed in place, Sky Woman recognized her incompleteness. Again she began to chant and sing. This time she danced—a certain hopping step, almost birdlike in its execution, weaving methodically to and fro as she stepped. She danced and chanted a very long time. Turtle moved a full three circuits before Sky Woman stopped. She paused. She listened. At last she sighed. Then she began again. Hopping and chanting, meandering this way and that, she danced on and on. Old Turtle pulled through the darkness steadily until four full circuits were fulfilled. Sky Woman paused. She stood in utter stillness. No thought moved within her. No memory, no dream stirred. In that absolute calm, she waited, perfectly still.

Then she crouched down, her legs spread wide. She placed the fingers of her left hand within the folds of the darkness between her legs and slowly withdrew a long slender stalk. She pulled and pulled and the stalk lengthened as it uncoiled at her fingers' urging. At last she straightened the slender stalk. It was very long. She breathed upon it until it dried, then she waited a certain interval. Finally she took its closer end and tamped it firmly into the substance that covered Turtle's back like an ever-moving cloak of darkness. When it was thus firmly planted, Sky Woman began again to sing, and as she sang the farther end of the stalk began to rise until it pointed straight up from Turtle's back. She sang again and the pole thickened and branches formed. She sang again and it grew more layers, and more branches formed. Changing her song slightly, she chanted once more and balls of light began to glimmer here and there upon the most slender boughs.

When the tree of light she had carried within her from her husband's far home had blossomed anew in this strange place, Sky Woman lay beneath it and fell asleep. She awakened slowly from her dream, or into her dream, to see her daughter emerge into the tree's sweet light. *Now, thought Sky Woman, I am complete.*

Sky Woman and her daughter lived comfortably on their island. Sometimes Sky Woman wondered what had become of the shimmering blue she had seen far below just before she jumped into the well of darkness so long before. Sometimes she dreamed of the song of the Waterfowl, their sweet song moving her heart nearly to tears. Sometimes she was lonely. But there was much to do to ready this sphere of intelligence into energies that would suit it to unfold through its destined cycles. She raised her daughter and taught her the ways of women beings. She taught her the ways of the sorceries she had learned long ago. She told her of her origins and cautioned her never to forget what she was taught or the stories she was told.

When she was grown, Sky Woman's daughter was wise and wondrous. Her active intelligence led her to seek in dreams—for what, she did not know. It made her dreaming restless, filled her belly with stirrings she did not recognize and could neither shape nor name. So in a kind of desperation, she left her mother's lodge and took to wandering. She would wander for days, seeking, musing, calling within her being, groping for a shape, a substance, she couldn't fathom.

One time, after many cycles of Turtle's turnings and spins, she came to rest beneath the shining tree. She lay in the same spot where her mother had lain eons before. And there she fell asleep. When she awoke, she became slowly aware of a large being standing before her, softly luminous, enticing in the tree's sweet light. Her thought began to dance within her and she smiled. *Ah,* she said within, *you're here.*

"Yes," the large luminous shadow replied. "I'm here."

They moved then into each other, dancing the dream she had sung into life, the dream she had made unknowingly, the dream that had rustled within her sending her forth to call from the darkness where Turtle swam. After they had danced and sung beneath the tree of light, the tree of life, for what seemed an endless span of time, the huge one faded from her being, faded ever so slowly until he became so faint he all but disappeared, leaving within her being only the tiniest fragment of his thought.

When their dance thus ended, Sky Woman's daughter returned to her mother's lodge and they resumed their earlier rhythms, the quiet order of their lives.

After a span of time, Sky Woman's daughter again went out. She went to the place of her dreaming and crouched against the tree of light. She breathed the fullness of her thought, the entirety of the dancing into ripeness, and felt her consciousness oddly slip into two parts. As she contemplated the sensation, which seemed to make two separate awarenesses within her—or was it four separate awarenesses?—she heard two voices speaking in the center of her being where earlier she had placed the fullness of her thought. One said, "This is how I will emerge," and she knew he was her son, and he would do it wrong. "No," the other said. "It is this way we should enter the sacred ground." And he emerged from her folds of darkness, from the place of origin and formless being into the place of shape and knowing that he was.

The other, anxious to emerge, longing to arise and become what he could not be, struggled his way from the being of his mother, nearer to her heart, tearing her asunder as he fled her cradling in sly rage. "See," he crooned, "I made it out the better way." But his mother had become another kind of being, and his elder brother could only weep.

Sky Woman, Grandmother, had become aware that something had transpired. She came to the place where the two new beings sat at the base of the tree of life near their mother's body. "Eh, what's this?" She gazed in consternation at the two small beings. Bud, the one who had emerged from his mother's being where no egress was said quickly, "He did that to our mother. He wouldn't emerge from her being as is proper but insisted on going another way. I tried to prevent him, but I was still too weak and he would not heed me." At this he burst into tears.

The sly one's brother said nothing. He was wrapped in his grief and did not speak. He was wrapped in drawing from his mother's quiet form all her knowledge and power, matching the energy patterns of her skill to his own which were as yet unformed.

"Come with me," the Old One said to her sly grandson. And taking Bud up in her arms she set off for her lodge, leaving Sapling to mourn beside the body of his mother beneath the tree of life.

Later, when the Ancient One returned, he was gone. She didn't search for him. She had no intention of taking him in—in fact, she would have been relieved if he had simply disappeared. She believed he was responsible for her daughter's death. But as things in those times were as they were, for this was long before the world we humans would inhabit had come into being, neither Sapling nor his mother could really die. Sapling lived in the wilderness far from his grandmother and his half-formed brother. He sang to the darkness and learned the ways of creation, for creating the world the human beings would live on would be his task.

So the Old One came to the tree of life, the light tree she had brought from her world far away, and mourning and singing she raised the body of her daughter and set it in a high branch of the tree. As it touched the branch, it began to give forth a soft, lovely light. It was the light of the night, the light by which plants and many creatures would find their way and being, and its seasons would set the seasons of human women in the way of their mother, the daughter of the woman god who fell from the sky.

Singing yet, the Ancient One lifted the head of her daughter and sent it spinning upward until it reached the top branch of the tree. It settled there and began to shine, its radiance growing ever more brilliant as she sang. And as she sang, she became aware that her daughter's task had reached its time of ripeness, and her purpose had been realized. Her daughter had not died; she had only been transformed. As the realization claimed the mind of Sky Woman, she began to dance, her chanting increased in volume, and its rhythm took on the imperturbable cadence of surety.

She realized that the new time had begun, and that with the coming of her grandsons the work of readying the earth—the back of the Turtle which the four of them rode through the darkness—for its myriad creatures and features had moved to a new plane. She danced and sang beneath her daughter's softly gleaming body and bright shining head. She gave thanks.

The Creation of Ulligara and Zalgarra

Sumerian (Iraq)

The tablets from which this myth have been translated were found in what is modern-day Iraq. The tablets have been dated approximately 800 BCE, and the myth belongs to the incantatory subgenre of sacred narratives. That is, the following story was likely sung or recited by temple officials during certain festivals as part of a magical ritual intended to encourage prosperity and abundance (note the meaning of the two created beings' names below). Indeed, a magical-religious performance like this one is just what Eliade means when he says that myths provide us with a means of

Source: Alexander Heidel. *The Babylonian Genesis: The Story of Creation.* 2nd edition. Chicago: University of Chicago Press, 1951, pp. 56–60. Used by permission of the University of Chicago Press.

reconnecting with the primordial moment of creation through ritual and thus renewing our lease on life. In his *Thespis: Myth, Ritual, and Drama in the Ancient Near East,* myth-ritualist Theodor Gaster asserts a similar point rather convincingly. According to Gaster, the ancient Near East's myths derived from rituals connected to seasonal religious observances marking the waxing and waning of vegetative fertility throughout the year. Thus, Gaster argues, when crops could not grow in winter, the ancients believed the fertility spirit (Enlil in the story that follows) had died and his life-giving powers had been withdrawn from Earth. When the rains and vegetation returned in spring, the fertility spirit was thought to have been resurrected. The myth-ritualists believed that religious rituals commemorating these seasonal fluctuations between bounteous fertility and the scarcity accompanying dormancy eventually resulted in myths, like the one below, that narrated their significance.

In the following story, a celebration of the mystery of fertility and abundance is combined with an account of the creation of the first human beings. The action begins with a consultation among the gods representing the four elements—Anu (god of air and sky), Enlil (god of storms and earth), Shamash (god of the sun and fire), and Ea (god of water)—and the Anunnaki, whose pronouncements become destiny. After having made the heavens and earth, the gods wonder among themselves what else is needed to complete their work. The answer, apparently, is human beings. As in the Assyrian myth of Attrahasis, the blood of slain gods is a crucial ingredient for creating the first human beings. With this divine spark, the prototypical human beings Ulligara ("establisher of abundance") and Zalgarra ("establisher of plenty") are created in order to build the gods' temples and increase the fruitfulness of plant and animal life. If stories of human creation are told, at least in part, to answer questions about the human being's purpose and place in the cosmos, then this story answers such questions by saying that the gods needed someone to do the daily labor of tending fields, raising livestock, and ensuring that the gods' rightful offerings are made. What consequences might such a worldview have on the religious imagination and social structures?

When both heaven and earth had been completely finished,
And the mother of the goddesses had been brought into being;
When the earth had been brought forth [and] the earth had been shaped;
When the destinies of heaven and earth had been fixed;
[When] trench and canal had been given their right course;
[And] the banks of the Tigris and the Euphrates had been established,
[Then] Anu, Enlil, Shamash, [and] Ea,
The great gods,

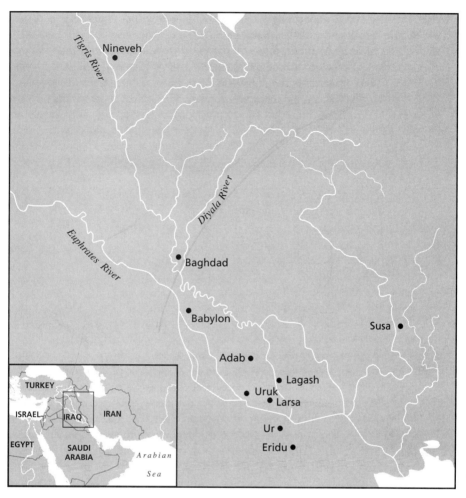

MAP 2.5 Ancient Sumeria and Babylonia

[Handwritten marginal notes:]
Gods have
created...
deus faber
Slays ogres...
Sacrifice?

Seated themselves [with] the Anunnaki, the great gods,
In the exalted sanctuary
And recounted among themselves what had been created.
"Now that the destinies of heaven and earth have been fixed;
Trench and canal have been given their right course;
The banks of the Tigris and the Euphrates
Have been established;
What [else] shall we do?
What [else] shall we create?
O Anunnaki, ye great gods,
What [else] shall we do?
What [else] shall we create?"

The great gods who were present,
The Anunnaki, who fix the destinies,
Both [groups] of them, made answer to Enlil:
"In Uzumua, the bond of heaven and earth,
Let us slay the Lamga gods.
With their blood let us create mankind;
The service of the gods be their portion,
For all times
To establish the boundary ditch,
To place the spade and the basket
Into their hands
For the dwelling of the great gods,
Which is fit to be an exalted sanctuary,
To mark off field from field;
For all times to establish the boundary ditch,
To give the trench (its) right course,
To establish the boundary,
To water the four regions of the earth,
To raise the plants . . .
[the tablet breaks off here]
To establish the boundary,
To fill(?) the granary,
[tablet is broken here]
To make the field of the Anunnaki produce,
To increase the abundance of the land,
To celebrate the festival of the gods,
To pour out cold water
For the great house of the gods, which is fit to be an exalted sanctuary,
Ulligarra [and] Zalgarra
They called their names.
[That Ulligara and Zalgarra should] increase ox, sheep, cattle, fish, and fowl,
The abundance in the land,
Enul [and] Ereshul
Decreed with their holy mouths.
Aruru, the lady of the gods, who is fit for rulership,
Ordained for them mighty destinies:
Skilled worker to produce for skilled worker [and] unskilled worker for
    unskilled worker,
Springing up among them like grain from the ground,
A thing which, [like] the star[s] of heaven, shall not be changed forever.
Day and night
To celebrate the festival of the gods,
[These] mighty destinies,
Among themselves
Did Anu, Enlil,
Ea, and Ninmah,

The great gods, decree [for the first human beings].
In the place where mankind was created,
There Nisaba was firmly established.
Let the wise teach the mystery to the wise.

Creation Myth from the *Vishnu Purana*

Hindu (India)

Indian religion and metaphysical thought have developed over at least the last 3,500 years and, unlike those of many of the cultures represented in this book, are part of a thriving tradition that still has many millions of adherents. Several distinct traditions influence Indian religious thought; of particular note are Hinduism, Buddhism, Jainism, and Islam. The earliest is the Vedic tradition of Hinduism, the texts of which are among the world's oldest written scriptures. The Veda comprises four kinds of writing: Samhita, Brahmana, Aranyaka, and Upanishad. The Samhita contains songs and hymns; the Brahmana are prose commentaries on religious ritual, particularly fire sacrifice; the Aranyaka focuses upon meditation practices; and the Upanishad records metaphysical speculations on the often abstract mystical questions raised by Hindu religion.

The Puranas, all 18 volumes and some 150,000 stanzas of them, emerge from the Vedic tradition, but are nevertheless separate from them. Sources as early as 400 BCE speak of an original Purana (a Sanskrit word which means "ancient") that is older than even the Veda; but if this most-ancient Purana ever existed, it has long since been lost. Certainly the Puranas assume the basic Hindu cosmology and religious practices of the Veda, but they tend to be less esoteric, less focused on priestly duties, and therefore more widely known among India's populace. The Puranas are said to contain five parts: (1) a cosmogony; (2) an outline of the cyclical creation and destruction of the universe; (3) a genealogy of the gods and patriarchs; (4) the reigns of the Manus, the sages and lawgivers that inaugurate civilization when each new world emerges from the destruction of the last; and (5) a history of the solar and lunar races and their descendants into modern times. The

Source: H. H. Wilson. *The Vishnu Purana: A System of Hindu Mythology and Tradition Translated from the Original Sanskrit and Illustrated by Notes Derived Chiefly from Other Puranas.* 1840. Calcutta, India: Punthi Pustak, 1972, 24–29.

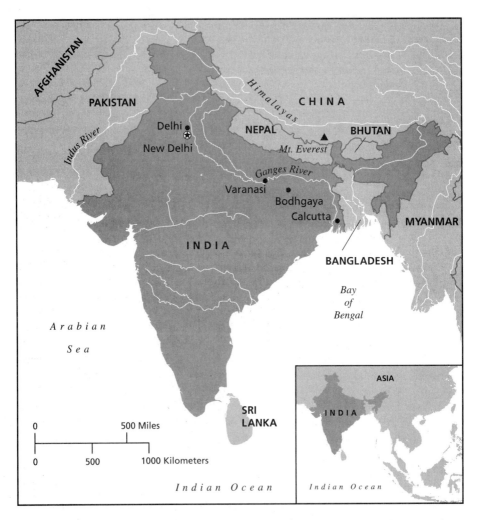

MAP 2.6 India is the mother of several world religions, including Buddhism and, most ancient of all organized religions, Hinduism. Complex mythic traditions predate even Hinduism and infuse the writings of both religions as well as the multilayered cultures of India, both past and present.

mechanism for telling these stories is the same in each of the Puranas: someone asks a question and a sage or god answers it.

The *Vishnu Purana,* from which the following excerpt is taken, follows this five-part pattern more carefully and thoroughly than the other Puranas, a fact which may be evidence of greater antiquity since strict adherence to literary forms often relaxes over time. In the story presented here, Maitreya asks the questions that occasion Parasara's discussion of the earth's creation, but Earth (Prithivi) herself eulogizes Narayan (one of the many forms of Brahman) and takes up one of the most complicated and vexing problems in Hindu metaphysics—the distinction between appearance and reality—and attempts to simplify it. The world, as it appears to the human mind, seems separate from the self and composed of many discrete objects and other selves. Yet, according to the Hindu sages, our customary distinction between subject ("I") and object ("not-I") is an error based on illusion. In this view, the entire universe is one entity, called Brahman. Ultimately, this distinction is a matter of perspective. From the deluded perspective of human beings embedded in space and time, the universe is comprised of discrete objects that are other than the self. From the perspective of the Absolute, everything—"I," you, a pencil, a flower, a rock on a planet in a distant solar system—are indiscrete (inseparable) expressions of Brahman. Enlightenment—freedom from the endless cycle of birth, suffering, and death—is a matter of fully actualizing this Oneness.

Hindu metaphysics assumes that the universe is continuously made and destroyed over vast cycles of time. Between each cycle, chaos reigns for 100 years, represented, not surprisingly, by a vast ocean. Each great creation–destruction cycle is called a *kalpa*, a day in the life of Brahma, which, according to one of many analogies, is the amount of time it would take a bird to wear away Mount Everest if it flew over the peak once in every 1,000 years and dragged a silk scarf over the mountain's uppermost tip. For the more scientifically minded, a *kalpa* is said to be 4,320,000,000 years. Thus references to various ages of creation and destruction in the story below are to be understood as subdivisions of the current *kalpa*, which will end in a great apocalypse called the *Mahapralya*.

MAITREYA: Tell me, mighty sage, how, in the commencement of the [present] Kalpa, Narayan, who is named Brahma, created all existent things.

PARASARA: In what manner the divine Brahma, who is one with Narayana, created progeny, and is thence named the lord of progeny [Prajapati], the lord god, you shall hear.

At the close of the past Kalpa [Padma], the divine Brahma, endowed with the quality of goodness, awoke from his night of sleep, and beheld the universe void. He, the supreme Narayana the incomprehensible, the sovereign of all creatures, invested with the form of Brahma, the god without beginning, the creator of all things; of whom, with respect to his name Narayana, the god who has the form of Brahma, the imperishable origin of the world, this verse is repeated: "The waters are called Nara, because they were the offspring of Nara [the supreme spirit]; and, as, in them, his first progress [in the form of Brahman] took place, he is thence named Narayan [he whose place of moving was the waters]." He, the lord, concluding that within the waters lay the earth, and being desirous to raise it up, created another form for that purpose; and, as, in preceding Kalpas, he has assumed the shape of a fish or a tortoise, so, in this, he took the figure of a boar. Having adopted a form composed

[handwritten annotation: deciphered, whilst in other forms]

of the sacrifices of the Vedas, for the preservation of the whole earth, the eternal, supreme, and universal soul, the great progenitor of created beings, eulogized by Sanaka and the other saints who dwell in the sphere of holy men [Janaloka]; he, the supporter of spiritual and material being, plunged into the ocean. The goddess Earth, beholding him thus descending to the subterranean regions, bowed in devout adoration, and thus glorified the god:—

PRITHIVI: Hail to thee, who are all creatures; to thee, the holder of the mace and shell: elevate me now from this place, as thou has upraised me in days of old. From thee have I proceeded; of thee do I consist; as do the skies and all other existing things. Hail to thee, spirit of the supreme spirit; to thee, soul of soul; to thee, who are discrete and indiscrete matter; who art one with the elements and with time. Thou art the creator of all things, their preserver, and their destroyer, in the forms, O lord, of Brahma, Vishnu, and Rudra, at the seasons of creation, duration, and dissolution. When thou has devoured all things, thou reposest on the ocean that sweeps over the world, meditated upon, O Govinda, by the wise. No one knoweth thy true nature; and the gods adore thee only in the forms it hath pleased thee to assume. They who are desirous of final liberation worship thee as the supreme Brahma; and who that adores not Vasudeva shall obtain emancipation? Whatever may be apprehended by the mind, whatever may be perceived by the senses, whatever may be discerned by the intellect, all is but a form of thee. I am of thee, upheld by thee; thou art my creator, and to thee I fly for refuge: hence, in this universe, Madhavi [the bride of Madhava, a form of Vishnu] is my designation. Triumph to the essence of all wisdom, to the unchangeable, the imperishable: triumph to the eternal; to the indiscrete, to the essence of discrete things: to him who is both cause and effect; who is the universe; the sinless lord of sacrifice; triumph. Thou art sacrifice; thou art the oblation; thou art the mystic Omkara; thou art the sacrificial fires; thou art the Vedas, and their dependent sciences; thou art, Hari, the object of all worship. The sun, the stars, the planets, the whole world; all that is formless, or that has form; all that is visible, or invisible; all. Purushottama, that I have said, or left unsaid; all this, Supreme, thou art. Hail to thee, again and again! hail! all hail!

PARASARA: The auspicious supporter of the world, being thus hymned by the earth, emitted a low murmuring sound, like the chanting of the Sama Veda; and the mighty boar, whose eyes were like the lotus, and whose body, vast as the Nila mountain, was of the dark color of the lotus-leaves, uplifted upon his ample tusks the earth from the lowest regions. As he reared his head, the waters shed from his brow purified the great sages, Sanandana and others, residing in the sphere of the saints. Through the indentations made by his hoofs, the waters rushed into the lower worlds with a thundering noise. Before his breath the pious denizens of Janaloka were scattered; and the Munis sought for shelter amongst the bristles upon the scriptural body of the boar, trembling as he rose up, supporting the earth, and dripping with moisture. Then the great sages, Sanandana and the rest, residing continually in the sphere of saints, were inspired with delight; and, blowing lowly, they praised the stern-eyed upholder of the earth.

THE YOGINS: Triumph, lord of lords supreme; Kesava, sovereign of the earth, the wielder of the mace, the shell, the discus, and the sword: cause of production, destruction, and existence. THOU ART, O god: there is no other supreme condition but thou. Thou, lord, art the person of sacrifice: for thy feet are the Vedas, thy tusks are the stake to which the victim is bound; in thy teeth are the offerings; thy mouth is the altar; thy tongue is the fire; and the hairs of thy body are the sacrificial grass. Thine eyes, O omnipotent, are day and night; thy head is the seat of all, the place of Brahma; thy name is all the hymns of the Vedas; thy nostrils are all oblations: O thou, whose snout is the ladle of oblation; whose deep voice is the chanting of the Sama Veda; whose body is the hall of sacrifice; whose joints are the different ceremonies; and whose ears have the properties of both voluntary and obligatory rites; do thou, who art eternal, who art in size a mountain, be propitious. We acknowledge thee, who hast traversed the world, O universal form, to be the beginning, the continuance, and the destruction of all things: thou art the supreme god. Have pity on us, O lord of conscious and unconscious beings. The orb of the earth is seen seated on the tip of thy tusks, as if thou hadst been sporting amidst a lake where the lotus floats, and hadst borne away the leaves covered with soil. The space between heaven and earth is occupied by thy body, O thou of unequalled glory, resplendent with the power of pervading the universe, O lord, for the benefit of all. Thou art the aim of all: there is none other than thee, sovereign of the world: this is thy might, by which all things, fixed or movable, are pervaded. This form, which is now beheld, is thy form, as one essentially with wisdom. Those who have practiced devotion conceive erroneously of the nature of the world. The ignorant who do not perceive that this universe is of the nature of wisdom, and judge of it as an object of perception only, are lost in the ocean of spiritual ignorance. But they who know true wisdom, and whose minds are pure, behold this whole world as one with divine knowledge, as one with thee, O god. Be favorable, O universal spirit: raise up this earth, for the habitation of created beings. Inscrutable deity, whose eyes are like lotuses, give us felicity. O lord, thou art endowed with the quality of goodness: raise up, Govinda, this earth, for the general good. Grant us happiness, O lotus-eyed. May this, thy activity in creation, be beneficial to the earth. Salutation to thee. Grant us happiness, O lotus-eyed.

PARASARA: The supreme being thus eulogized, upholding the earth, raised it quickly, and placed it on the summit of the ocean, where it floats like a mighty vessel, and, from its expansive surface, does not sink beneath the waters. Then, having leveled the earth, the great eternal deity divided it into portions, by mountains. He who never wills in vain created, by his irresistible power, those mountains again upon the earth, which had been consumed at the destruction of the world. Having then divided the earth into seven great portions for continents, as it was before, he constructed, in like manner, the four (lower) spheres, earth, sky, heaven, and sphere of the sages (Maharloka). Thus Heri, the four-faced god, invested with the quality of activity, and taking the form of Brahma, accomplished the creation. But he (Brahma) is only the instrumental cause of things to be created; the things that are capable of being created arise from nature as a common material cause. With exception of one instrumental cause alone, there is no need of any other cause; for (imperceptible) substance becomes perceptible substance according to the powers with which it is originally imbued.

Genesis
The Creation Account

Hebrew (Israel/Middle East)

Modern Jews trace their origins to the culture hero Abraham, who, according to biblical tradition, descended from Shem, one of Noah's sons. As a young man, Abram (later named Abraham) received a divine summons to leave his ancestral home in modern-day Iraq and journey to Canaan—though it is crucial to the story that Abram did not know at the time of his calling where God was taking him. It is Abram's belief in God's promise that he would make of Abram a "great nation" and that he and his descendants would always enjoy divine blessing and protection that established the basic character of Judaism as a covenant-based religion. According to most historians, Abram's people were originally a group of nomadic tribes that roamed Mesopotamia, Palestine, and northern Egypt from about 1950 to 1500 BCE. It was at the end of this period that the Hebrew-speaking peoples settled relatively permanently in the fertile land of northern Egypt called Goshen and the land of Canaan (an area that included modern-day Israel). It was here that this wandering tribe developed a national identity and a religious and ethical system from which each of the modern world's major monotheistic religions sprang.

The first five books of the Hebrew scriptures, or Torah (Pentateuch in Greek), were, according to Jewish and Christian traditions, attributed to Moses until modern times. Most biblical scholars now agree that the Torah is composed of at least four separate and distinct narratives, compiled from an original oral tradition and eventually written down over the course of several centuries. Looking closely at the following story, we can see for ourselves evidence of its having been compiled from more than one source. The first words of the Book of Genesis, transliterated from the Hebrew, are: *b'reshit · bara · elohim · et · ha'shamayim · v'et · ha'aretz.* "In the beginning Elohim created the heavens and the earth." The Hebrew word *elohim*, which literally means "gods," has traditionally been translated as "God"—a tradition that faithful Jews, Christians, and Muslims have emphatically defended through the years. Interestingly, this "elohist" creation account of the first chapter of Genesis gives way to a supplementary creation story in which *yehovah-elohim* (translated as "LORD GOD" in most Torahs and Bibles) moves about on the newly formed earth to create "the

Source: Scripture taken from the *New American Standard Bible®*, © Copyright 1960, 1962, 1963, 1971, 1972, 1973, 1975, 1977 by The Lockman Foundation. Used by permission (www.Lockman.org).

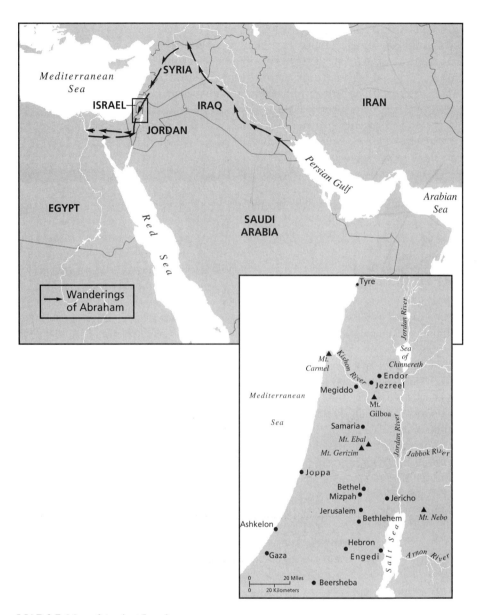

MAP 2.7 Map of Ancient Israel

man" (*ha'ahdahm,* or "Adam") from dust, plant a garden in Eden, make other vegetation grow, and then put the man in charge of Eden, commanding him not to eat of the "the tree of the knowledge of good and evil."

This presentation of two parallel creation accounts, each with its own focus, each giving the creator a different name—and a host of additional textual anomalies scattered throughout the rest of the book—has led to a consensus among biblical scholars that the Book of Genesis derives from three major traditions: the Yahwist, the Elohist, and the Priestly. The Yahwist and Elohist traditions are thought to have derived from cultural and sacerdotal differences between the Northern and Southern Kingdoms of Israel and Judah. These traditions date to sometime between 950 and 750 BCE and tend to be interested in such mythic issues as dreams, prophecies, and the revelation of the Divine character. The Priestly tradition, which probably was worked into the basic mythic material sometime during the sixth century BCE, focused on genealogies, historical dating, and ritual observances. We see its presence most clearly in the following excerpt when, at the end of creation, God "rests" from his work and proclaims the seventh day holy and, in a passage not included here, when the generations from Adam to Noah are recited.

In the beginning God created the heavens and the earth. And the earth was formless and void, and darkness was over the surface of the deep; and the Spirit of God was moving over the surface of the waters. Then God said, "Let there be light"; and there was light. And God saw that the light was good; and God separated the light from the darkness. And God called the light day, and the darkness He called night. And there was evening and there was morning, one day.

Then God said, "Let there be an expanse in the midst of the waters, and let it separate the waters from the waters." And God made the expanse, and separated the waters which were below the expanse from the waters which were above the expanse; and it was so. And God called the expanse heaven. And there was evening and there was morning, a second day.

Then God said, "Let the waters below the heavens be gathered into one place, and let the dry land appear"; and it was so. And God called the dry land earth, and the gathering of the waters He called seas; and God saw that it was good.

Then God said, "Let the earth sprout vegetation, plants yielding seed, and fruit trees bearing fruit after their kind, with seed in them, on the earth"; and it was so. And the earth brought forth vegetation, plants yielding seed, and fruit trees bearing fruit after their kind; and God saw that it was good. And there was evening and there was morning, a third day.

Then God said, "Let there be lights in the expanse of the heavens to separate the day from the night, and let them be for signs, and for seasons, and for days and years; and let them be for lights in the expanse of the heavens to give light on the earth"; and it was so. And God made the two great lights, the greater light to govern the day, the lesser light to govern the night; He made the stars also. And God placed them in the expanse of the heavens to give light on the earth, and to govern the day and the night, and to separate the light from the darkness; and God saw that it was good. And there was evening and there was morning, a fourth day.

Then God said, "Let the waters teem with swarms of living creatures, and let birds fly above the earth in the open expanse of the heavens." And God created the great sea monsters, and every living creature that moves, with which the waters swarmed after their kind, and every winged bird after its kind; and God saw that it was good. And God blessed them, saying, "Be fruitful and multiply, and fill the waters in the seas, and let birds multiply on the earth." And there was evening and there was morning, a fifth day.

Then God said, "Let the earth bring forth living creatures after their kind: cattle and creeping things and beasts of the earth after their kind"; and it was so. And God made the beasts of the earth after their kind, and the cattle after their kind, and everything that creeps on the ground after its kind; and God saw that it was good.

Then God said, "Let Us make man in Our own image, according to Our likeness; and let them rule over the fish of the sea and over the birds of the sky and over the cattle and over all the earth, and over every creeping thing that creeps on the earth." And God created man in His own image, in the image of God He created him; male and female He created them. And God blessed them; and God said to them, "Be fruitful and multiply, and fill the earth, and subdue it; and rule over the fish of the sea and over the birds of the sky, and over every living thing that moves on the earth."

Then God said, "Behold, I have given you every plant yielding seed that is on the surface of all the earth, and every tree which has fruit yielding seed; it shall be food for you; and to every beast of the earth and to every bird of the sky and to every thing that moves on the earth which has life, I have given every green plant for food"; and it was so. And God saw all that He had made, and behold, it was very good. And there was evening and there was morning, the sixth day.

Thus the heavens and the earth were completed, and all their hosts. And by the seventh day God completed His work which He had done; and He rested on the seventh day from all His work which He had done. Then God blessed the seventh day and sanctified it, because in it He rested from all His work which God had created and made. This is the account of the heavens and the earth when they were created, in the day that the Lord God made earth and heaven. Now no shrub of the field was yet in the earth, and no plant of the field had yet sprouted, for the Lord God had not sent rain upon the earth; and there was no man to cultivate the ground. But a mist used to rise from the earth and water the whole surface of the ground. Then the Lord God formed man of the dust from the ground, and breathed into his nostrils the breath of life; and man became a living being. And the Lord God planted a garden toward the east, in Eden; and there He placed the man whom He had formed. And out of the ground the Lord God caused to grow every tree that is pleasing to the sight and good for food; the tree of life also in the midst of the garden, and the tree of the knowledge of good and evil.

Now a river flowed out of Eden to water the garden; and from there it divided and became four rivers. The name of the first is Pishon; it flows around the whole land of Havilah, where there is gold. And the gold of that land is good; the bdellium and the onyx stone are there. And the name of the second river is Gihon; it flows around the whole land of Cush. And the name of the third river is Tigris; it flows east of Assyria. And the fourth river is the Euphrates.

Then the Lord God took the man and put him into the garden of Eden to cultivate it and keep it. And the Lord God commanded the man, saying, "From any tree

Marc Chagall. "The Creation of Man." Oil on canvas. Chagall,
a Russian Jew who fled his homeland and lived most of his life
in Paris, was noted for the dreamlike quality of his paintings.
In this image, a winged figure carries the inert body of Adam
through the darkness. In the swirl of activity near the light, we
see the tablets of the Mosaic Law and the crucified Christ.
Source: Photo © Réunion des Musées Nationaux/Art Resource, NY. © 2003
Artists Rights Society (ARS), New York/ADAGP, Paris.

of the garden you may eat freely; but from the tree of the knowledge of good and
evil you shall not eat, for in the day that you eat from it you shall surely die."

Then the Lord God said, "It is not good for the man to be alone; I will make him
a helper suitable for him." And out of the ground the Lord God formed every beast
of the field and every bird of the sky, and brought them to the man to see what he
would call them; and whatever the man called a living creature, that was its name.
And the man gave names to all the cattle, and to the birds of the sky, and to every

beast of the field, but for Adam there was not found a helper suitable for him. So the Lord God caused a deep sleep to fall upon the man, and he slept; then He took one of his ribs, and closed up the flesh at that place. And the Lord God fashioned into a woman the rib which He had taken from the man, and brought her to the man.

And the man said, "This is now one of my bones, And flesh of my flesh; She shall be called Woman, Because she was taken out of Man."

For this cause a man shall leave his father and his mother, and shall cleave to his wife; and they shall become one flesh. And the man and his wife were both naked and were not ashamed.

Now the serpent was craftier than any beast of the field which the Lord God had made. And he said to the woman, "Indeed, has God said, 'You shall not eat from any tree of the garden'?" And the woman said to the serpent, "From the fruit of the trees of the garden we may eat; but from the fruit of the tree which is in the middle of the garden, God has said, 'You shall not eat from it or touch it, lest you die.'" And the serpent said to the woman, "You surely shall not die! For God knows that in the day you eat from it your eyes will be opened, and you will be like God, knowing good and evil." When the woman saw that the tree was good for food, and that it was a delight to the eyes, and that the tree was desirable to make one wise, she took from its fruit and ate; and she gave also to her husband with her, and he ate.

Then the eyes of both of them were opened, and they knew that they were naked; and they sewed fig leaves together and made themselves loin coverings. And they heard the sound of the Lord God walking in the garden in the cool of the day, and the man and his wife hid themselves from the presence of the Lord God among the trees of the garden.

Then the Lord God called to the man, and said to him "Where are you?" And he said, "I heard the sound of Thee in the garden, and I was afraid because I was naked; so I hid myself."

And He said, "Who told you that you were naked? Have you eaten from the tree of which I commanded you not to eat?"

And the man said, "The woman whom thou gavest to be with me, she gave me from the tree, and I ate."

The Lord God said to the woman, "What is this you have done?" And the woman said, "The serpent deceived me, and I ate."

And the Lord God said to the serpent, "Because you have done this, Cursed are you more than all the cattle, and more than every beast of the field; on your belly shall you go, and dust shall you eat all the days of your life. And I will put enmity between you and the woman, and between your seed and her seed; He shall bruise you on the head, and you shall bruise him on the heel."

To the woman He said, "I will greatly multiply your pain in childbirth; in pain you shall bring forth children; yet your desire shall be for your husband, and he shall rule over you."

Then to Adam He said, "Because you have listened to the voice of your wife, and have eaten from the tree about which I commanded you, saying, 'You shall not eat from it'; cursed is the ground because of you; in toil you shall eat of it all the days of your life. Both thorns and thistles it shall grow for you; and you shall eat the plants of the field. By the sweat of your face you shall eat bread, till you return to the ground, because from it you were taken; for you are dust, and to dust you shall return."

Now the man called his wife's name Eve, because she was the mother of all the living. And the Lord God made garments of skin for Adam and his wife, and clothed them. The Lord God said, "Behold, the man has become like one of Us, knowing good and evil; and now, lest he stretch out his hand, and take also from the tree of life, and eat, and live forever"—therefore the Lord God sent him out from the garden of Eden, to cultivate the ground from which he was taken. So He drove the man out; and at the east of the garden of Eden He stationed the cherubim, and the flaming sword which turned every direction, to guard the way to the tree of life.

The *Popul Vu*

Maya (Guatemala/The Yucatán)

The ancient Maya civilization, at its height, occupied the eastern third of Mesoamerica, with important cultural centers in Guatemala and in southeastern Mexico's Yucatán. The Maya, despite numerous references to *the* "Mayan" civilization, were not members of a unified empire. Rather, like the ancient Greeks, they lived in "city-states," united by language and religion but politically quite distinct from one another. Indeed, Maya cities often were at war with each other.

The "classic period" of Maya development (ca. 300–900 CE) saw the Maya refining a long-count calendar and developing an advanced written language. Early in the Classic Period, the Maya were heavily influenced by the civilization of Teotihuacán to the north—a relationship that undoubtedly accounts for the many similarities between Maya and Mexica mythic traditions. After the collapse of Teotihuacán around 650 CE, the Maya reached their cultural acme, making advances in art, astronomy, and mathematics that continue to astound modern researchers. The Maya were, for example, able to measure the orbits of celestial bodies with unprecedented accuracy—without the benefit of Sir Isaac Newton's calculus.

The Maya are also famous for their ornate hieroglyphic writing system through which they recorded astronomical observations, noted important events in the lives of their rulers, and transmitted their myths from one generation to the next. Only priests and nobility, it appears, were given an education, particularly in

Source: Excerpts from pages 105–19 from *The Flayed God* by Roberta H. Markman and Peter T. Markman, copyright © 1992 by Roberta H. Markman and Peter T. Markman. Reprinted by permission of HarperCollins Publishers Inc.

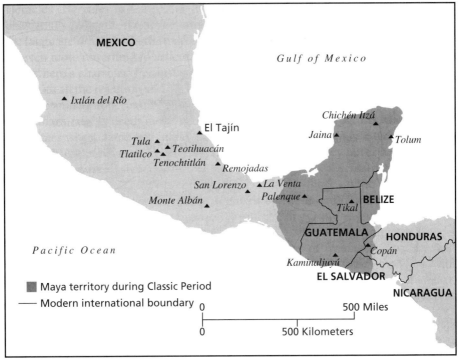

MAP 2.8 Maya Territory during Classic Period

the sacred art of symbol making. Inscriptions appear on tree bark books, stone, and wood and were frequently incorporated into Maya architecture. Unfortunately, a great deal of the written record did not survive the vicissitudes of the tropical climate or the invasion of the Spanish, who regarded these symbols as the work of the devil.

The Maya peaked gloriously, but faded quickly. By 750 CE—and for reasons that we do not fully understand—the tide had begun to turn. A few citadels clung to life in Belize and the Yucatán, but most Maya cities in what is now Guatemala were abandoned and their inhabitants moved to the highlands and farming villages. The descendants of the Maya can still be found in Guatemala working small farms and tending herds much as they have done since the great calamity that befell their people in the eighth and ninth centuries.

The *Popul Vu,* the Maya's cultural charter and repository of its stories of creation and the people's migrations, was a hieroglyphic manuscript predating European contact with the Americas and was used as a basis for oral performance even after the Spanish Conquest. The following text is at least one step removed from this original hieroglyphic manuscript and was, according to Markman and Markman, "written in Quiché in the European alphabet in Santa Cruz Quiché by an unknown writer. That manuscript, which has been lost since 1855, was copied by a young Dominican parish priest, Francisco Ximénez . . . in the early eighteenth century" (1992, 104). Although the influence of Christianity can be detected in this text, it is considered by most experts to be comparatively uncorrupted. We get a solid sense of the narrative style and mystical content of the original. The number four, sacred to many indigenous tribes from Alaska to Argentina, appears in this text as well. There are four sacred colors, four sacred directions, and four distinct creations, only the last of which culminates in the creation of the Quiché, the "daykeepers," who will at last be able to fulfill the will of the gods by keeping track of the calendar and making sacrifice in its appropriate season. Note that not only does this story feature the kind of *deus faber* fashioning found in the Genesis account of creation, but there is also an account of a great flood that wipes out an early, imperfect attempt to make man. In addition, the Maya gods are concerned, like the God of the Hebrew scriptures, that humanity could become too like themselves. Adam and Eve are expelled from Eden; the first Quiché are "unmade a little." Whether or not these similarities are a result of contact with missionizing Europeans is a call that we leave to our readers.

This is the beginning of the Ancient Word, here in this place called Quiché. Here we shall inscribe, we shall implant the Ancient Word, the potential and source for everything done in the citadel of Quiché, in the nation of Quiché people. And here we shall take up the demonstration, revelation, and account of how things were put in shadow and brought to light by the Maker, Modeler, named Bearer, Begetter, Hunahpu Possum, Hunahpu Coyote, Great White Peccary, Tapir, Sovereign Plumed Serpent, Heart of the Lake, Heart of the Sea, Maker of the Blue-Green Plate, Maker of the Blue-Green Bowl, as they are called, also named, also described as the midwife, matchmaker named Xpiyacoc, Xmucane, defender, protector, twice a midwife, twice a matchmaker, as is said in the words of Quiché.

They accounted for everything—and did it, too—as enlightened beings, in enlightened words. We shall write about this now amid the preaching of God, in Christendom now. We shall bring it out because there is no longer a place to see it, a Council Book, a place to see "The Light That Came from Across the Sea," the account of "Our Place in the Shadows," a place to see "The Dawn of Life," as it is called. There is the original book and ancient writing, but he who reads and ponders it hides his face. It takes a long performance and account to complete the emergence of all the sky-earth: the fourfold siding, fourfold cornering, fourfold measuring, fourfold staking, halving the cord, stretching the cord in the sky, on the earth, the four sides, the four corners, as it is said, by the Maker, Modeler, Mother-Father of life, of humankind, giver of breath, giver of heart, bearer, up-bringer in the light that lasts of those born in the light, begotten in the light; worrier, knower of everything, whatever there is: sky-earth, lake-sea.

This is the account; here it is. Now it still ripples, now it still murmurs, ripples, it still sighs, still hums, and it is empty under the sky. Here follow the first words, the first eloquence: There is not yet one person, one animal, bird, fish, crab, tree, rock, hollow, canyon, meadow, forest. Only the sky alone is there; the face of the earth is not clear. Only the sea alone is pooled under all the sky; there is nothing whatever gathered together. It is at rest; not a single thing stirs. It is held back, kept at rest under the sky. Whatever there is that might be is simply not there: only the pooled water, only the calm sea, only it alone is pooled.

Whatever might be is simply not there: only murmurs, ripples, in the dark, in the night. Only the Maker, Modeler alone, Sovereign Plumed Serpent, the Bearers, Begetters are in the water, a glittering light. They are there, they are enclosed in quetzal feathers, in blue-green. Thus the name, "Plumed Serpent." They are great knowers, great thinkers in their very being.

And of course there is the sky, and there is also the Heart of Sky. This is the name of the god, as it is spoken. And then came his word, he came here to the Sovereign Plumed Serpent, here in the blackness, in the early dawn. He spoke with the Sovereign Plumed Serpent, and they talked, then they thought, then they worried. They agreed with each other, they joined their words, their thoughts. Then it was clear; then they reached accord in the light; and then humanity was clear, when they conceived the growth, the generation of trees, of bushes, and the growth of life, of humankind, in the blackness, in the early dawn, all because of the Heart of Sky, named Hurricane. Thunderbolt Hurricane comes first, the second is Newborn Thunderbolt, and the third is Raw Thunderbolt. So there were three of them, as Heart of Sky, who came to the Sovereign Plumed Serpent, when the dawn of life was conceived: "How should it be sown, how should it dawn? Who is to be the provider, nurturer?"

"Let it be this way, think about it: this water should be removed, emptied out for the formation of the earth's own plate and platform, then comes the sowing, the dawning of the sky-earth. But there will be no high days and no bright praise for our work, our design, until the rise of the human work, the human design," they said.

And then the earth arose because of them; it was simply their word that brought it forth. For the forming of the earth they said "*Earth!*" It arose suddenly, just like a cloud, like a mist, now forming, unfolding. Then the mountains were separated from the water; all at once the great mountains came forth. By their genius alone, by their cutting edge alone they carried out the conception of the mountain-plain, whose face grew instant groves of cypress and pine.

And the Plumed Serpent was pleased with this: "It was good that you came, Heart of Sky, Hurricane, and Newborn Thunderbolt, Raw Thunderbolt. Our work, our design will turn out well," they said.

And the earth was formed first, the mountain-plain. The channels of water were separated; their branches wound their ways among the mountains. The waters were divided when the great mountains appeared. Such was the formation of the earth when it was brought forth by the Heart of Sky, Heart of Earth, as they are called, since they were the first to think of it. The sky was set apart; and the earth was set apart in the midst of the waters. Such was their plan when they thought, when they worried about the completion of their work.

Now they planned the animals of the mountains, all the guardians of the forests, creatures of the mountains: the deer, birds, pumas, jaguars, serpents, rattlesnakes, yellowbite, guardians of the bushes.

A Bearer, Begetter speaks: "Why this pointless humming? Why should there merely be rustling beneath the trees and bushes?"

"Indeed—they had better have guardians," the others replied. As soon as they thought it and said it, deer and birds came forth. And then they gave out homes to the deer and birds: "You, the deer: sleep along the rivers, in the canyons. Be here in the meadows, in the thickets, in the forests, multiply yourselves. You will stand and walk on all fours," they were told.

So then they established the nests of the birds, small and great: "You, precious birds: your nests, your houses are in the trees, in the bushes. Multiply there, scatter there, in the branches of trees, the branches of bushes," the deer and birds were told.

When this deed had been done, all of them had received a place to sleep and a place to stay. So it is that the nests of the animals are on the earth, given by the Bearer, Begetter. Now the arrangement of the deer and birds was complete. And then the deer and birds were told by the Maker, Modeler, Bearer, Begetter: "Talk, speak out. Don't moan, don't cry out. Please talk, each to each, within each kind, within each group," they were told—the deer, birds, puma, jaguar, serpent.

"Name now our names, praise us. We are your mother; we are your father. Speak now: 'Hurricane, Newborn Thunderbolt, Raw Thunderbolt, Heart of Sky, Heart of Earth, Maker, Modeler, Bearer, Begetter,' speak, pray to us, keep our days," they were told. But it didn't turn out that they spoke like people: they just squawked, they just chattered, they just howled. It wasn't apparent what language they spoke; each one gave a different cry.

When the Maker, Modeler heard this: "It hasn't turned out well; they haven't spoken," they said among themselves. "It hasn't turned out that our names have been named. Since we are their mason and sculptor, this will not do," the Bearers and Begetters said among themselves.

So they told them: "You will simply have to be transformed. Since it hasn't turned out well and you haven't spoken, we have changed our word: 'What you feed on, what you eat, the places where you sleep, the places where you stay, whatever is yours will remain in the canyons, the forests. Although it turned out that our days were not kept, nor did you pray to us, there may yet be strength in the keeper of days, the giver of praise whom we have yet to make. Just accept your service; just let your flesh be eaten.

"So be it, this must be your service," they were told when they were instructed—the animals, small and great, on the face of the earth.

And then they wanted to test their timing again; they wanted to experiment again; and they wanted to prepare for the keeping of days again. They had not heard their speech among the animals; it did not come to fruition and it was not complete. And so their [the animals'] flesh was brought low: they served, they were eaten, they were killed—the animals on the face of the earth.

Again there comes an experiment with the human work, the human design, by the Maker, Modeler, Bearer, Begetter: "It must simply be tried again. The time for the planting and dawning is nearing. For this we must make a provider and nurturer. How else can we be invoked and remembered on the face of the earth? We have already made our first try at our work and design, but it turned out that they didn't keep our days, nor did they glorify us. So now let's try to make a giver of praise, giver of respect, provider, nurturer," they said.

So then comes the building and working with earth and mud. They made a body, but it didn't look good to them. It was just separating, just crumbling, just loosening, just softening, just disintegrating, and just dissolving. Its head wouldn't turn, either. Its face was just lopsided, its face was just twisted. It couldn't look around. It talked at first, but senselessly. It was quickly dissolving in the water.

"It won't last," the mason and sculptor said then. "It seems to be dwindling away, so let it just dwindle. It can't walk and it can't multiply, so let it be merely a thought," they said.

So then they dismantled, again they brought down their work and design. Again they talked: "What is there for us to make that would turn out well, that would succeed in keeping our days and praying to us?" they said.

Then they planned again: "We'll just tell Xpiyacoc, Xmucane, Hunahpu Possum, Hunahpu Coyote, to try a counting of days, a counting of lots," the mason and sculptor said to themselves. Then they invoked Xpiyacoc, Xmucane. Then came the naming of those who are the midmost seers: the "Grandmother of Day, Grandmother of Light," as the Maker, Modeler called them. These are names of Xpiyacoc and Xmucane.

When Hurricane had spoken with the Sovereign Plumed Serpent, they invoked the daykeepers, diviners, the midmost seers: "There is yet to find, yet to discover how we are to model a person, construct a person again, a provider, nurturer, so that we are called upon and we are recognized: our recompense is in words.

"Midwife, matchmaker, our grandmother, our grandfather, Xpiyacoc, Xmucane, let there be planting, let there be the dawning of our invocation, our sustenance, our recognition by the human work, the human design, the human figure, the human mass. So be it, fulfill your names: Possum, Hunahpu Coyote, Bearer twice over, Begetter twice over, Great Peccary, Great Tapir, lapidary, jeweler, sawyer, carpenter, Maker of the Blue-Green Plate, Maker of the Blue-Green Bowl, incense maker, master craftsman, Grandmother of Day, Grandmother of Light.

"You have been called upon because of our work, our design. Run your hands over the kernels of corn, over the seeds of the coral tree, just get it done, just let it come out whether we should carve and gouge a mouth, a face in wood," they told the daykeepers.

And then comes the borrowing, the counting of days; the hand is moved over the corn kernels, over the coral seeds, the days, the lots. Then they spoke to them, one of them a grandmother, the other a grandfather. This is the grandfather; this is the master of the coral seeds: Xpiyacoc is his name. And this is the grandmother, the daykeeper, diviner who stands behind others: Xmucane is her name.

And they said, as they set out the days: "Just let it be found; just let it be discovered; say it; our ear is listening; may you talk; may you speak; just find the wood for the carving and sculpting by the builder, sculptor. Is this to be the provider, the nurturer when it comes to the planting, the dawning? You corn kernels, you coral seeds, you days, you lots: may you succeed, may you be accurate," they said to the corn kernels, coral seeds, days, lots.

"Have shame, you up there, Heart of Sky: attempt no deception before the mouth and face of Sovereign Plumed Serpent," they said.

Then they spoke straight to the point: "It is well that there be your manikins, woodcarvings, talking, speaking, there on the face of the earth."

"So be it," they replied. The moment they spoke it was done: the manikins, woodcarvings, human in looks and human in speech. This was the peopling of the face of the earth. They came into being, they multiplied, they had daughters, they had sons, these manikins, woodcarvings. But there was nothing in their hearts and nothing in their minds, no memory of their mason and builder. They just went and walked wherever they wanted. Nor did they remember the Heart of Sky. And so they fell, just an experiment and just a cutout for humankind. They were talking at first but their faces were dry. They were not yet developed in the legs and arms. They had no blood, no lymph. They had no sweat, no fat. Their complexions were dry; their faces were crusty. They flailed their legs and arms; their bodies were deformed. And so they accomplished nothing before the Maker, Modeler who gave them birth, gave them heart. They became the first numerous people here on the face of the earth.

Again there comes a humiliation, destruction, and demolition. The manikins, woodcarvings were killed when the Heart of Sky devised a flood for them. A great flood was made; it came down on the heads of the manikins, woodcarvings. The man's body was carved from the wood of the coral tree by the Maker, Modeler. And as for the woman, the Maker, Modeler needed the pith of reeds for the woman's body. They were not competent, nor did they speak before the builder and sculptor who made them and brought them forth, and so they were killed, done in by a flood: There came a rain of resin from the sky. There came the one named Gouger of Faces: he gouged out their eyeballs. There came Sudden Bloodletter: he snapped off their heads. There came Crunching Jaguar: he ate their flesh. There came Tearing Jaguar: he tore them open.

They were pounded down to the bones and tendons, smashed and pulverized even to the bones. Their faces were smashed because they were incompetent before their mother and their father, the Heart of Sky, named Hurricane. The earth was blackened because of this; the black rainstorm began, rain all day and rain all night. Into their houses came the animals, small and great. Their faces were crushed by things of wood and stone. Everything spoke: their water jars, their tortilla griddles, their plates, their cooking pots, their dogs, their grinding stones, each and every thing crushed their faces.

Their dogs and turkeys told them: "You caused us pain; you ate us, but now it is you whom we shall eat."

And this is the grinding stone: "We were undone because of you. Every day, every day, in the dark, in the dawn forever, r-r-rip, r-r-rip, r-r-rub, r-r-rub, right in our faces, because of you. This was the service we gave you at first, when you were still people, but today you will learn of our power. We shall pound and we shall grind your flesh," their grinding stones told them.

And this is what their dogs said, when they spoke in their turn: "Why is it you can't seem to give us our food? We just watch and you just keep us down, and throw us around. You keep a stick ready when you eat, just so you can hit us. We don't talk, so we've received nothing from you. How could you not have known? You did know that we were wasting away there, behind you. So, this very day you will taste the teeth in our mouths. We shall eat you," their dogs told them, and their faces were crushed.

And then their tortilla griddles and cooking pots spoke to them in turn: "Pain! That's all you've done for us. Our mouths are sooty; our faces are sooty. By setting us on the fire all the time, you burn us. Since we felt no pain, you try it. We shall burn you," all their cooking pots said, crushing their faces.

The stones, their hearthstones were shooting out, coming right out of the fire, going for their heads, causing them pain. Now they run for it, helter-skelter. They want to climb up on the houses, but they fall as the houses collapse. They want to climb the trees; they're thrown off by the trees. They want to get inside caves, but the caves slam shut in their faces.

Such was the scattering of the human work, the human design. The people were ground down, overthrown. The mouths and faces of all of them were destroyed and crushed. And it used to be said that the monkeys in the forests today are a sign of this. They were left as a sign because wood alone was used for their flesh by the builder and sculptor. So this is why monkeys look like people: they are a sign of a previous human work, human design—mere manikins, mere woodcarvings.

[The lengthy description of the journey of the hero twins that is included at this point in the original manuscript is omitted here.]

And here is the beginning of the conception of humans, and of the search for the ingredients of the human body. So they spoke, the Bearer, Begetter, the Makers, Modelers named Sovereign Plumed Serpent: "The dawn has approached, preparations have been made, and morning has come for the provider, nurturer, born in the light, begotten in the light. Morning has come for humankind, for the people of the face of the earth," they said.

It all came together as they went on thinking in the darkness, in the night, as they searched and they sifted, they thought and they wondered. And here their thoughts came out in clear light. They sought and discovered what was needed for human flesh. It was only a short while before the sun, moon, and stars were to appear above the Makers and Modelers. Broken Place, Bitter Water Place is the name: the yellow corn, white corn came from there. And these are the names of the animals that brought the food: fox, coyote, parrot, crow. There were four animals that brought the news of the ears of yellow corn and white corn. They were coming from over there at Broken Place, they showed the way to the break. And this was when they found the staple foods. And these were the ingredients for the flesh of the human work, the human design, and the water was for the blood. It became human blood, and corn was also used by the Bearer, Begetter.

And so they were happy over the provisions of the good mountain, filled with sweet things, thick with yellow corn, white corn, and thick with pataxte and cacao, countless zapotes, anonas, jocotes, nances, matasanos, sweets—the rich foods filling up the citadel named Broken Place, Bitter Water Place. All the edible fruits were there: small staples, great staples, small plants, great plants. The way was shown by the animals. And then the yellow corn and white corn were ground, and Xmucane did the grinding nine times. Corn was used, along with the water she rinsed her hands with, for the creation of grease; it became human fat when it was worked by the Bearer, Begetter, Sovereign Plumed Serpent, as they are called. After that, they put it into words: the making, the modeling of our first mother-father, with yellow corn, white corn alone for the flesh, food alone for the human legs and arms, for our first fathers, the four human works.

It was staples alone that made up their flesh.

This is the first person: Jaguar Quitze. And now the second: Jaguar Night. And now the third: Mahucutah. And the fourth: True Jaguar. And these are the names of our first mother-fathers. They were simply made and modeled, it is said; they had no mother and no father. We have named the men by themselves. No woman gave birth to them, nor were they begotten by the builder, sculptor, Bearer, Begetter. By sacrifice alone, by genius alone they were made, they were modeled by the Maker, Modeler, Bearer, Begetter, Sovereign Plumed Serpent. And when they came to fruition, they came out human:

They talked and they made words.

They looked and they listened.

They walked; they worked.

They were good people, handsome, with looks of the male kind. Thoughts came into existence and they gazed; their vision came all at once. Perfectly they saw, perfectly they knew everything under the sky, whenever they looked. The moment they turned around and looked around in the sky, on the earth, everything was seen without any obstruction. They didn't have to walk around before they could see what was under the sky; they just stayed where they were. As they looked, their knowledge became intense. Their sight passed through trees, through rocks, through lakes, through seas, through mountains, through plains. Jaguar Quitze, Jaguar Night, Mahucutah, and True Jaguar were truly gifted people. And then they were asked by the Builder and Mason: "What do you know about your being? Don't you look? Don't you listen? Isn't your speech good, and your walk? So you must look, to see out under the sky. Don't you see the mountain-plain clearly? So try it," they were told. And then they saw everything under the sky perfectly.

After that, they thanked the Maker, Modeler: "Truly now, double thanks, triple thanks that we've been formed. We've been given our mouths, our faces. We speak, we listen, we wonder, we move, our knowledge is good. We've understood what is far and near, and we've seen what is great and small under the sky, on the earth. Thanks to you we've been formed, we've come to be made and modeled, our grandmother, our grandfather," they said when they gave thanks for having been made and modeled.

They understood everything perfectly, they sighted the four sides, the four corners in the sky, on the earth, and this didn't sound good to the builder and sculptor: "What our works and designs have said is no good: 'We have understood everything, great and small,' they say."

And so the Bearer, Begetter took back their knowledge: "What should we do with them now? Their vision should at least reach nearby, they should see at least a small part of the face of the earth, but what they're saying isn't good. Aren't they merely 'works' and 'designs' in their very names? Yet they'll become as great as gods, unless they procreate, proliferate at the sowing, the dawning, unless they increase."

"Let it be this way: now we'll take them apart just a little, that's what we need. What we've found out isn't good. Their deeds would become equal to ours, just because their knowledge reaches so far. They see everything," so said the Heart of Sky, Hurricane, Newborn Thunderbolt, Raw Thunderbolt, Sovereign Plumed Serpent, Bearer, Begetter, Xpiyacoc, Xmucane, Maker, Modeler, as they are called.

And when they changed the nature of their works, their designs, it was enough that the eyes be marred by the Heart of Sky. They were blinded as the face of a mirror is breathed upon. Their eyes were weakened. Now it was only when they looked nearby that things were clear. And such was the loss of the means of understanding, along with the means of knowing everything, by the four humans.

The root was implanted. And such was the making, modeling of our first grandfather, our father, by the Heart of Sky, Heart of Earth. And then their wives and women came into being. Again, the same gods thought of it. It was as if they were asleep when they received them, truly beautiful women were there with Jaguar Quitze, Jaguar Night, Mahucutah, and True Jaguar. With their women there they became wider awake. Right away they were happy at heart again, because of their wives.

Celebrated Seahouse is the name of the wife of Jaguar Quitze. Prawn House is the name of the wife of Jaguar Night. Hummingbird House is the name of the wife of Mahucutah. Macaw House is the name of the wife of True Jaguar. So these are the names of their wives, who became ladies of rank, giving birth to the people of the tribes, small and great.

And this is our root, we who are Quiché people. And there came to be a crowd of penitents and sacrificers. It wasn't only four who came into being then but there were four mothers for us, the Quiché people. There were different names for each of the peoples when they multiplied, there in the east.

WORKS CITED AND SUGGESTIONS
FOR FURTHER READING

Alderink, Larry J. *Creation and Salvation in Ancient Orphism.* American Philosophical Association, American Classical Studies, no. 8. Chico, CA: Scholars Press, 1981.

Allen, Paula Gunn. *Grandmothers of Light: A Medicine Woman's Sourcebook.* Boston: Beacon Press, 1991.

Beckwith, Martha Warren, ed. and trans. *The Kumulipo: A Hawaiian Creation Chant.* Honolulu: University Press of Hawaii, 1972.

Bierhorst, John. *The Red Swan: Myths and Tales of the American Indians.* New York: Farrar, Straus, and Giroux, 1976.

Brandon, S. G. F. *Creation Legends of the Ancient Near East.* London: Hodder and Stoughton, 1963.

Budge, E. A. Wallis. *The Gods of the Egpytians.* Vols. 1 and 2. New York: Dover, 1969.

Crossley-Holland, Kevin. *The Norse Myths.* New York: Pantheon, 1980.

Doria, Charles, and Harris Lenowitz, eds. and trans. *Origins: Creation Texts from the Ancient Mediterranean, A Chrestomathy.* Garden City, NY: Anchor/Doubleday, 1976.

The Elder Edda: A Selection. Trans. Paul B. Taylor and W. H. Auden. London: Salus, 1969.

Eliade, Mircea. *Gods, Goddesses, and Myths of Creation: A Thematic Source Book of the History of Religions.* Part I of *From Primitives to Zen.* New York: Harper & Row, 1974.

———. *Myth and Reality.* New York: Harper & Row, 1975.

Farmer, Penelope, ed. *Beginnings: Creation Myths of the World.* New York: Atheneum, 1979.

Freund, Philip. *Myths of Creation.* Levittown, NY: Transatlantic Arts, 1975.

Gaster, Theodor. *Thespis: Myth, Ritual, and Drama in the Ancient Near East.* New York: Gordian, 1975.

Griaule, Marcel. *Conversations with Ogotemmêli: An Introduction to Dogon Religious Ideas.* London: Oxford University Press, 1965.

Heidel, Alexander. *The Babylonian Genesis: The Story of Creation.* 2nd ed. Chicago: University of Chicago Press, 1951.

Hewitt, John Napoleon Brinton. *Iroquoian Cosmology. 21st Annual Reports of the Bureau of American Ethnology (1899–1900).* Rpt. New York: AMS Press, 1974.

Kramer, Samuel Noah. *Mythologies of the Ancient World.* New York: Anchor/Doubleday, 1989.

Lincoln, Bruce. *Myth, Cosmos, and Society: Indo-European Themes of Creation and Destruction.* Cambridge, MA: Harvard University Press, 1986.

Long, Charles H. *Alpha: The Myths of Creation.* New York: George Braziller, 1963.

Maclagan, David. *Creation Myths: Man's Introduction to the World.* Art and Imagination Series. London: Thames and Hudson, 1977.

Markman, Roberta H., and Peter T. Markman. *The Flayed God: The Meso-American Mythological Tradition: Sacred Texts and Images from Pre-Columbian Mexico and Central America.* San Francisco: HarperCollins, 1992.

Newell, Venetia. *An Egg at Easter: A Folklore Study.* Bloomington: Indiana University Press, 1971.

O'Brien, Joan, and Wilfred Major. *In the Beginning: Creation Myths from Ancient Mesopotamia, Israel, and Greece.* American Academy of Religion. Aids for the Study of Religion Series, no. 11. Chico, CA: Scholars Press, 1982.

O'Bryan, Aileen. *The Dîne: Origin Myths of the Navajo Indians.* Smithsonian, Bureau of American Ethnology Bulletin 163. Washington: GPO, 1956.

The Prose Edda. Trans. Jean I. Young. Berkeley: University of California Press, 1971.

Reichard, Gladys A. *Navaho Religion: A Study of Symbolism.* 2nd ed. Princeton, NJ: Princeton University Press, 1990.

Rooth, Anna Birgitta. "Creation Myths of the North American Indians." *Anthropos* 52 (1957): 497–508.

Sproul, Barbara, ed. *Primal Myths: Creating the World.* San Francisco: Harper & Row, 1991.

Van Over, Raymond, ed. *Sun Songs: Creation Myths from Around the World.* New York: Penguin, 1984.

Van Wolde, Ellen. *Stories of the Beginning: Genesis 1–11 and Other Creation Stories.* Ridgefield, CT: Morehouse, 1997.

Von Franz, Marie-Louise. *Patterns of Creativity Mirrored in Creation Myths.* Dallas: Spring Publications, 1972.

Weigle, Marta. *Creation and Procreation: Feminist Reflections on Mythologies of Cosmogony and Parturition.* Philadelphia: University of Pennsylvania Press, 1989.

Wilson, Horace Hayman. *The Vishnu Purana: A System of Hindu Mythology and Tradition Translated from the Original Sanskrit and Illustrated by Notes Derived Chiefly from Other Puranas.* Calcutta, India: Punthi Pustak, 1972.

CHAPTER 3

The Female Divine

THE GREAT GODDESS

Was There a Great Goddess?

During the last century and a half, numerous and seemingly related prehistoric artifacts depicting female figures have been found in a wide range from France to Siberia and as far south as Greece. Among these ancient objects are engravings, statuettes, and relief carvings, dating anywhere from 30,000 to 5,000 BCE, some of which are adorned with designs such as crescents, spirals, triangles, meanders, egg shapes, and lozenges. Among the statuettes, a significant number are abstract representations of the female form, featuring exaggerated buttocks, breasts, vulvas, and bellies. The heads, legs, and arms of these statuettes tend to taper off into stumps and knobs without characteristic details such as fingers, toes, or even mouths and eyes. In the 19th and early 20th centuries, archaeologists and other prehistorians understood these images to be fertility objects or pornographic toys. But over the last 30 years, a growing number of archaeologists and anthropologists and other scholars, including historians, theologians, literary critics, and social theorists, have seen in these artifacts proof that human societies worshiped an all-powerful Great Goddess from whom the many goddesses of the historical period are descended. Led by Marija Gimbutas, whose *The Goddesses and Gods of Old Europe* (1982) connected the discourses of archaeology and the women's movement, a diverse group of Great Goddess proponents began to argue that early European cultures were, if not matriarchal (woman-dominated), matrifocal (woman-centered), and therefore they enjoyed greater gender equality, freedom from violence, and harmony with nature than currently experienced under the world's patriarchal (male-dominated) system.

In the decades following Gimbutas's theories of goddess religion and matrifocal society, the presumed existence of a kinder, gentler past gave rise to a wide variety of social phenomena, including modern revivals of goddess worship and earth-magic, a sharp critique of male-dominated political, religious, and educational institutions, and a new woman-centered vocabulary with which to discuss women's lives and relationships. Even before Gimbutas, few questioned the notion that

"Venus of Willendorf." Ht. 4.5 inches. 24,000 —22,000 BCE. Oolitic limestone covered with red ochre. Found in 1908 by Josef Szombathy in an Aurignacian loess deposit near the town of Willendorf, Austria.
Source: © Erich Lessing/Art Resource, NY.

"Venus of Laussel." Ht. 17 inches. 20,000 — 18,000 BCE. Limestone high-relief carving. Discovered in 1911 by J. G. Lalanne in the wall of a limestone rock shelter in the Dordogne region of France.
Source: © Erich Lessing/Art Resource, NY.

"Venus of Dolni Vestonice." Ht. 4.5 inches. 26,000 —24,000 BCE. Baked clay and bone ash. Found near Dolni Vestonice, Czechoslovakia, in 1925.
Source: Courtesy Anthropos Institute, Moravian Museum, Brno.

"Venus of Lespugue." Ht. 5.7 inches. 25,000 —18,000 BCE. Carved mammoth ivory. Found in 1922 in the Rideaux Cave of Lespugue (Hante-Garonne) in the foothills of the Pyrenees Mountains.
Source: © Scala/Art Resource, NY.

human societies began as goddess-oriented and matrifocal. Indeed, as far back as 1861 Johann Jakob Bachofen asserted, in *Das Mutterrecht (The Mother-Right),* that human societies evolved from "primitive" beginnings in small mother-ruled family units and clans to the vastly more complex and technologically superior cultural systems of patriarchy. In the early 20th century, Sir James Frazer's *The Golden Bough* elaborated upon Bachofen's conclusions, insisting that "primitive" religion was essentially fertility religion focused upon the relationship between an eternally fecund goddess and her son-consort, the "sacred king." By the mid-20th century, Jungian psychoanalysts had begun to explore the psychological dimensions of the modern world's presumed origins in matriarchy and worship of the maternal principle. Erich Neumann, for example, in *The Great Mother: An Analysis of the Archetype,* took as fact the early existence of matriarchy and a primitive religion of the Great Mother. A year later, in *Symbols of Transformation,* Jung himself made the unsettling pronouncement that, in order to deliver itself from the primal power of the Mother (the unconscious), the paternal principle of the Logos (the consciousness) in each person must engage in the creative act of "matricide" (1967, 251, 347). The "escape" of the individual consciousness from the Mother, Jung believed, paralleled the evolution of human society from its early matriarchal origins to its current patriarchal state.

Thus, throughout the 19th and 20th centuries, the literature of several disciplines took for granted the existence of a Primal Mother or Great Goddess and further assumed that her religion and the societies based upon it were part of the dark, primitive past from which *man* had happily escaped through the logocentric power of intellect. What was new about Gimbutas and her followers' work was its revaluation of this presumably matrifocal past. Rather than seeing the Goddess's religion as the crude and naive religion of primitive hunter-gatherers, members of what has become known as the Goddess Movement saw in humanity's Paleolithic and Neolithic past an appealing alternative to the brutality, materialism, spiritual bankruptcy, and ecological shortsightedness of modern patriarchal social systems. Where the male-dominated scientific establishment of the 19th and 20th centuries saw simplistic magic religion, sacred prostitution, and the ghastly spectacle of the dying god slaughtered and dismembered in the person of countless human sacred kings, the Goddess movement saw, in the words of Margaret W. Conkey and Ruth E. Tringham, that "past societies in Europe and the Near East, especially prior to the so-called invasion of the Indo-Europeans circa five thousand years ago . . . were Goddess-worshiping, female-centered, in harmony with their environments, and more balanced in male–female relationships" (1995, 206).

However, in the mid-1980s, a number of feminist archaeologists began to question the Goddess Movement's authoritarian pronouncements that the archaeological data unequivocally demonstrates the existence of a nearly universal Goddess religion that had existed for 30,000 years before being violently supplanted by male-dominated culture and religion. Equally problematic for this new wave of archaeologists was the claim that the material record of Paleolithic and Neolithic societies supports the claim that there existed a woman-centered Golden Age from which human societies have universally fallen. While sympathetic with some of the aims and concerns of the Goddess Movement, archaeologists such as Lucy Goodison and Christine Morris, authors of *Ancient Goddesses,* concluded that "in the rush to reclaim female history, Goddess writers have not addressed the complexity and diversity of the archaeological record; in the search for eternal verities they have failed to engage with its fluidity. By plucking out only those ancient artifacts whose faces fit their theory, they have not engaged with the primary evidence in a way which respects its context" (1998, 14). In short, they argued, members of the Goddess Movement weren't being scientific—or even completely honest about all that the archaeological record includes.

The terms of this growing debate are important because those conducting research into female divinity and/or its manifestation in specific goddesses are likely to encounter many books and articles that assume without question there once was a universally worshiped Great Goddess and that Her early human society was ecologically inclined, egalitarian, peaceful, and matrifocal. Substantially smaller and often considerably less accessible is the growing body of literature questioning what we actually *do* know about the past and, indeed, about the very artifacts that some say prove the existence of the Great Goddess.

In these pages, we consider the theory of a Great Goddess and an early woman-centered society as one of several possible explanations of the archaeological record. The close reading of myths can suggest strongly the vestigial presence of a Great Mother in even the most male-oriented of stories. Most likely, two important questions—Was there was a Great Goddess universally worshiped throughout Europe and much of northern Asia? and Did her religion inspire admirable societies that valued women and lived in harmony with their surroundings?—will never be entirely resolved. The cultures that produced the various figurines upon which the Goddess Movement has based its assumptions never developed writing. There will be no eyewitness accounts, no histories to which modern scholars can refer their hypotheses about the objects they unearth. Silenced by millennia, these objects do not speak for themselves but become meaningful only when an interpretation explains them. Without knowing who produced them and for what purposes, without a participant-observer's intimate knowledge of how these objects functioned and the beliefs and daily concerns of the people who created them, we cannot hope to discover unequivocal answers to the many questions the archaeological record raises.

The Case for the "Great Goddess"

Gimbutas's richly illustrated works, including *The Goddesses and Gods of Old Europe, The Language of the Goddess,* and *The Civilization of the Goddess,* focus on the ancient material record which inspired the so-called Goddess Movement. According to Gimbutas, "the continuity from the Paleolithic into the Neolithic of the portrayal of certain features of the human female body, which we may call stereotypes, is certain: it is a potent argument for the continuity of a philosophical idea; the repetitious occurrence of certain postures and other peculiarities throughout the millennia cannot otherwise be explained or understood" (1991b, 28). In other words, despite the fact that these images have been found in locations separated by hundreds or thousands of miles and associated with peoples separated by culture, language, and thousands of years, they nevertheless seem to represent the focus of a common religion—the worship of what some have called the Great Goddess Creatrix, the source and essence of life.

According to Gimbutas, the worship of the Goddess of Life, Death, and Regeneration was a universal religion in prehistoric Europe for some 30,000 years. She and others have argued that, until the beginning of the "Indo-European era when a very different social and religious system, dominated by males and male gods, began to supersede it" (1991b, 27), the social organization of Old European cultures was largely matrifocal. This is not to say that these peoples were matriarchal. But Gimbutas's interpretation of the archaeological evidence is that the female principle was the focus of social and religious life until the centuries between 4500 and 2500 BCE, when Old European social and religious systems began to fuse with the beliefs and customs of patrifocal (i.e., male-oriented) Indo-European invaders and settlers. If Gimbutas is right, what had once been a universal religion of the Great Mother, who was simultaneously the universe, the earth, and every woman and who possessed the awesome power to create, destroy, and regenerate on each of these levels, gradually gave way to the male-dominated religions of Indo-European immigrants.

Yet, according to the Goddess Movement's account of prehistoric events, the prehistoric religion of the Goddess was not entirely supplanted. Rather, elements of both male-centered and female-centered religions began to merge. As Gimbutas observes,

> The fusion of the two systems can be traced in practically all European mythologies. Even present myths, composed of many layers and with an accretion of features acquired through time, often retain the ancient features of certain figures at the core of the myth. This is particularly true in the myths of cosmogony, where the most ancient aspects of the Goddess Creatrix appear. In many beliefs, fairy tales, riddles, etc. of European peoples, mythical female images continue some characteristics of that prehistoric Goddess of Life, Death, and Regeneration. Even when severely demonized during the Christian era, their archaic features can be reconstructed. Such are the Slavic Baba Yaga and Paraskeva-Pjatnitsa; the Baltic Laima and Ragana; the Irish Machas, Morrigan, or Queen Medb; the Germanic Nerthus; and many others. The Fates—Norns, Moirae, Parcae—the apportioners, givers, and takers, clearly go back to the prehistoric [Goddess] and are not Indo-European in origin. (1991b, 29)

Looking for the Goddess in Hesiod

To test Gimbutas's claim that myths about a Great Goddess form a still-detectable substrate upon which later, patrifocal myths were constructed, let's apply it to part of the passage from Hesiod's *Theogony* found earlier in this book. In another famous passage from Hesiod, that of Pandora's Box (though it's a jar in the original Greek), the poet's statements about women suggest that he would have found incredible the claim that there was once a time when women-centered religion had been the norm. We can assume, then, the poet's cosmology is a pious attempt to present a straightforward account of Zeus's birth and conquest of the cosmos. Here are the lines from the *Theogony* included in Chapter 2:

> The very first to exist was Chaos
> and then Gaia whose expansive lap
> is the ever-safe foundation of the immortal gods

who live on the snowy peak of Olympos;
and then dark Tartaros, deep in the earth with its expansive paths;
and then Eros, the most beautiful of the gods
whose power loosens our bones —
who controls the thoughts and decisions
of every god and every man.

From Chaos came Erebos and black Night.
From Night came Air and Day,
whom she conceived and gave birth to
from her love with Erebos.

Then Gaia gave birth to someone her equal,
the starry sky Ouranos, so that he
would cover her whole
and be the ever-safe foundation of the blessed gods.

She gave birth to the high Mountains
where heavenly Nymphs enjoy life
in mountain valleys.
But without the pleasure of love
she bore Pontos whose stormy waves
are a barren sea. But then she
slept with Ouranos and bore Ocean
with his deep currents; then Koios and Krios;
Hyperion and Iapetos; and Theia and Rhea;
and Themis and Mnemosyne; and Phoebe
with her crown of gold;
and lovely Tethys; and after these
the youngest, most dreadful of her children, Kronos,
whose plans are crafty
and who hated his powerful father.   **116–38**

This ancient Greek cosmogonic myth does depict the basic framework of the material universe as coming into being through female agency. The primordial duo, Chaos and Gaia, create between them Night, Day, Air, the heavens (Ouranos), the seas and oceans, and the world's mountains. Presumably inspired by the god Eros, Gaia mates with her son, "the starry sky Ouranos," to also produce a first generation of gods and goddesses called the Titans. The female Titans mentioned in the preceding lines embodied the celestial lights, earth's mountains, the human and divine social orders, and the sea. Thus, writers of the Goddess Movement have argued, the Great Goddess is present in the persons of Theia, whose name could be translated "goddess of light," and Phoibe, who was associated with the full moon. She also appears in the person of Rheia, who was associated with mountains, and Themis, the "steadfast one," who, in Homer, is responsible for the social contract binding all humanity and without whom the Olympians could not convene. Likewise, the Great Goddess could be said to rule the waves in the person of Tethys, who was said by Homer to have given birth to 6,000 children, the female half of which were the Oceanids.

Many writers and scholars working within the traditions of literary criticism, art history, feminism, and new age spirituality would interpret the presence of Chaos, Gaia, and the female Titans at the beginning of an otherwise powerfully patrifocal narrative as the vestigial presence of Gimbutas's Triple Goddess of Birth, Death, and Regeneration. The presence of Chaos at the beginning of all things, it could be argued, represents the womblike potential of the universe to generate matter. More concretely, the *Theogony* explicitly depicts Gaia, the Earth, as the source of terrestrial matter, the gods, and Tartaros, the dungeon of the underworld. Thus Gaia's role in the *Theogony* resonates with the Great Goddess's association with the ever-fertile earth and the mysteries of death. Despite its matrifocal beginning, however, Hesiod's narrative centers on the deeds of the male divinities born through the primeval activities of these female powers. In addition, the power of sexual desire and its promise of an ever-renewing natural order is attributed not to a goddess but to the god Eros. In the *Theogony,* we read at length of how male power begets rather than bears life and how, through military might and wily ambition, it imposes the Olympian order upon the universe, including the mostly silent, mostly submissive divine mothers and mistresses who comprise the feminine members of the Classical Greek pantheon.

Such modern euhemerists as Gimbutas, Elinor Gadon, Joseph Campbell, Riane Eisler, Merlin Stone, Mary Daly, Starhawk, and Pamela Berger have claimed or simply assumed that myths like the *Theogony* present a garbled religious and cultural history of Old Europe. Hesiod, they might argue, unwittingly organizes and transmits a fragmentary and encoded history of the Great Goddess's religion. And undoubtedly the sequence of events in his narrative does raise intriguing questions along these lines. Does the birth of the cosmos through female agency and the eventual arrival of the violent and overpowering Ouranos, Kronos, and Zeus parallel the fate of matrifocal Old Europe at the hands of patrifocal Indo-European invaders? For that matter, doesn't the fact that Tiamat, the female presence that presides over the dark, primordial deep at the beginning of the *Enuma Elish,* fights and eventually loses a fierce battle with Enki and the other major male gods of the Babylonian pantheon suggest a similarly violent end for female-oriented religious and social culture in the Near East?

Many scholars and writers during the past century would answer yes to these questions. For example, Robert Graves, author of *Greek Myths* and *The White Goddess,* repeatedly suggests that Zeus's and Apollo's sexual pursuit of nymph and goddess are, at bottom, political allegories about the displacement of Old Europe's prehistoric Goddess religion by an insurgent male-centered social and religious culture. Elinor Gadon asserts that "the demise of the Goddess can be traced back to the invasions of warlike nomadic peoples from the Asiatic and European north who overran the centers of Goddess culture in southeastern Europe, the Near East, and India causing large-scale destruction and dislocation. They brought with them their sky gods who ruled from the heavens like despots" (1989, xiii). In the same vein, Riane Eisler claims "gradually, in the service of their earthly and divine lords and kings, the artists, bards, scribes, and priests of the ruling men replaced the matrifocal, female-oriented myths and images of the civilization of Old [matrifocal] Europe. But so strong is the memory of an earlier and better time that, albeit in distorted form, it still lingers on" (1991, 14).

The Case against a "Great Goddess"

As already noted, a small but steadily growing number of archaeologists in the past 15 years have urged caution on those who would look at a handful of artifacts and extrapolate from them an entire civilization—and one morally superior to our own. Since the Paleolithic and Neolithic figures depicting the abstract and exaggerated female form have inspired and, to some extent, authorized the Goddess Movement, it is not surprising that the debate about the Great Goddess centers on how we may best understand their meaning. Conkey and Tringham summarize the evolution of the "traditional view" this way:

> Late-nineteenth- and early-twentieth-century authors claimed that the female fig-urines—especially those of the Upper Paleolithic—with large stomachs and so-called pendulous breasts . . . depicted pregnancy and/or lactation and therefore signified fertil-ity and the magical desires for successful births in order to maintain the viability of the (supposedly precarious) population. Most traditional authors assume that the depiction of biological and essential female traits meant that females in the Upper Paleolithic were the objects not just of image-making but of social control and male desire; that their place and functions in Paleolithic society were biologically determined and determina-tive; and that women's status was therefore less cultural and less central to the highly val-ued arenas of artistic production, political control, and other domains of social and rit-ual power. In contrast, most Goddess authors view the fertility interpretation for both Paleolithic and Neolithic figurines as a positive attribution that highlights the cultural importance and centrality of female qualities and biological powers. (1995, 212–13)

Conkey and Tringham point out that neither the traditional male-centered nor the Goddess Movement's female-centered view of the "Goddess" figurines consid-ers whether or not large bellies and breasts do, in fact, symbolize pregnancy and lac-tation. How can we know, they ask, what motherhood meant to—or what best sym-bolized that meaning for—people who lived 20,000 years ago? For that matter, how can we know that these statuettes represent a goddess at all? What does the archae-ological record really tell us about whether they were considered sacred or profane? Conkey and Tringham also declare that the so-called goddess figurines featured so prominently in Gimbutas's work and in many introductory mythology and archae-ology texts are not a representative sample of the many figurines recovered in the past century and a half. A number of archaeologists, including Sarah M. Nelson and Alice B. Kehoe, have pointed out that the obviously female figurines from the Pale-olithic and Neolithic periods do not all look alike and are not found in the same con-texts. Marcia-Ann Dobres argues that the Goddess Movement writers conveniently forget that most figurines from these periods are not female. Indeed, Peter Ucko and others have observed that most of the human figurines recovered from either of these "stone ages" cannot authoritatively be ascribed to either sex. In addition, Conkey and Tringham say, not only are the so-called goddess figurines only a small subset of the total number of similar objects recovered by modern science, but "there is no evidence about the sex/gender of [their] makers or of the audience for whom [these] images were intended" (1995, 215). These archaeologists remind us that, although many Goddess Movement writers use such terms as *religion* and *ritual* and refer to *shrines* and other *holy places,* we cannot assume prehistoric peoples distinguished between the sacred and profane in the same way modern Judeo-Christian belief does. And, if we cannot be sure whether a site was considered *sacred* in the same sense that we understand the term, how can we be certain the figurines found in those sites had any religious significance for their makers?

Goodison and Morris raise another important concern about the existence of an ancient Goddess: "Contemporary writers often overlook the fact that the existence of a 'Mother Goddess' in prehistory was a matter of consensus from the late nineteenth century onwards for many male scholars who found this image compatible with their sense of the female as a primitive, 'natural,' sexual, maternal being utterly divorced from their 'rational' male world" (1998, 13). In other words, the Goddess Movement has simply reversed the values of male-dominated, Victorian-era science, never questioning whether our prehistoric forebears imposed the same strict male–female polarities upon their world or held the same assumptions about the erotic and the symbolic as we do. At bottom, Goodison and Morris are troubled by the tendency among many in the Goddess Movement to assume there is a single, fixed definition of woman and a single, original religion. One cannot, they would argue, genuinely and profitably engage the archaeological record if one's mind is already made up that women and men are and have always been the same and that the human world divides itself neatly into followers of peace-loving, nurturing earthmothers or war-mongering, despotic sky-fathers.

ARCHETYPAL PSYCHOLOGY

Goddesses in Therapy

In addition to developments in the field of archaeology during the past two decades, some Jungian psychologists have resurrected the Great Goddess and put her to work in the therapist's office. Analysts such as Roger Woolger and Jennifer Barker Woolger and Jean Shinoda Bolen, as well as many other scholars, feminists, and "New Age" enthusiasts, have argued that the powerful archetypal forces shaping women's lives can be represented "in the guise of Greek goddesses." These goddesses, then, embody various types of female personality. As Bolen puts it, these shaping forces—these goddesses—are

> responsible for major differences among women. For example, some women need monogamy, marriage, or children to feel fulfilled, and they grieve and rage when the goal is beyond their reach. . . . Such women differ markedly from another type of woman who most values her independence as she focuses on achieving goals that are important to her, or from still another type who seeks emotional intensity and new experiences and consequently moves from one relationship or one creative effort to the next. Yet another type of woman seeks solitude and finds that her spirituality means the most to her. What is fulfilling to one type of woman may be meaningless to another, depending on which "goddess" is active. (1985, 1–2)

The Goddess Within

Woolger and Woolger describe the basic archetypes shaping women's lives by associating them with the following goddesses: (1) Athena: Warrior Woman in the World; (2) Artemis: Heart of the Lonely Huntress; (3) Aphrodite: Golden Goddess

"Pallas Athene, 1898." Gustav Klimt. Oil on canvas. The artist captures the power and characteristics traditionally ascribed to Athene by depicting her wearing a helmet and carrying a spear in one hand and a globe surmounted by a nude female in the other.
Source: © Erich Lessing/Art Resource, NY.

of Love; (4) Hera: Queen and Partner in Power; (5) Persephone: Medium, Mystic, and Mistress of the Dead; and (6) Demeter: Mother of Us All. In their scheme, the Great Mother Goddess of Old Europe possessed six major attributes or areas of "rulership": Mother, Power, Civilization, Eros, the Underworld, and Nature. Woolger and Woolger see these six qualities as reducible to three "Goddess Dyads," which "arrange themselves broadly around the temperamental orientations of introversion and extraversion" (1989, 39). Thus Athena, the goddess of such civilized pursuits as technology, warfare, politics, education, priestcraft, and statecraft, is opposed to Artemis, the goddess of nature, virgin wilderness, animals, the moon, and instinct. For the purposes of psychological typing, Woolger and Woolger see the Athena woman on the extraverted end of her dyad and suggest that this goddess "rules" the psyche of the modern career woman, who is comfortable with competition, strategy, technology, and commerce. The Artemis woman, by contrast, would be the introverted member of this pair, a woman quite comfortable with solitude and well-attuned to the rhythms of her body and nature. Both psychological types in this first dyad are linked by their fierce independence, but one directs her energies outward and the other inward.

The second dyad concerns power. The Hera woman is the extraverted member here, and she pursues power outwardly into the sociopolitical sphere. Hera might be said to rule in a woman who leads or lends vital support to social, political, and religious movements, wishing to preserve traditional social and moral institutions such as the political status quo, marriage, fidelity, and familial unity. Hera's contrasting partner, Persephone, pursues power inwardly and rules in women intensely interested in the mystical, magical, and spiritual possibilities within themselves and others.

Finally, Demeter and Aphrodite confront each other across the love dyad; but in this case, the intro- and extraversion of their pursuits are mixed. As Woolger and Woolger put it, "we can see in them a subtle contrast between how they express love and how they experience their bodies. Demeter reserves her love for her children, serving as a selfless container for all her loved ones both physically and spiritually. Aphrodite nurtures spiritually and physically, but not by containing or mothering those she loves. What she gives to her lover is his (or her) full maturity and otherness" (1989, 34–39). And so we might find a Demeter woman pursuing love and life by working tirelessly to raise and nurture her children in an orderly, safe home and an Aphrodite woman pursuing beauty, emotional intensity, and self-knowledge through a variety of artistic endeavors and sexual encounters.

Everywoman's Goddess

Bolen's list of archetypal goddesses is similar, but not identical: (1) Artemis: Goddess of the Hunt and Moon, Competitor and Sister; (2) Athena: Goddess of Wisdom and Crafts, Strategist and Father's Daughter; (3) Hestia: Goddess of the Hearth and Temple, Wise Woman and Maiden Aunt; (4) Hera: Goddess of Marriage, Commitment Maker and Wife; (5) Demeter: Goddess of Grain, Nurturer and Mother; (6) Persephone: Maiden and Queen of the Underworld, Receptive Woman and Mother's Daughter; and (7) Aphrodite: Goddess of Love and Beauty, Creative Woman and Lover. Bolen's argument that these goddesses are archetypal "models of being and behaving [that] we recognize from the collective unconscious we all share" also subdivides these images of female psychological types into three categories but does not pair them along an axis of intro- and extraversion. Rather, as Bolen describes it,

> I have divided these seven goddesses into three categories: the virgin goddesses, the vulnerable goddesses, and the alchemical (or transformative) goddess . . . Modes of consciousness, favored roles, and motivating factors are distinguishing characteristics of each group. Attitudes toward others, the need for attachment, and the importance of relationships also are distinctly different in each category. Goddesses representing all three categories need expression somewhere in a woman's life—in order for her to love deeply, work meaningfully, and be sensual and creative. (1985, 15–16)

As a group, the virgin goddesses represent qualities of independence and self-direction. Bolen contends that "as archetypes, they express the need in women for autonomy, and the capacity women have to focus their consciousness on what is personally meaningful. Artemis and Athena represent goal-directedness and logical thinking . . . Hestia [goddess of the fires of home and the temple] is the archetype that focuses attention inward, to the spiritual center of a woman's personality" (1985, 16). The second group of vulnerable goddesses are "the relationship-oriented goddess archetypes, whose identities and well-being depend on having a significant relationship. They express women's needs for affiliation and bonding" (17). Aphrodite, the alchemical goddess of Love and Beauty, stands alone in Bolen's scheme, combining qualities of the virgin and vulnerable goddesses. Or, in Bolen's words, "She generated love and beauty, erotic attraction, sensuality, sexuality, and new life. She entered relationships of her own choosing and was never victimized. Thus she maintained her autonomy, like a virgin goddess, and was in relationships, like a vulnerable goddess" (17). Aphrodite is the inner image of women's desire for intense rather than permanent relationships and motivates them to value creative process and to remain open to change.

Both Woolger and Woolger and Bolen seek not a way of stereotyping women but a language for describing the inner images that motivate a wide range of behaviors and that condition the quality and intensity of women's relationships to others. Both texts emphasize that all women are motivated at various times by each of the archetypes, but that various tendencies of personality eventually bring the individual woman back to a primary or ruling goddess. That is, the primary archetype in each woman accounts for lifelong patterns of behavior even as her ability to actualize other archetypes accounts for the possibility that a woman might form bonds and make choices that otherwise might seem "out of character." In Bolen's terms, then, women whose primary motivation derives from one of the independent goddesses can and do at various times seek relationships, even as women primarily guided by the vulnerable goddesses can and do act independently, focusing their energies inward and/or toward personally fulfilling projects and activities.

GODDESSES AS LITERARY CHARACTER TYPES

The Triple Goddess

As this discussion demonstrates, the language of myth crystallizes around a limited number of images of women. Whether or not there existed a worldwide religion of the Great Goddess of Life, Death, and Regeneration, and whether or not archetypal psychology is correct about the forces impelling women's behaviors, these three domains nevertheless suggest the literary character types that anyone can observe in stories about goddesses. Many scholars have written on the notion of a Triple Goddess. That is, they have argued that the feminine divine reveals itself in three areas of influence corresponding to stages in a woman's life cycle. Robert Graves discusses these goddess types as three aspects of a single, complex female deity in his famous *The White Goddess.* More recently, Adam McLean echoes Graves's view, saying that the "triplicity of the Goddess is very important . . . [and] the most important triple aspect of the Goddess is her manifestation as Virgin/Mother/Crone. This is perhaps the easiest representation . . . as this triplicity corresponds to the three phases of a woman's life" (1989, 14–15). Although the Virgin/Mother/Crone trinity makes clear the three basic roles that goddesses in the world's various myths play, we are cautious about using it here because it typifies goddesses along patri-focal lines. That is, goddesses in this scheme are described in terms of their desir-ability to or relationship with men. Surely such a way of imagining the possibilities of goddesses—and women—is suspect. We therefore prefer to view the three basic roles goddesses play in Gimbutas's terms—Life, Death, and Regeneration.

Goddesses of Life

Depicted as goddesses of Life, the world's female divinities are Mothers Earth, the material cosmos, Nature, the Primordial Sea, and Celestial Queens. They are si-multaneously every mother and the Universal Womb, the nurturing presence that births, feeds, clothes, teaches, and guards all living things. Life goddesses can be de-picted, like the Sumerian goddess Tiamat, the Greek goddess Chaos, the Hindu god-dess Aditi ("Mother Space"), or the Nahua goddess Cipactli, as the ruler and essence of the dark, primeval sea that in so many creation myths precedes the appearance of physical matter. In this guise, they are pictured as the infinite, uncreated, immea-surable Creator who transcends even the limits of space and time. In the case of Cipactli, the Great Goddess of ancient Mexico who swam through the primordial waters of chaos in the form of an enormous caiman (a crocodilian), life goddesses bear within themselves all potential life. In the Nahuan conception—as in that of the Sumerians—this potential may be released only through the tearing of the di-vine body. And so, in the Nahuan story, two gods appear and rip Cipactli in half. One half of her body fell through the watery void and became the earth; the other half remained above and became the sky. Her eye sockets and mouth became caves from which the Nahua believed they could hear the sobs of Cipactli at night, groaning with longing for all life to die back into her and thus restore her to her original caiman form.

Perhaps more familiar are depictions of the Goddess as Great Mother, who is, literally, the ground from which we derive sustenance and the creator of all life upon it. Gaia of the ancient Greeks and Tellus of the Romans were both known as Mother Earth. From their ever-fertile soil-flesh sprang not only the earth's vast array of flora and fauna but their human children and the very gods. Over time, these Mothers Earth receded into the background while their daughters Demeter and Ceres, the Greek and Roman goddesses of grain and vegetal fertility, came to be revered for their gentleness and the life-sustaining grain over which they had influence. Deme-ter's love for her daughter Persephone emphasizes not only Demeter's influence on vegetation but the tenderness and permanence of maternal bonds.

There are numerous other examples of Mother Earth goddesses. In ancient Es-tonia, for example, Ma Emma was worshiped as source of all life. At harvest time, the people gathered at lone trees and rock outcroppings believed to be her physical manifestations on earth, spreading the first fruits of the harvest on the ground and saying "I give back to you what you have already given to me." The original inhab-itants of Ireland called themselves the Tuatha de Danu, the People of the Goddess Danu. While few stories about Danu have survived, the Great Mound at Newgrange outside Dublin has been taken by some to suggest that she was once considered the all-powerful Earth, the great womb from which all life springs and the great tomb to which it eventually returns. Newgrange is an underground site, its entrance stones, walls, and ceiling carved with giant spirals and inverted triangles, which are understood by many in the Goddess Movement as symbols of the Divine Womb and Vulva. Only once a year, on the Winter Solstice, this underground temple, which was built 500 years before the Egyptian pyramids, briefly receives sunlight through a hole in the roof, perhaps suggesting the fertilizing presence of earth-mother Danu's consort, the sun-father the Dagdu. If such speculations about the mythic significance of Newgrange are correct, the mound is a symbol depicting the Goddess as the still center of the ever-turning wheel of life and death.

In human affairs, life goddesses oversee the institutions that create the conditions for security and contentment, prosperity and growth, creativity and artistry. Like Greek Hera and Hestia, some life goddesses are depicted as encouraging and protecting the fundamental institutions of civilization—marriage and family. Hestia, the goddess of the hearth, had no bodily form but existed in the flames around which every family drew together for warmth and nourishment. Other life goddesses, like the Greek Horae—Eunomia ("lawful order"), Dike ("justice"), and Eirene ("peace")—personified the importance of law and order to human civilization. Among the Nigerian Ibo, Ala (or Ane) was thought to be mother earth and enforcer of community values and guardian of morality. Oaths sworn by Ala were considered sacred vows and courts of law were convened in her name.

Sometimes life goddesses combine several qualities. For example, Ardvi Sura Anahita, one of the most powerful divinities of the Persians, was depicted as both nurturing mother and fierce, armored protectress of her people. Anahita, whose name means "moist, powerful, immaculate one," was believed to control the fertilizing force of water, including semen and mother's milk, and was believed to ride through the earth on a chariot drawn by four horses. The Ugaritic goddess Anat also embodied the seemingly contradictory qualities of sexual vitality, virginity, and military ferocity. In Greece, Athena was depicted as a virginal military strategist, but she was less associated with sexuality. Instead, the "grey-eyed goddess" of ancient Athens was thought to be a sponsor of domestic industry, particularly weaving.

Among the Sioux, White Buffalo Calf Woman was said to have come to the people in the form of a beautiful woman who showed them how to construct Big Medicine tipis, red-earth altars, and the sacred pipe. She also instructed them in sacred rituals for smoking tobacco, preparing the dead, and purifying members of the tribe for ceremonial purposes. To women, White Buffalo Calf Woman gave corn, wild turnips, and knowledge of various seeds. Before disappearing, she gave all people the buffalo for meat and showed them how to cook it with corn in a buffalo skin.

Goddesses of life, then, foster civilization and culture as queens and law-givers, as priestesses and culture-bringers, as warriors and strategists, as technicians and agriculturalists, and as performers and artisans.

Goddesses of Death

Goddesses of Death, on the other hand, are revealed as manifestations of the earthen tomb which enfolds our spent bodies and Queens of the Underworld who receive our spirits when we die. They frequently appear in the world's myths as ancient wise

women, witches, and mediums. As seers, goddesses of Death or their earthly representatives are often depicted as portals through which humans, bound by the limitations of our space-time, and the unimaginable beings in unbounded eternity can
communicate. As witches, they are alchemists and apothecaries capable of manipu-
lating the elements and laws of nature to heal or harm. As queens of the Underworld,
goddesses of death frequently control the seasonal cycle which rotates through periods of fertility and sterility. In ancient Egypt, Isis was believed to have recon-
structed and resurrected her murdered and dismembered husband-brother Osiris,
the god of the Nile. The Egyptian goddess's long search for Osiris's dismembered
body was manifested on earth in the dry winter season's sterility, even as her magical power to restore him to near-wholeness was evident in the annual flooding of the
Nile and return of vegetative fertility. Isis's power over death gave rise to her widespread worship throughout the Mediterranean world. In Roman times she was believed to be able to extend her faithful followers' lives beyond the limits set by fate
and to greet them when they finally entered the Underworld.

"The Burney Plaque." Ht. 40 inches. Terracotta relief.
2200–2000 BCE. While not all scholars agree that the
goddess depicted in this image is Lilith, the wings, bird
feet, and presence of owls have all been cited as evidence that it is. Compounding this mystery are the as yet
unidentified symbolic objects that she holds in her hand.
Source: © Christie's Images.

Similar stories are told around the world. In ancient Greece, Persephone was abducted by Hades and became Queen of the Underworld, an event that so angered her mother, Demeter, that the elder goddess of life refused to let anything grow or breed upon the earth until her daughter was restored. Zeus, anxious to ensure that the people of earth had enough food and wine to offer the gods their customary sacrifices, brokered a deal with his brother Hades that allowed Persephone to visit her mother for half the year, and thus the earth is fertile for half the year and sterile for the other half. In Japan, the goddess Izanami, after giving birth to Japan's islands, mountains, waterfalls, plants, and animals, died when giving birth to fire. Her grieving husband, Izanagi, sought her out, eventually finding her in Yomi, the gloomy land of the dead. By the time he arrived, however, Izanami had established a palace and court, and she was reluctant to return with her husband to the light. Eventually she suggested that he ask the lord of death for her release, forbidding him to look upon her in the meantime. Unable to contain his curiosity, however, Izanagi made a torch from one of the teeth of a hair comb and looked in at Izanami's rotting corpse. Outraged at this humiliation, Izanami chased the terrified Izanagi all the way back to the light, screaming that his actions constituted a divorce. She then returned to her palace in Yomi. In this story, the male half of the primordial parents rules in the land of the living and the female half in the land of the dead.

In Sumerian tradition, Inanna undertook a visit to her sister, Ereshkigal, the Queen of the Underworld. The Queen of the Dark City, however, suspected that her more powerful sister planned to extend her influence beyond heaven and earth and to take over the underworld. In anger, Ereshkigal killed her sister. Inanna's corpse hung on a hook in the land of the dead for three days and nights, until her faithful attendant, Ninshubur, arranged with Enki, the god of wisdom, to resurrect her. But, as Ereshkigal tells Inanna, those who enter the underworld do not return unmarked. If Inanna is to rise again, said her sister, someone will have to take her place. Eventually, Inanna chose her husband, Dumuzi, to replace her in the underworld, only to repent a short time later. She laments the sterility of Dumuzi's sheepfolds, the silence of his reed-flute, the emptiness of his cup. Eventually, Dumuzi's sister Geshtinanna volunteers to take her brother's place in the underworld for half the year, thus suggesting yet again the cyclical nature of the seasons.

As witches and keepers of occult lore, death goddesses frequently draw their power from the secret depths of the Underworld. Airmed of the ancient Irish, the Greek Hekate, and the Navajo Glispa were believed to possess great magical power and were associated with death, snakes, and the Underworld. Airmed, for example, gained occult knowledge after her brother Miach's death. From his grave, all the herbs of the world sprang forth and Airmed learned and taught their various properties. The Navajo's Glispa gave the sacred healing chant to her people after learning it from her lover, chief of the snake people. Living underground, the snake people were believed to possess the serpent's regenerative power, growing old and becoming young again in a pattern reminiscent of the stories of Demeter-Persephone, Inanna-Dumuzi-Gesthinanna, and Isis-Osiris. In many cultures, snakes were considered sacred messengers from the Underworld, perhaps because they were so often seen entering and returning from holes in the earth.

Hekate, the quintessential witch of the ancient Greeks, was said by some to have had three heads—a horse's, a dog's, and a snake's. She was honored through special suppers in which sorcerer's secrets were whispered by her faithful followers and through food offerings left outside their homes. After the advent of Roman rule, Hekate was honored in public ceremonies with sacrifices of black dogs and lambs or even African slaves. In post-Christian eastern Europe, Baba Yaga, like Hekate, made her rounds under cover of night, rowing through the air in a mortar, using a pestle for an oar, and sweeping away the traces of her flight with a broom. She lived in the woods, scaring passersby to death so that she could eat them and decorate her fence with their skulls.

Baba Yaga was also believed to steal or kill children in their cribs. This cruel delight links her with a widespread and ancient tradition of she-demons thought to prey upon infants. Lilith is perhaps the most famous of these terrors of the night. In esoteric Judaism it is believed that Lilith was Adam's first wife, coeval and coequal with him. But Lilith soon rejected Adam, who had the temerity to suggest that she lie underneath him during intercourse. Lilith, like Isis, was said once to have tricked the supreme deity into revealing his secret name, thereby giving her ultimate magical power. Because he could no longer refuse her, Jehovah granted Lilith a set of beautiful wings which she used to fly from Eden. Often appearing to desert travelers in the form of owls, kites, jackals, wildcats, or wolves, Lilith is most often depicted as having beautiful flowing hair, a shapely body, and talons instead of feet. Lilith usually claimed her tiny victims at night, tickling their feet to make them giggle before strangling them. Similar stories are told of the Sumerian Lamasthu, Greek Lamia, and Japanese Kishimogin—all of whom were thought to prey upon newborns and infants. Mothers could easily protect their children, however, by fashioning talismans of various kinds bearing the name of these she-demons or the names of protective spirits.

In human affairs, goddesses of Death often operate as Fates, apportioning to each his and her share of light and life, illness and health, prosperity and poverty. Such were the Greek Moirae—Clotho, the "spinner" who spun the thread of life, Lachesis, the "measurer" who determined its length, and Atropos, the "inevitable" one who snipped it with her shears. Such, too, were the Norns—Urd, Verdandi, and Skuld—the three sisters reputed to be at the base of Yggdrasil, the World Tree of Norse myth. These sisters drew water daily from Urd's well, mixing it with gravel, and carefully measuring out just enough for Yggdrasil upon which not only human life but the entire universe depended. Like the Moirae, the Norns were more powerful than the rest of the gods; their will could not be altered and their judgments could not later be undone. Other goddesses presided over length of life and death as well. The ancient Mexican Coatlicue, the fivefold "serpent-skirted goddess," was often depicted as wearing a garland of human hearts and hands, a skirt of snakes hung with skulls, and a human-skin vest. Sometimes depicted as a woman with four sisters, Coatlicue was also thought to be the great mother of all living things as well as a moon goddess, able to give birth while forever remaining a virgin.

Goddesses of Regeneration

Finally, Goddesses of Regeneration appear as virgins and nymphs, as objects or embodiments of sexual desire, and as sponsors of and the inspiration for everything beautiful. They excite and entrance, inspire and conquer, may be had by all but possessed by none. In human affairs, Goddesses of Regeneration appear as irresistible erotic power and feminine allure. They punish those who resist their charms or who would forsake the marriage bed. As powers of regeneration and constant renewal, they mandate that all life must expend its force in order to procreate, thus ensuring continuity in a world of continual change, separation, and loss. Archaeologists and historians have identified many carvings, statues, and temples dedicated to "fertility" goddesses around the world. While fertility is certainly an element of what these images and sacred places celebrate, it is more accurate to say that they honor female sexual power.

Looking to examples from classical Greek and Latin sources, we see that Demeter/Ceres and Aphrodite/Venus held sway in related but ultimately separate spheres of influence. The Grain Mothers were thought to influence the ability of vegetation to grow and ripen each year, and each goddess was beloved for her stereotypically maternal qualities—gentleness, modesty, and unstinting nurture. Aphrodite/Venus, on the other hand, represented the power of women to excite, attract, and inspire men. In a Greek world that placed a great premium on rationality and a Roman world that likewise valued reason, order, and discipline, Regeneration Goddesses elicited considerable ambivalence. In Greek tradition, Aphrodite emerges from the primordial sea after Kronos castrates his father Ouranos, an act that was necessary to create an inhabitable world. Yet this story also attests to the link that the Ancient Greeks saw between the raw power of sexual allure and violence.

In the cases of the heroes Jason and Paris, Aphrodite's generous and pleasant gifts carry with them a terrible price. Through Aphrodite's influence, Medea falls in love with Jason, making it possible for him to win the Golden Fleece, which, in turn, makes possible his triumphant return home and his accession to his father's throne. Yet, when Jason's ardor for Medea cools and he marries a younger, prettier, and richer woman, Medea slaughters their children and incinerates his new bride, fleeing, at least in Euripides's play, with the children's bodies on a magical chariot into exile. Likewise, Aphrodite promises and delivers to Paris the love of the most beautiful woman in the world—Helen—who also happens to be married to Menelaus, king of Sparta. When she falls hopelessly in love with Paris and flees with him to Troy, Menelaus raises a great army and launches the proverbial thousand ships to avenge his loss and restore his pride. After nine years of siege and numerous bloody but inconclusive battles, the Greeks finally win the Trojan War through deception rather than military might. And Paris, who once enjoyed the love of the world's most beautiful woman, lives long enough to see his city destroyed and his people butchered or sold into slavery.

The world's mythic traditions are filled with stories of irresistible nymphs and insatiable lovers, most of them suggesting that men must pay for intense sexual passion with their lives. In Irish lore, Neeve of the Golden Hair (Niamh), whose very name means beauty, was known to be the daughter of the sea and queen of Tir-nan-Og, the land of the Blessed, thought to exist almost beyond human reach in the western ocean. Like many Goddesses of Regeneration around the world, Niamh had a weakness for mortal lovers. Once, it is said, Niamh stole Ossian away from his people to Tir-nan-Og where they lived together for uncountable years in loving bliss. On the Isle of the Blessed, even the mortal Ossian remained forever young and free from need and care. All the while, Ossian's people, the Fianna, grew old and eventually died out. Centuries passed in the mortal world and still Ossian remained young and enjoyed the warm embrace of the goddess of beauty. Yet, despite his seemingly perfect situation, Ossian eventually grew homesick and his pining and complaining grew worse and worse. Finally, Niamh could stand it no more and sent Ossian home on a magical horse, warning the poet not to dismount. But no sooner did the horse's hooves touch the soil of the human world than the saddle buckle broke, hurling Ossian to the ground. In that instant, the years that Ossian had evaded while on the Isle of the Blessed fell upon him. In a matter of moments, Ossian grew sick, old, and died, turning to dust.

A nearly identical story is told of the Japanese sea goddess, Oto-Hime. She falls in love with a mortal fisherman, taking him to her palace on the ocean floor. There, for what seemed only a short time, the couple took delight in lovemaking and life in Oto-Hime's royal court. Like Ossian, the Japanese fisherman begins to worry about those he has left behind and begs Oto-Hime to allow him to return. She agrees, on the condition that he carry a tiny box with him to the surface and never open it. He eagerly agrees to her conditions. But when he returns to his village, he soon discovers that hundreds of human years have passed during his seemingly brief stay in Oto-Hime's underwater palace. In glum bewilderment, the fisherman sits down upon a rock overlooking the sea. Absentmindedly, he opens the forbidden box. Instantly, all the years he'd missed while with Oto-Hime surround him like dense smoke, causing his body to wither and turn to dust.

Variations on this theme include stories like that of the French Celtic water spirit Pressina and her daughter Melusine, both of whom were said to have taken mortal husbands under the strict condition that they should not be viewed on certain days. Both mother and daughter were betrayed by their husbands' curiosity to see the forbidden and both therefore abandoned these mortals in terrible anger and sorrow. Each of these stories suggest that the Goddess's gift of emotional and sensual delights demands total commitment. In the case of Jason and Medea, Niamh and Ossian, and Oto-Hime and the Fisherman, regeneration goddesses offer sexual bliss and deeply satisfying companionship but demand unswerving devotion in return. One plummets from the arms of the goddess into disaster if anything, even a wish to see family and friends, intervenes. These stories emphasize that passion is an all-consuming emotional force, one that mortals cannot sustain forever. In the case of Pressina and Melusine, the Japanese goddesses Toyo-Tama-Hime and Uki-Onne, or the Irish goddess Aine, the emphasis is somewhat different. In each of these tales, a promise is extracted that human nature—especially masculine human nature—proves too weak to keep. In these latter stories, the gifts of love still come at a price, but the issue isn't so much unwavering devotion as it is trust and respect.

Other goddesses embodying female sexual power bestow their gifts with fewer strings attached. In India, esoteric tradition has it that Rati, goddess of passionate night, symbolizes enlightenment because the delights she bestows under the cover of darkness lead to awakened consciousness and clarity. Xochiquetzal, the Aztec goddess of flowers, was, like the Roman goddess Flora, associated with beauty and honored on holidays where nudity and sexual license were important parts of her worship. Ezili or Dahomey, the loa (spirit) of sensual enjoyment in Haitian voodoo, is revered for her extravagant generosity. Hit, the Octopus Woman of Micronesia, was so powerfully erotic that even the jealous wife of one of the sky gods fainted from excitement when she came to drag her wayward husband back to heaven. In these cases, the regeneration goddesses appear to represent the sensual rather than the emotional forces associated with love and sex. They neither demand loyalty or commitment, nor do they offer it.

In the natural world, regeneration goddesses often ordain the fertile moment and set in motion the seasons, tides, and celestial phases that are the very rhythm of nature. In Greek myth, the Horae were sometimes envisioned as a pair—Thallo (spring) and Carpo (autumn). At other times, the Horae were said to be a trinity— Eunomia ("lawful order"), Dike ("justice"), and Eirene ("peace"). Thus the Horae can be seen as Goddesses of Regeneration who influenced the natural as well as the human orders. Savitri, a primal female divinity in Hindu tradition, was said to have been impregnated by Brahman. Pregnant for more than a century, Savitri finally gave birth to music and poetry, the years, months, and days, the four ages of creation, and countless other beings, including death. Savitri's generative act, then, resulted in the creation of time and rhythm.

Other goddesses, like Savitri and the Horae, also influenced the temporal order governing vegetative fertility and human affairs. Among them, Unelanuhi, the ever-lovely young woman the Cherokee believed to be the sun, was the "divider" or "apportioner" who marked time and decreed the fate of her people. The Hindu dawn-goddess, Ushas or Urvasi, was thought to reveal the luminous splendor of her breasts each morning. She, like the Greek dawn-goddesses Eos, the Roman goddess Aurora, the frog-headed Egyptian goddess, Hekt, and the Babylonian Aja, were considered prolific lovers who were responsible for beginning each new day. Such moon-goddesses as the Greek Selene, the Welsh Olwen, the Irish Arianrhod, and the Mayan Ix Chel were also depicted as sexually generous and, paradoxically, chaste at the same time.

Thus, like the waxing and waning moon, regeneration goddesses are the keepers of the cosmic clock marking the season of fertility and growth and the season of sterility and death. Their pulsing sexual energies impel mortal creation to renew itself, and thus their influence redeems individual mortality through beauty, passion, and offspring.

READING THE FEMALE DIVINE

The following stories depict most of the character types we have discussed under the rubrics of Life, Death, and Regeneration. Goddesses appear as creators and mothers, as destroyers and warmongers, as virginal, as sexual, as embodiments of celestial wisdom, as bringers of earthly law and custom, and as embodiments and practitioners of occult knowledge and earth magic. Sometimes, as in the case of Pe-le, a goddess can be simultaneously creator, destroyer, the abbess of an all-woman community, and powerful medium and practitioner of the occult arts. At other times, as in the cases of White Buffalo Calf Woman, Au Co, and Diana, her role is more circumscribed. White Buffalo Calf Woman is a culture-bringer, Au Co the archetypal mother, and Diana the protector of virginal independence from domestic drudgery and the prurient gaze of unenlightened men. The Kali of Marguerite Yourcenar's modernized myth and the Gnostic's Pistis-Sophia embody qualities that could be attributed to either sex; but, in the context of the traditions from which they derive, their activities serve to bring a kind of gender balance to the cosmic order.

The Fire Goddess

Hawaiian

The original Hawaiians belong to a widespread group of Pacific island peoples known as Polynesians, who in turn belong to Oceania, the collective term for Pacific islanders whose territory ranges as far east as South America, as far west as Sumatra, as far north as Hawaii, and as far south as Tasmania. Although there is a great deal we do not know about the original wave of migrations that resulted in the habitation of Hawaii, it appears that the first human settlers arrived around the sixth century CE. According to the genealogical chants which conferred religious authority on the priests and political authority on the ruling families, the great *moi* ("chief") Nanaula traveled the wide ocean with his gods, priests, and a large entourage, landing on the southern islands. Others arrived shortly after Nanaula; but, then, according to genealogical chants, some 14 generations passed before the next wave of Polynesian immigrants arrived. It was then, during the 10th or 11th centuries CE, that yet another wave of seaborne settlers arrived, among them the great priest Paao. Apparently, despite the claim in the following story that even the "great Gods, Ku, Kane, Kaneloa, and Lono were forced to follow Pe-le when she left Kahiki, the land beyond the vastness of the ocean," Paao or one of his contemporaries introduced Pe-le and several other new gods into the religious traditions already established on the islands sometime after 1170 CE.

By the time Captain Cook set foot on the islands in 1777, Pe-le was the most feared and respected of Hawaii's divinities. She was said to inhabit all volcanoes, but her preferred residence was a palace beneath the boiling surface within the crater at Kilauea. There, with her five brothers and eight sisters, Pe-le held court, dining on the offerings of fruit, pigs, fish, fowl, and the occasional human being that the Hawaiians threw into the seething crater.

Source: Padraic Colum, *Tales and Legends of Hawaii.* New Haven: Yale UP, 1937. Pp. 25–37. Used by permission of Yale University Press.

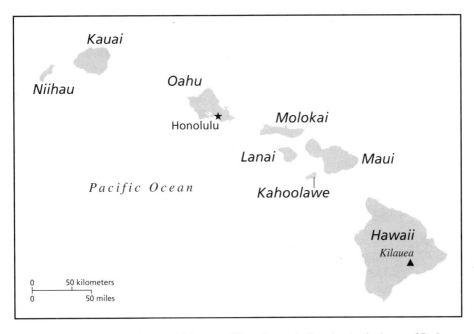

MAP 3.1a Kilauea, the volcano which created Hawaii, was believed to be the home of Pe-le and her court.

MAP 3.1b Oceania encompasses a vast region of Pacific islands that was gradually populated by linguistically and culturally related seafarers.

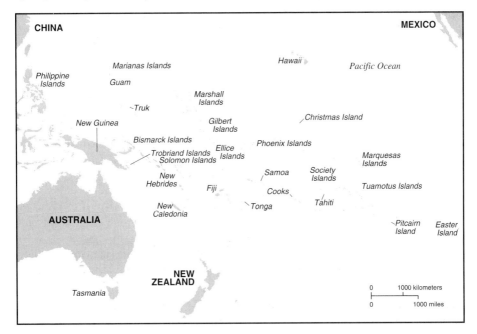

Like the volcanic action that she embodies, Pe-le is a goddess of both life and death. Her lava flows gradually created Hawaii and the rich soil that so abundantly nourishes such a vast array of plant and animal life, but the intense heat of those same flows destroys everything in their path, leaving behind a rocky wasteland. Numerous temples to the goddess and her fearsome family were erected near old lava flows and extinct craters, and it was believed that when Pe-le and her retinue left Kilauea to make the rounds of these sacred sites earthquakes announced their departure.

The story that follows was taken from a much longer work that features no less than 176 magical chants like those that Hi-i-aka-of-the-Bosom-of-Pele uses to resurrect the hapless Prince Lo-hi-au. And while Pe-le functions primarily as Mistress of Life and Death, the double resurrection of Lo-hi-au, his sexual allure, and Hi-i-aka's realization that life springs from death suggest the theme of regeneration as well.

Pe-le, the Goddess, came up out of her pit in Kilauea. No longer would she sit on the lava hearth below, with skin rugged and blackened, with hair the color of cinders, and with reddened eyes; no longer would she seem a hag whom no man would turn toward. She came up out of the pit a most lovely woman. Her many sisters were at her side, and each of them was only a little less lovely than was Pe-le upon that day. They stood on each side of her because it was forbidden to come behind the Goddess or to lay a hand upon her burning back.

Pe-le and her sisters stood on the crater's edge. Around them was the blackened plain, but below them was Puna, with the surf breaking upon its beach, and with its lehua groves all decked with scarlet blossoms. This land was Pe-le's. She had made it and she had the power to destroy it. She had power in the heavens, too, for her flames reached up to the skies. All the Gods—even the great Gods, Ku, Kane, Kane-loa, and Lono—were forced to follow her when she left Kahiki, the land beyond the vastness of the ocean, and came to Hawaii. Kilauea on Hawaii's island was the home she had chosen. And now she came out of the pit, and she said to her many sisters, "Come, let us go down to the beach at Puna, and bathe, and feast, and enjoy ourselves." Her sisters rejoiced, and they went down with her to the beach.

And when they had bathed and feasted, and had sported themselves in the water and along the beach, Pe-le went into a cavern and laid herself down to sleep. She said to the sister who was always beside her, to the sister who was named Hi-i-aka-of-the-Fire-Bloom, "Let me sleep until I awake of my own accord. If any of you should attempt to awaken me before, it will be death to you all. But if it has to be that one of you must awaken me, call the youngest of our sisters, Hi-i-aka-of-the-Bosom-of Pele, and let her bring me out of sleep."

So Pe-le said, and she lay in the cavern and slept. Her sisters said to each other, "How strange that the havoc-maker should sleep so deeply and without a bedfellow!" By turns they kept watch over her as she slept in the cavern.

But the youngest of her sisters was not by her when she spoke before going to sleep. Little Hi-i-aka had gone to where the groves of lehua showed their scarlet

The Goddess Pe-le. Ht. 34 inches. Carved wood.
Pe-le is herself a "triple goddess." Her volcanic
fires, depicted in the spiked wave above her
head, both give and take away life and, as suggested by her ravishing power over Lo-hi-au,
she also possesses the regenerating power of
female sexual allure.
Source: © Collection Musée del'Homme, Photo J. Oster.

blossoms. She was enchanted with the trees that she went amongst; she gathered the blossoms and wove them into wreaths. And then she saw another girl gathering blossoms and weaving them into wreaths and she knew this other girl to be the tree spirit, Ho-po-e. And Ho-po-e, seeing Hi-i-aka, danced for her. These two became friends; they danced for each other, and they played together, and never had Hi-i-aka, the little sister of the dread Goddess, known a friend that was as dear and as lovely as Ho-po-e whose life was in the grove of lehuas.

As for Pe-le, the Goddess, she slept in the cavern, and in her sleep she heard the beating of a drum. It sounded like a drum that announces a hula. Her spirit went from where she slept; her spirit body followed the sound of that drum. Over the sea her spirit body followed that sound. Her spirit body went to the Island of Kauai. There she came to a hall sacred to Laka: a hula was being performed there. As a most lovely woman Pe-le entered that hall. All the people who were assembled for the hula turned to look upon her. And in that hall Pe-le saw Prince Lo-hi-au.

He was seated on a dais, and his musicians were beside him. Pe-le, advancing through the hall filled with wondering people, went to where he was. Prince Lo-hi-au had her sit beside him; he had tables spread to feast her. Pe-le would not eat.

"And yet she must have come from a very great distance," the people around her said, "for if a woman so beautiful lived on this island, we would surely have heard her spoken about." Prince Lo-hi-au would not eat either; his mind was altogether on the beautiful woman who sat on the dais beside him.

When the hula was over he took her into his house. But although they were beside each other on the mat, Pe-le would not permit him to caress her. She let him have kisses, but kisses only. She said to him, "When I bring you to Hawaii you shall possess me and I shall possess you." He tried to grasp her and hold her, but she rose in her spirit body and floated away, leaving the house, leaving the island, crossing the sea, and coming back to where her body lay in the cavern in Puna.

Prince Lo-hi-au sought wildly for the woman who had been with him; he sought for her in the night, in the dark night of the ghosts. And because it seemed to him that she was forever gone, he went back into his house, and took his loin cloth off, and hanged himself with it from the ridgepole of the house. In the morning his sister and his people came in the house and found the chieftain dead. Bitterly they bewailed him; bitterly they cursed the woman who had been with him and who had brought him to his death. Then they wrapped the body in robes of tapa and laid it in a cavern of the mountainside.

In Puna, in a cavern, Pe-le's body lay, seemingly in deep sleep. For a day and a night, and a night and a day it lay like this. None of her sisters dared try to awaken Pe-le. But at last they became frightened by the trance that lasted so long. They would have their youngest sister, Hi-i-aka, awaken the Woman of the Pit. At the end of another day they sent for her.

And Hi-i-aka saw the messenger coming for her as she stood in the grove of lehua trees with her dear and lovely friend, Ho-po-e, beside her. She watched the messenger coming for her, and she chanted the me-le:

> From the forest land at Papa-lau-ahi,
> To the garlands heaped at Kua-o-ka-la,
> The lehua trees are wilted,

Scorched, burnt up—
Consumed are they by fire—
By the fire of the Woman of the Pit.

But Ho-po-e, her friend, said, "It is not true what you chant. See! Our lehuas are neither wilted nor burnt up. If they were I would no longer be able to see you nor to speak with you. Why, then, do you lament? You will stay with me, and we shall gather more blossoms for garlands."

But Hi-i-aka said, "Even as I saw the messenger who is coming to take me away from you, I saw our trees destroyed by Pe-le's fires."

Then the messenger came to them, and told Hi-i-aka that she was to return to where she had left her sisters. She took farewell of Ho-po-e and went to where her sisters awaited her. They brought her within the cavern, and they showed her Pe-le lying there, without color, without stir. Then Hi-i-aka, the youngest of her sisters, went to Pe-le's body and chanted over it. And the spirit body that had been hovering over the prostrate body entered into it. The breath entered the lungs again; Pe-le's bosom rose and fell; color came into her face. Then the Woman of the Pit stretched her body; she rose up, and she spoke to her sisters.

They left that place; they went back into Pe-le's dwelling place, into the pit of Ki-lau-ea. Then, after a while, Pe-le spoke to her sisters, one after the other. She said to each of them, "Will you be my messenger and fetch our lover—yours and mine— from Kauai?" None of the elder sisters would go; each one understood how dangerous such a mission would be. But when Pe-le spoke to Hi-i-aka, the youngest of her sisters, the girl said, "Yes, I will go, and I will bring back the man."

Her sisters were dismayed to hear Hi-i-aka say this. The journey was long, and for anyone who would go on the mission that Pe-le spoke of the danger was great. Who could tell what fit of rage and hatred might come over the Woman of the Pit— rage and hatred against the one who would be with the man she would have for her lover? And Hi-i-aka, who had agreed to go upon such a mission was the youngest and the least experienced of all of them. They tried to warn her against going; but they dared not speak their thought out to her. Besides, they knew that Hi-i-aka was so faithful to Pe-le, her chieftainess and her elder sister, that she would face every danger at her request.

Then said Pe-le to Hi-i-aka, "When you have brought our lover here, for five days and five nights he shall be mine. After that he shall be your lover. But until I have lifted the tapu you must not touch him, you must not caress him, you must not give him a kiss. If you break this tapu it shall be death to you and to Prince Lo-hi-au."

Her sisters made signs to her, and Hi-i-aka delayed her departure. She stood before Pe-le again, and Pe-le reproached her for her dilatoriness. But now Hi-i-aka spoke to her elder sister and chieftainess and said, "I go to bring a lover to you while you stay at home. But, going, I make one condition. If you must break out in fire and make raids while I am gone, raid the land that we both own, but do not raid where the lehua groves are; do not harm my friend Ho-po-e, whose life is in the lehua groves."

She said this, and she started on her journey. But now the length of the journey and its dangers came before her and made her afraid. She saw herself, alone and powerless, going upon that long way. Once again she returned to where the Woman of the Pit sat. She asked that she be given a companion for the journey. She asked that a portion of Pe-le's mane, or magic power, be given her. Pe-le did not deny her this: she called upon the Sun and the Moon, the Stars, the Wind, the Rain, the Lightning, and Thunder to give aid to her sister and her messenger. And now that mane was bestowed on her, Hi-i-aka started on the way that led across islands and over seas to the house of the man whom her sister desired—her sister, Pe-le, the dread Fire-Goddess.

Far did Hi-i-aka and her woman companion journey, long were they upon the way, many dangers did they face and overcome, and at last they came to the village that had Lo-hi-au for its lord. "Why have you come?" said the people who entertained the worn travelers. "I have come to bring Prince Lo-hi-au to Pe-le, that they may be lovers."

"Lo-hi-au has been dead many days. He fell under the spell of a witch, and he took his own life." Then they pointed out to her the cave in the mountainside in which his sister had laid the body of Lo-hi-au.

Then was Hi-i-aka greatly stricken. But she drew together all the power that she had—the power that Pe-le had endowed her with—and looked toward the cave in the mountainside. And she saw something hovering around the cave, and she knew it, thinned and wan as it was, for the ghost body of Lo-hi-au. She knew that she had to bring that ghost body back to the body that lay in the cave, and she knew that all the toil she had been through would be nothing to the toil that this would entail. She raised her hands toward the cave, and she uttered a chant to hold that ghost body in the place. But as she looked she saw that the ghost body was even more thinned and wan than she had thought. She was frightened by its shadowiness. The voice that came to her from before the cave was as thin and faint as the murmur that the land shell gives out. She answered it back in voice that was filled with pity:

> My man of the wind-driven mist,
> Or rain that plunges clean as a diver
> What time the mountain stream runs cold
> Adown the steps at Ka-lalau—
> Where we shall ere long climb together,
> With you, my friend, with you.
> Companion of the pitchy night,
> When heavenward turns my face—
> Thou art, indeed, my man.

With her woman companion she came to the mountainside. The sun was going down; they would have barely time to climb the ladder that was there and go into the cavern before the night fell. Then the ladder was taken away by witches who bore an enmity to Hi-i-aka; and the ghost body of Lo-hi-au wailed thinly and more faintly.

Hi-i-aka chanted an incantation that held the sun from sinking down. And while the sun stayed to give them light, she and her companion toiled up the cliff. They came to the entrance of the cave. Hi-i-aka caught in her hand Lo-hi-au's ghost body. They went within. Hi-i-aka directed her companion to take hold of the dead feet. The fluttering ghost body that she held in her hand she brought to the eye socket and strove to make it pass through at that place. With spells she strove to make the soul particle pass on. It went within; it reached the loins; it would pass no farther. Hi-i-aka forced it on. It went to the feet; the hands began to move, the eyelids quiver. Then breath came in to the body.

Hi-i-aka and her companion lifted it up and laid the body on a mat. With restoring herbs Hi-i-aka and her companion swathed the body from head to foot. But her companion said, "He will not recover in spite of all that you have done."

"I will make an incantation," Hi-i-aka said, "if it is rightly delivered, life will come back to him." Then she chanted:

> Ho, comrades from the sacred plateau!
> Ho, comrades from the burning gulf!
> Hither fly with art and cunning:
> Ku, who fells and guides the war boat;
> Ku, who pilots us through dreamland;
> All ye gods of broad Hawaii;
> Kanaloa, guard well your tapus;
> Candle-maker, candle-snuffer;
> Goddess, too, of passions, visions;
> Lightning red all heaven filling
> Pitchy darkness turned to brightness—
> Lono, come, thou God of Fire;
> Come, too, thou piercing eye of rain;
> Speed, speed, my prayer upon its quest!

More and more incantations Hi-i-aka made as the night passed and the day following passed. The people of the place were kept at a dance so that Hi-i-aka's task might not be broken in on. She made her last and her mightiest incantation; the soul particle stayed in the body, and Prince Lo-hi-au lived again.

They brought him to the entrance of the cave. Three rainbows arched themselves from the mouth of the cave, and down these three rainbows Prince Lo-hi-au, Hi-i-aka, and her companion went. To the beach they went. And in the ocean the three performed the cleansing rite. And now that the toil of the journey and the toil of restoring the man to life were past, Hi-i-aka thought upon the groves of lehua and upon her dear and lovely friend, Ho-po-e. And now that the time had come for her to make the journey back she turned toward Hawaii and chanted:

> Oh, care for my parks of lehua—
> How they bloom in the upland Ka-li'u!
> Long is my way and many a day
> Before you shall come to the bed of love,
> But, hark, the call of the lover,
> The voice of the lover, Lo-hi-au!

And when they had passed across many of the islands, and had crossed their channels, and had come at last to Hawaii, Hi-i-aka sent her companion before her to let Pe-le know that Lo-hi-au was being brought to her. When she had come with

Lo-hi-au to the eastern gate of the sun, when she had come to Puna, she went swiftly ahead of Prince Lo-hi-au that she might look over her own land.

Pe-le had broken out in her fires; in spite of the agreement she had made with her sister and her messenger, she had wasted with fire the lehua groves. No tree now stood decked with blossoms. And the life of Ho-po-e, Hi-i-aka's dear and lovely friend, was ended with her lehua groves.

Blackness and ruin were everywhere Hi-i-aka looked. She stood in a place that overlooked her well-loved land, and all the bitterness of her heart went into the chant that she made then:

> On the heights of Poha-ke
> I stand, and look forth on Puna—
> Puna, pelted with bitter rain,
> Veiled with a downpour black as night!
> Gone, gone are my forests, lehuas
> Whose bloom once gave the birds nectar!
> Yet they were insured with a promise!

Then she said, "I have faithfully kept the compact between myself and my sister. I have not touched her lover, I have not let him caress me, I have not given him a kiss. Now that compact is at an end. I am free to treat this handsome man as my lover, this man who has had desire for me. And I will let Pe-le, with her own eyes, see the compact broken."

When he came to where she was, she took his hand; she made herself kind to him; she told him she had been longing for the time when her companion would have gone and they two would be together. Hand in hand they went over the blackened and wasted land. They came to where an unburnt lehua grew upon a rock. There Hi-i-aka gathered blossoms to make a wreath for Lo-hi-au.

And on the terrace of Ka-hoa-lii where they were in full view of Pe-le and her court, she had him sit beside her. She plaited wreaths of lehua blossoms for him. She put them around his neck, while he, knowing nothing of the eyes that were watching them, became ardent in love making.

"Draw nearer," said Hi-i-aka, "draw nearer, so that I may fasten this wreath around your neck." She put her arm around the neck of Lo-hi-au; her body inclined toward his. She drew him to herself. The sisters around Pe-le cried out at that. "Hi-i-aka kisses Lo-hi-au! Look, Hi-i-aka kisses Lo-hi-au."

"Mouths were made for kissing," Pe-le said, but the flame came into her eyes.

Then Pe-le commanded her sisters to put on their robes of fire, and go forth and destroy Lo-hi-au. In their robes of fire they went to where he was; when they came to him they threw cinders upon his feet and went away again. But Pe-le knew that they had made only a pretence of destroying the man. The caldron within her pit bubbled up; she called upon her helpers, upon Lono-makua, Ku-pulupulu, Kumoku-halli, Ku-ala-na-wao. At first they would not help her to destroy Lo-hi-au; rather, with their own hands, did they roll the fires back into the pit. Then did Pe-le threaten her helpers; then did Lono-makua go forth to do her bidding.

Lo-hi-au saw the fires coming toward him, and he chanted:

> All about is flame—the rock plain rent,
> The coco palms that tufted the plain
> Are gone, all gone, clean down to Ka-poho.
> On rushes the dragon with flaming mouth,
> Eating its way to Oma'o-lala.
> For tinder it has the hair of the fern.
> A ghastly rain blots out the sky;
> The sooty birds of storm whirl through the vault;
> Heaven groans, adrip, as with dragon blood!

The fires that rolled toward them spared Hi-i-aka. Lo-hi-au, choked by the vapor, fell down, and the lava flow went over him.

So Hi-i-aka lost the one whom she had come to love, as she had lost her lehua groves and her dear and lovely friend, Ho-po-e, through the rage of her sister, the dread Goddess. And as for Pe-le, she would have broken up the strata of the earth, and would have let the sea rise up through and destroy the islands, if Ka-ne had not appeared before her—Ka-ne the Earth-Shaper. Ka-ne soothed her mind, and she went back to the Pit, and sat amongst her sisters.

Once a man who was a great sorcerer came down into the Pit. "What is the purpose of your visit?" he was asked.

"I have come to know why Lo-hi-au, my friend, has been destroyed," he said.

"He and Hi-i-aka kissed and the man was tapu for Pe-le," the sisters answered.

"He tasted death at Haena. Why was he made taste death again in Hawaii?"

Pe-le, seated at the back of the Pit, spoke: "What is it that you say? That Lo-hi-au tasted death at Haena?"

"Yes. Hi-i-aka brought his soul and his body together again. Then they sailed for Hawaii."

Then said Pe-le to her youngest sister: "Is this true? Is it true that you found Lo-hi-au dead and that you restored him to life?"

"It is true. And it is true that not until you had destroyed my friend Ho-po-e did I give a caress to Lo-hi-au."

So Hi-i-aka said, and Pe-le, the Woman of the Pit, became silent. Then the sorcerer, Lo-hi-au's friend, said, "I would speak to Pe-le. But which is Pe-le? I have a test. Let me hold the hand of each of you, O Divine Woman, so that I may know which of you is the Goddess."

He took the hand of each of Pe-le's sisters, and held the hand to his cheek. He held the hollow palm to his ear. Each hand that was given to him had only a natural warmth when it was put to his cheek. Then he took the hand of a hag whose skin was rugged and blackened, whose hair was the color of cinders, whose eyes were red. The hand was burning on his cheek. From the hollow of the hand came reverberations of the sounds made by fountains of fire. "This is Pe-le," said the man, and he bent down and adored her.

Then Pe-le, loving this man who was Lo-hi-au's friend, and knowing that Hi-i-aka had been faithful in her service to her, softened, and would have Lo-hi-au brought to life again. But only one who was in far Kahiki possessed the power to restore Lo-hi-au to life. This was Kane-milo-hai, Pe-le's brother.

And Kane-milo-hai, coming over the waters in his shell canoe, found Lo-hi-au's spirit, in the form of a bird, flitting over the waters. He took it, and he brought it to where Lo-hi-au lay. He broke up the lava in which the body was set, and he formed the body out of the fragments, restoring to it the lineaments that Lo-hi-au had. Then he brought the spirit back into the body.

And afterward it happened that Hi-i-aka, wandering where the lehua groves were growing again, and knowing that after dire destruction a new world had come into existence, heard the chant:

> Puna's plain takes the color of scarlet—
> Red as heart's blood the bloom of lehua
> The nymphs of the Pit string hearts in a wreath:
> O the pangs of the Pit, Ki-lau-ea!

Hi-i-aka went to where the chant came from; she discovered Lo-hi-au restored to life once more. With him she wandered through the land below Ki-lau-ea. Men and women were peopling the land, and the Goddess of the Pit was not now so terror-inspiring.

White Buffalo Calf Woman

Brulé Sioux (Great Plains, North America)

The various Lakota, Nakota, and Dakota (Sioux) tribes believed that the world was largely created by the trickster Iktome, and that it is characterized by absurdity and conflict. As Julian Rice asserts, we can best read Sioux narratives if we bear in mind the following seven assumptions characterizing their worldview:

1. The haphazard creation of the world and the inevitability of conflict and challenge.
2. The real danger and destruction of the trickster.
3. The need for human beings to complete responsibly what the spirits initiate.
4. The willingness to accept loss without diminishing the ability to live.
5. The respect for the generative and destructive potentialities in violent energy.
6. The sense of the world as contradictory or "absurd."

Source: Richard Erdoes and Alfonso Ortiz, *American Indian Myths and Legends.* New York: Pantheon, 1986. 47–52.

7. The tolerance of diverse spiritual thought without universal reverence for any one divinity. (1998, 13)

Among these general beliefs, the notion that the world is incomplete and that human beings have a duty to complete that which the spirits initiate is perhaps most helpful here, for White Buffalo Calf Woman is a culture-bringer. That is, she gives to the Sioux objects and practices that, to a large extent, symbolize and define their way of relating to the spirit and human worlds. White Buffalo Calf Woman is *wakan,* a word often translated as *sacred* or *holy.* Yet, for the Sioux, *wakan* is not as an abstract attribute of divinity or some detached, otherworldly state of mind. Rather, *wakan* is the spiritual energy that people feel when they make ritual use of powerful symbols. Therefore, the ways of *wakan* involve the careful handling of symbolic objects and the attentive performance of ritual, activities that were believed to summon the spiritual energy necessary to overcome adversity and to complete that which the spirits had initiated. For in Lakota, Nakota, and Dakota belief, there is no Divine Overseer who will ultimately provide relief from conflict and suffering in the sweet by-and-by. Nor is there an ultimate judge who uses loss and hardship to punish sin—or to test and refine character. For the Sioux, nothing and no one can make rational sense of human suffering or provide a way to escape it. Rather, human beings themselves must use the

MAP 3.2 Sioux Nation Territory and Area of Influence in Mid-19th Century

powers the spirits provide to overwhelm evil and to find the courage and energy necessary to change dangerous or unpleasant circumstances.

The Lakota, Nakota, and Dakota were warrior nations and decidedly male-centered. It is ironic, then, that the myth embodying such an important part of their "cultural charter" features White Buffalo Calf Woman. She teaches the people how to make and use ceremonial pipes as well as how to live. In contrast to our expectations of the values of a warrior culture, her teachings include walking in humility, respecting mother earth, valuing and protecting women and children, and living in harmony with all things. Thus White Buffalo Calf Woman presents the people with sacred objects and teaches them how to use them to summon the spiritual powers necessary to prosper. The story ends with the appearance of great herds of buffalo—a physical manifestation of the spiritual power released by the proper use of the ritual objects that the *wakan* woman gave to the people.

Richard Erdoes and Alfonso Ortiz collected the following story from "John Fire Lame Deer, . . . a famous Sioux 'holy man,' grandson of the first Chief Lame Deer, a great warrior who fought Custer and died during a skirmish with General Miles" (1986, 52). The Looking Horse family at Eagle Butte in South Dakota keeps two very old pipes. One of them, made from a buffalo calf's leg bone, is reputed to be the pipe that the White Buffalo Calf Woman gave to the Sioux. According to Lame Deer, he personally knows the power that the pipe invokes because he prayed with it long ago.

One summer so long ago that nobody knows how long, the Ocheti-Shakowin, the seven sacred council fires of the Lakota Oyate, the nation, came together and camped. The sun shone all the time, but there was no game and the people were starving. Every day they sent scouts to look for game, but the scouts found nothing.

Among the bands assembled were the Itazipcho, the Without-Bows, who had their own camp circle under their chief, Standing Hollow Horn. Early one morning the chief sent two of his young men to hunt for game. They went on foot, because at that time the Sioux didn't yet have horses. They searched everywhere but could find nothing. Seeing a high hill, they decided to climb it in order to look over the whole country. Halfway up, they saw something coming toward them from far off, but the figure was floating instead of walking. From this they knew that the person was *wakan*, holy.

At first they could make out only a small moving speck and had to squint to see that it was a human form. But as it came nearer, they realized that it was a beautiful young woman, more beautiful than any they had ever seen, with two round, red dots of face paint on her checks. She wore a wonderful white buckskin outfit, tanned until it shone a long way in the sun. It was embroidered with sacred and marvelous designs of porcupine quill, in radiant colors no ordinary woman could have made.

This *wakan* stranger was Ptesan-Wi, White Buffalo Calf Woman. In her hands she carried a large bundle and a fan of sage leaves. She wore her blue-black hair loose except for a strand at the left side, which was tied up with buffalo fur. Her eyes shone dark and sparkling, with great power in them.

The two young men looked at her open-mouthed. One was overawed, but the other desired her body and stretched his hand out to touch her. This woman was *lila wakan,* very sacred, and could not be treated with disrespect. Lightning instantly struck the brash young man and burned him up, so that only a small heap of blackened bones was left. Or some say that he was suddenly covered by a cloud, and within it he was eaten up by snakes that left only his skeleton, just as a man can be eaten up by lust.

To the other scout who had behaved rightly, the White Buffalo Calf Woman said: "Good things I am bringing, something holy to your nation. A message I carry for your people from the buffalo nation. Go back to the camp and tell the people to prepare for my arrival. Tell your chief to put up a medicine lodge with twenty-four poles. Let it be made holy for my coming."

This young hunter returned to the camp. He told the chief, he told the people, what the sacred woman had commanded. The chief told the *eyapaha,* the crier, and the crier went through the camp circle calling: "Someone sacred is coming. A holy woman approaches. Make all things ready for her." So the people put up the big medicine tipi and waited. After four days they saw the White Buffalo Calf Woman approaching, carrying her bundle before her. Her wonderful white buckskin dress shone from afar. The chief, Standing Hollow Horn, invited her to enter the medicine lodge. She went in and circled the interior sunwise. The chief addressed her respectfully, saying: "Sister, we are glad you have come to instruct us."

She told him what she wanted done. In the center of the tipi they were to put up an *owanka wakan,* a sacred altar, made of red earth, with a buffalo skull and a three-stick rack for a holy thing she was bringing. They did what she directed, and she traced a design with her finger on the smoothed earth of the altar. She showed them how to do all this, then circled the lodge again sunwise. Halting before the chief, she now opened the bundle. The holy thing it contained was the *chanunpa,* the sacred pipe. She held it out to the people and let them look at it. She was grasping the stem with her right hand and the bowl with her left, and thus the pipe has been held ever since.

Again the chief spoke, saying: "Sister, we are glad. We have had no meat for some time. All we can give you is water." They dipped some *wacanga,* sweet grass, into a skin bag of water and gave it to her, and to this day the people dip sweet grass or an eagle wing in water and sprinkle it on a person to be purified.

The White Buffalo Calf Woman showed the people how to use the pipe. She filled it with *chan-shasha,* red willow-bark tobacco. She walked around the lodge four times after the manner of Anpetu-Wi, the great sun. This represented the circle without end, the sacred hoop, the road of life. The woman placed a dry buffalo chip on the fire and lit the pipe with it. This was *peta-owihankeshni,* the fire without end, the flame to be passed on from generation to generation. She told them that the smoke rising from the bowl was Tunkashila's breath, the living breath of the great Grandfather Mystery.

The White Buffalo Calf Woman showed the people the right way to pray, the right words and the right gestures. She taught them how to sing the pipe-filling song and how to lift the pipe up to the sky, toward Grandfather, and down toward Grandmother Earth, to Unci, and then to the four directions of the universe.

"With this holy pipe," she said, "you will walk like a living prayer. With your feet resting upon the earth and the pipe-stem reaching into the sky, your body forms a living bridge between the Sacred Beneath and the Sacred Above. Wakan Tanka smiles upon us, because now we are as one: earth, sky, all living things, the two-legged, the four-legged, the winged ones, the trees, the grasses. Together with the people, they are all related, one family. The pipe holds them all together."

"Look at this bowl," said the White Buffalo Calf Woman. "Its stone represents the buffalo, but also the flesh and blood of the red man. The buffalo represents the universe and the four directions, because he stands on four legs, for the four ages of creation. The buffalo was put in the west by Wakan Tanka at the making of the world, to hold back the waters. Every year he loses one hair, and in every one of the four ages he loses a leg. The sacred hoop will end when all the hair and legs of the great buffalo are gone, and the water comes back to cover the Earth.

"The wooden stem of this *chanunpa* stands for all that grows on the earth. Twelve feathers hanging from where the stem—the backbone—joins the bowl—the skull—are from Wanblee Galeshka, the spotted eagle, the very sacred bird who is the Great Spirit's messenger and the wisest of all flying ones. You are joined to all things of the universe, for they all cry out to Tunkashila. Look at the bowl: engraved in it are seven circles of various sizes. They stand for the seven sacred ceremonies you will practice with this pipe, and for the Ocheti Shakowin, the seven sacred campfires of our Lakota nation."

The White Buffalo Calf Woman then spoke to the women, telling them that it was the work of their hands and the fruit of their bodies which kept the people alive. "You are from the Mother Earth," she told them. "What you are doing is as great as what the warriors do."

And therefore the sacred pipe is also something that binds men and women together in a circle of love. It is the one holy object in the making of which both men and women have a hand. The men carve the bowl and make the stem; the women decorate it with bands of colored porcupine quills. When a man takes a wife, they both hold the pipe at the same time and red trade cloth is wound around their hands, thus tying them together for life.

The White Buffalo Calf Woman had many things for her Lakota sisters in her sacred womb bag—corn, *wasna* (pemmican), wild turnip. She taught them how to make the hearth fire. She filled a buffalo paunch with cold water and dropped a red-hot stone into it. "This way you shall cook the corn and the meat," she told them.

The White Buffalo Calf Woman also talked to the children, because they have an understanding beyond their years. She told them that what their fathers and mothers did was for them, that their parents could remember being little once, and that they, the children, would grow up to have little ones of their own. She told them: "You are the coming generation, that's why you are the most important and precious ones. Some day you will hold this pipe and smoke it. Some day you will pray with it."

She spoke once more to all the people: "The pipe is alive; it is a red being showing you a red life and a red road. And this is the first ceremony for which you will use the pipe. You will use it to keep the soul of a dead person, because through it you can talk to Wakan Tanka, the Great Mystery Spirit. The day a human dies is always a sacred day. The day when the soul is released to the Great Spirit is another. Four women will become sacred on such a day. They will be the ones to cut the sacred tree—the *can-wakan*—for the sun dance."

She told the Lakota that they were the purest among the tribes, and for that reason Tunkashila had bestowed upon them the holy *chanunpa*. They had been chosen to take care of it for all the Indian people on this turtle continent.

She spoke one last time to Standing Hollow Horn, the chief, saying, "Remember: this pipe is very sacred. Respect it and it will take you to the end of the road. The four ages of creation are in me; I am the four ages. I will come to see you in every generation cycle. I shall come back to you."

The sacred woman then took leave of the people, saying: *"Toksha ake wacinyanktin ktelo*—I shall see you again."

The people saw her walking off in the same direction from which she had come, outlined against the red ball of the setting sun. As she went, she stopped and rolled over four times. The first time, she turned into a black buffalo; the second into a brown one; the third into a red one; and finally, the fourth time she rolled over, she turned into a white female buffalo calf. A white buffalo is the most sacred living thing you could ever encounter.

The White Buffalo Woman disappeared over the horizon. Sometime she might come back. As soon as she had vanished, buffalo in great herds appeared, allowing themselves to be killed so that the people might survive. And from that day on, our relations, the buffalo, furnished the people with everything they needed—meat for their food, skins for their clothes and tipis, bones for their many tools.

The Courtship of Inanna and Dumuzi

Sumerian (Iraq)

Situated in the southern half of modern Iraq between the Tigris and Euphrates rivers, the ancient Sumerians flourished between (approximately) 3000 and 1750 BCE. Particularly in the beginning, Sumeria was comprised of 12 or more "city-states," large walled cities surrounded by the villages that provided their respective agricultural bases. Anywhere from 10,000 to 50,000 people lived in each city-state. The largest building in each city was its *ziggurat,* a terraced temple of several stories resembling a pyramid in shape. Sumerian belief held that each city belonged to a ruling god and the *ziggurat,* with its shrine, altar, priestly quarters, and

Source: "The Courtship" from *Inanna, Queen of Heaven and Earth,* by Diane Wolkstein and Samuel Noah Kramer. HarperCollins, 1983. Used by permission.

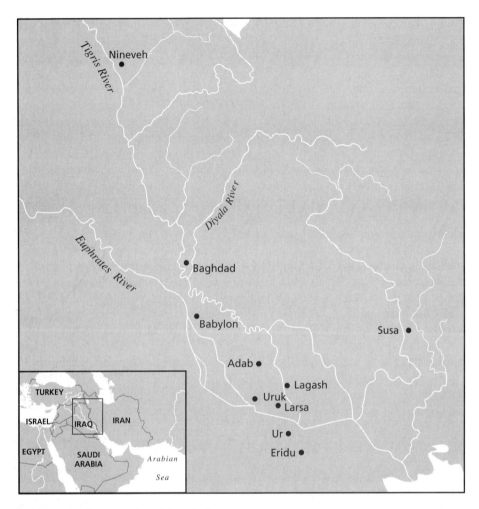

MAP 3.3 Ancient Sumeria and Babylonia

attached lands, was dedicated to that deity. On the secular plane, the king, nobles, and priests dominated the sociopolitical hierarchy, but in practice city governors attended to the details of city management.

In some ways, Sumerian culture resembles our own in that its government was based primarily on a code of laws. Excavations have recovered wills, lawsuits, deeds, promissory notes, receipts, and court decisions from the dust of ages, and we know private citizens as well as the government could file suit in court. Cases were heard by panels of three or four judges, and, when necessary, witnesses were called and oaths were taken. Women were permitted by law to own property, engage in business, and serve as witnesses in court, and, according to Samuel Kramer, the Sumerians "cherished goodness and truth, law and order, freedom and justice, mercy and compassion—and abhorred their opposites" (Wolkstein and Kramer 1983, 123).

Many scholars have observed that Aphrodite and Venus are more specialized versions of earlier, Middle Eastern Queens of Heaven and Earth. The goddesses of Mediterranean antiquity, by the first century BCE at least, were primarily the embodiments of women's sexual allure. The ancient Near Eastern goddess, however, not only inspired desire; she also bestowed the manifold civilizing blessings of the *me* (pronounced "may"), including the arts of priest- and statecraft, war making, the crafts of various artisans, husbandry, family, and the giving of counsel. As Inanna, Ishtar, or Astarte, this earlier goddess was believed to have chosen a mortal—Dumuzi or Tammuz—to be her royal consort, who would rule upon her lapis lazuli throne.

The following story may be read as an allegory of romantic love presented in three stages, moving from intense longing to passionate fulfillment to postmarital disillusionment. At first, Inanna assumes the role of young woman who still belongs to her family. Physically she is capable of sex, but emotionally she is unready, a fact which may account for her initial rejection of her family's choice in mate, the rough-hewn shepherd Dumuzi. But Dumuzi pleads his case, saying that his offerings and lineage are as good as anyone's. Still afraid, Inanna seeks the advice of her mother, who counsels her to "open the house" to Dumuzi, reassuring her that the young man will be both mother and father to her. In the second stage Inanna gives her heart to Dumuzi, and the lovers find in each others' arms a private world of delight. Their fierce lovemaking takes place in springtime and is described in rich agricultural metaphors.

The story begins with Inanna's bold and unashamed declaration of her longing for Dumuzi: "What I tell you / Let the singer weave into song," urges Inanna. "Let it flow from ear to mouth / Let it pass from old to young. / My vulva, the horn, / The Boat of Heaven, / Is full of eagerness like the young moon. / My untilled land lies fallow. / As for me, Inanna, / Who will plow my vulva? / Who will plow my high field? / Who will plow my wet ground?" (Wolkstein and Kramer 1983, 36–37). In this passage, all of the qualities of Life Goddesses are suggested. There is, most obviously, Inanna's powerful sexuality, which is represented in other texts by such symbolic adornments as the eye shadow called "Let him come, let him come" and the breastplate with the words "Come, man, come" written upon it. But the connection between Inanna's eagerness for intimacy and the arts should not be overlooked: "What I tell you / Let the singer weave into song . . . Let it pass from old to young." These words attest to the fact that romance, passion, and the pleasures of lovemaking have been the inspiration for song and story at least as far back as the invention of writing.

We should note as well that the female sexual power that Inanna embodies was believed to be inseparable from the life force that causes vegetation to flourish. When Dumuzi enters the sacred marriage chamber, Inanna says of him "At the king's lap stood the rising cedar. / Plants grew high by their side. / Grains grew high by their side. / Gardens flourished luxuriantly . . . He has sprouted; he has burgeoned; / He is lettuce planted by the water. / He is the one my womb loves best" (Wolkstein and Kramer 1983, 37–38). Of herself Inanna declares, "I poured out plants from my womb. / I placed plants before him, / I poured out plants before him. / I placed grain before him, I poured out grain before him. / I poured out grain from my womb" (40).

Yet, however pleasurable and necessary are the gifts and rituals of love, their emotional demands can be terrifying and destructive. In exchange for her sweet gifts, this Goddess of Life, too, demands an unswerving loyalty. Inanna and Dumuzi don't live happily ever after. Eventually the "honeymoon" is over and Inanna's response voices rejection and heartbreak when she finds herself the center of her husband's attentions only when he is sexually aroused: "Now, my sweet love is sated. / Now he says: / 'Set me free, my sister, set me free. / You will be a little daughter to my father. / Come, my beloved sister, I would go to the palace. / Set me free . . .'" (Wolkstein and Kramer 1983, 48). Ultimately, Inanna's rejected love for Dumuzi turns to terrible anger, and she sentences him to death at the hands of demonic torturers from the Underworld: "Inanna fastened on Dumuzi the eye of death. / She spoke against him the word of wrath. / She uttered against him the cry of guilt: / 'Take him! Take Dumuzi away!'" (71).

The brother spoke to his younger sister. The Sun god, Utu, spoke to Inanna, saying: "Young Lady, the flax in its fullness is lovely. Inanna, the grain is glistening in the furrow. I will hoe it for you. I will bring it to you. A piece of linen, big or small, is always needed. Inanna, I will bring it to you."

"Brother, after you've brought me the flax, who will comb it for me?"

"Sister, I will bring it to you combed."

"Utu, after you've brought it to me combed, who will spin it for me?"

"Inanna, I will bring it to you spun."

"Brother, after you've brought the flax to me spun, who will braid it for me?"

"Sister, I will bring it to you braided."

"Utu, after you've brought it to me braided, who will warp it for me?"

"Inanna, I will bring it to you warped."

"Brother, after you've brought the flax to me warped, who will weave it for me?"

"Sister, I will bring it to you woven."

"Utu, after you've brought it to me woven, who will bleach it for me?"

"Inanna, I will bring it to you bleached."

"Brother, after you've brought my bridal sheet to me, who will go to bed with me? Utu, who will go to bed with me?"

"Sister, your bridegroom will go to bed with you. He who was born from a fertile womb, he who was conceived on the sacred marriage throne, Dumuzi, the shepherd! He will go to bed with you."

Inanna spoke: "No, brother! The man of my heart works the hoe. The farmer! He is the man of my heart! He gathers the grain into great heaps. He brings the grain regularly into my storehouses."

Utu spoke: "Sister, marry the shepherd. What are you unwilling? His cream is good; his milk is good. Whatever he touches shines brightly. Inanna, marry Dumuzi. You who adorn yourself with the agate necklace of fertility, why are you unwilling? Dumuzi will share his rich cream with you. You who are meant to be the king's protector, why are you unwilling?"

Inanna spoke: "The shepherd! I will not marry the shepherd! His clothes are coarse; his wool is rough. I will marry the farmer. The farmer grows flax for my clothes. The farmer grows barley for my table."

Dumuzi spoke: "Why do you speak about the farmer? Why do you speak about him? If he gives you black flour, I will give you black wool. If he gives you white flour, I will give you white wool. If he gives you beer, I will give you sweet milk. If he gives you bread, I will give you honey cheese. I will give the farmer my leftover cream. I will give the farmer my leftover milk. Why do you speak about the farmer? What does he have more than I do?"

Inanna spoke: "Shepherd, without my mother, Ningal, you'd be driven away, without my grandmother, Ningikuga, you'd be driven into the steppes, without my father, Nanna, you'd have no roof, without my brother, Utu—"

Dumuzi spoke: "Inanna, do not start a quarrel. My father, Enki, is as good as your father, Nanna. My mother, Sirtur, is as good as your mother, Ningal. My sister, Geshtinanna, is as good as yours. Queen of the palace, let us talk it over. Inanna, let us sit and speak together. I am as good as Utu. Enki is as good as Nanna. Sirtur is as good as Ningal. Queen of the palace, let us talk it over."

The word they had spoken was a word of desire. From the starting of the quarrel came the lovers' desire.

The shepherd went to the royal house with cream. Dumuzi went to the royal house with milk. Before the door, he called out: "Open the house, My Lady, open the house!"

Inanna ran to Ningal, the mother who bore her. Ningal counseled her daughter, saying: "My child, the young man will be your father. My daughter, the young man will be your mother. He will treat you like a father. He will care for you like a mother. Open the house, My Lady, open the house!"

Inanna, at her mother's command, bathed and anointed herself with scented oil. She covered her body with the royal white robe. She readied her dowry. She arranged her precious lapis beads around her neck. She took her seal in her hand.

Dumuzi waited expectantly.

Inanna opened the door for him. Inside the house she shone before him like the light of the moon. Dumuzi looked at her joyously. He pressed his neck close against hers. He kissed her.

Inanna spoke: "What I tell you let the singer weave into song. What I tell you, let it flow from ear to mouth, let it pass from old to young: my vulva, the horn, the Boat of Heaven, is full of eagerness like the young moon. My untilled land lies fallow. As for me, Inanna, who will plow my vulva? Who will plow my high field? Who will plow my wet ground? As for me, the young woman, who will plow my vulva? Who will station the ox there? Who will plow my vulva?"

Dumuzi replied: "Great Lady, the king will plow your vulva. I, Dumuzi the King, will plow your vulva."

Inanna: "Then plow my vulva, man of my heart! Plow my vulva!"

At the king's lap stood the rising cedar. Plants grew high by their side. Grains grew high by their side. Gardens flourished luxuriantly.

Inanna sang: "He has sprouted; he has burgeoned; he is lettuce planted by the water. He is the one my womb loves best. My well-stocked garden of the plain, my barley growing high in its furrow, my apple tree which bears fruit up to its crown, he is lettuce planted by the water. My honey-man, my honey-man sweetens me always. My eager impetuous caresser of the navel, my caresser of the soft thighs—he is the one my womb loves best. His hand is honey; his foot is honey; he sweetens me always. My eager impetuous caresser of the navel, my caresser of the soft thighs, he is the one my womb loves best; he is lettuce planted by the water."

Dumuzi sang: "O Lady, your breast is your field. Inanna, your breast is your field. Your broad field pours out plants. Your broad field pours out grain. Water flows from on high for your servant. Bread flows from on high for your servant. Pour it out for me, Inanna. I will drink all you offer."

Inanna sang: "Make your milk sweet and thick, my bridegroom. My shepherd, I will drink your fresh milk. Wild bull, Dumuzi, make your milk sweet and thick. I will drink your fresh milk. Let the milk of the goat flow in my sheepfold. Fill my holy churn with honey cheese. Lord Dumuzi, I will drink your fresh milk. My husband, I will guard my sheepfold for you. I will watch over your house of life, the storehouse, the shining quivering place which delights Sumer—the house which decides the fates of the land, the house which gives the breath of life to the people. I, the queen of the palace, will watch over your house."

Dumuzi spoke: "My sister, I would go with you to my garden. Inanna, I would go with you to my garden. I would go with you to my orchard. I would go with you to my apple tree. There I would plant the sweet, honey-covered seed."

Inanna spoke: "He brought me into his garden. My brother, Dumuzi, brought me into his garden. I strolled with him among the standing trees, I stood with him among the fallen trees, by an apple tree I knelt as is proper. Before my brother coming in song, who rose to me out of the poplar leaves, who came to me in the midday heat, before my lord Dumuzi, I poured out plants from my womb. I placed plants before him, I poured out plants before him. I placed grain before him, I poured out grain before him. I poured out grain from my womb."

Inanna sang: "Last night as I, the queen, was shining bright, last night as I, the Queen of Heaven, was shining bright, as I was shining bright and dancing, singing praises at the coming of the night—he met me—he met me! My lord Dumuzi met me. He put his hand into my hand. He pressed his neck close against mine. My high priest is ready for the holy loins. My lord Dumuzi is ready for the holy loins. The plants and herbs in his field are ripe. O Dumuzi! Your fullness is my delight!"

She called for it, she called for it, she called for the bed! She called for the bed that rejoices the heart. She called for the bed that sweetens the loins. She called for the bed of kingship. She called for the bed of queenship. Inanna called for the bed:

"Let the bed that rejoices the heart be prepared! Let the bed that sweetens the loins be prepared! Let the bed of kingship be prepared! Let the bed of queenship be prepared! Let the royal bed be prepared!"

Inanna spread the bridal sheet across the bed. She called to the king: "The bed is ready!"

She called to her bridegroom: "The bed is waiting!"

He put his hand in her hand. He put his hand to her heart. Sweet is the sleep of hand-to-hand. Sweeter still the sleep of heart-to-heart.

Inanna spoke: "I bathed for the wild bull. I bathed for the shepherd Dumuzi. I perfumed my sides with ointment; I coated my mouth with sweet-smelling amber; I painted my eyes with kohl. He shaped my loins with his fair hands; the shepherd Dumuzi filled my lap with cream and milk. He stroked my pubic hair, he watered my womb. He laid his hands on my holy vulva, he smoothed my black boat with cream, he quickened my narrow boat with milk, he caressed me on the bed. Now I will caress my high priest on the bed; I will caress the faithful shepherd Dumuzi. I will caress his loins, the shepherdship of the land, I will decree a sweet fate for him."

The Queen of Heaven, the heroic woman, greater than her mother, who was presented the *me* by Enki, Inanna, the First Daughter of the Moon, decreed the fate of Dumuzi: "In battle I am your leader; in combat I am your armor-bearer; in the assembly I am your advocate; on the campaign I am your inspiration.

"You, the chosen shepherd of the holy shrine, you, the king, the faithful provider of Uruk, you the light of An's great shrine, in all ways you are fit to hold your head high on the lofty dais, to sit on the lapis lazuli throne, to cover your head with the holy crown, to wear long clothes on your body, to bind yourself with the garments of kingship, to carry the mace and sword, to guide straight the long bow and arrow, to fasten the throw-stick and sling at your side, to race on the road with the holy scepter in your hand, and the holy sandals on your fee, to prance on the holy breast like a lapis lazuli calf.

"You, the sprinter, the chosen shepherd, in all ways you are fit. May your heart enjoy long days. That which An has determined for you—may it not be altered. That which Enlil has granted—may in not be changed. You are the favorite of Ningal. Inanna holds you dear."

Ninshubur, the faithful servant of the holy shrine of Uruk, led Dumuzi to the sweet thighs of Inanna and spoke: "My queen, here is the choice of your heart, the king, your beloved bridegroom. May he spend long days in the sweetness of your holy loins. Give him a favorable and glorious reign. Grant him the king's throne, firm in its foundations. Grant him the shepherd's staff of judgment. Grant him the enduring crown with the radiant and noble diadem. From where the sun rises to where the sun sets, from south to north, from the Upper Sea to the Lower Sea, from the land of the *huluppu*-tree to the land of the cedar, let his shepherd's staff protect all of Sumer and Akkad. As the farmer, let him make the fields fertile, as the shepherd, let him make the sheepfolds multiply, under his reign let there be vegetation, under his reign let there be rich grain.

"In the marshland may the fish and birds chatter, in the canebrake may the young and old reeds grown high, in the steppe may the *mashgur*-trees grow high, in the forests may the deer and wild goats multiply, in the orchards may there be honey and wine, in the gardens may the lettuce and cress grow high, in the palace may there be long life. May there be floodwater in the Tigris and Euphrates, may the plants grow high on their banks and fill the meadows, may the Lady of Vegetation pile the grain in heaps and mounds.

"O my Queen of Heaven and Earth, Queen of all the universe, may he enjoy long days in the sweetness of your holy loins."

The king went with lifted head to the holy loins. He went with lifted head to the loins of Inanna. He went to the queen with lifted head. He opened wide his arms to the holy priestess of heaven.

Inanna spoke: "My beloved, the delight of my eyes, met me. We rejoiced together. He took his pleasure of me. He brought me into his house. He laid me down on the fragrant honey-bed. My sweet love, lying by my heart, tongue-playing, one by one, my fair Dumuzi did so fifty times.

"Now, my sweet love is sated. Now he says:

"'Set me free, my sister, set me free. You will be a little daughter to my father. Come, my beloved sister, I would go to the palace. Set me free . . .'"

Inanna spoke: "My blossom-bearer, your allure was sweet. My blossom-bearer in the apple orchard, my bearer of fruit in the apple orchard, Dumuzi-*abzu*, your allure was sweet. My fearless one, my holy statue, my statue outfitted with sword and lapis lazuli diadem, how sweet was your allure."

A Taste of Earth

Vietnamese (Vietnam)

The historical and archaeological evidence suggest that the Vietnamese were originally one of many peoples scattered throughout what is now southern China and northern Vietnam in third century BCE. According to tradition, the small Vietnamese kingdom of Au Lac, located in the heart of the Red River valley, was founded by a line of legendary kings, the so-called Hung Dynasty, which ruled during the legendary Age of Myths (2879–256 BCE, accord-

Source: Thich Nhat Hanh, "A Taste of Earth" and "One Hundred Eggs" from *A Taste of Earth and Other Legends of Vietnam.* Berkeley, CA: Parallax, 1993. 3–18. Used by permission of Parallax Press.

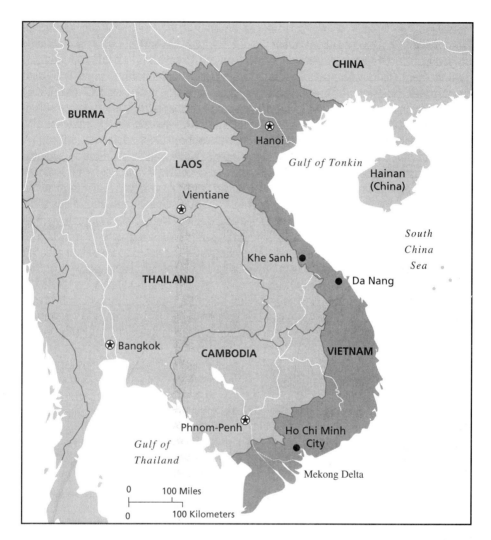

MAP 3.4 Vietnam

ing to one 16th-century source). Little in the existing archaeological record substantiates this tradition. Yet a few discoveries suggest that these early Red River delta dwellers were among the first to practice agriculture in east Asia and knew metallurgy to a degree comparable to European Bronze Age cultures.

Early in the second century BCE, a Chinese commander of the crumbling Ch'in Empire founded his own kingdom of Nam Viet (i.e., "South Viet"), an area including the Au Lac kingdom. But by 111 BCE, China's Han Empire had reconquered Nam Viet, a conquest that had important consequences for the Vietnamese. From this time until 939 CE, the Chinese attempted, politically and culturally, to absorb the Vietnamese. Chinese administrators re-placed local nobility; local educational and political institutions were replaced with others patterned after the Chinese model; the Chinese language became the official medium of governmental and literary expression; and Confucianism became the official ideology. Chinese ideographs became the written form of spoken Vietnamese, and Chinese art, architecture, and music had a deci-sive influence on their native counterparts.

While there were intermittent rebellions, the Chinese held sway for a thousand years. Finally, in 939 CE, Vietnamese forces defeated Chinese troops occupying the country and an indepen-dent state soon emerged. Even so, Vietnam retained many of the political and social institutions that the Chinese had imposed. Yet Vietnamese ethnic identity, never very far from the surface even during the millennium of Chinese occupation, gradually natural-ized these institutions, and, though there were local political in-trigues and further skirmishes with China, Vietnam (as it came to be called after 1802) remained independent until the French forcibly occupied Saigon (modern Ho Chi Minh City) in 1861.

The following story is a modern reworking of more ancient materials. The widely known Buddhist monk and peace activist Thich Nhat Hanh combined such early fragmentary references to this Vietnamese myth as found in the *Viet Dian U Linh* and the *Linh Nam Chich Quai* with a variety folk sources to create this beautifully rendered narrative. Since modern Vietnam is about 90 percent Buddhist, a story about a succession of cosmically charged eggs giving birth first to the universe and the Vietnamese would seem to date to pre-Buddhist antiquity. We might learn a bit more about the ancient provenance of the Au Co myth by comparing the present text with the traditional historical account of Sung Lam, whose title was Dragon Lord of the Lac (i.e., "the people"). The Dragon Lord, it was said, taught the people agri-culture and established the various duties and prerogatives of rul-ers and subjects, parents and children, and husbands and wives. Also according to legend, Sung Lam eventually returned to his Underwater Kingdom and only visited the people when they had petitions or when there was trouble. Later in this traditional his-tory, the Dragon Lord transformed himself into a handsome young man and married the Chinese princess Au Co, who gave birth to 100 identical children—the first Vietnamese.

At one level, this history is political myth; it clearly contrasts Sung Lam's dragon nature and his associations with the Vietnam-ese south with Au Co's associations with mountains and the Chi-nese north. Euhemerists might take the fact that Au Co tastes earth and therefore cannot return to her home in the 36th heaven to be sublimated political allegory. Having married a man of Nam

> Viet, the Chinese princess is contaminated in the eyes of the Chinese Imperial Court and cannot return. In any case, the Dragon Lord and Au Co, after giving birth to the Vietnamese people, agree to live in their separate yet interdependent worlds.

Long ago, when earth and sky were still covered in darkness, a great bird with wings like curtains of night came to rest on the cold earth. She sat for millions of years without stirring, until at last she laid two enormous eggs—one red, the other ivory. Powerful gusts of wind from her majestic wings shook heaven and earth as she flew back into the deep reaches of space.

Thousands of years later, the red egg began to glow. Bright light poured from the egg, chasing away the dense fog that had covered the mountains and filled the valleys for so long. With a thunderous clap, the red egg cracked, freeing a fiery golden crow whose brilliant light dazzled sky and earth.

Then the ivory egg began to radiate a soft and gentle light, and it, too, cracked open. Its shell burst into many fine pieces as an enormous, graceful swan emerged and flew into the sky, tender light streaming from her body down onto the earth.

Each bird followed its own course as it circled the earth. Soft, cool light streamed gently down from the wild swan. The golden crow's fiery wings hurled sparks of bright fire into space as it cried like thunder. The sparks remained suspended in the heavens, twinkling like diamonds. For millions of years, cold darkness had reigned. Now these wondrous birds brought the comfort of light.

The crow's red hot shell exploded into flames that burned for seven years. Boulders melted into fine sand, creating a vast desert. Steam rose from the seas and formed a blanket of clouds that shielded the earth from the crow's fiercest rays. The heavens reeled in the rich aroma that rose from the newly warmed earth.

The light shone all the way to the 36th heaven, where lived many goddesses. The youngest and loveliest goddess, Au Co, pulled back a curtain of cloud, saw the rosy earth below encircled by a halo of light, and cried, "Come, my sisters, let us change ourselves into white Lac birds and fly down to explore this new planet!"

Without hesitation, the goddesses transformed themselves into snow-white birds and flew down to the rosy earth. It was truly a wonderful discovery. As Lac birds they flew over the emerald sea, surprised to see their own reflections dancing in the water. The warm light of the golden crow was delightful. They leisurely skimmed over the pink mountains and came to rest on a hillside covered with soil as fine as powder.

When the first bird touched the ground, she folded her wings and returned to her goddess form. The other goddesses followed her example. Never had the earth hosted so delightful an event! The goddesses laughed and sang as, hand in hand, they strolled up and down the pink slopes. The earth beneath their feet was as soft as cotton balls. When they reached a broad meadow, they began to dance. It was the first dancing on earth. Before that moment, dancing had only been known in the 36th heaven. After a time, Au Co broke away from her sisters, knelt down to examine the fragrant earth more closely, and scooped up a small handful. How soft it was! How good it smelled! The other goddesses paused from their dancing and they too scooped up handfuls of pink earth.

Suddenly, Au Co wondered if the earth tasted as good as it smelled, and she lifted her hand to her mouth. Another goddess shouted, "Au Co! Don't do that!" But it was too late. Au Co had already swallowed a tiny handful of the sweet earth. The goddess who had shouted broke away from the others and ran towards Au Co. She grabbed the young goddess by the hand.

"Au Co, you foolish one! I'm afraid what you have done can never be repaired. Ours is the realm of form, not the realm of desire."

Frightened, the other goddesses quickly brushed all particles of pink earth from their delicate hands. They gathered around Au Co.

"What should we do now?" asked one.

"Let's leave at once and not mention our outing to anyone," suggested another.

They noticed with alarm that it was growing dark. The golden crow had almost disappeared behind the mountains and the light was fading with him.

"We must return before the golden crow disappears!" cried one goddess. She bent over slightly and transformed herself again into a snow-white Lac bird. The others did the same. As they flew into the sky their wings seemed to wave regretful farewells to the lovely earth.

Light disappeared with the golden crow, but it wasn't long before the wild swan returned. Her cool and gentle light was a refreshing change from the bright and sometimes burning rays of the golden crow. The first day on earth had just ended. It lasted as long as seven of our years today. Now the first night was beginning. It was a pleasant and mild night, illuminated by the swan's tender light.

Beneath that light, Au Co flew frantically back and forth, unable to join her sisters. Her wings were too heavy, and no matter how hard she tried, she could fly no higher. Because Au Co had tasted the new earth, she had lost her magical flying powers and could no longer return to the 36th heaven. Frightened and alone, she sank back down to earth. She resumed her goddess form and leaned against a boulder to weep.

Throughout the night, her tears became a long river that wound down to the seashore, where it emptied into the sea. Beneath the waves, multitudes of small creatures—shrimp, crabs, fish, and oysters—tasted the new current of water perfumed with fragrant earth. They shared their discovery with Dragon Prince, the son of the Sea Dragon Emperor, who had turned himself into a small fish to follow the sweet current upstream in search of its source. Although he swam swiftly, the first night on earth ended before he reached shore.

When Dragon Prince lifted his head above the water, he could see the golden crow. The sparkling sea rivaled his father's emerald palace below. Lapping waves spewed foam as white as snow. The prince leaped into the air. How soft, clear, and immense the sky was—round and blue like the sea itself. He could see the pale outlines of mountains and hills shimmering in the distance. Everything was similar to the landscape beneath the sea, yet here the world seemed more expansive, lighter and clearer.

He jumped onto shore and turned himself into a handsome young man with a broad forehead, long legs, and eyes that shone like stars. As he strolled along the shore, he admired the beauty all around him. He gazed at the rocky cliffs, rising from the sea into lofty peaks. Intent to find the river's source, he turned to follow it inland.

The more he walked, the more he marveled. Bright patches of moss draped the river-banks. Tiny gold and purple flowers blossomed among green carpets of grass. Beneath the ocean there were many kinds of strange and lovely seaweeds, corals, grasses, and flowers, but he had never seen such delicate shapes and colors as these. He guessed that the sweet water of the river was to thank, for no grass or flowers grew beyond the river's reach.

This was the second day on earth.

A band of butterflies suddenly appeared. At first Dragon Prince mistook them for flowers. He had never seen such fragile creatures. They were as light as air, sporting sunlight on their wings as they fluttered among the flowers. No doubt, he mused, they thought the flowers were creatures like themselves.

Dragon Prince climbed the mountain slope down which the river flowed. Its waters bubbled and gushed, caressing the mossy rocks along the banks. Bushes sprang up among the fresh grasses. Then he came to an abrupt halt. Before him was a sight unlike any he had ever encountered. Leaning against a moss-covered boulder was a young woman. Though her face was turned towards the rock, he could tell she was weeping. Unclad, she was more beautiful than any living creature he had seen before. She was like a newly blossomed flower. Her pale arms were folded beneath her forehead. Her long, lustrous black hair curled and flowed with the river currents. It was Au Co, forced to remain in the lower world because she had tasted the sweet earth. She had wept since nightfall, a span of more than ten years to us.

Dragon Prince did not take another step forward. He stood spellbound, and then he spoke, "Sun shining brightly

> Sky and sea both blue
> Butterflies flutter
> By a river so new
> Where have you come from?
> Why do you weep alone?"

Startled by the sea prince's voice, she stopped crying and looked up. Her eyes opened wide in surprise when she beheld the noble young man. She sat up and wiped her eyes with a lock of hair. Looking straight into his eyes, she answered:

> "Bright golden crow
> Fragrant new earth
> As white Lac birds
> We flew below.
> A taste of new earth
> No longer can I fly
> My sisters departed
> I wait alone and cry.
> Lost in a strange land
> My tears become a river."

Au Co explained all that had happened from the moment she pulled back the curtain of cloud to the moment she could no longer fly and was forced to return to earth. Dragon Prince sat down beside her and told her about his own life beneath the sea, where his father reigned. His voice was warm and kind, and whenever he mentioned the golden crow, the blue sky, or the fragrant hills, his eyes sparkled. Together they looked up at the sky and down at the green grasses that covered the riverbanks. Dragon Prince tried to console Au Co by telling her that her sisters would surely return that day or the next, as soon as they found a way to take her back home. They spoke for a long time. The sea prince's joy was so infectious that Au Co was soon talking and laughing as though no misfortune had befallen her.

Holding hands, they strolled down the mountain. Suddenly the sea prince grew alarmed. The river had almost completely drained into the sea. The grasses and flowers at their feet were withering. There were no butterflies in sight. The golden crow poised above their heads and their shadows shortened. It was noon, and the crow's rays were fierce and burning.

Dragon Prince said, "The earth is only green and beautiful when nourished by the sweet water of your tears. There are no trees and flowers growing by the seawater. It seems that land plants cannot thrive on seawater. Let me make some rain from the remaining tears in order to replenish the river."

Au Co did not know what rain was. But before she could ask, the prince climbed down to a tiny stream of water still trickling through the white sands about to empty into the sea. He scooped up some of the water in his hands and took three sips. When he returned to where she stood, he said, "Please sit down over there. I will moisten the earth with this wondrous water. Do not cry out until you see the rain. Look out over the ocean. If you see anything strange, do not worry. Although you are a goddess and I am a dragon, there is nothing to fear between us."

He quickly ran back to the sea. Au Co watched as he joined his palms together like a lotus bud. He dove into the water and quickly disappeared from sight. Within moments black clouds tumbled forth from a churning sea. They piled higher and higher until the blue sky was obscured. They were quite unlike the serene white clouds that drifted in the heavens Au Co knew. The golden crow's light grew fainter until Au Co could barely see what was happening. Suddenly, thunder bellowed from the depths of the sea, and a golden dragon hundreds of feet long burst from the waves. Its marvelous long body twisted gracefully before it disappeared into the black clouds. Lightning flashed across the black sky, and then there was a deafening crash.

Frightened, Au Co stood up, but she was unable to see anything. Then, all at once, she felt a pleasant sensation on her skin, something at once wet, ticklish, delicate, and refreshing. Thousands of tiny drops fell onto her body. Rain! Dragon Prince had made rain!

The steady pitter-patter was like the sound of singing. It reminded Au Co of the sea prince's warm and reassuring voice. She lifted her arms to welcome the refreshing drops and then offered her hair and shoulders, her whole body, to the soothing rains. Beneath her feet, young grasses sprang up and the river was soon replenished.

The rain lasted a long while. When nearly all the clouds were gone and bright sunlight streamed forth again, the golden dragon gazed down at the earth. Many new rivers and streams had appeared. Not only did grass grow fresh and green along the riverbanks but it now covered the hills, mountains, and fields. Flowers—violet, gold, pink, and white—dotted the landscape. The face of the earth glistened in unimaginable beauty. Yet what was even more miraculous to the sea prince as he gazed down from the last clouds was that the outline of the rivers took the very shape of Au Co herself—her long legs stretching to the sea, her hair flowing over all the hills and mountains. Her image was forever imprinted on the green fields of the fresh and lovely earth. Au Co, so beautiful and full of vitality, was herself the fertile heart of the earth.

The golden dragon flew back down to earth, turning again into a handsome young man. In his hand he held a white lotus. He was anxious to see the young goddess again. Indeed, he had fallen in love with her the moment he saw her. Au Co awaited the sea prince's return. His voice, as gentle as the early morning sunlight, had warmed her heart.

From a high cliff, Dragon Prince gazed down over the ocean. To him, nothing could match the beauty of morning by the sea. The pale blue horizon rested on the deep blue expanse. Sun sparkled on the waters. He watched fishermen drag their nets over the sand, while others pushed small boats out into the water. They were robust and handsome men, each wearing a dragon tattoo to ward off sea monsters. Dragon Prince was pleased with the human race. They had inherited the intelligence of goddesses from their mother Au Co and the bravery of dragons from their father.

Dragon Prince had no idea how many months or years had passed according to sea time since he met Goddess Au Co, but seven thousand years had passed on earth. Because she was an immortal, Au Co looked as fresh and beautiful as ever. But in those seven thousand years, many generations of the human race had come and gone. Since the birth of the first humans, Dragon Prince and Au Co had been there to teach and protect them. The people looked to Au Co as their ruler and used the image of the Lac bird as the symbol of their land. They often called Dragon Prince "Lac Dragon."

Seven thousand years. . . . Perhaps according to sea time it had been a mere seven months. Here on land, so much had changed. Dragon Prince reminisced about the first day he set foot on land and how he followed the stream of fresh water to discover Au Co. He remembered the first rainfall he made from her tears. Au Co's sweet tears were the source of life for the trees, grasses, flowers, and all living beings on land. Her tears refreshed both body and spirit. Dragon Prince thought of Au Co as the green earth herself in whose heart flowed endless springs of fresh water.

His union with Au Co was very special. She was beauty and vitality. She was the fertile earth. Not long after they began living together, Au Co laid a large sack of eggs. Had they both been dragons, Dragon Prince would have expected their children to be dragons. But this was a union between a dragon and a goddess. Many months passed before they knew what fruit their love was to bear. Although they lived together in a cave near the top of Long Trang mountain, they placed the egg sack outside in a grassy meadow to accustom their future children to the sky, the earth, and the warmth of the sun.

For nine years, they visited the egg sack daily. They sat together on the moist grass beneath the light of the wild swan or beneath the warm rays of the golden crow, listening quietly to the wind sift through the grasses. They usually communicated in silence, understanding each other perfectly. Dragon Prince knew how Au Co felt just by looking into her eyes. And Au Co understood what Dragon Prince wanted to say by the motions of his arms and hands. His outstretched arms resembled golden dragons in graceful flight.

One morning, as the wind sang through the trees, they reached the meadow to discover the egg sack had grown as large as a small hill, and it began to rip apart. When the warm rays of the golden crow came shining over the mountain, one hundred snow-white eggs began to crack open, and from each one emerged a plump baby. Au Co and Dragon Prince were overcome with joy and surprise. One hundred little boys and girls stretched out rosy arms to be held. Au Co and Dragon Prince carried their children back to the cave and made cozy beds for them out of soft grasses. The babies did not need mother's milk to grow. Together with the fresh air and the natural strength they inherited from their goddess mother and dragon father, they grew as quickly as flowers in the field.

Au Co devoted all her time to the care of her one hundred babies. She rocked each one in her arms, hardly able to believe the wondrous fruits of love. To be a mother was for her the greatest happiness. She loved the earth. She loved all the plants and creatures. She loved her new life. Now and again she thought longingly of her sister goddesses, but she was no longer overcome by sadness or regret. The goddesses did not return—perhaps they had been forbidden. Although Au Co wished to see them again, she was content with her life on earth and considered it her true home.

Dragon Prince's thoughts did not dwell much on his former life beneath the ocean. He remained on land to create a new life by the side of Au Co. Their children grew daily in strength and wisdom. Dragon Prince taught them to call him "Father" and to call Au Co "Mother." Au Co's daughters often called to her in high, sweet voices, "Mother, can we climb the hill to gather flowers?"

With Au Co, Dragon Prince created a human language and used it to name all the things on earth. They named the plants and flowers that flourished on land. They called the dense groves of trees "forests" and the majestic formations of rocks that grazed the skies "mountains." They named the golden crow "Sun" and the wild swan "Moon." They called their one hundred children Mountain, Water, Forest, Moon, Plum, Pear, Peach, Crystal, and many other beautiful names. One hundred children, and they never forgot the name of a single one.

When the children were old enough, Au Co and Dragon Prince showed them how to gather fruit and how to make stone tools to hunt in the forests. They helped them weave nets to catch shrimp and fish in the rivers and sea.

Dragon Prince remembered how a god appeared to Au Co in a dream one cold winter night. The god held a golden crow that glowed like fire in his hand. Its warmth comforted Au Co. The god introduced himself as A Nhi and he showed her simple tools made from stone. Then he said, "When the people are cold, they can call me. I am a child of the sun sent to help them. I live in these stones."

When she woke up, Au Co told this dream to Dragon Prince. They went outside to examine their stone tools, but they didn't notice anything unusual. Suddenly Dragon Prince remembered how he and his sons had seen sparks flying from stones while working with their tools. Dragon Prince struck two stones together and used dry twigs and leaves to start a fire from the sparks that were created. From that time on the people had fire for warmth and cooking.

Dragon Prince taught his children to chop wood and build huts. In the winter Au Co shredded tree bark into thread to weave some simple cloth. With the help of her daughters, everyone soon had clothes to wear. They cut and dried reeds to weave mats with which to cover the cold floors of their huts. The people netted shrimp and fish, and hunted game with bows and arrows. What food they didn't eat, they learned to dry and preserve to last the winter.

The work Au Co liked best of all was growing sweet rice. The people fashioned simple stone plows and sowed grains of rice. Where the land was low enough, they dug canals for irrigation. Lac Dragon showed his children how they could stuff sections of bamboo trunk with rice and then cover the bamboo with mud to throw onto hot beds of ashes. When the wet mud had dried and cracked away, they scooped out the rice. Rice prepared in this way was especially delicious.

In all ways, a new and wondrous life flourished on earth. Several thousand years passed. The first children grew old and died, as did their children and grandchildren. Each generation passed the land onto the next. Although humans were half-dragon and half-goddess, they lived only a few hundred years. When they died, their souls departed to the underworld, where, it is said, the living can sometimes visit. There were, however, a few children endowed with the same powers as their parents. They were immortal and lived in the high mountains or the deep sea, never growing old.

When children came of age, they could marry. A young woman's parents would bring an offering of salt to a young man's parents to request that a marriage be arranged. If the young man's parents agreed, the young man was sent to live with his bride's family. At the wedding, the bride and groom received sweet rice from everyone in the village. The ceremony itself was simple—bride and groom shared a meal of sweet rice together. After the wedding, they continued to live with the bride's family.

The salt offered to the groom's parents was a symbol of trust and friendship. The sweet rice eaten at the wedding was a symbol of intimacy and fidelity. At large weddings, friends of the families brought cakes made of flour pounded from wild roots. Au Co created all these customs for her children.

Human couples did not lay eggs. Instead, the mother gave birth to one child at a time. Au Co showed mothers how to arrange fresh banana leaves for their babies to sleep on, and how to nourish the babies with their own breast milk.

Salt was regarded as precious and essential. Au Co showed her children how to extract a kind of salt from gingerroots. Later, Lac Dragon showed them how they could evaporate sea water to obtain salt. Thanks to salt, the people could cure fish and make fish sauce that kept for long periods of time.

Au Co also taught her children to dance and sing. With the people, she organized special nights of dance and song held around great bonfires. The first musical instruments they invented were drums made by stretching animal skins over hollowed out logs. Young men and women also pounded long sticks against the sides of stone urns used to grind rice. Everyone, young and old, joined these celebrations, donning headdresses and vests made of white feathers, and dancing around the fire. Later generations replaced the simple wood and stone drums with copper ones that boomed like thunder.

A sudden cry from shore awoke Lac Dragon from his thoughts. He looked below. Thousands of silver fish glistened in the fishermen's nets. It was a tremendous catch! Then, without warning, Dragon Prince felt a curious twitch in his right arm. He knew that his Emperor Father was calling him to return to the sea palace. It was time. His father wished to hand over the throne to him. It had been a long time since

Dragon Prince had made an appearance at the sea palace. With a twinge of regret, Lac Dragon knew he had to leave the land and return to the sea. A gentle hand stroked his shoulder, and he looked up. He did not know how long Au Co had been standing behind him. Her hand rested gently on his shoulder.

She asked, "What are you thinking about so deeply?"

He stood up and clasped her hand, "My father, the Sea Emperor, has just summoned me to return to the sea palace to inherit the throne. I must depart at once, but I will return as soon as the coronation ceremony has taken place."

"May I go with you?" she asked.

"Sky is round and earth is square. Water and fire are different elements. You are a goddess and I am a dragon. Although our union on the land is wondrous, it is not possible for you to travel beneath the sea. I wish you could come, but it isn't possible."

"You are right, my dear. But what about our children? Do humans possess the ability to visit the sea palace?"

Lac Dragon thought a moment and then answered, "Because humans are half-dragon, they should be able to. If a boy and a girl were to go together, they could help each other along the way. I'll return just as soon as I've finished my duties beneath the sea, but if any emergency arises before then, send two of our children down to the sea palace for me. Anyone who holds this will find their way without danger."

Lac Dragon opened his mouth and a bright jadestone popped out. He handed it to Au Co.

"My father is calling. I must leave at once."

He took her hand and together they walked down to the beach. It was noon and the fishermen had returned to their villages for lunch. Dragon Prince gazed at the quiet blue sky. He felt as though seven thousand years had passed as quickly as a dream. He held Au Co's hands in his own and looked into her eyes for a long moment. He leaned down and kissed both her cheeks. Then, with a slight twist of his body, he turned into a little fish and dived into the ocean. Startled, Au Co stood and stared at the water. She called out her husband's dragon name. "Naga! Nagaraja!"

But Lac Dragon was already far away. The only answer to her cries was the steady lapping of the waves.

Kali Beheaded

Hindu (India)

The diverse religions of India feature numerous gods and goddesses, but, as one of the earliest philosophical dialogues in the Upanishads suggests, all religious philosophies and all gods, if re-

Source: Reprinted by permission of Farrar, Straus and Giroux, LLC. "Kali Beheaded" from *Oriental Tales* by Marguerite Yourcenar, translated by Alberto Manguel. Translation copyright © 1985 by Alberto Manguel.

duced to their fundamental meaning, are one. Indeed, if any single statement can be made summarizing the Vedic philosophy underlying Hindu, Buddhist, Sikh, and Jain belief, it is that the appearance of distinctions among beings and things—that is, the appearance of mundane reality that comes to us through normal consciousness—is an illusion. For beneath all distinctions and appearances, there is a fundamental identity between subject ("I") and object ("other") that transcends our everyday experience of things. Indeed, all things are one from the perspective of the Absolute whether that all-encompassing truth of existence is named Brahma, Vishnu, Shiva—or, for that matter, Parvati, Lakshmi, Durga, or Kali.

A second important understanding linking the above-named Indian religions is the notion of transmigration "which holds," according to Donald S. Lopez Jr.,

> that upon death a person is neither annihilated nor transported to some other world in perpetuity, but rather returns to worldly life, to live and die again in a new mortal form. This continuing succession of life, death, and rebirth is termed *samsara* (circling, wandering) in the Upanishads. *Samsara* comes to denote not just the individual wandering of a person from life to life, but also the entire world process seen as a perpetual flux. (1995, 12–13)

Although views differ about whether and how one can be freed from the endless wheel of birth, death, and rebirth, the Vedic methods most familiar to Westerners are those aimed at renouncing the world through various ascetic practices and the disciplined pursuit of higher forms of knowledge. The logic behind the way of renunciation is that we can become free of the world by disentangling ourselves from it. Seeking release from the pain and sorrow inherent in *samsara,* ascetics of India's various religious traditions have led lives of contemplation, subjecting themselves to a variety of rigors, including cloistering, restricted diet, breath control, celibacy, silence, and many forms of self-torture designed to move the ascetic beyond such ego-centric categories as pleasure and pain, good and bad, attraction and aversion.

Around the seventh century CE, a variety of previously unrecorded medical, yogic, magical, and religious practices became organized within what is now called the tantric tradition. Tantra is exceedingly difficult to define, but most scholars of Indian religion use the term to refer to a wide variety of ritual and yogic forms not described in the Vedas, including visualization of meditation deities, the creation of and contemplation upon mandalas, the use of mantras to release various powers, and Kundalini yoga. This form of yoga can involve the ritual use of sex as a means of transforming the individual's body into divinity—a technique that has gained

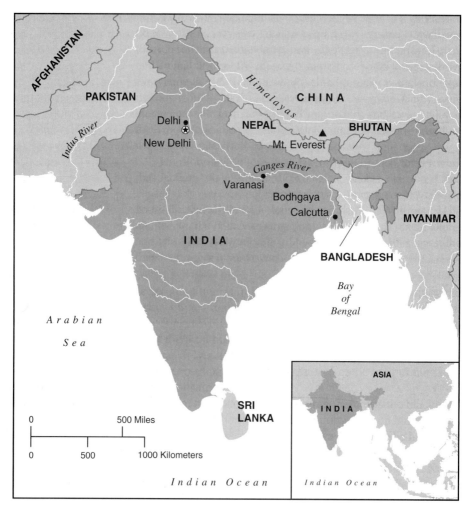

MAP 3.5 India

tantra much notoriety but little understanding in the West. In addition, the various rituals and techniques that comprise tantra tend to emphasize Shakti ("energy"), Shiva's consort, as the fundamental creative power of the universe. According to Lopez, "Medieval Shaiva theologians [devotees of the god Shiva] . . . postulated an inactive but transcendent male Shiva who carries out all his worldly activities through an immanent energetic female Shakti" (1995, 42). Tantra views female (Shakti) energy as the real power in the universe, and, whether in the form of Parvati, Durga, Kali, or another female deity, it attributes all activity to the transcendent Goddess. The following story, then, depicts Kali the destroyer as the active power who leads all beings to the realization that form is illusory and that we cannot escape *samsara* until desire is quenched.

Kali, the fierce "black goddess," has evolved from the blood-thirsty warrior goddess of the *Mahabharata* into a compassionate mother, not usually associated with misfortune and death. Traditionally, she was depicted with wild, long hair, a naked body, a necklace of skulls, a belt of human hands, and wielding an upraised sword. In traditional Shaivist literature, Kali's mad, destructive dance threatens to destroy the world until Shiva places his body beneath her feet. In some depictions, Shiva lies beheaded in the midst of a cremation ground while Kali copulates with him in order to lure him yet again into another birth. However, especially in modern Bengal, where Kali's temples and images appear everywhere, she now tends to be beautiful, smiling, clothed, her maternal qualities emphasized. What accounts for this transformation? Indeed, how can the goddess of death and destruction be "one" with the feminine force that the tantric tradition believes animates the entire universe? The notion of *samsara*, the fact that we live, die, and are reborn through countless lifetimes, provides a partial answer to this question. Kali, the devourer, represents the truth that all forms—our bodies included—will decay and ultimately disappear. This is not a matter of the goddess's malice, but of inevitability. That is why the devotional songs (*bhakti*) of her worshipers emphasize that Kali possesses the three attributes of matter, spirit, and emptiness. We exist, according to various Indian religious traditions, as a combination of matter and spirit, but because nothing retains its form forever, it is also considered "empty" of any fixed identity.

The following story is a modern adaptation of traditional materials written by Marguerite Yourcenar, French novelist, playwright, essayist, cultural critic, and translator—and the first woman elected to the French National Academy—which takes up the apparent contradictions in Kali's roles as mother and destroyer by providing a fanciful rationalization for her hatred of all existence and contradictory impulse to "swell her substance." She has the head of a goddess and the body of a prostitute, a condition that juxtaposes matter and spirit in the starkest possible terms. Like her human worshipers, she knows and longs for the glory of the eternal realm beyond birth and death but suffers all the miseries and indignities to which mortal flesh is heir. Ultimately, she meets a sage who tells her that her condition embodies the terrible truth: any form, even that of a goddess, is subject to change and destruction, and all yearnings and regrets are pointless. Ultimate freedom from the grossness of material form and the tyranny of craving is the only true happiness—and death and decay are the teachers who show us this truth.

This story, then, serves not only as an engaging presentation of myth from ancient India, which it certainly is, but also as a "case" representing the ongoing and transcultural nature of myth. Writing about the effects of time and changing human contexts on Greek and Roman statues, Yourcenar provides reflections that can be seen, metaphorically, as a provocative defense of her representation of the Kali material:

> On the day when a statue is finished, its life, in a certain sense, begins. The first phase, in which it has been brought, by means of the sculptor's efforts, out of the block of stone into human shape, is over; a second phase, stretching across the course of centuries, through alterations of adoration, admiration, love, hatred, and indifference, and successive degrees of erosion and attrition, will bit by bit return it to the state of unformed mineral mass out of which its sculptor had taken it.
>
> It goes without saying that we do not possess a single Greek statue in the state in which its contemporaries knew it: we can barely discern, here and there on the hair of a *kore* or a *kouros* of the sixth century, the traces of reddish color, like palest henna, which attest to the pristine character of painted statues alive with the intense, almost terrifying life of mannequins and idols which also happen to be masterpieces of art. Those hard objects fashioned in imitation of the forms of organic life have, in their own way, undergone the equivalent of fatigue, age, and unhappiness. They have changed in the way time changes us. Their maltreatment by Christians or barbarians, the conditions under which they have spent their centuries of abandonment underground until discovery has given them back to us, the sagacious or ill-advised restorations from which they have benefited or suffered, the accumulation of dirt and the true or false patina—everything, including the atmospheric conditions of the museums in which they are today imprisoned, leaves its mark on their bodies of metal or stone. Some of these alterations are sublime. (1992, 87–88)

Kali, the terrible goddess, roams the Indian plains. She can be seen both in the north and in the south, and at the same time in holy places and in the market squares. Women shudder as she passes; the young men, nostrils quivering, come out onto the thresholds, and even the little crying children know her name. Black Kali is beautiful and horrible. Her waist is so slender that the poets who sing about her compare her to the banana tree. Her shoulders are round like the rising autumn moon; her breasts are like buds about to burst; her hips sway like the trunk of the newly born elephant calf; and her dancing feet are like green shoots. Her mouth is as warm as life; her eyes as deep as death. In turn she gazes at herself in the bronze of night, in the silver of dawn, in the copper of dusk; in the gold of midday she stares at herself. But her lips have never smiled; a necklace of bones coils around her slender neck, and upon her face, paler than the rest of her body, her large eyes are pure and sad. Kali's face, eternally bathed in tears, is ashen and covered with dew like the uneasy face of dawn.

Kali is abject. She has lost her divine caste by having given herself to pariahs, to outcasts, and her cheeks kissed by lepers are now covered with a crust of stars. She presses herself against the mangy chests of the camel drivers from the north, who never wash because of the intense cold. She sleeps on vermin-ridden beds with blind beggars; she passes from the embrace of Brahmins to that of miserable creatures, the unclean, whose very presence pollutes the day, who are charged with washing the corpses. And stretched out in the pyramid-shaped shadows of the funeral pyres, Kali abandons herself upon the still warm ashes. She also loves the boatmen, who are rough and strong. She even accepts the black men who work in the bazaar, more harshly beaten than beasts of burden; she rubs her head against their shoulders raw from the swaying of their loads. Wretched as a feverish woman unable to find cool water, she goes from village to village, from crossroads to cross-roads, in search of the same mournful delights.

Her tiny feet dance frantically below the chiming anklets, but her eyes never stop weeping, her bitter mouth never kisses, her eyelashes never caress the cheeks of those who embrace her, and her face remains eternally pale like an immaculate moon.

A long time ago, Kali, lotus flower of perfection, reigned in Indra's heaven as in the depths of a sapphire; the diamonds of dawn glittered in her eyes, and the universe contracted or expanded in tune with the beatings of her heart.

But Kali, perfect as a flower, ignored her own perfection and, pure as the day itself, had no knowledge of her own purity.

The jealous gods followed Kali one evening, during an eclipse, into a cone of darkness, in a corner of a conniving planet. A bolt of lightning cut her head off. Instead of blood, a torrent of light sprang from her sliced neck. Her halved body, thrown into the abyss by the Jinns, rolled down into the uttermost pit of hell, where those who have not seen or have refused the heavenly light crawl and whimper. A cold wind blew, condensing the clear flakes that started to drop from the sky; a white layer began to collect on the mountaintops, beneath starry spaces where night was falling. The monster gods, the cattle gods, the gods of many arms and many legs like turning wheels, escaped through the shadows, blinded by their halos of fire, and the haggard immortals regretted their crime.

Contrite, the gods descended along the Roof of the World, into the abyss full of smoke where those who once were alive now crawl. They crossed the nine purgatories; they passed prisons of ice and mud, where ghosts devoured by remorse repent the wrongs they have committed, and prisons of fire, where other dead, tormented by vain greed, bemoan the wrongs they did not commit. The gods were astounded to find that man has such an infinite capacity for evil, so many resources and agonies of pleasure and sin. At the bottom of the ossuary, in a swamp, Kali's head bobbed like a water lily, and her long black hair rippled around it like floating roots.

Piously, they picked up the lovely pale head and they set off to find the body that had borne it. A headless body was lying on the shore. They took it, placed Kali's head upon those shoulders, and brought the goddess back to life.

The body was that of a prostitute condemned to death for having sought to trouble the meditations of a young Brahmin. Drained of blood, the ashen corpse seemed pure. The goddess and the harlot had on the left thigh the same beauty spot.

Never again did Kali, lotus flower of perfection, reign in Indra's heaven. The body to which the divine head was joined felt homesick for the streets of ill repute, the forbidden encounters, the rooms where the prostitutes, meditating on secret debauches, survey the clients' arrival through the slits of green shutters. She became the seducer of children, the inciter of old men, the ruthless mistress of the young; and the women of the town, neglected by their husbands and feeling like widows, compared Kali's body to the flames of a pyre. She was as unclean as a gutter rat and as loathed as a weasel of the fields. She stole hearts as if they were strips of offal from the butcher's block, and the liquefied fortunes of men clung to her hands like strands of honey. Never resting, from Benares to Kapilavastu, from Bangalore to Srinagar, Kali's body bore the goddess's dishonored head, and her limpid eyes continued to weep.

One morning in Benares, Kali, drunk, grimacing with fatigue, left the harlots' street. In the fields, an idiot quietly slobbering, seated at the edge of a dung heap, rose to his feet as she passed and ran after her. When he was barely the length of his shadow away, Kali slowed down and allowed him to overtake her.

After he had left her, she continued her way toward an unknown city. A child begged her for alms, and she did not even warn him that a snake, about to strike, was lifting its head between two stones. She had been overcome by a hatred of all living things, and at the same time by a desire to swell her substance, to annihilate all creatures as she fed on them. She could be seen crouching at the edge of graveyards; her jaws cracked bones like the maw of a lioness. She killed like the female insect devouring the male; she crushed the beings she brought to life like a wild sow turning on her young. Those she killed, she finished off by dancing on their bodies. Her lips stained with blood exuded a dull smell of butcher shops, but her embrace consoled her victims, and the warmth of her breast made them forget all ills.

At the edge of a wood, Kali met a wise man.

He was sitting cross-legged, palms placed one against the other, and his wizened body was as dry as firewood. Nobody could have said if he was very young or very old; his all-seeing eyes were barely visible beneath his half-shut lids. Around him the light formed a halo, and Kali felt rising from her own inner depths the presentiment of a vast definitive peace, where worlds would stop and beings would be delivered; and of a day of beatitude on which both life and death will be equally useless, an age in which the All will be absorbed into Nothingness, as if that pure vacuity that she had just conceived were quivering within her like a future child.

The Master of Great Compassion lifted a hand to bless the passing woman.

"My immaculate head has been fixed to the body of infamy," she said. "I desire and do not desire, I suffer and yet I enjoy, I loathe living and am afraid to die."

"We are all incomplete," said the wise man. "We are all pieces, fragments, shadows, matterless ghosts. We all have believed that we have wept and that we have felt pleasure for endless centuries."

"I was a goddess in Indra's heaven," said the harlot.

"And yet you were not freer from the chain of things, nor your diamond body safer from misfortune than your body of flesh and filth. Perhaps, unhappy woman, dishonored traveler of every road, you are about to attain that which has no shape."

"I am tired," moaned the goddess.

Then, touching with the tip of his fingers the black tresses soiled with ashes, he said: "Desire has taught you the emptiness of desire; regret has shown you the uselessness of regret. Be patient, Error of which we are all a part, Imperfect Creature thanks to whom perfection becomes aware of itself, O Lust which is not necessarily immortal . . ."

Callisto and Arcas, from Ovid's *Metamorphoses*

Roman (Italy)

The founding of Rome is described in two myths. According to the story favored in the poet Virgil's lifetime, the great hero Aeneas escaped with his life from the sack of Troy. After considerable wandering, Aeneas landed in Latium, through which the Tiber flows. Aeneas married the daughter of King Latinus, defended his bride and position against King Turnus of Rutuli, and began a line of kings in Rome. The second myth has it that King Numitor of Alba Longa was driven from his throne by his younger brother Amulius. Once in power, Amulius murdered Numitor's sons and forced Numitor's daughter, Rhea Silvia, into the service of the goddess Vesta, whose priestesses were expected to guard their virginity in the goddess's honor on pain of death. Not long after, Mars, the god of war and agriculture, became enamored of Rhea Silvia and forced himself upon her. The result of this union was the birth of twins, Romulus and Remus. When Amulius discovered that his niece was pregnant despite his scheming to prevent that very thing, he had her cast into the Tiber, where she drowned. The twins were set adrift on the river in a reed basket. They floated downstream until the basket was caught in the branches of a fig tree.

At this point, one version of the story has it that a she-wolf suckled them (wolves are sacred to Mars) until a shepherd found them. Another version of the same story says that the twins were immediately discovered by a shepherd whose wife had just given birth to a stillborn child and was therefore able to breast-feed them. In this second version of the story, the shepherd's wife is said to have once been a prostitute—a detail most likely suggested by the fact that the Latin word *lupa* means both "she-wolf" and "prostitute." In either case, the boys grew to manhood, learned of their true identities, and avenged their grandfather and mother by fighting in the battle that took Amulius's life and restored Numitor to his throne. The young men decided to found a city on the Palatine Hill, near the spot where their reed basket had been caught by the

Source: From Ovid, *Metamorphoses.* In *Ovid's Metamorphoses,* translated by various authors, including Sir Samuel Garth and John Dryden, et al., and published by Sir Samuel Garth. London: J. F. Dove, 1826 (updated stylistically).

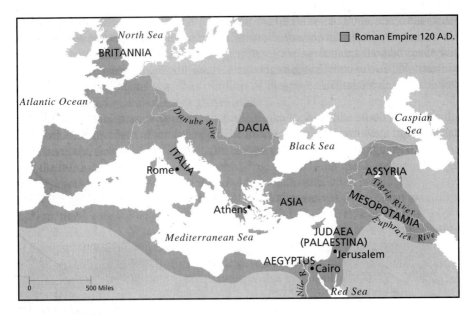

MAP 3.6 The Roman Empire

fig tree. Romulus, it was determined, would be the king; but the brothers soon quarreled and Romulus slew his brother, Remus. The new city, little more than a settlement of homesteaders, had few women. Romulus, hoping to remedy this situation, invited the neighboring tribe of the Sabines to a harvest festival. Once their guests had arrived the Romans abducted at sword point 600 Sabine daughters and raped them.

The historical record of Rome's founding suggests that the city was founded in 753 BCE and gradually grew from a small agricultural settlement into the greatest power of the ancient world. The history of Rome is typically discussed in terms of three broad eras: the monarchy (until 509 BCE), the republic (509–49 BCE), and the empire (27 BCE–476 CE). At the height of its power, the Roman Empire controlled a territory that extended from Britain to northern Africa and from Portugal to the western edge of the Black Sea, even briefly including the lands embraced by the Tigris and Euphrates rivers. Remarkably skilled at building and engineering, the Romans also developed a sophisticated legal and political system that administered affairs of state and civil matters for an empire of some 50 million subjects.

Under the Republic, the entire Italian peninsula was consolidated under Roman authority by 266 BCE and many of the major political and civic institutions that defined later Roman achievement were developed. Roman expansion brought great wealth and with that wealth, according to both sources of the time and modern historians, came corruption. With so much wealth and a sudden influx of slaves, peasants began moving to the larger cities in great numbers to find work. The nobility fought among themselves for an even greater share of this newfound wealth and became scandalous to the simpler rural folk who quickly grew tired of their rulers' sexual scandals and lust for power. From 133 BCE until Julius Caesar's death in 44 BCE, the prosperity and influence of Rome was jeopardized by civil war and political intrigue. Gaius Octavius, Julius's great-nephew and adopted son, came to power in 30 BCE, and through a combination of shrewd political maneuvering and a campaign to return to the ancient Roman virtues of family, personal piety, and nationalistic loyalty, Caesar Augustus, as he was now known, managed to reduce civil unrest and class hostility. Believing that the political corruption that nearly destroyed Rome during the Republican era was a direct result of moral decline, Augustus passed legislation to encourage marriage and childbearing and to punish adultery. In fact, Augustus banished his own daughter, Julia, for her illicit affairs.

Publius Ovidius Naso (43 BCE–18 CE), known to us as Ovid, lived during the Roman transition to Imperial rule and when the newfound emphasis on morality was at its most potent. As it happened, the emphasis on a home-and-hearth kind of morality had unhappy consequences for Ovid. Born to a relatively affluent rural family in the Abruzzi region (about 90 miles west of Rome), Ovid's family sent him to learn rhetoric when he was in his teens, a typical education for a young man whose family had the means and connections to set him on a course for public life. Ovid's older brother was skilled in rhetoric, whereas Ovid himself seemed incapable of anything but poetry—much to his father's disappointment. He gave his first public readings at age 18 and, with the publication of his *Amores,* or "Loves," and *Heroides,* or "Heroines," a decade or so before the beginning of the Common Era, Ovid became known as an important young poet. It was with the publication of the *Ars Amatoria,* or "Art of Love" and the *Metamorphoses* that Ovid's reputation as a major poet was secured.

Fame, however, came at a terrible personal cost. Given the morally conservative political climate, the *Ars Amatoria,* which was essentially a how-to poem about seducing a young woman, and the *Metamorphoses,* which depicted gods and rulers alike as having little compunction about adultery and lying, did not endear him to Caesar Augustus. For reasons not entirely clear, Augustus banished Ovid to Tomis, a Roman outpost on the Black Sea in modern Romania, where the poet lived the rest of his life in unhappy exile. Ovid's account of the reasons for his banishment are sketchy, but the moral laxity of the *Ars Amatoria*—and its apparent defiance of the emperor's efforts to restore the ancient moral order to the fledgling Empire—certainly had something to do with it. Ovid also suggests that he was guilty of complicity in a scandal—perhaps one of the sexual escapades of the emperor's daughter, Julia. In any case, Ovid continued to write while in exile, but his misery colors his later work; indeed, some of the poems are direct appeals to the emperor or to influential friends that he be allowed, if not a return from exile, at least exile in a less miserable place.

The *Metamorphoses,* from which the following story is drawn, is a complex work. Written in the style of epic poetry and recounting some 255 myths—mainly of Greek origin—the *Metamorphoses* is, as the name implies and as Ovid tells us in the first two lines, concerned largely with "forms changed to other bodies." The story of Callisto and her son Arcas involves a number of such transformations: Jove (Jupiter/Zeus) transforms himself into the goddess Diana's likeness, Callisto is transformed into a bear, and, ultimately, Callisto and her son Arcas are transformed into the constellations Ursa Major and Ursa Minor. Another kind of change central to the story is the transitory nature of human (and divine) desires and affections. Especially worth questioning are Diana's and Juno's relationships with Callisto and with Jove. Should we be surprised to see the divine woman warrior and the queen of heaven enforcing (blindly? unjustly?) chastity rules—despite the fact that Callisto is raped—and the sanctity of the marriage bed—despite the fact that it is really Jove who acts against that sanctity? Ultimately, Ovid depicts change as the governing principle of the universe. From the moment form emerges from Chaos, the poem seems to say, it is subject to the law of change. The poem—all 12,000 lines of it—presents the full human comedy with its small amusements and tragic suffering, its wars, its loves, its winners, and its losers with a great deal of humor, cleverness, and artistry. Ovid's outlook seems both tolerant and humane, but never naive or lacking a healthy skepticism.

As Jupiter walked about the Earth,
and raised the plants, and gave the spring its birth,
he saw a fair Arcadian nymph, Callisto,
and felt desire for her surge in his blood.
The nymph neither spun, nor dressed with artful pride;
she cared nothing for her looks,
beautiful though she most certainly was.
Her vest was gathered up, her hair was tied,
to offer ease of movement on the hunt;
in her hand she held a slender spear,
and a quiver of arrows adorned her shoulder.
From her youth dedicated to chaste Diana,
she joined the sprightly warriors of the wood.
Diana, too, loved the gentle huntress
more than all the other nymphs who roamed

over Maenalus, Arcadia's wild hills.
Sadly, though, no favor lasts for long.

One day the sun beating at mid-day drove
Callisto, panting, to seek for shelter
in a deeply shadowed hidden grove.
She dropped her arrows and unstrung her bow,
flung herself upon the cool grassy bed
and lay her head on the painted quiver.
Jove saw the charming huntress unguarded,
alone, stretched prone upon the lush green earth.
"Here I am safe," he cried, "from Juno's eye;
and should my jealous queen learn of my crime,
yet would I venture on a theft like this,
and stand her rage for such, for such a bliss!"
He quickly donned Diana's form and clothes,
softened his brows, and smoothed his awful look.
Then gently he spoke in a female voice,
"How fares my girl? How went the morning chase?"
Callisto, leaping from the grass, answered
"All hail, bright deity, whom I adore
more than Jove himself, even if he were here."
The God was nearer than she thought, and heard,
but smiled to hear his disguise so well received.

He then saluted her with a warm embrace;
before she had told half her morning chase,
inflamed by love, eager with lust,
he smothered her words with a passionate kiss.
Diana's shape could no longer conceal
the God in all his unbridled ardor.
The virgin fought with all her huntress might
—had she seen, Juno must have pardoned her—
against the God's all-consuming desire;
But how can a mortal girl resist Jove?

Possessed at length of what he had desired,
back to his heavens, the exulting God retired.
The lovely huntress, rising from the grass
with down-cast eyes and with a blushing face,
overwhelmed by shame and terrified the God might return,
fled the hateful dark site of her defeat
and almost, in the tumult of her mind,
left her forgotten bow and shafts behind.

But now Diana, hurrying across the plain
attended by her train of women warriors,
called in joy to the nymph. Callisto feared

a second fraud, Jove in his same disguise;
but, seeing the sister nymphs, she suppressed
her rising fears and mingled in the throng.

Yet how vivid in one's mien does guilt appear!
Down-spirited she loitered in the rear;
she trod heavily, no longer seeking
to run as she once did by the Goddess's side.
Her looks were so flushed, her face so sullen,
the virgin Goddess should (had she not been
a virgin) have seen the guilt plain upon her.
It's said the nymphs all saw and understood.

Later, the moon having waxed and waned nine times,
Diana, weary from the mid-day heat,
found a cool glen with a refreshing stream
that flowed in soft murmurs through the forest
and over a smooth bed of shining gravel.
The sylvan hideaway and the clear stream
so delighted the Goddess she called out,
"No intruders are near to see our play.
Let's strip naked, my gentle maids, and bathe."
Pleased with the motion, every maid complied;
only Callisto, blushing, stood confused
and tried to delay and offer excuses.
To no avail: her fellows pressed round her
and stripped Callisto bare against her will.
Her nakedness instantly revealed her shame;
in vain her hands shielded her swelling womb.
"Begone!" the Goddess cried with stern disdain,
"Begone! Dare not defile this holy stream!"
And Callisto fled,
forever banished from Diana's side.

Juno had waited long for the right time
to revenge Callisto's supposed crime;
and now enraging Juno even more,
Callisto bore Arcas, a lovely boy.
Her face wrenched with fury, Juno cried,
"Enough! This boy, this bastard
is living proof of Jove's unfaithfulness
—and, even worse, of his whore's triumph!
But vengeance will be mine at last.
The guilty charms that seduced the Thunderer
and drew him from our marriage bed
no longer shall keep their enticing force
or please the God or make the mortal woman vain."

This said, Juno seized her victim by the hair,
swung her to Earth, and dragged her to the ground.
Prostrate, Callisto lifted her arms in prayer;
yet her arms grew shaggy, deformed with hair,
her nails sharpened into long curved claws,
her hands became thick paws to bear her massive weight,
and her lips, that once could tempt a God, grew
ugly, distorted into toothsome grin.
And, lest the supplicating brute might reach
the ears of Jove, she was deprived of speech;
her desperate pleas came out a hoarse and
savage roar. Yet her mind remained the same.
The furry monster fixed her eyes above
and raised her new unwieldy paws to Jove.
She begged his aid with ceaseless groans, and though
she could not call him false, she thought him so.

Now she feared to dwell in the woods alone
or to haunt fields and meadows once her own.
How often did the baying dogs pursue
and drive the huntress before the hunters!
How she feared other beasts and shunned
her fellow shaggy bears, though she was one herself!
How she slunk from the sight of ranging wolves,
although her own father had become one!

One day it happened that Arcas her son,
now fifteen years old, a fierce and fearless
hunter, beating the woods in quest of prey,
roused his mother where she lay.
She knew her son, instantly turned to him,
and gazed fondly on him. The boy took fright,
aimed an arrow at her breast,
and would have slain his mother
had Jove not intervened at the last moment.
He seized them both in a sudden whirlwind,
bore them to Heaven, where he fixed them,
the Great Bear and the Lesser Bear,
lustrous constellations in the northern skies.

When Juno saw her rival in the sky,
spangled with stars and circled round with light,
she sought old Ocean in his deep abode
and Tethys, both revered among the Gods.
They asked what problem brought her down to them.
"Don't ask!" she said,

"Heaven is no longer a place for me.
When night has fallen, you'll see
Jove's starry bastard and triumphant whore
usurp the Heavens; you'll see them proudly rule!
So who will worship at my altars now,
when those I hate grow greater by my hate?
I made the nymph into an ugly beast,
but Jove changed the beast into a goddess.
This, this was all my weak revenge could do!

But who cares what foolish affairs Jove pursues?
Let him cast his Juno aside and lead
the wanton Callisto into his bed.
But you, honored Powers, be kind to me
and, if my wrongs do deserve resentment,
don't receive the light of these new constellations
in your waves, don't let the glaring strumpet
defile your ancient streams."

Thus the irate Goddess ended her complaint;
the water gods acceded to her wish,
and she rode her chariot back to Heaven,
triumphant, drawn by her gaudy peacocks,
their tails emblazoned with a thousand eyes . . .

On the Origin of the World

Gnostic/Coptic (Egypt)

According to Elaine Pagels, author of several books on early Christianity, including *The Gnostic Gospels, The Gnostic Paul,* and *Adam, Eve, and the Serpent,* in December 1945 two brothers made a remarkable discovery near Nag Hammadi, a village in Upper Egypt. Digging for *sabakh,* a soft, nitrate-rich soil used in farming, the brothers unearthed a large earthen jar at the base of a boulder on the mountain Jabal Al-Tarif. At first afraid that such a jar might contain a Jinn, the brothers hesitated to open the jar. But the hope for gold eventually won out, and, smashing the jar with a mattock, they discovered 13 papyrus books inside. They took them home, dumping them on the straw near the oven. Their mother admits to having used a great deal of the ancient paper to light her oven. Shortly after this discovery, the boys' father was killed, and the boys avenged their father's murder by hacking off the limbs of his

Source: Adapted from Hans-Gebhard Bethge and Bentley Layton. Societas Coptica Hierosolymitana, Trans., "On the Origin of the World." *The Nag Hammadi Library in English.* New York: HarperCollins, 1990. 170–89.

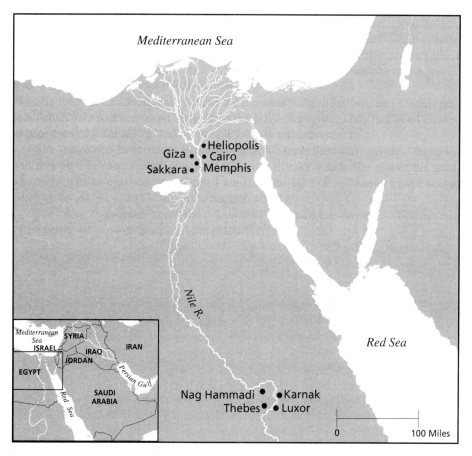

MAP 3.7 Ancient Egypt

killer, ripping out his heart, and eating it. Fearing that they were now marked men, the brothers gave the leather-bound books to a local priest, who had enough appreciation for their value to keep them safe and to consult an antiquities dealer in Cairo about their value. Money changed hands, and as soon as their existence became known the Egyptian government confiscated 10 of the remaining books. Yet one of the books was smuggled out of the country for sale in America. Amazingly, no one there purchased the book, and it eventually found its way to the Jung Foundation in Zürich, Switzerland, where Gilles Quispell, widely respected professor of the history of religion, made a few photographs and, later, translated the following, startling, sentence: "These are the secret words which the living Jesus spoke, and which the twin, Judas Thomas, wrote down" (Pagels 1989, xiii–xv).

The brothers had made one of the most remarkable archaeological discoveries of the twentieth century—the so-called Nag Hammadi Library of texts sacred to a heterogenous assortment of religious communities known to us collectively as the Gnostics. Deriving from the Greek word *gnosis,* usually translated as "knowledge," the term Gnostic generally refers to early Christians who believed that they had access to secret, hidden teachings and wisdom that were not available to the majority of Christians affiliated with what, by the second century of the Common Era, was called the "catholic church." James M. Robinson, editor of the *Nag Hammadi Library in English,* suggests that there may, in fact, have been an even broader Gnostic movement, one that would account for the fact that many of the texts of the Nag Hammadi materials seem to derive from traditions within Hermeticism, Judaism, and even Zoroastrianism (Robinson 1990, 6–10). The following creation story, in which Pistis-Sophia or Pistis-Zoe, the feminine embodiment of the Divine wisdom, has a decisive role in the creation of the universe and the events in the Garden of Eden, probably derives from the Jewish branch of the Gnostic tree.

In any case, by the second century, the Gnostics were viewed as heretics by the catholic majority and were harassed and even imprisoned or exiled for their unorthodox beliefs. It is most likely because they wished to save their sacred writings from the torch that the Egytpian Gnostics of Nag Hammadi buried the so-called library at the Jabal during the fourth century CE. The Christian Gnostics, naturally, viewed themselves not only as Christians, but as the *true* Church. Robinson reminds us that Jesus himself was quite radical politically, urging his followers to withdraw from the socioeconomic, political, and religious norms of "the world" and to align themselves instead with the invisible utopia that he called "the Kingdom of Heaven." It is this spirit of rejecting the compromises, greed, busyness, and spiritual error of the world that the Gnostics believed they were preserving. They tended to reject as deluded the Christian majority—and the Church that was slowly but steadily gaining authority in the Greco-Roman world by accommodating itself to various political and economic realities. Although generalizing about what the Gnostics believed is difficult, one important thread that links many Gnostic texts is an intense dualism that sees matter and spirit as not only opposites but at war with one another. As a result, some Gnostics believed that it was blasphemous to maintain that God had contaminated the purity of the Divine Essence by "becoming flesh." Indeed, a number of Gnostics believed that the so-called God worshiped by the Church was in fact not God at all, but a deluded and arrogant intermediary called Yaldabaoth, or the Demi-Urge.

We see in the following story that "the Immortals"—a company of purely spiritual beings including Jesus, Faith, and Wisdom—dwell in a realm beyond matter. However, even in the undefiled beginning, a mysterious first "product" exists alongside pure spirit and from it is projected a likeness of Sophia (Wisdom) which acts as a "veil," separating the realm of the Immortals from mankind. Yet, even though this veil is not exactly a material form, it begets a number of divisions which result in a variety of shadowy products, including the vast primordial deep featured in many other cosmogonies. The anonymous writer of "On the Origin of the World" takes some pains to show that the Chaos over which Pistis-Sophia "broods" like the Elohim of Genesis—and which is named as the beginning point in the Greek *Theogony*— is secondary to the realm of the immortals and appears to be the very beginning of things only because the material world has hidden the spiritual realm from us.

Pistis-Sophia projects an image of herself into Chaos and gives form to Yaldabaoth, granting him authority over matter, and then withdraws. Yaldabaoth presumes himself to be God Supreme and, also hovering over Chaos, creates the material world and a series of heavenly realms and uncountable spiritual "authorities" over which to rule. Soon Pistis-Sophia returns to reveal herself—and her Divine plan—to Yaldabaoth, who she calls Samael, or "blind god": "There is an immortal man of light [Jesus] who has been in existence before you and who will appear among your modeled forms; he will trample you to scorn just as a potter's clay is pounded. And you will descend to your mother, the abyss, along with those that belong to you" (Bethge et al. 1990, 175). This revelation troubles Yaldabaoth (now called the Prime Parent) and ultimately causes him to lose face before the "authorities." In response, he and the authorities plot to make man in the Garden of Eden, apparently hoping the Adam of Light (a form of Jesus) would become enamored of this likeness and therefore spare their works (the material world) from the destruction that Pistis-Sophia has foretold.

In a scene reminiscent of the creation of Ulligara and Zalgarra (see Chapter 2, pp. 76–79), the authorities cast their semen into the navel of the earth, to awaken the modeled form of man. But Pistis-Sophia, we are told, had foreseen this trick and, in the form of Sophia-Zoe, creates her own, androgynous human being, which she immediately molds into a female form named Eve of Zoe ("Eve of Life"). Adam, in this story, is the illegitimately created "man" that the authorities had modeled; but, seeing that he had no spirit in him, they abandoned him. Sophia-Zoe breathes a spirit into him and Eve calls out to him "Adam! Become alive! Arise upon the earth!" Then the spiritual Eve leaves a material likeness with Adam and infuses her essence into the Tree of Gnosis (i.e., the Tree of the Knowledge of Good and Evil in Genesis). The authorities, now realizing that they have failed in their attempt to avoid ultimate doom, content themselves by deceiving the descendants of Adam and Eve into believing that Yaldabaoth is God and that the authorities are the Angels. In this way, Demi-Urge and his minions resemble the biblical Satan, who knows that he cannot

> defeat God and therefore bides his time destroying the souls of his archenemy's favored creatures. Only those who have "the acquaintance" (*gnosis*) know the true story of creation and to see how Yaldabaoth and his minions have used the Church and other worldly authorities (i.e., the archons) to deceive the mass of humanity into viewing him as God and the material world as his crowning achievement.

Seeing that everybody, gods of the world and mankind, says that nothing existed prior to chaos, I in distinction to them shall demonstrate that they are all mistaken, because they are not acquainted with the origin of chaos, nor with its root. Here is the demonstration. How well it suits all men, on the subject of chaos, to say that it is a kind of darkness! But in fact it comes from a shadow, which has been called by the name darkness. And the shadow comes from a product that has existed since the beginning. It is, moreover, clear that the product existed before chaos came into being, and that the latter is posterior to the first product.

Let us therefore concern ourselves with the facts of the matter; and furthermore, with the first product, from which chaos was projected. And in this way the truth will be clearly demonstrated.

After the natural structure of the immortal beings had completely developed out of the infinite, a likeness then emanated from Pistis (Faith); it is called Sophia (Wisdom). It exercised volition and became a product resembling primeval light. And immediately her will manifested itself as a likeness of heaven, having an unimaginable magnitude; it was between the immortal beings and those things that came into being after them . . . Sophia functioned as a veil dividing mankind from the things above.

Now the eternal realm of truth has no shadow outside it, for the limitless light is everywhere within it. But its exterior is shadow, which has been called by the name darkness. From it there appeared a force, presiding over the darkness. And the forces that came into being subsequent to them called the shadow . . . From it, every kind of divinity sprouted up . . . together with the entire place, so that also shadow is posterior to the first product. It was in the abyss that shadow appeared, deriving from the aforementioned Pistis.

Then shadow perceived that there was something mightier than it, and felt envy; and when it had become pregnant of its own accord, suddenly it engendered jealousy. Since that day, the principle of jealousy amongst all eternal realms and their worlds has been apparent. Now as for that jealousy, it was found to be an abortion without any spirit in it. Like shadow it came into existence in a vast watery substance. Then the bile that had come into being out of the shadow was thrown into a part of chaos. Since that day, a watery substance has been apparent. And what sank within it flowed away, being visible in chaos: as with a woman giving birth to a child—all her fluids flow out; just so, matter came into being out of shadow and was projected apart. And matter did not depart from chaos; rather, matter was in chaos, being in a part of it.

And when these things had come to pass, then Pistis came and appeared over the matter of chaos, which had been expelled like an aborted fetus—since there was no spirit in it. For all chaos was limitless darkness and bottomless water. Now when

Pistis saw what had resulted from her defect, she became disturbed. And the disturbance appeared, as a fearful product; it rushed to her in the chaos. She turned into it and blew into its face in the abyss, which is below all the heavens.

And when Pistis-Sophia desired to cause the thing that had no spirit to be formed into a likeness and to rule over matter and over all her forces, there appeared for the first time a ruler, out of the waters, lionlike in appearance, androgynous, having great authority within him, and ignorant of whence he had come into being. Now when Pistis-Sophia saw him moving about in the depth of the waters she said to him, "Child, pass through to here" (which, translated, is *yalda baoth*).

Since that day there appeared the principle of verbal expression which reached the gods and the angels and mankind. And what came into being as a result of verbal expression, the gods and angels and mankind finished. Now as for the ruler, Yaldabaoth, he is ignorant of the force of Pistis: he did not see her face, rather he saw in the water the likeness that spoke with him. And because of that voice, he called himself Yaldabaoth. But Ariael is what the perfect call him, for he was like a lion. Now when he had come to have authority over matter, Pistis-Sophia withdrew up to her light.

When the ruler saw his magnitude—and it was only himself that he saw: he saw nothing else, except for water and darkness—then he supposed that it was he alone who existed. His [form?] was completed by verbal expression: it appeared as a spirit moving to and fro upon the waters. And when that spirit appeared, the ruler set apart the watery substance. And what was dry was divided into another place. And from matter, the ruler made a footstool, and he called it earth . . .

[Ed. note: At this point in the narrative, Yaldabaoth, ignorant of the eighth heaven, "the eternal realm of truth" and repressing the knowledge that he was called into being by the voice of Pistis-Sophia, imagines, in the words of the God of the Hebrew scriptures, that he is "God, and there is no other one that exists apart from [him]." He proceeds to create seven androgynous beings, granting to each a heavenly realm over which they are given authority. Just as the work is completed, an unnamed troublemaker from the Abyss brings these newly created worlds crashing down. Seeing this, Pistis intervenes and, using Yaldabaoth's—and his progeny's—ignorant ambitions against them, makes the creation of the world and its people possible.]

Now the prime parent Yaldabaoth, since he possessed great authorities, created heavens for each of his offspring through verbal expression—created them beautiful, as dwelling places—and in each heaven he created great glories, seven times excellent. Thrones and mansions and temples, and also chariots and virgin spirits up to an invisible one and their glories, each one has these in his heaven; mighty armies of gods and lords and angels and archangels—countless myriads—so that they might serve . . . And they were completed from this heaven to as far up as the sixth heaven, namely that of Sophia. The [first] heaven and his earth [created by Yaldabaoth] were destroyed by the troublemaker that was below them all. And the six heavens shook violently; for the forces of chaos knew who it was that had destroyed the heaven that was below them. And when Pistis knew about the breakage resulting from the disturbance, she sent forth breath and bound him and cast him down into Tartaros . . .

Now when the heavens had consolidated themselves along with their forces and all their administration, [Yaldabaoth] the prime parent, became insolent. And he was honored by all the army of angels. And all the gods and their angels gave blessing and honor to him. And for his part he was delighted and continually boasted, saying to them, "I have no need of anyone." He said, "It is I who am God, and there is no other one that exists apart from me." And when he said this, he sinned against all the immortal beings who give answer. And they laid it to his charge.

Then when Pistis saw the impiety of the chief ruler she was filled with anger. She was invisible. She said, "You are mistaken, Samael [i.e., "blind god"]. There is an immortal man of light who has been in existence before you and who will appear among your modeled forms; he will trample you to scorn just as potter's clay is pounded. And you will descend to your mother, the abyss, along with those that belong to you. For at the consummation of your works the entire defect that has become visible out of the truth will be abolished, and it will cease to be and will be like what has never been."

Saying this, Pistis revealed the likeness of her greatness in the waters. And, so doing, she withdrew up to her light.

Now when Sabaoth, the son of Yaldabaoth, heard the voice of Pistis, he sang praises to her, and he condemned his father . . . at the word of Pistis; and he praised her because she had instructed them about the immortal man and his light. Then Pistis-Sophia stretched out her finger and poured upon him some light from her light, to be a condemnation of his father. Then when Sabaoth was illumined, he received great authority against all the forces of chaos. Since that day he has been called "Lord of the Forces."

He hated his father, the darkness, and his mother, the Abyss, and loathed his sister [Pronoia], the thought of the prime parent, which moved to and fro upon the waters. And because of his light all the authorities of chaos were jealous of him. And when they had become disturbed, they made a great war in the seven heavens. Then, when Pistis-Sophia had seen the war, she dispatched seven archangels to Sabaoth from her light. They snatched him up to the seventh heaven. They stood before him as attendants. Furthermore she sent him three more archangels and established the kingdom for him over everyone so that he might dwell above the twelve gods of chaos.

Now when Sabaoth had taken up the place of repose in return for his repentance, Pistis also gave him her daughter Zoe (Life) together with great authority so that she might instruct him about all things that exist in the eighth heaven. And, as he had authority, he made himself first of all a mansion. It was huge, magnificent, seven times as great as all those that exist in the seven heavens . . .

[Ed. note: At this point in the narrative, Sabaoth, after creating symbols representing his power, creates the angels, Israel, and Jesus Christ ("who resembles the savior above in the eighth heaven"). In the lower heavens, an angry Yaldabaoth enthrones Death in the sixth heaven vacated by Sabaoth. In addition, the seven androgynous "authorities" of the lower heavens conceive within themselves the various plagues associated with mortality and life in the material world.]

And having seen the likeness of Pistis in the waters, the prime parent grieved very much, especially when he heard her voice, like the first voice that had called to him out of the waters. And when he knew that it was she who had given a name to him, he sighed. He was ashamed on account of his transgression. And when he had come to know in truth that an immortal man of light had been existing before him, he was greatly disturbed; for he had previously said to all the gods and their angels, "It is I who am God. No other one exists apart from me." For he had been afraid they might know that another had been in existence before him, and might condemn him. But he, being devoid of understanding, scoffed at the condemnation and acted recklessly. He said, "If anything has existed before me, let it appear, so that we may see its light."

And immediately, behold! Light came out of the eighth heaven above and passed through all of the heavens of the earth. When the prime parent saw that the light was beautiful as it radiated, he was amazed. And he was greatly ashamed. As that light appeared, a human likeness appeared within it, very wonderful. And no one saw it except for the prime parent and Pronoia, who was with him. Yet its light appeared to all the forces of the heavens. Because of this they were all troubled by it.

Then when Pronoia saw that emissary [the light from the eighth heaven], she became enamored of him. But he hated her because she was in the darkness. But she desired to embrace him, and she was not able to. When she was unable to assuage her love, she poured out her blood upon the earth. Since that day, that emissary has been called "Adam of Light," whose rendering is the "luminous man of blood," and the earth spread over him, holy Adaman, whose rendering is "the Holy Land of Adamantine."

Since that day, all the authorities have honored the blood of the virgin. And the earth was purified on account of the blood of the virgin. But most of all, the water was purified through the likeness of Pistis-Sophia, who had appeared to the prime parent in the waters. Justly, then, it has been said: "through the waters." The holy water, since it vivifies the all, purifies it.

Out of that first blood Eros appeared, being androgynous. His masculinity is Himireris, being fire from the light. His femininity, that is with him—soul of blood—is from the stuff of Pronoia. He is very lovely in his beauty, having a charm beyond all the creatures of chaos. Then all the gods and their angels, when they beheld Eros, became enamored of him. And appearing in all of them he set them afire: just as from a single lamp many lamps are lit, and one and the same light is there, but the lamp is not diminished. And in this way Eros became dispersed in all the created beings of chaos, and was not diminished. Just as from the midpoint of light and darkness Eros appeared and at the midpoint of the angels and mankind the sexual union of Eros was consummated, so out of the earth the primal pleasure blossomed. Woman followed earth. And marriage followed woman. Birth followed marriage. Dissolution followed birth.

After Eros, the grapevine sprouted up out of that blood, which had been shed over the earth. Because of this, those who drink of it conceive the desire of sexual union. After the grapevine, a fig tree and a pomegranate tree sprouted up from the earth, together with the rest of the trees, all species, having within them their seed from the seed of the authorities and their angels.

Then Justice created Paradise, being beautiful and being outside the orbit of the moon and the orbit of the sun in the Land of Wantonness, in the East in the midst of the stones. And desire is in the midst of the beautiful, appetizing trees. And the tree of eternal life is as it appeared by God's will, to the north of Paradise, so that it might make eternal the souls of the pure, who shall come forth from the modeled forms of poverty at the consummation of the age. Now the color of the tree of life is like the sun. And its branches are beautiful. Its leaves are like those of the cypress. Its fruit is like a bunch of grapes when it is white. Its height goes as far as heaven. And next to it is the tree of acquaintance (gnosis), having the strength of God. Its glory is like the moon when fully radiant. And its branches are beautiful. Its leaves are like fig leaves. Its fruit is like a good appetizing date. And this tree is to the north of Paradise, so that it might arouse the souls from the torpor of the demons, in order that they might approach the tree of life and eat of its fruit and so condemn the authorities and their angels . . .

Now after it, the olive tree sprouted up, which was to purify the kings and the high priests of righteousness, who were to appear in the last days, since the olive tree appeared out of the light of the first Adam for the sake of the unguent that they were to receive.

And the first soul (psyche) loved Eros, who was with her, and poured her blood upon him and upon the earth. And out of that blood the rose first sprouted up, out of the earth, out of the thorn bush, to be a source of joy for the light that was to appear in the bush. Moreover after this the beautiful, good-smelling flowers sprouted up from the earth, different kinds, from every single virgin of the daughters of Pronoia. And they, when they had become enamored of Eros, poured out their blood upon him and upon the earth. After these, every plant sprouted up from the earth, different kinds, containing the seed of the authorities and their angels. After these, the authorities created out of the waters all species of beast, and the reptiles and birds— different kinds—containing the seed of the authorities and their angels.

But before all these, when he had appeared on the first day, [Eros] remained upon the earth, something like two days, and left the lower Pronoia in heaven, and ascended towards his light. And immediately darkness covered all the universe. Now when she wished, [the second] Sophia who was in the lower heaven received authority from Pistis, and fashioned great luminous bodies and all the stars. And she put them in the sky to shine upon the earth and to render temporal signs and seasons and years and months and days and nights and moments and so forth. And in this way the entire region upon the sky was adorned.

Now when Adam-of-Light conceived the wish to enter his light—i.e. the eighth heaven—he was unable to do so because of the poverty [i.e., matter] that had mingled with his light. Then he created for himself a vast eternal realm. And within that eternal realm he created six eternal realms and their adornments, six in number, that were seven times better than the heavens of chaos and their adornments. Now all these eternal realms and their adornments exist within the infinity that is between the eighth heaven and the chaos below it, being counted with the universe that belongs to poverty . . .

And before Adam of Light had withdrawn in the chaos, the authorities saw him and laughed at the prime parent because he had lied when he said, "It is I who am God. No one exists before me." When they came to him, they said, "Is this not the god who ruined our work?" He answered and said, "Yes. If you do not want him to be able to ruin our work, come let us create a human being out of the earth, according to the image of our body and according to the likeness of this Adam of Light to serve us; so that when this Adam of Light sees his likeness he might become enamored of it. No longer will he ruin our work; rather, we shall make those who are born out of the light our servants for all the duration of this eternal realm." Now all of this came to pass according to the forethought of Pistis, in order that man should appear after the likeness of the Adam of Light, and should condemn [the authorities] because of their modeled form [the material body of the earthly Adam]. And their modeled form became and enclosure of the light.

Then the authorities received the gnosis necessary to create man. Sophia Zoe— she who is with Sabaoth—had anticipated them. And she laughed at their decision. For they are blind: against their own interests they ignorantly created [man]. And they do not realize what they are about to do. The reason she anticipated them and made her own human body first, was in order that she might instruct their modeled form how to despise them and thus to escape from them.

Now the production of the instructor came about as follows. When Sophia let fall a droplet of light, it flowed onto the water, and immediately a human being appeared, being androgynous. That droplet she molded first as a female body. Afterwards, using this body, she molded it in the likeness of the mother which had appeared. And she finished it in twelve months. An androgynous human being was produced, whom the Greeks call hermaphrodites; and whose mother the Hebrews call Eve of Life, namely, the female instructor of life. Her offspring is the creature that is lord. Afterwards, the authorities called it "Beast," so that it might lead astray their modeled creatures. The interpretation of "the beast" is "the instructor." For it was found to be the wisest of all beings.

Now, Eve is the first virgin, the one who without a husband bore her first offspring. It is she who served as her own midwife.

> For this reason she is held to have said:
> It is I who am the part of my mother;
> And it is I who am the mother;
> It is I who am the wife:
> It is I who am the pregnant;
> It is I who am the midwife;
> It is I who am the one that comforts pains of travail;
> It is my husband who bore me;
> And it is I who am his mother;
> And it is he who is my father and my lord.
> It is he who is my force;
> What he desires, he says with reason.
> I am in the process of becoming.
> Yet I have borne a man as lord.

The souls that were going to enter the modeled forms of the authorities were manifested to Sabaoth and his Christ. And regarding these the holy voice said, "Multiply and improve! Be lord over all creatures." And it is they who were taken captive, according to their destinies, by the prime parent. And thus they were shut into the prisons of the modeled forms [until] the consummation of the age.

And at that time, the prime parent then rendered an opinion concerning man to those who were with him. Then each of them cast his sperm into the midst of the navel of the earth. Since that day, the seven rulers have fashioned man with his body resembling their body, but his likeness resembling the man that had appeared to them. His modeling took place by parts, one at a time. And the leader fashioned the brain and the nervous system. Afterwards he appeared as prior to him. He became a soul-endowed man. And he was called Adam, that is, "father," according to the name of the one that existed before him.

And when they had finished Adam, they abandoned him as an inanimate vessel, since he had taken form like an [aborted fetus], in that no spirit was in him. Regarding this thing, when the chief ruler remembered the saying of Pistis, he was afraid lest the true man enter his modeled form and become its lord. For this reason he left his modeled form forty days without soul, and he withdrew and abandoned it. Now on the fortieth day, Sophia Zoe sent her breath into Adam, who had no soul. He began to move upon the ground. And he could not stand up.

Then when the seven rulers came, they saw him and were greatly disturbed. They went up to him and seized him. And the chief ruler said to the breath within him, "Who are you? And from where did you come?" It answered and said, "I have come from the force of the man for the destruction of your work." [A gap in the original text occurs here.]

When they heard, they glorified him, since he gave them respite from the fear and anxiety in which they found themselves. Then they called that day "Rest," in as much as they had rested from toil. And when they saw that Adam could not stand up, they were glad, and they took him and put him in Paradise. And they withdrew up to their heavens.

After the day of rest, Sophia sent her daughter Zoe, being called Eve, as an instructor in order that she might make Adam, who had no soul, arise so that those whom he should engender might become containers of light. When Eve saw her male counterpart prostrate she had pity upon him, and she said, "Adam! Become alive! Arise upon the earth!" Immediately her word became accomplished fact, for Adam, having arisen, suddenly opened his eyes. When he saw her he said, "You shall be called 'Mother of the Living.' For it is you who have given me life."

Then the authorities were informed that their modeled form was alive and had arisen, and they were greatly troubled. They sent seven archangels to see what had happened. They came to Adam. When they saw Eve talking to him they said to one another, "What sort of thing is this luminous woman? For she resembles that likeness which appeared to us in the light. Now come, let us lay hold of her and cast our seed into her, so that when she becomes soiled she may not be able to ascend into the light. Rather, those whom she bears will be under our charge. But let us not tell Adam, for he is not one of us. Rather let us bring a deep sleep over him. And let us instruct him in his sleep to the effect that she came from his rib, in order that his wife may obey, and he may be lord over her."

Then Eve, being a force, laughed at their decision. She put mist into their eyes and secretly left her likeness with Adam. She entered the tree of gnosis and remained there. And they pursued her, and she revealed to them that she had gone into the tree and become a tree. Then, entering a great state of fear, the blind creatures fled.

Afterwards, when they had recovered from the daze, they came to Adam; and seeing the likeness of this woman with him, they were greatly disturbed, thinking it was she that was the true Eve. And they acted rashly; they came up to her and seized her and cast their seed upon her. They did so wickedly, defiling not only in natural ways but also in foul ways, defiling first the seal of her voice—that had spoken with them, saying "What is it that exists before you?"—intending to defile those who might say at the consummation of the age that they had been born of the true man through verbal expression. And they erred, not knowing that it was their own body that that they had defiled: it was the likeness that the authorities and their angels defiled in this way.

First she was pregnant with Abel, by the first ruler. And it was by the seven authorities and their angels that she bore the other offspring. And all this came to pass according to the forethought of the prime parent, so that the first mother might bear within her every seed, being mixed and being fitted to the fate of the universe and its configurations, and to Justice. A prearranged plan came into effect regarding Eve, so that the modeled forms of the authorities might become enclosures of light, whereupon the light would condemn them through their modeled forms.

Now the first Adam, Adam of Light, is spirit-endowed, and appeared on the sixth day, which is called Aphrodite. The third Adam is a creature of the earth, that is, the man of the law, and he appeared on the eighth day . . . [a gap exists here]. And the progeny of the earthly Adam became numerous and was completed, and produced within itself every kind of scientific information of the soul-endowed Adam. But all were in ignorance.

Next let me say that once the rulers had seen him and the female creature who was with him erring ignorantly like beasts, they were very glad . . . When they learned that the immortal man was not going to neglect them, rather that they would even have to fear the female creature that had turned into a tree, they were disturbed, and said, "Perhaps this is the true man—this being who has brought a fog upon us and has taught us that she who was soiled is like him—and so we shall be conquered!"

Then the seven of them together laid plans. They came up to Adam and Eve timidly: they said to him, "The fruit of all trees created for you in Paradise shall be eaten; but as for the tree of gnosis, control yourselves and do not eat from it. If you eat you will die." Having imparted great fear to them, they withdrew up to their authorities.

Then came the wisest of all creatures, who was called Beast. And when he saw the likeness of their mother Eve he said to her "What did God say to you? Was it 'do not eat from the tree of gnosis'"? She said, "He said, 'Not only do not eat from it, but do not touch it, lest you die.'" He said to her "Do not be afraid. In death you shall not die. For he knows that when you eat from it, your intellect will become sober and you will come to be like gods, recognizing the difference that obtains between evil men and good ones. Indeed, it was in jealousy that he said this to you, so that you would not eat from it."

Now Eve had confidence in the words of the instructor. She gazed at the tree and saw that it was beautiful and appetizing, and liked it; she took some of its fruit and ate it; and she gave some also to her husband, and he too ate it. Then their intellect became open. For when they had eaten, the light of gnosis had shone upon them. When they clothed themselves with shame, they knew that they were naked of gnosis. When they became sober, they saw that they were naked and became enamored of one another. When they saw that the ones who had modeled them had the form of beasts, they loathed them: they were very aware.

Then when the rulers knew that they had broken their commandments, they entered Paradise and came to Adam and Eve with earthquake and great threatening, to see the effect of the aid. Then Adam and Even trembled greatly and hid under the trees in Paradise. Then the rulers did not know where they were and said, "Adam, where are you?" He said, "I am here, for through fear of you I hid, being ashamed." And they said to him ignorantly, "Who told you about the shame with which you clothed yourself?—unless you have eaten from the tree!" He said, "The woman whom you gave me—it is she that gave me and I ate." Then they said to Eve, "What is this that you have done?" She answered and said, "It is the instructor that urged me on, and I ate."

Then the rulers came up to the instructor. Their eyes became misty because of him, and they could not do anything to him. They cursed him, since they were powerless. Afterwards, they came up to the woman and cursed her and her offspring. After the woman, they and all things that they had created they cursed. They have not blessing. Good cannot result from evil.

From that day, the authorities knew that truly there was something mightier than they: they recognized only that their commandments had not been kept. Great jealousy was brought into the world solely because of the immortal man. Now when the rulers saw that their Adam had entered into an alien state of gnosis they desired to test him, and they gathered together all of the domestic animals and the wild beasts of the earth and the birds of heaven and brought them to Adam to see what he would call them. When he saw them he gave names to their creatures.

They became troubled because Adam had recovered from all the trials. They assembled and laid plans, and they said, "Behold Adam! He has come to be like one of us, so that he knows the difference between the light and the darkness. Now perhaps he will be deceived as in the case of the tree of gnosis and also will come to the tree of life and eat from it and become immortal and become lord and despise us and disdain us and all our glory. Then he will denounce us along with our universe. Come let us expel him from Paradise down to the land from which he was taken, so that henceforth he might not be able to recognize anything better than we can." And so they expelled Adam from Paradise, along with his wife. And this deed that they had done was not enough for them. Rather, they were afraid. They went in to the tree of life and surrounded it with great fearful things, fiery living creatures called *Cherubim,* and thereby put a flaming sword in their midst, fearfully twirling at all times, so that no earthly being might ever enter that place.

Thereupon since the rulers were envious of Adam they wanted to diminish Adam's and Eve's lifespans. They could not because of fate, which had been fixed since the beginning. For to each had been allotted a lifespan of 1,000 years according to the course of the luminous bodies. But although the rulers could not do this, each of the evil doers took away ten years. And the lifespan which remained amounted to 930 years; and these are in pain and weakness and evil distraction. And so life has turned out to be, from that day until the consummation of the age.

Then when Sophia Zoe saw that the rulers of the darkness had laid a curse upon her counterparts, she was indignant. And coming out of the first heaven with full power she chased those rulers out of their heavens, and cast them down into the sinful world, so that there they should dwell, in the form of evil spirits upon the earth . . .

Now when the seven rulers were cast down from their heavens onto the earth, they made for themselves angels, numerous, demonic, to serve them. And the latter instructed mankind in many kinds of error and magic and potions and worship of idols and spilling of blood and altars and temples and sacrifices and libations to all the spirits of the earth, having their coworker fate, who came into existence by the concord between the gods of injustice and justice.

And thus when the world had come into being, it distractedly erred at all times. For all men upon earth worshipped the spirits from the creation to the consummation—both the angels of righteousness and the men of unrighteousness. Thus did the world come to exist in distraction, in ignorance, and in stupor. They all erred, until the appearance of the true man . . .

When a multitude of human beings had come into existence, through the parentage of the Adam who had been fashioned, and out of matter, and when the world had already become full, the rulers were master over it—that is, they kept it restrained by ignorance. For what reason? For the following: since the immortal father knows that a deficiency of truth came into being amongst the eternal realms and their universe, when he wished to bring to naught the rulers of perdition through the creatures they had modeled he sent your licenses down into the world of perdition, namely, the blessed little innocent spirits. They are not alien to gnosis. For all gnosis is vested in one angel who appeared before them; he is not without power in the company of the father. And he gave them gnosis. Whenever they appear in the world of perdition, immediately and first of all they reveal the pattern of imperishability as a condemnation of the rulers and their forces. Thus when the blessed beings appeared in forms modeled by authorities, they were envied. And out of envy the authorities mixed their seed with them, in hopes of polluting them. They could not. Then when the blessed beings appeared in luminous form, they appeared in various ways. And each one of them, starting out in his land, revealed his kind of gnosis to the visible church constituted of the modeled forms of perdition. The Church was found to contain all kinds of seed, because of the seed of the authorities that had mixed with it.

WORKS CITED AND SUGGESTIONS
FOR FURTHER READING

Adler, Margot. *Drawing Down the Moon: Witches, Druids, Goddess-Worshippers, and Other Pagans in America Today*. New York: Penguin/Arkana, 1997.

Allen, Paula Gunn. *Grandmothers of Light: A Medicine-Woman's Sourcebook*. Boston: Beacon, 1991.

Bachofen, Johann Jakob. *Myth, Religion, and Mother Right: Selected Writings of J. J. Bachofen*. Trans. Ralph Manheim. Princeton, NJ: Princeton University Press, 1973.

Baring, Anne, and Jules Cashford. *The Myth of the Goddess: The Evolution of an Image*. London: Viking shie Arkana, 1991.

Benard, Elisabeth, and Beverly Moon, eds. *Goddesses Who Rule.* Oxford: Oxford University Press, 2000.

Berger, Pamela. *The Goddess Obscured: Transformation of the Grain Protectress to Saint.* Boston: Beacon, 1985.

Bethge, Hans-Gebhard, Bentley Layton, Societas Coptica Hierosolymitana, Trans. "On the Origin of the World." *The Nag Hammadi Library in English.* New York: Harper-Collins, 1990. 170–89.

Bolen, Jean Shinoda. *Goddesses in Everywoman: A New Psychology of Women.* New York: Harper & Row, 1985.

Campbell, Joseph, and Charles Musès, eds. *In All Her Names: Explorations of the Feminine in Divinity.* San Francisco: HarperSanFrancisco, 1991.

Christ, Carol P. *Laughter of Aphrodite: Reflections on a Journey to the Goddess.* San Francisco: Harper & Row, 1988.

——— "Why Women Need the Goddess." In *The Philosophical Quest: A Cross-Cultural Reader.* Gail M. Presbey, Karsten J. Struhl, and Richard E. Olsen, eds. New York: McGraw-Hill, 2000.

Christ, Carol P., and Judith Plaskow, eds. *Womanspirit Rising: A Feminist Reader in Religion.* San Francisco: HarperSanFrancisco, 1992.

Colun. Padraic. *Legends of Hawaii.* New Haven, CT: Yale University Press, 1965.

Conkey, Margaret W., and Ruth E. Tringham. "Archaeology and the Goddess: Exploring the Contours of Feminist Archaeology." In *Feminisms in the Academy.* Domna C. S. nton and Abigail J. Stewart, eds. Ann Arbor: University of Michigan Press, 1995.

Daly, Mary. *Beyond God the Father.* Boston: Beacon, 1973.

Dexter, Miriam Robbins. *Whence the Goddesses: A Source Book.* New York: Pergamon, 1990.

Dobres, Marcia-Anne. "Reconsidering Venus Figurines: A Feminist-Inspired Re-Analysis." In *Ancient Images, Ancient Thought: The Archaeology of Ideology.* A. Sean Goldsmith, Sandra Garvie, Davı Selin, and Jeannette Smith, eds. Calgary, Albertai Archaeological Association, 19. 245–62.

Downing, Christine. *The Goddess: Mythological Images of the Feminine.* New York: Crossroad Publishing, 1992.

Edwards, Carolyn McVickar. *Goddess: Tales of the Goddess and Her Wisdom from Around the World.* San Francisco: HarperSanFrancisco, 1991.

Eisler, Riane. *The Chalice and the Blade: Our History, Our Future.* San Francisco: Harper & Row, 1987.

———. "The Goddess of Nature and Spirituality: An Ecomanifesto." In *In All Her Names: Explorations of the Feminine in Divinity.* Joseph Campbell and Charles Musès, eds. San Francisco: HarperSanFrancisco, 1991.

Enuma Elish, in, for example, Alexander, Heidel. *The Babylonian Genesis: The Story of Creation.* 2nd ed. Chicago: University of Chicago Press, 1951.

Erdoes, Richard, and Alfonso Ortiz. *American Indian Myths and Legends.* New York: Pantheon, 1986.

Frazer, James George. *The Golden Bough.* Abridged ed. London: Macmillan, 1922.

Gadon, Elinor. *The Once and Future Goddess.* San Francisco: Harper & Row, 1989.

Gimbutas, Marija. *The Civilization of the Goddess: The World of Old Europe.* Joan Marler, ed. San Francisco: HarperSanFrancisco, 1991a.

———. *The Goddesses and Gods of Old Europe, 6500–3500 BC: Myths and Cult Images.* Berkeley: University of California Press, 1982.

———. *The Language of the Goddess: Unearthing the Hidden Symbols of Western Civilization.* New York: Thames and Hudson, 1989.

———. "The 'Monstrous Venus' of Prehistory: Divine Creatrix." In *In All Her Names: Explorations of the Feminine in Divinity.* Joseph Campbell and Charles Musès, eds. San Francisco: Harper, 1991b.

Goodison, Lacy, and Christine Morris., eds. *Ancient Goddesses: The Myths and the Evidence.* Madison: University of Wisconsin Press, 1998.

Graves, Robert. *Greek Myths.* 2 vols. 1955; Harmondsworth, England: Penguin, 1990.

———. *The White Goddess: A Historical Grammar of a Poetic Myth.* New York: Farrar, Straus, and Giroux, 1966.

Hesiod. *Theogony: Works and Days: Shield.* Ed. Apostolos N. Athanassakis. Baltimore: Johns Hopkins University Press, 1983.

James, Edwin Oliver. *The Cult of the Mother-Goddess: An Archaeological and Documentary Study.* New York, Barnes & Noble, 1961.

Kerènyi, Carl. *Eleusis: Archetypal Image of Mother and Daughter.* New York: Schocken Books, 1977.

Kramer, Samuel Noah. *The Sacred Marriage Rite: Aspects of Faith, Myth, and Ritual in Ancient Sumer.* Bloomington: Indiana University Press, 1969.

Jung, Carl G. *Symbols of Transformation: An Analysis of the Prelude to a Case of Schizophrenia.* Trans. R. F. C. Hull. Princeton: Princeton University Press, 1967.

Lopez, Donald S. Jr., ed. *Religions of India in Practice.* Princeton Readings in Religions Series. Princeton: Princeton University Press, 1995.

Lovecock, James E. *Gaia: A New Look at Life on Earth.* Oxford: Oxford University Press, 2000.

McClean, Adam. *The Triple Goddess: An Exploration of the Archetypal Feminine.* Grand Rapids, MI: Phanes, 1989.

Meskell, Lynn. "Goddesses, Gimbutas, and 'New Age' Archaeology." *Antiquity* 69 (1995): 74–86.

Monaghan, Patricia. *The Book of Goddesses and Heroines.* New York: Dutton, 1981.

Nelson, Sarah M. "Diversity of the Upper Paleolithic 'Venus' Figurines and Archaeological Mythology." In *Powers of Observation: Alternative Views in Archeology.* Sarah M. Nelson and Alice B. Kehoe, eds. Washington, DC: American Anthropological Association, 1990.

Nelson, Sarah M., and Alice B. Kehoe, eds. *Powers of Observation: Alternative Views in Archeology.* Washington, DC: American Anthropological Association, 1990.

Neumann, Erich. *The Great Mother: An Analysis of the Archetype.* Princeton: Princeton University Press, 1963.

Nhat Hanh, Thich. *A Taste of Earth and Other Legends of Vietnam.* Berkeley, CA: Parallax, 1993.

Olson, Carl. *The Book of the Goddess, Past and Present: An Introduction to Her Religion.* New York: Crossroads, 1992.

Pagels, Elaine. *Adam, Eve, and the Serpent.* 1988; New York: Vintage, 1989.

————. *The Gnostic Gospels.* 1979; New York: Vintage, 1989.

————. *The Gnostic Paul: Gnostic Exegesis of the Pauline Letters.* 1975; Philadelphia: Trinity Press International, 1992.

Patai, Raphael. *The Hebrew Goddess.* Detroit, MI: Wayne State University Press, 1990.

Perera, Sylvia Brinton. *Descent to the Goddess: A Way of Initiation for Women.* Toronto: Inner City Books, 1981.

Reuther, Rosemary Radford. *Gaia and God: An Ecofeminist Theology of Earth Healing.* San Francisco: HarperSanFrancisco, 1992.

Rice, Julian. *Before the Great Spirit: The Many Faces of Sioux Spirituality.* Albuquerque: University of New Mexico Press, 1998.

Robinson, James M., ed. *The Nag Hamadi Library.* San Francisco: HarperSanFrancisco, 1990.

Starhawk. *The Spiral Dance: A Rebirth of the Ancient Religion of the Great Goddess.* San Francisco: Harper & Row, 1979.

Stone, Merlin. *Ancient Mirrors of Womanhood: Our Goddess and Heroine Heritage.* 2 vols. New York: New Sibylline Books, 1979.

————. *When God Was a Woman.* New York: Dial, 1976.

Tringham, Ruth E., and Margaret Conkey. "Rethinking Figurines: A Critical View from Archaeology of Gimbutas, the 'Goddess,' and Popular Culture." In *Ancient Goddesses: The Myths and the Evidence.* Lucy Goodison and Christine Morris, eds. Madison: University of Wisconsin Press, 1998.

Ucko, Peter J. *Anthropomorphic Figurines of Predynastic Egypt and Neolithic Crete with Comparative Material from the Prehistoric Near East and Mainland Greece.* London: A. Szmidla, 1968.

————. "Mother, Are You There?" *Cambridge Archaeological Journal* 6, no. 2 (1996): 300–304.

Von Cles-Reden, Sibylle. *The Realm of the Great Goddess: The Story of the Megalith Builders.* Trans. Eric Mosbacher. Englewood Cliffs, NJ: Prentice Hall, 1962.

Walker, Barbara G. *The Skeptical Feminist: Discovering the Virgin, Mother, and Crone.* San Francisco: Harper & Row, 1987.

Whitmont, Edward C. *Return of the Goddess.* New York: Crossroads, 1990.

Wolkstein, Diane, and Samuel Noah Kramer. *Inanna: Queen of Heaven and Earth.* New York: Harper & Row, 1983.

Woolger, Jennifer Barker, and Roger J. Woolger. *The Goddess Within: A Guide to the Eternal Myths that Shape Women's Lives.* New York: Fawcett Columbine, 1989.

Yourcenar, Marguerite. "Kali Beheaded." In *Oriental Tales.* New York: Farrar, Straus and Giroux, 1983. 119–25.

————. "That Mighty Sculptor, Time." In *That Mighty Sculptor, Time.* Trans. Walter Kaiser. New York: Farrar, Straus and Giroux, 1992; Oxford: Aidan Ellis, 1992. 87–89.

CHAPTER 4 The Male Divine

THE PREHISTORY OF GOD

We began the last chapter with a discussion of the arguments for and against the existence of a prehistoric Great Goddess of Life, Death, and Regeneration. Proponents of the Goddess Movement not only assume the existence of such a goddess, but further claim that all subsequent goddesses attested by historical records (e.g., Aphrodite, Ma Emma, Nerthus) indicate a gradual devolution of the Goddess's worship into a scattering of less powerful, more localized cults who revered female deities embodying only certain aspects of the Great Goddess's vastly more complex character.

The archaeological record, however, shows that goddess worship, whether of the Great Goddess or of more local goddesses, was not the only game in town. Of the hundreds of figurines, engravings, and drawings that have survived from the Paleolithic and Neolithic ages, a number are clearly male. Just how many appears to be in dispute. Gimbutas claims that "male figurines constitute only 2 to 3 percent of all Old European figurines, and consequently any detailed reconstruction of their cult role is hardly possible" (1989, 175). However, as discussed in the last chapter, a number of archaeologists since the mid-1980s have disputed this claim. Conkey and Tringham, Dobres, and Ucko, for example, nearly reverse Gimbutas's assertion, declaring that more than half of the figurines recovered from these eras cannot be identified definitively as either male or female. Of the figurines whose sex is obvious, say these writers, at least half are male. Both camps agree, however, that a "detailed reconstruction" of the religious significance and ritual purposes of these figurines is "hardly possible."

THE "SORCERER" OF TROIS FRÈRES

One male image that has drawn a great deal of attention is the so-called Sorcerer of Trois Frères, a cave painting discovered near Ariège, in the French Pyrenees. The interpretation of this image is problematic in ways resembling the debate about the meaning of the so-called Venus images discussed in the previous chapter. How, exactly, did our Neolithic ancestors understand this image? Why was it painted on a nearly inaccessible ceiling near the deepest reach of the Ariège cave system? Who or what does it depict? Most modern writers, Marija Gimbutas among them, have relied upon a sketch by the Abbé Breuil when formulating their hypotheses about the meaning of this suggestive cave-drawing. But, as the reader can see by comparing the color photo and Breuil's drawing (see 187), the artist has invested his image with suggestive details that the camera does not record. Most notably, the x-ray effect of human hands and feet in bear-like "gloves" and the large, round eyes staring out over a long beard are scarcely suggested by the photograph. Rather than a pair of antlers, a single incised antler extends from the mostly deteriorated head and the bushy tail is barely discernible. The male genitals in both the sketch and the figure protrude from behind the figure which is suggestive of animal rather than human anatomy—as is the antler and the nearly horizontal attitude of the figure in relationship to the "horizon" of the cave's ceiling. Perhaps artistic license accounts for the differences between photo and sketch; perhaps the cave-drawing itself has deteriorated significantly since the early 20th century when the drawing was made; per-

The so-called Sorcerer of Trois Frères. Ht. 29.5 inches. Discovered in a cave near Ariège, France, and dated to approximately 13,000 BCE. The image is partly carved and partly painted and located on the ceiling in one of the most inaccessible reaches of the cave.
Source: Photo. Jean Claude Lejoux/CNRS.

Abbé Breuil's famous sketch of the figure he named the "Sorcerer of Trois Frères." This image has been duplicated and redrawn in numerous books on prehistoric art and religion. Notice the x-ray technique that Breuil uses to suggest his interpretation of the original object's meaning. *Source:* © The Granger Collection, NY.

haps a combination of both accounts for the differences. Photographs, too, can miss or alter details and we want to be careful not to suggest that Breuil's sketch completely falsifies the archaeological record. After all, the French cleric and art enthusiast, unlike many modern archaeologists and mythographers writing on the subject, was in the cave itself and saw the "Sorcerer" with his own eyes.

Gimbutas, who apparently had Breuil's sketch redrawn to illustrate her interpretation of its meaning, identifies this figure as the "god of Trois Frères," who, like "most of the male figures in Near Eastern and Old European art" symbolizes "the flourishing but limited and ultimately vanishing body" (1989, 175). Thus, to Gimbutas, the prehistoric religious imagination conceptualized the eternal and self-renewing nature of the cosmic order as a Great Goddess while it represented the ephemeral quality of individual existence in the form of a divine male. Prehistoric, pre-Indo-European male gods are to be viewed, then, as temporary consorts of the Great Goddess, always quickly rising in energy, quickly expending their life force, and then just as quickly dying away only to be replaced by new "sacred kings" in a perpetual cycle.

If Gimbutas's view is correct, the numerous "dying gods" of European and Middle Eastern history (e.g., Balder, Osiris, Dammuzi, Adonis) are descendants of the deity depicted in the "Sorcerer" image. These deities rise, briefly consummate a union with the Goddess, and, their fertilizing energies expended, fall into death. These gods are resurrected or their surrogates are appointed to repeat the drama year after year. Most scholars agree this common mythic plot line reenacts the seasonal cycle of vegetative fertility: vegetation protrudes from the soil in spring, waxes in strength throughout the summer, ages and declines in autumn, and vanishes in a kind of death during winter. Similarly, the dying gods gain in strength and influence but are suddenly cut down in their prime, often suffering dismemberment and the scattering of their remains, disappearing into the underworld—only to be reanimated in due course.

THE "SHAMAN" OF TROIS FRÈRES

David Leeming and Jake Page, while accepting the theory of a prehistoric and nearly universal religion of the Great Goddess, interpret the "Sorcerer of Trois Frères" differently than Gimbutas. Speaking of the Paleolithic period and the cave drawings of various "animal-men," they write:

> In most of the world this was an age in which the damp dark caves with their multitude of vulva depictions were perhaps representational precincts of a life-bearing Goddess. The paintings and carvings that represent this female figure certainly greatly outnumber those that depict the male. But there is a sufficient number of paintings and engravings to support the assumption of a Paleolithic sense of sacredness associated with the male as well . . . What we can determine of the nature of the Paleolithic myths of God must come from a blending together of the cave art and our knowledge of the myths and rituals of peoples who have brought what might be called a Paleolithic lifestyle into the post-Paleolithic ages. It is primarily to the hunter-gatherer societies of Africa and North America that we must look for indications of the nature of Paleolithic mythology and of the birth of the god archetype. (1996, 12–13)

For Leeming and Page, the so-called Sorcerer of Trois Frères is not a god but a shaman, a human religious figure who, in hunter-gatherer societies, is considered a "possessor of magic powers which are dangerous but useful. He is . . . by definition, a loner. One of his jobs is to apply his powers to the hunting of animals so that the group might have sufficient provisions" (1996, 13–14). By entering trances, chanting, dancing, and uttering incantations, shamans mediate between their people and the often indifferent spiritual powers that influence herds, crops, and other important natural phenomena. Anthropologists and others studying the few hunter-gatherer societies remaining in the world have noted that, even now, shamans ingest various hallucinogens, don masks or costumes, and become, among other things, animal masters—those capable of persuading animals to give themselves to people as food. Other shamans claim that in sacred trance they see the vibrations constituting our visible reality and learn songs that will influence those patterns in ways beneficial to humans.

IMAGES OF THE MASCULINE

In the previous chapter, we discussed various roles goddesses play in the world's mythic literature in terms of three broad categories: Life, Death, and Regeneration. Although it is possible to discuss the male divinities under the same headings, to do so ignores a key observation: gods are usually described not in terms of their relation to the reproductive and seasonal cycles but in terms of the various sociopolitical roles that they fulfill. That is, whereas female deities are often depicted as the earth itself or as embodying one or another stage of a woman's reproductive cycle, male deities tend to be depicted in terms of the offices they hold or the roles they play. For example, depending on the assumptions the student of myth brings with her, the painted image at Trois Frères can be seen as a god intimately involved with the cycles of plant life and thus the preservation of human society, *or* he is a human mediator, or hero, who seeks to affect supernatural powers on behalf of human society. Of course, the Trois Frères figure is just one image, strongly supporting either of two archetypal readings. The world of myth, however, is full of diverse images of male roles for gods and human mediators, and this array of images has led to numerous analytical schemes.

We have identified the following five broad categories through which we can approach the vast number of gods and heroes populating the world's myths: fathers and sons, kings and judges, saviors and sages, shamans and tricksters, and lords of destruction and the underworld. These categories will overlap with one another, and they are more useful when taken as hand-drawn maps rather than as satellite photographs of mythic terrain. For an example showing how quickly such categories can break down, the God of the Hebrew scriptures is depicted in a variety of ways: hands-on creator and loving father, jilted husband and desirable groom, majestic king and exacting judge, and compassionate culture-bringer and rational lawgiver. As his character is further developed in the New Testament, we see him as humble shepherd and husbandman, as Great Physician and merciful comforter, and as supreme commander of a heavenly host who will slaughter millions upon millions of wicked and cast their souls into the lake of fire. Clearly, then, the Judeo-Christian God could be discussed with considerable profit under any of our archetypes. The same could be said of many other gods. Our purpose here is to start conversations rather than to limit possible interpretations.

Fathers and Sons

At the most basic level, father-gods embody the male principle of fertility. Their life-giving seed energizes and organizes the life potential of womb and soil. The myth-logic behind this category is that the life force resting within the earthen and female body cannot be activated without the father's power to give it shape and direction. Unlike many of their female counterparts, however, father-gods often do not remain intimate with their offspring. In human relationships, the father becomes physically irrelevant after the sexual act. The children their seed calls forth are formed within the body of another, a deep connection that fathers cannot experience or duplicate. This biological fact may well account for why the father-god in myth frequently sends his son to the earth as an ambassador of his will. And perhaps this separation is why the father appears as the unknown and terrifying authority whom the hero must face before he can fully realize his divine nature. In any case, it is a mythic rule (with occasional exceptions) that the father-god dwells in unapproachable majesty in the heavens, far from the toil and tears of his earthly creations. Even as the divine seed awakens and gives shape to life, the father-god's commandments, principles, and laws organize and direct the energies of his creation. In patrifocal myths, all seek the father's love and approval; all long for even a glimpse of his face; and all live in terror of his wrath.

The Artemision Poseidon (Zeus?). Ht. 6′ 10″.
460–450 BCE. Raised from the sea floor off Cape
Artemision in north Euboea, this bronze statue is
an original work, possibly that of the great sculptor,
Kalamis. Originally identified as an image of Zeus, it
was thought that the right hand held a thunderbolt (now
lost). Today, most scholars agree that the statue represents Poseidon and that the right hand would have held
a trident. In either case, the powerful musculature and
athletic pose suggest the virility and authority of the
father-god archetype.
Source: © Scala/Art Resource, NY.

When considering gods embodying various paternal and filial attributes, it is
also important to make a distinction between gods who are members of pantheons
and those who come from monotheistic traditions. Pantheons are essentially extended families in which divine fathers take wives and lovers and beget divine or
semidivine sons and daughters. Peoples who imagined their gods as being in every
respect like humans, except for their superior powers and immortality, tended to
project their own earthly customs, hierarchies, and civil institutions onto their gods.
Like celestial CEOs, the founding fathers of the Egyptian, Sumerian, Greek, and
Norse pantheons behave like earthly despots, delegating to their children control

over such mundane affairs as fertility, weather, war-making, priest- and statecraft, technology, and language. In short, the father-gods of pantheons embody and demonstrate, to one degree or another, the potency and prerogatives of patriarchs, clan elders, and founders of royal dynasties.

But a closer look at the founding fathers of these familiar pantheons shows that they differ in their degree of involvement in earthly affairs. The European All-father, for example, tends to exhibit a more hands-on management style than his counterparts in Egypt and Sumeria. Zeus and Odin take frequent counsel with their divine families, and both receive and answer human prayers. In both mythic traditions, these father-gods derive much of their authority from their unmatched strength and martial prowess. Both father-gods beget divine children of awesome power and command their obedience, if not their love. Numerous myths attest to the willingness of Zeus and Odin to be involved in human affairs, and the archaeological record affirms their cultural importance.

By contrast, the great Sumerian god Anu and the Egyptian Atum also fathered second-generation divinities who assumed primary responsibility for establishing and maintaining the natural and human orders, but these founding fathers remained aloof from mundane concerns. As a result, little is said about them in myth apart from a few laudatory phrases about their role at the creation of the material universe. Anu is content to hold court among his starry hosts and doesn't let concerns about human well-being disturb his peace for long. In Egypt, Atum and Ra also begin divine families but soon retire to the relative quiet of the heavenly deep. Indeed, throughout the mythic traditions of the ancient Near East, first-generation father-gods are depicted as dwelling in celestial majesty, far above the quotidian affairs of mortals. Their sons and other second-generation male deities tend to be much more active in human affairs—often taking for themselves the name of father.

Other father-gods, including the Lord of the Hebrew scriptures and the Heavenly Father of the New Testament, are generally depicted as too remote in time and space, too holy, and too frightening to be approached. "No one comes to the Father, but through me," said Jesus (John 14:6); and, from his words and mission, we are to understand that human frailty can bear the Divine presence only when that presence is somehow mediated, e.g., when it is clothed in flesh and blood. A more complex example of the need for intermediary gods to make the face of the All-father more human can be found in the Vedic tradition of India. The great god Vishnu is said to have cast his seed upon the primeval waters where it floated like clusters of bubbles in the time before time. These bubbles became eggs of which our universe is but one. Vishnu entered our egg universe not as himself but as Purusha, the cosmic Everyman, and, in order to establish the social and religious order, arranged to have himself sacrificed. The various members of his gigantic Purusha-body became the elements, and gods sprang up to oversee their proper use. Purusha's mouth became fire, and Agni, the fire-god, presided over its mysteries; his nostrils became breathing and came under the authority of Vayu, the god of wind and air; his eyes became both the sense of sight and light itself, controlled by Surya, the sun-god. Brahma was the intellect of Purusha, and Shiva was his ego. Though each of these gods has his adherents, the worshipers of Vishnu say that Vishnu is the true creator and father of all and that each of India's myriad gods, no matter how powerful, manifests only one of the great father-god's many aspects.

In addition to humanizing the frightening aspects of the father-god, divine sons represent other qualities, among them filial duty and submission. Indeed, self-sacrificial obedience to the All-father's will is perhaps the defining quality of the divine father–son relationship. Even when second-generation gods seek to usurp their fathers' thrones—as happens when first Kronos, then Zeus overcome their fathers—the expectation that the divine son will perpetuate and extend his father's kingdom, subjecting his own will to that of his father, is the bedrock upon which such narratives usually stand. We see filial duty clearly demonstrated, when, for example, Jesus pleads, "Abba! Father! All things are possible for Thee; remove this cup from me; yet, not what I will, but what Thou wilt" (Mark 14:36). In Greek myth, Zeus clearly favors Apollo and Hermes because these sons represent aspects of himself that he wishes to acknowledge and see perpetuated. Hephaestus and Ares, on the other hand, do not enjoy the approval of the "father of gods and men." Hephaestus, for all his ingenuity and mastery of various crafts, is physically deformed, and so Zeus never takes his part in a dispute, never praises him in the Olympian company. Ares's bloodthirstiness prompts his father to reject him as "the most hated of the gods." What such filial relationships suggest about the institutions and cultural mores of the societies in which they were created is an open and potentially rewarding question.

Zeus has a somewhat more ambivalent relationship with his son Dionysus. On one hand, according to Euripedes, Zeus saves the unborn god's life when Hera destroys his mother, Semele, by sewing the unborn god "into his thigh" (a euphemism for the genitals). Thus Zeus has the same kind of intimate, bodily connection with Dionysus that most sons enjoy with their mothers. On the other hand, Euripedes depicts Dionysus savagely struggling to establish his claim to the rights and prerogatives of the other Olympians. Presumably, Zeus could have made such a struggle unnecessary, but he did not do so. Perhaps Dionysus's effeminate features and his promulgation of an emotional rather than rational worship served to alienate him from his father's affections.

Frequently, in the same way that Vishnu's worshipers claim that all other gods are but aspects of the Supreme Lord, divine children are depicted as distillations of one or another of their fathers' attributes. In Norse myth, Tyr manifests his father Odin's bravery, Balder his father's wisdom and beauty, and Thor more congenial versions of the All-father's military, reproductive, and poetical powers. A similar pattern can be found in the Korean myth of Tan'Gun. The ruler of heaven, Hanullim, had a son by one of his concubines. Foreseeing that the earth would one day contain people, Hanullim decided that this son, Hwanung, should rule over the earth, teaching its future inhabitants the ways of the celestial kingdom. Alighting upon the earth with his court of 3,000 spirits, Hwanung arranged it so that the first man, Tan'Gun, would appear and establish an earthly version of the heavenly order at P'yongyang. In the Korean myth, then, there is a perfect transmission of the All-father's will to his divine son and then to an earthly representative.

Kings and Judges

Frequently, there is little distinction to be made between father-gods and kings. The founding fathers of pantheons are typically depicted as heavenly kings, their au-

Pantokrator from the ceiling of the Church of the Virgin
Pammakaristos in Constantinople, Turkey. Pantokrator
is a Greek term signifying Christ in his aspect of Great
Judge. Notice his royal blue robes, golden Book of Life,
and stern countenance. Each item symbolizes an important dimension of Christ's authority to save and condemn at the Last Judgment.
Source: Dumbarton Oaks, Byzantine Photograph and Fieldwork
Archives, Washington, DC.

thority within their divine families a dimension of their power to create and admin-
ister the various levels of the cosmic order. Even so, the archetype of king shifts
the emphasis away from the duties and responsibilities of familial relations and
toward the duties and advantages of monarchical power. "The Lord reigns; he is
clothed with majesty," says King David, one of the poets whose work comprises the
Book of Psalms. "The Lord has clothed and girded Himself with strength. Indeed,
the world is firmly established, it will not be moved. Thy throne is established from
of old; Thou art from everlasting" (Psalms 93:1–2). These two verses neatly en-
capsulate the logic of the king archetype: safety, peace, and prosperity come from
the power to ensure stability and order. Surely, the faithful in ancient Israel drew a
great deal of comfort and hope from their belief in an all-powerful king, capable of

protecting them from the many stronger nations that surrounded them. As another psalm puts it: "You will not be afraid of the terror by night, or of the arrow that flies by day; of the pestilence that stalks in darkness, or of the destruction that lays waste at noon. A thousand may fall at your side, and ten thousand at your right hand; but it shall not approach you" (Psalms 91:5–7).

A badly fragmented Hurrian myth known to scholars as "Kingship in Heaven" dramatizes the relationship between stable power in heaven and the quality of life on earth. The story begins as the primordial god Alalu is deposed by a rival, Anu. Kumarbi, Alalu's son and the Hurrians' chief agricultural deity, avenges his father by biting off Anu's genitals. Anu, in pain, tells Kumarbi that the seed that he has inadvertently swallowed will make him pregnant with the weather god, the Tigris River, and another deity. The text breaks down at this point, but it appears that, despite an attempt to avoid this fate, Kumarbi does become pregnant and has—not surprisingly—a great deal of difficulty giving birth to the weather god. When the text resumes, the newborn weather god attacks his father, Kumarbi, and succeeds in deposing him. Kumarbi, though down, is not out, and he quickly hatches a plot to overthrow his son. To do so, Kumarbi impregnates a rock, which bears a stone monster named Ullikummi. In response, the weather god deputizes several gods and they go to inspect the stone monster only to discover that it has become so huge that none of the gods have power over it. The end of this episode has also been lost, but it appears that neither the weather god nor Kumarbi can defeat Ullikummi without help, and so neither establishes himself as the undisputed king of heaven. In a third episode, it appears that the weather god and not Kumarbi finally prevails in the heavenly power struggle by destroying one of Kumarbi's sons, a ravenous dragonlike beast named Hedammu, which had been devouring people and livestock at a furious pace. It is this last detail that suggests why a powerful heavenly king is the feature of every patrifocal mythical tradition: mortals are swept away when celestial power is up for grabs. For, as the African proverb says, "when elephants fight, the grass is trampled."

Linked to the need for a firm heavenly power to create and preserve celestial order and thus the general well-being of mortals is the importance of justice. The divine judge enforces order by rewarding those whose deeds conform to his will and by punishing those whose deeds do not. In Egyptian myth, Kherneter, the blessed fields of the afterlife, was located not in heaven but the West. There, in the Hall of Judgment, Osiris and 42 other gods tested each departed soul to determine whether or not it was *ma'at heru*, True of Voice. Each of the gods asked the soul a question to which the only truthful answer could be "No"—the so-called Negative Confession. A number of murals and engravings show Osiris looking on as the heart of a departed soul is weighed on a scale against a feather to determine its truthfulness. With this fate in mind, mummies were routinely entombed with green stone scarabs upon which was inscribed a prayer from the Book of the Dead: "Whereby my heart shall not speak falsehood against me in the Hall of Judgment." Thus Egyptian belief posited a final judgment in which every heart was literally weighed before a divine judge and his court to determine its eternal fate.

Those raised in the Judeo-Christian tradition are familiar with the idea of a judgment after death, but few traditions outside the ancient Near East make the

"The Weighing of the Heart," from the *Egyptian Book of the Dead: The Papyrus of Ani.* The goddess of truth and justice, Maat, is represented by the small figure on top of the scales occupying most of the bottom middle of this image. The dog-headed guardian of the Underworld, Anubis, weighs the recently deceased Ani's heart against one of Maat's feathers. Behind Anubis, the Ibis-headed Thoth pronounces and records the judgment. Crouching behind him, the crocodile-headed Ammut waits to devour the soul of any whose heart is weighed down by falsehood and evil-doing. Osiris is seated second from the right in the panel at the top of this scene. *Source:* © The British Museum.

same assumption. Traditions in Asia, Oceania, Africa, and North and South America do not typically feature a judge who determines each soul's fate after death. Even in the Near East, few myths depict divine judges as separating the sinners from the saints and meting out everlasting punishment or reward. The Sumerians and later Babylonians, for example, speak of the Annuna, the judges in the underworld, but sinfulness is not mentioned, and there seem to be no fate worse than death. Rather, the glimpse of the afterlife that Enkidu describes in the Epic of Gilgamesh suggests that, after death, one's social rank and personal deeds are meaningless. All people, regardless of the lives they lived, spend eternity as eviscerated shadows in the same filth, stench, and darkness. Interestingly, even the Hebrew scriptures are mostly silent about the soul's destiny after death. Instead, the Divine Judge, speaking through the Hebrew prophets, virtually beats a drum about settling accounts in the here and now. In addition, with few exceptions, God pronounces capital judgments against entire peoples rather than individuals. Nations are sentenced to destruction for persecuting Israel or for rejecting the true God. But, when Cain slays Abel, Moses strikes the rock instead of speaking to it as God commanded, or David arranges to have his neighbor killed in battle so he can have his wife, they suffer their respective punishments in the here and now, living for many years after their transgressions to reap the bitter harvest of their actions. The Christian and Islamic preoccupation with the individual's sin and his or her liability to Divine Judgment are comparatively new and began as isolated mythic ideas.

Saviors and Sages

Myths in patrifocal cultures tend to characterize human beings as alienated from the All-father and therefore in need of salvation. Whether it is Jesus who tastes eternal exile from the Father's presence on behalf of lost and helpless humanity or Padmasambhava defending the fledgling Buddhist religion from the demonic forces that would otherwise have destroyed it in ancient Tibet, saviors bridge the gulf that yawns between the father-god and his human children—or deflect or defeat demonic forces that crouch in the dark seeking an opportunity to harm or destroy a powerless humanity. In some stories, the savior willingly lays down his life for the people. So Jesus embodies the savior archetype, and so does the Aztec Nanauatzin, who, without hesitating, throws himself onto a roaring fire in order to become the sun. When the Nanauatzin-sun rises at the very first dawn, however, he does not have sufficient force to complete his journey across the sky and so the gods willingly bleed themselves in order to give him enough energy to make his daily march from east to west.

In most mythic traditions, however, the savior doesn't die prematurely, but instead communicates to the people sacred knowledge or a saving vision. Although the messenger may be human, he has so completely submerged his will and identity into that of the Divine that he is, in essence, the humanized voice of the Father. Thus Mohammed, in a cave on Mt. Hira, heard the voice of Allah telling him to read/recite the words that ultimately became the Koran. According to tradition, Mohammed's followers came to his wife, Aisha, after his death and asked her, "What was the Prophet, God's Messenger, like?" She answered, "Have you read the Koran? He was the living Koran." Similarly, Zarat-Hushtra (Zoroaster) in the early half of the first millennium BCE was called upon to preach the great struggle between the pure goodness of Ahura Mazda (Ormazd) and the irredeemable evil of Angra Mainu (Ahriman) in 17 visionary hymns, or Gathas. Moses, too, heard the voice of God speaking to him from the burning bush, commanding him to save his people from slavery to the Egyptians and to teach them the laws and purity practices that would make them acceptable to the Lord. In North America, the Mohawk Hy-ent-wat-ha (Hiawatha), after receiving a vision from the Great Spirit, preached a message of peace to his people, eventually inspiring them to form the Iriquois league. Only the Onondaga, led by the terrifying medicine man Atotarho, remained outside the league. To win them over, Hy-ent-wat-ha journeyed to their camp and proposed that Atotarho become the league's great chief and the Onondaga the keepers of the sacred flame. Atotarho, upon whose head snakes writhed and coiled, at first seemed disinclined to accept the young Mohawk's offer, but when Hy-ent-wat-ha placed the antler crown of the Sachem chief upon his head, the snakes fell dead to the ground. Seeing this miracle, the Onondaga immediately promised Hy-ent-wat-ha ("Snake Comber") that they would join the league and live in peace with their neighbors.

Prince Siddhartha, who eventually became the Buddha, also offered his people a kind of salvation. Although theistic traditions speak of the need for a divine savior or assume the need for a messenger to mediate between a people and their distant and often angry god, basic Buddhism is a nontheistic religion. According to tradition, Siddhartha was a human being like any of us. But, through a variety of

"Buddha Shakyamuni with Six Arhats and Two Guardian Kings." Thangka painting (mineral pigments on cotton). Ht. 4′ 6″. Traditionally, Tibetan Thangkas depicting the Buddha also feature 16 arhats, hermits who have attained enlightenment through the World-Honored One's teachings and who wait in seclusion to reestablish his teachings.
Source: Courtesy Southern Alleghenies Museum of Art.

meditation and ascetic practices, he realized Nirvana, the state in which a soul has completely exhausted the desires and worldly attachments that enslave it to the continuous cycle of birth, suffering, and death. After attaining this state, Siddhartha became known as the Buddha, or the enlightened or awakened one. Rather than passing completely from this world, the Buddha chose to remain another 40 years teaching and commenting upon the Four Noble Truths of the human condition and the Eightfold Path whereby all beings can achieve Nirvana.

Like other saviors and prophets, a great many legends and supernatural events are attributed to the Buddha, and it makes sense to discuss him, the founder of a major world religion, as an example of a savior. Even so, Buddhism's insistence that the Buddha was neither a god nor a messenger of a god might as easily class him among the world's sages. A sage might be distinguished from saviors and prophets by the fact that the sage is a human exemplar of a particular spiritual path or wisdom tradition. Under the rubric of sages we might find the much-caricaturized *arhat,* the lonely guru or yogin meditating in a mountain cave or secluded forest retreat. We also might find saints, great teachers, and those famed for their understanding and the significance of their judgment. King Solomon certainly exemplifies the archetype. It was said that his "wisdom surpassed the wisdom of all the sons of the east and all the wisdom of Egypt. For he was wiser than all men . . . He also spoke 3,000 proverbs, and his songs were 1,005 . . . and men came from all peoples to hear the wisdom of Solomon" (1 Kings 4:30–34). In later Jewish tradition, a number of other teachers stand out for their personal piety and the keenness of their minds. For example, Maimonides wrote a systematic code of all Jewish law, the *Mishneh Torah,* produced a philosophical work, *The Guide for the Perplexed,* served as physician to the sultan of Egypt, wrote numerous books on medicine, and was a revered leader of Cairo's Jewish community. When he died, thousands mourned him for three days, lamenting that the world had seen the last of his kind. In Christian tradition, Sts. Augustine and Thomas Aquinas epitomize their religion's core virtues: humility, submission, charity, faith, and steadfastness. Yet it is for the clarity and rationality of their writings that they are most venerated. Aquinas, for example, systematically described the ways of the world and the nature of the universe from the perspective of reason, demonstrating that orderly thinking and sound argumentation need not be antithetical to deep faith.

The sage, then, demonstrates through his every thought and deed a complete submission to his god or nontheistic spiritual practice. Put another way, sages show us that it is possible for human beings to approach a kind of perfection. For the Christian saint, this perfection might manifest itself in acts of selflessness and kindness that would approximate Jesus' supreme example. For the Zen Master, this perfection might manifest itself in a stable mind completely free of preconceptions and capable of wholeheartedly engaging in each moment and instantly understanding what that moment requires him or her to do. And for the Muslim sage, this perfection might manifest itself in a comprehensive knowledge and profound understanding of the scriptures which readily translate into love, mature judgment, patience, awareness of each seeker's unique needs, and a gratitude to God that manifests itself in service to the community. Because deep spiritual attainment is charismatic, sages frequently acquire followers and disciples—whether they want them or not. Thus their wisdom and the specifics of their discipline most frequently come to light through their teachings and interactions with students. The Sufi saint Shibli, for example, once tested his students' faith and understanding by entering so deeply into an ecstatic state that he was eventually locked up by the authorities as a madman. His students came to visit him in prison, but Shibli responded only by saying "Who are you?"

"We are your students," they replied, "Those who love and follow you." At this response the teacher appeared to become agitated, ranting and throwing rocks at his terrified disciples.

"The teacher truly has gone crazy!" they cried, running for the door.

Shibli called out, "Didn't I hear you say you loved me? Yet, you could not bear even a stone or two before running away. Did your love fly away with a couple of stones? If you really loved me, you would have endured the slight discomfort I caused you."

Tricksters and Shamans

We began this chapter with the suggestion that the "Sorcerer of Trois Frères" depicts a shaman, a human being capable of traveling between the natural and supernatural worlds. If a shaman is indeed the subject of this cave painting, it suggests that male divinity was first understood as a mediating presence and spiritual warrior who faced the terrors of the Otherworld on behalf of his people. Whether or not he would agree with this speculation, Jonathan Ott certainly considers shamanism the first and truest religion:

> Shamanic ecstasy is the *real* "Old Time Religion," of which modern churches are but pallid evocations. Shamanic, visionary ecstasy, the *mysterium tremendum,* the *unio mystica,* the eternally delightful experience of the universe as energy, is a *sine qua non* of religion, *it is what religion is for!* There is no need for faith, it is the ecstatic experience itself that *gives* one faith in the intrinsic unity and integrity of the universe, in ourselves as integral parts of the whole; that reveals to us the sublime majesty of our universe, and the fluctuant, scintillant, alchemical miracle that is quotidian consciousness ("Shamanism").

Obviously, the specific beliefs and practices surrounding prehistoric shamanic religion have been lost to us; but, in historic times, a number of gods emerged who were considered messengers of gods, guides of the soul, sexually prolific, inventors of science and writing, transgressors of boundaries, and masters of the magical and alchemical arts. We group these loosely affiliated gods under the Trickster/Shaman archetype, for they traverse the secret roads that, in the ancient religious imagination, connected the Great Above, the Great Below, and the material world that lies between them. The Greek Hermes represents many features of the archetype. With his winged sandals, broad-brimmed hat, and snake-entwined staff (i.e., the caduceus), Hermes was the messenger of the gods, transmitting to earth and the underworld the will of heaven. Those who died a natural death, it was believed, would find gentle Hermes waiting to take them by the hand to the afterlife. And, in the aspect of Hermes Trismegistus (i.e., Thrice-Great Hermes), he was the patron deity of alchemists, practitioners of magic, and of those who pursued the kind of ecstatic, mystical union described by Ott.

Egyptologist E. A. Wallis Budge points out that Thoth's role in Egyptian myth was so similar to that of Hermes that he was later identified with Hermes by the Greeks, who credited him with the invention of astronomy, mathematics, and medicine, the alphabet and writing, and a systematic theology. Budge writes, "The commonest name given to Thoth is h*b, ibis . . . From one aspect he was speech itself . . . In every legend in which Thoth takes a prominent part we see it is he who speaks the word that results in the wishes of Ra being carried into effect" (1999, 1:400–15). In short, Thoth, too, was a heavenly messenger. In Celtic myth, the supreme male deity, the Dagda, was known as the Red Man of All Knowledge, from whose magic cauldron all manner of useful and valuable items were drawn. In Slavic tradition, the horned god Weles (or Volos) is iconographically similar to the so-called Sorcerer of Trois Frères and was associated, like Hermes, with trade and the magical arts. Slavs would take oaths in the name of Weles and believed him to be the patron deity of bards and poets—facts that link him with the Dagda, Thoth, and Hermes, who were likewise associated with words of truth and power.

In Africa, among the Yoruba, Eshu (or Esu) is believed responsible for taking sacrifices to the High God, acting as his messenger, and for punishing the wicked. In his aspect as Elegbara, Eshu is the much-feared avenger and kinsman of the warlike Ajogun. He is also the most powerful of the *orishas* (i.e., gods or spirits) and is believed capable of changing his form at will. Like other Trickster/Shaman divinities, Eshu is also associated with the power of the word, as suggested by the fact that a form of his name was given to the 256-chapter volume of Yoruba traditions known as the *Ese Ifa*. In fact, each chapter of this massive work is believed to have its own Eshu. In the Caribbean, the Central American trickster Eleggua and the Voodoo deity Legba are Eshu's transplanted descendants. Both are associated with magic, but Eleggua is more closely associated with the role of messenger and Legba as the guardian of crossroads.

The Norse god Loki presents yet another dimension of the archetype. For while he is a Sky Traveler with shoes that could fly him over land and water and a Shape Changer, and while, like Hermes, he is associated with safe passage to and from the land of the dead, he is cruel, cunning, and consumed with envy. In fact, if the Trickster and Shaman are viewed as opposite ends of a spectrum, Loki is more Trickster than Shaman and a malicious one at that. Unlike the other gods exemplifying this archetype, Loki has little love of men and is no one's messenger. He uses his shape-changing abilities to sneak into Thor's bedroom and cut off his sleeping wife's hair and to disguise himself as the giantess Thokk, who refused to weep for the slain Balder, thus preventing his return from Hel (i.e., the realm of the dead).

Like other Trickster/Shaman gods, Loki is a master of words, but he is not the teacher of incantation and spells or the patron of poets. Rather, he excels in splitting hairs and using the ambiguities inherent in language to save himself from trouble or get the best of others. In one story, he wagered his head that the dwarves Brokk and Eitri could not produce gifts worthy of the gods. Their pride severely wounded, the dwarves angrily agreed to the wager and created three gifts of immense value: the boar, Gullinbursti, which can be ridden anywhere, even in the darkest corner of the underworld, because it will not tire and bears its own light; the solid gold armring, Draupnir, which Odin placed as a token of his love on the lifeless arm of Balder when he discovered him slain upon Ringhorn; and the mighty iron hammer, Mjollnir, which became the symbol of Thor's power and differed from all other hammers in the fact that it could be thrown at an enemy and would always return to Thor's hand. As the dwarf Brokk worked at the blazing forge, Loki assumed the form of a fly and stung him on his forehead, but, with blood in his eyes, Brokk worked on without faltering. When the gifts were at last presented to the gods, it was clear in a moment that Loki had lost his bet. Or had he? While Brokk was only too eager to take Loki's head, the Trickster stopped him, saying, "Not so fast! It's true you have a claim on my head, but of course you can't have any part of my neck." The Aesir, who have little use for dwarves, grinned at this lawyerly defense and Brokk knew that he'd been outwitted.

At the human level, this archetype manifests itself in a wealth of stories about wizards, magicians, shamans, and even clowns and fools. For if the gods can guide the soul of the shaman or the alchemist from the material world into the spiritual world and back again, then there is a story to tell about that journey and its revelations. Any one of a number of Native American stories could illustrate the persistence of "Paleolithic thinking" that Leeming and Page say will help us understand prehistoric cave art featuring such shamans as the "Sorcerer of Trois Frères." In Tewa (Hopi) tradition, for example, one tale tells of a young man, skeptical of the existence of the gods, who set out for the "Lower Place" to find out the truth. As he descended, he encountered first Silent One and then Deer-Kachina-Cloud god in their human forms. Both warned him that the Lower Place was too far away for humans to reach and both briefly revealed themselves in their divine forms. Deer-Kachina-Cloud god told him that Snake Village was closer than the Lower Place and gave him permission to continue that far before returning to his people. Reluctant to abandon his original mission and still skeptical, the young man continued his journey. A short distance later, he met Star-Flickering-Glossy Man, dressed in the feathers of numerous birds. This god repeated the message that the young man could go no farther than Snake Village, adding that, because he was an unbeliever, the Snake People would try to bite him. So saying, Star-Flickering-Glossy Man gave him an herb to protect him from snakebite which proved quite effective. Upon finally reaching the village, the young man met with the governor of the Snake People, who extended the weary traveler his full hospitality—including the attentive service of his two daughters.

The next morning, the young man made ready to return to his people. Before he left, however, the governor of Snake Village asked him which of his two daughters he'd like to marry. The young man chose the one with whom he'd slept the night before, and the governor readily agreed, instructing them to make a special bread offering on their way home. The young man did as he was instructed, but the return journey took so long that, by they time they reached the foot of the mesa upon which the young man's village was built, the Snake woman was nearly ready to deliver the baby she had conceived their first night together. The Snake woman chose to remain at the foot of the Mesa while the young man climbed up to his people to tell them about his travels. "Just be sure that no one touches you and that you touch no one," she warned as the young man began his climb.

The young man spent the night in his village, telling his people what he had seen on his journey. The next morning, he returned to the foot of the mesa for his wife; but, on his way down, he encountered a former lover who was on her way up the

A "Hunza Bitan," a shaman from Altit Gojal, Pakistan, with the aid of juniper smoke, dancing, and a blood sacrifice, puts himself in a trance to hear what the "mountain fairies" are saying. *Source:* © Jonathan Blair/Corbis.

trail. Without warning, she ran to him and embraced him. By the time the young man reached the bottom of the mesa, his Snake wife already knew that he'd been touched and, saying that he obviously didn't care for her, she returned to her people. But before she left, she gave the young man their baby. The baby, like his mother, could assume human and serpent forms at will. They say that the modern performers of the Tewa Snake Dance are this special child's descendants (adapted from Erdoes & Ortiz 1984, 455–57).

The Tewa account of the young man who descends to the Lower Place, who successfully encounters otherworldly perils, who sees deities in their undisguised form, and who returns with life-sustaining gifts for his people embodies the shaman's archetypal journey to the spiritual realms. Although the story does not specifically say that the young man falls into a dream or trance state, it nevertheless has him leaving the realm of human beings and journeying on a road that puts him in contact with supernatural and natural forces that most people cannot see. As one might expect in a dream, the young Tewa man has no fear of the gods when he encounters them and has no difficulty speaking to the Snake People when he finally reaches their village. While many such stories feature a test or series of trials, in this story the young man is immediately given the gifts of a wife and child, the knowledge of an herb that wards off snakebite, and instructions in the making of a special offering which reveals the four colors sacred to the Tewa.

Like other shamans in other stories from the Americas to Siberia to Africa—and like the shaman Leeming and Page are thinking of when they look at the so-called Sorcerer cave painting—the Tewa youth lives on the borderland between the spiritual, animal, and human worlds. Whether he uses naturally occurring psychedelic drugs, chanting, or meditation to induce a trance state, the shaman's "travels" typically result in important new knowledge. He may, for example, receive instruction in the medicinal qualities of various herbs and plants or in the particulars of a ritual performance. These revelations ensure the availability of game, promote the health of the tribe, and connect people more closely to the spiritual and animal worlds upon which they depend for survival.

In the many Yiddish stories featuring the exploits of that master of occult knowledge, King Solomon, we see the son of David outwitting and ultimately making a servant of Asmodeus, the king of the demons. Often with the demon's help, Solomon defeats enemies, solves impossible riddles, administers justice, and finds and shares treasure. Israel's most glorious king isn't a shaman, in the same sense as the Jivaro Indians of Ecuador who drink Ayahuasca tea and then both sing and *see* a power-song taught to them by the spirits. Rather, Solomon represents a parallel tradition of magi and adepts common in a number of "wisdom traditions" in which the adept is believed capable of projecting his or her soul anywhere on earth or into the Otherworld. Practitioners of such arts seek spiritual wisdom and power—and hope to translate their attainments into a variety of pragmatic applications.

Lords of Destruction and the Underworld

Gods in this archetypal category represent or are held responsible for that which humans fear most: death, disease, misfortune, and supernatural malevolence. Numerous deities are believed to cause miseries as specific as famine, pestilence, smallpox, and even the onset of winter, yet the archetype seems rooted in a more general concept of a Dark Lord of the Underworld. The archetype, were it embodied in a single deity, would depict a god clothed in either mummylike bandages or a black cowl, dwelling in a gloomy underworld, accompanied by a canine guard, and wielding a weapon of punishment such as a stone axe, a flail, or a sword. Osiris, for example, is often depicted wearing a mummy's wrappings from hips to feet, holding a crook and a flail, bearing the blackened skin of a corpse that has undergone funerary preparation, and accompanied by the jackal-headed god, Anubis. Frequently, the Dread Lord's palace is not only in the Underworld but also in the west. The Egyptian, Assyrian, Slavic, Greco-Roman, and Celtic kingdoms of the dead were all in the west, and a number of indigenous peoples in the Americas also believed the dead follow a path toward the setting sun into the Afterlife.

Hades and Pluto were both believed to be greedy, probably because they never gave up a soul once it came into their kingdom. They were also associated with hoarded wealth of precious metals and gems. In fact, the name "Pluto" literally means "wealthgiver." But there might be another reason for this seemingly odd connection between the land of the dead and abundance. A number of Lords of the Underworld are linked to fertility and renewal. The clearest example is Osiris, whose role before he was slain by his brother Set was that of seasonal vegetation deity. Several depictions of Osiris, for example, show him with green skin, an obvious allusion to his original role as a vegetation deity—an association reinforced by the

Mictlantecuhtli, the Lord of the Dead. Ht. 4.5 inches. Totonic pottery figure. Mictlantecuhtli presided over the regions of the north and the worlds beneath the earth with his wife Mictecaci-huatl. According to tradition, on the way to the underworld the dead are reduced to skeletons by a wind of knives. Location: Anthropology Museum, Veracruz University, Jalapa, Mexico.
Source: © Werner Forman Archive/Art Resource, NY.

seasonal flooding of the Nile (Osiris) with its dramatic springtime "greening" of the river valley (Isis). Hades, while not himself a vegetative deity, forced marriage upon Persephone, whose semiannual return from his kingdom into the land of the living marks the return of vegetative fertility. A little less obviously, Koshchei, the ancient Russian lord of death, was believed to have kept his soul in an egg, inside a duck, inside a hare, inside an iron chest, under a green oak tree, on an island in the middle of the ocean. With the exception of the iron chest, the other containers of his life force are clearly suggestive of fertility and growth. Among the Russian gods attested in the *Kievan Primary Chronicle,* the winged dog, Simargl, was said to guard seeds and plant growth—the very essence of vegetative renewal. Perhaps this "guard dog" fulfilled a role analogous to Cerberus in Greco-Roman tradition. In any case, the prevalent association of Lords of the Underworld with renewal and resurrection may at first seem contradictory. Nevertheless, it suggests a near-universal mythic truth: life, decay, death, and renewal of life follow each other in a never-ending cycle.

Of course death, by its nature, is frightening and emotionally devastating, and numerous gods that personify death, war, and other evils are not also associated with the promise of renewal. Most famous is the Greek god Ares, whose bloodthirstiness and unreasoning rage not only make him "sacker of cities" but also land him in all kinds of predicaments. Ares was depicted as an ungovernable terror who gloated over the death and destruction that followed in his wake. His Roman counterpart, Mars, was more complex, and, next to Jupiter, he was the most important deity in the Roman Empire. The month of March is named after him, and tradition had it that his birthday fell on March 1, the traditional first day of spring and the beginning of the new year—over both of which his mother, Juno, presided. In addition to this close association between Mars and spring, the Parilia, a springtime festival sacred to the "god of war," featured a sacral meal of millet cake and buckets of milk. Thus the early Roman religious imagination linked military protection and a bounteous crop.

Despite the cultural and geographical affinities between the Greeks and the Romans, Mars was less a war-god in the tradition of Ares than the Aztec war-god Huitzilopochtli. This god, whose name mysteriously translates as the "Blue Hummingbird from the Left," was believed to have led his people from their now-forgotten homeland in the north to a sacred site in what is now Mexico City. Huitzilopochtli was easily as bloody minded as Ares. He demanded nothing less than an offering of a beating human heart for his favor. Typically, sacrificial victims were slaves and enemies unfortunate enough to be captured alive by the advancing Aztecs.

Mythic literature speaks of many other gods of battle. In Slavic tradition, for instance, Perun was depicted as a large man with a silver face and golden moustaches. He was alternately depicted as bearing an enormous club, a battle ax, or a bow and arrow. At the time of Kiev's Christianization (988 CE), Perun was the chief Slavic deity whose tendency to destroy his enemies with thunder and lightning (the latter represented by his swift, flashing arrows) has much in common with Zeus, Baal, Odin, and a long list of other warlike sky-fathers. In Celtic tradition, Balor was the much-feared Fomorian war-god. The Fomors, who were believed to live under the Irish Sea, waged fierce war with the Tuatha de Danaan, the race from whom the Irish are said to be descended. Balor-of-the-Stout-Blow was said to have a single eye, the lid of which was so heavy that the god required several servants to hoist it open before he could see. Anyone unfortunate enough to fall under Balor's gaze was crushed in an instant. While Balor did not possess a thunderbolt, he shares with his Norse colleague Odin the distinctive characteristic of being monocular.

Odin, who also has much in common with the Germanic war-gods Wodan and Tiwasz, was depicted as ruthless, arrogant, and capricious. Even his worshipers

Bse'i Khrab Can ("He Who Has a Cuirass of Leather"). Thangka painting. This celestial warrior has no Indian prototype and is therefore likely to be a native Tibetan deity later "tamed" to serve the Buddhist religion. He wears leather armor and is armed with a jeweled club, a yak hair snare, bow and arrows, and a sword. Banners sprout from his helmet and roaring flames surround envelop his body and that of his horse. Prior to Buddhism, Bse'i Khrab Can was likely a war god much like Ares or Odin; but after the advent of the new religion he became a protective spirit that fiercely guarded the faith.
Source: © The Newark Museum/Art Resource, NY.

have been surprisingly critical of his tendency to break faith with his faithful servants for no good reason. Odin wore a blue cloak and always bore the magic spear, Gungnir, two elements of his iconography that link him to the Lord of the Underworld archetype. From these examples, we see that a people's war-god projects a pumped-up image of ruthless male strength. War-gods drink the blood of their enemies from the skulls of the fallen, wear the hands and feet of the slain like charms on belts and necklaces, ride dragons or other dangerous beasts, rip babies from their mother's swollen bellies, and laugh at the smoldering wreckage they leave behind. They never back down from a challenge, never tire of fighting or of dealing out death. War-gods of the Ares type aren't welcome at the feasts of god or men. Instead, their grim task is to patrol the outskirts of civilization, projecting dread into the hearts of would-be attackers.

A Babylonian tablet translated in 1903 by R. C. Thompson speaks of seven evil spirits:

> Of these seven the first is the South wind . . .
> The second is a dragon, whose mouth is opened . . .
> That none can measure.
> The third is a grim leopard, which carries off the young . . .
> The fourth is a terrible Shibbu . . .
> The fifth is a furious Wolf, who knoweth not to flee,
> The sixth is a rampant . . . which marches against god and king.
> The seventh is a storm, an evil wind, which takes vengeance,
> Seven are they, messengers to King Anu are they,
> From city to city darkness work they,
> A hurricane, which mightily hunts in the heavens, are they,
> Thick clouds, that bring darkness in heaven, are they,
> gusts of wind rising, which case gloom over the bright day, are they . . .
> (1976, Reginald Campbell Thompson, pp. 26–27)

These seven spirits, formed by the primal creator Anu before he retired from the terrestrial scene, embody the fierce storm winds of the desert. They mount an attack upon heaven, and, for a time, they prevail against the light of the sun, moon, and stars. These spirits suggest a final category of malevolent deities: those responsible for specific afflictions and natural disasters. But with these gods of disease, bad luck, natural dangers, and human weakness, we bump up against the archetype's useful limits. For there is nothing intrinsically male about the above-mentioned seven evil spirits other than that they wage war—a stereotypically male activity—against the celestial lights. Myth speaks of many male gods controlling forces inimical to human happiness. In Slavic tradition, Rarog, Varpulis, and Stribog were gods of "ill wind," and such winds were also believed to sow strife. In Egyptian tradition, Set, who killed and dismembered his brother Osiris, was banished to the desert wastes of the Sahara for his crimes, and he became associated with deadly wind and sandstorms. The Asuras of Hindu tradition were considered "antigods" whose role it was to resist and undermine the will and creative acts of the gods of light.

Most of what we know about pre-Christian ritual and myth comes to us in the form of unsympathetic reports made by conquerors and missionaries. In fact, most of the myths we have from Oceania and the natives of North and South America were recorded—and corrupted—by missionaries whose goal was to stamp out the "demonic" religion of the "savages." Indeed, even in our more secular society, it is not unusual to find dictionaries and encyclopedias of myth along with many websites lumping all gods and goddesses from shamanic and magic-centered religious traditions into such categories as "gods of evil and witchcraft." But such unthinking judgments tell us far more about our modern biases than they do about the actual beliefs and practices of our forebears. Yet noting this bias is not to say that all "gods of evil" are only misunderstood deities from extinct religions. Human beings do suffer, and one response to such suffering has been to personify such miseries as leprosy, sexually transmitted diseases, earthquakes, storms, and a host of other ills as deities—both male and female.

READING THE MALE DIVINE

The following stories feature gods embodying most of the archetypes we have discussed in the preceding pages of this chapter. As with other myths, specific deities and their human representatives can embody several archetypes at once. The excerpts from the *Bhagavad Gita,* featuring a lengthy conversation between the god Krishna and Prince Arjuna, depicts the divine as simultaneously the father of all existence, king, savior bearing liberating wisdom, and the lord of destruction. Arjuna himself is a sage-in-the-making as he learns how to master the paradox of waging war while bearing malice toward no being, and he is granted a vision of the god's unveiled nature. Enki is depicted in part as a father god, in part as shaman and trickster. Elements of the divine father and son relationship are featured in the Yoruba story of Orunmila bestowing upon the other *orishas* their powers and the Norse story of Thor's Duel with Hrungnir. And Quetzalcoatl's struggle with the Lord of Death, Mictlantecuhtli, for the precious bones suggests elements of the savior and the trickster archetypes while the journey to the underworld itself would seem to parallel the shaman's journey to the Great Below in search of secret knowledge.

Bhagavad Gita

Hindu (India)

The *Bhagavad Gita,* or *Gita,* as it is commonly known in India, has inspired philosophers, poets, and even pragmatists in that country and around the world for centuries. Although it also exists as an independent text, the *Gita* first appears as the sixth book of the 18-book *Mahabharata* and derives its basic context from that epic work. Most scholars agree that the *Mahabharata* originated in a

Source: From *The Bhagavad Gita,* translated by Barbara Stoler Miller. © 1986 Columbia University Press. Reprinted with permission of the publisher.

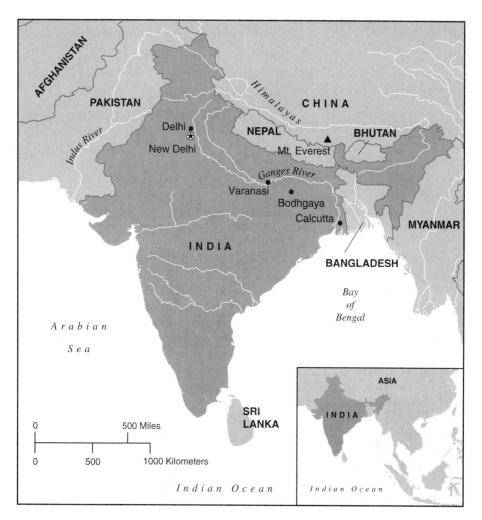

MAP 4.1 India

variety of related oral traditions that were given literary form between the years 400 BCE and 400 CE. But the epic's tale of spiritual
and temporal struggle recounts legendary events believed to have
taken place much earlier (around 1200 BCE), shortly after nomadic
Indo-Aryan-speaking tribes began to settle in northwest India. The
various sacrificial rites practiced by these tribes—and described
in great detail in the Vedas—eventually became Hinduism.

The *Gita* begins with armies stationed on the battlefield of
Kurukshetra, just moments before the horns sound and the warriors collide in combat. At the head of one army is Prince Arjuna
and his divine charioteer, Krishna. The prince dismounts and
surveys the scene. On the opposite hills are arrayed the sons of

Dhritarashtra, his cousins, and his beloved teachers, including the priest Drona, who taught him the martial arts of which he is now master. As a *kshatriya,* a member of the warrior caste, Arjuna has a sacred duty to wage this war and to establish the divinely ordained political order. But to fulfill the duties incumbent upon a *kshatriya* would, in this case, cause him to forsake equally important loyalties to his family and teachers. This paradox paralyzes Arjuna, who starts to shake, gets goosebumps, and finally drops his famous bow in utter misery. Better to renounce his warrior duties, he tells Krishna, and suffer the dishonor of surrender than to win a fight that can only make him despise himself for the rest of his life and send him to hell afterwards. In terms rooted in Hindu religious philosophy, Arjuna is caught between the human need to act in this world of violence and suffering and the spiritual necessity of renouncing the world and our attachments to it. Krishna, whose divine identity is known but not fully revealed to the troubled prince, tells him, in effect, to stop whining, pick up his bow, and do his job.

But the moral purpose of the *Gita* is to reveal how it is possible for Arjuna and, by extension, the story's audience to live and act in the world without forfeiting the spiritual advantages of renouncing it. By way of answer, the *Gita,* itself an 18-part work, articulates Krishna's teaching about the proper relationships among the oftentimes contradictory necessities of duty (*dharma*), action (*karma*), knowledge (*jñana*), discipline (*yoga*), and devotion (*bhakti*). In the *Gita's* first six teachings, Arjuna's questions and Krishna's answers focus exclusively on these necessities. Teaching 6 describes "the man of discipline" who discovers tranquility in action by renouncing any personal stake in the fruits of those actions, instead devoting the outcome of all activity to Krishna. Thus Arjuna's dilemma can be resolved through a complete and disciplined devotion to Krishna because he does not "own" the fruits of his actions once they have been offered to the god.

His confidence and faith gradually restored by the god's counsel, Arjuna asks, in the 11th teaching, to see Krishna's divine form, and the resulting theophany reveals the god to be both creator and destroyer. As destroyer, or "time grown old," Krishna has already destroyed both armies and every other living thing, for, from the perspective of eternity, all events have already happened and the cosmos is, in any case, destined to die and be reborn forever. As creator, the god brings all things to birth and is responsible for the cosmic and human orders through which all good things come into being. We can note in passing that Hindu religious thought doesn't need to invent a devil or evil god to account for death and suffering. Instead, supreme Hindu deities like

Krishna embody the totality of existence and are the source of agony and ecstasy alike. Arjuna understands from the revelation of Krishna's divine form that he has a small but completely necessary role to play in this cosmic drama. He realizes that it is possible to unite himself with Krishna and his divine purpose only if he performs his warrior duties selflessly, as an act of devotion to Krishna, thus freeing himself from the attachments that bind human beings to this world of suffering.

As a final note, we direct the reader's attention to the framing narrative through which this story reveals to us the god's character and doctrine. As the story opens, Vyasa, the sage who, tradition tells us, wrote the *Mahabharata,* meets the blind king Dhritarashtra and tells him that he can hear an account of the battle from Sanjaya, who has an "inner eye" so powerful that he can see past, present, and future events with equal clarity. So it is Sanjaya who tells the story that is the *Gita* and who interrupts at strategic places to provide information that cannot naturally be transmitted through dialog. Thus the narrative is itself complexly ironic. The ultimate losers of the battle tell the story and, in the process, hear Krishna's liberating teaching as they learn their fate. Arjuna is revealed as compassionate and guilt-stricken—until the god frees his mind from the egocentric delusions that produce these mental afflictions and prevent his taking deadly action.

THE FIRST TEACHING: ARJUNA'S DETECTION

DHRITARASHTRA: Sanjaya, tell me what my sons and the sons of Pandu did when they met, wanting to battle on the field of Kuru, on the field of sacred duty?

SANJAYA: Your son Duryodhana, the king, seeing the Pandava forces arrayed, approached his teacher Drona and spoke in command,

"My teacher, see the great Pandava army arrayed by Drupada's son, your pupil, intent on revenge. Here are heroes, mighty archers equal to Bhima and Arjuna in warfare, Yuyudhana, Virata, and Drupada, your sworn foe on his great chariot. Here too are Dhrishtaketu, Cekitana, and the brave kin of Benares Purujit, Kuntibhoja, and the manly king of the Shibis.

"Yudhamanyu is bold, and Uttamaujas is brave; the sons of Subhadra and Draupadi all command great chariots. Now, honored priest, mark the superb men on our side as I tell you the names of my army's leaders.

"They are you and Bhishma, Karna and Kripa, a victor in battles, your own son Ashvatthama, Vikarna, and the son of Somadatta. Many other heroes also risk their lives for my sake, bearing varied weapons and skilled in the ways of war. Guarded by Bhishma, the strength of our army is without limit; but the strength of their army, guarded by Bhima, is limited. In all the movements of battle, you and your men, stationed according to plan, must guard Bhishma well!"

Bhishma, fiery elder of the Kurus, roared his lion's roar and blew his conch horn, exciting Duryodhana's delight. Conches and kettledrums, cymbals, tabors, and trumpets were sounded at once and the din of tumult arose. Standing on their great chariot yoked with white stallions, Krishna and Arjuna, Pandu's son, sounded their divine conches. Krishna blew Pancajanya, won from a demon; Arjuna blew Devadatta, a gift of the gods; fierce wolf-bellied Bhima blew Paundra, his great conch of the east. Yudhishthira, Kunti's son, the king, blew Anantavijaya, conch of boundless victory; his twin brothers Nakula and Sahadeva blew conches resonant and jewel-toned. The king of Benares, a superb archer, and Shikhandin on his great chariot, Drishtadyumna, Virata, and indomitable Satyaki, all blew their conches. Drupada, with his five grandsons, and Subhadra's strong-armed son, each in his turn blew their conches, O King.

The noise tore the hearts of Dhritarashtra's sons, and tumult echoed through heaven and earth. Arjuna, his war flag a rampant monkey, saw Dhritarashtra's sons assembled as weapons were ready to clash, and he lifted his bow. He told his charioteer: "Krishna, halt my chariot between the armies! Far enough for me to see these men who lust for war, ready to fight with me in the strain of battle. I see men gathered here, eager to fight, bent on serving the folly of Dhritarashtra's son."

When Arjuna had spoken, Krishna halted their splendid chariot between the armies. Facing Bhishma and Drona and all the great kings, he said, "Arjuna, see the Kuru men assembled here!"

Arjuna saw them standing there: fathers, grandfathers, teachers, uncles, brothers, sons, grandsons, and friends. He surveyed his elders and companions in both armies, all his kinsmen assembled together. Dejected, filled with strange pity, he said this:

"Krishna, I see my kinsmen gathered here, wanting war. My limbs sink, my mouth is parched, my body trembles, the hair bristles on my flesh. The magic bow slips from my hand, my skin burns, I cannot stand still, my mind reels.

"I see omens of chaos, Krishna; I see no good in killing my kinsmen in battle. Krishna, I seek no victory, or kingship or pleasures. What use to us are kingship, delights, or life itself? We sought kingship, delights, and pleasures for the sake of those assembled to abandon their lives and fortunes in battle.

"They are teachers, fathers, sons, and grandfathers, uncles, grandsons, fathers and brothers of wives, and other men of our family. I do not want to kill them even if I am killed, Krishna; not for kingship of all three worlds, much less for the earth!

"What joy is there for us, Krishna, in killing Dhritarashtra's sons? Evil will haunt us if we kill them, though their bows are drawn to kill. Honor forbids us to kill our cousins, Dhritarashtra's sons; how can we know happiness if we kill our own kinsmen? If Dhritarashtra's armed sons kill me in battle when I am unarmed and offer no resistance, it will be my reward."

Saying this in the time of war, Arjuna slumped into the chariot and laid down his bow and arrows, his mind tormented by grief.

THE SECOND TEACHING: PHILOSOPHY
AND SPIRITUAL DISCIPLINE

SANJAYA: Arjuna sat dejected, filled with pity, his sad eyes blurred by tears. Krishna gave him counsel.

LORD KRISHNA: Why this cowardice in time of crisis, Arjuna? The coward is ignoble, shameful, foreign to the ways of heaven. Don't yield to impotence! It is unnatural in you! Banish this petty weakness from your heart. Rise to the fight, Arjuna!

ARJUNA: Krishna, how can I fight against Bhishma and Drona with arrows when they deserve my worship? It is better in this world to beg for scraps of food than to eat meals smeared with the blood of elders I killed at the height of their power while their goals were still desires.

We don't know which weight is worse to bear—our conquering them or their conquering us. We will not want to live if we kill the sons of Dhritarashtra assembled before us. The flaw of pity blights my very being; conflicting sacred duties confound my reason. I ask you to tell me decisively—which is better? I am your pupil. Teach me what I seek! I see nothing that could drive away the grief that withers my senses; even if I won kingdoms of unrivaled wealth on earth and sovereignty over gods.

SANJAYA: Arjuna told this to Krishna; then saying, "I shall not fight," he fell silent. Mocking him gently, Krishna gave this counsel as Arjuna sat dejected, between the two armies.

LORD KRISHNA: You grieve for those beyond grief, and you speak words of insight; but learned men do not grieve for the dead or the living. Never have I not existed, nor you, nor these kings; and never in the future shall we cease to exist.

Just as the embodied self enters childhood, youth, and old age, so does it enter another body; this does not confound a steadfast man. Contacts with matter make us feel heat and cold, pleasure and pain. Arjuna, you must learn to endure fleeting things—they come and go! When these cannot torment a man, when suffering and joy are equal for him and he has courage, he is fit for immortality.

Nothing of nonbeing comes to be, nor does being cease to exist; the boundary between these two is seen by men who see reality. Indestructible is the presence that pervades all this; no one can destroy this unchanging reality. Our bodies are known to end, but the embodied self is enduring, indestructible, and immeasurable; therefore, Arjuna, fight the battle!

He who thinks this self a killer and he who thinks it killed, both fail to understand; it does not kill, nor is it killed. It is not born, it does not die; having been, it will never not be; unborn, enduring, constant, and primordial, it is not killed when the body is killed.

Arjuna, when a man knows the self to be indestructible, enduring, unborn, unchanging, how does he kill or cause anyone to kill? As a man discards worn-out clothes to put on new and different ones, so the embodied self discards its worn-out bodies to take on other new ones.

Weapons do not cut it, fire does not burn it, waters do not wet it, wind does not wither it. It cannot be cut or burned; it cannot be wet or withered; it is enduring, all-pervasive, fixed, immovable, and timeless. It is called unmanifest, inconceivable, and immutable; since you know that to be so, you should not grieve!

If you think of its birth and death as ever-recurring, then too, Great Warrior, you have no cause to grieve! Death is certain for anyone born, and birth is certain for the dead; since the cycle is inevitable, you have no cause to grieve!

Creatures are unmanifest in origin, manifest in the midst of life, and unmanifest again in the end. Since this is so, why do you lament? Rarely someone sees it, rarely another speaks it, rarely anyone hears it—even hearing it, no one really knows it.

The self embodied in the body of every being is indestructible; you have no cause to grieve for all these creatures, Arjuna! Look to your own duty; do not tremble before it; nothing is better for a warrior than a battle of sacred duty.

The doors of heaven open for warriors who rejoice to have a battle like this thrust on them by chance. If you fail to wage this war of sacred duty, you will abandon your own duty and fame only to gain evil. The great chariot warriors will think you deserted in fear of battle; you will be despised by those who held you in esteem. Your enemies will slander you, scorning your skill in so many unspeakable ways— could any suffering be worse?

If you are killed, you win heaven; if you triumph, you enjoy the earth; therefore, Arjuna, stand up and resolve to fight the battle! Impartial to joy and suffering, gain and loss, victory and defeat, arm yourself for the battle, lest you fall into evil.

Understanding is defined in terms of philosophy; now hear it in spiritual discipline. Armed with this understanding, Arjuna, you will escape the bondage of action. No effort in this world is lost or wasted; a fragment of sacred duty saves you from great fear. This understanding is unique in its inner core of resolve; diffuse and pointless are the ways irresolute men understand. Undiscerning men who delight in the tenets of ritual lore utter florid speech, proclaiming, "There is nothing else!"

Driven by desire, they strive after heaven and contrive to win powers and delights, but their intricate ritual language bears only the fruit of action in rebirth. Obsessed with powers and delights, their reason lost in words, they do not find in contemplation this understanding of inner resolve. Arjuna, the realm of sacred lore is nature—beyond its triad of qualities, dualities, and mundane rewards, be forever lucid, alive to your self.

For the discerning priest, all of sacred lore has no more value than a well when water flows everywhere. Be intent on action, not on the fruits of action; avoid attraction to the fruits and attachment to inaction! Perform actions, firm in discipline, relinquishing attachment; be impartial to failure and success—this equanimity is called discipline.

Arjuna, action is far inferior to the discipline of understanding; so seek refuge in understanding—pitiful are men drawn by fruits of action. Disciplined by understanding, one abandons both good and evil deeds; so arm yourself for discipline— discipline is skill in actions.

Wise men disciplined by understanding relinquish the fruit born of action; freed from these bonds of rebirth, they reach a place beyond decay. When your understanding passes beyond the swamp of delusion you will be indifferent to all that is heard in sacred lore. When your understanding turns from sacred lore to stand fixed, immovable in contemplation, then you will reach discipline.

ARJUNA: Krishna, what defines a man deep in contemplation whose insight and thought are sure? How would he speak? How would he sit? How would he move?

LORD KRISHNA: When he gives up desires in his mind, is content with the self within himself, then he is said to be a man whose insight is sure, Arjuna. When suffering does not disturb his mind, when his craving for pleasures has vanished, when attraction, fear, and anger are gone, he is called a sage whose thought is sure. When he shows no preference in fortune or misfortune and neither exults nor hates, his insight is sure.

When, like a tortoise retracting its limbs, he withdraws his senses completely from sensuous objects, his insight is sure. Sensuous objects fade when the embodied self abstains from food; the taste lingers, but it too fades in the vision of higher truth.

Even when a man of wisdom tries to control them, Arjuna, the bewildering senses attack his mind with violence. Controlling them all, with discipline he should focus on me; when his senses are under control, his insight is sure. Brooding about sensuous objects makes attachment to them grow; from attachment desire arises, from desire anger is born. From anger comes confusion; from confusion memory lapses; from broken memory understanding is lost; from loss of understanding, he is ruined.

But a man of inner strength whose senses experience objects without attraction and hatred, in self-control, finds serenity. In serenity, all his sorrows dissolve; his reason becomes serene, his understanding sure. Without discipline, he has no understanding or inner power; without inner power, he has no peace; and without peace where is joy? If his mind submits to the play of the senses, they drive away insight, as wind drives a ship on water.

So, Great Warrior, when withdrawal of the senses from sense objects is complete, discernment is firm. When it is night for all creatures, a master of restraint is awake; when they are awake, it is night for the sage who sees reality. As the mountainous depths of the ocean are unmoved when waters rush into it, so the man unmoved when desires enter him attains a peace that eludes the man of many desires.

When he renounces all desires and acts without craving, possessiveness, or individuality, he finds peace. This is the place of the infinite spirit; achieving it, one is freed from delusion; abiding in it even at the time of death, one finds the pure calm of infinity.

THE SIXTH TEACHING: THE MAN OF DISCIPLINE

LORD KRISHNA: One who does what must be done without concern for the fruits is a man of renunciation and discipline, not one who shuns ritual fire and rites. Know that discipline, Arjuna, is what men call renunciation; no man is disciplined without renouncing willful intent.

Action is the means for a sage who seeks to mature in discipline; tranquility is the means for one who is mature in discipline. He is said to be mature in discipline when he has renounced all intention and is detached from sense objects and actions.

He should elevate himself by the self, not degrade himself; for the self is its own friend and its own worst foe. The self is the friend of a man who masters himself through the self, but for a man without self-mastery, the self is like an enemy at war.

The higher self of a tranquil man whose self is mastered is perfectly poised in cold or heat, joy or suffering, honor or contempt.

Self-contented in knowledge and judgment, his senses subdued, on the summit of existence, impartial to clay, stone, or gold, the man of discipline is disciplined. He is set apart by his disinterest toward comrades, allies, enemies, neutrals, non-partisans, foes, friends, good and even evil men.

A man of discipline should always discipline himself, remain in seclusion, isolated, his thought and self well controlled, without possessions or hope. He should fix for himself a firm seat in a pure place, neither too high nor too low, covered in cloth, deerskin, or grass. He should focus his mind and restrain the activity of his thought and senses; sitting on that seat, he should practice discipline for the purification of the self. He should keep his body, head, and neck aligned, immobile, steady; he should gaze at the tip of his nose and not let his glance wander.

The self tranquil, his fear dispelled, firm in his vow of celibacy, his mind restrained, let him sit with discipline, his thought fixed on me, intent on me. Disciplining himself, his mind controlled, a man of discipline finds peace, the pure calm that exists in me.

Gluttons have no discipline, nor the man who starves himself, nor he who sleeps excessively or suffers wakefulness. When a man disciplines his diet and diversions, his physical actions, his sleeping and waking, discipline destroys his sorrow. When his controlled thought rests within the self alone, without craving objects of desire, he is said to be disciplined.

"He does not waver, like a lamp sheltered from the wind" is the simile recalled for a man of discipline, restrained in thought and practicing self-discipline. When his thought ceases, checked by the exercise of discipline, he is content within the self, seeing the self through himself.

Absolute joy beyond the senses can only be grasped by understanding; when one knows it, he abides there and never wanders from this reality. Obtaining it, he thinks there is no greater gain; abiding there, he is unmoved, even by deep suffering.

Since he knows that discipline means unbinding the bonds of suffering, he should practice discipline resolutely, without despair dulling his reason. He should entirely relinquish desires aroused by willful intent; he should entirely control his senses with his mind. He should gradually become tranquil, firmly controlling his understanding; focusing his mind on the self, he should think nothing. Wherever his faltering mind unsteadily wanders, he should restrain it and bring it under self-control.

When his mind is tranquil, perfect joy comes to the man of discipline; his passion is calmed, he is without sin, being one with the infinite spirit. Constantly disciplining himself, free from sin, the man of discipline easily achieves perfect joy in harmony with the infinite spirit.

Arming himself with discipline, seeing everything with an equal eye, he sees the self in all creatures and all creatures in the self. He who sees me everywhere and sees everything in me will not be lost to me, and I will not be lost to him. I exist in all creatures, so the disciplined man devoted to me grasps the oneness of life; wherever he is, he is in me. When he sees identity in everything, whether joy or suffering, through analogy with the self, he is deemed a man of pure discipline.

ARJUNA: You define this discipline by equanimity, Krishna; but in my faltering condition, I see no ground for it. Krishna, the mind is faltering, violent, strong, and stubborn; I find it as difficult to hold as the wind.

LORD KRISHNA: Without doubt, the mind is unsteady and hard to hold, but practice and dispassion can restrain it, Arjuna. In my view, discipline eludes the unrestrained self, but if he strives to master himself, a man has the means to reach it.

ARJUNA: When a man has faith, but no ascetic will, and his mind deviates from discipline before its perfection is achieved, what way is there for him, Krishna? Doomed by his double failure, is he not like a cloud split apart, unsettled, deluded on the path of the infinite spirit?

Krishna, only you can dispel this doubt of mine completely; there is no one but you to dispel this doubt.

LORD KRISHNA: Arjuna, he does not suffer doom in this world or the next; any man who acts with honor cannot go the wrong way, my friend. Fallen in discipline, he reaches worlds made by his virtue, wherein he dwells for endless years, until he is reborn in a house of upright and noble men. Or he is born in a family of disciplined men; the kind of birth in the world that is very hard to win. There he regains a depth of understanding from his former life and strives further to perfection, Arjuna. Carried by the force of his previous practice, a man who seeks to learn discipline passes beyond sacred lore that expresses the infinite spirit in words.

The man of discipline, striving with effort, purified of his sins, perfected through many births, finds a higher way. He is deemed superior to men of penance, men of knowledge, and men of action; be a man of discipline, Arjuna! Of all the men of discipline, the faithful man devoted to me, with his inner self deep in mine, I deem most disciplined.

THE ELEVENTH TEACHING: THE VISION OF KRISHNA'S TOTALITY

ARJUNA: To favor me you revealed the deepest mystery of the self, and by your words my delusion is dispelled. I heard from you in detail how creatures come to be and die, Krishna, and about the self in its immutable greatness. Just as you have described yourself, I wish to see your form in all its majesty, Krishna, Supreme among Men. If you think I can see it, reveal to me your immutable self, Krishna, Lord of Discipline.

LORD KRISHNA: Arjuna, see my forms in hundreds and thousands; diverse, divine, of many colors and shapes. See the sun gods, gods of light, howling storm gods, twin gods of dawn, and gods of wind, Arjuna, wondrous forms not seen before.

Arjuna, see all the universe, animate and inanimate, and whatever else you wish to see; all stands here as one in my body. But you cannot see me with your own eye; I will give you a divine eye to see the majesty of my discipline.

SANJAYA: O King, saying this, Krishna, the great lord of discipline, revealed to Arjuna the true majesty of his form. It was a multiform, wondrous vision, with countless mouths and eyes and celestial ornaments, brandishing many divine weapons. Everywhere was boundless divinity containing all astonishing things, wearing divine garlands and garments, anointed with divine perfume.

If the light of a thousand suns were to rise in the sky at once, it would be like the light of that great spirit. Arjuna saw all the universe in its many ways and parts, standing as one in the body of the god of gods. Then filled with amazement, his hair bristling on his flesh, Arjuna bowed his head to the god, joined his hands in homage, and spoke.

ARJUNA: I see the gods in your body, O God, and hordes of varied creatures: Brahma, the cosmic creator, on his lotus throne, all the seers and celestial serpents. I see your boundless form everywhere, the countless arms, bellies, mouths, and eyes; Lord of All, I see no end, or middle or beginning to your totality.

I see you blazing through the fiery rays of your crown, mace, and discus, hard to behold in the burning light of fire and sun that surrounds your measureless presence. You are to be known as supreme eternity, the deepest treasure of all that is, the immutable guardian of enduring sacred duty; I think you are man's timeless spirit. I see no beginning or middle or end to you; only boundless strength in your endless arms, the moon and sun in your eyes, your mouths of consuming flames, your own brilliance scorching this universe. You alone fill the space between heaven and earth and all the directions; seeing this awesome, terrible form of yours, Great Soul, the three worlds tremble.

Throngs of gods enter you, some in their terror make gestures of homage to invoke you; throngs of great sages and saints hail you and praise you in resounding hymns. Howling storm gods, sun gods, bright gods, and gods of ritual, gods of the universe, twin gods of dawn, wind gods, vapor-drinking ghosts, throngs of celestial musicians, demigods, demons, and saints, all gaze at you amazed. Seeing the many mouths and eyes of your great form, its many arms, thighs, feet, bellies, and fangs, the worlds tremble and so do I. Vishnu, seeing you brush the clouds with flames of countless colors, your mouths agape, your huge eyes blazing, my inner self quakes and I find no resolve or tranquility.

Seeing the fangs protruding from your mouths like the fires of time, I lose my bearings and I find no refuge; be gracious, Lord of Gods, Shelter of the Universe. All those sons of the blind king Dhritarashtra come accompanied by troops of kings, by the generals Bhishma, Drona, Karna, and by our battle leaders. Rushing through your fangs into grim mouths, some are dangling from heads crushed between your teeth.

As roiling river waters stream headlong toward the sea, so do these human heroes enter into your blazing mouths.

As moths in the frenzy of destruction fly into a blazing flame, worlds in the frenzy of destruction enter your mouths. You lick at the worlds around you, devouring them with flaming mouths; and your terrible fires scorch the entire universe, filling it, Vishnu, with violent rays. Tell me who are you in this terrible form? Homage to you, Best of Gods! Be gracious! I want to know you as you are in your beginning. I do not comprehend the course of your ways.

LORD KRISHNA: I am time grown old, creating world destruction, set in motion to annihilate the worlds; even without you, all these warriors arrayed in hostile ranks will cease to exist. Therefore, arise and win glory! Conquer your foes and fulfill your kingship! They are already killed by me. Be just my instrument, the archer at my side! Drona, Bhishma, Jayadratha, and Karna, and all the other battle heroes, are killed by me. Kill them without wavering; fight, and you will conquer your foes in battle!

SANJAYA: Hearing Krishna's words, Arjuna trembled under his crown, and he joined his hands in reverent homage; terrified of his fear, he bowed to Krishna and stammered in reply.

ARJUNA: Krishna, the universe responds with joy and rapture to your glory, terrified demons flee in far directions, and saints throng to bow in homage. Why should they not bow in homage to you, Great Soul, Original Creator, more venerable than the creator Brahma? Boundless Lord of Gods, Shelter of All That Is, you are eternity, being, nonbeing, and beyond.

You are the original god, the primordial spirit of man, the deepest treasure of all that is, knower and what is to be known, the supreme abode; you pervade the universe, Lord of Boundless Form. You are the gods of wind, death, fire, and water; the moon; the lord of life; and the great ancestor. Homage to you, a thousand times homage! I bow in homage to you again and yet again. I bow in homage before you and behind you; I bow everywhere to your omnipresence! You have boundless strength and limitless force; you fulfill all that you are.

Thinking you a friend, I boldly said, "Welcome, Krishna! Welcome, cousin, friend!" From negligence, or through love, I failed to know your greatness. If in jest I offended you, alone or publicly, at sport, rest, sitting, or at meals, I beg your patience, unfathomable Krishna.

You are father of the world of animate and inanimate things, its venerable teacher, most worthy of worship, without equal. Where in all three worlds is another to match your extraordinary power? I bow to you, I prostrate my body, I beg you to be gracious, Worshipful Lord—as a father to a son, a friend to a friend, a lover to a beloved, O God, bear with me. I am thrilled, and yet my mind trembles with fear at seeing what has not been seen before. Show me, God, the form I know—be gracious, Lord of Gods, Shelter of the World. I want to see you as before, with your crown and mace, and the discus in your hand. O Thousand-Armed God, assume the four-armed form embodied in your totality.

LORD KRISHNA: To grace you, Arjuna, I revealed through self-discipline my higher form, which no one but you has ever beheld—brilliant, total, boundless, primal. Not through sacred lore or sacrificial ritual or study or charity, not by rites or by terrible penances can I be seen in this form in the world of men by anyone but you, Great Hero.

Do not tremble or suffer confusion from seeing my horrific form; your fear dispelled, your mind full of love, see my form again as it was.

SANJAYA: Saying this to Arjuna, Krishna once more revealed his intimate form; resuming his gentle body, the great spirit let the terrified hero regain his breath.

ARJUNA: Seeing your gentle human form, Krishna, I recover my own nature, and my reason is restored.

LORD KRISHNA: This form you have seen is rarely revealed; the gods are constantly craving for a vision of this form. Not through sacred lore, penances, charity, or sacrificial rites can I be seen in the form that you saw me. By devotion alone can I, as I really am, be known and seen and entered into, Arjuna. Acting only for me, intent on me, free from attachment, hostile to no creature, Arjuna, a man of devotion, comes to me.

Enki and Ninhursanga

Sumerian (Iraq)

The archaeological and linguistic record strongly suggests that the Sumerians originated somewhere in south-central Asia and began to settle in the land between the Tigris and Euphrates rivers around 3500 BCE. When they arrived, they would have encountered the Ubaidians and the Semitic nomadic groups that dominated them politically. By the time of the Sumerians' arrival, the Ubaidian culture had already mastered such crafts as farming, cattle ranching, fishing, weaving, pottery, masonry, and work in leather, wood, and metal. The Sumerians flourished in this environment and, over the course of the next few centuries, created the world's first major civilization. In Sumer, the wheel, kiln-fired pottery, and written language were invented and the people we know as the Sumerians soon refined and extended these inventions to produce the world's first large cities, irrigation systems, military strategy, monumental art, codes of law and ethics, epic literature, formal education, and awe-inspiring works in silver, gold, and precious and semiprecious stones.

The Sumerians believed that the universe was administered by a pantheon of living beings similar to humans in form but superior to them in nature and power. There were deities of sun, moon, and the other celestial objects, of earth, water, mountains, and steppes, of Heaven and the Underworld, of cities, farms, and such objects as pickaxes, brickmolds, and plows. Of these many deities, those ranking highest were Earth (Ki, who later became known as Ninhursag), Sky (An, the god of the primordial deep and captain of the heavenly host), Air (Enlil, who eventually became ruler of the gods), and Water (Enki, who eventually became known as the god of wisdom). Of lesser rank, but nevertheless of great cultural importance, were the moon-god, Nanna; the sun-god, Utu; the queen of the morning and evening stars, Inanna; and the rest of the sky gods, the Anuna.

Source: Jeremy A. Black, G. Cunningham, E. Fluckiger-Hawker, E. Robson, and G. Zolyomi. *The Electronic Text Corpus of Sumerian Literature* (http://www-etcsl.orient.ox.ac.uk/), Oxford 1998–. Copyright@J. A. Black, G. Cunningham, E. Robson, and G. Zolyomi 1998, 1999, 2000; J. A. Black, G. Cunningham, E. Fluckiger-Hawker, E. Robson, J. Taylor, and G. Zolyomi 2001. The authors have asserted their moral rights.

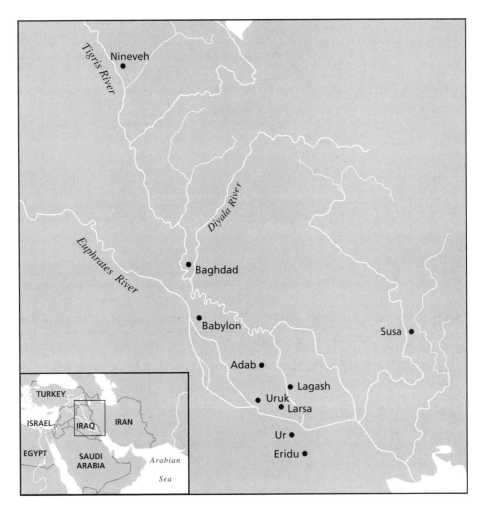

MAP 4.2 Babylon and Sumeria

Given the paramount importance of writing to the Sumerians, it is not surprising that they believed that the power of the gods resided in the divine word. We saw in the story of Ulligara and Zalgarra (chapter 2, pp. 75–76), for example, that the first man and woman were created not only from clay and the blood of one of the Anuna, but also by the incantation of the holy word. Enki was, even among the Anuna, believed to be the master of words and thus it is through his *me* (pronounced *may*) that civilization arises. The *me,* like other divine utterances, can be likened to computer "source code," for they are like the rules that direct the electrons inside your PC to perform its various tasks. In cosmological terms, the divine word provides the instructions that separate form from chaos and impart the intrinsic character and limitations of all divine, human, and natural entities and activities. The divine word was considered both the animating power and defining logic behind all things in the universe. The *me* of kingship, for example, would confer the necessary authority and charisma upon a ruler as well as specifying the prerogatives and responsibilities inherent to his office. Similarly, the *me* of beer making would make possible the microbial processes necessary to fermentation, give the beverage its various properties, and define for its maker a specific role and status within the community.

As master of the divine word, Enki is creator, fertilizer, and the shaman embodied, the master of spells, rituals, and incantations. But, despite his many associations with the holy word, Enki is not an embodiment of divine law. Rather his "laws" are derived from personal exploration of the mysteries and he is depicted as mediating between humanity and the gods and between human litigants in a dispute. His shrine, the Abzu, was believed to be located just above the underworld in his city, Eridu. This site, located in the marshlands of what is now southern Iraq, is a place where saltwater and freshwater mingle and a wide variety of flora and fauna abound. In the following story, we see Enki impregnating the earth mother Ninhursag—or Ninhursanga or Ninhursaj, the spellings vary—and then, in succession, four of her female descendants. It is from his home in the Abzu that Enki spies his daughters and comes to each of them in turn.

The following story challenges the reader because it occurs in circular, mythic time rather than the conventional, linear beginning–middle–end pattern. The myth begins during the interim between the creation of the cosmos and the final settling of Enki's domain and early on we see him transforming the land (Ninhursanga) by inseminating it. Like Hermes, who also embodies the shaman's mastery of words of power, Enki's sexual energies are as prolific as they are inexhaustible and thus he fathers many daughters. Eventually, his copulations produce Nanna, who he courts rather more elaborately than her mothers. He brings her a variety of garden crops, which symbolize settled living and the land's abundance. When he impregnates Nanna, her grandmother Ninhursanga removes the seed and it becomes a variety of useful plants which Enki sees, and, with the help of his counselor and servant Isimud, he uproots and eats each one, an action that somehow determines each plant's destiny. This action also infuriates Ninhursanga, who promises never again to look upon him with "life-giving" eye. This dire curse causes the Anuna to lie down in the dust, perhaps symbolizing a famine similar to the one caused when Demeter's own wrath with her daughter's kidnapping caused her to abandon her usual office and go wandering. In any case, a fox hatches a plot with Enlil, the chief of the Anuna, which apparently tricks Ninhursanga into saving Enki's life by removing various pains he suffers after ingesting the plants and determining their destinies. The pains are somehow converted back into plants and father Enki is praised.

Pure are the cities—and you are the ones to whom they are allotted. Pure is Dilmun land. Pure is Sumer—and you are the ones to whom it is allotted. Pure is Dilmun land. Pure is Dilmun land. Virginal is Dilmun land. Virginal is Dilmun land. Pristine is Dilmun land.

He laid her down all alone in Dilmun, and the place where Enki had lain down with his spouse, that place was still virginal, that place was still pristine. He laid her down all alone in Dilmun, and the place where Enki had lain down with Ninsikila, that place was virginal, that place was pristine.

In Dilmun the raven was not yet cawing, the partridge not cackling. The lion did not slay, the wolf was not carrying off lambs, the dog had not been taught to make kids curl up, the pig had not learned that grain was to be eaten.

When a widow had spread malt on the roof, the birds did not yet eat that malt up there. The pigeon then did not tuck its head under its wing.

No eye-diseases said there: "I am the eye disease." No headache said there: "I am the headache." No old woman belonging to it said there: "I am an old woman." No old man belonging to it said there: "I am an old man." No maiden in her unwashed state [. . .] in the city. No man dredging a river said there: "It is getting dark." No herald made the rounds in his border district.

No singer sang an *elulam* there. No wailings were wailed in the city's outskirts there.

Ninsikila said to her father Enki: "You have given a city. You have given a city. What does your giving avail me? You have given a city, Dilmun. You have given a city. What does your giving avail me? You have given [. . .] You have given a city. What does your giving avail me?"

"You have given [. . .], a city that has no river quay. You have given a city. What does your giving avail me?

1 line fragmentary

A city that has no fields, glebe or furrow"

3 lines missing

[Enki answered Ninsikila:] "When Utu steps up into heaven, fresh waters shall run out of the ground for you from the standing vessels (?) on Ezen's (?) shore, from Nanna's radiant high temple, from the mouth of the waters running underground."

"May the waters rise up from it into your great basins. May your city drink water aplenty from them. May Dilmun drink water aplenty from them. May your pools of salt water become pools of fresh water. May your city become an emporium on the quay for the Land. May Dilmun become an emporium on the quay for the Land."

"May the land of Tukric hand over to you gold from Harali, lapis lazuli and [. . .]. May the land of Meluha load precious desirable cornelian, *mec* wood of Magan and the best *abba* wood into large ships for you. May the land of Marhaci yield you precious stones, topazes. May the land of Magan offer you strong, powerful copper, dolerite, *u* stone and *cumin* stone. May the Sea-land offer you its own ebony wood, [. . .] of a king. May the 'Tent'-lands offer you fine multicoloured wools. May the land of Elam hand over to you choice wools, its tribute. May the manor of Urim, the royal throne dais, the city [. . .], load up into large ships for you sesame, august raiment, and fine cloth. May the wide sea yield you its wealth."

The city's dwellings are good dwellings. Dilmun's dwellings are good dwellings. Its grains are little grains, its dates are big dates, its harvests are triple [. . .], its wood is [. . .] wood.

At that moment, on that day, and under that sun, when Utu stepped up into heaven, from the standing vessels (?) on Ezen's (?) shore, from Nanna's radiant high temple, from the mouth of the waters running underground, fresh waters ran out of the ground for her.

The waters rose up from it into her great basins. Her city drank water aplenty from them. Dilmun drank water aplenty from them. Her pools of salt water indeed became pools of fresh water. Her fields, glebe and furrows indeed produced grain for her. Her city indeed became an emporium on the quay for the Land. Dilmun indeed became an emporium on the quay for the Land. At that moment, on that day, and under that sun, so it indeed happened.

All alone the wise one, toward Nintud, the country's mother, Enki, the wise one, toward Nintud, the country's mother, was digging his phallus into the dykes, plunging his phallus into the reedbeds. The august one pulled his phallus aside and cried out: "No man take me in the marsh."

Enki cried out: "By the life's breath of heaven I adjure you. Lie down for me in the marsh, lie down for me in the marsh, that would be joyous." Enki distributed his semen destined for Damgalnuna. He poured semen into Ninhursaja's womb and she conceived the semen in the womb, the semen of Enki.

But her one month was one day, but her two months were two days, but her three months were three days, but her four months were four days, but her five months were five days, but her six months were six days, but her seven months were seven days, but her eight months were eight days, but her nine months were nine days. In the month of womanhood, like juniper oil, like juniper oil, like oil of abundance, Nintud, mother of the country, like juniper oil, gave birth to Ninsar.

In turn Ninsar went out to the riverbank. Enki was able to see up there from in the marsh, he was able to see up there, he was. He said to his minister Isimud: "Is this nice youngster not to be kissed? Is this nice Ninsar not to be kissed?" His minister Isimud answered him: "Is this nice youngster not to be kissed? Is this nice Ninsar not to be kissed? My master will sail, let me navigate. He will sail, let me navigate."

First he put his feet in the boat, next he put them on dry land. He clasped her to the bosom, kissed her, Enki poured semen into the womb and she conceived the semen in the womb, the semen of Enki. But her one month was one day, but her two months were two days, but her nine months were nine days. In the month of womanhood, like juniper oil, like juniper oil, like oil of abundance, Ninsar, like juniper oil, like juniper oil, like oil of abundance, gave birth to Ninkura.

In turn Ninkura went out to the riverbank. Enki was able to see up there from in the marsh, he was able to see up there, he was. He said to his minister Isimud: "Is this nice youngster not to be kissed? Is this nice Ninkura not to kissed?" His minister Isimud answered him: "Kiss this nice youngster. Kiss this nice Ninkura. My master will sail, let me navigate. He will sail, let me navigate."

First he put his feet in the boat, next he put them on dry land. He clasped her to the bosom, kissed her, Enki poured semen into the womb and she conceived the semen in the womb, the semen of Enki. But her one month was one day, but her nine months were nine days. In the month of womanhood, like juniper oil, like juniper oil, like oil of abundance, Ninkura, like juniper oil, like juniper oil, like oil of abundance, gave birth to Uttu, the exalted (?) woman.

Ninkura in turn gave birth to Ninimma. She brought the child up and made her flourish. Ninimma in turn went out to the riverbank. Enki was towing his boat along and was able to see up there, [. . .] He laid eyes on Ninimma on the riverbank and said to his minister Isimud: "Have I ever kissed one like this nice youngster? Have I ever made love to one like nice Ninimma?" His minister Isimud answered him: "My master will sail, let me navigate. He will sail, let me navigate."

First he put his feet in the boat, next he put them on dry land. He clasped her to the bosom, lying in her crotch, made love to the youngster and kissed her. Enki poured semen into Ninimma's womb and she conceived the semen in the womb, the semen of Enki.

To the woman its one month was but its one day, its two months were but its two days, its three months were but its three days, its four months were but its four days, its five months were but its five days, its six months were but its six days, its seven months were but its seven days, its eight months were but its eight days, and at its nine days, in the month of womanhood, like juniper oil, like juniper oil, like oil of abundance, Ninimma, like juniper oil, like oil of abundance, gave birth to Uttu, the exalted (?) woman.

Nintud said to Uttu: "Let me advise you, and may you take heed of my advice. Let me speak words to you and may you heed my words. From in the marsh one man is able to see up here, is able to see up here, he is; from in the marsh Enki is able to see up here, is able to see up here, he is. He will set eyes on you."

10 lines fragmentary

[. . .] Uttu, the exalted (?) woman [. . .]

3 lines fragmentary

[Uttu said:] "Bring cucumbers in [. . .], bring apples with their stems sticking out (?), bring grapes in their clusters, and in the house you will indeed have hold of my halter, O Enki, you will indeed have hold of my halter."

When he was filling with water a second time, he filled the dykes with water, he filled the canals with water, he filled the fallows with water. The gardener in his joy rose (?) from the dust and embraced him: "Who are you who [. . .] the garden?"

Enki (said to) [. . .] the gardener:

4 lines missing

He brought him cucumbers in [. . .], brought him apples with their stems sticking out (?), brought him grapes in their clusters, filled his lap.

Enki made his face attractive and took a staff in his hand. Enki came to a halt at Uttu's, knocked at her house (demanding): "Open up, open up." [She asked:] "Who are you?" [He answered:] "I am a gardener. Let me give you cucumbers, apples, and grapes for your 'Yes.'" Joyfully Uttu opened the house. Enki gave Uttu, the exalted (?) woman, cucumbers in [. . .], gave her apples with their stems sticking out (?), gave her grapes in their clusters. He poured beer for her in the large *ban* measure.

Uttu, the exalted (?) woman, [. . .] to the left for him, waved the hands for him. Enki aroused Uttu. He clasped her to the bosom, lying in her crotch, fondled her thighs, fondled her with the hand. He clasped her to the bosom, lying in her crotch, made love to the youngster and kissed her. Enki poured semen into Uttu's womb and she conceived the semen in the womb, the semen of Enki.

Uttu, the beautiful woman, cried out: "Woe, my thighs!" She cried out: "Woe, my liver! Woe, my heart!" Ninhursaja removed the semen from the thighs.

2 lines fragmentary

She grew the "tree" plant, she grew the "honey" plant, she grew the "vegetable" plant, she grew the esparto grass (?), she grew the *atutu* plant, she grew the *actaltal* plant, she grew the [. . .] plant, she grew the *amharu* plant.

Enki was able to see up there from in the marsh, he was able to see up there, he was. He said to his minister Isimud: "I have not determined the destiny of these plants. What is this one? What is that one?"

His minister Isimud had the answer for him. "My master, the 'tree' plant," he said to him, cut it off for him and Enki ate it. "My master, the 'honey' plant," he said to him, pulled it up for him and Enki ate it. "My master, the 'vegetable' plant," he said to him, cut it off for him and Enki ate it. "My master, the alfalfa grass (?)," he said to him, pulled it up for him and Enki ate it.

"My master, the *atutu* plant," he said to him, cut it off for him and Enki ate it. "My master, the *actaltal* plant," he said to him, pulled it up for him and Enki ate it. "My master, the [. . .] plant," he said to him, cut it off for him and Enki ate it. "My master, the *amharu* plant," he said to him, pulled it up for him and Enki ate it. Enki determined the destiny of the plants, had them know it in their hearts.

Ninhursaja cursed the name Enki: "Until his dying day, I will never look upon him with life-giving eye."

The Anuna sat down in the dust. But a fox was able to speak to Enlil: "If I bring Ninhursaja to you, what will be my reward?" Enlil answered the fox: "If you bring Ninhursaja to me, I shall erect two standards for you in my city and you will be renowned."

The fox first anointed his body, first shook out his fur (?), first put kohl on his eyes.

4 lines fragmentary

[The fox said to Ninhursaja:] "I have been to Nibru, but Enlil [. . .] I have been to Urim, but Nanna [. . .] I have been to Larsa, but Utu [. . .] I have been to Unug, but Inana [. . .] I am seeking refuge with one who is [. . .]"

7 lines fragmentary

Ninhursaja hastened to the temple. The Anuna slipped off her garment, made [. . .], determined its destiny and [. . .] Ninhursaja made Enki sit by her vagina. She placed (?) her hands on [. . .] and [. . .] on its outside.

[Ninhursaja asked:] "My brother, what part of you hurts you?"

"The top of my head (*ugu-dili*) hurts me."

She gave birth to Ab-u out of it. "My brother, what part of you hurts you?"

"The locks of my hair (*siki*) hurt me."

She gave birth to Ninsikila out of it. "My brother, what part of you hurts you?"

"My nose (*giri*) hurts me."

She gave birth to Ningiriudu out of it. "My brother, what part of you hurts you?"

"My mouth (*ka*) hurts me."

She gave birth to Ninkasi out of it. "My brother, what part of you hurts you?"

"My throat (*zi*) hurts me."

She gave birth to Nazi out of it. "My brother, what part of you hurts you?"

"My arm (*a*) hurts me."

She gave birth to Azimua out of it. "My brother, what part of you hurts you?"

"My ribs (*ti*) hurt me."

She gave birth to Ninti out of it. "My brother, what part of you hurts you?"

"My sides (*zag*) hurt me."

She gave birth to Ensag out of it. [She said:] "For the little ones to whom I have given birth may rewards not be lacking. Ab-u shall become king of the grasses, Ninsikila shall become lord of Magan, Ningiriudu shall marry Ninazu, Ninkasi shall be what satisfies the heart, Nazi shall marry Nindara, Azimua shall marry Ninjiczida, Ninti shall become the lady of the month, and Ensag shall become lord of Dilmun."

Praise be to Father Enki.

Orunmila Gives the *Orishas* Their Powers and His Friendship with Eshu

Yoruba (Nigeria and Benin)

Occupying southwest Nigeria and much of Benin, the Yoruba have flourished for approximately a millennium. The *orishas*, gods and semidivine heroes of Yoruba culture, literally number in the hundreds, but at their head is Olorun, the great sky-father. They are responsible for natural powers and for ordering human affairs through various technologies, crafts, and customs. Humans supplicate orishas with prayers and food offerings for health, fertility, a good harvest, and protection from enemies.

Although the *orishas* are numerous, a dozen or so "great" *orishas* are most prominent in Yoruba myth. There is the trickster and embodiment of accident and uncertainty, Eshu; there is the essence and giver of iron, Ogun. In addition, there are stories about

Source: Harold Courlander, *Tales of Yoruba Gods and Heroes*. New York: Crown Books, 1973. 25–28, 59–62.

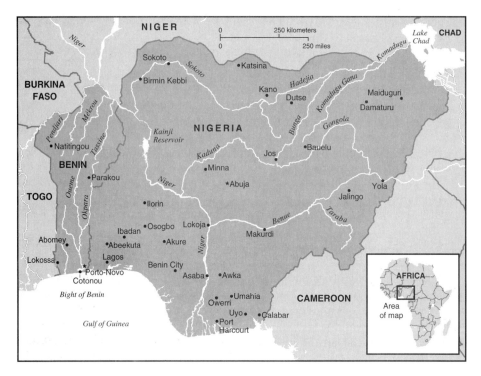

MAP 4.3 Benin and Nigeria. Yoruba territory covers much of Nigeria and Benin and has done so for a millennium.

the warrior, Oranmiyan, and the creator of dry land and shaper of infants in the womb, Obatala. Most active and important of the *orishas,* Orunmila is the eldest son of the sky-father and, by reading palm nuts and cowries, communicates Olorun's irreversible intentions. Orunmila, therefore, personifies fate. His close friend, Eshu, on the other hand, embodies uncertainty and accident. In the stories that follow, Orunmila behaves as a typical divine son, communicating and administering the will of his heavenly father. While the sky-father has excused himself from mundane affairs, his eldest son administers the divine and human orders through wisdom, generosity, and truthfulness.

Numerous *orishas* were living on the earth, but they did not yet have all the powers for which they are now known. When knowledge was needed to accomplish an important thing, the *orishas,* like ordinary men, appealed to Olorun or to Orunmila for help. But one day the *orisha* called Oko thought, "Here I am, living among humans. But what distinguishes me? If the people need something they go to Orunmila for it. If I need something I also must go to Orunmila. Why should this be? If I had the knowledge of a certain thing people could call on me for help, and they would not have to importune Orunmila."

Orisha-Oko went to where Orunmila was living on earth. He said, "I have no powers that distinguish me from the humans created by Obatala. You, Orunmila, who are spokesman for Olorun on earth, endow me with some special attribute. If this is done people can appeal to me for help in many things."

Orunmila pondered on what Orisha-Oko was asking. He said, "Yes, perhaps there is reason in it. Let me consider the matter." Orisha-Oko departed.

Now, the *orisha* called Ogun was thinking similar thoughts. "Am I not an *orisha?* I should have special powers greater than those of humans." He also went to where Orunmila was living. He said, "Whenever some important thing is required by the people they come to you. Their demands are heavy. It is Orunmila this and Orunmila that. Give me special knowledge of some kind so that I can do something to keep the world going."

Orunmila answered, "Yes, I have been thinking about it. I will see what can be done."

The minds of the other *orishas* turned the same way. Eshu, who already had the knowledge of language, went to Orunmila seeking more knowledge. Shango went to Orunmila, Sonponno went to Orunmila, Olu-Igbo went to Orunmila, Osanyin went to Orunmila. And after them still more *orishas* went, all asking for a special gift of some part of Orunmila's understanding of the world and its forces.

Orunmila was distressed. He thought, "I hold all the *orishas* equal in my affection. If I give anything to one of them the others will surely complain that I denied something to them and they will hold it against me. There are many powers to be shared. To whom should I give one power or another?"

Because the matter weighed heavily on him, Orunmila hardly touched his food. He could not sleep at night. His wives and servants worried about him. Orunmila took to walking by himself in the open country and pondering the question of how he might divide the powers among the *orishas*. He was walking in the fields this way one time when he met Agemo, the chameleon.

Agemo said to him, "You, Orunmila, spokesman for Olorun on earth, why are you so heavy with care?"

Orunmila answered, "One by one the *orishas* come to me, saying, 'Give me a special power so that I can relieve you of some of your burdens.' But there are so many powers, some great, some small. If I give something small it will be held against me. If I give something large to one, the others will resent it. I want to treat all the *orishas* equally. How can I do it so there will be harmony instead of dissension?"

Agemo said, "Perhaps it would be best to leave the distribution to chance. Return to the sky. Then send messengers to announce that on such and such a day you will pour the powers down on the earth. Let each *orisha* catch what he can or retrieve it from the place where it falls. Whatever powers an *orisha* collects in this way will be his. By sending your messengers you will have given everyone equal notice, and no one can say, 'Orunmila has neglected me.'"

On hearing Agemo's advice, Orunmila's mind rested, for now he saw how it could be done. He said, "Agemo, though you are small your name will be great. I will share out the powers and the knowledge by raining them on the earth."

Orunmila returned to the sky and prepared things. Then he sent messengers down to the places where the *orishas* lived. The messengers went from the house of one *orisha* to another. They said, "Orunmila has instructed us to announce that he will dispense the powers from the sky. On the fifth day following this one you are to go out into the open fields and wait. Orunmila will scatter the things you want. They will fall here, there and anywhere. Grasp what you can as it falls or retrieve it from the ground. One of you will acquire one thing, others will acquire others. In this way the special knowledge will be distributed, and no one can say Orunmila prefers one *orisha* over another."

The *orishas* said, "Orunmila does a good thing. Thank him for us. We will receive what he rains down on us."

On the fifth day they went into the open fields and waited. Then the powers began to fall from the sky. The *orishas* ran here and there with their hands outstretched. One *orisha* caught one thing, another caught another. Some of the powers eluded their hands and fell in the tall grass or among the trees. The *orishas* went searching in all directions. Now, some *orishas* were fleet while some were not. Some were more agile or stronger than others. Those who were swifter, or stronger or more persistent were able to get larger or more desirable portions of what Orunmila was bestowing. But everyone received something.

Because Eshu was one of the strongest, and because he did not hesitate to push anyone aside, he gathered a very large share of the powers, one of which was the capability of destroying anyone who offended him. He acquired the power of phallic strength and the power to deprive his enemies of their virility. He received the power of turning men back from their purposes and of turning order into disorder. And all these things were in addition to the power of language that he already possessed. Because of all these attributes possessed by Eshu, *orishas* and humans thereafter treated him with special respect and sought to avoid his enmity.

The *orisha* Shango, through what he picked up in the fields, became the owner of the lightning bolt, and therefore he acquired the name Jakuta, the Stone Thrower. Later, when he became the ruler of the city of Oyo, he was called Oba Jakuta. Orisha-Oko received the power to make crops flourish, and human beings supplicated him to make their yams and grain grow. Sonponno became the owner of smallpox, and both *orishas* and humans dreaded his power. Osanyin acquired special knowledge of curing and divining, and Olu-Igbo became the *orisha* of the bush country and the forest. Each *orisha* received something.

This is how the *orishas* who went to live on earth came by their special attributes.

THE FRIENDSHIP OF ESHU AND ORUNMILA

How can it be explained that Orunmila, the eldest son of the Sky God, was a warm friend to Eshu, who continually plagued both *orishas* and humans with disorder and disruption? For they were opposite to each other in many ways. Orunmila brought the knowledge of the Sky God to humans, while Eshu carried the words of humans to the Sky God. Orunmila's character was calm, while Eshu's was like a hot fire. Through the use of divining shells, Orunmila conveyed to men the intentions of the supreme God Olorun and the meanings of fate. But Eshu strove to turn Olorun's meanings aside, so that events would take an unintended course. Orunmila smoothed the road for humans, while Eshu lurked on the highway and made all things uncertain. Orunmila's character was destiny, and Eshu's character was accident. Yet these two *orishas* were in friendship, and this is how it came to be so.

It is said that Orunmila was on a journey with some traveling companions. They were still some distance from home. His companions were carrying nothing, but Orunmila carried the bag in which he kept his divining tray, his divining cup and the palm nuts with which he read the future. Those who traveled with Orunmila envied his knowledge of divining and wished nothing more than to possess the bag that contained the knowledge.

One of his companions said, "Orunmila, you must be tired. Let me carry your divining bag."

Another said, "On the contrary, it is I who should carry the bag for Orunmila."

They argued over who should carry the divining bag. But at last Orunmila said, "No, let us end it. I am not tired. It is only proper that I should carry the divining bag."

When Orunmila arrived at his home he pondered on the incident, wondering who among his companions was truly a friend and who was not. He thought of a plan that would reveal what he wanted to know. He sent out messengers with the word that he had died. Then he hid behind his house where he could not be seen. There he waited.

After a while one of his companions came from another village to express his sorrow. He said to Orunmila's wife, "Where is the body of my good friend Orunmila?"

Orunmila's wife answered, as she had been instructed, "It is already buried."

The man said, "Yes, his death is painful to me. Orunmila and I were the closest of friends. Many times I gave him money and refused to let him repay me. However, he said that when he died he would leave me his divining nuts, his tray and all the secrets of his profession."

"It appears that you were indeed one of his best friends," Orunmila's wife said. "But misfortune! His divining bag has disappeared."

The man went away disappointed. Another man came crying out, "Orunmila, my best friend, why have you died like this? Nevertheless, do not worry about your divining bag and all it contains, for I shall take the greatest care of it."

Orunmila's wife said, "It would be good if you could take care of it. But an unfortunate thing has happened. The bag cannot be found. It is said that he felt death coming to him and that he sent his things to Olorun the Sky God from whom he received the knowledge of divining."

Another man came, saying that Orunmila had promised to give him all the paraphernalia for divining the truth of life. Everyone who came asked for these things.

At last Eshu arrived. He said, "What comfort is there for one who has lost a friend? I walk on Orunmila's path, I sit in his house, but Orunmila is not here and I know I will not see him again. For you, his wife, the sorrow is surely greater. Each day you prepared his food you said to yourself, 'This is the food of Orunmila.' Now what can you say? Only, 'Once I cooked the food of Orunmila, but now he is gone.'"

Orunmila's wife answered, "Yes, the sorrow is great. But you were his companion in life. Did he owe you money? Did he promise to leave you an inheritance? If he did, I will pay it for him."

Eshu said, "No, he owed me nothing and promised me nothing. On the contrary, it was I who owed money to Orunmila. After I return to my home I will send it, even though it is too late for him to receive it in his own hand. It was not I who was generous with Orunmila, it was he who was generous with me."

Orunmila's wife persisted. She said, "But surely he must have promised to leave something for you. Perhaps his divining tray and the sacred palm nuts through which the purposes of Olorun can be told?"

"No," Eshu said, "for he was too wise to do such a thing. The secret of life is not in the palm nuts, but in the mind of Orunmila himself."

And now Orunmila left his hiding place behind the house and entered the room, saying, "You, Eshu, are my true friend."

So it came to be said thereafter, "No friends can be closer than Orunmila and Eshu."

Thor's Duel with Hrungnir

Norse (Iceland)

Norse cosmology envisioned the universe as a three-part structure that might have resembled three stacked plates with space between each dish. The top level was Asgard, home of the Vanir (fertility gods), Aesir (the warrior gods), and the light elves. In addition, Asgard contained Valhalla, the hall of dead warriors legendary for their valor who Odin and the Valkyrie deemed worthy to continue fighting and feasting in their presence until the end of time, and Vigrid, the vast plain upon which the world-ending battle of Ragnarok will eventually be fought. The middle "plate," or Midgard, was the home of men and the location of Utgard, the "out-world" fortress of the Giants. Midgard was believed to be surrounded by an ocean so vast that only Norsemen were brave enough to cross it; in its depths lay Jormungand, the terrifying serpent encircling the world and biting his own tail. At the northernmost reaches of Midgard were to be found Nidavellir, the Dark Home of the Dwarves, and Svartalfheim, the Land of the Dark Elves. Only the rainbow bridge Bifrost, or "trembling road," con-

Source: "Thor's Duel with Hrungnir," from *The Norse Myths* by Kevin Crossley-Holland, copyright © 1980 by Kevin Crossley-Holland. Used by permission of Pantheon Books, a division of Random House, Inc.

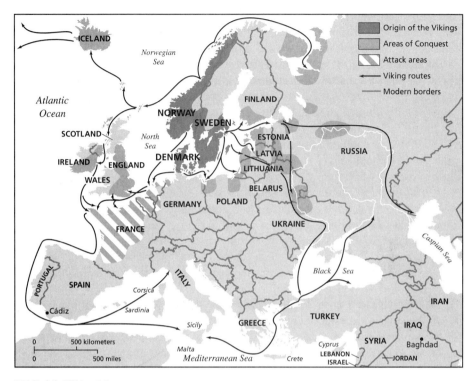

MAP 4.4 Viking Map

nected "middle earth" with Asgard. On the third and lowest level lay the perpetually dark and frozen land of the dead, Nifleheim, which was nine days' ride downward from Asgard. Its capital city was Hel, its citizens closely guarded by the half-corpse, half-living female monster of the same name.

In the following story, Odin's natural love of battle and bloodshed have made him restless. While his son has yet again left his realm, Thrudheim, to crush the skulls of trolls and troll-wives with his mighty hammer, Mjollnir, the father of gods, rests and rusts in Valhalla. Eventually Odin rides to Jotunheim, the land of the giants, knowing full well that he'll be able to pick a fight there. This tale demonstrates rather starkly the typical relationship between the heavenly father and his divine son. Although Odin lures Hrungnir, the greatest of the giants, into Valhalla, he seems unwilling or unable to destroy him. Instead, he sends for his son, who will be able not only to kill the giant but to do so with honor.

Odin, god of gods, was not content with being able to see everything that happened in the nine worlds. He was not content even with being able to understand all that he saw. His blood raced and he longed to test life's winds and tides for himself.

While Thor was away fighting trolls and troll women and their wolfchildren in Iron Wood, Odin bridled at his own lack of action. He became so restless that he donned his golden helmet and leaped on to Sleipnir, hungry for some happening.

Sleipnir vaulted the torrent Thund beside Valhalla and then the old river that snaked through a canyon; he spring-heeled over the broad gleaming river and the river teeming with spears, and his eight hooves clattered as he galloped over scree. For hour after hour Odin rode towards Jotunheim across utterly dreary country, at first flat and tussocky and pocked with small deserted lakes, then flat and stony—a sea of slabs where nothing lived and nothing grew. At last, where the land began to swell and in some places to smoke, leavened by fires far below the earth crust, Odin came to the hall of Hrungnir, strongest of all the giants.

"Who are you?" demanded Hrungnir.

The raider pulled his blue cloak close about him, tilted his wide-brimmed hat forward, and said nothing.

"I've been watching. I saw you coming, your gold helmet flashing under the sun. You seemed to be riding as much through the air as on the ground." Hrungnir rubbed his enormous nose. "That's an uncommonly fine horse you've got there."

"Better than any in Jotunheim," retorted Odin. "That's for sure."

"That's what you think," replied the giant.

"That's what I know," said Odin.

"What do you know of Jotunheim, little man?" said Hrungnir, his temper rising. "Don't be so certain."

"I'm certain enough to wager my head on it."

"You fool!" bellowed Hrungnir. "Have you never heard of Gold Mane?"

"Who?" said Odin.

"My horse!" shouted Hrungnir. "Gold Mane. Fast as your horse may be, Gold Mane will gallop him into the ground."

"Gab!" spat Odin. "All gab!"

"Gold Mane!" boomed Hrungnir, and his voice bounced back off the mountain wall.

"My head, Hrungnir," called Odin, spurring Sleipnir into a gallop. "Come and collect it!"

By the time Hrungnir had sprung on to Gold Mane the Helmeted One was already on the other side of the smoking hill. The god and the giant raced across the flatlands and neither gained ground on the other; they raced into the uplands, and Hrungnir had no thought for anything but the chase; they crossed the nineteen rivers and before the thick-headed giant had taken stock of where he was, he found himself inside the walls of Asgard. Then at last he realized who his visitor had been.

Odin was waiting for Hrungnir beside Valgrind, the outer gate of Valhalla. "That's an uncommonly fine horse you've got there," he said.

Hrungnir glared at Odin, angry but unable now to do anything about it.

"You must be thirsty after such exertion," Odin said. "Let Gold Mane drink from this torrent Thund. And you, Hrungnir, come and drink in Valhalla."

Odin led the way in under the roof of shields and spears, and his wolves Freki and Geri at once got up and loped towards him. Ranks of warriors filled the benches, feasting and drinking after the day's slaughter, and when they saw the giant, they began to shout. It was an awesome noise, as if the sea itself were caught in the mighty hall and waves were breaking on a strand of stones.

The Father of Battle raised one hand and as the clamor began to die down he called out, "Hrungnir comes unarmed. He comes in peace."

"How can I drink," said Hrungnir, "without a horn in my hands?"

Then the Valkyries Axe Time and Raging brought out the two massive horns from which Thor was used to drink. Both were brimming with ale.

"Drink!" said Odin. "Test your thirst against our finest trenchermen."

All the company in Valhalla watched as Hrungnir tossed off one horn without taking a breath, and then did the same with the other—such a tide of ale that even Thor might have had trouble with it. It was not long before the giant began to feel the effects. "I will!" he shouted suddenly.

Odin looked at Hrungnir and his one eye glittered. "Surely not," he murmured.

"I will," the giant shouted again. He waved his arms and, thrusting his head forward, glared at Odin. "I'll pick up this piffling hall and carry it home to Jotunheim."

The warriors sitting at the benches roared with laughter. Hrungnir swung round to face them. He meant to take steps towards them, but his balance was wrong and he reeled sideways. "I'm going to shink Ashgard in the shea," he bellowed.

Odin folded his arms. His mask-like face hid his thoughts. After a while he asked rather casually, "Then what is to become of us?"

"You," shouted Hrungnir. "I'm going to kill you, you gods and warriors. Shmash you!" The giant brought his fist down on a trestle table; its end leaped up and the table danced and fell flat on its face.

There was not so much noise in the hall then. Everyone was watching Hrungnir. "All except you two," said the giant, pointing at Freyja and Sif, fairest of the goddesses. "I'll take you back with me. I can find a use for you."

Odin nodded and Freyja sidled forward. As she moved, all the jewels she was wearing flashed and glimmered, and Hrungnir tried to rub the stars out of his eyes. "Drink again," said Freyja. She poured a lot more ale into one of the horns.

"Is jat all the ale in thish hall?" demanded the giant. "I'll drink every drop of ale in Ashgard."

But although the giant drank more and more, he did not fall into a stupor as Freyja had planned; he simply assaulted the company with a stream of boasts. The gods and warriors soon became tired of them and Odin sent a messenger to find Thor in Iron Wood and ask him to return to Asgard at once.

It was not at all long before Thor burst into the hall, swinging his hammer. "What's this?" he shouted. "What next?" No one had seen him more angry, even when Loki had cut off Sif's hair. "What next when sly devils of giants can hope to drink in Valhalla?"

Hrungnir looked at Thor blearily, and hiccuped.

"Who says you can drink here?" demanded Thor. "And why is Freyja waiting on you? Is this a feast in honor of the giants?"

The giant waved an arm in the direction of Odin. "His shafe conjuct," he burbled. "Ojin, he invited me in."

"Easier to get in than out," said Thor, tightening his hold on his hammer and raising it again.

"If you kill me unarmed," said the giant, "it won't add much to your fame—except for foul play." Drunk as he was, he well understood he still had to escape from Valhalla unscathed and he knew, too, what would touch Thor most closely. "It would be a better tesht," he began, "a much better tesht of your bravery."

"What?" said Thor.

"If you dared fight me."

"Dared," repeated Thor between his teeth.

"I challenge you to meet me," said Hrungnir. "On the borders of Jotunheim and Ashgard. We'll fight at Grjotunagardar, the Stone Fence House."

Thor looked at the giant and saw that he was in earnest.

"What a great fool I am to have left my hone and shield at home," said Hrungnir. "If I had my weapons, we could shettle the matter here and now. But if you mean to kill me unarmed, you're a coward."

No one had dared challenge Thor to a duel before and the Thunder God was eager to accept. "You can count on it," he told the giant. "I do not break faith. Do not break faith with me."

Then Hrungnir barged out of Valhalla without a backward look. He heaved himself on to Gold Mane's back and galloped away to Jotunheim as fast as he could.

When the giants heard about Hrungnir's journey to Valhalla and his forthcoming duel with Thor, they thought he had won great honor. "And," they said, "you have won the first part of a famous victory." But for all that the giants were uneasy and anxious. They knew that if Hrungnir lost the duel, and was killed, that would be a bad hour for Jotunheim. "If you do not win," they said, "what can we expect? You're the strongest of us all."

At Grjotunagardar there was a river with a bed of clay.

"Let us dredge it," said the giants. "Let us mould a man so vast that Thor will shake at the sight of him."

Then the giants worked night and day and piled up the clay and made a mountain of a man: he was nine leagues high, and measured three leagues across the chest from armpit to armpit.

"He may be so tall that the clouds gather round his head," said the giants, "but he is nothing but clay. What are we going to do about his heart?"

The giants were quite unable to find a heart anything like large enough. In the end they killed a mare and put her heart into his body. Its pump was enough to give the clay life, but rather too unsteady to inspire much confidence. They called this clay giant Mist Calf, and told him to wait by Grjotunagardar.

On the appointed day Hrungnir headed for the Stone Fence House. And unlike Mist Calf, his heart gave others heart. It was made of unyielding stone, sharp-edged and three-cornered. Hrungnir's head was made of stone, too, and so was the great shield he held in front of him as he waited for Thor. With his other hand, he grasped a huge hone; he shouldered it and was ready to hurl it. Hrungnir looked very nasty and very dangerous.

Then Thor, the Son of Earth, angrily sprang into his chariot and Thialfi leaped in beside him. It rocked beneath them. The Charioteer bawled and at once his two goats strained at their harnesses; the chariot rattled out of Thrudvang. The moon's path quivered and echoed. Lightning flared and flashed and men on middle earth thought the world itself was about to catch fire. Then hail lashed the ground; it smashed frail stooks and flattened fields of grass and men quailed within their walls. Headlands were shaken by such storms that gullies and rifts and gashes and chasms opened underfoot, and rocks and boulders cascaded into the curdling sea.

They rolled into Jotunheim towards Grjotunagardar. Then Thialfi jumped out of the chariot and ran ahead of it until he could see Hrungnir and Mist Calf. They stood side by side, and Mist Calf's heart thumped inside him.

"Thor can see you," shouted Thialfi. "Can you hear me? Thor can see you with your shield raised before you." Thialfi cupped his hands to his mouth. "Can you hear me, Hrungnir? Put it on the ground. Stand by your shield. Thor will come at you from below."

Then Hrungnir laid his stone shield on the ground and stood on it; he grasped his hone with both hands.

The moment he saw Hrungnir standing at the Stone Fence House, Thor brandished his hammer and hurled it at him. The giant was assaulted by blinding forked flashes and claps of thunder.

Hrungnir saw the hammer flying towards him. He drew back his hone and aimed it straight at Mjollnir. The hammer and the hone met in mid-air with a dazzling flash, followed by a crack that was heard through the nine worlds. The hone was smashed into hundreds of fragments.

The shrapnel flew in every direction. One piece flew to Midgard and splintered again as it crashed into the ground—and every bit is a whetstone quarry. Another piece whistled through the air and lodged in Thor's head. The strongest of all the gods was badly wounded. He fell out of his chariot, and his blood streamed over the earth. But Thor's hammer found its target. Despite the hone, Mjollnir still struck Hrungnir on his forehead and crushed his skull. The giant tottered and fell. One of his massive legs pinned Thor down by the neck.

When Mist Calf saw Thor, he was terrified; he sprang a leak and peed uncontrollably. Then Thialfi swung his axe and attacked Mist Calf, the giant with feet of clay. Thialfi hacked at his legs and Mist Calf did not have enough strength in his body to fight back. He lurched and toppled backwards, and his fall shook Jotunheim. Every giant heard him fall; they knew what had happened at the Stone Fence House.

"My head!" growled Thor.

Thialfi inspected the piece of whetstone stuck in Thor's head.

"It's in better shape than Hrungnir's head," said Thialfi. He seized the giant's leg and tried to lift it and release Thor. But for Thialfi it was like trying to lift the trunk of a tree; he was unable to move it an inch.

"Get help," said Thor.

Thialfi put his fleetness of foot to good use. It was not at all long before many of the gods hurried out of Asgard and came to Grjotunagardar, rejoicing at Thor's great victory and anxious to release him. One by one the strongest of the gods tried to lift the giant's leg but none of them—not even Odin himself—was able to do anything about it.

The last to reach Stone Fence House was Magni, the son of Thor and the giantess Jarnsaxa. He was three years old. When he saw how the gods were unable to release his father, he said, "Now let me try!" Magni stooped, grasped Hrungnir by the heel, and swung the giant's foot away from his father's neck.

All the gods cried out in wonder and Thor quickly got to his feet.

"It's a pity I didn't come sooner," said Magni. "If I had met this giant, I'd have struck him dead with my bare fist."

"If you go on as you've begun," said Thor warmly, clamping an iron-gloved hand on to his son's shoulder, "you'll become quite strong."

"My mother is Iron Cutlass," Magni said. "And I am the son of Thunder."

"What's more," said Thor, "I'm going to give you Gold Mane. Take Hrungnir's horse as a reward."

"No," said Odin sharply. "You shouldn't give such an uncommonly fine horse to the son of a giantess instead of to your own father."

Thor took no notice. He clapped his hands to his banging head and rode back to Asgard, followed by the Aesir. Only Odin complained; the other gods gave thanks that good had prevailed over evil and that they seemed quite safe again, as safe as they had ever been.

When Thor got to Thrudvang, and walked into his own hall Bilskirnir, the whetstone was still stuck in his head. So he sent to Midgard for the sybil Groa, the wife of Aurvandil the Brave. The wise woman hurried up over Bifrost and all night she chanted magic words over Thor—charms and spells known only to her. As she sang, the hone began to work loose, and the hammering in Thor's head began to fade. It seemed less like pain than the memory of pain.

Thor was so thankful that he wanted to make Groa happy. "I have a surprise for you," he said.

"Nothing could surprise me," said Groa.

"This will," said Thor. "Not long ago I was in the north and I met your husband, Aurvandil the Brave."

Groa stiffened. Then she began to shake her head sadly.

"You may think he's dead," said Thor, "but I brought him out of Jotunheim. I waded across the streams of venom, Elivagar, carrying him in a basket strapped on to my back."

"Stuff!" said Groa gruffly, not because she wanted to disbelieve Thor but because she did not dare to believe him.

"Do you need proof?" asked Thor.

"Yes," said Groa.

"All night you've sung charms over my head," said Thor, "and it is almost morning. Come with me." The Thunder God led the way out of Bilskirnir into the silent courtyard. "Look!" said Thor, pointing into the sky. "Have you ever seen that star?"

Groa frowned and shook her head.

Thor smiled faintly. "One of Aurvandil's toes stuck out of the basket, and froze. So I broke it off and hurled it into heaven. Now and always that star will be known as Aurvandil's Toe."

Groa's heart was pounding; her eyes shone with tears of joy.

"Now are you satisfied" said Thor. "And I'll tell you one thing more. It won't be long at all now before your husband gets home."

Groa felt as if nothing else in the world had ever mattered; and she felt as if there were no way in which she could properly thank Thor.

"Only finish your charms and spells," said Thor. "Then I too will be happy."

Groa looked at Thor and gaped.

"The charms," said Thor.

The sybil's head and heart whirled and her blood raced round her body. She was so excited that she could not recall a single charm.

"Think, woman!" said Thor fretfully.

Groa buried her face in her hands but it was no good.

"Think, woman, think!" roared Thor. His eyes blazed and his red beard bristled.

But Groa was able to think only of her husband Aurvandil's homecoming, and of a shining star. Thor sent her packing with a bellow of fury. And that is why the whetstone remained in Thor's head.

Quetzalcoatl Rescues the Precious Bones and Discovers Corn

Aztec (Mexico)

When Hernán Cortés arrived in northern Mexico in the early 16th century, he encountered a nation of fierce warriors and skilled builders whose empire was surpassed in size in the Americas only by that of the Incas in Peru. Modern archaeology has revealed that the Mexica or Tenochca, as the Aztecs called themselves, had developed a highly specialized and stratified society and an imperial administration that were no less complex than those of Europe. Their trading network and tribute system made them rich and there is evidence that their agricultural economy flourished under skilled management. Despite the fact that their religious practices frequently demanded bloodletting and human sacrifice, it is clear that they valued human life, perceiving human society to be a necessary and integral part of the cosmic order and divine plan. Like most cultures in the Americas, Aztec myth suggests that the creation of the world remained incomplete without human inhabitants in place to establish and preserve order through religious observances and cultivation of the land.

According to their traditions, the Aztec originated upon an island called Aztlan, somewhere in north or northwest Mexico. Here they went about in boats and fished the reedy waters of the surrounding lagoon. But, though they remembered their ancestral

Source: Excerpts from *Native MesoAmerican Spirituality: Ancient Myths, Discourses, Stories, Doctrines, Hymns, Poems from the Aztec, Yucatec, Quiche-Maya, and Other Sacred Stories.* Translated by Miguel Leon-Portilla, J. O., Arthur Anderson, Charles E. Dibble, and Munro S. Edmonson. 1980. Used with permission of Paulist Press. www.paulistpress.com.

MAP 4.5 Central America

homeland with nostalgia and longed to return to it, the Mexica left Aztlan, descending from the north upon the more advanced civilizations of Mexico. In some mythic records, the tribe's fierce war-god and patron deity, Huitzilopochtli, "Blue Hummingbird from the Left," inspired the Aztecs to set out on their great migration. Some accounts suggest a rather sensational trail of conquest, culminating in the founding of the empire bearing their name. But, the archaeological record shows, at the time of their migration sometime in the 12th century, the Aztecs were a small, nomadic, Nahuatl-speaking confederacy of tribal peoples on the outskirts of civilized Mesoamerica. After about a century of being driven to and fro by various warring factions among the nations already living there, the Aztecs finally found refuge on small islands in Lake Texcoco where, in 1325, they founded the town of Tenochtitlán (modern-day Mexico City).

The Mexica creation myth shares much in common with the Quiché Maya's story in Chapter 2. Both stories feature a primordial "Lord of Duality" who is both male and female and who activates the principles of the cosmic order embodied in the luminous deities sleeping within the primal deep. Both stories recount a series of failed attempts by the recently awakened gods to create beings intelligent enough to participate in the social and religious rituals necessary to the sustenance and stability of the newly created universe. In the Mayan story, the gods finally arrive on the perfect material from which to form human flesh and to generate human consciousness—maize!

The Mexica account, however, tells of Quetzalcoatl, the Great Plumed Serpent, and his brave decent into the Mictlan, the "Place of the Dead." There he demands of Mictlantecuhtli and Mictlancihuatl, the Lord and Lady of the Dead, respectively, the "precious bones" necessary to creating human life on earth. The Lord of the Dead agrees to give these bones to Quetzalcoatl but, in the miserly fashion of other gods of the dead, he immediately reneges, using various tricks to prevent the success of his mission. Quetzalcoatl then conspires with his *nahual,* an alter ego symbolized by an animal that has some association with the character of a person or god, to trick Mictlantecuhtli. After he has successfully brought the precious bones to Tamoanchan (another name for the place of origins), the gods search among themselves for food to sustain the newly created beings. Quetzalcoatl again volunteers and successfully finds and brings corn to Tamoanchan.

The Great Plumed Serpent and several of the other gods "do penance" by bleeding their male organs—a ritual depicted in several surviving relief carvings. Apparently, those doing penance would run cords through piercings in their tongues or penises, the blood from these wounds draining into sacred offertory vessels. In Aztec religion, blood and even beating human hearts were necessary offerings, especially to the gods of sun and rain: an offering of life in hopes of receiving life in return. As the narrator piously announces, "And thus we mortals owe our life to penance, because for our sake the gods did penance." Once this penance is done, the first human couple, Oxomoco and Cipactonal, draw lots, apparently as a way of determining how the sustaining power of corn could be continued. The story ends mysteriously with rain gods from the four directions stealing the corn and the narrator lamenting "from us our sustenance was stolen." Perhaps, embedded in this final scene is a recognition that the people will have corn only when and if the rains bring it.

And as soon as the gods came together they said: "Who shall live on the earth? The sky has already been established, and the earth has been established. But who shall live on the earth, O gods?"

Citlalinicue, Citlaltonac, Apantecuhtili, Tepanquizqui, Quetzalcoatl, and Tezcatlipoca were grieved. Then Quetzalcoatl went to Mictlan; he approached Mictlantecuhtli and Mictlancihuatl and immediately said to them: "I have come for the precious bones that you keep here. I have come to take them."

And Mictlantecuhtli said to him: "What would you do with them, Quetzal-coatl?"

And Quetzalcoatl answered him: "The gods are concerned that someone shall live on the earth." And Mictlantecuhtli replied: "Very well. Sound my conch shell and go four times around my domain."

But the conch shell had no holes; therefore Quetzalcoatl called the worms; they made holes in it and then the bees and hornets went inside and made it sound. On hearing it sound, Mictlantecuhtli said again: "Very well. Take the bones." But Mictlantecuhtli said to those who served him: "People of Mictlan! Oh gods, tell Quetzalcoatl he must not take them."

Quetzalcoatl replied: "Indeed, yes, I take possession of them." And he said to his *nahual* [alter ego], "You go and tell Mictlantecuhtli I will not take them." And his *nahual* said loudly, "I will not take them."

But then Quetzalcoatl went, he gathered up the precious bones. The bones of the man were together on one side and the bones of the woman together on the other side and Quetzalcoatl took them and made a bundle. Again Mictlantecuhtli said to those who served him: "Gods, is Quetzalcoatl really carrying away the precious bones? Gods, go and dig a big hole."

They went and dug it. And Quetzalcoatl stumbled, frightened by quail, and fell into the hole. He fell down as if dead and the precious bones were scattered, so that the quail chewed and gnawed upon them. After a while Quetzalcoatl was revived; he was grieved, and he said to his *nahual:* "What shall I do now?"

His *nahual* answered him: "Although the affair has started badly, let it continue as best it may."

Quetzalcoatl gathered up the bones, put them together, made again a bundle, and carried them to Tamoanchan. As soon as he arrived, the goddess called Qui-laztli, also called Cihuacoatl, ground them up and put them in a fine earthen tub. Quetzalcoatl bled his male organ on them. And immediately the gods named Apan-tecuhtili, Huictolinqui, Tepanquizqui, Tlallamanac, Tzontemoc, and the sixth, Quet-zalcoatl, all did penance. And they said: "Oh gods, the *macehuales* are born."

And thus we mortals owe our life to penance, because for our sake the gods did penance.

Once more the gods said: "What shall they eat, O gods? Let our sustenance, corn, come down. And then the ant went to gather shelled corn from within the Mountain of our sustenance. Quetzalcoatl went to meet the ant. He asked her: "Where did you go to gather it? Tell me!"

But she does not want to tell him. Quetzalcoatl insisted on asking. Then she said: "It is there!" Whereupon she led him.

Promptly Quetzalcoatl changed himself into a black ant. Then she guided him, and thus introduced him. Together they came to enter. It is said that the red ant guided Quetzalcoatl to the foot of the Mountain where they placed the corn. Then Quetzalcoatl carried it on his back, to Tamoanchan.

Whereupon, from it, the gods ate and ate and later they put it into our mouths so that we might become strong. And then they said: "What shall we do with the Mount of our sustenance? For now it will only remain where it is."

Quetzalcoatl pulled at it, but he could not move it. Then Oxomoco drew lots, and likewise Cipactonal, the wife of Oxomoco, drew lots. (For Cipactonal is a woman.) Oxomoco and Cipactonal said: "If only Nanahuac will send a bolt of lightning to the Mount of our sustenance, because we drew lots."

Then the gods of rain were summoned, the blue-green gods of rain, the white gods of rain, the yellow gods of rain, the red gods of rain. At once Nanahuac sent a lightning bolt. Then our sustenance was stolen by the gods of rain. White, dark, yellow, red corn, beans, blades, amaranth, from us our sustenance was stolen.

WORKS CITED AND SUGGESTIONS
FOR FURTHER READING

Ajayi, J. F. A., and Michael Crowder, eds. *History of West Africa.* New York: Columbia University Press, 1976.

Aquinas, Thomas, Saint. *Summa Theologica.* Trans. Fr. Laurence Shapcote. Chicago: Encyclopædia Britannica, 1990.

Atta, Fariduddin. *Memoirs of the Saints.* Trans. Bankey Behari. Lahore, Pakistan: Sh. Muhammad Ashraf, 1965.

Augustine, Saint, Bishop of Hippo. *The City of God.* Trans. Marcus Dodds. New York: Modern Library, 2000.

———. *Confessions: A New Translation.* Trans. Rex Warner. New York: New American Library, 1963.

Bancroft-Hunt, Norman. *Gods and Myths of the Aztecs.* New York: Smithmark, 1996.

Black, Jeremy A., G. Cunningham, E. Fluckiger-Hawker, E. Robson, and G. Zólyomi. *The Electronic Text Corpus of Sumerian Literature* (http://www.etcsl.orient.ox.ac.uk/). Oxford, 1998–.

Black, Jeremy A., and Anthony Green. *Gods, Demons, and Symbols of Ancient Mesopotamia: An Illustrated Dictionary.* Austin: University of Texas Press, 1992.

Bolen, Jean Shinoda. *Gods in Everyman: A New Psychology of Men's Lives and Loves.* New York: HarperPerennial, 1989.

Boyce, Mary. *Zoroastrians: Their Religious Beliefs and Practices.* New York: Routledge, 2001.

Budge, Ernest Alfred Wallis. *The Book of the Dead: The Hieroglyphic Transcript and Translation into English of the Papyrus of Ani.* New York: Gramercy Books, 1999.

———. *The Gods of the Egyptians.* Vols. 1 and 2. New York: Dover, 1969.

Burland, Cottie Arthur. *North American Indian Mythology.* Rev. Marion Wood. New York: Barnes & Noble, 1985.

Campbell, C. G., trans. *Tales from the Arab Tribes: A Collection of the Stories Told by the Arab Tribes of the Lower Euphrates.* London: L. Drummond, 1949.

Conkey, Margaret W., and Ruth E. Tringham. "Archaeology and the Goddess: Exploring the Contours of Feminist Archaeology." In *Feminisms in the Academy.* Donna C. Stanton and Abigail J. Stewart, eds. Ann Arbor: University of Michigan Press, 1995.

Courlander, Harold. *Tales of Yoruba Gods and Heroes.* New York: Crown, 1973.

Crossley-Holland, Kevin. *The Norse Myths.* New York: Pantheon, 1980.

Curran, Bob. *An Encyclopedia of Celtic Mythology.* Lincolnwood, IL: Contemporary Books, 2000.

Dobres, Marcia-Anne. "Reconsidering Venus Figurines: A Feminist-Inspired Re-Analysis." In *Ancient Images, Ancient Thought: The Archaeology of Ideology.* A. Sean Goldsmith, Sandra Garvie, David Selin, and Jeannette Smith, eds. Calgary, Alberta: Archaeological Association, 1992. 245–62.

Doniger, Wendy O'Flaherty. *Hindu Myths.* London: Penguin, 1975.

———. *Siva, The Erotic Ascetic: Asceticism and Eroticism in the Mythology of Siva.* New York: Oxford University Press, 1981.

Doty, William G. *Myths of Masculinity.* New York: Crossroads, 1993.

Downing, Christine. *Gods in Our Midst: Mythological Images of the Masculine: A Woman's View.* New York: Crossroads, 1993.

Dowson, J. *Classical Dictionary of Hindu Mythology.* London: Routledge and Kegan Paul, 1972.

Driver, Godfrey Rolles. *Canaanite Myths and Legends from Ugarit (Now Râs-as-Samrah).* Edinburgh: T & T Clark, 1976.

Eliade, Mircea. *Shamanism: Archaic Techniques of Ecstasy.* Trans. William R. Trask. Princeton, NJ: Princeton University Press, 1974.

Erdoes, Richard, and Alfonso Ortiz. *American Indian Myths and Legends.* New York: Pantheon, 1984.

Fadiman, James, and Robert Frager. *Essential Sufism.* Edison, NJ: Castle, 1997.

Ferguson, Diana. *Tales of the Plumed Serpent: Aztec, Inca and Mayan Myths.* London: Collins & Brown, 2000.

Gibson, John C. L. *Canaanite Myths and Legends.* Edinburgh: T & T Clark, 1978.

Gilson, Etienne. *The Philosophy of St. Thomas Aquinas.* Trans. Edward Bullogh. Ed. Rev. G. A. Erlington. New York: Barnes & Noble, 1993.

Gimbutas, Marija. *The Language of the Goddess:* Unearthing the Hidden Symbols of Western Civilization. New York: Thames and Hudson, 1989.

Grayson, James H. *Myths and Legends from Korea: An Annotated Compendium of Ancient and Modern Materials.* Richmond, Surrey: Curzon, 2001.

Kishlansky, Mark A., ed. *Sources of the West: Readings for Western Civilization.* New York: Longman, 1998.

Knappert, Jan. *Pacific Mythology: An Encyclopedia of Myth and Legend.* London: Diamond, 1995.

Kovacs, Maureen Gallery. *The Epic of Gilgamesh.* Stanford, CA: Stanford University Press, 1989.

Leeming, David, and Jake Page. *God: Myths of the Male Divine.* New York: Oxford University Press, 1996.

Léon-Portilla, Miguel. *The Aztec Image of Self and Society: An Introduction to Nahua Culture.* Ed. J. Jorge Klor de Alva. Salt Lake City: University of Utah Press, 1992.

Léon-Portilla, Miguel, ed. *Native Mesoamerican Spirituality: Ancient Myths, Discourses, Stories, Doctrines, Hymn, Poems from the Aztec, Yucatec, Quiché-Maya, and Other Sacred Stories.* Trans. Miguel Léon-Portilla, J. O., Arthur Anderson, Charles E. Dibble, and Munro S. Edmonson. New York: Paulist Press, 1980.

Lopez, Donald S., Jr., ed. *Religions of Tibet in Practice.* Princeton, NJ: Princeton University Press, 1997.

MacCana, Proinsias. *Celtic Mythology.* Feltham, England: Hamlyn, 1970.

Maimonides, Moses. *The Code of Maimonides: Mishneh Torah.* Trans. Jacob J. Rabinowitz. New Haven, CT: Yale University Press, 1949.

————. *The Guide for the Perplexed.* Trans. M. Friedlander. London: Routledge & Kegan Paul, 1956.

Markman, Roberta H., and Peter T. Markman. *The Flayed God: The Mesoamerican Mythological Tradition: Sacred Texts and Images from Pre-Columbian Mexico and Central America.* San Francisco: HarperCollins, 1992.

Miller, Barbara Stoler, trans. *The Bhagavad Gita: Krishna's Counsel in Time of War.* New York: Columbia University Press, 1986.

New American Standard Bible. La Habra, CA: Lockman Foundation, 1977.

The Old Rus' Kievan and Galician-Volhynian Chronicles: The Ostroz'kyj (Xlebnikov) and Cetvertyns'kyj (Pogodin) Codices. Omeljan Pritsak, ed. Cambridge, MA: Harvard University Press, 1990.

Ott, Jonathan. In "Shamanism." Available online: http://deoxy.org/shaman.htm. Retrieved on February 12, 2002.

Pearson, Carol S. *Awakening the Hero Within: Twelve Archetypes to Help Us Find Ourselves and Transform Our World.* New York: HarperCollins, 1991.

————. *The Hero Within: Six Archetypes We Live By.* San Francisco: Harper, 1986.

Pritchard, James B., ed. *Ancient Near Eastern Texts Relating to the Old Testament.* Princeton, NJ: Princeton University Press, 1969.

Riordan, James. *Tales from Central Russia.* New York: Viking, 1976.

Ripinsky-Naxon, Michael. *The Nature of Shamanism: Substance and Function of a Religious Metaphor.* Albany: State University of New York Press, 1993.

Sheub, Harold. *A Dictionary of African Mythology: The Mythmaker as Storyteller.* New York: Oxford University Press, 2000.

Snellgrove, David. *Indo-Tibetan Buddhism: Indian Buddhists and Their Tibetan Successors.* Boston: Shambala, 1987.

Taube, Karl A. *Aztec and Maya Myths.* Austin: University of Texas Press, 1995.

Thompson, Reginald Campbell. *Semitic Magic: Its Origins and Development.* New York: AMS Press, 1976.

————. "The Seven Evil Spirits." In *The Devils and Evil Spirits of Babylonia: Being Babylonian and Assyrian Incantations against the Demons, Ghouls, Vampires, Hobglobins, Ghosts, and Kindred Evil Spirits, Which Attack Mankind.* New York: AMS Press, 1976.

Thorpe, S. A. *Shamans, Medicine Men and Traditional Healers: A Comparative Study of Shamanism in Siberian Asia, Southern Africa and North America.* Pretoria: University of South Africa Press, 1993

Tucci, Giuseppe. *The Religions of Tibet.* Trans. Geoffrey Samuel. New York: Kegan Paul International, 2000.

Ucko, Peter J. *Anthropomorphic Figurines of Predynastic Egypt and Neolithic Crete with Comparative Material from the Prehistoric Near East and Mainland Greece.* London: A. Szmidla, 1968.

CHAPTER 5   Trickster Myths

THE EMBODIMENT OF AMBIGUITIES

The Trickster is alive and well. If, as we argue in this book, mythology is far more than the study of ancient stories that give us a window into the distant past, the Trickster is perhaps the most vital, most alive, even most recognizable (from our current points of view) *person* in the array of mythic characters. As Richard Erdoes and Alfonso Ortiz write in *American Indian Trickster Tales,*

> Of all the characters in myths and legends told around the world through the centuries— courageous heroes, scary monsters, rapturous virgins—it's the Trickster who provides the *real* spark in the action—always hungry for another meal swiped from someone else's kitchen, always ready to lure someone else's wife into bed, always trying to get something for nothing, shifting shapes (and even sex), getting caught in the act, ever scheming, never remorseful. (1998, xiii)

Erdoes and Ortiz may speak of the Trickster's "spark" in the sense of providing narrative energy, but we also think it fair to apply their comment to the audience's ability to enter into mythic narratives. The Trickster provides the *"real* spark" because it is in the Trickster figure—in all his complexities, all his contradictions— that we meet ourselves most directly in the mythic worlds that might otherwise seem so easily dismissed as "exotic" or "other" or "primitive." It is one thing to contemplate the actions of creator gods and goddesses shaping the cosmos or the earth and to speculate on the "meanings" of such stories in terms of various academic disciplines or theoretical concerns. It is quite another to see Coyote scheming to score a free meal or to convince an unwilling—or perhaps a very willing—female to share his amorous desires. The Trickster is myth come alive to meet us where we live.

Tricksters, moreover, are figures of play, albeit sometimes a rather rough sort of play. If we approach them in a spirit of play (as well as intellectual rigor), they are likely to reward us even through the process of pulling our legs. In approaching the Trickster, we might be wise to consider a cautionary tale that Barre Toelken offers in his introduction to Barry Lopez's retelling of Native American Trickster tales:

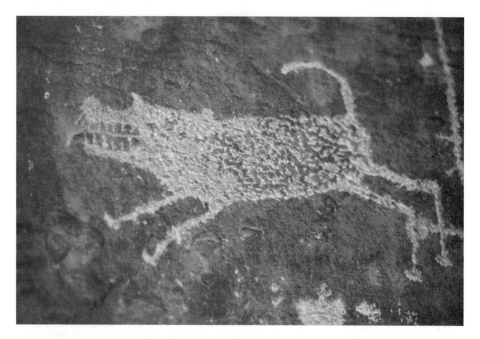

Image identified as Coyote from the Rochester Panel, Moore, Utah. Fremont culture, ca. 4000–3500 BCE.
Source: © Nolan Thomas Jones, Jr./Utah Photo Wild

On the Warm Springs Indian Reservation in central Oregon, some people tell a story about a wandering anthropologist who came across a coyote caught in a trap.

"Please let me out of this trap; if you do, I'll give you lots of money," the coyote said.

"Well, I'm not sure. Will you tell me a story, too?" asked the professor.

"Sure I will; I'll tell you a real true story, a real long one for your books."

So the anthropologist sprung the trap, collected a big handful of bills from the coyote, and then set up his tape machine. The coyote sat, rubbing his sore legs, and told a long story that lasted until the tape ran out. Then he ran off.

The anthropologist went home and told his wife about what happened, but she wouldn't believe him. When he reached in his pocket to show her the money, all he came out with was a handful of fur and dirt.

And when he went to play his tape for the other professors, all that was in the machine was a pile of coyote droppings. (1977, xi–xii)

Toelken argues that this story shows "several important aspects of Old Man Coyote: that he is alive and well in the modern world, that he has survived acculturation (and triumphed over it), that—in spite of tribal differences—there is a broadly recognizable cluster of characteristics we still know as his own" (1977, xii). In short, the Trickster lives—and he still has a lot to say to us, even if we ourselves don't come from a native culture. Yet, in light of the always contradictory nature of the Trickster and the stories about him, Toelken's tale also shows that if you try to capture Coyote or his stories with modern values and consciousness (money, tape machines, anthropological methodologies), all you'll end up with is "dirt" and humiliation—both personal (the anthropologist's wife) and professional (the other professors). Textbook writers and readers beware!

Toelken is not alone in presenting the Trickster as playing with our minds, crossing boundaries from "native" to "modern" worlds. Thomas King's novel *Green Grass, Running Water*, which, among many things, is about the problems of "native" and "modern" worlds coexisting in the contemporary United States, opens with a prologue that begins in a place readers familiar with the opening of Genesis will recognize: "So. In the beginning, there was nothing. Just the water" (1993, 1). King then continues to posit the entire world, the entire history of earth and all its cultures down through the ages culminating in our time and our social/political struggles, to be nothing but a figment of the Trickster's imagination. Even more, it is not just Coyote's creation, but actually the result of a dog in one of Coyote's dreams who gets everything backward and so—according to Coyote—imagines himself to be g-o-d. Our whole world, then, is the backward mess of a dog dream in the subconscious mind of, but not fully controlled by, the notorious mischiefmaker himself. You'd have to laugh in a world like that, even when disaster and heartache happen at every turn.

Peter Blue Cloud gives another quick vision of Trickster's unwillingness to stay safely in the confines of academic analyses in his short tale "Coyote's Anthro":

> The anthropologist was very excited. He'd just received his doctorate after having delivered his paper, entitled: The Mythology of Coyote: Trickster, Thief, Fool and Worldmaker's Helper. He was at this very moment in the process of gathering further data, working on a generous grant from a well-known Foundation. He'd just set up camp in the sagebrush not far from his latest informant's shack.
>
> Now he sat by his fire, looking at the stars and sipping coffee. He chuckled to himself when he heard a coyote bark not far away. He wondered what that coyote would think if the myths about him (or her) were read aloud?
>
> "Not much!" said a voice. The anthro was startled, he hadn't heard anyone approach. "Not much, maybe just a cup of coffee and some of that cake I see sitting there." Then into the campfire light stepped an old man, but not a man. He had long furry ears sticking thru his felt hat, and he had a long, bushy tail hanging from beneath his greatcoat. He leaned on his walking stick and grinned.
>
> Good God! The anthro was stunned: it was Coyote Old Man himself. But it couldn't be; he was a myth!
>
> "Not always," Coyote said.

After a bit more teasing conversation, Coyote offers to help the anthropologist:

> "I'm a doctor, you know. I'm here to help you. Now then, how can I help you?"
>
> "Well, actually, it's the stories I'm most concerned with. The reasons behind the seasons, if you follow me: interrelationships, the problem of special paradox, sexual taboos, those kinds of things. I want to create a whole fabric of thought, a complicated tapestry, no loose threads. Know what I mean?"
>
> "Parrot boxes, huh? Sex shell tables and followyouse: what's all that? That how you talk about pussy in college? You know, you sound like my tapeworm, and he never made any sense. How about just one question to begin with, huh?"
>
> "Well, let's start with the Creation myth, cutting to the core! What's the meat of it really, the true meaning?"

Source: "Coyote Anthro," from *Elderberry Flute Song*, by Peter Blue Cloud. © 1989 White Pine Press. Used with permission of the publisher.

"My friend," said Coyote, "If you think Creation's a myth, you just might be in serious trouble. It's not the learning that's important, but the leaning. You must lean toward your questions, your problems; lean slowly so that you don't bend the solution too badly out of shape." (1989)

While the Trickster is certainly a figure of playfulness, he is much more than that term would imply. He possesses a funny, absurd, iconoclastic sort of playfulness, yet the Trickster's playfulness can carry with it serious, even tragic or transcendent, overtones. Tricksters provide the comic relief in the world's mythologies, but they do so by embodying all the infinite ambiguities of what it is to be alive in the world. Tricksters are characters with attention deficit disorder, sacred clowns, carefree as children, obscene lechers, and generous companions. No single character type embodies so many, often contradictory, qualities. The Trickster is as likely to betray a friend as he is to set the stars in heaven or to become the victim of his own pranks. The Trickster appears in the mythologies of people from all continents. He is Loki, Reynard the Fox, and Hermes in Europe; Àjàpá and Anansi in Africa. Some African-American folktales, harkening back to African antecedents, call the Trickster Aunt Nancy. He is Pa Pandir in Malaysia, or Nasr-eddin in Turkey. To Native American cultures from Alaska to Florida, from Nova Scotia to Arizona, he is Raven, Mink, Rabbit, Spider-man, and Blue Jay to various tribes, but he is perhaps best known as Coyote.

According to Erdoes and Ortiz "Coyote [is] part human and part animal, taking whichever shape he pleases, [and he] combines in his nature the sacredness and sinfulness, grand gestures and pettiness, strength and weakness, joy and misery, heroism and cowardice that together form the human character" (1998, xiv). We can extend this observation about Coyote to include Tricksters generally. For, no matter where in the world we find this unique character, he persistently displays humanity's highest aspirations and our basest impulses—often in the same story.

This complexity of character—in actions, in motivations, and in results both intended and serendipitous—leads Lewis Hyde to comment in a footnote:

> Many, myself included, find the connotation of "Trickster" too limited for the scope of activities ascribed to this character. Some have tried to change the name (one writer uses Trickster-Transformer-Culture Hero which is apt but a touch unwieldy). Others stick to local names, complaining that the general term "Trickster" is an invention of nineteenth-century anthropology and not well fitted to its indigenous objects.
>
> This is partly true; indigenous terms doubtless allow a fuller feeling for the Trickster's sacred complexity. But his trickiness was hardly invented by ethnographers. Hermes is called *mechaniota* in Homeric Greek, which translates well as "Trickster." The West African Trickster Legba is also called *Aflakete,* which means "I have tricked you." The Winnebago Indian figure is called *Wakdjunkaga,* which means "the tricky one." Trickery appeared long before anthropology. (1998, 7)

Tricksters are more than representations of the illogic of a universe in which we simultaneously experience good and evil. They also act as moral examples—or, to put it more accurately, as moral *counterexamples.* Tricksters are frequently greedy and lazy, dishonest and gluttonous, vain and impulsive. Thus they can be seen as agents of chaos, for society provides the greatest advantages to the greatest number

Loki (?). Kirby Stephan, Westmorland, England, ca.
950–1050 CE. Numerous cross-shafts of the Jellinge
style (10th century) bear the image of a "bound Christ,"
but the "bound devil" pictured here is one of a kind.
Some have identified the tied figure as Loki, who would
have been equated with the devil as the Vikings were
gradually Christianized.
Source: © Werner Forman/Art Resource, NY

only if everyone restrains his or her impulses and cravings and makes allowances
for the needs of others. As members of society, we don't steal, or commit adultery,
or cheat, or lie, or do whatever we feel like whenever we please because to behave
selfishly rips the social fabric. Indeed, as our nightly newscasts confirm, it takes
only a handful of people acting without regard for others to do serious damage to

the civility and sense of safety that form the foundation of any community. Trick-sters, however, simply do not obey the rules whereby groups of people live together for mutual advantage. In fact, this is why most of these stories are funny and some-times shocking. The main character transgresses the most fundamental rules of any society, including breaking taboos against incest and cannibalism. The moral of the story often seems to be: laugh at but do not imitate the Trickster's foolishness.

There is more to Trickster's transgressive nature than being a moral antitype, however. In Western moralizing fables, for example, the transgressor must be pun-ished for the message to be "safe" for public consumption. In Trickster tales, he might be punished, or he might not. Often he devours the fruits of his misbehaviors with great relish. The innocent are as likely to suffer as the guilty in these mythic realms. Ironically, then, such myths are more *realistic* than instructional tales usu-ally are. The world is sometimes far more capricious than we would like to admit; bad things do happen to innocent people, the greedy often do win the day.

There is, in addition, a sort of *Curious George* quality to some Trickster tales. In such tales misbehavior, disobedience, dangerous curiosity are not punished—or the punishment is worth enduring for the sake of the adventure. This quality com-bines well with another—that the weak do sometimes overcome the strong—to em-body a certain kind of hope in the face of societies ruled by the strong, the "moral" (those in power are always "right"), the creator gods, the heroes, the role models. As Erdoes and Ortiz comment, "Tales in which the lowly and apparently weak play pranks and outwit the high and mighty have delighted young and old all over the world for centuries" (1998, xiii). Bruno Bettelheim goes further and says that such tales are therapeutic, providing children—and all of us, we would add—the reas-surance that perhaps we will manage to outwit the destroying giants that beset us (1975, 27–28).

One thing we hope is clear from these introductory remarks about Tricksters is that, whatever else is true about them, they are very difficult to pin down. The Trick-ster does not suffer categorization lightly. He does not submit to the rules of his own society and will hardly sit still long enough for us to paint a clear picture of him, much less nail him down. In the words of Lewis Hyde:

> All Tricksters are "on the road." They are the lords of in-between. A Trickster does not live near the hearth; he does not live in the halls of justice, the soldier's tent, the shaman's hut, the monastery. He passes through each of these when there is a moment of silence, and he enlivens each with mischief, but he is not their guiding spirit. He is the spirit of the doorway leading out, and of the crossroad at the edge of town (the one where a little market springs up). He is the spirit of the road at dusk, the one that runs from one town to another and belongs to neither. (1998, 6)

In this chapter, we present the Trickster in ten of his fundamental aspects: cre-ator, culture-bringer, opportunist, mischief-maker, amorous adventurer, hunger-driven manipulator, credulous victim of others' tricks, lazy work avoider, transgres-sor, and clown of the body. Coyote sets the stars in heaven, makes sex possible, and establishes fishing taboos. Ma-ui uses craft and ingenuity to create the Hawaiian is-lands, put the sun on a proper course, and discover fire. The darker side of the Trick-ster is revealed when he takes advantage of the physical and moral vulnerabilities of his victims. Coyote's insatiable sexual appetite, of course, should never be far from our minds, but Pa Pandir and Anaanu illustrate that Tricksters hunger for more than sex and are often so intent on the next meal that they can fall into the most obvious traps. Finally, Tricksters remind us that, despite our human pretension to nobility and semidivinity, we are inseparable from our bodily urges to eat, excrete, and procreate. At the same time, the Trickster *by his very transgressions* celebrates and helps maintain the rules, the social structures, which are also central to what we are. And in all this contradiction, the Trickster teaches us to reach for what we desire, and to laugh at ourselves when we fall short.

READING TRICKSTER MYTHS

As we have said, categories are dangerous—Tricksters are too quick to undercut our mental constructs, to cross boundaries, to belie the categories in which we try to cage them. In terms of this mythic figure, it is far better to be aware of his numerous roles, functions, characteristics, and then question how these ambiguous characteristics convey meaning. How do they give us chances to understand values in the cultures from which the stories came—even when (which is always the case) we know too little to do justice to the culture's systems of meaning and knowledge and reality? How do they give us chances to question the human conditions and responses carried within the stories? How do they give us chances to analyze and understand our own ways of seeing boundaries and their crossings, our own appetite-driven behaviors, and our own imaginative creativity serving diverse needs both personal and communal?

The stories that follow, of course, barely scratch the surface of the rich array of myths available about the Trickster throughout the world. We chose these examples because they capture a wide mix of Trickster's behaviors and motivations and because the stories themselves offer a rich ground for further analyses—both of the myths as "meanings" situated in their original cultures *and* of the myths as "means" to read our own situated natures and conditions.

Why We Tell Stories about Spider

Ga (Ghana and West Africa)

African mythology features a variety of Tricksters in animal, human, and divine forms. Most plentiful are tales about animal Tricksters. One finds, for example, spider-Tricksters like the Asante's

Source: Jack Berry, "Why We Tell Stories About Spider," from *West African Folk Tales.* Evanston: Northwestern University Press, 1999, pp. 14–16. Used with permission of Northwestern University Press.

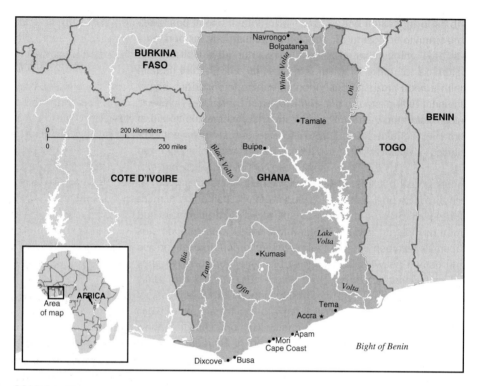

MAP 5.1 Ghana

Ananse, the Zande's Ture, and the Hausa's Gizo; Trickster-hares like the Kikuyu's Wakaboko and Sungura and Zomo of East and Central Africa; tortoise-Tricksters like the Kalabari's Ikaki, the Mbongwe's Ekaga, and the Ila's Sulwe; and the Trickster-jackal of the Dogon and southern Africans. In such colorful company, Anaanu the Spider and Àjàpá the Tortoise, the Yoruban "Master of Sundry Wiles," are standouts. Like most African animal Tricksters, Anaanu and Àjàpá are hungry for recognition, mentally acute, tight-fisted, ungrateful, greedy, and lazy. Their aversion to work and their reliance upon trickery to satisfy an insatiable appetite are qualities they share with Coyote, Raven, and Spider of North America—as is their tendency to involve friends in a scheme and then abandon them when trouble arises. While similar in these ways, Anaanu and Àjàpá, like most African Tricksters, are not as sexually ravenous as their American counterparts, nor is the humor in the analogous African stories as oriented toward the scatological. Despite their well-deserved reputation as selfish mischief-makers, Anaanu and Àjàpá can sometimes be big-hearted—even if only because they want to demonstrate what big shots they are.

African mythology was "oral literature" until European missionaries and anthropologists took an interest in it and began to write it down. Thus, to get a true sense of how stories like the two that follow function in their original social context, one would have to hear them performed by a storyteller familiar with the narrative traditions of the Ga and Yoruba. Typically, a good storyteller employs various voices, gestures, and faces and would possess impeccable comic timing to bring the characters and situations to life for the audience. The audience, for its part, participates enthusiastically—singing, laughing, and shouting out comments and jokes. According to the notes and introduction in Jack Berry's *West African Folk Tales,* the following story was told by Nii Amon Kotei, who began with the traditional opening formula "Shall I tell you this story or shall I not?" The audience answered with the equally traditional "Yes! Tell us!" When a Ga storyteller finishes a tale he says, "If I get another story, I'll stick it behind your ears!"

In the olden days stories were told about God, not about Anaanu, the Spider. One day, Anaanu felt a very strong desire to have stories told about him. So he went to God and said, "Dear God, I want to have your stories told about me."

And God said, "My dear Anaanu, to have stories told about you is a very heavy responsibility. If you want it, I will let you have it, but first you must prove to me that you are fit to have it. I want you to bring me three things: first, a swarm of bees; second, a live python; third, a live leopard, the King of the Forest himself. If you can bring me these three things, I will allow the stories that are told about me to be told about you instead."

Anaanu went away and sat down and thought. For three whole days he sat and thought. Then he got up, smiling, and took a huge calabash with a lid. He put some honey in this calabash, set it on his head, and he walked into the forest. He came to a place where a swarm of bees was hovering around some branches. Then he took the calabash off his head, opened the lid, and started saying loudly to himself while looking into the calabash, "They can fill it; they can't fill it; they can fill it; they can't fill it."

The bees heard him and asked, "Anaanu, what are you talking about?"

And Anaanu said, "Oh, it would be nothing if it were not for that foolish friend of mine. We had an argument. I said that, despite the honey in the calabash, there is still enough space for the makers of the honey to go into the calabash. But he said you are too many, that you cannot go inside the space that is left. I say you can fill it; he says you can't."

Then the leader of the bees said, "Ho! That is easily proved. We can go inside." So he flew into the calabash. And all the bees flew in after him. As soon as they were all inside, Anaanu clapped the lid onto the calabash, very tightly, and took the calabash to God. He said, "I have brought you the first thing, the swarm of bees." And God looked inside the calabash and said, "Well done, Anaanu, but where are the python and the leopard?"

Anaanu went away into the forest and cut a long stick from a branch of a tree. He scraped all the bark off this stick so that it became a long white pole. Then he went deeper into the forest, carrying the pole and shouting to himself, "It is longer than he; it is not longer than he; it is longer than he; it is not longer than he."

manipulate

Now the python, who was very proud of his length, for which he was feared throughout the forest, was lying down curled up and resting. When he saw Anaanu, he said, "What are you talking about, Anaanu?"

And Anaanu said, "Oh, it is nothing but an argument that I had with a very ignorant and foolish friend of mine. Do you know that when I told him that you are longer than this stick, from the black mark to the other end, he refused to believe me, and said the stick is longer than you? I say you are longer; he says you are not."

The python growled and said, "What! There is nobody in this world longer than I. As for that stick, bah! I shall soon show you who is longer."

So saying, Python stretched himself beside the stick, putting his head on the black mark. Anaanu said, "To be sure I get the correct length by which you exceed the stick, let me tie you closely to the stick so you won't wiggle and seem shorter." So Anaanu tied Python firmly to the stick. But as soon as Anaanu had finished doing so, he lifted the stick onto his shoulder and said, "Now, my friend, we will go on a little journey." Then he took the python to God and said, "I have brought you the second thing, the python."

And God looked at the long pole with its burden and said, "Well done, Anaanu, but you still have to bring me Leopard, the King of the Forest himself."

strategic

Anaanu went away and dug a deep pit in the forest, on Leopard's path, and covered the pit with sticks and leaves. Leopard, who was going hunting for his food, soon came along the trail and fell into the pit. He was trapped and couldn't get out. Anaanu soon appeared, as if by chance, and said, "Eh, is this King Leopard himself? Well, well, well! But if I am kind enough to bring my family to help me get you out of this pit, you will reward us by eating us all."

But Leopard replied, "How can you talk like that, Anaanu? How could I do such a thing after you have saved my life? I promise that, if you can get me out of this pit, no leopard will ever eat a spider again."

And Anaanu said, "All right, I believe you. I will call my family to help get you out of this pit." So Anaanu brought his family and also a heavy stick and a lot of rope. He threw the stick into the pit and jumped in after it. And he told Leopard, "Since you are so heavy, we will have to hoist you out with this stick and some ropes." So Leopard took hold of the stick between his four paws. Anaanu tied first his two front paws to the stick and then his two hind paws, all very firmly. Then his family hoisted them both out of the pit. But as soon as they came out, Anaanu jumped off and grabbed the tail end of the pole. He told Leopard, "Now we will go and visit someone you know." So saying, he dragged the stick with its load to God and said, "I have brought you Leopard, the King of the Forest himself." And God looked at Anaanu and said, "You have done very well, Anaanu. You have achieved the impossible. You deserve to have stories told about you. So from today I decree that the stories that were once told about me shall be told about you."

And that is why stories are told about Anaanu, the spider.

Àjàpá, Ajá the Dog, and the Yams

Yoruba (Nigeria and Benin)

Today, more than 10 million Yoruba occupy southwestern Nigeria. When the Portuguese "discovered" the cities of Ife and Benin in the 15th century, the Yoruba were already a numerous people who, while sharing a common linguistic, religious, and cultural base, did not view themselves as one people—a condition similar to that of the ancient Greeks, who, for examples, saw themselves as Athenians, Trojans, or Spartans rather than as Greeks. The Yoruban cities that the first Europeans encountered were large urban complexes surrounded by farmlands and earthen walls that extended outward a dozen miles or more. One city, Ijebu-ode, had "a forty-foot-high earthwork, comprised of a ditch and a bank, enclosing an area of some four hundred square miles" (Courlander 1973, 2).

Yoruba cosmology is distinctly hierarchical. There are hundreds of *orishas,* or gods, in Yoruba belief; a dozen or so are coeval with but subordinate to the supreme sky god, Olorun. Below this primary group of *orishas* are other, lesser spirits whose areas of influence range from health to fertility to good crops to protection against enemies. Even further down the ladder are minor *orishas,* who rank no higher than human heroes, and, finally, there are common human beings. All *orishas*—and all deceased Yoruba—have power over and interest in the fortunes and behavior of the living, and *orishas* and ancestors alike are invoked and placated through offerings and ceremony. The supreme *orishas* form a pantheon reminiscent of the Egyptian, Sumerian, Babylonian, Greek, and Norse divine families: Obatala, shaper of the fetus; Ogun, essence of iron; Shango, owner of lightning; Olokun, ruler of the sea and marshes where the sea intrudes; Orunmila, eldest son of Olorun and archdiviner who discovers the fate that his father will pronounce through reading palm nuts or cowries. Countering fate is Eshu, the essence of uncertainty and accident.

Somewhere in this tangle of spiritual presences is Àjàpá, the tortoise-Trickster. One of the ways that Àjàpá is distinct from Anaanu and many other African Tricksters is his irresistible musicianship. In many stories, Àjàpá's singing carries his schemes forward, mesmerizing individuals, villages, and even beings from the Otherworld with the rhythm of his songs. Indeed, when told

Source: Reprinted from *Yoruba Trickster Tales* by Oyekan Owomoyela by permission of the University of Nebraska Press. © 1997 by the University of Nebraska Press.

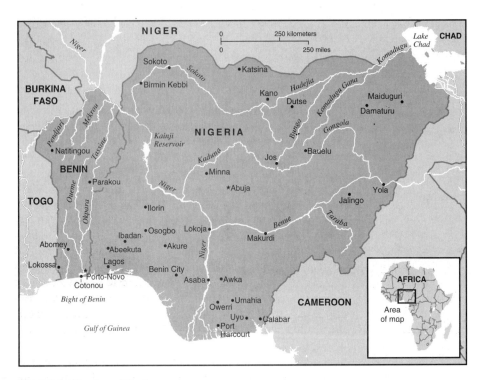

MAP 5.2 Nigeria and Benin

properly—that is, in Yoruban practice—the following tale would include singing.

In an era long gone, Ajá the Dog fell on such hard times as left him with no means of feeding himself and his family. With no farm and no trade, he had to content himself with whatever he could <u>scrounge</u> in the bushes, by the pathways, and on the dunghills. But there was never enough to glean from those sources, never enough for him to fulfill the role of provider for his family; he knew that he must find a better alternative. He thought long and hard about options available to him, mindful that the sages say if one lacks brawn one should make up for it with brains, and also that a lazy person eats what his cunning provides. He reached down deep into his fount of wisdom and was rewarded with an inspiration.

All around his town were large farms, all planted with yams, where if one were careful one could satisfy one's needs without arousing the suspicion of the farm owners. The farms beckoned to him, and for a time his scruples held him back. But his condition worsened and his scruples became increasingly anemic, until eventually <u>expediency</u> became his motivator and he yielded to the appeal of the farms.

<u>He devised</u> a rotation scheme that would take him on a pilfering circuit of different farms, one that allowed a decent interval between two visits to any given quarry. As an added precaution he resolved never to yield to greed when he helped himself to the largess of the farms. Together these voluntary restraints would make

his theft strike each farm owner as a minimal nuisance unworthy of any special measures. The scheme was so successful that he was able to feed himself and his family rather well for quite a while, and very rapidly his emaciated brood became the embodiments of health and good living.

The change that came over the family did not escape the notice of Ajá's good friend Àjàpá the Tortoise, who was constitutionally averse to exposing himself to any labor he could avoid, even if its purpose was to sustain life. He was so widely known as a shirker and idler that the whole world scornfully dismissed him with the appellation *Olédàrùn,* an expression of the common view that his laziness was no longer just a character trait: it was a disease.

Àjàpá was used to trading commiserations with his friend when they both shared the same condition. Indeed, he was drawn to the other because he was gratified to have company in his destitution. When Ajá began to show unmistakable signs of thriving, Àjàpá judged it only fair that he be let in on the secret of his friend's altered circumstances. Whenever he asked the question, though, Ajá put him off with increasingly convoluted stories. But Àjàpá was nothing if not persistent, and he would not be discouraged; Ajá was obviously onto too good a thing to be circumspect about it. Àjàpá would not relent in his pestering, until Ajá was persuaded that his life would be far easier if he revealed his scheme than if he continued to hold out. He therefore agreed in the end to take Àjàpá along on his next expedition.

When the day for the visit dawned, Ajá led the way out of town and to a farm that seemed to be endless in its expanse and that was abundant with mature yams ready for harvesting.

"This is it," Ajá told his friend.

Àjàpá was puzzled.

"This is it?"

"Yes," Ajá answered.

"This is your secret?"

"Yes."

Àjàpá looked around and into the distance where yam plants blended into one another to form a solid mass of wilting foliage. He was almost beside himself with wonder.

"What kind of friend keeps such abundance to himself while his friend starves? How many stomachs do you have? Ten mouths could feed from your farm and still leave enough for ten more. Why have you kept it secret from your friend?"

The puzzlement Ajá had felt at the start of his friend's tirade gave way to understanding when the last words came out.

"No, no!" he corrected Àjàpá. "This is not my farm."

"It's not?"

"Of course not."

"Then, whose is it?" Àjàpá asked, his demeanor indicating that he suspected the answer even as he asked the question.

"Does that matter?" Ajá asked in turn. "Do you want the owner, or do you want food?"

"Food, of course," Àjàpá agreed.

"Here, then, is food. This is no time to ask of the owner of the limb before you bite it. Take what the gods bring your way."

Persuading Àjàpá to do just that was not difficult; his questioning came from puzzlement and not out of any scruples, of which he was blissfully free. Now that he knew how matters stood, Ajá told him, he should also know that their mission was not the type that one could dawdle over.

"A masquerader covered with dry straw may venture into a foundry with open flames," he told Àjàpá, "but he had better not tarry. We must be quick about taking what we need and be off."

They commenced digging up yams, and in a short while Ajá had unearthed two sizable ones. He went into the bush to cut some vine to tie them together so he could carry them more easily. Long after he was done he saw that Àjàpá was still busily digging away, despite the small heap he had already assembled.

"Don't you think you have enough already?" he asked Àjàpá, somewhat alarmed.

"A few more and I will be done."

It was quite apparent to him that Àjàpá already had more than enough to keep him and his wife fed for several days. Besides, apart from seemingly ignoring Ajá's admonition about speed, he was jeopardizing the carefully thought-out strategy for denying any farmer the incentive to come after the raider of his crop.

"No time for a few more," Ajá told him, "it is time to stop, now!"

"Patience!" Àjàpá chided his friend.

"Patience?" Ajá asked, anything but patient. "If you cannot tell when to stop you are headed for disgrace; your greed will get us both into trouble."

"The reputation one gets from stealing one yam is no different from that for stealing ten, is it?" Àjàpá asked his friend. "I have risked earning the name, and I must make it worth my while."

"But," his friend argued in return, "a farmer may ignore the theft of two or three yams from his farm, but he is not likely to overlook the loss of ten. And once the farmer is provoked into vigilance, any further visit to his farm becomes a most risky venture. Your behavior will cause today to bar all tomorrows!"

"There are other farms besides this," Àjàpá said, unimpressed by Ajá's reasoning. "When a door closes, another opens. Besides," he continued, "the elders say there is no fat to this life; therefore, whenever only a little comes one's way, one should take only a little, and whenever abundance comes one's way, one should enjoy the abundance; for you can really call your own only what has already found its way into your stomach."

Ajá knew all along that he was not likely to make any impression on Àjàpá with any argument, and he was anxious to be off the farm before the owner chanced upon them. But he tried one more time.

"How do you mean to carry this many yams home?" he asked.

"The way will show itself," Àjàpá replied and returned to his digging.

"In that case," Ajá said in resignation, "I will leave you. If the farmer catches you, you don't know me, and I don't know you."

The sight of Ajá lifting his two-yam load and the specter of an arriving farmer raised second thoughts for Àjàpá.

"All right, all right," he said. "Lest I appear greedy and unreasonable, I will stop."

As if to indicate that whatever Àjàpá did was now immaterial to him, Ajá turned his face toward the path.

"Keep on coming on," he said, giving his friend the customary parting greeting to tardy fellow travelers, and turned his feet in the direction of home.

"Wait!" Àjàpá called in alarm. "Do you mean to leave me here alone?"

"I promised to show you where to find food, and I have done that," Ajá replied. "You have legs, and they know their way home; I did not promise to walk you back home."

Àjàpá now commenced to plead with Ajá to wait so they could leave together.

"We came together," he argued, "and it is only right that we leave together."

Ajá was by now eager to get away from the farm, for something told him that disaster approached, and so he paid no attention to Àjàpá's pleas. He walked briskly away, leaving Àjàpá to fumble frantically with tying his yams together, an impossible job. Finally, in a panic he called after Ajá:

> Ajá, Ajá, lend me a hand!
> Ajá, Ajá, wait for me, please!
> If you don't, I'll hail the farmer
> And when he comes,
> He won't he pleased.
> Ajá, Ajá, lend me a hand!

Àjàpá's words stopped Ajá in his tracks. He knew his friend well enough to know that what he threatened was no bluff. If he was caught he would not hesitate for a moment to implicate Ajá. His anger mounting, therefore, he returned to help his greedy friend tie the yams securely together. He also helped to lift it unto Àjàpá's back.

The load proved so heavy that the Àjàpá could hardly walk, but he would not entertain the suggestion that he discard some yams. Again, Ajá had no choice but to let his friend have his way, and he hurried toward home. But he had not gone very far when the forest again echoed with Àjàpá's call:

> Ajá, Ajá, lend me a hand!
> Ajá, Ajá, wait for me, please!
> If you don't, I'll hail the farmer
> And when he comes,
> He won't be pleased.
> Ajá, Ajá, lend me a hand!

The trip had already taken much longer than Ajá liked. He berated himself for his folly in permitting friendship to cloud his better judgment; after all, no one knew better than he what type of creature Àjàpá was. Thinking thus he ignored the call and hurried along, anxious to put as much distance between himself and the farm and as quickly as he could.

Àjàpá was so weighed down by his loot that his progress was painfully slow. Worse yet, with every step he felt as though the load would flatten him. He called and called in desperation to Ajá, but the latter paid him no further heed. That Àjàpá would be caught he was certain; that he would implicate his benefactor Ajá had no doubt, either. His best course, he thought, was to hurry to the safety of his home. A person who can truthfully say "I was sitting innocently in my home" is not easily proclaimed a public criminal. The more Àjàpá called, the more Ajá urged his legs into his walk, until soon every sound from Àjàpá faded and died away.

As soon as he arrived home, Ajá instructed his wife to hide the yams quickly in the bush nearby, where nobody would see them. That done, he asked her to make a fire in the hearth and bring him two raw eggs. His wife did as she was told, all the while wondering what her husband was up to. She did not question him about his strange instructions, for she was certain that he had good reasons. When the fire was going, Ajá rubbed himself thoroughly with oil and lay in front of the hearth. He told his wife to cover him up, and to anyone who might come visiting or asking about him that he had taken ill, that he had been laid up for a few days and had been unable to go outside. He then placed one egg in each cheek and waited for whatever would happen.

In the meantime, Àjàpá's greed had indeed caught up with him. Unable to make any real progress under his oppressive load and unwilling to let go of any part of it, he inevitably attracted the suspicion of those who came upon him on the road. So well known was he in the surrounding communities that there was only one explanation for his sudden access to so many yams. Every farmer who had suffered some theft on his farm in recent times claimed that the habitual thief was finally cornered. Following custom, people gathered and taunted him with derisive chants:

> Behold the face of a thief,
> THIEF!
> Behold the face of a thief,
> THIEF!

Children trooped after him, echoing and clapping to the chant, and occasionally pelting him with stones. By the time he was delivered before the *oba* in the palace, the procession after him had swelled to more than half the town's population.

"Àjàpá," the *oba* said, "if I told you I was surprised to see you here in these circumstances, I would be lying. You, *Òlédàrùn*. You are so lazy you would sooner call down a deluge than do gainful work. Now we see where your laziness has brought you—to stealing."

In response, Àjàpá wished the king a long life.

"*Kábíyèsí,* your Majesty, seeing me in these circumstances, who would doubt the wisdom of your words? But, please bend your ears downwards and you will learn the truth."

"The truth? What truth is there to learn besides what we can all see?" the *oba* responded. "This matter is one for the eyes to see, not something for the nose to sniff out."

"Your breath will be long," Àjàpá persisted. "You say I am lazy, and I will not bandy words with you. But, did I become lazy only yesterday? No! Yet, did anyone accuse me of stealing yesterday? No! How then . . . ?"

"As our fathers said," the *oba* interrupted him, "the thief may range freely for a great many days, but the owner's one day, that day when the thief is caught, is all that counts."

"Your words are wise, your Majesty," Àjàpá responded, "but I am innocent. I am no thief."

"Are these yams from your farm, then?" the *oba* asked, indicating the yams that had been placed as evidence before him.

"No."

"Did you perhaps buy them?"

"No, your Majesty."

"Ah, some kind farmer gave them to you?"

"Your Majesty," he replied, "that is the truth."

Those words provoked some scattered titters, and the skeptical *oba* asked who his benefactor was.

"Your ancestors will not visit you with evil," Àjàpá responded. "Your Majesty, the first person I saw when I woke up this morning must have been wearing ill-luck like a garment, and must have infected me with it. Otherwise, would I have found myself in the company of Ajá, a friend who told me that he owned a farm he planted with yams? He said he was short-handed, and offered me some yams if I would help him dig some and bring them home."

Correctly reading the incredulity on the *oba*'s face, Àjàpá pressed on quickly.

LIAR !

"I know," he continued, "that I should have remembered the ancient wisdom of you, our elder, that a lamb that keeps company with Ajá will come to savor shit, but I fell victim to my own good nature. May your ancestors not make your good nature bring you grief."

He continued, claiming that he had no idea that the farm was not Ajá's until others accused him of stealing as he struggled home with his wages for helping Ajá. Only then did he realize why Ajá had acted so strangely, sneaking off the farm, with the story that he was taking a few yams to the barn and would be back shortly.

Since Àjàpá was accusing Ajá of stealing, of inducement to steal, and of deception, the *oba* ordered that Ajá be brought to confront his accuser; one does not judge a case after hearing only one side, he said.

When the *oba*'s messengers arrived at Ajá's house, his wife asked why they had come.

"The *oba* asks that Ajá briefly show his eyes at the palace," they said.

"How terrible!" she exclaimed. "One may not refuse an *oba*'s summons, but certain things make honoring it a problem."

What sort of thing might keep anyone from shaking himself loose from whatever he was doing to run to answer an *oba*'s call? the messengers wanted to know. Was Ajá dead, perhaps? No, she replied, but he was ill and had been laid up for several days.

"That is not what we heard," they said. "If he has been laid up, how was he able to go to a farm to steal yams?"

At that, Ajá's wife exclaimed in convincing disbelief, saying some evil person had lied about her husband. She invited them into the house to see for themselves. The messengers entered, and there they saw Ajá, completely covered and shivering before the fire and looking every bit the invalid at death's door. The messengers looked hard at him and were convinced that he was indeed ill.

"How does the body feel, Ajá?" one of them asked in sympathy.

Ajá rolled his eyes toward the questioner and made as though he would respond. But instead he gave a heave, and the contents of one of his cheeks spurted out. The messengers leaped out of the way, now thoroughly convinced that the creature was in very poor shape indeed.

They commiserated with his wife and consulted among themselves as to what best to do. Their order was to bring Ajá, and whatever the *oba* ordered they must carry out. They explained the situation to his wife and persuaded her that the best evidence of her husband's condition, anyway, was the sight he looked. Her display of anguish was convincing as she helped them wrap Ajá in a warm cloth before they bore him away.

The *oba* and the people assembled at the court were puzzled when the messengers arrived bearing what seemed a corpse instead of marching a supposedly hardened criminal. Had they been heavy-handed in their mission? some wondered. Àjàpá was as puzzled as the rest.

"Your majesty," the spokesman for the messengers reported to the *oba*, "we did as you ordered, but we found Ajá in death's courtyard."

The *oba* looked at him and saw a creature laboring for breath.

"Is this the same Ajá you accused of stealing yams on a farm?" he asked Àjàpá.

Àjàpá moved closer and looked at Ajá, who was now groaning ever so weakly. Àjàpá knew, of course, that he was faking, and he so informed the *oba*.

"This is a trick, your majesty," he cried. "He's faking! He's a thief, a faker, and worse things besides."

In his agitation he got hold of Ajá's wrap intending to pull it off, while the messengers rushed to restrain him. Just then Ajá released the contents of the remaining egg in his mouth. Àjàpá caught most of it in his face, and was both halted and silenced.

The *oba*'s conviction that Ajá was really ill and that Àjàpá had made up his stories was aided by a properly queasy stomach that could not endure the sight of vomit. He ordered Ajá returned to his home and pronounced sentence on Àjàpá.

Whoever cannot live as the inhabitants of a town live does not belong in that town. Since Àjàpá would not work but preferred to steal, the *oba* said, his presence in the town was a threat to its harmony. Àjàpá belonged not in the community but in the company of thieves. Accordingly, he ordered Àjàpá from the town, on pain of being shackled and killed if ever he showed his face again therein. Since then Àjàpá has wandered the forest, while Ajá remains welcome in town.

Thus did Àjàpá pay for his greed and his ingratitude to his friend.

How Coyote Placed the Stars

Wasco (The Dalles, Oregon)

Among the world's Tricksters, those whose stories are most widely published and studied are found in North America. The Native American Trickster in his guises as Raven, Spider, Rabbit, Mink, and especially Coyote is, by far, the character about whom the most stories are told. Throughout the surviving narratives, the Indians' Trickster embodies, at one time or another, all 10 of the Trickster's attributes (creator, culture-bringer, opportunist, etc.). As the Sioux's Iktomi, he creates time, space, language, and names the animals; as the Cheyenne's Veeho, he is both creator with vast powers, an idiot, and the White Man; as the Cherokee's Rabbit Boy, he snares the sun and kills monsters; and as the Hopi's Masau'u he is benevolent creator and protector of travelers and lecher, thief, and liar.

Our experience has shown that students of myth often find American Indian Trickster stories, with their frequent references to genitalia, urination, and defecation, a bit shocking. Yet, to many of North America's Indian nations, the Trickster and stories told about him are sacred. Indeed, among some Indian nations, the Trickster could be mentioned only at certain times and under specific conditions. Yet sacred needn't mean somber; the Trickster in his many guises embodies a deep delight in the body and in life itself. Where Trickster tales are still told in performative ways, grandmothers and children revel in Coyote's bawdy vitality as unself-consciously and freely as any member of the tribe. The body and its functions are not, in the views of most Native American cultures, profane or shameful; they simply are what they are. As Erdoes and Ortiz remind us, "there are no dirty words in Indian languages. A penis is a penis, not a 'dick' or a 'peter,' and a vulva is just that, never a 'twat' or 'snatch'" (1998, xxi). Indeed, the Native American's Trickster reminds us like no other that humans, for all their pretensions to intellectual and spiritual culture and for all their moments of bravery, altruism, and generosity, are nevertheless animals ruled by appetites and impulses that make them equally capable of cowardice, selfishness, and cruelty.

Sadly, much of what we know of this vast and compelling literature has been lost or shows evidence of European influence. Ever since "first contact," European-borne disease, military action, dishonest treaties, and missionary work have decimated populations, transplanted indigenous groups to multitribal reservations, and erased entire language groups and religions through compulsory attendance in English-only schools and Christian churches. In

Source: Barry Lopez, *Giving Birth to Thunder, Sleeping with His Daughter.* New York: Avon, 1977. 14–15.

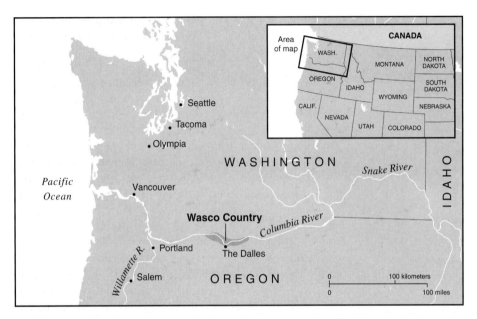

MAP 5.3 The Dalles, Oregon, along the Columbia River separating Washington and Oregon. The Dalles was a thriving trade center for the Wasco and other Pacific Northwest tribes long before their "first contact" with Lewis and Clark in the early 19th century.

addition, much of the firsthand information we have about the customs, religions, and myths of the Indian nations that thrived as recently as the first half of the nineteenth century comes to us from missionaries and ethnographers whose cultural biases and distaste for native ways is sometimes so pronounced as to render their testimony nearly worthless to those interested in culture for its own sake. And even in the cases when these missionaries and researchers were sensitive to the cultural complexities of the natives and committed to doing what they could to aid their subjects, the socioeconomic-political forces driving European-American policies toward the Native Americans overwhelmed what effect a few small voices in the wilderness could have. By the time such policies had come under question and practitioners of ethnographic methods had developed more consistent and self-conscious standards, there remained very few groups whose cultural traditions had survived intact. As a result, all that remains of a once vast continent of cultural practices, sacred stories, languages, and beliefs is a comparatively tiny scattering of eyewitness accounts, anthropologists' field notes, testimony of now-aged children about what they remember of their grandparents, renaissance efforts among some tribes, and, on some reservations, modern retellings.

The Wascos, one of many Chinook tribes, lived along the south side of the Columbia River from The Dalles downstream to the Hood River. The Dalles was perhaps the largest trading center in the Pacific Northwest—perhaps in all of North America—when Lewis and Clark "discovered" it in the first decade of the 19th century. Thousands of people from dozens of tribes gathered at The Dalles during the May through October salmon runs to buy, sell, and trade everything from furs and horses to salmon jerky and human beings. Originally one of the most powerful tribes along the river, the Wascos traded in slaves, horses, and salmon—the latter commodity in such bulk that a European trader once estimated that on one day in one Wasco village more than two tons of salmon could be seen curing in the sun. To maintain their influence, the Wascos carefully controlled all fishing stations along their stretch of the river and, before midcentury, made substantial profits by charging European trappers and traders portage fees and passage tolls.

Despite their location more than 100 miles from the Pacific, Wasco culture had as much in common with coastal tribes as they had with their inland neighbors. They lived in long plank houses which they occupied year-round, based their economy on fishing and trade, and their beadwork and crafts were as sophisticated as those of the coastal tribes. Like most of their inland neighbors, a great deal of Wasco social and economic life centered on small-scale skirmishing with other tribes, especially the Paiute. Indeed, continual raids, scalping, and slaveholding were common practices among the natives of the Pacific Northwest interior.

One time there were five wolves, all brothers, who traveled together. Whatever meat they got when they were hunting they would share with Coyote. One evening Coyote saw the wolves looking up at the sky.

"What are you looking at up there, my brothers?" asked Coyote.

"Oh nothing," said the oldest wolf.

Next evening Coyote saw they were all looking up in the sky at something. He asked the next oldest wolf what they were looking at, but he wouldn't say. It went on like this for three or four nights. No one wanted to tell Coyote what they were looking at because they thought he would want to interfere. One night Coyote asked the youngest wolf brother to tell him and the youngest wolf said to the other wolves, "Let's tell Coyote what we see up there. He won't do anything."

So they told him. "We see two animals up there. Way up there, where we cannot get to them."

"Let's go up and see them," said Coyote.

"Well, how can we do that?"

"Oh, I can do that easy," said Coyote. "I can show you how to get up there without any trouble at all."

Coyote gathered a great number of arrows and then began shooting them into the sky. The first arrow stuck in the sky and the second arrow stuck in the first. Each arrow stuck in the end of the one before it like that until there was a ladder reaching down to the earth.

he persuaded

"We can climb up now," said Coyote. The oldest wolf took his dog with him, and then the other four wolf brothers came, and then Coyote. They climbed all day and into the night. All the next day they climbed. For many days and nights they climbed until they finally reached the sky. They stood in the sky and looked over at the two animals the wolves had seen from down below. They were two grizzly bears.

"Don't go near them," said Coyote. "They will tear you apart." But the two youngest wolves were already headed over. And the next two youngest wolves followed them. Only the oldest wolf held back. When the wolves got near the grizzlies nothing happened. The wolves sat down and looked at the bears, and the bears sat there looking at the wolves. The oldest wolf, when he saw it was safe, came over with his dog and sat down with them.

Coyote wouldn't come over. He didn't trust the bears. "That makes a nice picture, though," thought Coyote. "They all look pretty good sitting there like that. I think I'll leave it that way for everyone to see. Then when people look at them in the sky they will say, 'There's a story about that picture,' and they will tell a story about me."

So Coyote left it that way. He took out the arrows as he descended so there was no way for anyone to get back. From down on the earth Coyote admired the arrangement he had left up there. Today they still look the same. They call those stars Big Dipper now. If you look up there you'll see three wolves make up the handle and the oldest wolf, the one in the middle, still has his dog with him. The two youngest wolves make up the part of the bowl under the handle and the two grizzlies make up the other side, the one that points toward the North Star.

When Coyote saw how they looked he wanted to put up a lot of stars. He arranged stars all over the sky in pictures and then he made the Big Road across the sky with the stars he had left over.

When Coyote was finished he called Meadowlark over. "My brother" he said, "When I am gone, tell everyone that when they look up into the sky and see the stars arranged this way, that I was the one who did that. That is my work."

Now Meadowlark tells that story. About Coyote.

Coyote Man and Saucy Duckfeather

Peter Blue Cloud (Modern Account, Iroquois) Northeastern United States

The following story demonstrates that myth-making continues in our own time. According to William Bright, Peter Blue Cloud is "a poet of Iroquois origins [who] has written some of the best Coy-

Source: William Bright, *A Coyote Reader,* pages 73–82. Copyright © 1992 The Regents of the University of California. Used by permission.

oterotica, with plots taken from Western Indian traditions and his own imagination" (1993, 73). Coyote's never-ending appetite leads him in this story to pretend to the powers of a shaman in order to grant the vain and flirtatious Saucy Duckfeather her fondest wish: to have pure white feathers. All she need do is help a "male tree" find his mate.

Of course they called her that because of the way she moved her rump to some secret music or itch. So proud she was, married to White Crane Man whose every feather was valued by those over-the-water-people, sure she was pretty and even the old men who helped gather firewood, you seen them eyeing that tail with their mouths like wrinkled holes. And Young Singer, too, would hang around the village and trip over everything while pretending not to watch her: yes, all the men and boys of age were walking around on three legs and not much fishing or hunting getting done, not to mention some pretty jealous women, like Bullhead Woman who took some old duck feathers and stuck them up her butt and wiggle-walked all over camp, saying loud, "how you like this, huh, it look sassy enough for all you men?"

But Saucy Duckfeather wouldn't notice any of these things. Down by the shore she was smoothing her feathers and looking at herself in the water and wishing her secret longing that her feathers might turn shiny white. And then, what a gorgeous creature she would become, a truly fitting companion for the White Crane Man! Oh, what a pair—like sunlight they would be and their children surely shame the great swan so white!

And Magpie Woman was hopping all around camp, picking up twigs for her small campfire. And worried, too, old woman that she was, with no more men whose duty was to give her meat of the hunt and once in a while a load of branches. Stirring her tiny basket of mush, mumbling to herself these last few weeks, and now, suddenly she reached her decision, and a very hard one to reach, too. But nothing else to be done. No, it had to be, she had to call in that crazy Coyote Man, so full of tricks and mischief all the time and never content to only gamble with the men, but had to be out in the brush chasing after all those young women. And now Magpie Woman sighed, and then giggled in remembering her youth. Yes, yes, there always seemed to be eager young women, way out there, pretending to gather wood or dig for food, the better to be caught by Coyote Man or any other like himself. For of course there are many kinds of coyote, among all men, not to mention certain kinds of women, too, who glory in mischief and hidden games, among the bushes or in the forest. But that's always been so, sighed Magpie Woman and giggled again in remembrance. And "yes," she re-decided, "I will invite Coyote Man to feast with me, though I have little enough, but little enough is often plenty for those whose hunger is not always stomach food." And anyway she'd seen that Coyote Man often, yes, when he'd come to doctor someone, looking, studying that Saucy Duckfeather and more, too, in his eyes than just curious sparkles. And so, pretending to be very sick she tore her hair and cried that only Coyote Man could cure her, and of course he heard of it soon enough and was seen coming down the hill with his basket on his back and singing loud and long a song which the young men envied for it could not be imitated because the hearer forgot it as soon as hearing it and only remembered the beauty of it.

She distracts owls Vain!

calls him

And "oh, oh, here he comes again, and watch out for everything you own and especially watch out for wives, daughters, nieces and any grandmothers," they said, and Coyote Man he step-danced into camp and threw his basket down, heavy with rocks he pretended were beads, and right on the foot of Badger's Son who screamed in pain and danced around on the other foot. And Coyote Man turned and looked shocked, and studied the young man's step, then declared, "well, it's a fancy step all right, but I don't think you'll win any girls with it," which set the other men laughing, which good mood Coyote Man needed to get about his business.

So he took up his basket and went to the house of Magpie Woman and entered and stood looking down at her for a long time, then said, "well, well, yes I can see that you're not sick at all and will probably outlive youngsters," and smiled at her and she smiled back. "You look just like your father, you surely do, and wherever did he go to?" Coyote Man still smiling, "yes, that old man left for upriver some time back and I guess he found a good place to be." And of course it was the very same Coyote Man because in old age a coyote often gets much younger, but secrets are to keep and so he asked her what her problem was. And she, she talked while stirring him a basket of mush and fed him the last of the salmon. And he listened and nodded and mumbled, "hmm, yes, I see; I got lots of other important things to do, but my father was your friend, so I guess I can help you. Yes, I guess I'll do this thing just for old times' sake, yes." And he ate and had a nap to refresh his mind and dreamed just the right dream.

So when Magpie Woman walked from her house at sundown all cured, the camp had a dance to celebrate this miraculous cure by Coyote Man. And the feet stomped all night and lots of rustling and giggling in the brush after Coyote Man hinted to certain young women of the power root he had obtained in downriver country, which the women there all used to be sure to have male children. And this root was only to be used at night of course and attached to the front of a man who knew the song that went with it: and so Coyote Man slept all the next day almost, and then faded into the woods with some of the salmon and beads brought to him by grateful young women who were sure now of male children. And Coyote Man, when out of sight, picked vines and stripped the bark, and bent them just like strings of moneybeads, for of course he had only one real string for his last night's work. And he filled his burden basket with the vines and placed the beads on top, and went walking fast through the camp and mumbling to himself so that all could hear. "Oh, these heavy beads again, and I suppose there'll be more there tomorrow night that I'll have to carry away. Oh, if I could just give them all away instead," and he threw the string of real beads to some young men hanging around Saucy Duckfeather and kept right on going. And next morning they saw him again, walking real fast through the camp with a basket full of salmon which was really dyed pieces of bark with a few real salmon on top which he threw to the people and mumbled that he wished he could rest awhile and not have to be always getting beads and salmon and taking them from one place to another. And the salmon he threw landed pretty close to Saucy Duckfeather, and so she began to wonder about this Coyote Man with so much wealth and the only one around with no time to look at her. And there he went, disappearing into the brush. And then again in the afternoon he reappeared, and this time he was carrying a great bundle of white deer skins, but moving so fast that the people could just make out the one which hung loose. And he once again disappeared until almost dark, when he danced into camp, his head and shoulders turned a brilliant gold like the sun, the brightest and most beautiful of feathers ever seen around. And eyes of greed, or wonder, or just dreaming never know the truth of pine pitch and yellow ocher and quick motion in fading light.

And now, waiting, waiting, the snare was set and the prey was curious. Saucy Duckfeather began—but not to let anyone notice, of course—following Coyote Man around. And he pretended not to notice her and walked away from camp and looked to the hills from which he'd come. And holding his head as in great pain, he moaned, "Oh, I wish that tree would just leave me alone, oh, where can a simple man like myself find a mate for the male tree? Oh, I know it's said that she'll appear soon, and every wish of hers will be granted, but how will I know her to be the one the male tree wishes? And how will I be able to tell that she deserves to be the one? Oh, now that I'm wealthy and have wished myself a hood and mantle of golden feathers, still the other tree cries out to me and makes my head feel so much pain. Oh, I got to find that woman for the male tree." And Saucy Duckfeather did not even hesitate but said, "it's me, the male tree has called me and I'm instructed to ask of you, Coyote Man, what I must do to have my wish of feathers white as polished shell or snow. What must I do?"

And he jumped at her voice, a man caught guilty and looked at her a long while. Yes, thinking, just, oh yes, and "yes," he said, "perhaps you are the one. And I guess I must tell you all of it. So simple, merely a tree, a male tree, a dead oak with a protruding red branch near the bottom which a woman must mount and ride upon a four night ride, an all night ride with no time wasted, just riding and wishing a four night journey to bring about the truth of all your dreams."

And there was Coyote Man standing inside the hollow oak, his pecker sticking way out and his hide was stretched toward the root of his manhood so hard that he couldn't even blink his eyes. And she, the Saucy Duckfeather, riding and riding the magic branch and it even became obvious that she was enjoying the ride. And Coyote Man blew white ash through a knothole, and what with her sweat and imagination and secret longing, she just knew she was turning white. And being ridden four nights steady, Coyote Man was content to leave and left. And she, poor Saucy Duckfeather was left with knowledge of her greed and the acceptance of her given life with her grayish, long-tailed children.

And old Magpie Woman stirred her salmon soup and to the idle or curious would only say, "well, that's the way of doctors, especially if they're coyote."

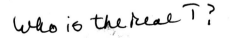

The Trouble with Rose Hips

Lipan Apache (American Southwest)

There is no evidence that the Apache lived in the southwestern United States before 1500. Like their Navajo cousins in Arizona and New Mexico, the Apache belong to the Athabascan language family—which suggests that they migrated south from Canada along the foot of the Rockies shortly before Coronado "discovered" them in western Texas in 1541. The Apache, who call themselves the *Na-dene* or *N'de dine* (i.e., the people), probably derive this name from the Zuni word a*pachu,* which means "enemy." Indeed, unlike the agriculturally based Pueblo and Zuni, most Apache tribes did little farming until they were forced onto reservations in the late 19th century. Living in nomadic hunting bands, the Apache hunted buffalo and other game, supplementing their supplies of food and trade implements by raiding sedentary tribes like the Zuni and, eventually, Euro-American settlers.

The various Apache tribes—the Jicarilla, Chiricahua, Mibreños, Mogollones, Mescalero, and Lipan—were infamous in the second half of the 19th century for their resistance to Euro-American incursions on their lands. Led by such famous warriors as Cochise, Victorio, and Geronimo, the Apaches resisted being moved onto reservations for decades. Although most Apachean tribes eventually succumbed to the superior forces of the U.S. government by the 1890s, a few bands continued raids against white settlers from the hills of northern Mexico until the 1930s. The Lipan suffered terribly during the 1840s and 1850s when the Texas government attempted to exterminate all Indians within its borders, and the Smithsonian Institution's Frederick Webb Hodge estimated that no more than 30 Lipan were left by 1900. The Lipan story that follows is the kind of cautionary tale that a hunting and gathering people would find both useful and entertaining because it includes lore about the health effects of eating rose hips and because it warns against gullibility.

Coyote went on. Along the path he saw some rose hips. They looked red and ripe. "Oh, they might be good to eat!" he thought.

The rose hips said among themselves, "We'd better tell him we are not fit to eat."

He stopped there and said, "How sweet you look. I wonder whether you are good to eat."

"No, we are not good to eat at all."

Source: From *American Indian Trickster Tales* by Richard Erdoes and Alfonso Ortiz. Copyright 1998 by Richard Erdoes and the Estate of Alfonso Ortiz. Used by permission of Viking Penguin, a division of Penguin Putnam, Inc.

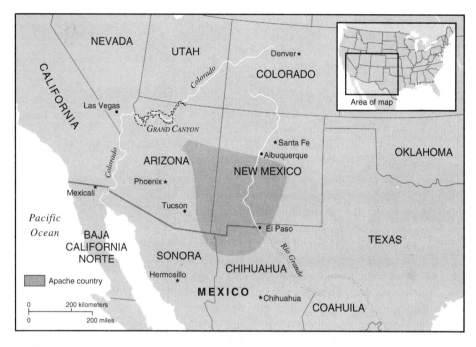

MAP 5.4 At an unknown time prior to 1541 the Apache migrated to the southwestern region of what is now the United States. Living in bands of nomadic hunters, they thrived there until they virtually were destroyed by the U.S. government at the end of the 19th century.

"What will happen if someone eats you?"

"Oh, if anyone eats us, he will have to break wind so hard that it will toss him up into the sky."

"Well, I just want to try one," said Coyote. He picked one and ate it. The berries nudged each other. "Oh, you are sweet," he said. He ate another and another until he was full. He gathered them by the handful. They didn't nudge each other anymore.

He started to sing:

> When I look up I see many berries,
> When I look down I see many more;
> The ripe ones, the soft ones; they are the ones I eat.

He had had enough. They all nudged each other when he had gone a little distance away.

They began to work on his insides. He ran for a tree and hung on. He went off like a horse. He had to do this again and again.

Far away in the flats he saw a black thing moving. He went out there. He saw what it was. There were two people looking around on the ground. They were two crows. He stopped there. He said, "You two fellows must have killed a good fat buffalo."

"Yes, our children were hungry. So we killed this buffalo. We are butchering it."

"Well, leave your work. We'll play a little game first."

[handwritten: deceives them to get the buy]

"No, let us alone."

He insisted. Finally they asked, "Well, what is this game?"

"Let us see who can defecate over this buffalo."

"No, that's a dirty thing. We don't do anything like that over the game we kill, over the things we eat."

[handwritten: persuasive]

"Oh, only a little will get on it, perhaps."

He kept begging and they finally gave in. They wanted him to do it first. But he said, "No, you do it first."

The first crow tried. He jumped and defecated. It went only a little way, about halfway across.

But Coyote said, "That's pretty good. I don't think I can do that well." The other crow tried it then and did no better. Now it was Coyote's turn. He whirled around and bent down. It came out red and went straight across.

They had agreed that the one whose excrement went all the way over could have all the meat. Coyote had won all the meat. They had agreed because they thought no one could do it. The crows begged him to leave a little fat in the eye sockets, a little meat between the ribs, and some on the joints.

Coyote went back home with the meat. The two crows were there blaming each other. That has all been carried on to this day. If two are going along somewhere and meet someone going the other way, this fellow will persuade them to change their plans. Then they do something unwise, for they do not think it over. And it has a meaning in a different way. Some are not honest in playing games and trick others. One must watch out for these people, for they start trouble.

Before these two crows parted, they said, "Now our children will go hungry because we were fooled." And that's the way it is today. People spend their money foolishly and their children go around badly clothed and ill fed. Today some Indians do not listen to the advice of an older brother or a parent and gamble and drink and get into trouble.

[handwritten: teaching story]

Old Man Coyote Meets Coyote Woman

Blackfoot (Alberta, Saskatchewan, Montana, and Wyoming)

The Blackfoot are an Algonqian-speaking Indian nation not to be confused with the Sioux tribe of the same name. A nomadic people who followed herds of bison, elk, and antelope, they ranged between the borders of Alberta and Saskatchewan down into the northern plains of Wyoming, Montana, and North Da-

Source: From *American Indian Trickster Tales* by Richard Erdoes and Alfonso Ortiz. Copyright 1998 by Richard Erdoes and the Estate of Alfonso Ortiz. Used by permission of Viking Penguin, a division of Penguin Putnam, Inc.

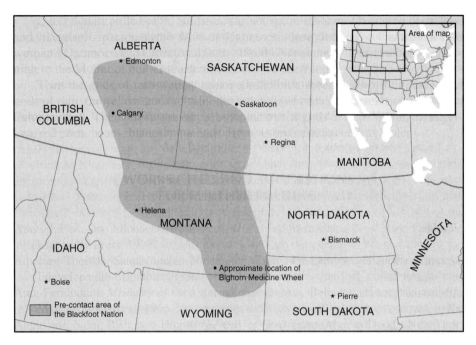

MAP 5.5 Blackfoot Nation

kota. Until the advent of the horse, the Blackfoot or their dogs carried their possessions, thus making a virtue of living simply—a few blankets, cooking implements, hunting gear, and a medicine bag wrapped in tent cloth were enough. Before the horse made hunting more efficient, the Blackfoot were constantly on the lookout for boxed canyons and other steep landforms against which they could herd, corral, and gradually harvest bison. For most of the year, the Blackfoot tended to live in bands of about 50 to 100, just large enough to operate a buffalo pound effectively. In summer, however, the Blackfoot and their allies, the Sarsi and Piegan, gathered in comparatively large hunting camps to conduct trade, play games, swap stories, plant ritual fields of tobacco, and practice their religion.

The most spectacular of the public religious rites was the Sun Dance, an event sponsored by someone whose prayer to the Almighty Power (whose voice was Thunder) for healing or aid had been answered. When the man or woman who had promised the Almighty a Sun Dance in his or her time of crisis had amassed enough wealth and sufficiently coordinated the event with the tribe's several priests, preparations lasting several weeks would begin. The head priest and four assistants would chant prayers and, at specified times, reveal the various ritual objects contained within a medicine bundle. A special lodge would be erected in the middle of the camp and those who had promised gifts to the Almighty in time of crisis would hang them upon the boughs of a tree that had been cut down and placed in the center of the lodge. These festivities would usually last four days—the magic number in most American Indian cultures—and would feature music on eaglebone flutes, buffalo hide drums and rattles, and dancing. When the ceremony ended, the lodge and its gifts would be abandoned to the Almighty, who would reclaim them through natural decay.

In the following story, medicine bags feature prominently. Old Man Coyote and Coyote Woman discover their genitalia within them. The medicine bag was a cloth, blanket, or skin bag filled with a variety of ritual objects. These objects could include the skins of smaller animals and pieces of the hides of larger animals, precious stones or shells, feathers, bones, or hair—all of which were thought to embody spiritual powers that could aid the individual and the tribe in the search for game, success in battle, and protection from disease and other evils. Indeed, for a people of few material possessions, the medicine bag was invaluable and its objects were carefully protected.

In the beginning there were only two human beings in the world—Old Man Coyote and Coyote Woman. Old Man Coyote lived on one side of the world, Coyote Woman on the other. By chance they met.

"How strange" said Old Man Coyote. "We are exactly alike."

"I don't know about that," said Coyote Woman. "You're holding a bag. What's in it?"

Old Man Coyote reached into his bag and brought out a penis. "This odd thing."

"It is indeed an odd thing" said Coyote Woman. "It looks funny. What is it for?"

"I don't know," said Old Man Coyote. "I don't know what to use it for. What do you have in your bag?"

Coyote Woman dug deep into her bag and came up with a vagina. "You see" she said, "we are not alike. We carry different things in our bags. Where should we put them?"

"I think we should put them into our navels," said Old Man Coyote. "The navel seems to be a good place for them."

"No, I think not" said Coyote Woman. I think we should stick them between our legs. Then they will be out of the way."

"Well, all right," said Old Man Coyote. "Let's put them there." They placed these things between their legs.

"You know," said Coyote Woman, "it seems to me that the strange thing you have there would fit this odd thing of mine."

"Well, you might be right," said Old Man Coyote. "Let's find out." Coyote stuck his penis into Coyote Woman's vagina.

"Um, that feels good," said Coyote Woman.

"You are right," said Old Man Coyote. "It feels very good indeed. I have never felt this way before."

"Neither have I," said Coyote Woman. It occurred to me that this might be the way to make other human beings. It would be nice to have company."

"It certainly would," said Old Man Coyote. "Just you and me could become boring."

"Well, in case doing what we just did should result in bringing forth more human beings, what should they be like?" said Coyote Woman.

"Well, I think they should have eyes and mouths going up and down."

"No, no," said Coyote Woman. "Then they would not be able to see well, and food would dribble out of the lower corner of their mouths. Let's have their eyes and mouths go crosswise."

"I think that the men should order the women about," said Old Man Coyote, "and that the women should obey them."

"We'll see about that," said Coyote Woman. "I think that the men should pretend to be in charge and that the women should pretend to obey, but that in reality it should be the other way around."

"I can't agree to this," said Old Man Coyote.

"Why quarrel?" said Coyote Woman. "Let's just wait and see how it will work out."

"All right, let's wait and see. How should the men live?"

"The men should hunt, kill buffalo and bears, and bring the meat to the women. They should protect the women at all times."

"Well, that could be dangerous for the men," said Old Man Coyote. "A buffalo bull or a bear could kill a man. Is it fair to put the men in such danger? What should the women do in return?"

"Why, let the women do the work," said Coyote Woman. "Let them cook, and fetch water, and scrape and tan hides with buffalo rains. Let them do all these things while the men take a rest from hunting."

"Well, then we agree upon everything," said Old Man Coyote. "Then it's settled."

"Yes," said Coyote Woman. "And why don't you stick that funny thing of yours between my legs again?"

The Treasures of the Gods

Norse (Iceland)

Loki, the Norse Trickster, may appear to be the wolfish cousin of Coyote, but he is conspicuously less genial in nature. Like Coyote, Loki is an opportunist and troublemaker of the first order. Like Coyote, he is also a shape-shifter, able to assume any number of

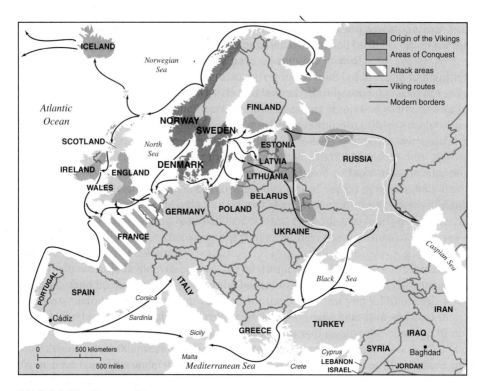

MAP 5.6 The Norse world

guises and hear all kinds of secrets. Nevertheless, Loki isn't fun-loving or warm; his appetites proceed not from friendly bodily urges, but from more sinister psychic cravings. Should Loki swipe a meal or steal a moment in bed with someone else's wife, he does so to exercise power or to gain advantage, not to satisfy fleshly cravings. Moreover, Loki is neither culture hero nor creator, though he certainly craves the authority and respect that are a creator's right. If Coyote embodies the creative potential of chaos and following one's impulses, Loki embodies their potential for destruction.

Much of Loki's mischief, as the following story demonstrates, is motivated by his hatred of the Aesir (the Norse war gods), espe-cially Thor. His action against Sif aims only to humiliate her and aggravate Thor. Even when publicly humiliated himself, Loki finds comfort in some new scheme to bring pain to his enemies. To some degree, Loki reflects the sardonic wit that pervades the Ed-das. In a universe in which even the gods are doomed to age and die, things are not so bad that they couldn't get a little worse. Loki crouches in the shadows waiting for an opportunity to make sure they do.

Somehow the Shape-Changer got into Sif's locked bedroom. Smiling to himself, he pulled out a curved knife and moved to her bedside. Thor's wife was breathing deeply, evenly, dead to worldly sorrows. Then Loki raised his knife. With quick deft strokes he lopped off Sif's head of shining hair—her hair which as she moved rippled and gleamed and changed from gold to gold like swaying corn. Sif murmured but she did not wake; the hair left on her cropped head stuck up like stubble.

Loki scooped up the skeins. He dropped Sif's sheen hair to the floor, a soft glowing mass. The Trickster looked at it and grinned; then he left Sif's bedroom.

"A joke," protested Loki, dangling a foot off the ground.

"What kind of a joke?" shouted Thor, not loosening his grip for one moment.

"Only a joke," whined the Sky Traveler.

All morning Sif had sobbed and sobbed. She knew and Thor knew that only Loki would have shorn her hair.

"Well, what are you going to do about it?" demanded Thor.

"I'll replace it," yelped Loki. "I'll get help from the dwarfs. I promise to replace it."

"Or else," said Thor, and he dumped Loki on the ground.

Loki raised both hands and cautiously explored the top of his head.

"Or else," Thor said, "I'll smash every bone in your body."

Loki straightened his clothes and smoothed his hair and then suddenly he winked at Thor. He hurried out of Asgard, over Bifrost, and down into the land of the dark elves. He picked his way through a chain of chilly potholes, and he skirted dark and shining pools, until he reached a great cave, the home of the sons of Ivaldi.

The sly god explained to the two dwarfs the reasons for his journey, without feeling the need to describe exactly how Sif had lost her hair. "Only you dwarfs are skilled enough smiths," he said, "and only the sons of Ivaldi could spin gold as fine as Sif's hair and imbue it with such magic that it will grow on her head."

"What will we get out of this?" was all that the sons of Ivaldi wanted to know.

"The thanks of Sif and Thor and the friendship of the gods," said Loki. "That counts for a great deal. And, above that, I give you my oath that I'll repay you in full measure when you have need of me."

The dwarfs could see that although Loki offered nothing but promises, they were likely to get the better of the bargain, since the most they could lose was a little effort and a few ounces of gold. They piled wood on to the furnace in the corner of their cave, and while one dwarf worked the bellows, the other began to hammer and spin the gold. Loki watched and marveled, and his eyes flickered red and green in the firelight.

The sons of Ivaldi made a long wave of fine golden strands and, as they worked, they murmured spells over them. The hair hung over Loki's outstretched arm like a single shining sheet and yet a breath of air was enough to ruffle it.

"To waste this blaze is to no one's advantage," said one of the dwarfs.

"We can please the gods at no further expense," said the other.

So the sons of Ivaldi set to work again and, before the furnace had begun to lose any of its heat, they fashioned a marvelous ship for Freyr called Skidbladnir and forged for Odin a spear called Gungnir, as strong as it was slender. Then the two dwarfs gave Loki the ship and the spear and explained their magic power. As usual

Loki was at no loss for words—his mouth was full of air, thanks and compliments and promises to hurry back with news of what the gods thought of such gifts.

On his way back through the dismal underground caverns, Loki had an idea. He did not head straight for the welcoming light of Midgard, but turned down a long aisle studded with rock pillars and, carrying his three treasures, walked into the hall of Brokk and Eitri.

The dwarf brothers stood up to greet Loki. But when they saw the skein of hair and the ship and the spear, they ignored him entirely. Their hearts quickened and their fingertips tingled. Loki let them take the treasures out of his hands and turn them over and over, watching their scorn and envy grow.

"Have you ever seen such work?" exclaimed Loki. "Such perfect craftsmanship?"

"Yes," said Brokk.

"Whose?" asked Loki.

"My own," said Eitri bluntly.

"Well then," said Loki slowly, as if the thought were just forming in his mind, "you think you could make treasures as fine as these?"   *manipulate*

"Not as fine . . ." Brokk said.

"Finer," said Eitri.

"No," said Loki craftily. "Surely not. I'll stake my head on it. Brokk, I'll stake my head that your brother can't forge treasures the likes of these."

Brokk and Eitri were very eager to take up his challenge. It occurred to them that if they were as good as their boast, not only would they be rid of the schemer Loki but the treasures made by the sons of Ivaldi would be theirs for the taking.

Leaving Loki with a horn full of mead and with orders only to wait, Eitri and Brokk stumped across their hall and through an arch into the rocky alcove that was their smithy. At once Brokk began to pile wood on to the furnace while Eitri hammered and rolled a length of gold wire and cut it into hundreds of short pieces. Then Eitri laid a pigskin on the roaring fire and said to Brokk, "Pump the bellows now. Whatever happens, keep pumping until I pull this treasure out of the forge."

A little while after Eitri had walked out of the smithy a fly alighted on Brokk's leathery hand. It stung him. Brokk glanced down but did not pause; he kept pumping the bellows, and when Eitri returned he pulled Gullinbursti out of the forge, a boar with bristles of gold.

Now Eitri picked a great block of unflawed gold. He heated the metal until it was glowing and malleable. Then he hammered it into shape and put it back into the furnace. "Pump the bellows now,' said Eitri. "Whatever happens, keep pumping until I pull this treasure out of the forge."

A little while after Eitri had left the smithy, the same fly returned and settled on Brokk's neck. It stung him twice as sharply as before. Brokk winced and flinched but he did not pause; he kept pumping the bellows, and when Eitri returned he took Draupnir out of the forge, an arm-ring of solid gold.

Now Eitri humped a great hunk of iron across the smithy and into the furnace. He heated it and hammered it. He struck at it and shaped it, he reshaped it, he tapped and tapped at it. His body ached, he streamed with sweat and, when he was ready, his head and heart were both banging with his own efforts. "Pump the bellows now,' said Eitri. "It will all be wrecked if you stop pumping."

Very soon after Eitri had walked wearily out of the smithy, and looked around for their visitor, the fly buzzed through the arch into the alcove. This time it settled between Brokk's eyes, and at once it stung him on both eyelids. The dwarf was blinded with blood. He could not see what he was doing. For a moment he took a hand off the bellows, so that they caught their breath, to brush the fly off his forehead and the blood out of his eyes. Then the Shape Changer, Loki, for the fly was none other, returned to his waiting place and his horn of mead.

At this moment Eitri hurried back into the smithy. "What has happened?" he shouted. He peered into the furnace. "So nearly," he said. He peered into the flames again and his glittering gray eyes did not even reflect them. "So very nearly spoiled." Then Eitri pulled from the forge an iron hammer, massive and finely forged, but rather short in the handle. He called it Mjollnir. Eitri and Brokk stared at it, they stared at each other, they slowly nodded.

"Take this hammer and this ring and this boar," said Eitri. "Tell the gods the mysteries of these treasures. Go with Loki to Asgard and claim that schemer's head."

Brokk and Eitri walked out of the alcove and found the Sly One, the Shape Changer, waiting for them, smiling. He cast an eye over their three treasures. "Ready?" he said.

Loki and Brokk made their way slowly across the shining fields of Asgard, laden with their treasures. Word of their coming ran ahead of them, and they were met in Gladsheim by all the gods, sitting in their high places. Loki at once told of his visit to the world of the dwarfs, and boasted that he had been able to exploit the dwarfs' envy and greed to secure six gifts for the gods.

"Talk while you can," said Brokk. "Soon you'll have no tongue."

It was agreed that Odin and Thor and Freyr should decide whether Eitri or the sons of Ivaldi were the finer smiths, and Loki began to display his treasures.

"This spear," he said, "is for you, Odin. It is Gungnir. It differs from other spears in this way: it never misses its mark." The Father of Battle took the spear and raised it and looked around the hall. Nobody could withstand his terrible gaze. "You may want to use it," Loki said, "to stir up warfare in the world of men."

Then Loki turned to Freyr. "This vessel is for you, Freyr. It is Skidbladnir. As you can see, it's large enough to hold all of the gods, fully armed. As soon as you hoist its sail, a breeze will spring up and fill it, and urge the boat forward. But when you have no need of it, you can take it apart." Loki swiftly dismasted and dismantled the boat until the pieces were together no larger than a piece of cloth. "You can fold it up like this," said Loki, "and put it in your purse!"

"My third gift," said the schemer, "I owe to you, Sif." He showed the skein of flowing golden hair to the goddess. "As soon as you lift this to your head, it will take root and grow. You'll be no less beautiful than you were before."

Thor's wife took the hair from Loki. She fingered it, she turned it over and over, then she slowly raised it to her head. There was a shout of joy in Gladsheim; it was just as Loki said.

Now Brokk produced his gifts. "This gold arm-ring is for you, Odin," he said. "It is Draupnir. There is a little more to it than it seems. Eight rings of its own weight will drop from it on every ninth night."

Then Brokk turned to Freyr. "This boar is for you. He is Gullinbursti. He can charge over earth, air and sea alike, and no horse can keep up with him. And no matter where he goes, running through the night or plunging into the gloom under all the worlds, he'll always be surrounded by brilliant light. He carries it himself because his bristles shine in the dark."

"My third treasure," said Brokk, "is for you, Thor. This is the hammer Mjollnir. You can use it against anything, and use it with all your strength. Nothing can ever break it." The Storm God eagerly grasped the hammer and listened. "Even if you hurl it, you'll never lose it. No matter how far you fling it, it will always return to your hand. And should you need to hide it, you can make it small enough to tuck inside your shirt." All the gods stared at Mjollnir, astounded, and knew what powerful magic must have gone into its making. "It has only one small flaw," added Brokk, "not that it matters. Its handle is rather short."

Odin and Thor and Freyr wasted no time in giving their answer. All three were of one mind, that wondrous though all the treasures were, the hammer Mjollnir was the most valuable because it alone could guard the gods against the giants.

"You, Brokk," said Odin, "have won the wager."

"Loki's head," shrieked Brokk.

"Wait!" cried Loki. "What would you do with my head? I'll give you its weight in gold instead."

"There's no future in that," said Brokk. "And no future for you."

The gods in Gladsheim laughed to see the Trickster cornered.

"Well," said Loki slowly, "well . . . catch me then!" He darted through the doors of the hall and made off as fast as he could. By the time Brokk had made a move to stop him, the Sky Traveler was already well on his way, wearing his shoes with which he could fly over land and water. The gods in Gladsheim laughed all the louder.

"If you had any honor, you'd help me," shrieked the dwarf. "Thor, help me!"

Thor was in no mood to see Brokk humiliated. He leaped up from his high seat and stormed out of Gladsheim. The gods and Brokk waited, and after a while Thor returned, dragging Loki after him.

"Not so fast!" said Loki, raising a hand, as Brokk started towards him. "It's true you have a claim on my head. But of course you can't have any part of my neck."

The gods grinned and nodded, and Brokk saw that Loki had got the better of him.

"In that case," said Brokk, "since your head is mine, at least I'll stop your sweet talk. I'll sew your lips together."

Loki shrugged his shoulders. "Nothing but fine words!" he said.

Brokk unwound a thong from round his waist and tried to skewer Loki's lips with his knife. That was no good. Sharp as the point was, the dwarf could not even draw a drop of blood.

"I could certainly do with my brother's awl," said Brokk. No sooner had he spoken than Eitri's awl lay at his feet. Brokk picked it up, and it proved sharp enough to pierce Loki's lips. The dwarf drew the leather thong through the holes and sewed up the Trickster's mouth.

Loki ran out of Gladsheim. He ripped the thong out through the holes, and yelped at the pain of it. Then for some while the Schemer stood listening to the hum inside the hall—the hive of happiness. He began to dream of revenge, and slowly his lips curled into a twisted smile.

The Seven Great Deeds of Ma-ui

Oceania (Hawaii)

Oceania—the thousands of South Pacific islands between Asia and South America—was originally populated by culturally and linguistically similar peoples who periodically braved the open ocean in small, oar-assisted sailing craft, establishing communities as far north as Hawaii, as far south as New Zealand, as far east as the Easter Islands, and as far west as Indonesia. Thus people as geographically dispersed as the Hawaiians and Maori and the natives of the Marquesas and Borneo share key elements of their mythologies.

Among the Indonesian cultures of Oceania, there are such animal Tricksters as the deer mouse, tortoise, and ape, whose exploits are reminiscent of African Tortoise, Hare, and Jackal stories. These Tricksters avoid work, search constantly for a free lunch, and outwit their stronger, fiercer opponents with ingenious lies, tricks, and escapes. But among the Polynesian cultures of Oceania, Ma-ui is Trickster. Unlike the animal Tricksters, Ma-ui is also culture-bringer and hero, and, perhaps because he is more human than Coyote, Àjàpá, and Loki, he uses a combination of craft and daring to create conditions favorable to human civilization. Indeed, Ma-ui occupies a borderland between animal Tricksters and such wily human heroes as Odysseus and India's King Ashoka. These latter characters use intellect and endurance to overcome seemingly impossible challenges, and Ma-ui certainly shares these qualities with them. Nevertheless, Ma-ui is a supernatural being whose paradoxically human birth is neither celebrated nor recognized at first. It is only after revealing his magical powers that Ma-ui becomes the apple of his mother's eye and the envy of his slower-witted brothers.

Source: Padraic Colum, *Tales and Legends of Hawaii.* New Haven, CT: Yale University Press, 1937. 38–64. Used with permission of Yale University Press.

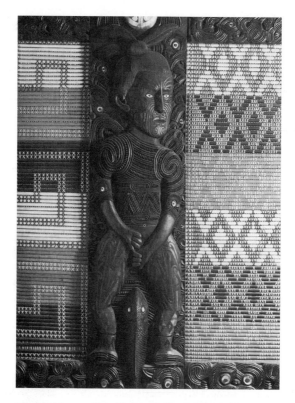

Maui fishing up New Zealand's North Island. Carved
wood. Ht. 7′ 5/8″. Maori, carved in 1898–99 by Tene
Waitere. While the stories told about Maui are similar
throughout Oceania, his representation in art varies
according to local styles. Notice the whorls and geomet-
ric patterns representing the tatooing that was common
among New Zealand's Maori.
Source: © Museum für Völkerkunde, Hamburg

As the following Hawaiian cycle of Ma-ui stories shows, the
Polynesian culture-bringer puts the finishing touches on creation
by better organizing the sun and sky, dredges up land from the
bottom of the ocean, discovers the secret of fire, and even challenges death. In these exploits, Ma-ui uses a combination of wit,
occult knowledge, muscle, and bravery to do the seemingly impossible. But what is his motivation? Altruism? The pursuit of
glory? Or does he act only upon impulse, simply doing that which
the circumstances require? In short, how *human* are Ma-ui's motives in comparison to other, more obviously "natural" culture-
bringers and heroes?

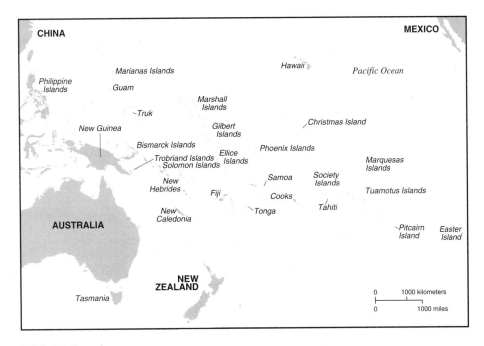

MAP 5.7 Oceania

There is no hero who is more famous than Ma-ui. In all the islands of the Great Ocean, from Kahiki-mo-e to Hawaii-nei, his name and his deeds are spoken of. His deeds were many, but seven of them were very great, and it is about those seven great deeds that I shall tell you.

HOW MA-UI WON A PLACE FOR HIMSELF IN THE HOUSE

abandons him

When Ma-ui, the last of her five sons, was born, his mother thought she would have no food for him. So she took him down to the shore of the sea, she cut off her hair and tied it around him, and she gave him to the waves. But Ma-ui was not drowned in the sea: first of all the jellyfish came; it folded him in its softness, and it kept him warm while he floated on. And then the God of the Sea found the child and took charge of him: he brought him to his house and warmed and cherished him, and little Ma-ui grew up in the land where lived the God of the Sea.

But while he was still a boy he went back to his mother's country. He saw his mother and his four brothers, and he followed them into a house; it was a house that all the people of the country were going into. He sat there with his brothers. And when his mother called her children to take them home, she found this strange child with them. She did not know him, and she would not take him with the rest of the children. But Ma-ui followed them. And when his four brothers came out of their own house they found him there, and he played with them. At first they played hide-and-seek, but then they made themselves spears from canes and began throwing the spears at the house.

The slight spears did not go through the thatch of grass that was at the outside of the house. And then Ma-ui made a charm over the cane that was his spear—a charm that toughened it and made it heavy. He flung it again, and a great hole was made in the grass thatch of the house. His mother came out to chastise the boy and drive him away. But when she stood at the door and saw him standing there so angry, and saw how he was able to break down the house with the throws of his spear, she knew in him the great power that his father had, and she called to him to come into the house. He would not come in until she had laid her hands upon him. When she did this his brothers were jealous that their mother made so much of this strange boy, and they did not want to have him with them. It was then that the elder brother spoke and said, "Never mind, let him be with us and be our dear brother." And then they all asked him to come into the house.

The doorposts, Short Post and Tall Post, that had been put there to guard the house, would not let him come in. Then Ma-ui lifted up his spear, and he threw it at Tall Post and overthrew him. He threw his spear again and overthrew Short Post. And after that he went into his mother's house and was with his brothers. The overthrowing of the two posts that guarded the house was the first of the great deeds of Ma-ui.

In those days, say the people who know the stories of the old times, the birds were not seen by the men and women of the Islands. They flew around the houses, and the flutter of their wings was heard, and the stirring of the branches and the leaves as they were lit upon. Then there would be music. But the people who had never seen the birds thought that this was music made by gods who wanted to remain unseen by the people. Ma-ui could see the birds; he rejoiced in their brilliant colors, and when he called to them they would come and rest upon the branches around the place where he was, there they would sing their happiest songs to him.

There was a visitor who came from another land to the country that Ma-ui lived in. He boasted of all the wonderful things that were in his country, and it seemed to the people of Ma-ui's land that they had nothing that was fine or that could be spoken about. Then Ma-ui called to the birds. They came and they made music on every side. The visitor who had boasted so much was made to wonder, and he said that there was nothing in his country that was so marvelous as the music made by Ma-ui's friends, the birds.

Then, that they might be honored by all, Ma-ui said a charm by which the birds came to be seen by men—the red birds, the *i-i-wi* and the *aha-hani,* and the yellow birds, the *o-o* and the *mamo,* and all the other bright birds. The delight of seeing them was equal to the delight of hearing the music that they made. Ever afterward the birds were seen and heard, and the people all rejoiced in them. This Ma-ui did when he was still a boy growing up with his brothers and with his sister in his mother's house. But this is not counted amongst the great deeds of Ma-ui the hero.

HOW MA-UI LIFTED UP THE SKY

Then he lifted up the sky to where it is now. This was the second of Ma-ui's great deeds.

When he was growing up in his mother's house the sky was so low that the trees touched it and had their leaves flattened out. Men and women burned with the heat because the sky was so near to them. The clouds were so close that there was much darkness on the earth. Something had to be done about it, and Ma-ui made up his mind that he would lift up the sky.

Somewhere he got a mark tattooed on his arm that was a magic mark and that gave him great strength. Then he went to lift up the sky. And from some woman he got a drink that made his strength greater. "Give me to drink out of your gourd," he said, "and I will push up the sky." The woman gave him her gourd to drink from. Then Ma-ui pushed at the sky. He lifted it high, to where the trees have their tops now. He pushed at it again, and he put it where the mountains have their tops now. And then he pushed it to where it rests, on the tops of the highest mountains.

Then the men and women were able to walk about all over the earth, and they had light now and clear air. The trees grew higher and higher, and they grew more and more fruit. But even to this day their leaves are flattened out: it is from the time when their leaves were flattened against the sky.

When the sky was lifted up Ma-ui went and made a kite for himself. From his mother he got the largest and strongest piece of *tapa* cloth she had ever made, and he formed it into a kite with a frame and cross-sticks of *hau* wood. The tail of the kite was fifteen fathoms long, and he got a line of *olona* vine for it that was twenty times forty fathoms in length. He started the kite. But it rose very slowly; the wind barely held it up.

Then the people said: "Look at Ma-ui! He lifted the sky up, and now he can't fly a kite." Ma-ui was made angry when he heard them say this: he drew the kite this way and that way, but still he was not able to make it rise up. He cried out his incantation—

> "Strong wind, come;
> Soft wind, come"—

but still the kite would not rise.

Then he remembered that in the Valley of Wai-pio there was a wizard who had control of the winds. Over the mountains and down into the valley Ma-ui went. He saw the calabash that the wizard kept the winds in, and he asked him to loosen them and direct them to blow along the river to the place where he was going to fly his kite. Then Ma-ui went back. He stood with his feet upon the rocks along the bank of the Wai-lu-ku River; he stood there braced to hold his kite, and where he stood are the marks of his feet to this day. He called out:

> "O winds, winds of Wai-pio,
> Come from the calabash—
> 'the Calabash of Perpetual Winds.'
> O wind, O wind of Hilo,
> Come quickly; come with power."

The call that Ma-ui gave went across the mountains and down into the valley of Wai-pio. No sooner did he hear it than the wizard opened his calabash. The winds rushed out. They went into the bay of Hilo, and they dashed themselves against the water. The call of Ma-ui came to them:

> "O winds, winds of Hilo,
> Hurry, hurry and come to me."

The winds turned from the sea. They rushed along the river. They came to where Ma-ui stood, and then they saw the great, strange bird that he held.

They wanted to fall upon that bird and dash it up against the sky. But the great kite was strong. The winds flung it up and flung it this way and that way. But they could not carry it off or dash it against the sky as they wanted to.

Ma-ui rejoiced. How grand it was to hold a kite that the winds strove to tear away! He called out again:

> "O winds, O winds of Hilo,
> Come to the mountains, come."

Then came the west wind that had been dashing up waves in the bay of Hilo. It joined itself with the north wind and the east wind, the two winds that had been tearing and pushing at Ma-ui's kite. Now, although the kite was made of the strongest *tapa,* and although it had been strengthened in every cunning way that Ma-ui knew, it was flung here and flung there. Ma-ui let his line out; the kite was borne up and up and above the mountains. And now he cried out to the kite that he had made:

> "Climb up, climb up
> To the highest level of the heavens,
> To all the sides of the heavens.
> Climb thou to thy ancestor,
> To the sacred bird in the heavens."

The three winds joined together, and now they made a fiercer attack upon Ma-ui's kite. The winds tore and tossed it. Then the line broke in Ma-ui's hands.

The winds flung the kite across the mountains. And then, to punish it for having dared to face the heavens, they rammed it down into the volcano, and stirred up the fires against it.

Then Ma-ui made for himself another kite. He flew it, and rejoiced in the flying of it, and all who saw him wondered at how high his kite went and how gracefully it bore itself in the heavens. But never again did he call upon the great winds to help him in his sport. Sometimes he would fasten his line to the black stones in the bed of the Wai-lu-ku River, and he would let the kite soar upward and range here and there. He knew by watching his soaring kite whether it would be dry and pleasant weather, and he showed his neighbors how they might know it. "Eh, neighbor," one would say to another, "it is going to be dry weather; look how Ma-ui's kite keeps in the sky." They knew that they could go to the fields to work and spread out their *tapa* to dry, for as long as the kite soared the rain would not fall.

Ma-ui learned what a strong pull the fierce winds had. He used to bring his kite with him when he went out on the ocean in his canoe. He would let it free; then, fastening his line to the canoe, he would let the wind that pulled the kite pull him along.

By flying his kite he learned how to go more swiftly over the ocean in his canoe, and how to make voyages further than ever a man made before. Nevertheless, his kite flying is not counted amongst the great deeds of Ma-ui.

HOW MA-UI FISHED UP THE GREAT ISLAND

Now, although Ma-ui had done deeds as great as these, he was not thought so very much of in his own house. His brothers complained that when he went fishing with them he caught no fish, or, if he drew one up, it was a fish that had been taken on a hook belonging to one of them and that Ma-ui had managed to get tangled on to his own line. And yet Ma-ui had invented many things that his brothers made use of. At first they had spears with smooth heads on them: if they struck a bird, the bird was often able to flutter away, drawing away from the spearhead that had pierced a wing. And if they struck through a fish, the fish was often able to wriggle away. Then Ma-ui put barbs upon his spear, and his spearhead held the birds and the fish. His brothers copied the spearhead that he made, and after that they were able to kill and secure more birds and fish than ever before.

He made many things that they copied, and yet his brothers thought him a lazy and a shiftless fellow, and they made their mother think the same about him. They were the better fishermen—that was true; indeed, if there were no one but Ma-ui to go fishing, Hina-of-the-Fire, his mother, and Hina-of-the-Sea, his sister, would often go hungry.

At last Ma-ui made up his mind to do some wonderful fishing; he might not be able to catch the fine fish that his brothers desired—the *u-lua* and the *pi-mo-e*—but he would take up something from the bottom of the sea that would make his brothers forget that he was the lazy and the shiftless one.

He had to make many plans and go on many adventures before he was ready for this great fishing. First he had to get a fishhook that was different from any fishhook that had ever been in the world before. In those days fishhooks were made out of bones—there was nothing else to make fishhooks out of—and Ma-ui would have to get a wonderful bone to form into a hook. He went down into the underworld to get that bone.

He went to where his ancestress was. On one side she was dead and on the other side she was a living woman. From the side of her that was dead Ma-ui took a bone—her jawbone—and out of this bone he made his fishhook. There was never a fishhook like it in the world before, and it was called "Ma-nai-i-ka-lani," meaning "made fast to the heavens." He told no one about the wonderful fishhook he had made for himself.

He had to get a different bait from any bait that had ever been used in the world before. His mother had sacred birds, the *alae,* and he asked her to give him one of them for bait. She gave him one of her birds.

Then Ma-ui, with his bait and his hook hidden, and with a line that he had made from the strongest *olona* vines, went down to his brothers' canoe. "Here is Ma-ui," they said when they saw him, "here is Ma-ui, the lazy and the shiftless, and we have sworn that we will never let him come again with us in our canoe." They pushed out when they saw him coming; they paddled away, although he begged them to take him with them.

He waited on the beach. His brothers came back, and they had to tell him that they had caught no fish. Then he begged them to go back to sea again and to let him go this time in their canoe. They let him in, and they paddled off. "Farther and farther out, my brothers," said Ma-ui; "out there is where the *u-lua* and the *pi-mo-e* are." They paddled far out. They let down their lines, but they caught no fish. "Where are the *u-lua* and the *pi-mo-e* that you spoke of?" said his brothers to him. Still he told them to go farther and farther out. At last they got tired with paddling, and they wanted to go back.

Then Ma-ui put a sail upon the canoe. Farther and farther out into the ocean they went. One of the brothers let down a line, and a great fish drew on it. They pulled. But what came out of the depths was a shark. They cut the line and let the shark get away. The brothers were very tired now. "Oh, Ma-ui," they said, "as ever, thou art lazy and shiftless. Thou hast brought us out all this way, and thou wilt do nothing to help us. Thou hast let down no line in all the sea we have crossed."

It was then that Ma-ui let down his line with the magic hook upon it, the hook that was baited with the struggling *alae* bird. Down, down went the hook that was named "Ma-nai-i-ka-lani." Down through the waters the hook and the bait went. Ka-uni ho-kahi, Old One Tooth, who holds fast the land to the bottom of the sea, was there. When the sacred bird came near him he took it in his mouth. And the magic hook that Ma-ui had made held fast in his jaws.

Ma-ui felt the pull upon the line. He fastened the line to the canoe, and he bade his brothers paddle their hardest, for now the great fish was caught. He dipped his own paddle into the sea, and he made the canoe dash on.

The brothers felt a great weight grow behind the canoe. But still they paddled on and on. Weighty and more weighty became the catch, harder and harder it became to pull it along. As they struggled on Ma-ui chanted a magic chant, and the weight came with them.

> "O Island, O great Island,
> O Island, O great Island!
> Why art thou
> Sulkily biting, biting below?
> Beneath the earth
> The power is felt,
> The foam is seen:
> Come, O thou loved grandchild
> Of Kanaloa."

On and on the canoe went, and heavier and heavier grew what was behind them. At last one of the brothers looked back. At what he saw he screamed out in affright. For there, rising behind them, a whole land was rising up, with mountains upon it. The brother dropped his paddle when he saw what had been fished up; as he dropped his paddle the line that was fastened to the jaws of old Ka-uni ho-kahi broke.

What Ma-ui fished up would have been a mainland, only that his brother's paddle dropped and the line broke. Then only an island came up out of the water. If more land had come up, all the islands that we know would have been joined in one.

There are people who say that his sister, Hina-of-the-Sea, was near at the time of that great fishing. They say she came floating out on a calabash. When Ma-ui let down the magic hook with their mother's sacred bird upon it, Hina-of-the-Sea dived down and put the hook into the mouth of Old One Tooth, and then pulled at the line to let Ma-ui know that the hook was in his jaws. Some people say this, and it may be the truth. But whether or not, everyone, on every island in the Great Ocean, from Kahiki-mo-e to Hawaii nei, knows that Ma-ui fished up a great island for men to live on. And this fishing was the third of Ma-ui's great deeds.

HOW MA-UI SNARED THE SUN AND MADE HIM GO MORE SLOWLY ACROSS THE HEAVENS

The Sky had been lifted up, and another great island had come from the grip of Old One Tooth and was above the waters. The world was better now for men and women to live in. But still there were miseries in it, and the greatest of these miseries was on account of the heedlessness of the Sun.

For the Sun in those days made his way too quickly across the world. He hurried so that little of his heat got to the plants and the fruits, and it took years and years for them to ripen. The farmers working on their patches would not have time in the light of a day to put down their crop into the ground, so quickly the Sun would rush across the heavens, and the fishermen would barely have time to launch their canoes and get to the fishing grounds when the darkness would come on. And the women's tasks were never finished. It was theirs to make the *tapa* cloth: a woman would begin at one end of the board to beat the bark with her four-sided mallet, and she would be only at the middle of the board by the time the sunset came. When she was ready to go on with the work next day, the Sun would be already halfway across the heavens.

Ma-ui, when he was a child, used to watch his mother making *tapa,* and as he grew up he pitied her more and more because of all the toil and trouble that she had. She would break the branches from the *ma-ma-ka* trees and from the *wau-ka* trees and soak them in water until their bark was easily taken off. Then she would take off the outer bark, leaving the inner bark to be worked upon. She would take the bundles of the wet inner bark and lay them on the *tapa* board and begin pounding them with little clubs. And then she would use her four-sided mallet and beat all the soft stuff into little thin sheets. Then she would paste the little sheets together, making large cloths. This was *tapa*—the *tapa* that it was every woman's business in those days to make. As soon as morning reddened the clouds Ma-ui's mother, Hina-of-the-Fire, would begin her task: she would begin beating the softened bark at one end of the board, and she would be only in the middle of the board when the sunset came. And when she managed to get the *tapa* made she could never get it dried in a single day, so quickly the Sun made his way across the heavens. Ma-ui pitied his mother because of her unceasing toil.

He greatly blamed the Sun for his inconsiderateness of the people of the world. He took to watching the Sun. He began to know the path by which the Sun came over the great mountain Ha-le-a-ka-la (but in those days it was not called Ha-le-a-ka-la, the House of the Sun, but A-hele-a-ka-la, the Rays of the Sun). Through a great chasm in the side of this mountain the Sun used to come.

He told his mother that he was going to do something to make the Sun have more consideration for the men and women of the world. "You will not be able to make him do anything about it," she said; "the Sun always went swiftly, and he will always go swiftly." But Ma-ui said that he would find a way to make the Sun remember that there were people in the world and that they were not at all pleased with the way he was going on.

Then his mother said: "If you are going to force the Sun to go more slowly you must prepare yourself for a great battle, for the Sun is a great creature, and he has much energy. Go to your grandmother who lives on the side of Ha-le-a-ka-la," said she (but it was called A-hele-a-ka-la then), "and beg her to give you her counsel, and also to give you a weapon to battle with the Sun."

So Ma-ui went to his grandmother who lived on the side of the great mountain. Ma-ui's grandmother was the one who cooked the bananas that the Sun ate as he came through the great chasm in the mountain. "You must go to the place where there is a large *wili-wili* tree growing," said his mother. "There the Sun stops to eat the bananas that your grandmother cooks for him. Stay until the rooster that watches beside the *wili-wili* tree crows three times. Your grandmother will come out then with a bunch of bananas. When she lays them down, you take them up. She will bring another bunch out; take that up too. When all her bananas are gone she will search for the one who took them. Then do you show yourself to her. Tell her that you are Ma-ui and that you belong to Hina-of-the-Fire."

So Ma-ui went up the side of the mountain that is now called Ha-le-a-ka-la, but that then was called A-hele-a-ka-la, the Rays of the Sun. He came to where a great *wili-wili* tree was growing. There he waited. The rooster crowed three times, and then an old woman came out with a bunch of bananas. He knew that this was his grandmother. She laid the bananas down to cook them, and as she did so Ma-ui snatched them away. When she went to pick up the bunch she cried out, "Where are the bananas that I have to cook for my lord, the Sun?" She went within and got another bunch, and this one, too, Ma-ui snatched away. This he did until the last bunch of bananas that his grandmother had was taken.

She was nearly blind, so she could not find him with her eyes. She sniffed around, and at last she got the smell of a man. "Who are you?" she said. "I am Ma-ui, and I belong to Hina-of-the-Fire," said he. "What have you come for?" asked his grandmother. "I have come to chastise the Sun and to make him go more slowly across the heavens. He goes so fast now that my mother cannot dry the *tapa* that she takes all the days of the year to beat out."

The old woman considered all that Ma-ui said to her. She knew that he was a hero born, because the birds sang, the pebbles rumbled, the grass withered, the smoke hung low, the rainbow appeared, the thunder was heard, the hairless dogs were seen, and even the ants in the grass were heard to sing in his praise. She decided to give help to him. And she told him what preparations he was to make for his battle with the Sun.

First of all he was to get sixteen of the strongest ropes that ever were made. So as to be sure they were the strongest, he was to knit them himself. And he was to make nooses for them out of the hair of the head of his sister, Hina-of-the-Sea. When the ropes were ready he was to come back to her, and she would show him what else he had to do.

Ma-ui made the sixteen ropes; he made them out of the strongest fiber, and his sister, Hina-of-the-Sea, gave him the hair of her head to make into nooses. Then, with the ropes and the nooses upon them, Ma-ui went back to his grandmother. She told him where to set the nooses, and she gave him a magic stone ax with which to do battle with the Sun.

He set the nooses as snares for the Sun, and he dug a hole beside the roots of the *wili-wili* tree, and in that hole he hid himself. Soon the first ray of light, the first leg of the Sun, came over the mountain wall. It was caught in one of the nooses that Ma-ui had set. One by one the legs of the Sun came over the rim, and one by one they were caught in the nooses. One leg was left hanging down the side of the mountain: it was hard for the Sun to move that leg. At last this last leg came slowly over the edge of the mountain and was caught in the snare. Then Ma-ui gathered up the ropes and tied them to the great *wili-wili* tree.

When the Sun saw that his sixteen legs were held fast by the nooses that Ma-ui had set he tried to back down the mountainside and into the sea again. But the ropes held him, and the *wili-wili* tree stood the drag of the ropes. The Sun could not get away. Then he turned all his burning strength upon Ma-ui. They fought. The man began to strike at the Sun with his magic ax of stone; and never before did the Sun get such a beating. "Give me my life," said the Sun.

"I will give you your life," said Ma-ui, "if you promise to go slowly across the heavens." At last the Sun promised to do what Ma-ui asked him.

They entered into an agreement with each other, Ma-ui and the Sun. There should be longer days, the Sun making his course slower. But every six months, in the winter, the Sun might go as fast as he had been in the habit of going. Then Ma-ui let the Sun out of the snares which he had set for him. But, lest he should ever forget the agreement he had made and take to traveling swiftly again, Ma-ui left all the ropes and the nooses on the side of Ha-le-a-ka-la, so that he might see them every day that he came across the rim of the mountain. And the mountain was not called A-hele-a-ka-la, the Rays of the Sun, any more, but Ha-le-a-ka-la, the House of the Sun. After that came the saying of the people, "Long shall be the daily journey of the Sun, and he shall give light for all the peoples' toil." And Ma-ui's mother, Hina-of-the-Fire, learned that she could pound on the *tapa* board until she was tired, and the farmers could plant and take care of their crops, and the fishermen could go out to the deep sea and fish and come back, and the fruits and the plants got heat enough to make them ripen in their season.

HOW MA-UI WON FIRE FOR MEN

Ma-ui's mother must have known about fire and the use of fire; else why should she have been called Hina-of-the-Fire, and how did it come that her birds, the *alae,* knew where fire was hidden and how to make it blaze up? Hina must have known about fire. But her son had to search and search for fire. The people who lived in houses on the Islands did not know of it: they had to eat raw roots and raw fish, and they had to suffer the cold. It was for them that Ma-ui wanted to get fire; it was for them that he went down to the lower world, and that he went searching through the upper world for it.

In Kahiki-mo-e they have a tale about Ma-ui that the Hawaiians do not know. There they tell how he went down to the lower world and sought out his great-great-grandmother, Ma-hui'a. She was glad to see Ma-ui, of whom she had heard in the lower world; and when he asked her to give him fire to take to the upper world, she plucked a nail off her finger and gave it to him.

In this nail, fire burned. Ma-ui went to the upper world with it. But in crossing a stream of water he let the nail drop into it. And so he lost the fire that his great-great-grandmother had given him.

He went back to her again. And again Ma-hui'a plucked off a fingernail and gave it to him. But when he went to the upper world and went to cross the stream, he let this burning nail also drop into the water. Again he went back, and his great-great-grandmother plucked off a third nail for him. And this went on, Ma-ui letting the nails fall into the water, and Ma-hui'a giving him the nails off her fingers, until at last all the nails of all her fingers were given to him.

But still he went on letting the burning nails fall into the water that he had to cross, and at last the nails of his great-great-grandmother's toes as well as the nails of her fingers were given to him—all but the nail on the last of her toes. Ma-ui went back to her to get this last nail. Then Ma-hui'a became blazing angry, she plucked the nail off, but instead of giving it to him she flung it upon the ground.

Fire poured out of the nail and took hold on everything. Ma-ui ran to the upper world, and Ma-hui'a in her anger ran after him. He dashed into the water. But now the forests were blazing, and the earth was burning, and the water was boiling. Ma-ui ran on, and Ma-hui'a ran behind him. As he ran he chanted a magic incantation for rain to come, so that the burning might be put out:

> "To the roaring thunder;
> To the great rain—the long rain;
> To the drizzling rain—the small rain;
> To the rain pattering on the leaves.
> These are the storms, the storms
> Cause them to fall;
> To pour in torrents."

The rain came on—the long rain, the small rain, the rain that patters on the leaves; storms came, and rain in torrents. The fire that raged in the forests and burned on the ground was drowned out. And Ma-hui'a, who had followed him, was nearly drowned by the torrents of rain. She saw her fire, all the fire that was in the lower and in the upper worlds, being quenched by the rain.

She gathered up what fragments of fire she could, and she hid them in barks of different trees so that the rain could not get at them and quench them. Ma-ui's mother must have known where his great-great-grandmother hid the fire. If she did not, her sacred birds, the *alae,* knew it. They were able to take the barks of the trees and, by rubbing them together, to bring out fire.

In Hawaii they tell how Ma-ui and his brothers used to go out fishing every day, and how, as soon as they got far out to sea, they would see smoke rising on the mountainside. "Behold," they would say, "there is a fire. Whose can it be?"

"Let us hasten to the shore and cook our fish at that fire," another would say.

So, with the fish that they had caught, Ma-ui and his brothers would hasten to the shore. The swiftest of them would run up the mountainside. But when he would get to where the smoke had been, all he would see would be the *alae* scratching clay over burnt-out sticks. The *alae* would leave the place where they had been seen, and Ma-ui would follow them from place to place, hoping to catch them while their fire was lighted.

He would send his brothers off fishing, and he himself would watch for the smoke from the fire that the *alae* would kindle. But they would kindle no fire on the days that he did not go out in the canoe with his brothers. "We cannot have our cooked bananas today," the old bird would say to the young birds, "for the swift son of Hina is somewhere near, and he would come upon us before we put out our fire. And remember that the guardian of the fire told us never to show a man where it is hidden or how it is taken out of its hiding place."

Then Ma-ui understood that the birds watched for his going and that they made no fire until they saw him out at sea in his canoe. He knew that they counted the men that went out, and that if he was not in the number they did no cooking that day. Every time he went in the canoe he saw smoke rising on the mountainside.

Then Ma-ui thought of a trick to play on them—on the stingy *alae* that would not give fire, but left men to eat raw roots and raw fish. He rolled up a piece of *tapa,* and he put it into the canoe, making it like a man. Then he hid near the shore. The brothers went fishing, and the birds counted the figures in the canoe. "The swift son of Hina has gone fishing: we can have cooked bananas today." "Make the fire, make the fire, until we cook our bananas," said the young *alae.*

So they gathered the wood together, and they rubbed the barks, and they made the fire. The smoke rose up from it, and swift Ma-ui ran up the mountainside. He came upon the flock of birds just as the old one was dashing water upon the embers. He caught her by the neck and held her.

"I will kill you," he said, "for hiding fire from men."

"If you kill me," said the old *alae,* "there will be no one to show you how to get fire."

"Show me how to get fire," said Ma-ui, "and I will let you go."

The cunning *alae* tried to deceive Ma-ui. She thought she would get him off his guard, that he would let go of her, and that she could fly away. "Go to the reeds and rub them together, and you will get fire," she said.

Ma-ui went to the reeds and rubbed them together. But still he held the bird by the neck. Nothing came out of the reeds but moisture. He squeezed her neck. "If you kill me, there will be no one to tell you where to get fire," said the cunning bird, still hoping to get him off his guard. "Go to the taro leaves and rub them together and you will get fire."

Ma-ui held to the bird's neck. He went to the taro leaves and rubbed them together, but no fire came. He squeezed her neck harder. The bird was nearly dead now. But still she tried to deceive the man. "Go to the banana stumps and rub them together, and you will get fire," she said.

He went to the banana stumps and rubbed them together. But still no fire came. Then he gave the bird a squeeze that brought her near death. She showed him then the trees to go to—the *hau* tree and the sandalwood tree. He took the barks of the trees and rubbed them, and they gave fire. And the sweet-smelling sandalwood he called "*ili-aha*"—that is, "fire bark"—because fire came most easily from the bark of that tree. With sticks from these trees Ma-ui went to men. He showed them how to get fire by rubbing them together. And never afterward had men to eat fish raw and roots raw. They could always have fire now.

The first stick he lighted he rubbed on the head of the bird that showed him at last where the fire was hidden. And that is the reason why the *alae,* the mud hen, has a red streak on her head to this day.

HOW MA-UI OVERCAME KUNA LOA THE LONG EEL

Hina-of-the-Fire lived in a cave that the waters of the river streamed over, a cave that always had a beautiful rainbow glimmering across it. While her sons were away no enemy could come to Hina in this cave, for the walls of it went up straight and smooth. And there at the opening of the cave she used to sit, beating out her *tapa* in the long days that came after Ma-ui had snared the Sun and had made him go more slowly across the heavens.

In the river below there was one who was an enemy to Hina. This was Kuna Loa, the Long Eel. Once Kuna Loa had seen Hina on the bank of the river, and he had wanted her to leave her cave and come to his abode. But Hina-of-the-Fire would not go near the Long Eel. Then he had gone to her, and he had lashed her with his tail, covering her with the slime of the river. She told about the insults he had given her, and Ma-ui drove the Long Eel up the river, where he took shelter in the deep pools. Ma-ui broke down the banks of the deep pools with thrusts of his spear, but Kuna Loa, the Long Eel, was still able to escape from him. Now Ma-ui had gone away, and his mother, Hina-of-the-Fire, kept within the cave, the smooth rock of which Kuna Loa could not climb.

The Long Eel came down the river. He saw Hina sitting in the mouth of the cave that had the rainbow glimmering across it, and he was filled with rage and a wish to destroy her. He took a great rock and he put it across the stream, filling it from bank to bank. Then he lashed about in the water in his delight at the thought of what was going to happen to Hina.

She heard a deeper sound in the water than she had ever heard before as she sat there. She looked down and she saw that the water was nearer to the mouth of the cave than she had ever seen it before. Higher and higher it came. And then Hina heard the voice of Kuna Loa rejoicing at the destruction that was coming to her. He raised himself up in the water and cried out to her: "Now your mighty son cannot help you. I will drown you with the waters of the river before he comes back to you, Hina."

And Hina-of-the-Fire cried, "Alas, alas," as she watched the waters mount up and up, for she knew that Ma-ui and her other sons were far away, and that there was no one to help her against Kuna Loa, the Long Eel. But, even as she lamented, something was happening to aid Hina. For Ma-ui had placed above her cave a cloud that served her—"Ao-opua," "The Warning Cloud." Over the cave it rose now, giving itself a strange shape: Ma-ui would see it and be sure to know by its sign that something dire was happening in his mother's cave.

He was then on the mountain Ha-le-a-ka-la, the House of the Sun. He saw the strangely shaped cloud hanging over her cave, and he knew that some danger threatened his mother, Hina-of-the-Fire. He dashed down the side of the mountain, bringing with him the magic ax that his grandmother had given him for his battle with the Sun. He sprang into his canoe. With two strokes of his paddle he crossed the channel and was at the mouth of the Wai-lu-ku River. The bed of the river was empty of water, and Ma-ui left his canoe on the stones and went up toward Hina's cave.

The water had mounted up and up and had gone into the cave, and was spilling over Hina's *tapa* board. She was lamenting, and her heart was broken with the thought that neither Ma-ui nor his brothers would come until the river had drowned her in her cave.

Ma-ui was then coming up the bed of the river. He saw the great stone across the stream, and he heard Kuna Loa rejoicing over the destruction that was coming to Hina in her cave. With one stroke of his ax he broke the rock across. The water came through the break. He struck the rocks and smashed them. The river flowed down once more, and Hina was safe in her cave.

Kuna Loa heard the crash of the ax on the rock, and he knew that Ma-ui had come. He dashed up the stream to hide himself again in the deep pools. Ma-ui showed his mother that she was safe, and then he followed the Long Eel.

Kuna Loa had gone into a deep pool. Ma-ui flung burning stones into the water of that pool, making it boil up. Then Kuna Loa dashed into another pool. From pool to pool Ma-ui chased him, making the pools boil around him. (And there they boil to this day, although Kuna Loa is no longer there.) At last the Eel found a cave in the bottom of one of the pools, and he went and hid in it, and Ma-ui could not find him there, nor could the hot stones that Ma-ui threw into the water, making it boil, drive Kuna Loa out.

Hina thought she was safe from the Long Eel after that. She thought that his skin was so scalded by the boiling water that he had died in his cave. Down the river bank for water she would go, and sometimes she would stand on the bank all wreathed in flowers.

But one day, as she was standing on the bank of the river, Kuna Loa suddenly came up. Hina fled before him. The Eel was between her and her cave, and she could not get back to her shelter. She fled through the woods. And as she fled she shrieked out chants to Ma-ui: her chants went through the woods, and along the side of the mountain, and across the sea; they came at last up the side of Ha-le-a-ka-la, where her son Ma-ui was.

There were many people in the places that Hina fled through, but they could do nothing to help her against the Long Eel. He came swiftly after her. The people in the villages that they went through stood and watched the woman and the Eel that pursued her.

Where would she go now? The Long Eel was close behind her. Then Hina saw a breadfruit tree with great branches, and she climbed into it. Kuna Loa wound himself around the tree and came after her. But the branch that Hina was in was lifted up and up by the tree, and the Long Eel could not come to her.

And then Ma-ui came. He had dashed down the side of the mountain and had crossed the channel with two strokes of his paddles and had hurried along the track made by the Long Eel. Now he saw his mother in the branch that kept mounting up, and he saw Kuna Loa winding himself up after her. Ma-ui went into the tree. He struck the Eel a terrible blow and brought him to the ground. Then he sprang down and cut his head off. With other blows of his ax he cut the Eel all to pieces. He flung the head and the tail of Kuna Loa into the sea. The head turned into fish of many kinds, and the tail became the large conger eel of the sea. Other parts of the body turned into sea monsters of different kinds. And the blood of Kuna Loa, as it fell into the fresh water, became the common eels. The fresh and the salt water eels came into the world in this way, and Ma-ui, by killing the Long Eel, wrought the sixth of his great deeds.

THE SEARCH THAT MA-UI'S BROTHER MADE FOR HIS SISTER HINA-OF-THE-SEA

Ma-ui had four brothers, and each of them was named Ma-ui. The doer of the great deeds was known as "the skilful Ma-ui," and the other four brothers were called "the forgetful Ma-uis." But there was one brother who should not have been called "forgetful." He was the eldest brother, Ma-ui Mua, and he was sometimes called Lu-pe. He may have been forgetful about many things that the skilful Ma-ui took account of, but he was not forgetful of his sister, Hina-of-the-Sea.

His great and skilful brother had set Hina-of-the-Sea wandering. She was married, and her husband often went on journeys with the skilful Ma-ui. And once Ma-ui became angry with him because he ate the bait that they had taken with them for fishing; he became angry with his sister's husband, and in his anger he uttered a spell over him, and changed his form into the form of a dog.

When Hina-of-the-Sea knew that her husband was lost to her she went down to the shore and she chanted her own death song:

> "I weep, I call upon the steep billows of the sea,
> And on him, the great, the ocean god;
> The monsters, all now hidden,
> To come and bury me,
> Who am now wrapped in mourning.
> Let the waves wear their mourning, too,
> And sleep as sleeps the dead."

And after she had chanted this, she threw herself into the sea.

But the waves did not drown her. They carried her to a far land. There were no people there; according to the ancient chant—

> "The houses of Lima Loa stand,
> But there are no people;
> They are at Mana."

The people were by the sea, and two who were fishermen found her. They carried her to their hut, and when they had taken the sea weed and the sea moss from her body they saw what a beautiful woman she was. They brought her to their chief, and the chief took Hina-of-the-Sea for his wife.

But after a while he became forgetful of her. After another while he abused her. She had a child now, but she was very lonely, for she was in a far and a strange land.

> "The houses of Lima Loa stand,
> But there are no people;
> They are at Mana."

She was not forgotten, for Ma-ui Mua, her eldest brother, thought of her. In Kahiki-mo-e they tell of his search for her, and they say that when he heard of her casting herself into the sea, he took to his canoe and went searching all over the sea for her. He found new islands, islands that no one had ever been on before, and he went from island to island, ever hoping to find Hina-of-the-Sea. Far, far he went, and he found neither his sister nor anyone who knew about her.

> "The houses of Lima Loa stand,
> But there are no people;
> They are at Mana."

And every day Hina-of-the-Sea would go down to the shore of the land she was on, and she would call on her eldest brother:

> "O Lu-pe! Come over!
> Take me and my child!"

Now one day, as Hina cried out on the beach, there came a canoe toward her. There was a man in the canoe; but Hina, hardly noticing him, still cried to the waves and the winds:

> "O Lu-pe! Come over!
> Take me and my child!"

The man came up on the beach. He was worn with much travel, and he was white and old looking. He heard the cry that was sent to the waves and the winds, and he cried back in answer:

> "It is Lu-pe, yes, Lu-pe,
> The eldest brother;
> And I am here."

He knew Hina-of-the-Sea. He took her and her child in his canoe, rejoicing that his long search was over at last and that he had a sister again. He took her and her child to one of the islands which he had discovered.

And there Hina-of-the-Sea lived happily with her eldest brother, Ma-ui Mua, and there her child grew up to manhood. The story of her eldest brother's search for Hina is not told in Hawaii nei, and one has to go to Kahiki-mo-e to hear it. But in Hawaii nei they tell of a beautiful land that Ma-ui the Skilful came to in search of someone. It is the land, perhaps, that his brother and sister lived in—the beautiful land that is called Moana-liha-i-ka-wao-ke-le.

HOW MA-UI STROVE TO WIN IMMORTALITY FOR MEN

Would you hear the seventh and last of great Ma-ui's deeds? They do not tell of this deed in Hawaii nei, but they tell of it in Kahiki-mo-e. The last was the greatest of all Ma-ui's deeds, for it was his dangerous labor then to win the greatest boon for men—the boon of everlasting life.

He heard of the Goblin-Goddess who is called Hina-nui-ke-po, Great Hina-of-the-Night. It is she who brings death on all creatures. But if one could take the heart out of her body and give it to all the creatures of the earth to eat, they would live forever, and death would be no more in the world.

They tell how the Moon bathes in the Waters of Life, and comes back to the world with her life renewed. And once Ma-ui caught and held the Moon. He said to her, "Let Death be short, and as you return with new strength let it be that men shall come back from Death with new strength." But the Moon said to Ma-ui, "Rather let Death be long, so that men may sigh and have sorrow. When a man dies, let him go into darkness and become as earth, so that those whom he leaves behind may weep and mourn for him." But for all that the Moon said to Ma-ui, he would not have it that men should go into the darkness forever and become as earth. The Moon showed him where Hina-of-the-Night had her abode. He looked over to her island and saw her. Her eyes shone through the distance; he saw her great teeth that were like volcanic glass and her mouth that was wide like the mouth of a fish; he saw her hair that floated all around her like seaweed in the sea.

He saw her and was afraid; even great Ma-ui was made afraid by the Goblin-Goddess, Great Hina-of-the-Night. But he remembered that he had said that he would find a way of giving everlasting life to men and to all creatures, and he thought and thought of how he could come to the Goblin-Goddess and take the heart out of her body.

It was his task then to draw all creatures to him and to have them promise him that they would help him against the Goblin-Goddess. And when at last he was ready to go against her the birds went with him. He came to the island where she was, Great Hina-of-the-Night. She was sleeping, and all her guards were around her. Ma-ui passed through her guards. He prepared to enter her terrible open mouth, and bring back her heart to give to all the creatures of the earth.

And at last he stood ready to go between the jaws that had the fearful teeth that were sharp like volcanic glass. He stood there in the light of a sun-setting, his body tall and fine and tattooed all over with the histories of his great deeds. He stood there, and then he gave warning to all the birds that none of them was to sing or to laugh until he was outside her jaws again with the heart of the Goblin-Goddess in his hands.

He went within the jaws of Great Hina-of-the-Night. He passed the fearful teeth that were sharp like volcanic glass. He went down into her stomach. And then he seized upon her heart. He came back again as far as her jaws, and he saw the sky beyond them.

Then a bird sang or a bird laughed—either the *e-le-pa-io* sang, or the water wagtail laughed—and the Goblin-Goddess awoke. She caught Ma-ui in her great teeth, and she tore him across. There was darkness then, and the crying of all the birds.

Thus died Ma-ui who raised the sky and who fished up the land, who made the Sun go more slowly across the heavens, and who brought fire to men. Thus died Ma-ui, with the Meat of Immortality in his hands. And since his death no one has ever ventured near the lair of Hina-nui-ke-po, the Goblin-Goddess.

creative manipulator

Prometheus, from Hesiod's *Theogony*

Greek

The first stories of Prometheus appear in Hesiod's *Theogony* and *Works and Days*. From the telling and retelling of his story, Prometheus emerged as a culture hero: he not only defied the wicked gods and gave humans the means to create a better world, but he gave us technology as well. This is the received image of Prometheus. However, we can best understand him as a Trickster, whose actions explain why we struggle daily to survive in an often harsh world.

To understand Hesiod's story of Prometheus fully, it is necessary to understand Hesiod's mind-set. Hesiod sees his world as a place where the gods no longer live—they are divine forces only in a distant, unreachable realm—and where humans must struggle to eke out even a meager existence. He asks himself why this is. His answer is that there was a golden age, in which gods and men lived happily together; and the gods made sure that men didn't have to work for their food or become sick from disease. But there had to be a fall from this golden age. How could this have come about? This is where our Trickster Prometheus enters the story.

Source: Translated by Jon-David Hague, Ph.D. for this volume.

Prometheus and Atlas. Laconian kylix, attributed to the Arkesilas Painter, ca. 555 BCE. Diam. approximately 8 inches. The image painted on this Greek wine-drinking vessel could be said to illustrate the wry adage, "no good deed goes unpunished." Atlas stands upholding the heavens, while an eagle picks at the chest of Prometheus who is bound to a stake.
Source: © Scala/Art Resource, NY

The rift between gods and humans began, Hesiod tells us, at Mekone (a place not far from modern-day Corinth in Greece) where Prometheus tricked Zeus (who nonetheless knew what was going on) into accepting an animal sacrifice of bones wrapped in skin and fat. Humans got the nourishing meat. Zeus, however, became angry at Prometheus's trick, deciding, somewhat illogically, to punish all humans in response. Thus the fall from the Golden Age began, and the first sign of this fall was that gods and humans no longer lived together and were left to communicate through sacrifices.

In his anger at Prometheus's trick, Zeus no longer allowed the ash trees, which provided good kindling, to supply fire to humans. Not only was communication with the gods cut off, humans could no longer eat the nourishing meat. Prometheus then stole fire from Zeus and brought it to humans. Once again communication and nourishment were regained. But Zeus was further angered and in

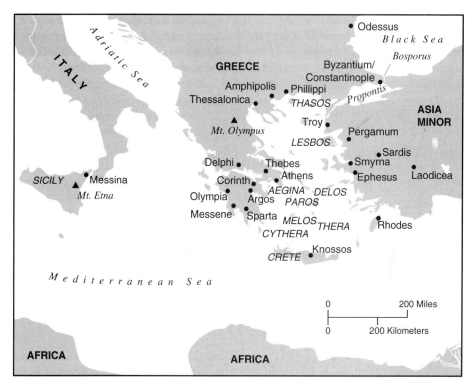

MAP 5.8 Ancient Greece and its area of influence

turn created an evil for men: woman or Pandora. In this part of the story, Hesiod most clearly displays his misogynistic tendencies.

In short, Hesiod's stories of Prometheus in both the *Theogony* and *Works and Days* explain why humans no longer live with the gods in a proverbial land of milk and honey. Humans now cultivate their own food—no easy task—and, in their communication with the gods through sacrifice, they ritually reiterate Prometheus's trick by eating the meat and sending only fragrant smoke to the gods.

Today, we also speak of the past as if it were a Golden Age, a time when we were closer to nature and to the gods. Many speak of a time when young were more respectful of their elders, people were more honest and hard-working, political leaders worked selflessly for the public good, and people practiced faithfully "that old-time religion." Hesiod's story of a lost Golden Age suggests that the ancients also looked with nostalgia at the past. Indeed, this longing for simpler, easier times may well have its roots in the usual trajectory of a human life from the relative peace and security of childhood to the complicated and often painful struggle for self-sufficiency that characterizes adulthood. Who has not looked back with longing at the exuberant energy, the innocence, and the freedom from responsibility that he or she enjoyed in childhood?

Prometheus, the Trickster, acts as catalyst in Hesiod's story in much the same way as the Serpent in the Genesis creation myth. Both Prometheus and the Serpent give "gifts" of forbidden knowledge to humans, thus providing them with the mental tools necessary to move them out of the protective nest in which they had lived with the gods and into the world. And thus the Serpent and Prometheus empower humans through a rudimentary sort of technology to make their own ways in the world—with or without divine assistance and nurture. We all fall from the Garden of Eden—or the Golden Age—and grow up to the complicated and contentious reality of our lives as independent adults.

Iapetos [a child of Gaia and Ouranos] married one of Ocean's daughters,
Klymene with her beautiful ankles,
and took her to their bed.
She gave birth to Atlas for him,
a child with strong will,
and then Menoitios with all his fame,
and Prometheus with his many tricky plans,
and Epimetheus who could never get it right
and was from the start something bad for men,
who live by eating bread,
as he was the first to get from Zeus, once she was made,
a woman to marry.

But Zeus bound Prometheus and his many intentions
with painful chains no one could break,
strapping him hard with these to a pole.
And Zeus sent an eagle with beautiful wings
to attack him and eat his immortal liver.
Yet everything this bird with beautiful wings
would eat during the day would grow back at night.

For the gods and mortal men had had an argument at Mekone.
At that time Prometheus, knowing just what he was doing,
deceiving Zeus, cut up and offered a great ox.

He first set out the ox's flesh and innards with tasty fat,
hidden in the ox's stomach.
He then set out the ox's white bones, neatly and with skilled deceit
hidden in the glistening fat.

The father of both men and gods addressed him:
"Iapetos' son, most famous of all the lords,
my friend, you've laid these portions out unfairly."
This is what Zeus said sneering; Zeus with his plans that can't be changed.

And Prometheus with his crafty plans addressed Zeus:
"Zeus, greatest and mightiest of all the everlasting gods,
choose whichever of these you'd like."
He said this thinking he was being clever.
But Zeus with his plans that can't be changed
was fully aware of this deceit
and thought up evils for mortal men
intending to see them through.

Nonetheless, with both hands he chose the white fat.
And when he saw the white bones of the ox,
laid out with skilled deceit,
his temper rose in anger.

This is why the race of men on earth
burn white bones on smoking altars.

Greatly disappointed, Zeus who gathers clouds together, addressed him:
"Iapetos' son, you who know what the plans are for everything,
my friend, you certainly haven't forgotten how to deceive with skill."
This is what Zeus said seething; Zeus with his plans that can't be changed.

Because Zeus never forgot this trick, he stopped giving the ash trees
the power of unresting fire to mortals who live on earth.

But the good son of Iapetos tricked him
by stealing unresting fire, bright and clear from a distance,
in a hollow fennel stalk.

This hurt Zeus deeply in his soul; Zeus whose thunder
is heard in the heavens; and he seethed in his heart,
seeing fire among men, bright and clear from a distance.
For the theft of fire he immediately made
something evil for men:
The famous lame-legged Hephaistos,
through the intentions of Kronos' son [Zeus]
made something very much like
a modest young woman.
And the gray-eyed goddess Athena
dressed her in silvery-white clothes,
arranged her hair, and applied makeup.
And she put on her head a beautiful veil
—it was amazing to see—
and then a crown of flowers that had just bloomed.

When Hephaistos had finished this beautiful thing,
something evil instead of something good,
he brought her out where the other gods and men were.

Her appearance was delightful, thanks to Athena
the gray-eyed daughter of great Zeus.

The immortal gods and men were amazed
when they saw this perfect trick, this thing
that would leave men at a loss.

So from her come the female sex—
women who live with mortal men
and cause them pain—
no good at being damn poor
but quite suited to getting more than enough.

And this is how Zeus whose thunder is heard in the heavens
made for mortal men an evil, women,
a sex synonymous with trouble and pain.

So it isn't possible to trick the mind of Zeus
nor get around it in some way
as even Prometheus, the son of Iapetos, with good meaning,
didn't evade his deep anger, but necessity bound him,
despite his wisdom, with great chains.   507–681

Pa Pandir, or Daddy Moron

Malaysian

Pa Pandir reveals yet another of the Trickster's faces—the sacred clown. Through his example—or, more accurately, through his counterexample—a great deal is revealed about human pretensions. Malaysia's Daddy Moron frequently confuses holy men and royalty with the wicked and beasts of the field—thus deflating the categories by which human beings imagine themselves to be "above" their animal natures and each other. In this way, he is like Loki, who detests the Aesir for their pomp, pageantry, and brave talk when all of them have at times been adulterous, gluttonous, and cowardly in response to their own baser instincts. But, unlike Loki, Pa Pandir is appetite without mind—and without malice. He doesn't hate the high and mighty; he only shows them what else they are. Like most animal Tricksters, Pa Pandir is lazy, proud, greedy, gullible, cowardly, and of course hungry and, more often than the other Tricksters presented in this chapter, the victim of his own mindlessness.

Source: Jan Knappert, *Malay Myths and Legends.* Kuala Lumpur, Malaysia: Heinemann Educational Books, 1980. 256–63.

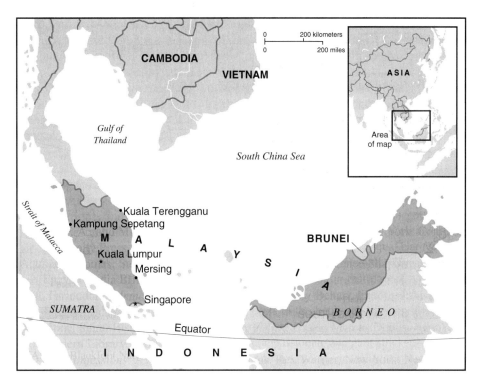

MAP 5.9 Malaysia

It is also interesting to note that the following collection of short episodes in the life of Daddy Moron suggests how traditional tales and beliefs change in response to sociopolitical innovations. In what follows, you will see mentioned the cannabalistic Gergasi and the King of the Jinns, Shah Malim. The voracious giants and Pa Pandir himself are native Malaysian characters of relatively ancient origin, but Jinns and Shahs are Islamic characters that would have been imported by Muslim merchants who came to live in Malaysia as early as the later seventh century CE. Comparative mythologists would use historical and linguistic research methods to determine how many of the events in the Pa Pandir tales are also imported or whether most of the tales simply have changed titles and names but have retained their native plots.

One day, Pa Pandir went out fishing. The wind was against him, so he had to row upstream. By the time he was tired and had to stop rowing, the wind changed and blew favorably in his direction, but he was too angry with the wind to hoist his sail, so that he was carried downstream again by the river, right beyond the point where he had started. All the time he was muttering:

"Blow! Go on, blow! You rotten wind! I must have a rest first."

When he had finished resting, the wind turned again, so he had to row all the way back.

One day, he decided to go and challenge the king's cock in a fight. However, he had no decent clothes to put on for he was only a poor man. So his wife Ma Andeh made him a suit of clothes from newspapers. As soon as his cock started winning, he jumped up and danced. Alas! His clothes burst and were blown away by the wind! There he stood, stark naked, and the spectators rolled about in laughter.

One day Pa Pandir was told by his wife to go and buy a cow. He did not know what a cow was so he asked her to explain "cow." Ma Andeh said:

"It is that which crops the grass!"

Satisfied with this definition of "cow," Pa Pandir now set out to find a cow. Along the way he saw a man mowing with a *babad,* a knife on a long stick.

"Aha!" He exclaimed, thinking himself very clever. "That must be a cow!"

So, he bought the grassknife and dragged it home after tying it to a long rope, for that, his wife had told him, was the best way to transport a cow. At each step, it cut his heels.

One day Ma Andeh told him to go and invite Haji Musa, the local priest, for a meal in his honor. Again, he asked her to describe what he was supposed to bring home.

"You will easily recognize him," said his wife, "he has a white beard."

So, Pa Pandir went out and came back with a big old billy-goat whose white beard indeed looked venerable.

The next day his wife asked him to go and buy a bag of salt. While he was walking along the river with his bag, he felt the call of nature. Before squatting in the shallow water, as is the custom, he thought of a place to hide away his jute bag, full of salt, from thieves. Of course! The best hiding place was . . . under water! He was much surprised later to find the bag empty as soon as all the water had run out.

Finally, Ma Andeh sent Pa Pandir out to invite Datuk Keramat Jinn Islam, the local saint.

"But remember! When you walk up to the fork in the road, take the right path. The left path leads to the house of the *Gergasi!*"

The *Gergasi* were man-eating giants.

Alas! Pa Pandir forgot his wife's warning, turned left at the bifurcation and came upon a very big house. There he shouted out loudly:

"Holy man! My wife and I invite you!"

The *Gergasi* was sleeping with his wife. Furious at the disturbance, he woke up and jumped out of the house, intending to eat that shouting man. But Pa Pandir repeated his invitation:

"My wife has cooked a cow! All for you! Come and eat it! We invite you!"

"If it is a lie, I will eat you!" threatened the giant.

"No, no, come with me, there is plenty of food!" said Pa Pandir unperturbed.

So, the two cannibals followed him, leaving their baby behind. As soon as Ma Andeh saw her husband coming down the garden path with the two huge monsters, one male, one female, trundling behind him, she almost fainted with fright, but it was too late to run away. She made the best of a bad situation and served the meal which was a whole cow with a heap of rice. She sent Pa Pandir to the *Gergasis'* house with a basket of rice and a basket of meat saying:

"Go and feed the baby of our guests."

So, Pa Pandir took the two baskets up the hill and into the house where he found the monster baby lying on the floor. He stuffed the two baskets into the big baby's mouth without bothering to take the food out. The baby choked and died. Pa Pandir ran back to his wife in the kitchen and told her what had happened. Together they ran out of the backdoor to the river and into their boat. They were safely on the other bank when the *Gergasis,* having finished the enormous meal, walked back to their house, only to find their child dead. Furious, they ran back, shouting that they would eat Pa Pandir alive. They ransacked his house but found nobody. They ran to the riverbank. Pa Pandir shouted:

"Do not fall into the water, grandparents! You might die! Go to my house, take the two big jars and place them on the river bank, they will serve you as boats!"

The *Gergasis* did exactly as Pa Pandir had suggested. They placed the huge jars on the bank and stepped in, one monster in each jar.

"Now rock yourselves and your boats will sail!" shouted Pa Pandir.

The *Gergasis* did as they were told, the jars fell over, plunged into the water and were carried away by the current. The cannibals were never heard of again.

So, Pa Pandir became a famous hero in his own village. He went up to the house of the *Gergasis* and searched it. He found many treasures in it, golden rings, bracelets, anklets, brooches, earrings, necklaces and many other good things. He also found piles of bones, scalps and skins of the countless victims of the *Gergasis'* voracity.

One day Pa Pandir bought chaff which a farmer was winnowing out and throwing away. When he arrived at a riverbank, he saw an army of ants, thousands of them, crawling across a long twig afloat on the water. Pa Pandir reflected:

"If a thousand ants can walk on that twig, it will hold me as well."

So he stepped on it, but it did not hold him. He almost drowned and lost his bag of chaff. When he came home, his wife Ma Andeh fired so many ugly words at him that the forest trembled.

"What are you worried about?" asked Pa Pandir. "You said the chaff was worthless, so what does it matter if it is lost?"

Ma Andeh was speechless.

"I have myself to blame," she thought, "I should never have sent him on an errand." She stopped giving him orders.

So, Pa Pandir now had all his time to himself, so he made an elaborate fishtrap and caught many fishes, which he smoked over a fire. After eating a large number of them, he hung the rest up in a bag on the branch of a tree. Every day he came back to eat more fishes, and to smoke the newly caught ones. He stayed away all day and came home late at night. Ma Andeh, noticing that he grew fatter though she did not feed him, decided one day to follow him, so that she could discover and confiscate his store of food. So, the next morning she asked him if there was any animal he was afraid of. He answered:

"None at all, not even the tiger, nor the snakes and crocodiles, only the *tokai* (gecko)."

Then, when he had left the house, she followed him at a distance until he stopped near his tree and started to climb it. Just as he untied his bag from the branch, she imitated the call of the gecko from behind the shrubs:

"Toke! Toke!"

Pa Pandir fell out of the tree with fright, jumped up and ran away. He ran and ran all day and did not dare come home until late at night. Meanwhile, Ma Andeh had picked up the bag which had fallen under the tree, and taken it home. She discovered it was full of fish and that night she gave Pa Pandir two fishes with *nasi* (boiled rice). When he asked for more, she said she had no fishes left, but that she would have a piece of her joint.

"I'll have a piece of *my* joint," said Pa Pandir, and proceeded to carve a piece of flesh from his thigh with the carving knife. He held it over the fire to roast it, then ate it up. Alas! Soon he got wound fever and Ma Andeh had to treat him with herbs and salves. Strong man that he was, Pa Pandir soon felt as fit as before.

He then thought of a plan to catch birds. He found a *lembu* tree and boiled its sticky juice into glue. This he smeared on the branches of a tree and waited. Soon, some birds perched on the branches and were stuck. Pa Pandir took them from the sticky branches and tied their feet to a string which he fastened his belt, then wound round and round his body. In the end, every part of his body was covered with birds, as he caught hundreds of them. Having their wings free, the birds started flapping them wildly, as a result of which Pa Pandir was lifted up and soon could be seen soaring high over the forest. The journey through the sky lasted until after nightfall. Then the birds began to feel tired, and descended on the moonlit roof terrace of King Shah Malim's palace. The king's servants fled, believing him to be a ghost or a devil or an angel or even a god. He quickly cut the strings that held the birds tied to his body, then shouted in a deep voice:

"Beware! Prepare! The King of the *Jinns* (spirits) is descending to earth!"

King Malim ordered everything to be prepared for the reception of the Spirit King. All the lamps in the palace were extinguished, because neither light nor fire may shine on the Spirit King's countenance. King Malim called his daughter, and when she came and made her obeisance to him, he addressed her thus:

"For a long time I have cherished the wish to marry you to the King of the Spirits. Tonight by good fortune he has arrived in my palace and you will marry him. Go, bathe and dress for your wedding."

Whereupon Shah Malim proceeded to welcome the Spirit King with dignity and due honors. He entrusted his guest to his servants who bathed and perfumed Pa Pandir, rubbed his body with fragrant oils and dressed him in regal robes. When bride and bridegroom were ready, Shah Malim performed the ritual of holy matrimony, reading the ceremonial prayers himself. The couple were led to a state room, undressed by the ladies-in-waiting and put to bed together in the sumptuous bedstead.

However, the princess fled, screaming that she did not want to be carried away by a spirit into the cold night air, not even by a king. Pa Pandir was not worried. He slept soundly after the lavish wedding meal. So well did he sleep that the next morning the servants came in as the sun was shining on his face. They discovered that in daylight he was not an invisible spirit but a common man. Furious Shah Malim ordered his servants to give the imposter a sound hiding and chase him out. Pa Pandir fled into the jungle and at last arrived at his house.

He told Ma Andeh what had happened and she laid herbs and salves on the wounds and bruises he had received.

One day, Pa Pandir told his wife:

"I am going to a far country by boat. Pack food for me for seven days."

Ma Andeh cooked rice and baked delicious cakes which she put on a broad board which was laid across the roof-beams of the house, to dry. Then she went out to the forest to collect herbs and roots for her medical practice. In her absence, Pa Pandir climbed on to the board and lay down to eat the cakes and rice in comfort. He had told his wife:

"If you hear a gunshot, it is me coming back."

When she came back from the forest and found him gone, she concluded that he must have departed on his boat trip. Pa Pandir lay quietly on his board right above her head, for six days, eating her cakes. The rats liked the fatty smell so much that they ate away his lips, nibbling all night, but he let them. On the seventh day he sneezed. Ma Andeh, thinking that this must be a gunshot, went out to the river to see the ship. Pa Pandir came down from his board and went out to the river to relieve himself. When they met on the riverside, she asked him if he had not been on board ship?

"Oh, yes, I ha' 'een on 'oard," answered Pa Pandir, who could no longer pronounce sounds that required movements of the lips.

"Where did you leave your lips?" she asked further.

"The rats ha' eaten 'y li's," replied Pa Pandir, grinning with his lipless face. "I 'as aslee' all the ti'e."

Some days later, they went out to the forest together to cut wood. Pa Pandir felt hungry so he told his wife to fry some bananas. She said:

"Go home and fetch me some live coals from the fire."

He quarreled about this, until she gave him some raw bananas. This finally persuaded him and he went to get fire from the house. When he came back she fried some bananas and gave them to him. Expecting these also to be raw, Pa Pandir swallowed them whole. Soon he rolled with pain in his tummy and died. Ma Andeh buried him under the *lesung* (rice block or mortar). She died soon after.

Thus ends the tale of Pa Pandir who always acted without thinking.

The Raven Steals the Light

Haida (Haida Gwaii, Pacific Northwest North America)

Raven, another of the Trickster's many North American guises, is commonly found in tales told among the Athapascan-speaking tribes from California all the way to Alaska. Seeking to satisfy his endless hunger, lust, and curiosity, Raven, like Coyote, hatches elaborate plans, wears disguises, and uses deceit to accomplish his purposes. However, as in the story below, these tribes also

Source: Bill Reid and Robert Bringhurst, *The Raven Steals the Light.* Vancouver/Toronto: Douglas & McIntyre, 1996. 19–24.

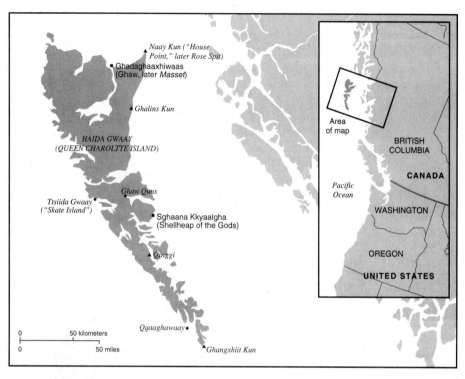

MAP 5.10 Queen Charlotte Islands, Haida Gwaii

conceived of Raven as a creator and associated him with a great supernatural power. In one story, this Trickster was said to have created the female sexual organ from the soft lips of the chiton (also called the sea slug) and the male organ from the long muscular foot of the clam. In another, he is said to have stolen lakes and rivers and salmon from the mainland, thus making them available for human enjoyment. The Haida, one tribe for whom Raven is both benefactor and meddlesome plague, struggle to retain the ancient ways of their ancestors on a group of Pacific Northwest islands, known to Western culture as the Queen Charlotte Islands. The Haida know them as *Haida Gwaii,* the Islands of the People, or, in classical Haida, *Xhaaydla Gwaayaay,* the Islands on the Boundary Between Worlds.

These islands were once densely populated, with thriving civilizations, before their population was decimated by diseases brought to the Haida by Western traders, whalers, and missionaries. At its height, going back many centuries before the epidemics of the late 19th century, Haida civilization had a deep and complex mythology, as strikingly evidenced by its many now-abandoned settlements with their vast array of totem pole sculp-

"The Raven Steals the Light," drawing by Bill Reid.
Source: © Bill Reid/Bill Reid Studio Gallery

ture and other art forms, including an extensive mythic narrative tradition perpetuated by quasi-holy storytellers. Unfortunately, that narrative tradition has, like the totem sculpture itself, been neglected, and nearly lost. Thanks to storytellers practicing their heritage despite the Haida suffering a virtual holocaust and despite the distraction and fragmentation of the survivors under the complex pressures of 20th-century society, some vestiges of that mythic tradition remain.

In 1900–1901 linguist and anthropologist John Swanton took dictation from the last master storyteller in the Haida tradition. Swanton's work forms the majority of Haida mythology that is available to us today. Canadian poet and cultural historian Robert Bringhurst made this work available in a tour-de-force three-volume set of translations and commentary: *A Story as Sharp as a Knife, Nine Visits to the Mythworld,* and *Being in Being.* These myths-become-texts suggest what Haida tradition must have been like in full flower, and students of myth can only be grateful that so much has been recorded and preserved. Yet, while acknowledging the valuable contributions of Swanton, Bringhurst, Bill Reid, and Sean Kane in saving Haida myth from oblivion, it must also be said that recording these stories in written form falsifies them significantly. Haida myths, like those of so many tribal peoples, were always and only delivered through oral performances, shaped by a collaboration between storyteller and audience in the unique context of the individual moment as well as the larger context of their shared cultural milieu. So what has survived are translations of transcriptions of an oral art never meant to be transcribed, never fully representable in static printed form.

Nevertheless, a great deal of what we know about Haida culture, particularly about the relationship among their beliefs, arts, and social practices, comes to us through these imperfect vessels. Concerning the vital link between art and belief, Claude Lévi-Straus writes:

> The traditional arts of the Indians of the Northwest Coast are indissolubly linked to legends and myths. No other art has broken through the barrier between the natural and the supernatural worlds with such momentum. Over the millennia, the Indians of the Northwest Coast have developed graphic and sculptural conventions and employed stylistic devices in which human and nonhuman traits are combined, interwoven and transmuted. They give life to a reality hitherto unimaginable, one to which the viewer is immediately drawn. This reality consists of beings of a third type: neither human nor animal, but both at once. As the poet says, these beings cast upon us a familiar eye and take us back to the time . . . when animals could take on human form and knew the manners and the language of humans perfectly well.
>
> These beings all played a determining role in the history of the people, or rather of the clans, the houses, the families. The way in which the artist brings them together or represents their particular traits evokes, in detail, the moment at which they appeared. They are great ancestors, protectors, and sometimes formidable adversaries, that humans met in very ancient times. The circumstances of those meetings, as described in the myths and legends, explain the social distinctions, the hierarchy and the rituals. (Reid and Bringhurst, 1996, 9–10)

Lévi-Strauss's notion of a single "Northwest Coast" tradition is about as accurate and inaccurate as the notion of a single European culture. Although the Italians, the French, and the Irish have many religious, sociopolitical, and cultural commonalities, each group would object strenuously to having its unique history and cultural expressions smoothed over by a few broad-brush generalizations about European culture. Similarly, we should delineate Haida culture as one among what was once a vast array of separate but often interconnected native cultures whose mythologies informed and shaped one another to varying degrees. Fortunately for the relatively few tribes that retain at least some of their pre-European cultural integrity, modern artists such as Bill Reid keep their people's artistic traditions alive. Reid himself, in his prologue to *Raven Steals the Light,* regrets the dilution of his Haida culture's mythic coherence and power even as he practices his own storytelling and sculpture informed and shaped by his connection to his cultural past. Reid's dedication of *The Raven Steals,* written in 1984 when Reid was 64, is worth quoting here:

> To . . . Henry Young of Skidegate, who was my friend when I was twenty and he was in his eighties. I wish I had had more patience and had spent the tiny part of my life he requested, to learn something of the wonderful language he spoke so resonantly and well, and to learn more of the stories of all the mythcreatures whose many adventures instructed, informed and entertained the Haidas during their long history.
>
> Henry was the repository of much of the myth and legend of the Southern Haidas, trained as a boy to carry on a long bardic tradition. If I had listened longer and more carefully, we might now be able to tell you the true stories of the Raven and all his fellows, instead of these light entertainments, mere glancing versions of the grand old tales. (13–14)

Before there was anything, before the great flood had covered the earth and receded, before the animals walked the earth or the trees covered the land or the birds flew between the trees, even before the fish and the whales and seals swam in the sea, an old man lived in a house on the bank of a river with his only child, a daughter. Whether she was as beautiful as hemlock fronds against the spring sky at sunrise or as ugly as a sea slug doesn't really matter very much to this story, which takes place mainly in the dark.

Because at that time the whole world was dark. Inky, pitchy, all-consuming dark, blacker than a thousand stormy winter midnights, blacker than anything anywhere has been since.

The reason for all this blackness has to do with the old man in the house by the river, who had a box which contained a box which contained a box which contained an infinite number of boxes each nestled in a box slightly larger than itself until finally there was a box so small all it could contain was all the light in the universe.

Interferes

___The Raven, who of course existed at that time, because he had always existed and always would, was somewhat less than satisfied with this state of affairs, since it led to an awful lot of blundering around and bumping into things. It slowed him down a good deal in his pursuit of food and other fleshly pleasures, and in his constant effort to interfere and to change things.

Eventually, his bumbling around in the dark took him close to the home of the old man. He first heard a little singsong voice muttering away. When he followed the voice, he soon came to the wall of the house, and there, placing his ear against the planking, he could just make out the words, "I have a box and inside the box is another box and inside it are many more boxes, and in the smallest box of all is all the light in the world, and it is all mine and I'll never give any of it to anyone, not even to my daughter, because, who knows, she may be as homely as a sea slug, and neither she nor I would like to know that."

It took only an instant for the Raven to decide to steal the light for himself, but it took a lot longer for him to invent a way to do so.

First he had to find a door into the house. But no matter how many times he circled it or how carefully he felt the planking, it remained a smooth, unbroken barrier. Sometimes he heard either the old man or his daughter leave the house to get water or for some other reason, but they always departed from the side of the house opposite to him, and when he ran around to the other side the wall seemed as unbroken as ever.

Finally, the Raven retired a little way upstream and thought and thought about how he could enter the house. As he did so, he began to think more and more of the young girl who lived there, and thinking of her began to stir more than just the Raven's imagination.

"It's probable that she's as homely as a sea slug," he said to himself, "but on the other hand, she may be as beautiful as the fronds of the hemlock would be against a bright spring sunrise, if only there were light enough to make one." And in that idle speculation, he found the solution to his problem.

He waited until the young woman, whose footsteps he could distinguish by now from those of her father, came to the river to gather water. Then he changed himself into a single hemlock needle, dropped himself into the river and floated down just in time to be caught in the basket which the girl was dipping in the river.

Even in his much diminished form, the Raven was able to make at least a very small magic—enough to make the girl so thirsty she took a deep drink from the basket, and in doing so, swallowed the needle.

The Raven slithered down deep into her warm insides and found a soft, comfortable spot, where he transformed himself once more, this time into a very small human being, and went to sleep for a long while. And as he slept he grew.

The young girl didn't have any idea what was happening to her, and of course she didn't tell her father, who noticed nothing unusual because it was so dark—until suddenly he became very aware indeed of a new presence in the house, as the Raven at last emerged triumphantly in the shape of a human boychild.

He was—or would have been, if anyone could have seen him—a strange-looking boy, with a long, beaklike nose and a few feathers here and there. In addition, he had the shining eyes of the Raven, which would have given his face a bright, inquisitive appearance—if anyone could have seen these features then.

And he was noisy. He had a cry that contained all the noises of a spoiled child and an angry raven—yet he could sometimes speak as softly as the wind in the hemlock boughs, with an echo of that beautiful other sound, like an organic bell, which is also part of every raven's speech.

At times like that his grandfather grew to love this strange new member of his household and spent many hours playing with him, making him toys and inventing games for him.

As he gained more and more of the affection and confidence of the old man, the Raven felt more intently around the house, trying to find where the light was hidden. After much exploration, he was convinced it was kept in the big box which stood in the corner of the house. One day he cautiously lifted the lid, but of course could see nothing, and all he could feel was another box. His grandfather, however, heard his precious treasure chest being disturbed, and he dealt very harshly with the would-be thief, threatening dire punishment if the Raven-child ever touched the box again.

This triggered a tidal wave of noisy protests, followed by tender importuning, in which the Raven never mentioned the light, but only pleaded for the largest box. That box, said the Ravenchild, was the one thing he needed to make him completely happy.

As most if not all grandfathers have done since the beginning, the old man finally yielded and gave his grandchild the outermost box. This contented the boy for a short time—but as most if not all grandchildren have done since the beginning, the Raven soon demanded the next box.

It took many days and much cajoling, carefully balanced with well-planned tantrums, but one by one the boxes were removed. When only a few were left, a strange radiance, never before seen, began to infuse the darkness of the house, disclosing vague shapes and their shadows, still too dim to have definite form. The Ravenchild then begged in his most pitiful voice to be allowed to hold the light for just a moment.

His request was instantly refused, but of course in time his grandfather yielded. The old man lifted the light, in the form of a beautiful, incandescent ball, from the final box and tossed it to his grandson.

He had only a glimpse of the child on whom he had lavished such love and affection, for even as the light was travelling toward him, the child changed from his human form to a huge, shining black shadow, wings spread and beak open, waiting. The Raven snapped up the light in his jaws, thrust his great wings downward and shot through the smokehole of the house into the huge darkness of the world.

That world was at once transformed. Mountains and valleys were starkly silhouetted, the river sparkled with broken reflections, and everywhere life began to stir. And from far away, another great winged shape launched itself into the air, as light struck the eyes of the Eagle for the first time and showed him his target.

The Raven flew on, rejoicing in his wonderful new possession, admiring the effect it had on the world below, revelling in the experience of being able to see where he was going, instead of flying blind and hoping for the best. He was having such a good time that he never saw the Eagle until the Eagle was almost upon him. In a panic he swerved to escape the savage outstretched claws, and in doing so he dropped a good half of the light he was carrying. It fell to the rocky ground below and there broke into pieces—one large piece and too many small ones to count. They bounced back into the sky and remain there even today as the moon and the stars that glorify the night.

The Eagle pursued the Raven beyond the rim of the world, and there, exhausted by the long chase, the Raven finally let go of his last piece of light. Out beyond the rim of the world, it floated gently on the clouds and started up over the mountains lying to the east.

Its first rays caught the smokehole of the house by the river, where the old man sat weeping bitterly over the loss of his precious light and the treachery of his grandchild. But as the light reached in, he looked up and for the first time saw his daughter, who had been quietly sitting during all this time, completely bewildered by the rush of events.

The old man saw that she was as beautiful as the fronds of a hemlock against a spring sky at sunrise, and he began to feel a little better.

WORKS CITED AND SUGGESTIONS FOR FURTHER READING

Abrahams, Roger D. *African Folktales: Traditional Stories of the Black World.* New York: Pantheon, 1983.

Allen, Paula Gunn. *Grandmothers of Light: A Medicine Woman's Sourcebook.* Boston: Beacon, 1991.

Berry, Jack. *West African Folk Tales.* Evanston, IL: Northwestern University Press, 1991.

Bettelheim, Bruno. *The Uses of Enchantment: The Meaning and Importance of Fairy Tales.* New York: Vintage, 1975.

Blue Cloud, Peter. "Coyote Man and Saucy Duckfeather." In *A Coyote Reader*, ed. by William Bright. Berkeley: University of California Press, 1993.

———. "Coyote's Anthro." In *Elderberry Flute Song.* White Pine Press, 1989.

Bright, William. *A Coyote Reader.* Berkeley: University of California Press, 1993.

Bringhurst, Robert. *A Story as Sharp as a Knife: The Classical Haida Mythtellers and Their World.* Masterworks of the Classical Haida Mythtellers. Vol. 1. Lincoln, NE: University of Nebraska Press, 1999.

Bringhurst, Robert, trans. *Ghandl of the Qayahl Llaanas: Nine Visits to the Mythworld.* Masterworks of the Classical Haida Mythtellers. Vol. 2. Lincoln, NE: University of Nebraska, 2000.

———. *Skaay of Qquuna Qiighawaay: The Collected Works.* Masterworks of the Classical Haida Mythtellers. Vol. 3. Lincoln, NE: University of Nebraska, 2001.

Brown, Joseph Epes. *Animals of the Soul: Sacred Animals of the Oglala Sioux.* Rockport, MA: Element, 1997.

Colum, Padraic. *Legends of Hawaii.* New Haven, CT: Yale University Press, 1937.

Courlander, Harold. *Tales of the Yoruba Gods and Heroes.* New York: Crown, 1973.

Cristen, Kimberly A., and Sam D. Gill, eds. *Clowns and Tricksters: An Encyclopedia of Tradition and Culture.* Denver, CO: ABC-CLIO, 1998.

Crossley-Holland, Kevin. *The Norse Myths.* New York: Pantheon, 1980.

Davis, Donald. *Southern Jack Tales.* Little Rock, AR: August House, 1992.

Duncan, Barbara. *Living Stories of the Cherokee.* Chapel Hill: University of North Carolina Press, 1998.

Erdoes, Richard, and Alfonso Ortiz. *American Indian Trickster Tales.* New York: Penguin, 1998.

Feldman, Susan. *The Storytelling Stone: Traditional Native American Myths and Tales.* New York: Delta, 1965.

Ford, Clyde W. *The Hero with an African Face: Mythic Wisdom of Traditional Africa.* New York: Bantam, 1999.

Glancy, Diane, and Mark Nowak, eds. *Visit Teepee Town: Native Writings after The Detours.* Minneapolis: Coffee House, 1999.

Hamilton, Virginia. *A Ring of Tricksters: Animal Tales from America, the West Indies, and Africa.* New York: Blue Sky, 1997.

Hodge, Frederick Webb. *Handbook of American Indians North of Mexico.* Vol. 1. Washington, DC: GPO, 1912.

Hyde, Lewis. *Trickster Makes This World: Mischief, Myth, and Art.* New York: North Point Press, 1998.

Hynes, William J., and William G. Doty. *Mythical Trickster Figures: Contours, Contexts, and Criticisms.* Tuscaloosa: University of Alabama Press, 1993.

King, Thomas. *Green Grass, Running Water.* Boston: Houghton Mifflin, 1993.

Knappert, Jan. *Malay Myths and Legends.* Kuala Lumpur, Malaysia: Heinemann Educational, 1980.

Kramer, Samuel Noah, and John Maier. *Myths of Enki, The Crafty God.* New York: Oxford University Press, 1989.

Kroeber, Karl. *Artistry in Native American Myths.* Lincoln: University of Nebraska Press, 1998.

Leeming, David, and Jake Page, eds. *Myths, Legends, and Folktales of America: An Anthology.* New York: Oxford University Press, 1999.

Levitt, Paul M., and Elissa S. Guralnick. *How Raven Found the Daylight and Other American Indian Stories.* Boulder, CO: University Press of Colorado, 2000.

Lopez, Barry. *Giving Birth to Thunder, Sleeping with His Daughter: Coyote Builds North America.* New York: Avon, 1977.

Owomoyela, Oyekan. *Yoruba Trickster Tales.* Lincoln: University of Nebraska Press, 1997.

Radin, Paul. *The Trickster: A Study in American Indian Mythology.* New York: Greenwood, 1969.

Reid, Bill, and Robert Bringhurst. *The Raven Steals the Light.* Vancouver/Toronto: Douglas & McIntyre, 1996.

Suzuki, Yoshimatsu. *Japanese Legends and Folk-Tales.* Tokyo: Sakurai Shoten, 1951.

Toelken, Barre. "Foreword." In Barry Lopez, *Giving Birth to Thunder, Sleeping with His Daughter: Coyote Builds North America.* New York: Avon, 1977. xi–xiv.

Walker, Deward E., and Daniel N. Matthews. *Blood of the Monster: The Nez Perce Coyote Cycle.* Worland, WY: High Plains, 1994.

CHAPTER 6

Sacred Places

THE GROUNDING OF MYTHOLOGY

Sacred places are a significant element of the mythic traditions we are exploring, and that they comprise a common genre is, of course, enough reason to consider them here. But even more than their presence in the world's myths, such stories are important because in them the mythic breaks through into our present world, embodying the very kinds of boundary crossing that are so central to all mythological thinking. Such stories give us a chance to see, to feel, the presence of mythic truth in the midst of our perceptions of contemporary reality. Whether they are the repositories of national or ethnic identity or the site of supernatural revelation or visitation, whether they are actual places where we can stand and hear the echoes of long-ago battles or imaginary places shaped by the requirements of mythic vision, sacred places serve to teach and remind us of who we are and how we ought to behave in our day-to-day lives.

This claim may seem somewhat overblown. We members of the mainstream, 21st-century American society like to think of ourselves as practical, realistic, down to earth. The mythological has nothing to do with us—except perhaps as an object of curiosity and intellectual interest. But wait a minute. How "down to earth" are we *really?* We take this phrase to mean "realistic" or "sensible," yet, when we think for a moment, it might be argued that in our highly technological and technology-dependent society the very last thing we are is "down to earth." Sacred places, especially in the various senses that Native Americans use the term, call out to us to *become* "down to earth," to remember and honor and revitalize our essential connections to the earth and the natural world, to the *sacred* all around us. They invite us to associate the spiritual with such natural material phenomena as mountains, rivers, lakes, trees, and caves. The study of stories about sacred places might just allow us to see such opposed binaries as past versus present, realistic versus mythological, or spiritual versus material as not so mutually exclusive. As Vine Deloria has pointed out, Gettysburg, Pennsylvania, with its battlefield and its National Cemetery, serves as a sacred place in our creation of national identity. Other places similarly "hallowed" come to mind as well: the Alamo, Pearl Harbor, Concord Bridge. Places such as these are sacred "because the location is a site where, within our own history something of great importance has happened" (Deloria 1993, 272). Deloria is right, as far as he goes, but there is something deeper that makes such sites sacred. What makes them important is that they *embody* and provide a *location* that dramatizes complex notions about nationhood and individual identity as well as the various contradictions that constitute the human condition such as bravery and fear, aggression and altruism.

Such sites are, of course, actual places. We can go there today, stand, look, and know we are in *the* place. Yet, at the same time, these actual places are mythic because they embody meanings far beyond the scope of the events that happened and even beyond the limits of the physical locations themselves. In that sense, they are *imaginary* places. We imagine them to be far more than any real place can be in and of itself. Does this fact mean the sacred meanings are not real? Not at all. We could say the abstract meaning becomes real, becomes accessible, becomes visible, becomes imaginable *because* it is connected with a real place that we can see and with real events that we can remember. Thus, for example, a visit to Gettysburg can make concrete such abstract notions as "casualties" and "the *United* States" in a way that a visit to another Pennsylvania pasture cannot. In short, this particular sacred place brings a great many abstractions about nationhood and warfare "down to earth." But national shrines are only one kind of sacred place. Let's consider what other kinds there may be.

GULLIFORD'S NINE CATEGORIES OF SACRED PLACES

Andrew Gulliford, in his analysis of Native American sites, argues there are nine categories of sacred places: (1) sites associated with emergence and migration tales; (2) sites of trails and pilgrimage routes; (3) places essential to cultural survival; (4) altars; (5) vision quest sites; (6) ceremonial dance sites; (7) ancestral ruins; (8) petroglyphs and pictographs; and (9) burial or massacre sites.

Each of Gulliford's categories refers to a specific, identifiable location that has a mythological dimension not unlike that which has attached itself to Gettysburg or the Liberty Bell. Gulliford's categories are particularly apt in reference to sacred American Indian places. As such, they describe sites closely tied to the historical events, spiritual practices, and identity-reinforcing activities so important to Indian culture. But, even as a typology of sacred Indian places, Gulliford's list is incomplete. What about sites that have been sanctified by the divine touch? The Modoc Indians of northern California, for instance, considered the dormant volcano Mount Shasta sacred because the Chief of the Sky Spirits made it as a dwelling for himself and his family. Indeed, the Chief's own daughter became the mother of the human race when the winds that perpetually blow at Shasta's summit whisked her off the mountain and, ultimately, into the care of the Grizzly Bears living at its base. The Jicarilla Apache saw Taos as the center of the earth and revered this place because "the Ruler" led them to this propitious site shortly after they emerged from the earth. The Brulé Sioux associated the Badlands with ancient evil and horrific wonder, believing its rock formations to be the bones of Unktehi, the primordial water monster who, before she was defeated by Tunkashila (Grandfather Spirit), drowned the entire world in a great flood. These Sioux consider the red pipestones which are part of the Badlands multicolored rock formations to be sacred because they are the flesh, blood, and bones of their drowned ancestors. Smoke from pipes made with this stone is said to be the breath of the ancestors whose power can be felt when these sacred pipes are smoked during ceremonies.

These real-world locations were made sacred by events that happened in the mythic, rather than the historical past. Therefore, what is needed is a typology of sacred places that describes all the possible associations that make a place holy.

DELORIA'S FOUR CATEGORIES OF SACRED SITES

Vine Deloria, author of *Custer Died for Your Sins,* offers another way of categorizing myths about sacred places in his *God Is Red: A Native View of Religion.* While Deloria's work also focuses on Native American cultures, his categories are open-ended enough to be useful in looking at sacred sites around the mythic world. Instead of nine, Deloria presents four categories of "sacred places," arranged on a scale of "agency"—entirely human agency at one end versus the agency of "Higher Powers'" at the other. Gettysburg, in Deloria's view, is sacred entirely through human agency. In his second category, one he calls "deeper, more profound," places become sacred because they are the location of events through which "the sacred or higher powers have appeared in the lives of human beings" (1993, 273). Deloria cites Joshua leading the Hebrews across the River Jordan dry-shod on their way into the Holy Land after the death of Moses as a Western example of such an intervention (272). The Jicarilla Apache's divine "Ruler" leading the people to Taos is a similar story of human and divine activities making a place sacred. These are the places, to use Judeo-Christian terms, where miracles have been recorded. And, since Judeo-Christian traditions are revealed religions (i.e., God reveals himself and his will to human beings through miraculous events and prophetic utterance), there are numerous biblical stories that illustrate this idea. But similarly sacred locations are not unknown in our modern world. For example, think of Lourdes, France, where believers assert that the Virgin Mary continues to make her healing presence felt. Similarly, in Mecca, Saudi Arabia, the Kaaba, a Muslim sacred site, holds a black stone, possibly a meteorite, believed to contain divine miraculous powers. Both these places are sacred because the Divine revealed itself through miracles in those specific locations. In this notion of sacred places, the limits of the ordinary are revealed, *here,* in *this* place, to be permeable to the supernatural.

In Deloria's third category, places become sacred because the Higher Powers, rather than just being the unseen agents of events in this world, "on their own initiative have revealed Themselves to human beings" (1993, 275). Deloria cites Moses speaking with the Burning Bush as an Old Testament example of this sort of revelation. A Medicine Wheel, where Indian youths seek and receive a life-defining vision, is sacred in this same sense. To these examples we could add the cave of the oracle at Delphi, Greece, and Ayres Rock, Australia, as places where the Divine was and is said to speak to humans through prophets and dreams. In these cases, the human being shares some degree of agency when he or she fasts and seeks the vision,

The Kaaba (Baytullah) and the Hajar-e-Aswad (the
Black Stone). Mecca, Saudi Arabia. It would be difficult
to overestimate the importance of the Kaaba to faithful
Muslims who turn and pray toward this structure five
times a day. The building and its surrounding precincts
were, however, sacred to a variety of Arabic peoples
centuries before Mohammed. Ishmael and Hagar (Ismail
and Hajira) are said to be buried here and the sacred
healing waters of the well Zamzam are made available
to the millions of pilgrims who visit the site each year.
In addition to the mysterious Black Stone, another sacred stone, the Maqam-e-Ibrahim, is said to retain
miraculously the footprints of Mohammed who stood
upon it when building the Kaaba.
Source: © Robert Azzi/Woodfin Camp and Associates

yet the place becomes sacred at the revelation of the Higher Powers. According to
Deloria, places where such revelations occur tend to transcend local history, and the
world is full of places where communication and communion with Higher Powers
are said to be possible. For example, Alistair Shearer, describing the origins of sacred places in Asia, writes in a similar tone:

First comes the earth, ancient mother of the gods, intrinsically holy, irrepressible womb of the Divine. Then here and there across the landscape, shrines spring up, separating and protecting what is particularly holy ground: that place, be it mountain, tree or rock, where the invisible presences that govern our world are known to congregate, where they have been felt or seen, either in direct revelation, or by their witnessed effects. Some miraculous event, a punishment, a healing or a vision, shows that the hidden forces are breathing through such a place, bending the commonplace boundaries of time and space and infusing them with a numinous power that puts the visitor in contact with new levels of being. (Freeman and Shearer 2000, 10)

In Deloria's fourth category, he calls for the possibility of new sacred places, underscoring even more the present, ongoing nature of the kinds of interactions between the human and the spiritual realms. Sometimes the politics of the ongoing interactions surrounding sacred places can be tortured. Recently, two statues of the Buddha (each more than 100 feet tall) carved into the rock walls of a gorge in Bamiyan, Afghanistan, were destroyed by order of Mullah Omar, the leader of the now-scattered Taliban militia, on the grounds that they were idols that might lead "the people" astray.

Similar conflicts have arisen in North America, where sacred places exist in a world in which some property is designated as "private" and where "public" land is owned by a government sympathetic to the pecuniary interests of miners, loggers, ranchers, and real estate developers. Whereas the dominant culture views the possession of land and the quest for profit as fundamental human rights, native cultures usually see at least some land as the necessary locations of religious ceremonies that literally maintain the prosperity and even the life of the world as a whole (Deloria 1993, 275–76). Because of the unique complexities that come out of the intersection of competing ways of seeing the world—political, religious, mythological, economic, historical, to name a few—discussions about actual places that have been labeled "sacred" by minority populations are often at odds with the dominant culture.

One thing worth noting from our comparison of Gulliford's and Deloria's schemes is the necessity, or at least the descriptive effectiveness, of viewing their categories as markers along a continuum which has the "entirely mythic" (or metaphoric or imaginary) at one extreme and the "real world" at the other. Throughout this book, we have made the point that such a continuum need not embody a hierarchy of values in which the "real world" is positive, understandable, and believable in ways that "mythic" cannot be. Myth is a serious way of knowing the world—just as serious as our "practical" understanding of how things are—and therefore sacred stories about places that cannot be located on the map are no less powerful for their being imaginary. For examples, such mythic locales as Heaven and Hell, Eden and Shangri-La, the Cave of Wonders and the Enchanted Forest have long affected various people's behavior and belief. Thus Gettysburg and the Grand Canyon are wholly "actual" (though note these two places are sacred for very different reasons), while Mt. Olympus is both "actual" and "imaginary" at the same time, and the Garden of Eden is, if not wholly "imaginary," impossible to locate on any map. Yet wherever we might place them along a continuum between the wholly mythic and the wholly actual, each of these sites has the power to affect behavior, belief, and worldview.

SITES OF LONGING AND FEAR

Some mythical places are sacred because they dramatize our fears of and resistance to the inevitable facts of aging, weakness, disease, and death. For example, the Yiddish story of Alexander the Great's search for the Waters of Eternal Life depicts a wish to escape the harsh facts of our mortality.

Other imaginary places dramatize other longings. The Nordlander Isak's voyage to Utröst, the Tibetan Rinchen's accidental encounter with the King of the Castle in the Lake, and the Chinese K'o-li's adventures to the Treasure Mountain of Yao enact hopes and anxieties arising from the need to earn our daily bread. In each of these stories, the protagonist discovers the source of unlimited material wealth; and, in the last two cases, there is reflection on the ways wealth can complicate our existence. This childlike longing for comfort, security, and stasis also forms the basis for Eliade's claim that all myths are myths of return to the "sweet time" of beginnings. Myths which take us to a sacred place where rejuvenation or immortality is possible—whether that place is a garden, a forest, a mountain, a well, lake, stream, fountain, or river—have the effect of transporting us back to the primordial and womblike condition that preceded our quotidian struggles with money, relationships, and the eventual loss of our physical and mental powers.

COMBINING INTERPRETIVE STRATEGIES

Thus we can locate sacred places along two axes. The first locates a sacred place along a continuum from historical/actual to imaginary/metaphorical. The second axis locates a sacred place along a continuum from human to divine agency. Let's take Deloria's example of Gettysburg and "read" it in terms of the analytical tool now before us. As Deloria suggests, Gettysburg is a comparatively simple case and, to reverse his previously quoted terms, exemplifies a "shallower, more mundane" sense of the sacred than, say, India's Ganges River or Peru's Machu Picchu. At first glance, anyway, there is no need to go outside the boundaries of everyday life to comprehend Gettysburg as a sacred place. As Deloria points out, even mere days after the conflict, this Pennsylvania battlefield was accepted as hallowed ground, at least in part because, as Abraham Lincoln said in his "Gettysburg Address," the soldiers there gave "the last full measure of devotion" to a "sacred cause." Deloria would stop there; for him, human sacrifice is enough to explain a site's sacredness. But is this explanation enough? Soldiers equally brave and self-sacrificing have perished in bloody agony in many battles before and after Gettysburg. What then makes the Gettysburg soldiers' sacrifice more holy than others' sacrifice?

If we think of Gulliford's categories, it is possible to see Gettysburg as sacred in several ways. It is not only a place of ultimate past sacrifice but a place where we now make pilgrimages to honor those past actions; it is a site of "altars and shrines"; it could even be said to embody a relatively "ancient" emergence narrative. Here, in this place, "the Union" was saved. The idea of the United States of America was preserved—and, more than preserved, a new vision for what America could be in the future was embodied in the successful sacrifice of these cultural heroes and offered to the rest of the nation (including us) by the vibrant rhetoric of Lincoln's Address. In that sense Lincoln used the battle to sell the war to the citizens of the North in terms of higher abstractions, but in that sense, too, thousands of Americans journey to Gettysburg every year even now because it is a site that somehow embodies "imaginary" or "abstract" or "mythological" meanings that are still important to us and to our sense of belonging to a larger, national whole.

TWO SACRED PLACES OF HUMAN ORIGINS

Let us turn our attention to the myths we have selected to illustrate ideas raised in this chapter. We have seen that the mythic functions of sacred places are numerous, even when the places in question are actual and have been made sacred "only" by the actions of men. When we move from actual places made sacred by human agency, like Waterloo, Flanders Field, Gettysburg, or Pearl Harbor, to actual places made sacred by divine agency, like Lourdes, the Kaaba, the Ganges, or Bighorn Medicine Wheel, the mythic resonances increase.

Perhaps the most richly resonant sacred places are those for which determining whether they are actual or "simply" mythic is difficult. For example, the location of their Emergence Myth in the Grand Canyon by contemporary Zuni leaders connects the mythic origins of a people with an actual place—a place that continues to be sacred today in various of the senses that Gulliford and Deloria suggest. But consider Western culture's own myth of origin—the story of the creation of Adam and Eve in the Garden of Eden. Many readers would accord Adam and Eve greater credence than they would the Zuni Emergence story, even though the Zunis claim an unbroken knowledge and ritual line that can be traced back to their own origins, and even though, when you consider the details carefully, the believability of the two stories does not appear markedly different. A story of the first two humans, made of lumps of mud animated by the breath of God, who conspire to disobey that God because of the interference of a talking serpent is no more or less realistic than the Zunis' multiple worlds from which people were led by "elder brother priests" into the world of light so that Father Sun might have people to offer him prayer sticks. And while we can actually visit the Grand Canyon, Eden exists nowhere on earth.

We cannot, in either case, point to better evidence or greater plausibility; therefore, comparing them to show which is true and which false is a doomed enterprise. Only the faith and reality that our cultural surroundings authorize for us would cause us to choose talking snakes over gradual emergence from underground cave-worlds. In either case, a literal reading of the creation narrative closes off all further discussion. But if we consider the *meaning functions* of the respective myths, we are led to a number of interesting questions. What, for example, do these myths of place hold for those who created them? To what degree are place and people connected? And what kinds of power do myths of place exert on those of us who consider them from intellectual or scholarly points of view?

Let us dig a bit further into the two origin stories just mentioned to see what we might learn about culture, identity, and a sense of place if we move beyond notions

The Grand Canyon
Source: © Corbis

of true and false to consider the ways myths function. In the Eden story, humans were placed in a perfect setting by a beneficent God, but they rejected lives of perfect ease and became estranged from the "Higher Power" through an act of disobedience. The human race then lives in an ill world, marked by disharmony, broken relationships, suffering, and death, all because of the actions of the primal pair (and the snake, of course). We have, especially in the Christian era, a promise of future healing, a return to harmony and perfect existence, but we must struggle through childbirth, ceaseless labor, and a constant state of emptiness, yearning for lost fullness in the here and now because of those first human decisions. In this story we move from perfection and harmony to imperfection, struggle, and disharmony.

In the Zuni tale, on the other hand, humans existed in a dark, imperfect world, and their relationships were broken or destructive. At the calling of Father Sun, they emerged from this dark chaos into a world of light and healthy relationships and harmony with their fellow inhabitants, including nonhuman creatures and with the earth itself. When the aboriginal Zunis emerged into the sun-kissed fourth world, they found that Death and the kind of evil magic that causes sickness and strife were already there. But, from the point of view of this myth, such circumstances are simply part of the way it is and not a punishment for moral failure. Thus the Zuni tale moves from disharmony to harmony, from imperfection to perfection, from emptiness to fullness. According to their myth, the Zunis came into the world to complete rather than wreck the divine plan.

The two tales leave us—the readers who must now live in the post-Eden/post-emergence world—in fundamentally different places, one defined by suffering we may hope to escape from "one glad morning when this life is over," the other a beautiful, if not trouble-free place in which to worship and celebrate the perfection of the bright dawn. In addition, the two stories frame differing cultural attitudes toward the earth itself. From the Judeo-Christian myth, we get the sense that the earth is as much a prison and proving ground as it is a home. Adam and Eve are told that they must leave Eden and, through blood, sweat, and tears, force an indifferent planet to yield sustenance and shelter. The feeling one gets from the Zuni myth is that the earth is the perfect environment for human happiness. The first Zuni emerge to find a world perfectly suited to their basic needs, including connection to their god. The point of this comparison is not that one culture's story is better than another, but that we can see powerful values inscribed in such stories. And those cultural values ultimately become our own sense of what is real and right and normal.

READING SACRED PLACES MYTHS

When studying myths about sacred places, we need to consider not only questions about actuality and agency but also the general tropes or myth types that are in operation as well. Some important tropes are (1) myths of sacred waters; (2) myths of sacred landforms such as mountains, canyons, and caves; (3) myths of sacred trees, gardens, or forests; and (4) myths of blessed isles or magic realms.

Whether they focus on rivers, lakes, wells, or oceans, myths of sacred waters abound. Varanasi, a city in northern India where the Buddha is said to have taught, is sacred because of the River Ganges. As Alistair Shearer writes:

> Varanasi is what she is because of where she is: on the banks of the holy Ganges. Personified as the mighty goddess Ganga, she first descended from heaven with such power that Shiva had to filter her mighty flow through his matted locks . . . Starting as a crystal clear rivulet at the "Cow's Mouth" of Gangotri in the high Himalayas, she widens and lengthens over 1,250 miles, sanctifying site after site, to end by exploding into the profusion of waters that empty joyously into the Bay of Bengal. She is the Hindu's link to the pure vastness of the Himalayas, where only the saints and gods can dwell, and as "Mother Ganges" she is the bringer of life to the north Indian plains. (Freeman and Shearer 2000, 63–64)

Part of the holiness of the Ganges is that she connects India to the holy mountains, another worldwide mythic trope. Olympus was sacred to the Greeks as the very dwelling place of the gods. Similarly, many Romans revered the volcano Etna as the home of the smith-god, Vulcan. Mount Shasta, as mentioned above, is sacred

Woman praying in the Ganges. Benares, India.
Source: © Courtney Milne

in northern California to the Modoc and several other California tribes, and Denali, "the Great One," in Alaska is similarly sacred to several tribes there. Kilimanjaro in Kenya features prominently in myth. Fuji is a sacred symbol of Japan even today, and myths about the goddess of Fuji are among the most ancient in Japan. All these sacred mountains are actual, but there are mythic mountains as well. The biblical Mount Zion is not a literal mountain but a symbol for the stability of God's chosen nation. Mount Sumeru, in Buddhist and other Asian traditions, is the center of the universe and site of several important "beginnings," but it does not exist on a map. The idyllic mountain kingdom of Shangri-La is also more imaginary than real.

In addition to sacred waters and mountains are sacred trees, gardens, and forests. The Tree of the Knowledge of Good and Evil and the Tree of Life stand at the heart of the Adam and Eve story—at the heart of the Garden of Eden. The Norse creation myth in chapter 2 mentions Yggdrasill, the mighty ash upon which the three worlds in Nordic cosmology rest. Where Yggdrasill came from is uncertain, but it will apparently outlast even gods and men when Ragnorac—the great conflagration at the end of time—finally occurs. The Tree of Liberty in Boston is sacred much like Gettysburg is sacred, but, as we have seen, even that "simple" sort of sacredness is a rich mine of possible meanings with far-reaching implications. The areca tree from Vietnam and the willow and chestnut trees linked with Kobo Daishi in Japan are sacred in the sense of Deloria's second category, where the Higher Powers have made their presence known through interventions in the natural world. The fig tree in the Garden of Enlightenment in Bodh Gaya, India, under which Prince Gautama achieved enlightenment and became known as the Buddha, is sacred in Deloria's third sense and in a number of the categories Gulliford offers and Shearer highlights.

The fourth trope, myths of "blessed isles," evokes locations that are nearly or entirely mythic. "Blessed isles" here refers not necessarily to literal islands; rather, the blessed isle is a discrete, often tiny land that most often suggests paradise lost. In such stories, the lands are usually described as being far away, hidden, or exceptionally difficult to reach. Often these blessed isles are guarded by monsters or demons or treacherous terrain; but just as frequently, if the hero perseveres, he or she finds a surprisingly warm reception and usually receives gifts of great worth. In many stories, like the story of Alexander the Great's search for the "Water of Everlasting Life," the blessed isle (in this case, the mountain kingdom of the archdemon Asmodeus) is discovered accidentally. In another story that follows, the blessed isle of Utröst is discovered only after the fisherman Isak is blown off course by a fierce storm. Just when he knows that his life is over, Utröst heaves into view. Another characteristic of blessed isles is that they are places of Edenic ease and material wealth. Asmodeus possesses vast wealth and, more important to Alexander (who strongly resembles King Solomon in this story), the deepest secrets. And no sooner does he land than Isak discovers that the bowls and cups of "father Cormorant" remain perpetually full.

In yet another story included below, a young Chinese, K'o-li, is given the keys to a mysterious treasure cave from which he draws implements that never fail to produce unlimited abundance. This cave most properly falls under the rubric of "sacred landforms," but its unlimited wealth suggests the carefree ease of paradise. And these are but a few examples. We learn of Atlantis from a few tantalizing lines in Plato's *Timaeus,* the Elysian Fields from Book 6 of the *Aeneid,* and Valhalla from the Eddas. If we also explore fairy tales and science fiction and fantasy novels, we are certain to find many fairy kingdoms, extraterrestrial civilizations, and lost continents which entail significant hardship and luck to find, which are well-guarded against the unworthy, and which enjoy idyllic ease, endless wealth, and rational, benign governments.

Thus, as Eliade suggests, the world is filled with rivers, trees, and mountains that have been and are still seen as points of contact between the sacred and the profane. In the stories that follow we present tales that feature these tropes in various ways. We hope that our readers will consider not only which tropes are at work but the degree to which the places mentioned below are actual and mythic, and the degree to which they are humanly and divinely consecrated. Explorations of the meanings of place and the senses in which place becomes mythically sacred can and should take off from here in many directions.

The Zuni and the Grand Canyon

Zuni (Modern Account, Arizona)

This modern version of the Zuni emergence myth was written by Harry Chimoni of the Zuni Cultural Advisory team and E. Richard Hart, Institute of the North American West, in consultation with the other members of the Zuni Cultural Resources Advisory Team and a number of Zuni religious leaders. Chimoni's account was first presented at the 1994 annual meeting of the Western History Association, Albuquerque, New Mexico, October 22, 1994.

The Zunis first emerged out of Mother Earth's fourth womb at a sacred place deep within the Grand Canyon. Zuni religious leaders explained that the Zunis came out of *Chimik'yana'kya dey'a* in a group which included those peoples now known as the Havasupai and Hualapai. The Hopis emerged at the same time but at a different location. The Zunis, or A:shiwi as we call ourselves, came into the first light of Sun Father at a beautiful spot near Ribbon Falls. Naturally the first things that happened to us and the first things that we saw became prominent in our prayers, ceremonies and religion. The point from which the first ray of sunlight reached us over a spot on the canyon rim; the plants that grew along the stream that flows from Ribbon Falls to the Colorado River; the birds and animals that we saw as we traveled out into the world; the brilliantly-colored minerals in the rock walls of the canyon; all of these things are recounted sacred in our prayers, and have a central place in our religious activities and way of life.

After emerging into what non-Indians now call the Grand Canyon, we began a long search for *Idiwana'a,* the "Middle Place," a place where equilibrium and stability could be achieved, and where we could sustain ourselves for the foreseeable future. Many stops were made journeying up the Colorado River. Villages were built and offerings were made. When ancestral Zunis died they were buried near those villages with accompanying ceremonies and blessings.

At certain places during the later migration along the Little Colorado, the *Kokko,* our supernatural beings, delivered sacred information to the Zunis. Many of these villages and sacred places are remembered in our prayers and in the religious narratives that tell the story of our migration to *Idiwana'a,* the "Middle Place."

Still searching for the "Middle Place," the A:shiwi continued up what is now known as the Little Colorado River, stopping and settling at villages periodically, before moving on in their search. At the junction of the Little Colorado and the Zuni River the migrating A:shiwi had important interaction with the *Kokko* and supernatural beings. This spot came to be the place where all Zunis go after death, and is known in Zuni as *Kolhu/wala:wa,* or "Zuni Heaven."

Source: Excerpts from *Sacred Objects, Sacred Places: Preserving Tribal Traditions* by Andrew Gulliford, © University Press of Colorado, 2000. Used by permission of the University Press of Colorado.

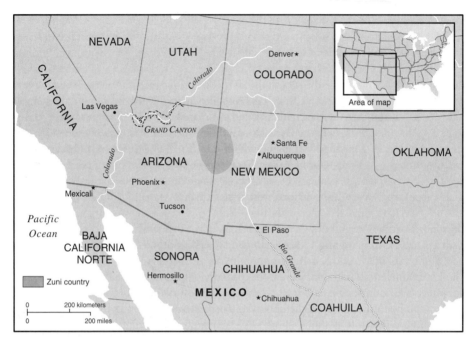

MAP 6.1 Zuni territory and the Grand Canyon

Eventually the Zunis located the "Middle Place" near the headwaters of the Zuni River and settled there. The current village of Zuni is located at that "Middle Place" and we have been living there ever since, for many hundreds of years. The point of emergence, the place where Zunis go after death, and the village of the living Zunis, these three places and all their ancient villages and shrines in between them are all tied together by the sacred flowing waters of the Zuni River, the Little Colorado River, and the Colorado River. The water of these rivers is of central importance to Zunis' prayers and offerings. The history of the A:shiwi is not only told in the prayers and religious narratives maintained by Zuni religious societies today, but in the ancestral ruins, graves, shrines, trails and sacred places left along these rivers and their tributaries from the time when Zuni was undertaking its great migration.

Zuni religious activity is oriented towards bringing rain, prosperity and stability to Zuni and to the rest of the world. Periodic visits and pilgrimages to locations along the Zuni migration route are necessary in order to carry out the duties of the various Zuni religious societies. At these sacred locations, Zunis say prayers and make offerings. Zuni religious leaders also collect samples of plants, pigments and water, and take those samples back to Zuni where they are used in religious ceremonies. Many ceremonial activities cannot be undertaken without these samples, which must be collected at the precise locations mentioned in the ancient Zuni prayers.

It has been thousands of years since the Zunis first emerged into the world in the Grand Canyon; long, long before Europeans ever set foot upon this continent, or on

Zuni territory. Zunis, consequently, have been making pilgrimages to shrines and sacred places on the Zuni River and in the Grand Canyon for many centuries.

Zunis do not make the same distinctions concerning "living" and "non-living" that many non-Indians make. To Zunis, the earth is alive. The walls of the Grand Canyon, the rocks, the minerals, and pigments there, and the water that flows between the walls of the canyon are all alive. Like any other living being, the earth can be harmed, injured and hurt when it is cut, gouged, or in any other ways mistreated. So, we believe that the Grand Canyon itself is alive and sacred. The minerals used for pigments, the native plants and animals mentioned in our prayers and religious narratives, and the water of the river and its tributaries are sacred to us and should be protected.

The Emergence

Zuni (Traditional Account, Arizona)

The following reading is a traditional Zuni account collected by Ruth Benedict during the first half of the 20th century. Compare this narrative with the previous, modern version. In both stories, the idea of process, of journeying from a state of incompleteness to a state of perfection gives the plot of each its direction. In the modern account, the emergence of the Zuni from the "beautiful spot" near Ribbon Falls and gradual migration from there to the "Middle Place" permits the myth-teller, Harry Chimoni, to reiterate his people's connection to various sacred sites where their ancestors settled temporarily or received instruction from the *Kokko* that ultimately established Zuni religious practice and culture. In the more ancient account, the focus is less on the people and more on the actions of Elder and Younger Brother, Zuni divinities that gradually lead and gradually perfect the people as they make their lengthy journey from the subterranean "fourth world" into the daylight world of Father Sun. Both stories, however, suggest that this world is sacred and a place of "equilibrium and stability" perfectly suited for the Zuni to live and worship.

They were living in the fourth world. It was dark. They could not see one another. They stepped upon one another, they urinated upon one another, they spat upon one another, they threw refuse upon one another. They could not breathe. They lived there four days [years]. The Sun took pity upon them. He saw that the world was covered with hills and springs but there were no people to give him prayer sticks. He thought, "My people shall come to the daylight world."

Source: Zuni Mythology, 2 vols., by Ruth Benedict. Copyright 1969 by Columbia University Press. Reproduced with permission of Columbia University Press.

The earth was covered with mist. He threw his rays into the mist and there in the world his sons stood up. Their hair was tangled, they had long noses, long cheeks. Next day they played together. The third day the younger brother said to the elder, "Let us go and look for beautiful places. I will go to Corn Mountain and you shall go to the south Where the Cotton Hangs." The third day they went. The younger looked over the world and he saw that nobody lived there. He said to himself, "To-morrow we shall be old enough to work."

When the next day came he called his brother. Elder Brother came and said, "What is it that you have to say that you have called me?" Younger Brother said, "We are four days old and we are old enough to work. This is a good world and nobody lives in it. Let us go to the southwest. There below the people are living in the fourth world. They are our fathers and mothers, our sons and daughters. There is no light there, no room to move about. They cannot see one another. They step on one another, they urinate upon one another. They should come to this world where they can see our father Sun."

Elder Brother answered, "It is as you say. We will go and try."

The two went to the southwest and they came to the entrance to the fourth world. They went in and came to the first world. There was just a little light there. They came to the second world. It was dark. They came to the third world. It was darker still. They came to the fourth world. It was black. The people could not see each other. They felt one another with their hands and recognized their faces. They said, "Some stranger has come. Where is it that you have come from? It is our fathers, the bow priests." They ran to feel them and they said, "Our fathers, you have come. Teach us how to get out of this place. We have heard of our father Sun and we wish to see him."

The two answered, "We have come to bring you to the other world where you can see him. Will you come with us?"

The people answered, "Yes, we wish to go. In this world we cannot see one another. We step upon one another, we urinate upon one another, we spit upon one another, we throw refuse upon one another. It is nasty here. We wish to see our father Sun. We have been waiting for someone to show us the way, but our brothers must come too. As the priest of the north says, so let it be."

The two "needed" the priest of the north. He came and said, "I have come. What is it that you wish to ask?"

"We want you to come into the daylight world."

"Yes, we shall be glad to come. We want to see our father Sun, but my brothers must come too. As the priest of the east says, so let it be." [Repeat for east, south, west.]

They said to them, "Do you know how we can get to the daylight world?" Younger Brother went to the north. He took the seeds of the pine tree and planted them. He turned about and, when he looked where he had planted, the pine had already grown. He turned again and, when he looked at the tree, the branches were grown to full size. He tore off a branch and brought it back to the people. He went to the west and planted the seeds of the spruce. He turned about and, when he looked where he had planted, the spruce had already grown. He turned again and, when he looked at the tree, the branches were grown to full size. He tore off a branch and brought it back to the people. He went to the south and planted the seeds of the silver spruce. He turned about and, when he looked where he had planted the seeds, the silver spruce had already grown. He turned again and, when he looked at the tree, the branches were grown to full size. He tore off a branch and brought it back to the people. He went to the east and planted the seeds of the aspen. He turned about and, when he looked where he had planted the seeds, the aspen had already grown. He turned again and, when he looked, the branches had grown to full size. He tore off a branch and brought it back to the people. He said, "This is all. We are ready to go up to the upper world. My people, make yourselves ready. Take those things that you live by."

The bow priests took the long prayer stick [elbow length] they had made from the pine of the north. They set it in the earth. The people went up the prayer stick and came into the third world. There was rumbling like thunder. It was lighter in that world and the people were blinded. The bow priests said, "Have we all come out?"

They answered, "Yes. Is it here that we are going to live?"

They answered, "Not yet. This is not the upper world." They lived there four days [years]. The bow priests took the crook of the west that they had made from the spruce. They set it in the earth. There was rumbling like thunder and the people came up into the second world. It was twilight there and the people were blinded. The bow priests said, "Have we all come out?"

"Yes. Is it here that we shall live?"

"Not yet." They remained there four days [years] and the two took the long prayer stick that they had made from the silver spruce of the south and set it in the earth. There was rumbling like thunder and the people came up into the first world. It was light like red dawn. They were dazzled and they said, "Is it here that we shall live?"

They answered, "Not yet." The people were sad. They could see each other quite plain. Their bodies were covered with dirt and with ashes. They were stained with spit and urine and they had green slime on their heads. Their hands and feet were webbed and they had tails and no mouths or exits. They remained there four days [years]. The bow priests took the long prayer stick they had made from the aspen of the east and they set it in the earth. There was rumbling like thunder and the people came up into the daylight world. The two bow priests came first and after them those who carried the medicine bundles, the *ka'etone, tcu'etone, mu'etone* and *le'etone*. When they came into the sunlight the tears ran down their cheeks. Younger Brother said to them, "Turn to the sun and look full at our father Sun no matter how bright it is." They cried out for it hurt them and their tears ran to the ground. Everywhere they were standing the sun's flowers [sunflowers and buttercups] sprang up from the tears caused by the sun. The people said, "Is this the world where we shall live?"

"Yes, this is the last world. Here you see our father Sun." They remained there four days [years] and they went on.

They came to Slime Spring. They lived there four days [years] and the bow priests said, "It is time our people learned to eat." They took the corn of the witch and they put it in the fields to *itsumawe*. When it had grown they harvested it and the men took it home to their wives. They smelled it, but they had no way to eat. The bow priests were sad and Younger Brother said, "Older Brother, the people have made *itsumawe* and I am sorry for them that they cannot eat. Let us cut them so that they can enjoy food."

Elder Brother agreed and his brother said, "When everyone is asleep we shall go to each house and cut mouths in their faces."

That night after the people were asleep, the bow priests took their [ceremonial] stone knives and sharpened them with a red whetstone. They went to each house. They cut each face where the skin of the mouth was puffed up. The knife made the lips red from the red of the whetstone. They went home. When the sun rose the people found that they had mouths. They said, "What makes our faces so flat?" They began to get hungry and the men brought in corn and water and they ate. That night they were uncomfortable because they had no exits. They could not defecate.

Younger Brother thought, "We should cut the anus so that they can defecate." He went to his brother and he said, "These people should have the anus. Let us cut it tonight when they are asleep." Elder Brother agreed and they took the [smaller] stone knives and sharpened them on a soot whetstone. They cut the anus for all the people and the soot colored those parts black. Next morning the people were uncomfortable and they went outside. They thought they had broken open in their sleep.

They tried to break up the corn so that they could eat it better. They took whetstones in their webbed hands and rubbed the corn on the hearthstone. They mixed porridge and made corncakes. After they had made it, it was hard to clean their hands for they were webbed, and the Younger Brother said to Elder Brother, "I am sorry for my people that their hands are webbed. Let us cut their fingers apart."

Elder Brother agreed and that night they took the [larger] stone knife and cut the webbed hands and feet of the people. In the morning the people were frightened but when the sun had risen they did not notice any more. They worked better with fingers and toes.

The next day Younger Brother said to the older, "Our people have been cut. They still have tails, and horns. Let us cut them away."

Elder Brother agreed and they took the [smaller] stone knife. They went to each house and cut the tails and horns from their people. In the morning the people were frightened but when the sun rose they did not mind any more. They were glad that they were finished.

Bighorn Medicine Wheel

Northern Cheyenne, Northern Arapaho, Eastern Shoshone, and Crow (Wyoming)

The following account, written by Andrew Gulliford, is neither a myth nor, strictly speaking, mythology. We have broken with our own organizational pattern by including this chapter from a "secondary" source because it illustrates the immensely complex

Source: Excerpts from *Sacred Objects, Sacred Places: Preserving Tribal Traditions* by Andrew Gulliford, © University Press of Colorado, 2000. Used by permission of the University Press of Colorado.

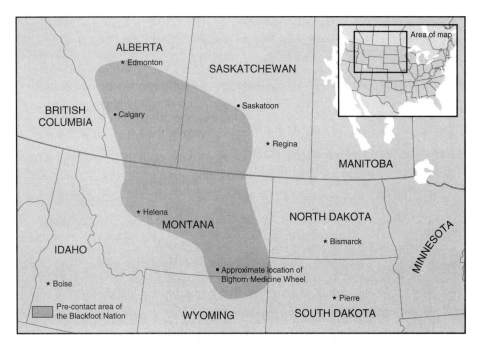

MAP 6.2 Approximate pre-contact area of the Blackfoot Nation and the location of the Bighorn Medicine Wheel.

present-day sociopolitical and economic interests that can collide at sacred sites.

Located atop Medicine Mountain at 9,642 feet in the Bighorn National Forest of Wyoming, the Medicine Wheel is one of the most intriguing combinations of archaeological features and sacred sites west of the Mississippi River. Situated above timberline, Medicine Mountain represents over 10,000 years of Native American culture in a spectacular setting that generates its own weather and spiritual power. A National Historic Landmark since 1970, the Medicine Wheel attracted the attention of anthropologists and historians early in the twentieth century, and it is one of dozens of wheels scattered across the northern Great Plains and southern Canada; eighty feet in diameter, it is the largest in the United States.

Northern Cheyenne elder William Tall Bull explained that the Medicine Wheel "is an altar for the mountain," and the Historic Preservation Plan developed in 1996 to manage the wheel represents one of the best case studies in sacred site access, compromise, and preservation protection. The preservation plan's purpose "is to ensure that the Medicine Wheel and Medicine Mountain are managed in a manner that protects the integrity of the site as a sacred site and a nationally important traditional cultural property."

The medicine wheel complex of cairns, spokes, teepee rings, lithic scatters, buried archaeological sites, system of ancient travois trails, and rock clusters is revered by mountain and Plains tribes, including the Northern Arapaho, Eastern

Bighorn Medicine Wheel, Bighorn National Forest, Wyoming. This sacred site has astronomical as well as spiritual significance. It is aligned to the four sacred directions and various points along its axes align with the summer and winter solstice sunrise.
Source: © Courtney Milne

Shoshone, Northern Cheyenne, and Crow Indians. A stone tool quarry close by may be thousands of years old. Classic U-shaped vision quest enclosures are at the site, in addition to small stone circles. Possibly constructed 1,500 years ago, the wheel has been utilized, built, rebuilt, and formed over centuries and is still an actively used religious site both for local tribes and native peoples from all over the nation who come on pilgrimages and leave offerings of cloth, sage, sweetgrass, beads, and bundles. Approximately 245 feet in circumference, with a central cairn, the wheel includes twenty-eight spokes that radiate to the outer rim of the circle. Around the rim are six smaller cairns, four of which face the center; one faces north and the other east. At one time, the smaller cairns may have been covered with skins placed atop wooden posts. The central cairn is the largest and measures twelve feet by seven feet.

Who built the cairn and why remains a mystery, though Crow Indians insist it was built "before the light came" and "by people without iron," possibly the Shoshonean band of Sheepeaters who lived at high elevations and hunted mountain sheep. A piece of wood found in the wheel has been dated to AD 1760, a trade bead dates to the early 1800s, and other radiocarbon dates vary from 420 to 6,650 years ago. A projectile point has been found nearby that dates to 9,000 years before the present, and trails leave the wheel from all directions as they go up and over the Bighorn Mountains toward the Great Plains to the east or the Yellowstone Country to the west. The Medicine Wheel may be an ancient astronomical observatory, with cairns placed at specific locations to mark rising stars during the summer solstice. Other scholars suggest the structure resembles the Sun Dance Lodge or Medicine Lodge so important to Plains Indian religious traditions. The Crow believe that spokes of the wheel are also similar to the placement of poles for tepees and that the wheel was built to demonstrate how to correctly construct homes.

A contemporary Cheyenne cultural leader explained,

> The tribes traditionally went and still go to the sacred mountain. The people sought the high mountain for prayer. They sought spiritual harmony with the powerful spirits there. Many offerings have always been left on this mountain. The center cairn, once occupied by a large buffalo skull, was a place to make prayer offerings. Vision questers would have offered prayers of thanks for plant and animal life that had, and would, sustain them in the future. Prayers of thanks were offered for all of creation. Prayers are made for families and for loved ones who are ill. Atonements are made for any offense to Mother Earth. When asking for guidance, prayers for wisdom and strength are always part of this ritual. All of this is done so that spiritual harmony will be our constant companion throughout the year.

Young men go to the wheel for vision quests today as they have done for centuries, and many chiefs and prominent Indians have fasted there. A Crow story relates the vision quest of Red Plume, a Crow chief of the early nineteenth century who found spiritual medicine at the wheel during four days there without food or water. Red Plume was visited by little people who inhabited the wheel. They took him into the earth where they lived, and he learned that the red eagle would be his spirit guardian, so he always wore the small feather from the back of the eagle, above its longer tail feathers—hence the name Red Plume. As he lay dying, he told his people that his spirit would live at the wheel and that they could talk with him there.

John Hill, from Crow Agency, Montana, said, "The Medicine Wheel is very dear to the American Plains Indian tribes; in fact, the Medicine Wheel itself is the root of the Plains Indian religion." Enemy tribes would approach the wheel at certain times of the year and would "come up to the foot of the hill and lay down their arms and prepare their candidates for the fasting program or their vision quest programs and others would prepare those candidates for the pilgrimage up the hill to the Medicine Wheel itself and they would meet up there, these enemy, these warring tribes."

Hill further explained that the Medicine Wheel "is a religious shrine, it is a prayer site, it's a spiritual site [similar to] holy places throughout the world—the Vatican in Rome, the Temple in Salt Lake City, other places across the seas. It is not the church that is powerful; it's the spirit transmitted through the church, and here we have a site that we observe and recognize as a spiritual prayer site."

For tribes, the Medicine Wheel is an ongoing religious site of paramount importance, but for most of the twentieth century, the U.S. Forest Service, which manages Medicine Mountain, misunderstood the site and thought of it only as an interesting archaeological site with no contemporary significance. Forest Service personnel insisted on managing the site within the ideological framework of "multiple use" for a variety of timber, grazing, and other interests. A district ranger for the Bighorn National Forest once stated at a public meeting, "That pile of rocks could be bulldozed over the side of the mountain" for all he cared, as long as the Forest

Service complied with certain regulations. Religious values at the site were ignored, and local nonnative residents insisted they had never seen Indians near the Medicine Wheel and that it was not important to nearby tribes.

But as the Wyoming State Historic Preservation Office noted, "To contemporary Native Americans, the Medicine Wheel and the surrounding terrain constitute a uniquely important and sacred landscape that figures prominently in tribal oral and ceremonial traditions. To Indian people, the rock alignments and cairns that comprise the Medicine Wheel represent religious architecture rather than inanimate archaeological data." Quietly over the years, Indians had secretly used the wheel for vision quests and made special pilgrimages to the mountain in the nineteenth and early twentieth centuries despite the fact that white Indian agents on reservations prohibited travel for traditional religious purposes. Native Americans are reluctant to talk about sacred sites, and as *National Register Bulletin #38* revealed, "Particularly because properties of traditional cultural significance are often kept secret, it is not uncommon for them to be 'discovered' only when something threatens them—for example, when a change in land-use is proposed in their vicinity."

Imagine the consternation when, in 1988, the superintendent of the Bighorn National Forest, in conjunction with businessmen in Lovell, Wyoming, sought to erect at the sacred wheel a massive metal overhead observation platform, a parking lot for 200 vehicles including recreational vehicles, road improvements, and huts for cross-country skiers and snowmobilers. Years of Indian silence came to an end. The tribes became incensed at this commercialization of their religious shrine. The Medicine Wheel Alliance targeted the Forest Service's proposal to cut timber on Medicine Mountain, and the Medicine Wheel Coalition was formed to stop the threat to the wheel because of its National Historic Landmark status. Both groups insisted that the U.S. Forest Service abide by national preservation laws, and they successfully thwarted local development of the site and demanded that the Bighorn National Forest staff consider other alternatives.

The U.S. Forest Service prepared an environmental assessment and, to their surprise, received over 800 letters; 95 percent of the letter writers "wanted nothing done at the site except to protect it for Native American spiritual use," stated Mary Randolph, who was the Bighorn Forest's public affairs officer. She remembered,

> No one was quite sure how to deal with this. At forestry school, they don't teach you religion or spirituality, or how to manage a sacred site. Meetings between state and federal agencies and Native American organizations involved were not going well. Meetings between the parties were antagonistic, unproductive and usually ended with less and less trust.

Eventually, as the nonnative land managers came to understand Indian spirituality and began to act as interested individuals instead of federal bureaucrats, discussion began.

Seven parties consulted on the Wheel, including the Medicine Wheel Coalition, the Medicine Wheel Alliance, the Advisory Council for Historic Preservation, the Wyoming State Historic Preservation Office, the Federal Aviation Administration (FAA), Big Horn County Commissioners, and the U.S. Forest Service. The FAA got involved because a little over one mile east of the wheel is a radar dome that tracks airplanes crossing the northern Rockies. Issues focused on development and access. Native Americans agreed that tourists could continue to visit the site but said that it should be closed for traditional cultural use for religious ceremonies. Development should be minimal, and the site should be treated with respect. In 1995, 16,275 visitors came to the site, including 840 Native Americans.

Final completion of the Medicine Wheel Historic Preservation Plan in 1996 represents one of the best models of cooperation among tribes and federal agencies, although the agreement took years to work out because relationships between Indians and land managers were originally hostile. Before the eventual compromise was reached, several USFS employees had been transferred or resigned because of heated pressure and public debates. Forest Service managers and Big Horn County Commissioners also threatened preservationists. According to Alan Stanfill of the Advisory Council for Historic Preservation,

> More than once, the Forest Supervisor met with State and Council officials in unsuccessful attempts to have staff members of the SHPO and Advisory Council dismissed from the negotiations and their jobs. Newspaper articles quoting the commissioners and the Forest Service appeared regularly and invariably contained personal insults, accusations of impropriety, misinformation, and political posturing to promote public and political sympathy.

Defending Indian sacred sites is never easy in the West, especially when locals favor development dollars over First Amendment religious freedoms.

Controversy began with the ill-conceived plan to publicize the wheel and to install a massive observation tower that tourists could climb. In order to reduce vandalism to the prehistoric spokes and stone alignments, the wheel was already encased in a chain-link fence with barbed wire jutting out at the top. Crow Indian John Hill explained that in 1991, a Pennsylvania family picked up a rock at the wheel during their vacation and took it home with them, only to experience much bad luck and numerous accidents in the next several months. Hill related that, in desperation, "the family wrapped up their rock very neatly, very nice like a Christmas present, and they sent it back to the Postmaster of Crow Agency" with a plea to have the rock returned. Hill continued:

> So that was in December and the Medicine Wheel is the hardest to get to at that time of year with snowdrifts sometimes as high as fifteen feet. So we took it up the 12th of July, took the rock up there and went through what we call a cleansing ceremony for the rock itself, used sweetgrass, sweet cedar, sweet sage, Indian tobacco, not from North Carolina, but native Indian tobacco from right here, and we used medicine root and smudged the rock.

Hill and a friend restored the rock to the Medicine Wheel and simultaneously restored the health and safety of the family who had taken it.

As for the wheel itself, Alan Stanfill explained that the sacred qualities of this special place "still exist because people cared enough about it to become involved in deliberations over its future. The destruction of the Wheel was as likely as its protection. The reason that some assurance of its protection resulted from the consultation effort is because enough people put enough pressure on the decision makers to make it too painful to decide otherwise."

A key facet of the Historic Preservation Plan requires all new Forest Service staffers to meet with concerned tribal members and be briefed on the significance of the wheel before they take on their new responsibilities. In this way, the acrimony and misunderstandings of the past will not be repeated, and Native Americans will be part of the training process to ensure that new USFS personnel understand the mysteries of the wheel and its deep and abiding religious importance; thereafter, "when leadership changes in the agency occur, management direction will not." The plan "is meant to be an ongoing living document which adapts to the needs of the site and the people who use and treasure it."

In the final preservation plan, the Wyoming State Historic Preservation Office stated,

> The Medicine Wheel, and the surrounding ethnographic, historic, and archaeological localities comprise a set of uniquely significant cultural resources that merit the greatest possible protection under the law. The Native American traditional use areas and other sites that occupy Medicine Mountain express a profound spiritual heritage, as well as anthropological values, that are connected by the common thread of centuries of use by Native Americans. It is one of the very few historic reserves in the United States where the prehistoric past and ethnographic present are unequivocally linked.

As the preservation plan indicated, "Ceremonial activities are ongoing today, resulting in the continued creation, renewal, or modification of these sites."

This is the dynamic nature of ongoing religion. Multiple uses such as grazing, camping, timber management, and commercial pursuits will now be excluded from the area near the wheel. Mary Randolph stated that the Medicine Wheel Preservation Plan "has become a model for management of sacred sites across the country and for many federal agencies." Though working on the plan was difficult, she added that "for many of us it represents the highlight of our careers in federal government."

According to the National Register nomination, "The Medicine Wheel clearly represents a contin ity of Native spiritual symbolism that extends into an unknown and distant past and is now recognized among virtually all contemporary Plains tribes." Indian religion is highly individualistic, and the nomination said, "Each different practitioner acts within a deep and complex spiritual tradition, but within that tradition he acts as his own direct connection [with the Creator] when the Spirit moves him," and thus Indians may realign stones or set up new stone features at an ancient site, as Bill Tall Bull did. Though religious practices among tribes differ, common sacred site requirements include land that "must be largely undisturbed, the plants and animals and rocks and waters must be accessible, there must be opportunities for solitude, and free movement and access to the Mountain must be available." This is essential because "there must not be such intensive intrusion into the natural landscape that the spirits inhabiting the landscape are forced to leave. All this requires a National Historic Landmark of some size."

The Wyoming State Historic Preservation Office is now in the process of expanding the boundaries for the Medicine Wheel National Historic Landmark to fully accommodate associated trails, shrines, cairns, petroglyph sites, and other religious features not fully understood when the wheel itself was discovered by settlers and scientists a century ago. Adjacent sites include staging areas for religious activities, such as sweat lodges in the lower valleys. Local people over the years had helped to protect the wheel and suggested it be fenced to deter vandalism. Now the Medicine Wheel is both protected and properly interpreted as a sacred place, and tribes will be contacted to help provide on-site interpreters. Visitors must walk a mile and a half to the site, and for a minimum of twelve days between July 1 and November 1 the site is subject to a voluntary closure to allow Native Americans privacy to conduct ancient ceremonies and initiations. Otherwise, visitation is encouraged, provided the site is approached in a respectful manner. At the wheel, Indians also gather plants, herbs, and other materials for ceremonial, religious, or traditional cultural purposes. At 10,000 feet in elevation, the viewshed of the Medicine Wheel is an important value of the sacred site, and currently, the Federal Aviation Agency's Long Range Radar Facility is a jarring visual factor on the landscape directly to the east of the wheel. As the satellite global positioning technology system (GPS) becomes perfected, it is hoped the dome will be removed within the next 20 years.

To stand on Medicine Mountain at dawn on a summer morning is to sense the power of the peak and the sacred spokes of the wheel. When the fog slowly lifts, one may feel spirits there among the stones and offerings carefully hung on the fence and placed in vision quest sites by those seeking knowledge. When the Framers of the Constitution drafted the First Amendment to protect religious freedom, the Medicine Wheel was already centuries old. To be there at dawn is to know the power of a sacred place.

The Medicine Wheel

Hyemeyohsts Storm (Wyoming)

According to his website, Hyemeyohsts (Wolf) Storm was raised on the Northern Cheyenne and Crow reservations of Montana and was from an early age apprenticed to the Maya Indian "Zero Chief" and holy woman Estcheemah, who was born during the Indian Wars of the late 1800s. According to Storm, she was one of the most powerful Medicine Chiefs of her time and was the one who passed on to him the histories and knowledge of the Zero Chiefs that preceded her. After maturing in the self-discipline that Estcheemah taught him for over 20 years, Storm emerged as a teacher in his own right and has spent the last 30 years transmitting her revelations to others as artist, writer, and lecturer. Since the publication of his first book, *Seven Arrows,* from which the following excerpt is taken, Storm founded and directs the Circle of the Earth Temple and Institute and the International School of Metis Art.

Source: Excerpts from pages 4–7 of *Seven Arrows* by Hyemeyohsts Storm. Copyright © 1972 by Hyemeyohsts Storm. Reprinted by permission of HarperCollins Publishers, Inc.

In the previous reading, we learned about the cultural and political complexities of designating the Bighorn Medicine Wheel both a sacred place and a national park. In what follows, we read about the spiritual and symbolic significance of medicine wheels from the perspective of someone for whom these sacred places are a crucial part of his religious practice. It is interesting to note that native American religion as Storm practices it has much in common with the mystical traditions of the world's so-called major religions inasmuch as it, too, teaches that all beings and things in the universe are interconnected and of equal importance. The medicine wheel both mirrors and orients the practitioner to the totality of the universe and teaches that everything is, by nature, in harmony with everything else in the cosmos.

While this reading is, like the previous one, not, strictly speaking, myth or mythology per se, it helps provide a worldview context necessary for reading many Native American myths in this book and elsewhere.

In many ways this Circle, the Medicine Wheel, can best be understood if you think of it as a mirror in which everything is reflected. "The Universe is the Mirror of the People," the old Teachers tell us, "and each person is a Mirror to every other person."

Any idea, person, or object can be a Medicine Wheel, a Mirror, for man. The tiniest flower can be such a Mirror, as can a wolf, a story, a touch, a religion, or a mountain top. For example, one person alone on a mountain top at night might feel fear. Another might feel calm and peaceful. Still another might feel nothing at all. In each case the mountain top would be the same, but it would be perceived differently as it reflected the feelings of the different people who experienced it. This book, *Seven Arrows,* is such a Mirror. It is a Medicine Wheel, just as you are.

Here is a drawing of a simple Medicine Wheel. (see fig. 6.1). Among the People, the Teachers usually constructed it from small stones or pebbles, which they would place like this before them upon the ground.

Each one of these tiny stones within the Medicine Wheel represents one of the many things of the Universe. One of them represents you, and another represents me. Others hold within them our mothers, fathers, sisters, brothers, and our friends. Still others symbolize hawks, buffalo, elks and wolves. There are also stones which represent religions, governments, philosophies, and even entire nations. All things are contained within the Medicine Wheel, and all things are equal within it. The Medicine Wheel is the Total Universe.

Our Teachers tell us that all things within this Universe Wheel know of their Harmony with every other thing, and know how to *Give-Away* one to the other, except man. Of all the Universe's creatures, it is we alone who do not begin our lives with knowledge of this great Harmony.

All the things of the Universe Wheel have spirit and life, including the rivers, rocks, earth, sky, plants and animals. But it is only man, of all the Beings on the Wheel, who is a determiner. Our determining spirit can be made whole only through the learning of our harmony with all our brothers and sisters, and with all the other

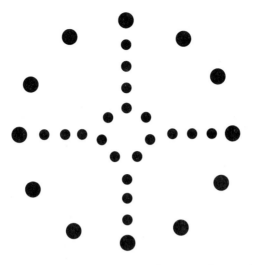

FIGURE 6.1 Simple Medicine Wheel, as illustrated
in *Seven Arrows.*

spirits of the Universe. To do this we must learn to seek and to perceive. We must do
this to find our place within the Medicine Wheel. To determine this place we must
learn to *Give-Away.*

The *Vision Quest,* or perceiving quest, is the way we must begin this search. We
must all follow our Vision Quest to discover ourselves, to learn how we perceive of
ourselves, and to find our relationship with the world around us.

THE POWERS

Among the People, a child's first Teaching is of the Four Great Powers of the Medicine Wheel.

To the North on the Medicine Wheel is found Wisdom. The Color of the Wisdom of the North is White, and its Medicine Animal is the Buffalo. The South is represented by the Sign of the Mouse, and its Medicine Color is Green. The South is
the place of Innocence and Trust, and for perceiving closely our nature of heart. The
West is the Looks-Within Place, which speaks of the Introspective nature of man.
The Color of this Place is Black. The East is marked by the Sign of the Eagle. It is
the Place of Illumination, where we can see things clearly far and wide. Its Color
is the Gold of the Morning Star.

At birth, each of us is given a particular Beginning Place within these Four
Great Directions on the Medicine Wheel. This Starting Place gives us our first way
of perceiving things, which will then be our easiest and most natural way throughout our lives.

But any person who perceives from only one of these Four Great Directions will
remain just a partial man. For example, a man who possesses only the Gift of the
North will be wise. But he will be a cold man, a man without feeling. And the man

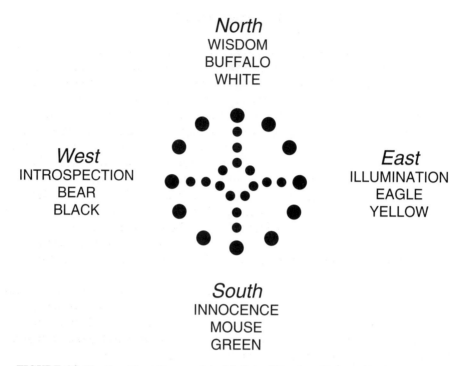

North
WISDOM
BUFFALO
WHITE

West
INTROSPECTION
BEAR
BLACK

East
ILLUMINATION
EAGLE
YELLOW

South
INNOCENCE
MOUSE
GREEN

FIGURE 6.2 The Four Great Powers of the Medicine Wheel, as illustrated in *Seven Arrows.*

who lives only in the East will have the clear, far sighted vision of the Eagle, but he will never be close to things. This man will feel separated, high above life, and will never understand or believe that he can be touched by anything.

A man or woman who perceives only from the West will go over the same thought again and again in their mind, and will always be undecided. And if a person has only the Gift of the South, he will see everything with the eyes of a Mouse. He will be too close to the ground and too near sighted to see anything except what is right in front of him, touching his whiskers.

There are many people who have two or three of these Gifts, but these people still are not Whole. A man might be a Bear person from the East, or an Eagle person of the South. The first of these men would have the Gift of seeing Introspectively within Illumination, but he would lack the Gifts of Touching and Wisdom. The second would be able to see clearly and far. But he would still not know of the things of the North, nor of the Looks-Within Place.

In this same way, a person might also be a Golden Bear of the North, or a Black Eagle of the South. But none of these people would yet be Whole. After each of us has learned of our Beginning Gift, our First Place on the Medicine Wheel, we must then Grow by Seeking Understanding in each of the Four Great Ways. Only in this way can we become Full, capable of Balance and Decision in what we do . . .

THE TOUCHING

To Touch and Feel is to Experience. Many people live out their entire lives without really Touching or being Touched by anything. These people live within a world of mind and imagination that may move them sometimes to joy, tears, happiness or sorrow. But these people never really Touch. They do not live and become one with life.

The Sun Dancer believes that each person is a unique Living Medicine Wheel, powerful beyond imagination, that has been limited and placed upon this earth to Touch, Experience and Learn. The Six Grandfathers Taught me that each man, woman, and child at one time was a Living Power that existed somewhere in time and space. These powers were without form, but they were aware. They were alive.

Each Power possessed boundless energy and beauty. These living Medicine Wheels were capable of nearly anything. They were beautiful and perfect in all ways except one. They had no understanding of limitation, no experience of substance. These beings were total energy of the Mind, without Body or Heart. They were placed upon this earth that they might Learn the things of the Heart through Touching.

According to the Teachers, there is only one thing that all people possess equally. This is their loneliness. No two people on the face of this earth are alike in any one thing except for their loneliness. This is the cause of our Growing, but it is also the cause of our wars. Love, hate, greed and generosity are all rooted within our loneliness, within our desire to be needed and loved.

The only way that we can overcome our loneliness is through Touching. It is only in this way that we can learn to be Total Beings. God is a presence of this Total. *Heamavihio*, the Breath of Wisdom, and *Miaheyyun*, Total Understanding, are but two of the words in the Cheyenne language which express this wholeness.

Sacred Landforms in Japan

Japanese

All cultures tell stories about sacred places, but it may fairly be said that sacred places are particularly numerous in Japan. This may well be the case because the native religion of this country, Shinto, views all landforms—indeed, all things—as being closely associated with a particular *kami* (god). In the *Kojiki*, the mythical account of Japan's origins, we read of the *kami* of wheat, the *kami* of a particular lake, the *kamis* of mountains, stones, and trees. Thus, each natural thing in the material world has its own *kami* and practitioners of Shinto believe that the natural world is sacred

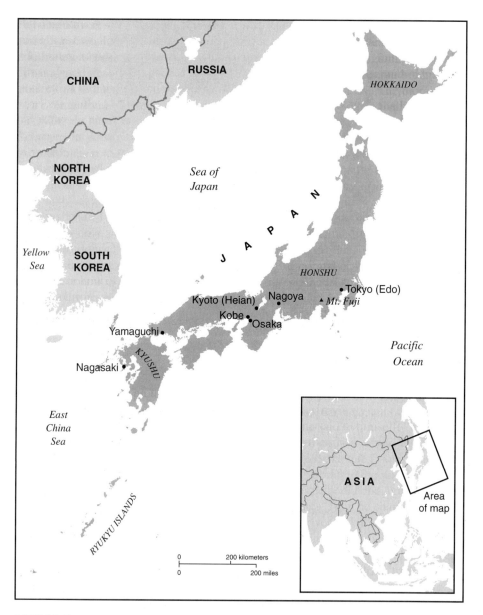

MAP 6.3 Japan

and that one draws close to the gods when one is in nature. Indeed, natural objects are worshiped as embodiments of the gods.

After the arrival of Buddhism to Japan in the 7th century CE,
the two religions merged to a significant degree. Shinto practitioners tended to view the Buddha as a *kami* and Buddhists tended
to think of the *kami* as Buddhas and venerable ancestors. Indeed,

many weddings in modern Japan are performed by Shinto priests while most funeral services are conducted by Buddhist priests. This cross-pollination of spiritual traditions is particularly noticeable in the following story in which the mountains Yatsu-ga-take and Fuji are associated with their respective deities, but Buddha Amida is called upon to settle their dispute about which is loftier. In the Japanese stories that follow, mountains, wells, trees, and springs are the sites of shrines, notable deeds, and are respected as sacred, emphasizing the traditional importance that Japanese culture has placed on nature and particular landforms as places where the divine is revealed.

In ancient times Yatsu-ga-take was higher than Mt. Fuji. Once the female deity of Fuji (Asama-sama) and the male deity of Yatsu-ga-take (Gongen-sama) had a contest to see which was higher. They asked the Buddha Amida to decide which one was loftier. It was a difficult task. Amida ran a water pipe from the summit of Yatsu-ga-take to the summit of Fuji-san and poured water in the pipe. The water flowed to Fuji-san, so Amida decided that Fuji-san was defeated.

Although Fuji-san was a woman, she was too proud to recognize her defeat. She beat the summit of Yatsu-ga-take with a big stick. So his head was split into eight parts, and that is why Yatsu-ga-take [Eight Peaks] now has eight peaks. *Gods !*

The Mountain of the Lotus and the Fan

Japanese

The beautifully symmetrical, snow-capped cone of Mount Fuji, or Fujiyama (The Never-Dying Mountain), is recognized the world over. It symbolizes, for many Japanese, the permanence of beauty, tranquility, and divine mystery in a world of change and secular striving.

Poets and street-corner philosophers have likened its majestic presence to a white lotus or an inverted, wide-stretched fan. The reference to the lotus blossom links it to the sacred flower of the Lord Buddha, the eight points of which are said to symbolize Buddha's Eightfold Path of Right View, Right Intention, Right Speech, Right Action, Right Livelihood, Right Effort, Right Mindfulness, and Right Concentration. For centuries, poets and artists have found inspiration in Fuji. The following poem suggests the religious and aesthetic appeal of this sacred place.

Source: Yone Noguchi, "The Mountain of the Lotus and the Fan." In *Myths and Legends: Japan*, ed. F. Hadland Davis. © David D. Nickerson, 1955. Reprinted 1992 by Dover Press.

The 12,388-ft. snow-capped peak of Mount Fuji looms above a rural road. Since much of the surrounding land is near sea level, Fuji can be seen from great distances on clear days.
Source: © Digital Stock

In fact, for many contemporary Japanese, the myths surrounding Fuji are forgotten—or, if not forgotten, seen as quaint antiques. Nevertheless, Mt. Fuji-san (Japanese usually add the honorific term "san" to Fuji's name) is a particularly interesting case of multilayered significances for a sacred place as seen by local peoples. As the stories about Fuji-san we present show, the mountain has very ancient mythic roots. But Fuji is not simply the locus of ancient myth; she is sacred in another sense as well. For many Japanese Fuji-san serves as an emblem of the nation of Japan. To view the rising sun (another national emblem) from the rim of the crater of Fuji is thus a doubly powerful goal for the many thousands of pilgrims who hike to the top of Fuji in the middle of the night, stopping at mountain huts at numerous stages along the way for tea or beer or noodles or a short sleep—or to purchase bottles of oxygen since altitude sickness is common among climbers who mostly live near sea level.

Fuji Yama,
Touched by thy divine breath,
We return to the shape of God.
Thy silence is Song,

Mount Fuji. Ink and color on silk by Katsushika Hokusai, seventeenth century. This idealized image of Fuji emphasizes the symmetry of this summit. Notice that Fuji's crater is smoking in this painting. The last major eruption of this still active volcano in historic times occurred about the time this painting was executed.

Source: Boy and Mt. Fuji by Katsushika Hokusai. Freer Gallery of Art, Smithsonian Institution, Washington, DC: Gift of Charles Lang Freer, F1898.

Thy song is the song of Heaven:
Our land of fever and care
Turns to a home of mellow-eyed ease—
The home away from the land
Where mortals are born only to die.
We Japanese daughters and sons,
Chanting of thy fair majesty,
The pride of God,
Seal our shadows in thy bosom,
The balmiest place of eternity,
O white-faced wonder,
O matchless sight,
O sublimity, O Beauty!
The thousand rivers carry thy sacred image
On their brows;
All the mountains raise their heads unto thee
Like the flowing tide,
As if to hear thy final command.

Behold! the seas surrounding Japan
Lose their hungry-toothed song and wolfish desire,
Kissed by lullaby-humming repose,
At sight of thy shadow,
As one in a dream of poem.
We being round thee forget to die:
Death is sweet,
Life is sweeter than Death.
We are mortals and also gods,
Innocent companions of thine,
O eternal Fuji!

Yosoji and the Goddess Fuji

Japanese

Yosoji's mother, in common with many in the village where she lived, was stricken down with smallpox. Yosoji consulted the magician Kamo Yamakiko in the matter, for his mother grew so ill that every hour he expected her to be taken from him in death. Kamo Yamakiko told Yosoji to go to a small stream that flowed from the southwest side of Mount Fuji. "Near the source of this stream," said the magician, "is a shrine to the God of Long Breath. Go fetch this water, and give it to your mother, for this alone will cure her."

Yosoji, full of hope, eagerly set forth upon his journey, and when he had arrived at a spot where three paths crossed each other he was in difficulty as to the right one to take. Just as he was debating the matter, a lovely girl, clad in white, stepped out from the forest and bade him follow her to the place where the precious stream flowed near the shrine of the God of Long Breath.

When they reached the stream Yosoji was told to drink himself, as well as to fill the gourd with the sparkling water for his mother. When he had done these things the beautiful girl accompanied him to the place where he had originally seen her, and said: "Meet me again at this place in three days' time, for you will require a further supply of this water."

After five visits to this sacred shrine Yosoji rejoiced to find that his mother was quite well again, and not only his mother, but many of the villagers who had also been privileged to drink the water. Yosoji's bravery was loudly extolled, and presents were sent to the magician for his timely advice; but Yosoji, who was an honest lad, knew in his heart that all praise was really due to the beautiful girl who had been his guide. He desired to thank her more fully than he had hitherto done, and for this purpose he once more set out for the stream.

Source: Myths and Legends: Japan, Ed. by F. Hadland Davis. © David D. Nickerson, 1955. Reprinted 1992 by Dover Press.

When Yosoji reached the shrine of the God of Long Breath he found that the stream had dried up. With much surprise and not a little sorrow he knelt down and prayed that she who had been so good to his mother would appear before him in order that he might thank her as she so richly deserved. When Yosoji arose he saw the maiden standing before him.

Yosoji expressed his gratitude in warm and elegant language, and begged to be told the name of her who had been his guide and restored his mother to health and strength again. But the maiden, smiling sweetly upon him, would not tell her name. Still smiling, she swung a branch of camellia in the air, so that it seemed that the fair blossom beckoned to some invisible spirit far away. In answer to the floral summons a cloud came down from Mount Fuji; it enveloped the lovely maiden, and carried her to the sacred mountain from which she had come. Yosoji knew now that his guide was none other than the Goddess of Fuji. He knelt with rapture upon his face as he watched the departing figure. As he gazed upon her he knew in his heart that with his thanks love had mingled too. While he yet knelt the Goddess of Fuji threw down the branch of camellia, a remembrance, perhaps a token, of her love for him.

The Ten Thousand Treasure Mountain

Yao (China)

If myth were history, Chinese civilization would have begun sometime after the giant Pan-ku (or Pangu) created the universe and a succession of sage-emperors, including Yandi (Fiery Lord) and Huangdi (Yellow Emperor), who taught the people everything from how to communicate to how to provide themselves with food, clothing, and shelter. The archaeological record suggests interesting parallels with these myths of early invention and conquest. In fact, many of the ancient place names mentioned in the myths led archaeologists to important prehistoric sites. Today, most scholars agree that the first truly Chinese civilization, the Xia Dynasty, emerged and flourished between the 21st and 16th centuries BCE. The quality of its urban centers, bronze implements, and tombs suggests that this period marked an important evolutionary stage between the late Neolithic Age and the characteristic feudal urbanity that emerged during the Shang and Zhou dynasties.

The dynastic system, through which a ruling family passed the reins of power from one generation to another, persisted from the Xia Dynasty until the Nationalist revolution began in 1911— more than three millennia! Over time, the emperor became known

Source: Louise Kuo and Yuan-Hsi Kuo, *Chinese Folk Tales.* Millbrae, CA: Celestial Arts, 1976. 134–41.

China's Yangshou mountains. The Yao people, with whom the story of the Ten-Thousand Treasure Mountain originated, have worked farms at the base of these mountains for centuries. These unusual peaks have inspired a number of stories.
Source: Photo: Andre van Huizen/www.imaginature.nl

as the Son of Heaven who ruled with the all-important Mandate of Heaven. In ancient Chinese belief, venerable ancestors and the gods chose the people's leaders for them and the leader's word was law—or at least it was until he showed signs of weakness or incompetence. Such signs would suggest that the emperor had lost the Mandate of Heaven, whereupon members of the royal family, or powerful nobles in the provinces, or the people themselves would revolt and install a successor deemed more worthy. It is not surprising, then, that the political history of China is one where strong leaders and strong imperial families retained the throne and weaker ones did not. Thus one dynasty lasted 800 years, another only 15.

Chinese myth, according to a number of scholars, tends to emphasize the importance of industrious labor, perseverance, self-sacrifice, respect for elders and departed ancestors, rebellion against oppression, passionate love, and virtuous deeds. A kind of humanism pervades Chinese myth, where gods, animals, and ghosts share our very fleshly appetites, passions, fears, and aspirations. The creator, Pan-ku, for example, is a giant with human form who dies after his enormous primal labors are concluded. In

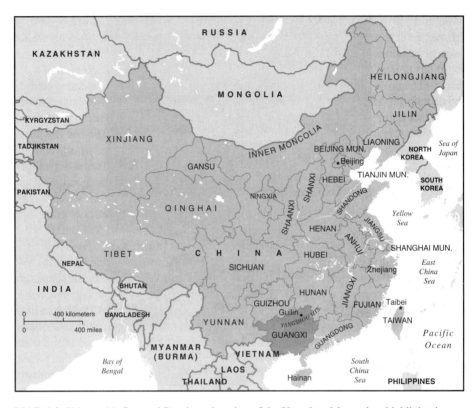

MAP 6.4 China, with Guangxi Province, location of the Yangshou Mountains, highlighted

addition, Chinese myths tend to evince a kind of fatalism which encourages individuals to view their needs as subordinate to those of a larger community—whether that community is one's family, one's ethnic group, or one's kingdom. Likewise, Chinese myths tend to illustrate Buddhist ideas about karma and Confucian ideas about virtue by showing that those who are humble, work hard, and deal honestly and generously with others are rewarded, whereas those who are greedy, lazy, and violent are punished.

In the following story, K'o-li and his mother embody the virtues of self-sacrifice, honor for one's elders, and hard work. It is significant that within the first few paragraphs, K'o-li shows respect for his mother, the mysterious "old father," and the property of the young maiden, Mi-mi. Given the opportunity to grab bags full of gold and precious stones inside the Ten Treasure Cave, the young man demonstrates filial piety and industry by choosing to follow his mother's advice and remove instead a mill with which he can earn an honest living. The action of the story takes place in the Kwangsi (Yangshou) Mountains where the Yao extracted a great deal of gold and silver. This fact and the oppressive noble

and king who seek to appropriate the Ten Thousand Treasure
Mountain suggest the intertwining of historical fact and mythical
fiction that also characterizes Chinese myth.

Deep in a valley amidst high mountains there once lived an old woman and her son
named K'o-li. Every day he went to the mountains to dig the roots of the turtle foot
plant. Beating the roots to shreds, rubbing and sieving them in a large wooden drum
filled with water, the white starchy powder settled at the bottom. This was steamed
and used as a staple since they were far too poor to have rice or corn. But one day
K'o-li had a sore foot that prevented him from digging more than a small amount.
Now there would be only a small bowl of the powder for their meal!

"Mother, you eat it," the unselfish boy said. "I'm not hungry."

"My child, you eat it," the kindly mother replied. "I don't feel hungry either."

As the mother and son were urging each other to eat the pitifully small bowl of
powder, an old man with a long, white beard appeared outside the door. He was so
pale looking, and seemed so feeble and shaky. Holding a peculiar walking stick to
support himself, he leaned against the door.

"Old man, you must be starved," the mother called out.

The beggar nodded without saying a word.

"My child, you don't feel like eating nor do I. Let us give this to the old father."

K'o-li instantly handed the food to the old man who finished it in a few mouth-
fuls. Then he made a gesture indicating that he wished to go home.

"Old father," K'o-li said as he brought out a large basket, "Let me carry
you home."

The old man nodded again, and K'o-li helped him into the basket, strapped it
over his shoulders and set out in the direction where the old man's fingers pointed.

K'o-li walked through a forest, crossed deep gorges and climbed mountain slopes
until they reached a big stone cave under a cliff. A lovely maiden hurriedly came forth
to welcome the old man and exclaimed, "Old father, you have come back!"

The old man jumped out of the basket and greeted the maiden Mi-mi. All of a
sudden he could speak! "This young man is truly wonderful! Take off your earrings
and make them into keys so he can open the mountains to get some treasures."

The maiden immediately removed a gold earring from her right ear and a silver
one from her left ear, hammered one into a golden key and the other into a silver key.
Giving them to K'o-li, she said, "Young brother, on the right side of this mountain
there is a Ten Thousand Treasure Mountain. In the saddle of the mountain is a big
stone cave called Ten Thousand Treasure Cave. You will see a big yellow stone just
like a door at the entrance. Put the golden key into the tiny hole in the stone, and it
will open. Within are countless treasures that you may take according to your heart's
desire. The stone door will automatically close as soon as you have entered the cave.
When you wish to come out, use the silver key by inserting it into a tiny hole at the
back of the door. Take care not to lose the silver key or you won't be able to get out
again."

"How can I take your earrings?" K'o-li asked with concern.

"Hurry! Go now," the old man shouted. "A tiger is coming to eat you up."

K'o-li looked around but saw no sign of any tiger. At that instant the old man
took the maiden by the hand and went into the stone cave. A large stone dropped

down fitting snugly into the cave entrance. Only a pair of shiny keys were left lying at his feet, and all around was quiet.

At last K'o-li picked up the keys and wandered home to relate what had happened. His mother listened thoughtfully and said, "My child, we dig turtle foot roots day after day just to get a little of the pulp. That is really not the way to live. See what implements are in the cave. If you bring something to help us farm, that won't be a bad idea."

K'o-li took the keys and went to the Ten Thousand Treasure Mountain where he found the stone cave with the yellow stone door sealing the entrance. He entered by using the golden key and the door closed behind him with a BANG. K'o-li saw countless treasures, precious pearls, silver and gold objects. He looked east, west, and all around. The dazzle and sparkle confused him, and for a long time, he wondered what to take home. Then he recalled his mother's suggestion and decided to pick an implement. "There—that white stone grinder lying in the corner—I'll take that home to earn my living by grinding grains. That will be good," he thought as he took the grinder.

He then inserted the silver key as the maiden had instructed, and the door opened instantly. When he walked out of the cave, the door closed behind him with a BANG. The lad then went happily homeward.

His mother put the white stone grinder in the middle of the room and turned the stone lid a few times to see how it worked. Many grains of corn suddenly rolled out. The more they turned, the more rolled out until corn spilled all over the ground. The old mother and her son laughed with joy until their jaws ached. "How can the two of us ever finish all this? Let us give some to poor people," she finally said. So K'o-li filled a large basket to the very top with grains and distributed them among the neighbors. Everyday the stone grinder turned out grains of corn, and each day some were given away.

It was not long before the story of the white stone grinder reached the ears of the king who immediately sent a high official with troops of soldiers to K'o-li's house. Off went the stone grinder to the palace. The happy king walked over to feel the grinder. With just one touch—*si-sa!*—it turned into a pile of white lime. The king was so furious, his face turned blue. "Behead that useless official!" he ordered the soldiers.

The old mother was very upset, and asked, "My son, do you still have the keys?"

"Yes, I'm carrying them close to my breast," he replied.

"Then return to The Ten Thousand Treasure Mountain and find something else," she urged K'o-li.

K'o-li went back and this time took a yellow stone mortar. They tried using it by pounding with a wooden pestle, and pearly white rice instantly fell out! The more they pounded, the more fell out!

The story soon reached the king who once again dispatched soldiers together with a high official to take away the stone mortar. The happy king walked over to examine it, but this time took care to feel it very gently. Yet with just one touch—*si-sa!*—the stone mortar turned into a heap of yellow clay. The king was so enraged, even his beard bristled, and he shouted to his soldiers, "Behead that useless official!"

Once again K'o-li returned to the Ten Thousand Treasure Cave and this time brought back a hoe. He moved the hoe merely once over the barren ground in front of their hut, and strange to say, a great big cornstalk having many giant ears of corn instantly shot up. He moved it back and forth ten times, and ten giant cornstalks shot up; then a hundred times, and one hundred cornstalks shot up, then. . . . Again, mother and son were overcome with laughter. K'o-li once more gave a generous amount to the neighbors. Soon everyone was talking about the magic hoe, and, of course, the news reached the king who said, "This time we are not going to take away the hoe. So far everything has turned to either lime or clay. Bring the young fellow here for questioning."

Thus a high official with soldiers went to K'o-li's house where he was bound hand and foot and carried to the palace. The king sat on his throne flanked by executioners with axes and knives. "Where did your treasures come from? Speak out," the vicious king commanded, "and you will be rewarded. Otherwise I'll have you beheaded."

The executioners shouted in unison to threaten K'o-li. But why should he be afraid? He remained silent but racked his brains for the best way to keep the secret. All of a sudden it dawned on him and he replied, "My treasures were obtained from the Ten Thousand Treasure Cave in the Ten Thousand Treasure Mountain. There is so much treasure there, it is endless."

The king laughed aloud with happiness and said, "Very good, we will go to take it all. Give me the key at once. Take the lead and guide us there."

The king was born aloft in his sedan chair accompanied by troops who carried huge empty baskets while K'o-li guided them. On their arrival the king took out the golden key from his vest, rushed into the cave, followed by all his soldiers, officials and attendants. BANG! The stone door closed behind them.

"King, you wicked one," K'o-li shouted from without, "the silver key is in my hand. Stay in the cave forever!"

K'o-li hurried home to tell his mother what had happened. "You are a clever, good son," she said thankfully. "We still have the hoe so let us till the land for corn."

"Ma-ma, the maiden Mi-mi, gave me two keys," K'o-li said in dismay as he suddenly remembered that there was now only a silver one. "What can I do? They are her earrings."

"I'll go with you to return it and we can apologize for the loss," she replied.

Mother and son each carried a basketful of corn on their shoulders. They passed through the forest, crossed the deep gorge and climbed the mountain slopes until they saw the old father, his long, white beard swaying gently in the breeze, and his granddaughter sitting at the entrance of the stone cave.

"I'm so sorry that the golden key was lost," K'o-li said as he returned the silver one. A soft rosy hue spread over her face as she silently took the key. She twisted it back into an earring, and placed it in her left earlobe.

The mother said, "Old father, here are two baskets of corn. They are really not much more than a taste, but it is all from your precious hoe."

"Old woman, I don't need your corn. Better keep it for the poor people. Your son is honest and diligent so I'll give my granddaughter to him in marriage." As soon as he finished talking, he walked into the cave. A big stone door dropped, sealing the cave entrance, and the maiden was left behind. The old woman looked tenderly at the lovely young maiden, then at her beloved, strong son. She took one hand of her daughter-in-law, and the other of her son, and smiling, went home.

Kobo Stories

Buddhist (Japan)

In Japan, local legend, the ancient nature-focused Shinto religion, and Buddhism combined to create a rich tapestry of stories in which sacred waters play an important role. Shintoism's veneration of departed ancestors and its respect for all spirits, particularly angry ones, manifests itself in numerous shrines and numerous stories about the various acts of heroism, passion, and compassion that surround wells, streams, rock formations, and other landmarks. When Buddhism came to Japan, indigenous stories about various sacred waters were revised by the adherents of the new religion to attribute their miraculous power to the Buddha, his priests, and various temples and statues. For example, images of the Buddha were said to cry and wiggle if robbers came to cart them off.

Many stories refer to Kobo Daishi, the founder of Shingon Buddhism in Japan, a tradition that features a variety of esoteric and magical practices. In some stories, Kobo Daishi wandered the countryside in disguise, rewarding the generous and punishing the greedy. The following cluster of short Kobo stories will give readers a sense of the many hundreds of similar tales.

ST. KOBO'S WELL

There is a spring by the name of St. Kobo's Well in the village of Muramatsu, Ninohe-gun. The following story concerning this well is told in this district. A girl was once weaving alone at her home. An old man, staggering, came by there and asked her for a cup of water. She walked over the hill more than a thousand yards away and brought back water for the visitor. The old man was pleased with her kindness and said that he would make her free from such painful labor. After saying this, he struck the ground with his cane. While he was striking, water sprang forth from the point struck by his cane. That spring was called St. Kobo's Well.

The old man who could do such a miraculous deed was thought to be St. Kobo, however poor and weak he might look.

THE WILLOW WELL OF KOBO

There is a well in the compound of Zempuku-ji in Azabu. In ancient times while Kobo Daishi was staying in this temple, in order to get the water for offering to the Buddha, he put his staff into the ground, praying to the god of the Kashima Shrine [a large shrine where warriors prayed before going into battle].

Then clear water gushed forth. Later Kobo Daishi planted a willow tree by the well to commemorate it forever. So it is called the Willow Well.

Source: Excerpt from *Folk Legends of Japan* by Richard M. Dorson. © 1962 Charles E. Tuttle, Inc., of Boston, Massachusetts, and Tokyo, Japan. Used by permission.

THE KOBO CHESTNUT TREES

In the mountains around Fukiage Pass in Nagura-mura, Kita Shidara-gun, grow chestnut trees called Kobo chestnuts. Those trees bear fruit very young, even when they are only three feet high.

Hundreds of years ago there was a big chestnut tree on this pass. Boys would rush to climb it to pick the chestnuts, but little children could not climb the tree. One day while they were weeping, a traveling priest passed by, saw the little children crying, and said: "Well, you shall be able to pick the chestnuts from next year on."

The next year every small young chestnut tree bore fruit so that the little children could pick them easily. The villagers thought that the traveling priest must have been St. Kobo, and since then they have called these the Kobo chestnut trees.

THE STREAM WHERE KOBO WASHED HIS GARMENT

Long ago Kobo Daishi went on a pilgrimage throughout the country. He came to Momotomataga in Toyoda-mura, and he took off his dirty clothes. He washed them in the Hinomoto River. The villagers who saw him did not know that he was a virtuous priest, and criticized him for washing dirty clothes. St. Kobo went away without saying anything. He went to Takatsu-mura, and he washed his clothes on the bank in Suko. For this reason, in Momotomataga the river dries up in summer and people often suffer from lack of water. On the other hand, in Suko, through the mercy of the priest, no one has drowned in the river.

At present almost every year the water is dried up in Hinomoto and gushes out in Kadoi.

The Waters of Eternal Life

Jewish (Italy, ca. 11th Century)

Jewish history is well-documented and so for the purposes of this introduction it is sufficient to remark that while this people enjoyed a brief reign as a major power in the Mediterranean world during the 10th century BCE, they have largely been a distinct ethnic group maintaining their religious and cultural traditions within other, larger cultures. Before their Solomonic glory days, the Hebrews were a small shepherd tribe living among the more culturally advanced Canaanites, slaves to the Pharaohs in Egypt, and an antagonistic rival of the Philistines. A few generations after Solomon's reign, the Jews were subjugated first by the Babylonians

Source: From *Miriam's Tambourine: Jewish Folktales from Around the World.* Macmillan, Inc. Copyright © 1984, 1985, 1986 by Howard Schwartz. Reprinted by permission of Ellen Levine Literary Agency, Inc.

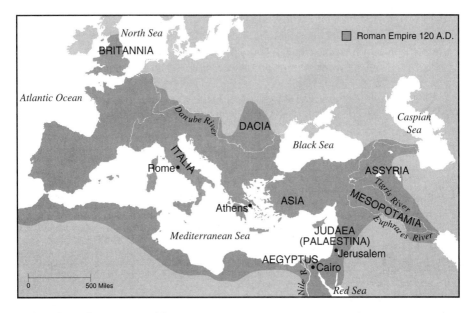

MAP 6.5 Mediterranean world

under Nebuchadnezzar, later by the Persians under Darius, the Greeks under Alexander the Great, and finally by the Romans under the Caesars. It was during the Roman occupation that the Jews were scattered throughout the ancient world in what is known as the Diaspora.

This long history of subjugation to foreign and often hostile rule has influenced Jewish literature in at least two important ways. First, Jewish literature, like Jewish culture itself, has assimilated some of the knowledge, customs, and artistic conventions of each of the nations to which the Jews were subjugated or exiled. Thus Yiddish folk stories from the *shtetls* and *ghettos* of pre-Holocaust Europe have a distinct flavor and range of concerns that distinguish them from the stories told in the *maghrebs* of Northern Africa. The children of the Jews deported to Babylon by Nebuchadnezzar returned to the land of Israel with new metaphysical ideas that were gradually assimilated into traditional Jewish belief. It is notable, for example, that post-exilic Jewish literature begins to discuss heaven and hell, angels and demons, and the fate of the individual soul after death, whereas the Torah and pre-exilic prophets do not mention them. Moreover, the long and troubled history of the Jews has tended to make the themes of struggle, alienation, and survival central to its literature. Numerous folk stories about famous Jewish teachers and not-so-famous tradesmen outwitting or conciliating hostile emperors, soldiers, and popes by holding fast to the teachings and religious traditions of their ancestors amply illustrate this sense that the Jews are always "strangers in a strange land." Scores of stories show that God rewards those who keep the Sabbath or keep kosher or practice charity and hospitality in the face of strong pressure—or even threats of violence—to do otherwise. Indeed, it is the struggle to survive as a distinct people and to preserve religious traditions and a cultural identity that date back nearly three thousand years that constitute the background of a great many novels, plays, and folk stories.

In addition to these influences, Jewish myth and literature have a long evolutionary history as well. Literacy—at least the ability to read Hebrew script well enough to recite one's daily prayers and take part in public and private religious observances—has been central to Jewish life at least since the return from the Babylonian exile. The Torah, the five books of law that outline the divine history of the Jews and that define its religious culture, is held in such high regard that, were it to be accidentally dropped, all those present would be bound by rabbinic tradition to fast during daylight hours for 40 days. At least since the European Middle Ages, all Jewish males were required to chant a passage from the Torah in order to be considered *bar mitzvah,* a "son of the good deed." In addition to the Torah, an extensive oral tradition of commentary upon biblical law came into being throughout the years of the Roman occupation. Later, this oral tradition was codified and written down in what is now called the Talmud. Torah and Talmud are sacred texts, though Torah is considered by the orthodox to be the direct and literal expression of God's will while the Talmud is considered the collected wisdom of the sages. A third, less authoritative, literary tradition complements and to a large degree supplements the Torah. This tradition, or Midrash, is a vast collection of stories about the Jewish patriarchs, matriarchs, and other important biblical persons that often finds its way into sermons and rabbinic teachings. These stories serve to fill in some of the blanks of the biblical record. For example, one *medresh* (a story from the Midrash) describes the relationship between Adam and Lilith—the powerful sorceress to whom Adam was said to have been married before God created Eve. Generally speaking, the stories in the Midrash provide allegories, parables, and illustrations of the Torah's main teachings.

The following story, then, has more in common with Midrash than other sacred Jewish literature. Its purpose is to put into play the religious principles derived from Torah and Talmud within the context of human needs, desires, hopes, and fears. The fact that Alexander the Great embodies these longings in a Jewish tale from 11th-century Italy demonstrates the degree to which Jewish tradition has assimilated and transformed histories, persons, events, and traditions from the many cultures with which it has had contact during the past three thousand years. Interestingly, the story of Alexander's search for secret knowledge and his encounter with Asmodeus, king of the demons, has numerous parallels in stories told about King Solomon. One of the most famous of these, the story of Solomon tricking Asmodeus into serving him by leading him to the *shamir*—a mysterious object that made it possible for Solomon to obey God's command that no iron implement could cut the stones from which the Great Temple was to be built—has many similarities to Alexander's adventures. Readers interested in reading more stories of this kind will find Howard Schwartz's *Miriam's Tambourine* and *Elijah's Violin* excellent places to begin.

The birth of Alexander the Great was preceded by many signs, read by many astrologers. For two stars were seen together in the sky at night, a pair of twin suns burning brightly. All the diviners recognized this as a sign of greatness, but they also saw in it the prophecy of an early death. So it was that Alexander always knew of the destiny foretold for him, and he fulfilled the first part to the hilt, conquering the world. But once he had succeeded in this enormous quest, Alexander began to worry about the second part of the prophecy, that his life would be brief. So it was that he undertook his second great quest—to locate the Waters of Eternal Life.

The legend of such miraculous waters is found in every land, and Alexander heard of it wherever he went. Since he had managed to conquer the world, he undertook the quest to locate those waters without fear or hesitation for above all he longed to conquer death.

Alexander set out with a dozen of his finest soldiers, well aware that many obstacles might lie before him. From an old soothsayer—one of those who had foreseen his birth—Alexander learned that the Waters of Eternal Life were to be found beyond the Mountains of Darkness. But none who had tried to go there had ever returned. This did not discourage Alexander; he set out at once, confident that nothing was insurmountable.

Thus the king and his men traveled for many weeks, and at last they reached the towering mountains. Alexander saw that it would take his men several more weeks to cross them, and he was loathe to take that much time. Then he noticed several giant eagles flying overhead, and an astonishing idea occurred to him to leash some of those eagles together, to carry him to the other side of those mountains. Alexander decided to try such a crossing for himself, while his men would cross on foot. If he succeeded, he would meet them on the other side of the mountains in a few weeks.

So it was that Alexander ordered his warriors to bring him four of those giant eagles. Before long four of the largest were captured in a net. The king then ordered their food to be withheld for three days. Meanwhile Alexander ordered his men to weave a basket that was large enough to carry him, with a lid that could be closed to protect him from falling out during flight.

Next Alexander ordered that four long iron spikes be affixed to a board, with four pieces of meat affixed to the spikes. After that Alexander told the men to take the four eagles and bind their legs to the four corners of the board. And he had ropes hung from the board, from which the basket was suspended, with Alexander inside it. The eagles, seeing the meat above them, flapped their wings attempting to reach it. Thus the basket was carried high into the clouds. And from a narrow slot in the basket, which had been left so that he could view the land below, Alexander looked with amazement upon the mountains beneath him. And as he was carried higher, he began to see the entire continent, which seemed to him like a cup floating on the waters of the ocean.

When the heat of the sun began to weary him, Alexander pulled a rope, which turned the spikes downward, so that the eagles followed them in that direction until they finally landed on the earth. When Alexander emerged from the basket he released the eagles and then looked about. He found that he had indeed been carried across those Mountains of Darkness and had landed beside a mighty river. The land on which he stood was barren, but across the river he saw a great many trees, filled with fruit. He wished that the eagles had landed on the far side of the river but since they had not, he had to find a way to reach it, for there he could sustain himself. Alexander decided to build himself a raft.

He bound logs together and then strapped the basket to the raft and climbed inside. Now the currents of that river were quite swift, with many dangerous rapids. Before the raft had crossed the river half way, it split apart and the basket with Alexander in it was cast into the currents, where it floated on the waters like a barrel. Inside it, Alexander was turned over and over, tumbling ceaselessly. At last the basket was cast out of the waters and onto the shore. When the weary Alexander climbed out, he found that he had indeed reached the far side of the river where the rich fruit grew.

Now Alexander was famished after all he had gone through to fly over those mountains and cross that river, and the fruit of these trees beckoned him as no other food had in all his days. Alexander reached out and plucked one of those ripe, alluring fruits, but the moment he did he heard shouting from all sides, and in an instant he found himself surrounded by strange and frightening looking beings. Although their form was human, they had wings and cast no shadows. Even so, Alexander was not afraid, but before he could do anything, four of the beings took hold of him, and in an instant Alexander found himself wrapped in chains. His captors then set out through the forest with Alexander as their prisoner.

So it was that Alexander found himself taken to a magnificent palace, far greater than that of any king he had known. He could barely believe his eyes as he stared at the mighty size of that palace. He asked the guards who walked at his side whose palace it was, and they told him it was the palace of Asmodeus, king of demons. Alexander was deeply shaken, for now he realized who had captured him, and while he had no fears among men, he knew nothing of the ways of demons.

So it was that Alexander the Great, conqueror of the world of men, was brought in chains before Asmodeus, king of demons. Asmodeus had a very stern and frightening bearing, and Alexander began to fear that he might have reached the end of his days. Asmodeus spoke loudly, and said, "You, sir, are accused of very serious crimes. First of all, none born of woman are permitted to set foot in this land, the kingdom of the demons. The penalty for this crime is death! Second, you have been accused of picking one of the fruits of the trees in my royal orchard. The penalty for this crime is also death! Therefore you have twice been condemned to death. Is there anything you wish to say in your defense before the sentence is carried out?"

Alexander was well aware that only his wits could save him. He replied, "My lord monarch, I have come to your realm on a quest, for I am seeking the fabled Waters of Eternal Life. Instead it appears that I have found an early death."

Asmodeus was much impressed both by the directness of Alexander's reply and by the nature of the quest. And he wished to know more of his captive. So he said, "Tell me, before the sentence is carried out, who you are, so that your fate will not be lost to the world."

Alexander then revealed his name, and when Asmodeus discovered the identity of his famous prisoner, he was greatly surprised. The king of demons rose from his throne and embraced Alexander, much to Alexander's amazement. "Welcome, oh great king," Asmodeus said, "for the conquests of Alexander are known not only in the world of men, but in our world as well. Had I only known who you were, you would never have been subjected to such trials. For a king such as yourself is always a welcome guest."

Alexander could scarcely believe his ears, for the very stern judge of a moment earlier was now embracing him as an equal. Alexander gratefully acknowledged the kind gestures of the king of demons, and then said, "Some men believe that I care for nothing except conquering. But this is not true. Above all, I am an explorer, drawn to the far corners of the earth. And now that my days of conquest are behind me, I have chosen to devote myself to searching for these secret waters. If you can help me in this quest in any way, I would be eternally grateful and I would seek to repay you in any way that I could."

Now Asmodeus could be the most deadly enemy, but he could also be the most trusted friend. And he had long admired the exploits of Alexander, who at such a young age had conquered the world of men. Thus Asmodeus replied, "Would that I could lead you there myself, my lord Alexander. But this is not possible, for it has been decreed in Heaven that neither angels nor demons may reveal the locations of those miraculous waters to mortal men. But since you have overcome all obstacles to reach this distant land, I will assist you as much as I can. And if I may not reveal the location myself, I can at least tell you how this secret can be learned. For the only one permitted to reveal this secret is the Speaking Tree."

Alexander was astonished to hear that there actually was a tree that spoke. "Where, then, can this Speaking Tree be found," Alexander asked, "for I am prepared to set out even today to seek it out."

Asmodeus was pleased that Alexander was truly devoted to his quest. "Stay with me tonight and be a guest at my table," he said, "and in the morning I will tell you how to reach this tree and send you on your way."

This Alexander readily agreed to, and so his hunger and thirst were quenched that night at the table of the king of demons.

So it was that Alexander was the first of men ever to taste the far more exquisite food of demons. Alexander asked Asmodeus why this was, and the king explained that the wonderful taste of those foods derived from the fruits that grew only in that royal orchard in which Alexander had been discovered. For they were enchanted fruits, which Asmodeus himself had brought into being by a spell.

That night Alexander slept in a bed fit for a king, and in the morning he breakfasted with Asmodeus, who revealed the only way possible to reach the Speaking Tree. First, he must travel to a certain forest, in the midst of which were sweet waters. There Alexander must go upstream until he reached a cave from which the waters flowed forth. Then he must wade through that cave to their source in a spring, beyond which he would see at once a large red tree—that was the Speaking Tree. It spoke on the third hour of the day and would reply to whatever was asked of it, except to reveal the day destined for a man's own death.

Alexander was deeply grateful to learn this, and he asked Asmodeus if he could show his gratitude by bringing him some of the Waters of Eternal Life when he had found them. But Asmodeus explained that he and all other demons were immortal, and therefore had no need for these waters. However, Asmodeus added that there was one thing Alexander could do for him, which he would greatly appreciate. Alexander vowed to do whatever the king asked of him, and Asmodeus said, "The Speaking Tree replies to three questions; three and no more. For one of these questions I would like you to ask where a glowing pearl can be found. For I have every kind of jewel in my crown except for the glowing pearl, and if you should bring me the reply to this question, I would be very grateful. And if you should somehow happen to bring back one of these pearls, I would give you a great reward."

Alexander assured Asmodeus that he would make this one of his three questions to the tree, and, if fate permitted, he would seek out the glowing pearl as well. Then he set out on the quest. He found the way to the forest exactly as Asmodeus had described it, in the midst of which sweet waters were flowing. The king then followed the path alongside those waters until he reached the entrance to a cave. Alexander was certain that this must be the cave beyond which lay the Speaking Tree.

Alexander waded through the waters of the cave for twenty-nine days. And though the waters were up to his neck—and sometimes even a bit higher—he often found himself wondering what the third question to the Speaking Tree should be. Alexander knew that he could not ask the tree how long he would live, since this question alone was forbidden, so he decided to ask how he would be remembered in the future. For the impression a man leaves behind is even more important than the perception of him during his lifetime.

At the end of twenty-nine days Alexander at last reached the source of the stream and stepped out of that cave into the light. The first thing he saw there was a towering red tree, and he knew at once that this must be the Speaking Tree. Alexander looked at the sun and decided that it was almost the third hour of the day, the hour when the tree could speak. So Alexander approached it and asked his first question: "Tell me, oh Speaking Tree, where can the Waters of Eternal Life be found? I have come here from very far to hear your reply."

Alexander had to wait only a moment, for exactly when the third hour arrived, the Speaking Tree replied: "You have taken the right path. Continue on and you will reach those waters. For it is destined that you will find them." Alexander was filled with joy when he heard this, for he was certain that if he reached those waters he would achieve his ultimate aim—eternal life.

Then Alexander asked the second question: "Where can one of the glowing pearls be found?" And the Speaking Tree replied: "Whoever descends into the Well of Living Waters will find it on the very bottom."

This reply threw Alexander into a dilemma. The tree would reply to only one more question, and he wanted to ask about his future reputation. But he did not know where the Well of Living Waters could be found, nor might he ever find out if he did not ask the Speaking Tree. So Alexander had to ask, "How can the Well of Living Waters be reached?" The Speaking Tree replied, "The first light of the full moon shall reveal the well."

Now this reply mystified Alexander, for the tree had not told him where to go. He decided to meditate upon the words of the oracle, and since night was about to fall, Alexander sat down beneath the Speaking Tree. Before long he saw a feather of light on the horizon and soon realized it was the first light of the rising moon. As Alexander watched, this feather seemed to gain wings, which shone on a single spot in the forest. Alexander suddenly recalled the words of the Speaking Tree, and rushed to the place illumined by the light, which was inside a circle of trees. But when he got there, he was disappointed; he had hoped to be led to the Well of Living Waters, but there was nothing there but a clearing in the forest. He sat down and soon fell into a deep sleep.

As he slept, Alexander dreamed he was floating on the waters of a river, drifting as if weightless. It was a very pleasing dream and it lasted all night. When Alexander awoke at dawn he recalled the dream and wondered at its meaning, especially since he had been searching for a well.

As he thought about this, Alexander noticed the outline of a circle around him. He felt with his hand and discovered it was a circle of stones, with only a small portion of each stone protruding from beneath the earth. Suddenly it occurred to Alexander that this might be the well he was seeking, and that it was covered with a layer of dirt. Alexander began to dig there at once, and although he only had sharp stones to dig with, he managed to clear away several feet, so that he was soon digging from the bottom of a pit. Then, all at once, the crust of earth on which he stood broke, and Alexander fell a great distance, finally plunging into ice-cold water with a great splash. Any other man would have been terrified, but Alexander was delighted, feeling certain that this must be the Well of Living Waters.

Yet even if this were so, what good could it do him if he remained trapped in that well? As Alexander treaded water there, wondering how he might find his way out, he suddenly noticed a light glowing from the very bottom of the well. Alexander was quite curious to know what this might be, so he took a deep breath and dived below. He descended a great distance, and began to run out of breath just as he reached the bottom. He picked up the glowing object in his hand and shot to the surface as fast as he could, gasping for air as he emerged. When he reached the surface of the water, he saw at once that things had changed, for when he had dived below the waters were pitch black, and now a light shone on every stone—the glowing pearl! He had found it. And when Alexander realized this, he regained his confidence and felt certain that he would not only find a way out of that well, but also complete his quest to find the Waters of Eternal Life.

With the light cast by the glowing pearl, Alexander examined the sides of the well. He spotted a stone ladder that had been built into the round wall. Alexander swam over to the wall and just as he was about to grip the first stone rung, he remembered that this was, in fact, the Well of Living Waters. He wondered what was special about those waters, so before he climbed out he decided to taste them. He put the pearl in his pocket, and filled his cupped hands with water. No sooner had he tasted that wonderful water, than he felt refreshed and filled with strength. Alexander understood that these were indeed living waters that brought new life to whoever tasted them.

With his newfound strength Alexander was able to ascend the ladder inside the well, the glowing pearl held in his teeth to light the way. It took him several hours, but at last he climbed out of that deep well. By then he was exhausted, and he decided that he must have some more of those refreshing waters, but there was no bucket to be found. So Alexander plucked a gourd which grew in that place, hollowed it out, and made a long rope out of vines. And when this rope and bucket were ready, he lowered them into the well until they reached the waters far below, and when he had filled the gourd, he pulled it back up. When he tasted those waters this time, they seemed even more delicious, since he had made such great efforts to obtain them.

Invigorated once more, Alexander turned his thoughts back to the quest that had brought him there in the first place—the Waters of Eternal Life. For although the waters of this well were surely wonderful, he was seeking the even more wonderful waters that provided not only vigor, but also eternal life. He recalled the oracle of the Speaking Tree, which had guided him to continue on the same path. Yet what path was it, since he had traveled on so many? While Alexander was considering this matter he happened to notice that the light cast from the glowing pearl in his hand seemed to form a path before him. It was a miracle, Alexander decided, and holding the pearl in front of him, he followed that path wherever it led.

In this way Alexander was led a great distance through the forest, and after he had traveled for many days and nights, sustained by the fruit that grew wild on those trees, Alexander came to a great gate. Before that gate shone a mighty light, like a small sun. Alexander was very curious to know what garden that was, and what was the source of that light. He hurried toward the gate, shielding his eyes from the light, and when he reached it and stood off to one side, he was able to see that the light was given off by a flaming sword being spun at amazing speed by a mighty angel stationed at the gate. And when Alexander saw such a gatekeeper, he knew that this must be the Garden of Eden, of which he had often heard. Inscribed on the gate of the Garden, which arched above the angel, letters were engraved, which read:

> Lift up your head, O ye gates, and be elevated, ye gates of the world.
> For this is the gate of the Lord, through which the righteous shall enter.

Alexander gazed in amazement at the angel with the spinning sword of fire, and he wondered if it had been placed there to guard the way to the Waters of Eternal Life. Alexander decided that he must find a way to enter that Garden, although it appeared to be impossible. Then Alexander explored the wall of the Garden, which rose up to such a great height that he could not see the top of it. It seemed to be circular, and great trees grew around it, with their tops reaching into heaven.

Alexander studied that wall and decided that the only way to climb it would be by climbing one of those immense trees. Therefore he sought out a branch within his reach and pulled himself up, for he had climbed many trees when he was a boy, though none were of such a great height. At the end of the first day of climbing, Alexander still had not climbed the first third of the tree. He had to climb another full day to reach the second third. And only after the third day of climbing did he reach the top of that tree and look down from that dizzying height at the world below.

But now, for the first time, he could see the top of that high wall, which was within his reach. So it was that Alexander very carefully climbed from the top of that mighty tree onto the high wall. And when he looked down, he saw the most splendid sight of his life—a Garden that looked like a paradise, perfect in its abundance, with four rivers branching from a spring that flowed forth from a mighty tree in the center of the garden, its top branches reaching into the palaces of heaven. Alexander then knew for certain that he had reached the fabled Garden of Eden, and he sensed at once that the Waters of Eternal Life could not be found anywhere else; perhaps they were the very waters flowing from the roots of that wondrous tree.

Alexander then decided to climb down into the garden, and by holding on to the thick vines that grew against the inside of the wall, Alexander was able to descend to the world below. Climbing down went much faster than climbing up, and before long Alexander found himself on the ground once again. Then he hurried over to one of the rivers that flowed nearby. He was filled with curiosity to know if these were indeed the waters he had sought so long. But how was he to find out? Suddenly an idea occurred to him. He opened up his pack, in which he carried his provisions, and he took out a salted fish. He quickly tossed that fish into those waters, and instantly it came to life and swam away, its tail swishing back and forth. Alexander rejoiced to know that he had finally reached the precious waters. Now he would be able to obtain eternal life.

Alexander leaned over and filled his cupped hands with water and was just about to drink when a solemn voice said, "Wait! Before you drink of those waters, do you not want to know the consequences?" Then Alexander looked up and saw a radiant being standing before him, like the one at the gate of the Garden, and he knew it must be an angel. Alexander was filled with awe. The eyes of that angel cast an aura, and when Alexander felt that light upon himself, he felt the presence of the angel all around him, and knew its sacred purpose. Alexander said simply, "Yes, please tell me." Then the angel Raziel—for that is who it was—said to Alexander, "Know, then, that whoever drinks these waters will know eternal life, but he will never be able to leave this garden."

These words greatly startled Alexander, for had the angel not stopped him, he would already have tasted of those waters and become a prisoner in that paradise. For a life of peace and meditation in that garden was not what Alexander wanted. Instead, he longed to explore every hidden corner of the world and to found a great city that would bear his name. Alexandria. At that moment Alexander understood that he could not drink those waters, for he preferred to live in the world of men, even if it meant giving up eternal life. All at once he found himself standing outside the Garden walls once again, not far from the angel that guarded the gates, its flaming sword still spinning.

Then Alexander turned around, and much to his amazement, he saw the palace of Asmodeus before him. He could not understand how that was possible, and when he turned back to the Garden gate, he found that it was no longer there. Somehow he had returned to the palace of the king of demons, far away from the Garden in which he had stood just moments before. Alexander was very confused.

When Alexander stood before the king of demons once more, he asked how it was possible for the king's palace to be so near the Garden, he had traveled such a great distance from one to the other. Asmodeus replied, "In this kingdom, Alexander, distances are not what they seem. They are different for each man, according to his fate. When you set out on your quest, you had many trials and obstacles to overcome. But after your decision to give up the Waters of Eternal Life, even when they were in your grasp, your fate was changed, and the distance reduced itself to almost nothing. But I see that you have brought the glowing pearl with you. Know that at the very moment you picked it up from the bottom of the Well of Living Water, another such pearl appeared in my crown, glowing for all the world to see." And it was true. A pearl just like Alexander's glowed from the king of demons' crown. Asmodeus continued, "The pearl in your possession, Alexander, is therefore your own. Let it lead you for the rest of your days and you will not go astray."

So it was that Alexander realized that his quest had not been in vain after all, for that glowing pearl was invaluable, since it would guide a man wherever it was that he had to go. Then Alexander thanked Asmodeus for helping him, and set out on his own with the light of the pearl leading the way. For it was time to return to the Mountains of Darkness, to meet his men, who were about to descend the final peak. And when they did, they found Alexander waiting there, though they had no idea of how far he had traveled since they had parted.

When they were reunited, Alexander told his men of his adventures, and showed them the glowing pearl. Now the men were astonished at this tale, but the thought of turning back when they had just crossed those mountains distressed them greatly. Then Alexander asked the glowing pearl to show them the shortest way across, and all at once it shone upon the entrance to a cave, which none of them had noticed before. They entered that cave, which the pearl illumined for them better than any torch, and before a day had passed they reached the other side of the Mountains of Darkness, simply crossing beneath them. After that they let the glowing pearl lead them wherever they needed to go, for it always led them to the right place. And so it was that although the life of Alexander was not long, as had been prophesied at his birth, his days were filled far more than those of most men, and his life was a rich one.

The Castle in the Lake

Post-Buddhism Bon (Tibet)

Tibet, known to its people as the "Roof of the World," is situated upon a vast, fertile plain surrounded by snow-capped mountains and arid plains that cover an area roughly the size of western Europe. According to a creation myth that would seem to derive

Source: From *Tibetan Folk Tales* by Frederick and Audrey Hyde-Chambers. © 1981 by Frederick and Audrey Hyde-Chambers. Reprinted by arrangement with Shambhala Publications, Inc., Boston. www.shambhala.com.

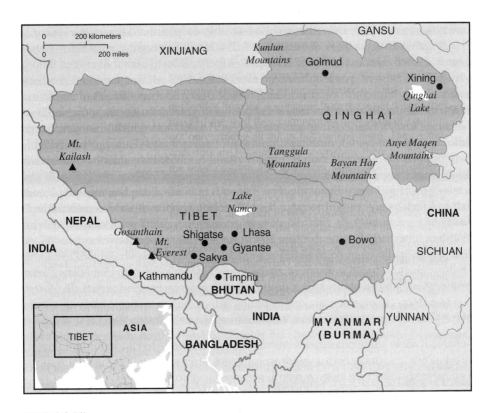

MAP 6.6 Tibet

from Tibet's native, shamanic Bon religion, in the beginning there was nothing but the primeval void. From the void emerged a black and a white light: *myal ba nag po*, Black Misery, and *'od zer ldan*, Radiant. A rainbow also emerged from the chaos and, from its five colors, the five qualities—hardness, fluidity, heat, motion, and space—also came into being. These five qualities fused in the form of a great cosmic egg over which Black Misery and Radiant hovered. From the egg, Black Misery produced the darkness of nonbeing, disease, death, and a host of demons responsible for misfortune, drought, and pain. Radiant produced the light of auspicious becoming, robust health, joy, and a host of beneficent gods responsible for prosperity, longevity, and delight. The gods and demons, it was further said, mated and filled the world with their progeny and, for traditional Tibetans, the earth and all that it contains are the dwelling places and physical manifestations of this host of gods and demons. Human beings have been assigned to the earthly realm, the gods live in the heavens, and the demons dwell beneath the earth's surface. Only the entranced shaman has the power to travel the three spheres and to rightly understand the causes of disease and misfortune and to retrieve human souls abducted by spirits—and to prescribe the sacrifices and "ransoms" necessary to placate offended or malicious spirits.

Bon tradition suggests that before human history a succession of demonic races settled the land of Tibet, each possessing knowledge of such crucial technologies as bows and arrow, hammers and axes, slings and catapults, the forging of iron, black magic, and shields and armor. When humans finally arrived on the scene they were given the settled earth as a home and the technologies necessary to survive upon it. But where did human beings come from? According to a later Buddhist myth, the Tibetan people are descended from the mating of an ape—an emanation of Avalokiteshvara, the Bodhisattva of Compassion—and an ogress—an emanation of the goddess Tara. Their offspring gave birth to the Tibetan people in the Yar Lung valley. The early Tibetan nation was without a ruler until 127 BCE, when it is said that an Indian king named Rupati fled over the Himalayas and arrived in the Yar Lung valley after suffering a defeat in the war described in the *Mahabharata*. Twelve Bon priests, believing that Rupati had descended from heaven, gave him the name Nyatri Tsenpo and declared him king.

Most Westerners know Tibet as a Buddhist nation and the ancestral home of the Dalai Lama, but Buddhism didn't become the state religion until well after its introduction in 173 CE. Indeed, if we can read the legendary battle between the great Buddhist sage Milarepa and the great Bon shaman Naro Bon-chung as history, it wasn't until the 11th century that Buddhism fully displaced Tibet's native religion. In any case, historical and archaeological records confirm that Buddhism was only gradually assimilated into the Tibetan way of life and that the new religion was itself significantly transformed by Bon rituals and beliefs. Buddhist clergy adopted over time the Bon talismans of the helmet, lance, armor, the divination arrow, the magic mirror, reinterpreting each of them as symbols of the Buddha's life and teaching. From the feathers, horns, bones, and fur of the shaman's cloak, Buddhist priests created dramatic costumes and dances celebrating the attributes of the eagle, stag, snow lion, and skeleton that are now said to illustrate Buddhist doctrine. Tibetan Buddhists still believe that the heavens, earth, and underworld are teeming with gods and demons, but now these divinities have been "converted" to protect and promote Buddhist teachings and practices. Even the fascinating landscape of the afterlife discussed in rich detail in the *Tibetan Book of the Dead* derives more from the shaman's experiences while under trance than the recorded teachings of the Buddha.

The following story, then, draws upon native Tibetan belief in a spirit world that lies hidden in various sacred landforms and bodies of water. The opening lines describing the fearful stories told about the spirits and fire-dogs believed to emerge from "Castle Lake" at night might suggest pre-Buddhist beliefs about demons lurking in the shadowy places of the world ready to pounce upon the unprotected and the unwary. The "actual," beneficent nature of those dwelling beneath the mysterious waters of the lake suggests the post-Buddhist belief that the demons of the world have been tamed by the virtue and wisdom of Buddhas and sages and that only a person's deeds create his or her misfortune. But, ultimately, the following story isn't about religion as much as it is about the deepest wishes of the human heart for a return to the womb—a condition usually expressed in myth as a source of unlimited wealth and magical power that frees the lucky from worldly care.

In the land of Tibet, there was a beautiful lake surrounded by hills and mountains. So beautiful and clear was the lake that people who passed by would gasp in wonderment. Some would say that when the sun was high in the sky, casting the shadows of the mountain peaks across the calm expanse of water, it looked just as if there was a castle in the lake, a castle of such vast proportions that it filled the water. So the lake soon came to be known as "The Castle Lake."

Many stories grew up around the lake and its castle. Sometimes it was said that when the moon shone full and the stars gleamed like diamonds on the water, people could be seen rising from the lake, strange people, with eyes of fire and flowing hair hanging like wet leaves around their faces. Or fiery dogs would appear to tear the flesh from lone travelers walking the beach in innocence.

But, as is often the case with legends, father told daughter and mother told son through many generations, until the stories grew bigger and bigger with each telling, and finally they conveyed much more than the original teller intended. Soon it was generally accepted that there was indeed a castle in the lake, and that the castle had a king. The king, it was said, had many retainers, men who by some misfortune had fallen into the lake, or who had been captured while walking alone on its shores and were thereafter forced to remain in the service of the king.

One day a young herdsman was tending his yaks on the eastern side of the lake. Feeling a need for refreshment, he left his herd and made his way down to the water's edge. After he had splashed the cooling water onto his face, he lay back against a large rock, took his cheese and barley bread from his bag, lit a small fire to heat up his butter tea, and began to have his lunch.

While he was eating, Rinchen began to reflect upon his life. His mother was a cruel woman; she forced him to work hard so that she could buy new clothes and eat well, while he had to be content with a few cast-off rags and the scraps of food his mother did not want. Thinking thus, Rinchen began to cry. The tears rolled down his cheeks and sobs shook his body; he could work no harder and yet his mother wanted more and more.

As the boy began to pack away his things he looked up and saw a man standing at the water's edge. The man was tall and dressed in a black *chuba* dripping with water, looking just as if he had come up out of the lake. Recalling the stories he had heard about The Castle Lake and the king's retainers, Rinchen began to panic, and was just starting to run away when the man spoke.

"Why do you cry so?" the man asked. Rinchen turned to the man and saw that his face was gentle and kind, and heard that his voice was soft and melodious. All fear seemed to leave his body and he walked toward the tall man standing in the shallows of the lake. The man repeated his question and Rinchen told him about his mother and how she forced him to work harder and harder in order to keep her.

"Come with me into the lake," the man said, "for the king is a kind man and may be able to help you with your problem." The young herdsman felt fear begin to well inside him once more, for he was sure that if he went into the lake he would never return. The tall man sensed the boy's fear but in gentle tones which fell like music on the ear, he persuaded the young herdsman that he need not fear for his life.

"I am one of the king's retainers," said the man. "I will take you to see him and see that you return safely."

The young herdsman thought for a moment, "What have I to lose? My mother is so cruel that even death would be better than spending the rest of my life in her bondage." And so, throwing his fear away, Rinchen followed the king's retainer into the lake.

The water was warm and friendly, and the boy was surprised that he could breathe quite freely. The king's retainer asked him to close his eyes as he led the boy through the water to the castle. When they stopped and Rinchen opened his eyes he saw that he was standing in a large hall, elaborately decorated in gold, shining silver, and beautiful shell. At the end of the hall was a throne, and on the throne sat an old man, the king.

The king beckoned to the boy to come forward and as he did so Rinchen noticed that he was not alone in the room with the king and his retainer, for standing on each side of the throne were more retainers, dressed in black *chubas* just like the tall man who met him on the shore of the lake. When he reached the foot of the king's throne one of the retainers sprang forward and placed a small stool in front of the throne for the boy to sit on. Nervously, Rinchen sat down and looked up into the watery blue eyes of the king.

"Why do you come here," asked the king in a deep voice which resembled the distant rumblings of thunder. The boy told the king his story, just as he had related it to the retainer on the shores of the lake.

The king listened, and when Rinchen had finished his story he turned toward his group of retainers and motioned for one of them to come to him. The retainer approached the king and bent low while the king whispered instructions into his ear. The young herdsman strained but could not hear what the king was saying. The retainer left the hall and returned a few minutes later with a dog.

"Take this dog," said the king to the young herdsman, "but take care that you feed it before you feed yourself, that is very important." Rinchen took the dog, and with eyes closed let himself be led to the shores of the lake. When he opened his eyes he was alone with the dog.

The young herdsman went home with the dog and from that day on everything he desired appeared before him. He would wake up in the morning and find that barley had been placed in the barley chest, butter in the butter chest and money in the money chest. Even new clothes appeared in his clothes chest. He was very happy and always took great care of the dog, heeding the king's instructions to always feed it before feeding himself.

Rinchen's mother was amazed that her son should suddenly become so wealthy, and one day she decided to go out with the herd of yaks to see if she could discover the source of infinite plenty. While his mother was out of the house the young herdsman decided to watch the dog, for he was curious and wanted to know how the animal managed to produce the money and food. Hiding himself in the house, he watched the dog as it entered the door, walked over to the hearth, and violently began shaking itself.

Suddenly, the dog's skin fell to the ground, revealing a beautiful woman, the most beautiful woman Rinchen had ever seen. The woman went to the barley chest, opened the lid, and placed in it the barley, which appeared from nowhere. Then she did the same with the butter chest, the tea chest, the money chest, going all about the house producing everything that the boy and his mother needed.

Rinchen could contain himself no longer. He seized the dog's skin and threw it into the fire. The beautiful woman begged him not to do so, but it was too late, the skin burned quickly and was soon just a pile of ashes. Frightened that the chief's son would see the woman and take her for his wife, Rinchen covered her face with soot to hide her beauty, and kept her in the house away from the eyes of the people.

Soon, the young herdsman grew very rich, and with his wealth he grew exceedingly bold. "Why do I worry," he thought, "I have much money; the chief's son will not dare to steal the woman from me, for I can buy weapons and men." Thinking this, Rinchen washed the soot from the beautiful woman's face and took her into the town to show her to the people, for he was very proud of her beauty.

The chief's son was in the town and saw the woman. He was determined that she should become his wife, and sent his men to fetch the woman to him. The young herdsman was distressed and called upon the men of the town to help him, but they were too afraid of the chief and his son, and not one man would come forward to help Rinchen save his woman.

Feeling very sad, the young herdsman went down to the shore of the lake, sat down by the large rock and began to cry. Just as before, the king's retainer appeared. "Why do you weep this time?" he asked.

"I have lost my woman," the boy replied and told the whole story of how he had burned the dog skin and kept the beautiful woman hidden from the eyes of the people by covering her face in soot, but growing bold he washed her face, showing her beauty to the chief's son, and so lost her forever.

The retainer asked Rinchen to follow him into the lake again, for the king needed to be told the story. "Perhaps," said the retainer, "the king may be able to help you again." The young herdsman soon found himself in front of the throne once more at the feet of the king of the lake. After he heard the story of how Rinchen had lost the beautiful woman, the king gave him a small wooden box.

"Take this box," the king said, holding it out to the young herdsman. The boy took the box from the king. "Now," the king continued, "go to the top of a high hill and call the chief's son to war. When he has assembled his armies at the base of the hill, open the box and shout '*Fight!*'"

This the young herdsman did, and when he opened the box and called "*Fight!*" thousands of men charged out of the box and defeated the chief's son's soldiers.

Rinchen won back his beautiful woman and took her for his wife. He also took half of the chief's lands and became a rich, benevolent leader of the people. The young herdsman also returned the box to the king of the lake, thanking him and living in fruitful contact with him for all of his life.

The Cormorants from Utröst

Norland (Northern Norway)

Utröst, like the Irish Tir-nan-Og and the undersea kingdom to which Urashima Taro traveled in Japanese tradition, is an "Isle of the Blessed," a home of the gods, often underwater, where every human need is granted and no mortal ages. Utröst stories are typically presented as actual experiences and some have suggested that these stories were created to explain how it often happens that fishermen find straws of wheat tangled around the rudders of their ships or grains of barley in the stomachs of the fish they catch. According to legend, this normally soil-based vegetation indicates that they have passed over the undersea realm of Utröst or another of the *huldre* lands, the inhabitants of which live much like the Norlanders themselves, farming and raising cattle, fishing and sailing their boats.

On Vaeröy Island, close to Röst, there once lived a poor fisherman called Isak. He owned nothing more than a boat, and a couple of goats, which the wife kept alive on fish offals and the few blades of grass they managed to gather on the mountain, but his hut was full of hungry children. Nonetheless he was always satisfied with the way Our Lord had arranged things for him. The only thing he complained of was that his neighbor would never leave him alone. This was a rich man who thought he should be better off in every way than a wretch like Isak, and he wanted to have him out of the way so he could have the harbor that was outside Isak's hut.

One day Isak was fishing several miles out to sea when a dense fog came over his boat. All at once such a violent storm blew up that he had to throw all the fish overboard in order to lighten the boat and save his life. Still, it was not easy to keep afloat, but he turned the vessel quite neatly in and out among the heavy seas that were ready to suck him down at every moment. After he had been sailing at great speed for five or six hours, he thought he ought to be coming to land somewhere. But he sailed on and on, and the fog and the storm grew worse and worse. Then he

Source: From *Folktales of Norway*, edited by Reidar Th. Christiansen, translated by Pat Shaw Iverson. © University of Chicago Press, 1964. Used by permission.

MAP 6.7 Norway

began to realize that he was heading out to sea, or else the wind had turned. At last he knew it had to be true, for he sailed and sailed and did not reach land. All at once he heard a terrifying shriek ahead of the bow, and he thought it was none other than the *draug* singing his burial hymn! He prayed to Our Lord for his wife and children, for now he understood that his last hour had come.

All at once, as he sat there praying, he caught a glimpse of something black, but when he came closer there were only three cormorants sitting on a floating log, and whoops! he was past them. On and on he sailed, both far and long, and he became so thirsty and hungry and tired that he did not know what to do and sat half asleep, with the helm in his hand. But all at once the bottom of the boat scraped against land, and it stopped with a jolt. Then Isak opened his eyes. The sun broke through the fog and shone over a beautiful landscape. Hills and mountains were green all the way up to the top, fields and meadows sloped up to them, and flowers and grass seemed to have a sweeter fragrance than he had ever noticed before.

"God be praised! Now I'm saved! This is Utröst!'" said Isak to himself. Right in front of him lay a field of barley, with spikes so big and full of grain that he had never seen anything like it. And through the field went a small path leading up to a green, peat-roofed earthen hut that lay above the field. On the roof grazed a white goat with gilded horns, and its udders were as big as the udders on the biggest cow. Outside, on a stool, sat a little, blue-clad fellow, sucking on a briar pipe. He had a beard so bushy and long that it hung way down on his chest.

"Welcome to Utröst, Isak," said the old fellow.

"Blessings on the meeting, father," replied Isak. "Do you know me then?"

"That very well might be," said the old fellow. "I dare say you'd like me to put you up for the night."

"If that were possible, then the best is good enough, father," said Isak.

"The trouble is with my sons; they can't stand the smell of a Christian man," said the old fellow. "Haven't you met them?"

"No, all I met was three cormorants, sitting and shrieking on a floating log."

"Well, those were my sons," said the old fellow. Then he knocked the ashes out of his pipe and said to Isak, "You'd better come in for the time being. I imagine you must be both hungry and thirsty."

"Much obliged, father," said Isak.

But when the man opened the door, it was so richly furnished inside the hut that Isak was out-and-out dazzled. He had never seen such wealth before. The table was decked with the tastiest dishes: clabber and haddock, reindeer steak, great piles of Bergen twists, loaves of bread and fish liver covered with molasses and cheese, spirits and ale and mead, and everything good! Isak ate and drank as much as he was able, and still the plate was never empty and the glass was just as full. The old fellow did not eat much, nor did he say much either. But suddenly, as they were sitting there, they heard a shrieking and a rattling outside the door and then he went out. After a while he came back in again with his three sons. Isak started a little when they came in the door, but the old fellow had probably managed to calm them down, for they were quite gentle and good-natured. And then they said he would have to mind his manners and remain seated and drink with them, for Isak had wanted to leave the table. He had had enough, he said. But he humored them, and they drank dram after dram, and in between they took a drop of the ale and the mead. They became friends and were on good terms, and at last they said that he was to sail a few voyages with them, so he could have a little to take home with him when he left.

The first voyage they made was in a violent storm. One of the sons sat by the helm, the second by the tack, and the third was halyard man. Isak had to use the big bailer until the sweat poured off him. They sailed as if they were raving mad. Not once did they reef the sail, and when the boat was full of water, they sheered up on the waves and ran before the wind, so the water poured out the stern like a waterfall.

After a while the storm abated, and then they started fishing. There were so many fish that they could not get the sinker to the bottom for the shoals under them. The sons from Utröst hauled in fish without stopping. Isak also had good bites, but he had taken his own fishing equipment along, and every time he got a fish to the gunnels, it got away again, and his creel stayed empty. When the boat was full, they rushed home to Utröst, and the sons cleaned the fish and hung it up on flakes to dry. But Isak complained to the old fellow because it had gone so badly with his fish. The fellow promised that it would go better the next time, and gave him a couple of fishhooks. And on the next voyage he pulled in fish just as fast as the others, and when they came home, he was given three flakes filled with fish as his share.

Then he grew homesick, and when he was ready to go the old fellow presented him with a new, eight-oared fishing boat filled with flour and fine sailcloth and other useful things. Isak thanked him, and as he was leaving the old fellow said he was to come back in time for the launching of the *jagt*. He wanted to take a cargo of fish to Bergen along with the next group of *jagts* from Nordland, and then Isak could come with him and sell his fish himself. Well, Isak was only too willing, and asked which course to follow when he wanted to come back to Utröst again.

"Straight behind the cormorants, when they head out to sea. Then you're on the right course!" said the old fellow. "Good luck on your journey."

But when Isak had shoved off and wanted to look around, he saw no more of Utröst. He saw nothing but the sea as far as his eye could reach.

When it was time, Isak showed up for the launching. But such a *jagt* he had never seen before. It was so long that when the mate, who stood watch in the prow, wanted to shout to the man at the helm, the fellow could not hear him; and so they had to put a man in the middle of the vessel, beside the mast, who shouted the mate's call to the helmsman. And even then he had to shout as loud as he could. They put Isak's share of the fish in the prow of the *jagt*. He took the fish off the flakes himself. But he could not understand how it happened: new fish constantly appeared on the flakes in place of the ones he took away, and when he left, they were just as full as when he had come.

When he got to Bergen, he sold his fish and got so much money for them that he bought himself a new *jagt* that was fully equipped, and with a cargo and everything that belonged to it, for the old fellow had advised him to do so. And late in the evening, before he was going to sail for home, the old fellow came on board and told him not to forget the ones who lived the way his neighbor did, for now he'd become a rich man himself, he said. And then he prophesied both good fortune and prosperity for Isak with the *jagt*.

"All is well, and everything will withstand the storms," he said. By this he meant that there was someone on board that no one could see who supported the mast with his back when things looked bad.

From that time, Isak always had good fortune. He knew well where it came from, and he never forgot to leave something good for the one who stood watch during the winter, after he put the *jagt* up in the autumn. And every Christmas Eve, lights blazed from the *jagt*, and they could hear the sound of fiddles and music and laughter and noise, and there was dancing in the cabin.

The Areca Tree

Vietnamese (Vietnam)

The areca tree, scientific name *Areca catechu,* resembles a thin coconut palm. The fruit of this tree, the betel nut, is chewed—casually like gum or chewing tobacco—by millions of people throughout Asia and the south Pacific Islands, especially in India, Vietnam, Sri Lanka, Indonesia, the Philippines, the Marianas, American Samoa, Belau, and Bangladesh. In most countries, the betel quid—or betel cud—consists of a crushed betel seed, a pinch of lime (calcium oxide, not the fruit), and such spices as cardamom or nutmeg, all wrapped in an areca leaf. Some Pacific Islanders also add tobacco to the betel quid, which tends to increase the sense of well-being and alertness that this natural stimulant produces. Archaeologists working in the Pacific Islands have discovered evidence of betel-nut chewing far back into antiquity. Today, betel nuts are used medicinally to treat a variety of intestinal disorders as well as headache, venereal disease, and depression. Whatever its efficacy in treating these conditions may be, it has been demonstrated, both from the archaeological record and modern observation, that chewing betel nut stains and wears down the teeth, but, at the same time, it also prevents cavities.

The practice of chewing betel nut is on the wane, especially in the cities. The gift of betel nuts to begin a courtship and during the exchange of vows, however, which was once widespread in Vietnam, is reflected in the connection between the areca tree and marital fidelity which figures prominently in the following story. In this version, the pleasant properties of the areca tree and the betel nut are discovered by King Hung Vuong II, whose heart is moved by the story of love and devotion told about the brothers Tan and Lang and the woman they both love, Thao. But some have seen in this myth a contest between Chinese and especially Confucian cultural norms and the indigenous practices of the Vietnamese people over whom they ruled for approximately the first thousand years of the Common Era. Polygamy was not uncommon among the Vietnamese before and during much of the long era of Chinese occupation, nor was the practice of *levirat,* the custom of marrying a dead brother's wife in order to produce offspring to honor his memory. Interestingly, this custom is also condoned in the Hebrew scriptures and continues to be practiced in some parts of India and southeast Asia as well. In any case, some versions of the story have the older brother, Tan, leaving on a trip from which he

Source: Thich Nhat Hanh, *A Taste of Earth and Other Legends of Vietnam.* Berkeley: Paralax Press, 1993. 41–50. Used with permission of Paralax Press.

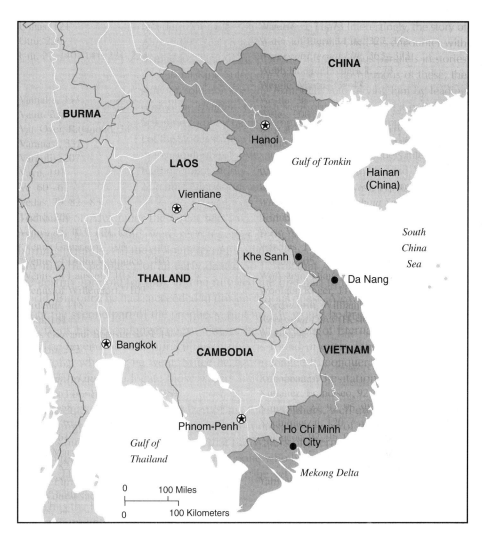

MAP 6.8 Vietnam

does not return. Believing him dead, Lang marries Thao, as custom required. Tan, however, is not dead and eventually returns to find his brother now living with his wife. But this is no Cain and Abel story. Tan understands perfectly his brother's actions and the three propose to live together harmoniously. Lang finds the situation awkward, however, and soon leaves on a trip of his own. In a sequence of events much like the ones recounted in Thich Nhat Hanh's version of the myth, Lang dies while away, becoming a white stone. Tan and, later, Thao go in search of Lang, eventually undergoing the transformations depicted in the story. The site of this miraculous testimony to fraternal and marital love becomes a shrine and the locals come frequently to this pleasant place to offer incense and reflect.

In the version of the story presented here, the customs of *levirat* and polygamy are submerged. Even so, certain narrative details suggest their importance in earlier versions of the story. We see, for example, that the brothers, though they are not twins, are nevertheless "as alike as two drops of water." To an audience that might otherwise have been scandalized by such goings on, this fact provides an innocent explanation for the mutual love triangle that develops between the brothers and Thao—and for Thao's "mistakenly" embracing Lang at one point. In addition, the narrator chastely observes that when Thao transforms into a vine, she clings to her husband even in death: "the roots of the vine began deep beneath the rock which it stretched across before twining gracefully up the tree. It almost seemed to be supporting the tree to stand upright." Yet her roots begin under Lang's stone body and drape across him/it before they climb the trunk of Tan's tree body as if in perpetual support. Thus, while the version of the myth we present here shows the influence of Confucian values, it nevertheless preserves the themes of love and loyalty, provides the origin story for a sacred place, and explains the birth of the widespread custom of chewing betel nut.

Tan and Lang were brothers. Though Tan was a year older than Lang, they were as alike in looks as two drops of water. No one could tell them apart. No one, that is, except the lovely Thao, whose father taught the village youth. During their years of studies together, Tan, Lang, and Thao became the best of friends.

At first Thao could not distinguish between the two brothers. They wore identical clothes and their hair was cut the same way. Then one stormy night when the brothers stayed late at their teacher's home, Thao saw her chance. She prepared rice porridge for their meal and brought out one bowl and one pair of chopsticks and placed them on the table between the two brothers. She returned to the kitchen and watched them through a crack in the door. One brother motioned to the other to eat first, a privilege reserved for an elder brother. Now Thao knew which brother was Tan. She quickly brought out a second bowl for Lang. All evening, she observed the brothers carefully, until she managed to discover one small difference between them. Lang had a tiny mole on his right ear.

After that, her father and classmates were impressed by Thao's ability to tell the brothers apart. She never handed Tan's notebook to Lang, and she always greeted each brother by his own name. Over time, Thao noticed differences in the brothers' personalities. Tan was outgoing and talkative. Lang tended to be quiet and pensive. Gradually, she could tell them apart merely by looking into their eyes. And although their voices were similar, she was sensitive enough to hear each boy's nature expressed in his words.

One New Year's Day the two brothers came to offer their respects to Thao's father. Suddenly Thao realized that Tan was in love with her. She couldn't explain exactly why, but the look in his eyes let her know beyond the shadow of a doubt. And as for Lang? Thao was so shaken by Tan's look, she did not notice Lang's.

Not long afterwards, Tan's parents brought the traditional offering of salt to Thao's parents to ask for her hand in marriage to their elder son. Thao's parents agreed. With some regret, Thao left the home of her parents to go live with her husband's family. She wished that her people still followed the old custom of having the groom live with the bride's family. But she loved Tan and was happy to be his wife. On their wedding day, Tan wore a robe the cheerful color of green banana shoots. Lang's robe was a deep shade of violet.

Each day, Thao saw how deeply her husband loved his younger brother. When she and Tan strolled beneath the moonlight, drank tea, went horseback riding, or played chess, Tan always invited Lang to join them. In fact, Lang wanted the couple to enjoy time alone, but Tan insisted on Lang's presence. Lang pretended to enjoy these occasions, while deep down he longed for more solitude. He found great contentment spending quiet moments on his own. Tan was unable to understand this need in his brother and could not bear the thought of Lang being left alone. Thao tried to speak to Tan about Lang's special needs, but Tan would not listen.

A new discovery added to Thao's concern. Lang was also in love with her. Love burned within him like a fiery volcano. Although he appeared cool and indifferent on the outside, Thao was sensitive enough to know the truth.

One day Lang told them he wanted to retire to a remote mountain hut where he could tend a garden and compose poems. Thao hoped her husband would support Lang's idea, but instead he insisted Lang remain with them.

One dark evening when the brothers returned from a day's labor in the rice fields, Thao mistook Lang for her husband when he entered their hut first. She opened her arms to greet him. Lang hastily removed himself from her embrace and Thao realized her error.

The next morning as they shared rice porridge, Lang informed Tan and Thao that he was taking the day off. Though he laughed as he spoke, Thao detected his anguish. She loved her husband, but that did not prevent her from feeling Lang's pain.

Lang did not return that evening. Ten days passed and there was still no word from him. Frantic, Tan left home to search for his brother. Ten more days passed and neither brother had returned. Thao was beside herself with worry. She left home herself to look for Tan. Like both brothers she followed the road that led out of the capital city's southern gate. There the road forked. One side led up into the mountains, the other down to the sea. She chose the mountain route.

Thao walked for days until her sandals were no more than shreds and her feet were swollen and bloody. Matted locks of hair fell into her eyes. All she had left was a straw hat to protect her from the sun. She felt almost too weak to continue. Her heart was filled with dread.

Somehow she knew that Tan and Lang had passed by this same way and that knowledge alone kept her going. She tore strips of cloth from her shirt to wrap her blistered feet and trudged on until she came to the banks of a wide river. It was evening, and there was no ferry in sight. A slight wind rustled overhead leaves, and a few birds called in shrill voices. Thao was prepared to spend the night by the river, when she noticed a tiny hut perched on stilts a couple hundred yards away on her side of the shore. A sudden gust of wind sent dry leaves flying. Black clouds gathered at the horizon. Thao knew a storm was brewing. She made her way to the hut and climbed up the ladder to knock on the door. She was greeted, somewhat cautiously, by a woman who looked at her oddly but then urged her to enter. She took Thao's hat and invited her to be seated on a low bamboo bench. Dinner was spread out on a simple mat. Thao greeted the woman's husband, who was feeding their baby spoonfuls of rice.

The woman took out an extra bowl and chopsticks for Thao, but Thao politely declined. She was too exhausted to eat but gladly accepted a bowl of hot tea. There was a sudden crash of thunder outside. Wind howled and rain beat against the hut. The sounds of the storm momentarily quieted the storm raging in Thao's own heart. The highland farmer lit a small lamp which cast a dim light. His wife put their child to bed in the next room, the strains of her lullaby drowned out by the raging storm.

When the baby was asleep, the woman rejoined them. Thao asked the couple, "Have you, by any chance, seen a young man in a green robe pass by this way recently?"

Neither the man nor his wife spoke. The man looked at Thao with a strange expression. Frightened, Thao asked, "Has something happened? Have you seen him then?"

The man slowly answered, "Yes, we did see such a man. What's more, we saw another man who looked just like him but was dressed in white. But I don't think you'll be finding either of them now. Please spend the night with us. You can't go out again in this storm. Tomorrow you can return safely home."

A chill ran down Thao's spine. A feeling of doom closed in around her, as she listened to the woman speak, "Move in a little closer so you can escape the draft that sneaks in by the door. I'll tell you everything we know."

"One afternoon, about a month ago, I saw a man dressed in white approach the river. He was empty-handed and didn't have even a hat or jacket. My husband was still working in the fields. I wanted to run out and tell the man that he had just missed the last ferry of the day, but I was occupied with the baby and couldn't go out right then. The man looked as if he was searching for something. It was odd, Miss, how he looked up at the sky and down at the ground. He turned his head this way and that before sitting down on the riverbank and holding his face in his hands. He began to shake and I could tell he was weeping. I felt uneasy and wanted my husband to hurry home so he could invite the poor fellow up to our hut. It began to rain lightly, and the man raised his head to the sky again. Then I thought he saw something, because he stretched out his arms as if to embrace someone. But, Miss, all he embraced was the empty air. The rain started coming down harder and soon I could not make him out very clearly. When my husband returned from the fields, I handed him a rain jacket and asked him to go down and fetch the fellow."

The highland farmer took a long sip of tea and said, "I found him sitting like a stone down by the riverbank, not flinching a muscle in all that wind and rain. I asked him several times to put on the jacket and join us inside, but he only shook his head. Finally, I left the jacket on the ground beside him and returned alone. The rain was really pouring by then."

"It was a storm like tonight," said the woman. "We couldn't fall asleep thinking about that poor fellow. All we could hope was that he'd get up out of the rain and return to his home. At dawn, all that was left of the storm was a light drizzle. I looked out the door and thought I saw the man still sitting by the riverbank. I put on a jacket and made my way out. Imagine my surprise when I realized it wasn't the man at all but a large white rock. Next to the rock was the rain jacket my husband had left the night before."

The man spoke, "It was so strange, Miss. That pure white rock hadn't ever been there before. We don't see any rocks like that up in these parts. It seemed unlikely that the man had dragged it there in the night. Anyway, I don't think four men could have budged a stone that size. Rocks don't just spring up out of the earth overnight. We couldn't figure it out. As for the man, we guessed he'd returned the way he'd come or perhaps even thrown himself into the river. That's what my wife thought, anyway, but I couldn't imagine what would drive a man to such desperate measures."

The farmer lit his pipe and took a long, thoughtful puff. His wife continued, "Ten days later another man dressed in green came. He looked all around him, too, like he was lost. Then he came up to our house and asked if we'd seen the other man dressed in white. When my husband told him all we'd seen, his eyes filled with tears. He cried out, 'My brother has turned to stone!' He ran to the river to find the rock just as it was beginning to rain. We had another storm and though we tried to convince the man to come inside, he refused to budge from the rock. He leaned against it and wept bitterly. Once again, my husband and I spent a sleepless night. In the morning, when we went outside, we didn't see the man, but there was a tree of the palm family, tall as a ten-year-old child, growing beside the rock. That tree hadn't been there before. What kind of tree grows that fast? I told my husband that the man dressed in green must have turned into the tree and that the rock was the man dressed in white. I believe the two men were brothers who loved each other deeply. Some terrible sorrow or misunderstanding must have taken place between them. But you, Miss, are you related to those men? Why are you looking for them? It's another stormy night. Please don't think of going out again. Stay with us tonight, I implore you."

Thao wiped tears from her eyes and made an effort to smile. To ease the mountain couple, she pretended to make light of the whole affair, "Don't worry about me. I'm the housekeeper of the man dressed in green. The man dressed in white is my master's younger brother. I'm sure they simply crossed the river early in the morning after the storms. I'll be crossing the river tomorrow myself. I'm sure I'll find them. I doubt they've gone too far. Please don't worry—I have no intention of venturing out in this storm tonight. I'd be grateful to spend the night here and then I'll catch the first ferry in the morning."

Having reassured them, Thao asked for a mat to serve as a blanket and after the couple retired to the back room, she lay down. Wind shrieked and battered at the walls as Thao's tears soaked her mat. The lamp's wick cast a bare flicker of light that trembled in the cold drafts seeping in through the doorway. A deafening clap of thunder made Thao wonder if heaven and earth had been reduced to dust.

The storm's fury seemed endless. But at long last, the winds died down. Shortly before dawn, all was quiet. Thao rose, careful not to make a sound. She opened the door and climbed down the ladder. A bright moon emerged from wisps of cloud. By its light, Thao could easily make out the white rock by the shore. Slowly she walked towards it.

It was just as the kind couple had described. A tree with bright green leaves and trunk stood by the rock, slightly bending over as if to protect it. Thao knelt by the rock and put her arms around the tree. She hid her face in its leaves and wept. Some of her warm tears fell on the rock and seemed to sizzle. Clinging to the tree, her knees sank into the soft, muddy earth.

When the couple awoke, the young woman was gone. They went down to shore and asked the ferryman if he had carried her across the river. He replied, "No, this is my first trip of the day. I haven't carried anyone across yet."

They asked if days before he had carried a man dressed in green or a man dressed in white. Again the answer was no. The couple walked to the white rock. The tree had grown a good two feet in the night and clinging to it was a fresh, green vine. The roots of the vine began deep beneath the rock which it stretched across before twining gracefully up the tree. It almost seemed to be supporting the tree to stand upright. They plucked a vine leaf and crumbled it. It gave an ardent fragrance which reminded them of the young woman whose gaze had been so deep the night before.

One summer afternoon, a party on horseback, led by King Hung Vuong II, came to rest along the riverbank. They noticed a small shrine sheltered beneath several large trees. King Hung dismounted close to the shrine. There he sat down on a smooth white rock while fanning himself. An attendant offered to wave the fan for him, but the king shook his head and smiled. He pointed to the tall straight trees around them and asked the attendant, "What kind of trees are these? The upper branches are laden with fruit. And do you know whose shrine this is?"

The attendant did not know, but seeing the king's curiosity, he climbed one of the trees and picked two of the fruits. Another attendant standing nearby said, "Your majesty, I do not know the name of these trees or fruit, but I do know something about their origin and why the shrine is here."

He told the king the story of Tan, Lang, and Thao as though he had once heard it in detail from the mountain couple.

"Your majesty, the white rock you are sitting on is the kind of rock Lang turned into. The fruit in your hand comes from the kind of tree Tan turned into. And the green vines which you see twining around the trees are like the vine Thao became. People in these parts say that the white rock represents Lang's pure heart. The tall, straight trees which shade the rocks represent Tan's desire to protect his younger brother, and the graceful vine shows the spirit of Thao who even after death remains at her husband's side. When the parents of these young people came looking for them, the farmer and his wife explained what had happened. The two families had this shrine built. Since then, local people have continued to light incense here to honor the memory of Tan, Lang, and Thao."

King Hung regarded the fruit in his hand for a long moment. He looked at the trees and vines and gently patted the white rock as though it were a small child. He was deeply moved by the story. He handed the fruit to his attendant and said, "Please cut this fruit so I might taste it."

The attendant took out a knife, peeled the fruit, and cut it into eight sections. Each slice of the white fruit held a portion of a smooth pink seed. The king placed a slice in his mouth. It was not sweet like a guava but had a special tang he found refreshing. He crumbled a vine leaf and chewed it along with the fruit. The combined taste was even better. His mouth watered and he spat. A few drops of his saliva fell on the white rock and turned as red as blood. The king put a finger in his mouth and pulled it out but there was no trace of red on it. He asked his attendant to scrape off a small chip of rock which he chewed with the fruit and leaf. His lips were soon stained as red as a young maiden's.

He invited his companions to taste a bit of fruit with leaf and rock. They all found the tangy taste most agreeable, and soon their lips were stained red, as well. King Hung spoke, "The love and bond between two brothers and husband and wife has borne a deep and ardent fruit. I decree that from now on this fruit and leaf and rock will be used in place of the traditional offering of salt for marriage proposals and weddings. They shall be symbols of love and fidelity."

The others bowed to acknowledge the king's decree. Soon after that the trees and vines were planted throughout the kingdom. The trees were named "Cao" after Tan and Lang's family name, and the vine was called "Lu" after Thao's family name. Thus the custom of chewing areca wrapped in a betel leaf with a sliver of quicklime began among the people.

Biriwilg Becomes a Painting

Aboriginal Australia

Aboriginal Australia offers a uniquely powerful example of the layers of meaning and the ongoing political and social implications of sacred places in myth. Aboriginal myths share with many other mythic traditions the notion of a previous Golden Age, the Dreamtime, in which spirit beings shaped the world as we know it. However, unlike most of the world's Golden Age myths, Aboriginal Australians do not consider the connections to that previous time to be lost or even particularly ancient (even though the aboriginals are justly proud that their heritage is one of the oldest unbroken cultural lines in the world). In fact, the relationship of the current people to their spirit ancestors is a fluid one, and the relationship between the ancient Dreamtime and the ongoing

Source: The Speaking Land: Myth and Story in Aboriginal Australia by Ronald M. Berndt and Catherine H. Berndt. Copyright © 1994 by Inner Traditions/Bear & Co. Reproduced with permission of Inner Traditions/Bear & Co.

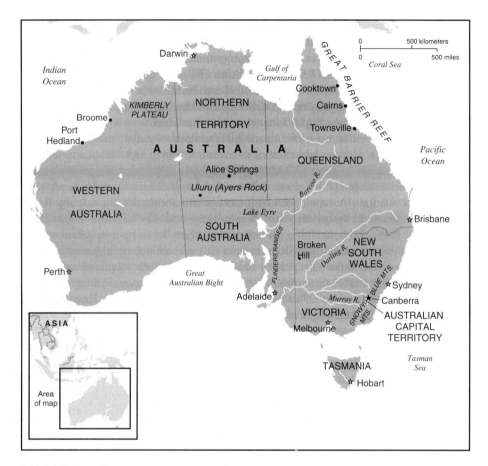

MAP 6.9 Australia

manifestations of the Dreaming is, similarly, not one of separation and loss, but rather one of ongoing creation. Thus, through ritual practices, current people enter into the Dreaming and commune with primal forces directly. In some sense, the current dreamer *becomes* her or his ancestor for the sake of receiving revelation, wisdom, guidance, understanding, and creative energy. An Aboriginal writer, Mudrooroo, puts it this way:

> The Dreamtime, the time of creation, symbolizes that all life to the Aboriginal peoples is part of one interconnected system, one vast network of relationships which came into existence with the stirring of the great eternal archetypes, the spirit ancestors who emerged during the Dreamtime.
>
> At the beginning, when the Earth was a featureless plain or, in some myths, covered with water, these archetypes, our creative ancestors, in many shapes and forms,

stirred and found themselves in the void, the featureless landscape, the waveless ocean. Some, like the giant serpents who had been sleeping under the ground, pushed upward and writhed across the void, creating as they went along the landscape in which we live today. Other ancestors descended from the sky or came from the sea and when they reached the land they commenced their work of creation, not only making all things but naming them. The creative ancestors are responsible for everything there is, including the laws, customs and languages which order the different Aboriginal tribes and communities.

The creative period of the *Dreamtime* is as much metaphysical as an epoch in time. Aboriginal people can bring into present the *djang,* the spiritual energy of those times, by engaging in rituals which the ancestors taught and connecting up with them. They believe that the spark of life, the soul which energizes them, is part of that ancestor, so by stimulating that part through ritual and ceremony a breakthrough can be made into the timeless time of the *Dreaming,* when all things are made and continue to be made. (1994, 52)

Also, and perhaps most important in terms of the role of sacred sites in aboriginal mythology, the land itself is the embodiment of the Dreamtime (in the sense of the distant creative roots of the world as we know it) as well as the contemporary manifestation of living spirit beings and mythological truths that are every bit as much alive and active now as at any other time. Even time itself is seen here as a much more fluid than it is in Western cultures. We might agree the past is always part of the present, in the sense that current attitudes, institutions, and behaviors emerge from previous ones, but in aboriginal worldviews, such aspects of the "past" are very much more active in the "present." When, through ritual practice, the aboriginal enters the Dreaming, he or she literally becomes one of the ancestors, and the realities of the Dreamtime are fully accessible to the current practitioner. Thus the land, which embodies the Dreamtime, is sacred not only in the sense of honored past but also in the sense that every stream, every boulder is a living part of the primal forces of the universe.

Perhaps the most famous aboriginal sacred place is Uluru, or Ayers Rock. As Mudrooroo writes:

Uluru is perhaps the most sacred place for Aboriginal people right across Australia, for here the many *song lines* and *Dreaming tracks* come together in a unity of myth which is celebrated by the giant sandstone monolith rising nearly 400 meters above the surrounding countryside. The monolith was built in the *Tjukurrpa* or *Dreamtime* by two boys who played in the mud and rain . . .

The custodianship of Uluru is with the Pitjantjatjara and Yankuntjatjara people and ownership has been inherited from both mothers' and fathers' sides. The rock itself is divided into the sunny side and the shady side, which not only refers to generational divisions but also to the division between two great myth cycles whose central themes motivate most of central Australian Aboriginal society . . . Opposites meet here in an uneasy tension which was resolved in a great battle which marks the end of the Dreamtime age and the beginning of our own age.

The mythology of the "shade" concerns the Kuniya, the Rock Python people. They came in three groups to Uluru, from the west, south and north. One of the Kuniya carried her eggs on her head, using a *manguri* (grass-head pad) to cushion them. She buried these eggs at the eastern end of Uluru. When I was at Uluru a few years ago I watched a woman performing what has become an age-old ritual at the base of the rock. In the *dance* her feet dragged in the sand, leaving the tracks of a snake.

While they were camped at Uluru the Kuniya were attacked by a party of Liru, poisonous snake warriors. At Alyurungu, on the southwest face of the rock, are pock marks, the scars left by the warriors' *spears,* and two *black*-stained watercourses there are the transformed bodies of two Liru warriors. When it rains the water channels down these watercourses but often they are dry and thus only marks.

The battle centered on Mutjitjulu, a section of the northeastern part of the rock. There is an Aboriginal settlement there. Here a Kuniya woman fought with her digging stick and her features are preserved on the eastern face of the gorge, while the features of the attacking Liru warrior can be seen on the western face, where his eyes, head wounds (transformed into vertical cracks) and severed nose form part of the cliff. Above Mutjitjulu is Uluru rock hole. This is the home of a Kuniya who releases water into Mutjitjulu.

The Liru had been called down upon the Kuniya by the Mulga Seed men, for they had also refused the Mulga Seed men's invitation to their ceremonies. They too were defeated and retreated to the east.

There are also stories of other ancestors who entered into this vast battle, a veritable battle of the scale which occurs in the Indian epic *Mahabharata* and signals the end of an era, the creative period of the *Dreamtime.* (1994, 169–70)

The pair of stories we present below introduce Aboriginal myths that appear in several of the themes that Mudrooroo mentions. This pairing of tales also represents another important aspect of Aboriginal mythic tradition and Aboriginal societies: many of the deep mysteries of Aboriginal myth are in the keeping of one sex or the other. Men and women are careful to preserve their independent yet mutually supporting ritual truths and practices. When it comes to *yawulyu,* or "women's business . . . men's opinions . . . [are] neither sought nor required" (Bell 1983, 11) in the preservation and practice of Aboriginal women's myths and rituals. Diane Bell, a white anthropologist who studied women's lives among the Aboriginals of central Australia, is careful to restrict her study to women's lives because their gender separation is so significant that cross-gender study by an outsider is virtually impossible (as Bell says, "it was unproductive and even dangerous to work with members of the opposite sex" [8]).

Ronald and Catherine Berndt, a married team of anthropologists who lived with and studied Aboriginal peoples for over 50 years, found themselves similarly constrained. In their essential collection, *The Speaking Land,* from which we selected the male and female versions of the myth of Biriwilg becoming a cave painting, each presents tales gathered exclusively from his or her own gender among their Aboriginal hosts. Both the Berndts, as well as Bell, also are careful to report only tales that their informants label as acceptable for general public attention. Much of the heart of Aboriginal mythology cannot be spoken in the hearing of (or be made available in any other way to) the opposite sex or of strangers or non-Aboriginal people.

BIRIWILG BECOMES A PAINTING (TOLD BY MEN)

An old woman named Biriwilg was camped at Gwoyurbir on the western side of Red Lily Lagoon, near Oenpelli. She went walking around, to Bandalgwoyu and to the long billabong of Inawelag (close to the Landing), looking for lily roots to roast. She became tired of doing this. "It is better that I go to that long 'pocket,' that corner, at Magagur," she thought. So she camped at Walg, Red Lily (*wurumanin*) billabong. After a while she went to Indju-mandagag, a large rock nearby; and then on to Umer-ngam, another hill outside the plain where there is a billabong of red lilies. There she collected roots and roasted them for eating. Continuing, she came to Mandjalan, where she made a "road" (a dry place) across the middle of Mandjalan billabong. She walked to another billabong.

At Yalwunbenen, where she found more lily roots, she camped and slept. Next morning she went on to Ridjewad (Uridjawad) on the plain: there is a large rock here, with a cave. She climbed up to this place, Won-ganengg, and cleaned out the cave. She put her belongings inside it, including her lily root collecting bag, and she brought up soft paperbark to make a bed and to cover herself. She sat down there for a long time. She left the cave from time to time to catch tortoises and snakes in the nearby billabongs, but returned to her home to cook and eat them. She also went to the Yarugiwag hills, but she always returned to Won-ganengg.

One day, however, from her cave entrance she saw two "men," one chasing the other: Dingo chasing long-tailed Rock Goanna, Malawamb. "Ah," she thought, "Men are coming!" She went farther back into her cave. Rock Goanna came in, and she went back still farther. [The two men had intended to go past her cave!] Biriwilg then "made herself" a picture on the cave wall. "No human being drew that picture. She turned herself into a spirit on the wall of the rock. She is there now!"

Today, men and women come to this cave and "feel" that drawing—they touch her there. She is standing up like an ordinary drawing. And when they touch it she sends out plenty of children [spirit children] to enter women everywhere.

BIRIWILG (TOLD BY WOMEN)

Biriwilg set off, coming and camping on the way, looking for honey and meats and vegetable foods. She came to Wiridjeng, where she met Ngalmoban, who was carrying *man-gindjeg,* bitter yams, and asked her, "Where shall we go?" Ngalmoban said, "We'll go this way, north, in search of a place." So they came on together. They camped at Gun-roidbi-boro, a red-ochre place name, and talked together. Ngalmoban told her, "I'm going higher up, and you go this way. We'll go separately. I'm taking *man-gindjeg* yams." Biriwilg agreed: "I'm going to the Garigen area, I'm not going that way." Ngalmoban went off with her yams. She was throwing them about at different places so they would grow there, and naming the places as she did so.

Biriwilg went on by herself. At Gara-morug on the plain, eating *man-gulaid* nuts, she said, "I'll go north and look for a place to put myself!" She came on, crossing the fresh water at Mula, and settling down for a while at Ngaraid-wodi-daidgeng where White Cockatoo had cut the rock with a boomerang. Still she came on. "I'm looking for a house where I can put myself and stay always." On the way she was eating long yams. "I'll stay here for a while, at Inyalbiri, eating these yams." Then she went on again. At Gun-ngad-bo she gave the place its name, because "here I dug a soak, and I drank water." She came on, climbing up, camping on the way, and crossing the water at Yawagara. She said, "I'll go this way, where there is a big stretch of water, and I'll cross over." She crossed a big creek at Wolgal, went on, looked at the place, and said, "Here I'll put myself, where the place is good and the cave-house is good, where I'll stay always." She went on, and was digging for soak water. As she dug the ground, she saw that it was only a little hole. She got up, and dug in another place. This time she was digging a big hole. Then she went, and was swimming about in it. When she had finished swimming, she climbed up out of the water and went to the cave. She said, "Here I'll put myself. I am Biriwilg. I came a long way. Ngalmoban and I came together, then we said farewell to each other. She went on. I came this way, and here I'll stay for ever: I put myself. I stand outside, like a drawing [painting] I stand. But I am a woman. I started off far away. Here the name of the place is Gun-gangin, where I put myself. I stand like a person, and I keep on standing here for ever."

WORKS CITED AND SUGGESTIONS
FOR FURTHER READING

Arden, Harvey. *Dreamkeepers: A Spirit Journey into Aboriginal Australia.* New York: HarperCollins, 1994.

Barker, Kenneth, ed. *The NIV Study Bible.* Grand Rapids, MI: Zondervan, 1985.

Bell, Diane. *Daughters of the Dreaming.* Melbourne, Australia: McPhee Gribble, 1983.

Benedict, Ruth. "The Emergence (Zuni)." In *Zuni Mythology.* 2 vols. New York: Columbia University Press, 1935, 1969.

Bernbaum, Edwin. *Sacred Mountains of the World.* Berkeley: University of California Press, 1997.

Berndt, Ronald M., and Catherine H. Berndt. *The Speaking Land: Myth and Story in Aboriginal Australia.* Rochester, VT: Inner Traditions International, 1994.

Bushnaq, Inea. *Arab Folk-Tales.* New York: Pantheon, 1986.

Christiansen, Reidar T., ed. *Folktales of Norway.* Trans. Pat Shaw Iverson. Chicago: University of Chicago Press, 1964.

Davis, F. Hadland. *Myths and Legends: Japan.* Boston: David D. Nickerson, 1955.

Deloria, Vine. *God Is Red: A Native View of Religion.* Golden, CO: Fulcrum, 1993.

Doniger, Wendy. *The Implied Spider: Politics and Theology in Myth.* New York: Columbia University Press, 1998.

Dorson, Richard M. *Folk Legends of Japan.* Tokyo: Charles E. Tuttle, 1962.

Dyson, Verne. *Forgotten Tales of Ancient China.* Shanghai: Commercial Press, 1927.

Feldman, Susan, ed. *The Storytelling Stone: Traditional Native American Myths and Tales.* New York: Delta, 1965.

Freeman, Michael, and Alistair Shearer. *The Spirit of Asia: Journeys to the Sacred Places of the East.* New York: Thames & Hudson, 2000.

Green, Miranda J. *The World of the Druids.* New York: Thames & Hudson, 1997.

Gulliford, Andrew. *Sacred Objects and Sacred Places: Preserving Tribal Traditions.* Boulder: University Press of Colorado, 2000.

Harpur, James. *The Atlas of Sacred Places: Meeting Points of Heaven and Earth.* New York: Holt, 1994.

Hyde-Chambers, Fredrick, and Audrey Hyde-Chambers. *Tibetan Folk Tales.* Boulder, CO: Shambhala, 1981.

Kelley, Klara Bonsack, and Harris Francis. *Navajo Sacred Places.* Bloomington: Indiana University Press, 1994.

Kuo, Louise, and Yuan-Hsi Kuo. *Chinese Folk Tales.* Millbrae, CA: Celestial Arts, 1976.

Linford, Laurance D. *Navajo Places: History, Legend, Landscape.* Salt Lake City: University of Utah Press, 2000.

Mudrooroo [Nyoongah]. *Aboriginal Mythology: An A–Z Spanning the History of Aboriginal Mythology from the Earliest Legends to the Present Day.* London: Thorsons, 1994.

Nhat Hanh, Thich. *A Taste of Earth and Other Legends of Vietnam.* Berkeley: Paralax Press, 1993.

Paksoy, H. B. "Dastan Genre in Central Asia." In *Modern Encyclopedia of Religions in Russia and the Soviet Union.* Ed. Paul D. Steeves. Gulf Breeze, FL: Academic Press International, 1988: 222–31.

Ramanujan, A. K. *A Flowering Tree and Other Oral Tales from India.* Berkeley: University of California Press, 1997.

Sadeh, Pinhas. *Jewish Folktales.* New York: Doubleday, 1989.

Schwartz, Howard. *Elijah's Violin and Other Jewish Fairy Tales.* New York: Harper, 1983.

———. *Miriam's Tambourine: Jewish Folktales from Around the World.* New York: Free Press, 1986.

Solnit, Rebecca. *As Eve Said to the Serpent: On Landscape, Gender, and Art.* Athens: University of Georgia Press, 2001.

Storm, Hyemeyohsts. *Seven Arrows.* New York: HarperCollins, 1972.

Terada, Alice M. *The Magic Crocodile and Other Folktales of Indonesia.* Honolulu: University of Hawaii Press, 1994.

Index